MANAGING THE STRATEGY PROCESS

A Framework for a Multibusiness Firm

Balaji S. Chakravarthy
The Curtis L. Carlson School of Management
University of Minnesota

Peter Lorange
The Norwegian School of Management and
The Wharton School
University of Pennsylvania

PRENTICE HALL
Englewood Cliffs, New Jersey 07632

Library of Congress Cataloging-in-Publication Data

Chakravarthy, Balaji S.
  Managing the strategy process : a framework for a multibusiness
firm / Balaji S. Chakravarthy, Peter Lorange.
    p.   cm.
  Includes bibliographical references (p.   ) and index.
  ISBN 0–13–284589–X
  1. Strategic planning.   2. Conglomerate corporations—Management
3. Conglomerate corporations—Planning.   I. Lorange, Peter.
II. Title.
HD30.28.C44   1991
658.4′012—dc20   90–26004
                                                                  CIP

To our families

Acquisitions editor: Alison Reeves
Editorial/production supervision: Peggy M. Gordon
Interior design: Karen Buck
Cover design: Bruce Kenselaar
Prepress buyer: Trudy Pisciotti
Manufacturing buyer: Robert Anderson

© 1991 by Prentice-Hall, Inc.
A Division of Simon & Schuster
Englewood Cliffs, New Jersey 07632

Printed in the United States of America
10 9 8 7 6 5 4 3 2 1

ISBN 0-13-284589-X

Prentice-Hall International (UK) Limited, *London*
Prentice-Hall of Australia Pty. Limited, *Sydney*
Prentice-Hall Canada Inc., *Toronto*
Prentice-Hall Hispanoamericana, S.A., *Mexico*
Prentice-Hall of India Private Limited, *New Delhi*
Prentice-Hall of Japan, Inc., *Tokyo*
Simon & Schuster Asia Pte. Ltd., *Singapore*
Editora Prentice-Hall do Brasil, Ltda., *Rio de Janeiro*

BRIEF CONTENTS

CONTENTS

ACKNOWLEDGMENTS

We received our first systematic exposure to the strategy process perspective at the Harvard Business School. The important work done in this area by Joseph Bower, Alfred Chandler, Charles Christenson, Paul Lawrence, Richard Vancil, and their colleagues has guided our own research. The contributions of these and other scholars to the conceptual frameworks presented in this book are duly acknowledged in the notes and references at the end of each chapter. The bibliography lists books that have had a broader influence on our work.

We are equally thankful to the numerous senior managers in organizations throughout the world who have helped us understand how the strategy process can be managed. They provided the empirical data from which we developed our conceptual frameworks. In particular, we would like to thank Harry Faulkner of Alfa-Laval; Kaspar Kieland of Elkem; Worth Loomis, James Mayerhofer, and the late John Vrabel of Dexter Corporation; Pietro Sighicelli of Fiat-Hitachi; James Castle of Infotron Systems Corporation; and William Dircks, Guy Cunningham III, and Edward B. Blackwood of the U.S. Nuclear Regulatory Commission. Case studies on their organizations are included in the book.

The manuscript itself has been slow in developing and has benefited along the way from the thoughtful comments of our colleagues at the Carlson School, the Wharton School, INSEAD (where Professor Chakravarthy spent his sabbatical), and the Stockholm School of Economics (where Professor Lorange spent his sabbatical). Gilbert Probst of the University of Geneva, Sumantra Ghoshal of INSEAD, Lourent Jacque of the Carlson School, and Howard Perlmutter of the Wharton School shared their insights with us on how a multinational business can be managed. Stefanie Lenway of the Carlson School and Peter Ring of Loyola Marymount also offered useful advice on Part III of the book. Andrew Van de Ven and Larry Cummings helped shape some of the ideas in Part IV of the book. We are especially thankful to Edward Bowman of the Wharton School, Yves Doz of INSEAD, John Grant of the University of Pittsburgh, Odd Nordhaug of the Norwegian School of Economics and Business Administration, and the anonymous reviewers engaged by Prentice Hall for their comprehensive and helpful reviews. The research support provided by the Strategic Management Research Center at the University of Minnesota; the Reginald H. Jones Center for Management Policy, Strategy, and Organization; and the William F. Wurster Center for International Management Studies at the Wharton School is gratefully acknowledged.

The book is enriched by the case studies that were contributed by Francis Aguilar (Norton Company), Christopher Bartlett (Procter & Gamble), and Richard Vancil (Vick International Division), all of the Harvard Business School; Ralph Biggadike (Becton Dickinson and Company, Parts 1 and 2) of Becton Dickinson and Company and formerly of the Colgate Darden School, University of Virginia; William Boulton (Texas Instruments Incorporated: MODPLAN) of Auburn University; and Sumantra Ghoshal (Scandinavian Airlines System) of INSEAD, France. We are grateful to these authors and their institutions for permitting us to use their cases.

We also appreciate the detailed comments that our graduate students have offered us on several aspects of this book. Johan Roos of the Stockholm School, Seog Kwun of the Carlson School, and Bente Loewendahl of the Wharton School deserve special mention in this regard. Our research assistants, Bari Abdul, Celia Kapsomera, Anne Murphy, and Barry Neal—all graduates of the University of Pennsylvania—helped us with our own case-writing efforts.

Alison Reeves, our acquisitions editor at Prentice Hall, kept us moving patiently and yet firmly. Barbara Bernstein of Prentice Hall and Peggy Gordon managed the production of this book with the utmost competence. John Pipkin at the Carlson School and Heidi Brown at the Wharton School provided outstanding word-processing support. In addition, Heidi served cheerfully as the manager of this project, helping us keep in touch often across continents. Without the help of these individuals, this book would not have been possible.

Finally, our deepest gratitude goes to our wives, Kiran and Liv, who really made the sacrifice and provided the encouragement to make us persevere when it was so tempting to quit.

Although so many have helped, we alone remain responsible for whatever shortcomings this book may still have.

Balaji S. Chakravarthy
Peter Lorange

INTRODUCTION

BEYOND ANALYSIS

Strategic management has benefited enormously in the past two decades from the development of new analytical techniques. The appendix to this book provides a brief review of some of the common techniques that are used today.[1] Although superior analytical approaches are invaluable aids to top management for *evaluating* a firm's strategies, these approaches are not as helpful in either *forming* or *implementing* the firm's strategies. In this book we focus primarily on the process through which strategies are formed and implemented in a multibusiness firm, and on how that process can be managed better.

In a multibusiness firm, it is difficult for top management to play the strategist in all the firm's diverse businesses. Often individual business managers are more expert at this. Moreover, the bulk of the information required by top management to evaluate the strategies proposed by the firm's business managers is typically provided by the evaluees. This information asymmetry between top management and the firm's business managers can be a potential problem, unless the firm's administrative context encourages the open and full sharing of all business information across its managerial hierarchy.[2]

Also, the multiple strategists in a diversified firm can disagree on the goals that should be pursued. For example, the relative emphasis that should be placed on short-term profitability versus long-term growth can be a bone of contention; or in a multinational corporation, the corporate need for global integration can be in conflict with the more parochial interests of country managers.[3] In the case of new organizational forms, such as joint ventures and cooperative networks, the multiple stakeholder groups that are involved can have opposing claims. Goal incongruence is another serious challenge for top management in a multibusiness firm.

This book describes how top management can use the strategy process to minimize the problems of both information asymmetry and goal incongruence.[4]

The key role of top management as envisaged here is not one of making strategic decisions per se,[5] but rather of managing the administrative context[6] within which the firm's strategies are formed and implemented.

The administrative context of a firm is defined by its organizational structure, its strategy process, and its informal organization. The literature on organizational structure and how it influences a firm's administrative context is voluminous.[7] We have chosen to de-emphasize this aspect of the administrative context because most multibusiness firms are organized similarly—in a divisional structure.[8] We have also chosen not to elaborate on the very important role played by a firm's informal organization, including its organizational culture, in shaping its administrative context. The literature on this topic is rich and diverse,[9] and we felt that it deserves more than a token mention.

This book seeks primarily to describe how the strategy process can shape the administrative context of a multibusiness firm and the critical role that top management can play in managing this process. We include in the firm's strategy process its strategic planning; monitoring, control, and learning; incentives; and staffing systems. We will address, where appropriate, the important links between these systems and a firm's formal and informal organizations.

BASIS OF THE BOOK

The book is based largely on our own research on multibusiness firms. The perspective we provide has been drawn from the experiences of over fifty well-managed multibusiness firms, a dozen of which we studied in depth.[10] In addition, we interviewed senior managers from twenty other firms to complement the data we had on them from the research of our academic colleagues. Case studies on several of these firms are included in this book. Although some of our ideas were also tested on a larger sample of firms, the frameworks that we offer here are essentially descriptive. They provide useful starting points for managing a firm's strategy process. For presentation purposes, however, the book is written in a normative style.

ABOUT THE BOOK

This book has three major themes: (1) identifying the critical elements in the strategy process, (2) emphasizing tailormaking and alignment, and (3) managing change and adaptation.

Identifying the Critical Elements in the Strategy Process

As we noted earlier, the strategy process consists of four management systems (Figure I-1). The strategic planning system is commonly referred to as the firm's strategy-making subprocess, and the other three systems are collectively called its

strategy implementation subprocess. Although we will use this distinction to introduce our framework, we see the distinction as an arbitrary one. Strategy making
and implementation are not sequential but highly interactive.

The strategic planning system attempts to articulate and communicate the
corporate objectives to the firm's managers, to negotiate a common understanding
among them of the intended strategy for each of the firm's businesses, and to help
delineate the managers' responsibilities in developing and implementing the intended strategies. The monitoring, control, and learning system assists in monitoring the actual implementation of the chosen strategies and in sensitizing the firm to

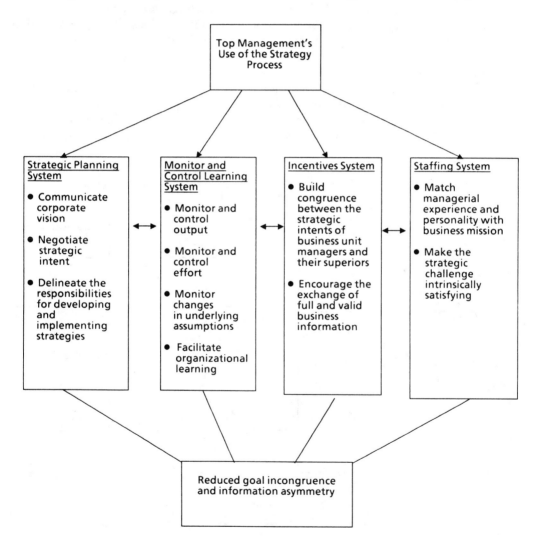

Figure I-1   **The Strategy Process**

changes in the underlying assumptions behind these strategies. Thus the monitoring, control, and learning system helps both validate and implement the chosen strategies. The incentives system attempts to encourage the exchange of full and valid information within the firm. The staffing system seeks to reduce goal incongruence by staffing the firm with managers whose experience and personality are consistent with the intended strategies for the firm's businesses.

The four management systems described above span the four organizational levels at which strategy is shaped in a typical multibusiness firm (Figure I-2). The strategy process must ensure that the plans pursued by the functional departments of a multibusiness firm—such as operations, marketing, and engineering—are consistent with the strategies of the firm's business units. Business strategies should in turn be consistent with the strategies pursued at the divisional level. Finally, the divisional strategies of a firm must support its corporate strategy. These *interactions* are shown by the thick solid lines in Figure I-2.

The thin, solid lines show another set of communication channels that connect the four management systems. These represent the frequent *iterations* that are needed between the systems. Based on actual developments (shown by circles in Figure I-2) against plans (shown by crosses), the firm's plans as well as the underly-

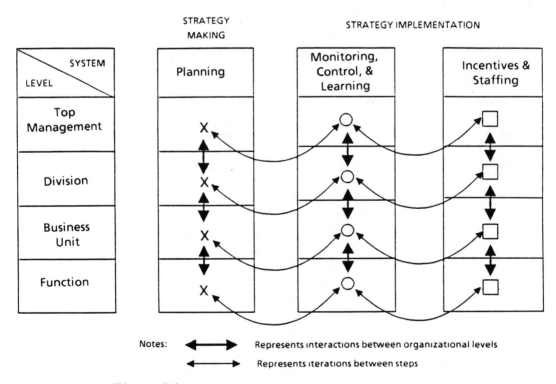

Figure I-2   **A Skeletal Framework for the Strategy Process**

ing objectives may have to be modified or even abandoned. As we discuss at length in Part II, a strategy cannot always be fully planned; it has to evolve in many contexts through several incremental steps of trial-and-error learning.[11] Based on the performance of a function, business unit, or division (shown by squares in Figure I-2), the incentives that have to be awarded to the managers can be determined. It may be necessary under some circumstances, depending on the observed performance variances, even to change the staffing of these organizational units.

We describe how the four organizational levels are linked by the strategy process in greater detail in Part I. The roles of top management are to tailor this process to suit the context of the firm and to ensure that the four systems that constitute the process are well aligned with each other.

Emphasizing Tailormaking and Alignment

Tailormaking and alignment are two important themes of this book. A tailormade management system is one that is specifically designed to meet the contextual pressures that confront an organizational unit. Many of the ills of management systems in the past may be attributed to their failure to adapt to the changing needs of the corporation and its subunits.

Strategic planning, in particular, has been criticized in both the business and the academic press for being bureaucratic, for stifling creativity, and for causing analytic detachment among senior managers.[12] Although there is some truth to this criticism, what is offered as an alternative is also clearly unworkable in a multibusiness firm. Managing by "wandering about" or aping Japanese management practices is not a valid prescription. The former ignores, for example, the diversity that has to be coped with by top management, and the latter assumes that the informal aspects of the administrative context on which the Japanese seem to rely so heavily can easily be replicated in Western firms. Also, although strategy must indeed emerge through trial and error in some business contexts, it can be planned in others. What is therefore required is a strategy process that varies in its formality depending on the business context.

A related issue is the compartmentalized view of planning that still seems to exist in many firms,[13] whose strategy processes are consequently misaligned. It is not uncommon to have a firm's strategic planning system designed and managed by the strategic planner; its monitoring, control, and learning system by the controller; and its incentives and staffing systems by the human resource manager—in isolation from each other.

We argue that unless the close interdependence between a firm's management systems is recognized by its top management and other senior line and staff managers, the firm's performance will suffer. After all, strategy is shaped not only by the strategic planning system but also by the other three systems. The personal profiles of a firm's strategists, how their performance is measured and evaluated, and how they are rewarded are important determinants of the strategic alternatives that they will consider. Alignment describes how well the four systems reinforce each other (see Figure I-1).

We discuss in Part II how the strategy process can be tailored and aligned to suit the context of a business unit. In Part III, we focus on the distinct problems of tailormaking and alignment in multinational businesses and strategic alliances. In Part IV, we discuss how the strategy process can be tailored to suit different corporate contexts.

Managing Change and Adaptation

Tailormaking and alignment are important concepts, but they can breed inertia. As the environment of a firm changes, its strategies should change. Strategies also can change because of alterations in a firm's resources or simply because of a new top management vision. At some point in this change trajectory, the strategy process in use by the firm stops being useful and can become a hinderance. Changing the strategy process to facilitate the continuous strategic adaptation of a firm is another important theme that is addressed in this book. We examine in Part IV how the process can get entrenched and explore some useful features that can help the process become self-adapting.

ORGANIZATION OF THE BOOK

In Part I, we introduce the strategy process perspective. We provide in Chapter 1 a conceptual framework for understanding the strategy process, and discuss in Chapter 2 the critical areas in which top management intervention can be helpful to the process.

In Part II, we focus entirely on how the strategy process can be designed to suit the context of a business unit. In Chapter 3, we provide a classification scheme to distinguish between various business contexts and specify a strategic planning system that is appropriate to each. Then in Chapter 4, we elaborate the design of a monitoring, control, and learning system to suit each of these contexts. Finally in Chapter 5, we discuss how the incentives and staffing systems can be aligned with the other two systems.

In Part III, we focus on special business contexts. Chapter 6 deals with some of the distinct challenges in designing a strategy process for a multinational business. In Chapter 7, we describe a process for instituting and maintaining strategic alliances with other organizations.

In Part IV, we shift the discussion to the corporate level. In Chapter 8, we discuss various approaches to sharing responsibilities for business strategies with divisional general managers. Then in Chapter 9, we deal with the fundamental challenge of ensuring the relevance of the strategy process over time, even as the context of a firm changes.

The Appendix provides a brief overview of some of the common analytical approaches that are available for evaluating both business and corporate strategies.

A NOTE TO OUR READERS

This book is intended primarily for graduate students in strategic management who wish to understand how the strategy process is managed in successful multibusiness firms. In addition, the book should be of interest to senior line and staff managers within multibusiness firms who seek a framework for evaluating the strategy process used by their firms.

The book offers a set of complex case studies, several of them developed especially for it. Although the cases are segregated in certain parts of the book to highlight concepts that are advanced in those parts, they are far richer than what any single conceptual scheme can capture. It is our hope that the reader will move back and forth between the text and the case materials in various parts of the book and thus acquire a richer appreciation of how the strategy process can be managed in a multibusiness firm. The cases cover a wide range of firms that vary in size and nationality of ownership.

In Part I we present three cases. The first, Scandinavian Airlines System, describes how a clear corporate vision and a matching organizational context helped the airline come up with innovative strategies to improve its performance dramatically. The next case, on the U.S. Nuclear Regulatory Commission, illustrates the importance of managing the key stakeholders of an organization in order to bring about strategic change. The third case in Part I describes the challenges faced by a growing high-technology firm, Infotron Systems Corporation, in establishing an organizational context in which strategic decisions can be delegated by the Chief Executive Officer to other managers within the firm.

Part II of the book contains four cases. The case on the Vick International Division provides a rich description of the strategic planning and control system used by the Latin America/Far East (LA/FE) division of Richardson-Merrell and how its design was influenced by the business context of the firm. The next case, on Texas Instruments' computer-assisted planning system (MODPLAN), provides yet another detailed description of a planning system and how it can be linked to a firm's information system. The other two cases in this part provide an excellent description of the challenges faced by Becton Dickinson in designing a monitoring, control, and learning system; an incentives system; and a staffing system to support the business strategies that top management had chosen for the various business units of the firm.

Part III contains three cases. The case on Elkem describes the challenges faced by this Norwegian multinational firm in integrating its worldwide operations that, for reasons of resource and energy availability, had to be dispersed. The next case, on Procter & Gamble, discusses that company's struggle in moving its strategy in Europe from a national to a transnational focus. Finally, the case on the

FiatGeotech-Hitachi strategic alliance provides the backdrop to discuss how alliances of this type can be managed.

The six cases in Part IV illustrate the four options that are available to a multibusiness firm for managing its corporate strategy: the central planning process at the ITT Corporation under Harold Geneen, the corporate portfolio management process at the Norton Company under Robert Cushman, the divisional portfolio management process at the Dexter Corporation under Worth Loomis, and the transition from a self-renewal process at Texas Instruments after Pat Haggerty's retirement. These cases also provide a good description of how various analytical aids like the PIMS model and value-based planning and control are used in multibusiness firms. The challenges in adapting the strategy process used by a firm to its changing context are described in the cases on the ITT Corporation, Texas Instruments, and Alfa-Laval.

The book is partial to large, for-profit, manufacturing organizations. It offers only one case on a not-for-profit organization (Case 2 on the U.S. Nuclear Regulatory Commission) and one case on a service sector firm (Case 1 on the Scandinavian Airlines System). Nevertheless, the text portion of the book can be usefully extended to these other organizational settings as well.

NOTES

1. For an excellent discussion of these techniques, see A. C. Hax and N. S. Majluf, *Strategic Management: An Integrative Perspective* (Englewood Cliffs, NJ: Prentice Hall, 1984), 108–240.

2. For a discussion on how the administrative context of a multibusiness firm can force business managers to hold back bad news, see R. G. Hamermesh, "Responding to Divisional Profit Crises," *Harvard Business Review* 55 (Mar.–Apr. 1977): 124–130. For a model that explains how such behavior can trigger a vicious cycle of events that further distorts the information that is made available to top management, see C. Argyris, "Double-Loop Learning in Organizations," *Harvard Business Review* 55 (Sept.–Oct. 1977): 115–125.

3. See C. K. Prahalad and Y. Doz, *The Multinational Mission: Balancing Local Demands and Global Vision* (New York: Free Press, 1987).

4. This responsibility of top management can be modeled as an agency problem. For example, see M. Jensen and W. Meckling, "Theory of the Firm: Managerial Behavior, Agency Costs, and Ownership Structure," *Journal of Financial Economics* 3 (1976): 305–360. Top management, the principal, must structure a context within which the business manager, the agent, can be made to behave in a manner consistent with management's goals. The strategy process is an important mechanism for minimizing the problems of both moral hazard and adverse selection in such a principal/agent relationship.

5. See H. A. Simon, *Administrative Behavior* (New York: Macmillan, 1945). This author was one of the first to make this important distinction between making a decision and managing the premises for a decision.

6. For a rich description of the context-setting role of senior managers, see J. L. Bower, *Managing the Resource Allocation Process* (Boston: Harvard Business School, 1968). For a description of the evolution of such a context-setting role, see F. W. Gluck, S. P. Kaufman, and A. S. Walleck, "The Four Phases of Strategic Management," *The Journal of Business Strategy* 2 (Winter 1982): 9–21.

7. See H. Mintzberg, *The Structuring of Organizations* (Englewood Cliffs, NJ: Prentice-Hall, 1979). Of the six structural configurations described by Mintzberg, a multibusiness firm typically uses the divisionalized form, although its subunits may exhibit some of the other configurations.

8. This association has been empirically demonstrated by many studies. For theoretical justifications, see the following: A. Chandler, *Strategy and Structure* (Cambridge, MA: MIT Press, 1962); and O. E. Williamson, *Markets and Hierarchies* (New York: Free Press, 1975).

9. For example, see the following: M. Beer et al., *Managing Human Assets* (New York: Free Press, 1984); T. E. Deal and A. A. Kennedy, *Corporate Culture* (Reading, MA: Addison-Wesley, 1982); and E. H. Schein, *Organizational Culture and Leadership* (San Francisco: Jossey-Bass, 1985).

10. The list of companies that we studied includes Alfa-Laval, ARA Services, Becton Dickinson, Corning Glass, Cummings Engine, Dexter, Digital Equipment, Dupont, EG&G, Elkem, Fiat, General Motors, General Electric, Hewlett Packard, Honeywell, IBM, Infotron, ITT, IU International, Mead, Norton, P&G, Rohm & Haas, SAS, Siam Cement, Thomson, Thorn-EMI, and Unilever.

11. This alternate view of the strategy process has been articulated by the following: H. Mintzberg and J. A. Waters, "On Strategies, Deliberate and Emergent," *Strategic Management Journal* 6 (1985): 257–272; and J. B. Quinn, *Strategies for Change: Logical Incrementalism* (Homewood, IL: Richard D. Irwin, 1980).

12. For a sampling of this critique in the business press, see the following: "The New Breed of Strategic Planner," *Business Week* (Sept. 17, 1984): 62–67; and T. J. Peters and R. H. Waterman, *In Search of Excellence* (New York: Harper and Row, 1982). For examples of the criticism in academia, see the following: Mintzberg and Waters, "Of Strategies"; R. H. Hayes and W. J. Abernathy, "Managing Our Way to Economic Decline," *Harvard Business Review* 58 (July–Aug. 1980): 67–77; R. Hayes, "Strategic Planning: Forward in Reverse?" *Harvard Business Review* 85 (Nov.–Dec. 1985): 111–119; R. T. Lenz and M. Lyles, "Paralysis by Analysis: Is Your Planning System Becoming Too Rational?" *Long Range Planning* 18 (Aug. 1985): 64–72; H. Mintzberg, "What Is Planning Anyway?" *Strategic Management Journal* 2 (July–Sept. 1981): 319–324; and H. Mintzberg, J. P. Brunet, and J. Waters, "Does Planning Impede Strategic Thinking? The Strategy of Air Canada 1937–1976," in *Advances in Strategic Management* 4 (Greenwich, CT: JAI Press, 1986), 3–41.

13. See J. B. Quinn, H. Mintzberg, and R. M. James, *The Strategy Process* (Englewood Cliffs, NJ: Prentice Hall, 1988).

REFERENCES

Bowman, E. H., "Concerns of the CEO," *Human Resources Management* 25 (Summer 1986): 267–285.

Gordon, T. J., and O. Helmer, "Report on Long-Range Forecasting Study" (Paper P-2982, Rand Corporation in Santa Monica, CA, Sept. 1964).

Huff, A. S., "A Review of Strategic Process Research," *Journal of Management* 13 (Summer 1987): 211–236.

Lorange, P., "Organization Structure and Process," in *Handbook of Business Strategy,* ed. W. D. Gruth (Boston: Warren, Gorham and Lamont, 1985), 1–31.

Mintzberg, H., "Organization Design: Fashion or Fit?" *Harvard Business Review* 59 (Jan.–Feb. 1981): 103–116.

Schwartz, H., and S. M. Davis, "Matching Corporate Culture and Business Strategy," *Organizational Dynamics* 10 (Summer 1981): 30–48.

Starbuck, W. H., "Organizations and their Environments," in *Handbook of Industrial and Organizational Psychology,* ed. M. D. Dunette (Chicago: Rand McNally, 1976), 1069–1124.

Waterman, R. H., Jr., "The Seven Elements of Strategic Fit," *The Journal of Business Strategy* 2 (Winter 1982): 69–73.

Chapter 1

A CONCEPTUAL FRAMEWORK

In this chapter, we present a framework for understanding the key elements of the strategy process.[1] We describe how the four systems associated with the process—planning; monitoring, control, and learning; incentives; and staffing—are related to each other. Also, we introduce some of the critical elements in these four systems, around which the process can be tailored to suit the context of a multibusiness firm. First we discuss the four levels in a firm's organizational hierarchy that are spanned by its strategy process; each of these levels is responsible for a distinct type of strategy. Then we describe the five important steps through which these strategies are formed and implemented. We conclude with a discussion of how the four organizational levels are linked through the strategic planning steps.

ORGANIZATIONAL LEVELS AND STRATEGY TYPES

Figure 1-1 is a simplified organizational chart of a typical multibusiness firm. This is a skeletal description of a divisional structure. As noted in the Introduction, firms pursuing a multibusiness strategy commonly are organized in this fashion. Each hierarchical level in the organizational chart is responsible for a distinct type of strategy.

The corporate level consists of the Chief Executive Officer (CEO) and his or her top management team. These executives are concerned with *corporate strategies*. They determine in which businesses the firm will compete and the relative emphasis that will be placed on each business in the firm's portfolio. By allocating strategic resources to the firm's businesses, top management ensures that the cumulative expected returns from these investments, after discounting for the associated risks, provide a satisfactory return to the firm's stockholders. When necessary, top management may seek acquisitions, mergers, alliances, and divestitures to strengthen the firm's business portfolio. The logic behind such restructur-

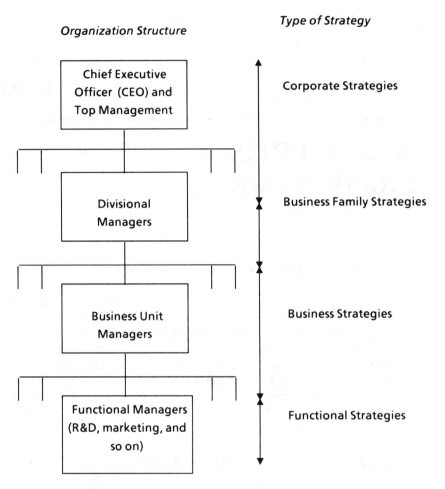

Figure 1-1   **Organizational Levels and Types of Strategies**

ing must be clearly signaled, however, to all of the firm's stakeholders. Internally this signalling sets the direction for the strategies that are pursued at lower levels in the organization, and externally it helps the firm's stakeholders evaluate the firm's actions better.[2]

The next level in the organization is the division. Divisional managers are responsible for *business family strategies*. A business family is a collection of businesses that have either a common mission or common customers or activities and therefore are housed organizationally within the same division.[3] There are important advantages to such an arrangement. For example, between its various business units, the division may be able to derive economies through joint marketing campaigns, common distribution facilities, shared brand names, shared sales force, common research, and joint manufacturing. Even if none of these economies is possible, a common mission can help business units learn from one another and thus contribute to the division's efficiency. The role of a division manager in shaping business family strategies can vary among multibusiness firms. In Chapter 8, we describe four such distinct roles.

The third level in the organization houses the firm's business unit managers, who are responsible for ensuring that their business units have profitable and defensible *business strategies.* A business unit incorporates a group of products/ services that share common customers and competitors, rely on common technologies, and have common success factors. In an ideal divisional structure, each business unit is self-contained in the functions that are required to support its strategy. However, it is more common that a business unit shares one or more functions with other business units within its division in order to achieve economies of scale. Occasionally the sharing of functional resources can extend beyond divisional lines. In Chapter 8, we describe such a matrixlike structure that is used by some multibusiness firms.

The fourth level in the organization represents the managers of the firm's functional departments: operations, marketing, sales, engineering, and so forth. These managers are responsible for the firm's *functional strategies.* The functional elements within an organization are critical to strategy making and implementation because most of the specialized resources of the firm rest within these departments. However, the primary role of functional managers is to lend support to and facilitate the implementation of business family and/or business unit strategies. Autonomous functional initiatives and freestanding functional plans must therefore be discouraged.

The strategy process used by a firm must make certain that the strategies pursued at all levels in the organization are consistent, with the high organizational levels influencing the strategies pursued at the lower levels. Corporate strategies, for example, should provide the umbrella under which business family strategies are formulated. Business strategies in turn should be shaped by business family strategies, and functional strategies must be consistent with the needs of business strategies.

STEPS IN THE STRATEGY PROCESS

In the previous section, we described the four distinctive types of strategies, each associated with a different organizational level. In this section, we describe the steps through which these strategies are conceived, detailed, and executed. There are five distinct steps in the strategy process (Figure 1-2). The first three steps involve the strategic planning system; the final two steps cover the role of the monitoring, control, and learning system and the incentives and staffing systems, respectively.

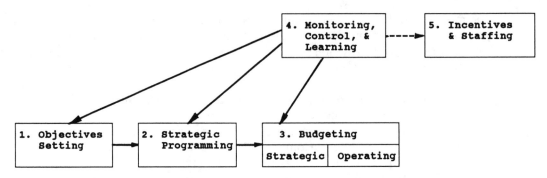

Figure 1-2   **The Five Steps in the Strategy Process**

The Strategic Planning System

The strategic planning system (Figure 1-3) facilitates the negotiation of strategic intent and the search for strategic alternatives, helps narrow these into an optimal choice, and details action plans and budgets for implementing the chosen strategy. It is important to note that the number of strategic alternatives that are considered in the objectives-setting step and how quickly these are narrowed in the subsequent planning steps are both critical elements in the design of a strategic planning system. Figure 1-3 illustrates two distinct profiles: The outer profile characterizes an adaptive planning system, and the inner-shaded profile characterizes an integrative planning system. The former is useful for new business development, and the latter is more appropriate for a mature business. We describe these two ideal types in greater detail in Chapter 3.

The purpose of the first step in the planning system, *objectives setting,* is to determine a strategic direction for the firm and each of its divisions and business units. Objectives setting calls for an open-ended reassessment of the firm's business environments and its strengths in dealing with these environments. At the conclusion of this step, there should be agreement at all levels of the organization on the goals that should be pursued and the strategies that will be needed to meet these goals. It is worth differentiating here between objectives and goals. Objectives refer to the strategic intent of the firm in the long run. An example of an objective would be General Electric's intent to be the primary contender in the markets in which it competes. Goals, on the other hand, are more specific statements of the achievements targeted for certain deadlines—goals can be accomplished, and when that happens the firm moves closer to meeting its objectives. Objectives represent a more enduring challenge.

The second step, *strategic programming,* develops the strategies that were identified in the first step and defines the cross-functional programs that will be needed to implement the chosen strategies. Cross-functional cooperation is essential to this step. At the end of the strategic programming step a long-term financial plan is drawn for the firm as a whole and each of its divisions, business units, and

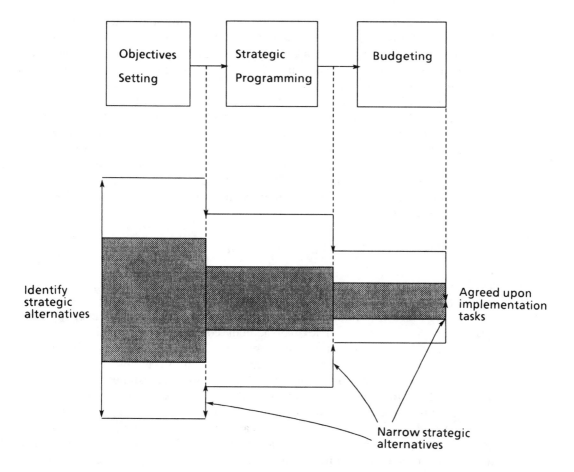

Figure 1-3   **The Strategic Planning System**

functions. On top of the financial projections from existing operations, the long-term financial plan overlays both the expenditures and revenues associated with the approved strategic programs of an organizational unit. The time horizon for these financial plans is chosen to cover the typical lead times that are required to implement the firm's strategic programs. A five-year financial plan is, however, very common. The purpose of the five-year financial plan is to ensure that the approved strategic programs can be funded through either the firm's internally generated resources or externally financed resources.

The third step, *budgeting,* defines both the strategic and operating budgets of the firm. The strategic budget helps identify the contributions that the firm's functional departments, business units, and divisions will be expected to make in a given fiscal year in support of the firm's approved strategic programs. It incorporates new product/market initiatives. The operating budget, on the other hand, provides resources to functional departments, business units, and divisions so that they can sustain their existing momentum. It is based on projected short-term activity levels, given past trends. Failure to meet the operating budget will hurt the firm's short-term performance, whereas failure to meet the strategic budget will compromise the firm's future. Clearly performance against both budgets is critical. Strong operating performance helps generate resources internally for funding a firm's strategic budget, and strong performance against the strategic budget creates the potential for strong operating performance in future years. We have more to say on these two budgets in Chapter 4.

The Monitoring, Control, and Learning System

The fourth step in the strategy process (see Figure 1-2) is *monitoring, control, and learning.* The monitoring, control, and learning system, as envisaged here, goes beyond the more traditional management control system that has been well described in the literature.[4] The management control system monitors progress against operating budgets; the system proposed here, on the other hand, also monitors progress against strategic budgets, strategic programs, and objectives. Here the emphasis is not on output but on meeting key milestones in the strategic budget and on adhering to planned spending schedules. Strategic programs, like strategic budgets, are monitored for the milestones reached and for adherence to spending schedules. In addition, the key assumptions underlying these programs are validated periodically. As a natural extension to this validation process, even the agreed-on goals at various levels are reassessed in the light of changes to the resources of the firm and its business environment. We discuss the learning aspects of this system in detail in Chapter 4.

The Incentives and Staffing Systems

The fifth and final step in the strategy process is *incentives and staffing.* One part of this is the award of incentives as contracted to the firm's managers. If the incentives system is perceived to have failed in inducing the desired performance, redesigning the incentives system and reassessing the staffing of key managerial positions are considered at this step. As we noted in the Introduction, goal incongruence and information asymmetry are two troublesome problems for a multibusiness firm. Well-designed strategic planning and control systems can solve these problems partially; the rest has to be dealt with through the use of tailor-made incentives and the careful staffing of the various managerial positions. We have more to say about these two systems in Chapter 5.

LINKING ORGANIZATIONAL LEVELS AND STEPS IN STRATEGIC PLANNING

An effective strategy process must allow for interactions between the organizational levels and iterations between the process' steps. Figure 1-4 describes some of these interactions and iterations in the strategic planning steps. The formal interactions in the process are shown in the figure by the solid line that weaves up and down through the organizational levels and across the three steps. The informal interactions that complement the formal interactions are shown by dotted loops. The

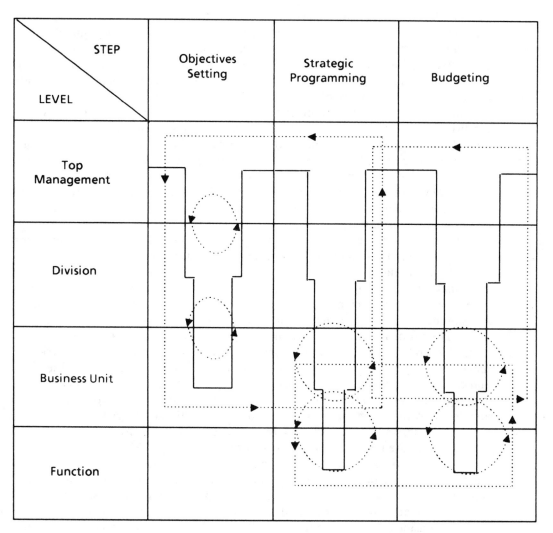

Figure 1-4   **Interactions and Iterations in the Strategy Process**

figure also shows some dotted boxes that represent the iterations that are necessary between the strategy-making and strategy implementation steps of the process. Our purpose here is to describe the typical links between levels and steps in the strategy process, but the nature of the interactions and iterations in the strategy process can vary from firm to firm. In fact, as we show in the following chapters, an important approach to tailoring the strategy process is through influencing the interactions and iterations within it.

Objectives Setting

The first formal step of the strategy process (see Figure 1-4) commences soon after top management reaffirms or modifies the firm's objectives at the beginning of each fiscal year. Embedded in these objectives should be the vision of the chief executive officer (CEO) and his or her top management team. Top management's vision helps specify what will make the firm great. An elaboration of this vision can be done through a formal statement of objectives. However, it is not the formality of a firm's objectives but rather the excitement and challenge that top management's vision can bring to a firm's managers that is important to the strategy process.

Along with its communication of corporate objectives, top management must provide a forecast on key environmental factors. Assumptions on exchange rates, inflation, and other economic factors—as well as projections on the political risks associated with each country—are best compiled centrally so as to ensure objectivity and consistency. These objectives and forecasts are then discussed with a firm's divisional and business unit managers.

Once the corporate objectives are decided, top management negotiates, for each division and business unit in the firm, goals that are consistent with these objectives. The nature of these negotiations can vary. In some firms, top management may wish to set goals in a top-down fashion; in others, it may invite subordinate managers to participate in the goal-setting process. Managers are encouraged to examine new strategies and modify existing ones in order to accomplish their goals. The proposed strategies are approved at each higher level in the organizational hierarchy, then eventually by top management. Top management tries to make certain that the strategies as proposed are consistent with the firm's objectives and can be supported with the resources available to the firm. Modifications, where necessary, are made to the objectives, goals, and strategies in order to bring them in alignment. Another important outcome of the objectives-setting step is to build a common understanding across the firm's managerial hierarchy of the goals and strategies that are intended for each organizational unit.

The objectives-setting step in Figure 1-4 does not include the functional departments. As we observed earlier, the primary role of these departments is a supporting one. They do not have a profit or growth responsibility, and their goals cannot be decided until the second step, when strategic programs in support of approved business unit goals begin to be formed. It is not uncommon, however, for key functional managers to be invited to participate in the objectives-setting step either as experts in a corporate task force or, more informally, as participants in the deliberations that are held at the business unit level.

It is important that divisional proposals be evaluated on an overall basis as elements of a corporate portfolio and not reviewed in a sequential mode. In the latter case, the resulting overall balance in the corporate portfolio would be more or less incidental, representing the accumulated sum of individual approvals. It makes little sense to attempt to judge in isolation whether a particular business family or business strategy is attractive to the corporate portfolio. That will depend on a strategy's fit with the rest of the portfolio and on the competing investment opportunities available to the firm in its business portfolio.

Various business portfolio matrices (see the Appendix at the end of the book) can be used for this purpose. Although the relevance of these matrices for formulating business and corporate strategies has been justifiably criticized, the matrices are invaluable aids for auditing a firm's business portfolio. Two case studies in this book illustrate such a use: The top management of Alfa-Laval (see Case 16) found the BCG growth-share matrix useful for framing the strategic challenges confronting it; similarly the Arthur D. Little matrix was the one that alerted Becton Dickinson's (see Case 6) top management to the fact that the company's financial problems were directly attributable to its deteriorating business portfolio.

The use of business portfolio matrices to audit a company's corporate strategy may be likened to an x-ray. If the matrices reveal that the company is healthy, the audit needs to be done only once a year, usually during the objectives-setting step. On the other hand, if the firm is in a turnaround mode, more frequent audits may help top management measure its accomplishments and recognize the unmet challenges.

Strategic Programming

This second step in the process has two purposes: (1) to forge an agreement between divisional, business unit, and functional managers on the strategic programs that have to be implemented over the next few years and (2) to deepen the involvement of functional managers in developing the strategies that were tentatively selected in the first step.

The strategic programming step begins with a communication from top management about the goals and strategies that were finally approved for the firm's divisions and business units. The divisional manager then invites his or her business unit and functional managers to identify program alternatives in support of the approved goals and strategies. Examples of strategic programs include increasing market share for an existing product, introducing a new product, and launching a joint marketing campaign for a family of divisional products. As in these examples, a strategic program typically requires the cooperation of multiple functional departments.

However, the functional specialties within a firm often represent different professional cultures that do not necessarily blend easily. Further, day-to-day operating tasks can be so demanding that the functional managers may simply find it difficult to participate in the time-consuming cross-functional teamwork. A key challenge for both divisional and business managers is to bring about this interaction.

The proposed strategic programs travel up the hierarchy for approval at each level. At the division level, the programs are evaluated not only for how well they support the approved strategies but also for how they promote synergies within the firm. Synergies can come from two sources: through economies of scale and/or economies of scope.[5] The creation of synergies based on economies of scale calls for a sharing of common functional activities—such as research and development (R&D), raw materials procurement, production, and distribution—so as to spread over a larger volume the overhead costs associated with these functions. The creation of economies of scope, on the other hand, requires a common approach to the market. Examples of such an approach include the development of a common trademark, the development of products/services that have a complementary appeal to a customer group, and the ability to offer a common regional service organization for the firm's diverse businesses.

At the corporate level, the proposed strategic programs provide an estimate of the resources that will be required to support the divisional and business unit goals. These goals, as well as their supporting strategies, are once again reassessed; and where needed, modifications are sought in the proposed strategic programs. As noted earlier, a long-term financial plan is drawn at this stage for the firm as a whole and each of its organizational units. The approved strategic programs are communicated to the divisions, business units, and functional departments at the beginning of the budgeting cycle.

Budgeting

When top management decides on the strategic programs that the firm should pursue, it has de facto allocated all of the firm's human, technological, and financial resources that are available for internal development. This allocation influences the strategic budgets that may be requested at each level in the organizational hierarchy.

Figure 1-5 describes how the strategic programs and the strategic budgets of a firm are linked. The solid horizontal arrows indicate strategic programs. The functional departments that are required to support a strategic program are indicated by circles. The broken vertical lines indicate the demands placed on a functional department by all of the firm's strategic programs. It is important to note that these are the demands placed on a functional department by currently approved strategic programs. It is unlikely that all these programs will be implemented in a given year. Budgeting is the step during which business unit managers negotiate with functional managers the contributions that they will make in any given budget year to the various programs associated with their business units. With reference to Figure 1-5, the strategic budget for a business unit consists of a portion of $F_{R\&D}$, $F_{PRODUCTION}$, F_{SALES}, and so on that is planned to be expended in a given budget year.

The strategic budgets, together with the operating budgets of the various organizational units, are consolidated and sent up for top management approval.

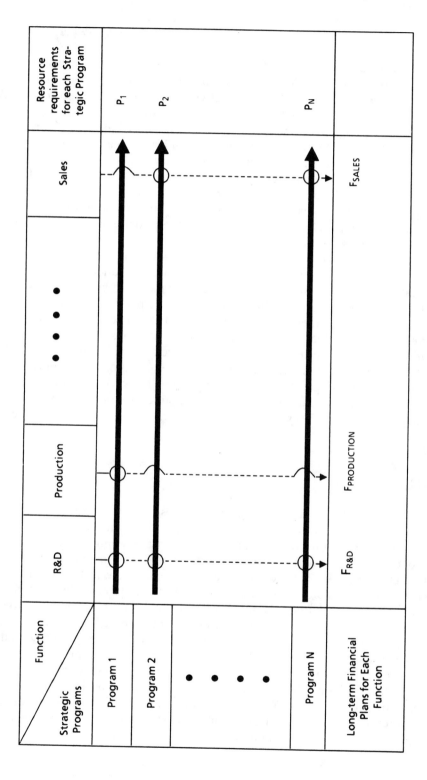

Figure 1-5 **Cross-functional Teams for Strategic Programming**

<u>NOTE</u>: *The annual strategic budget for each business unit is arrived at by cumulating the functional expenses and investments associated with the strategic programs of the business unit in that budget year.*

11

As we show in Chapter 4, it is prudent practice, however, to retain the identity of the two budgets in the consolidated budget presented to top management; otherwise, funds allocated to strategic budget activities risk being diverted to provide supplementary finance for activities in the operating budget.

When top management finally approves the budgets of the various organizational units, before the start of a new budget year, it brings to a close what can be a year-long journey through the three steps of the strategy-making subprocess. The strategy implementation subprocess is then set into motion. Even though the two subprocesses are described sequentially here, it is important to mention that even as the budget for a given year is being formed, the one for the prior year will be under implementation. Midcourse corrections to the prior year's budget can have an impact on the formulation of the current budget.

If the actual accomplishments fall short of the strategic budget, in particular, the negative variance may suggest that the firm's managers failed to implement its chosen strategy efficiently. But, as we describe in Chapter 4, it can also suggest that the strategic programs that drive this budget may have been ill conceived or even that the goals underlying these programs may have been specified incorrectly. The monitoring, control, and learning system provides continuous information on both the appropriateness of a strategic budget and the efficiency with which the budget is implemented. This information, based on the implementation of the prior year's strategic budget, can trigger another set of iterations between the three strategy-making steps calling into question the goals and strategies on which the current year's budget are based. These iterations are shown by the dotted rectangles in Figure 1-4.

SUMMARY

In this chapter, we described how the strategy process in a multibusiness firm spans four organizational levels—corporate, divisional, business unit, and functional—and covers five steps—objectives setting; strategic programming; budgeting; monitoring, control, and learning; and incentives and staffing. By managing the formal and informal interactions between managers at each of these levels, top management can ensure that the objectives, goals, and strategies pursued by the firm are consistent and widely shared. By managing the iterations between the process steps, it can ensure that the chosen strategies are implemented efficiently and are validated continuously for their relevance. The conceptual framework presented in this chapter is meant to introduce the key elements in the design of a strategy process. Each of these will be elaborated in the following chapters. Parts II and III discuss how the process can be tailored to suit the context of a business unit. In Part IV, we examine the distinct arrangements that multibusiness firms use, depending on their contexts, for sharing the responsibilities in strategy making and implementation between the corporate and divisional levels of an organization.

NOTES

1. This framework has been adapted from R. F. Vancil and P. Lorange, "Strategic Planning in Diversified Companies," *Harvard Business Review* 53 (Jan.–Feb. 1975): 81–90. The three levels and three steps framework first proposed by Vancil and Lorange was subsequently elaborated by P. Lorange, *Corporate Planning: An Executive Viewpoint* (Englewood Cliffs, NJ: Prentice Hall, 1980), into a three levels and five steps framework. The framework proposed here is a further extension of his 1980 framework. Others who have offered frameworks for strategic planning include: R. N. Anthony, *Planning and Control Systems: A Framework for Analysis* (Boston: Harvard Business School, 1965); and J. C. Camillus, *Strategic Planning and Management Control: Systems for Survival and Success* (Lexington, MA: D. C. Heath, 1986).

2. For an elaboration, see P. Harvey-Jones, *Making It Happen* (London: Collins, 1988).

3. For a summary of value-chain analysis, a technique that helps identify synergies across a division's businesses, see the Appendix to the book and also M. E. Porter, *Competitive Advantage* (New York: Free Press, 1985): 33–61.

4. For example, see R. Anthony and J. Dearden, *Management Control Systems* (Homewood, IL: Richard D. Irwin, 1980).

5. The distinction between economies of scale and economies of scope is made in W. J. Baumol, J. C. Panzar, and R. D. Willig, *Contestable Markets and the Theory of Industry Structure* (New York: Harcourt Brace Jovanovich, 1982).

REFERENCES

Camillus, J. C., "Evaluating the Benefits of Formal Planning," *Long Range Planning* 8 (June 1975): 33–40.

Gage, G. H., "On Acceptance of Strategic Planning Systems," in *Implementation of Strategic Planning,* ed. P. Lorange (Englewood Cliffs, NJ: Prentice-Hall, 1982), 171–182.

Cohen, M. D., and J. P. Olsen, "A Garbage Can Model of Organizational Choice," *Administrative Science Quarterly* 17 (1972): 1–25.

Frederickson, J. W., "The Strategic Decision Process and Organizational Structure," *Academy of Management Review* 8 (1983): 565–575.

Gluck, F. W., S. P. Kaufman, and A. S. Walleck, "The Four Phases of Strategic Management," *The Journal of Business Strategy* 2 (Winter 1982): 9–21.

Gray, D. H. "Uses and Misuses of Strategic Planning," *Harvard Business Review* 64 (Jan.–Feb. 1986): 89–97.

Hayes, R. H., "Why Strategic Planning Goes Awry," *New York Times* (Apr. 20, 1986): 2F.

Henderson, B. D., "The Product Portfolio," in *Perspectives* (Boston: Boston Consulting Group, 1970).

Miles, R. H., "Findings and Implications of Organizational Life Cycle Research: A Commencement," in *The Organizational Life Cycle,* ed. J. R. Kimberly and R. H. Miles (New York: Jossey-Bass, 1980), 430–450.

Mintzberg, H., "Patterns in Strategy Formation," *Management Science* 24 (May 1978): 934–948.

———, and J. A. Waters, "Of Strategies, Deliberate and Emergent," *Strategic Management Journal* 6 (July–Sep. 1985): 257–272.

Nutt, P. C., "Types of Organizational Decision Processes," *Administrative Science Quarterly* 29 (1984): 414–450.

Pascale, R. T., "Perspectives on Strategy: The Real Story Behind Honda's Success," *California Management Review* 26 (Spring 1984): 47–72.

———, "Our Curious Addiction to Corporate Grand Strategy," *Fortune* (Jan. 25, 1982): 115–116.

Quinn, J. B., "Strategic Goals: Process and Politics," *Sloan Management Review* 19 (Fall 1977): 21–37.

Ramanujam, V., N. Venkatraman, and J. C. Camillus, "Multiobjective Assessment of Strategic Planning Effectiveness: A Discriminant Analysis Approach," *Academy of Management Journal* 29 (June 1986): 347–372.

Weick, K. E., "Substitutes for Corporate Strategy," in *The Competitive Challenge: Strategies for Industrial Innovation and Renewal,* ed. D. J. Teece (Cambridge, MA: Ballinger, 1987), 221–234.

Chapter 2

MAKING THE PROCESS WORK

An important task for top management is to adapt the strategy process outlined in the previous chapter to the context of the firm. As noted in the Introduction, our primary focus is on this task. We examine in the next three parts of the book various aspects of tailoring the strategy process. However, in this chapter we address the critical support that top management must provide in the following six areas, regardless of the firm's context, to make the strategy process work well:

1. Providing a corporate vision
2. Satisfying all stakeholders
3. Nurturing strategic thinking
4. Encouraging organizational learning
5. Promoting intrafirm cooperation
6. Revitalizing the process

PROVIDING A CORPORATE VISION

A corporate vision articulates top management's strategic intent. It focuses the attention of the firm's managers and channels their energies toward a common purpose.[1] For example, Jan Carlzon's vision for Scandinavian Airlines System (SAS) as "the businessman's airline" (see Case 1) was a powerful catalyst for transforming that firm into a competitive and profitable airline.[2] A corporate vision also specifies the intrinsic values of the firm. These values may not guide strategy directly, but they circumscribe the space within which strategic decisions can be made and specify the means that its managers may use in pursuit of their goals. In Alfa-Laval (see Case 16), for example, top management expected subordinate managers to adhere to the core values of the firm, which were published for convenience in a little blue book. The corporate vision must be reaffirmed (or redefined if necessary) early in the objectives-setting step and updated for any changes throughout the strategy process.

Because this vision is expected to be more enduring than the firm's objectives and goals, it should normally be revised very infrequently.

The competitive successes of many firms, such as Canon against Xerox and Komatsu against Caterpillar, have been directly attributed to the clarity of their top management's strategic intent: "Beat the industry leader."[3] It may not always be easy to provide a clear vision at the corporate level, especially when the firm is highly diversified or when it is not playing catchup to an industry leader. However, even a broad statement of strategic intent can give the firm a sense of identity, define a set of challenges for its businesses, and guide its resource allocation. An example of such a statement is Jack Welch's vision of General Electric (GE) as a primary contender (number one or two in market share) in the world in all of its businesses. This vision has guided the company's acquisition and divestiture decisions, as well as its internal resource allocation decisions.[4]

A corporate vision not merely is a dream or ambition but also is a concise description of the direction in which a firm should head in order to survive and prosper. It therefore has to be shaped in part by a careful analysis of the opportunities and threats that are likely to confront the firm in the future and by a projection of the firm's strengths for dealing with these changes. However, the purpose of such an analysis is to make certain that the corporate vision is challenging without being impossible and not to specify the means of fulfilling this vision. Discovering alternate means of fulfilling the corporate vision is indeed a challenge that must be left for the organization to fulfill.

An analytical approach that is useful to visioning is scenario analysis. It represents a conscious effort by the firm's top management, together with outside experts as needed, to articulate alternative business scenarios for each set of environmental conditions that is likely to confront the firm. Royal Dutch Shell is one among several leading companies that have used scenario analysis for developing a sharper corporate vision.[5] Pierre Wack, a senior Shell executive, points out that the primary benefit from scenario analysis is not action but understanding; a business scenario is not a strategy but a helping aid in setting a firm's direction.

SATISFYING ALL STAKEHOLDERS

In many Western countries, a primary responsibility of top management in public corporations is to create value for the firm's stockholders.[6] When translating its vision into objectives, goals, and strategic programs through the first two steps of the strategy process, top management must ensure that the projected returns from the planned investments will be satisfactory to the firm's stockholders.[7] It must further follow these investments through implementation and confirm that the promised values are realized for the stockholders.

Value-based planning[8] is one approach that is available to top management. We describe this approach in the Appendix at the end of the book. In essence, the technique tries to quantify the impact on shareholder wealth of every major strategic move that is made by the firm. The importance of value-based planning in evaluating a merger, an acquisition, or a divestiture is widely recognized.[9] Some companies, such as Dexter Corporation (see Cases 13 and 14), have sought to extend that approach to an ongoing valuation of the firm's businesses. Although such a valuation is not very accurate (is "naïve," as the company itself calls it), it provides a useful benchmark for top management to judge the performance of its various businesses from a stockholder's perspective.

Enhancing the wealth of stockholders may sometimes be inconsistent with the needs of the firm's other stakeholders. Every firm engages in transactions with groups and individuals who can affect, or are affected by, the achievement of its goals. These groups and individuals are called stakeholders.[10] Top management must be sensitive to the conflicting demands of stakeholders and be skilled at balancing these demands. After all, it needs the cooperation of all of the firm's stakeholders and not merely its stockholders.[11] The study of the U.S. Nuclear Regulatory Commission (see Case 2) describes how top management's insensitivity to an organization's stakeholders can disrupt the implementation of its strategies.

Top management should from time to time examine its assumptions about a firm's stakeholders and help modify the firm's strategies, programs, and budgets where necessary (Figure 2-1).[12]

The first step in stakeholder management is to map a firm's stakeholders. This changing map must be understood by top management before it can formulate objectives for the firm. The next step is to understand the power and stake of the individual stakeholders and their impact on a firm's strategic programs. There can be a variety of expectations even among a seemingly homogeneous stakeholder group. For example, even among stockholders there can be different stakes. Top management must be aligned with the most powerful stockholder group. It must also recognize the multiple roles that a stakeholder can play. For example, the union representing an organization's employees may also be a stockholder (through the investment of its pension funds). Furthermore, different stakeholders of an organization can at times act in concert. The coalition between church groups and consumer groups to challenge Nestlé on its infant formula marketing strategy in Third World countries is a good illustration of how stakeholders can combine two or more power bases to challenge an organization.[13] In the strategic programming phase, either specific action plans must be drawn to deal with important stakeholder concerns or business plans must be modified to placate the stakeholders. The choice of action is obviously a function of the power of a firm's stakeholders.

The final step in managing stakeholders is to ensure that the budget of a business unit explicitly provides funds for stakeholder management activities. It is desirable to have the active involvement of business unit and functional managers in managing stakeholders. Although the public affairs, regulatory affairs, and consumer affairs experts in a firm can provide invaluable advice on dealing with specific stakeholders and their problems, business unit and functional managers are the ones who interact with stakeholders on a regular basis. They have the opportunity to spot stakeholder concerns early and so to prevent these concerns from hardening

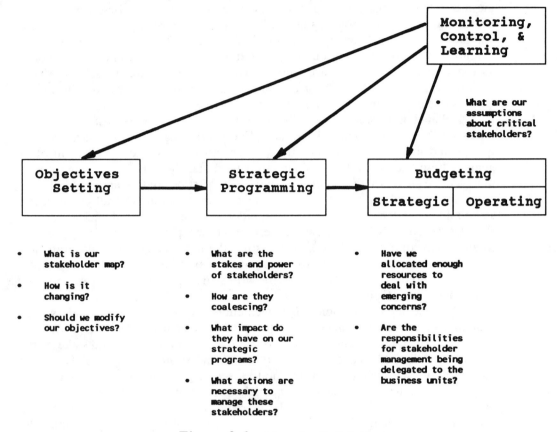

Figure 2-1   Managing Stakeholders

into positions hostile to the firm. However, these managers are unlikely to expend any resources on a stakeholder issue unless they have a separate budget for it and are monitored and rewarded for actions in this area.[14]

NURTURING STRATEGIC THINKING

Another important challenge for top management is to guarantee that strategic thinking remains fresh at all levels of the organization. Divisions and business units that have developed successful strategies in the past are especially prone to complacence. There is often a tendency among managers of these organizational units to become inward-focused in their thinking and to extrapolate their strategies from past actions rather than to shape these strategies based on changing environmental realities. And yet it is unlikely that top management can challenge the strategies proposed by their subordinate managers based on first-hand knowledge of their businesses. As we noted in the Introduction, information asymmetry is a serious problem in a multibusiness firm. What top management can resort to, however, is "strategic questioning"—a term used by Frank Carey, the ex-CEO of IBM.[15]

Strategic questioning is the process through which top management can persuade subordinate managers to consider additional alternatives without specifying any of them. Several of the analytical techniques that are described in the Appendix at the end of the book can be very helpful in this regard. For example, based on the data submitted in the business plan, top management can question the proposed strategy for its internal consistency or for its ability to withstand various competitive pressures. It also can challenge the strategy based on the position of a business on one of the analytical matrices popularized by management consultants or based on empirical models, such as the PIMS model. For example, Norton's president, Robert Cushman (see Case 12), challenged the strategy of modest-growth proposed by his manager for the coated abrasives business, with a suggestion of modest-harvest using the PIMS model and divest using the BCG growth-share matrix. The motivation behind such a challenge is not to second-guess the business unit manager but to force him or her to explore several alternatives before recommending a strategy.

In some firms, business strategies are challenged on a routine basis not only by top management but also by the peers of business unit managers. Two distinct approaches—dialectic inquiry and devil's advocacy—are the formal methods used for this purpose.[16] In the former approach, also called the strategic assumption analysis,[17] a select team of managers is charged with the responsibility of providing a set of counter-recommendations based on a set of assumptions different from that made by the business manager. The two opposing sets of assumptions and the strategic decisions that flow out of them are debated by the managers, until a new pool of assumptions is mutually agreed on by the debating parties; then they unite to develop recommendations based on those assumptions. The devil's advocacy is a less exacting approach by comparison. In this approach, a select group of peer managers is required to critique the assumptions and strategies that are proposed by a business manager. However, these "devil's advocates" do not have to provide an alternate set of recommendations, as in the dialectic inquiry approach. It is left to the business manager to modify his or her proposal suitably based on the criticisms provided by the devil's advocate and offer the modified recommendations for further criticism until all the substantive criticisms have been dealt with to the satisfaction of the critics. What is important to note about both of these approaches is the recognition that there is a real danger of building an escalating commitment to a pet strategy. Unless the assumptions and logic that underlie the strategy are formally challenged, new facts and patterns will go unrecognized.[18]

Another useful approach to nurturing strategic thinking is competitive benchmarking.[19] Top management initiates this process by identifying a number of critical capabilities that it feels a particular business must have in order to succeed. Examples of these capabilities include manufacturing quality, cost effectiveness, and superior distribution. Then management compares the firm's strengths in each of these functions with what it considers to be best practice—first relative to other departments within the firm itself; then in comparison with the strongest competitors to the business being analyzed; and finally with the firms that are the strongest in these functions, regardless of the businesses in which they participate. After this analysis, areas in which a business unit can strengthen its position can be identified.

The recent advances in information technology offer yet another potent avenue for strengthening strategic thinking within the firm.[20] The ability to update and manipulate large masses of data speedily and accurately has freed managers from some of the computational drudgery associated with the strategy process and helped them concentrate more on its creative aspects. The first Texas Instruments study (see Case 5) provides an early example of how firms have used computer-based decision support systems to strengthen their strategy process.

Superior communication technology also has helped enrich the interactions and iterations in a firm's strategy process. Rapid and reliable transmission of data over computer networks, telefaxing, and televideoconferencing helps managers to overcome the logistical barriers imposed by geographic diversification.

Another promising development is the recent work on managerial expert systems.[21] Such a system tries to replicate the decision-making heuristics used by expert managers. Although strategic decisions are not easy to model, at least for a subset of these decisions, expert systems can provide invaluable support to decision makers. For instance, an expert system can help a manager monitor changes in the critical success factors associated with a strategy, identify areas in which the strategy has to be modified, and evaluate strategic alternatives. An expert system cannot as yet help managers formulate strategies, but it can enhance their capacity to learn and deal with complex issues, to act faster, and to draw more explicitly on all of the information available to the firm.

Top management should champion the use of information technology, because this technology is an important complement to its efforts in nurturing strategic thinking. By mechanizing the routine aspects of strategic decision making and by strengthening interactive communication with the firm, top management can help a firm's business unit managers spend more time on the creative aspects of strategy making.

ENCOURAGING ORGANIZATIONAL LEARNING

A business unit that is well adapted to its environment is unlikely to change until it encounters failure.[22] Even when failure occurs, the unit's managers are more likely to modify existing operating procedures than to question the fundamental strategy that caused that failure.[23] Instead, if top management can simulate various environmental changes in a controlled fashion and force the business unit to cope with these changes, it can set up a useful trial-and-error learning process.

A successful trial will open new growth opportunities for the business unit, and even a failed trial may provide useful learning on its vulnerability to certain environmental conditions.[24] Moreover, because the trials are conducted by the business unit under controlled conditions, they do not have the same disastrous consequences as those imposed by an unpredictable change in its environment.

Lawrence and Dyer[25] propose a useful framework for how a business unit can learn through trial and error. They found in a number of industry settings that the ability of an organization to design new strategies is a function of the resource scarcity and the information complexity of its environment. Resource scarcity is a composite measure of the difficulties encountered by an organizational unit when accessing its essential resources. Information complexity, on the other hand, is the degree of competitive, product, market, technological, and regulatory variations in a business unit's relevant environment. A business unit's learning capacity increases, according to these authors, when both resource scarcity and information complexity are at moderate levels and decreases when either of them becomes too high or too low.

Top management can simulate resource scarcity in the budgeting step. For example, a cut in the funding of a business unit's strategic budget can force its managers to explore creative options for protecting their strategic programs. It is useful to remember that such budget cuts do not need to be motivated by a real resource scarcity but must have the effect of simulating resource scarcity.

Similarly top management can also manage a business unit's informational complexity by the strategies that it encourages the business unit to pursue. A cautious approach to experimenting with new environments is through geographic or related diversification.[26] In either of these diversification efforts, a business unit needs only a small incremental investment to make initial entry. If the trial should prove to be unsuccessful, the cost of exit is correspondingly low. However, each trial provides an opportunity for the business unit to manage a different set of stakeholders and to acquire a new capability. Acquisition, mergers, and alliances provide another approach either to learn new strategies or to build new capabilities.[27] As we noted in the previous section, a business unit can also learn directly from the experiences of others through competitive benchmarking.

The essence of learning is the willingness to question the status quo, the humility to admit that there may be better strategies than the one currently in use, and the supportive internal environment in which first-time errors are forgiven. Top management must nurture such a learning environment within the firm.

PROMOTING INTRAFIRM COOPERATION

Corporate diversification often is justified as being in the best interests of the firm's stockholders because of top management's ability to exploit synergies between the firm's businesses.[28] Synergy is a concept that describes how, by sharing their capabilities, two or more businesses can help strengthen each of their competitive positions. The cumulative returns from these synergistic businesses should exceed what would be normally available to a stockholder if he or she had chosen to invest in them as stand-alone businesses. A major responsibility of top management is to ensure that all available synergies to the firm are exploited. We discussed in the previous chapter how interfunctional cooperation is critical to the successful development of a strategic program and that interbusiness cooperation within a division promotes economies of scale and scope. There are other synergies that can be exploited within the firm. In GE,[29] for example, semiconductors were not a major bought-out item for any single division. However, GE as a whole was a major consumer of semiconductors. Opportunities for joint research, shared development, joint manufacturing, and volume discounts had all been missed by the company, until top management began coordinating these efforts.

Similarly Dupont's top management realized that the sale of its products to large customers, such as General Motors and Ford, was uncoordinated.[30] Several Dupont divisions, each offering a piecemeal solution to its problems, served the same customer. The potential to provide a systemic solution to the customer's problems was completely missed. Dupont has since reorganized its sales efforts through what it calls "co-managed strategies," which represent a firm-wide concerted effort at servicing the needs of large customers.

These and other examples point to the need for top management to encourage more intrafirm cooperation. The basis of this cooperation will clearly differ from firm to firm, as we explain in Chapter 8. However, in all of these contexts, top management should focus on synergy at each step of the strategy process, calling for "co-managed strategies" in the objectives-setting step, supporting cross-divisional programs in the strategic programming step, and facilitating inter- and intradivisional cooperation in the budgeting step through appropriate transfer pricing mechanisms. Also, it should recognize and reward cooperative effort, subjective as some of these evaluations may have to be.

REVITALIZING THE PROCESS

As a way to illustrate the critical role of top management in this regard, we briefly discuss how one large multinational corporation, General Electric, has revitalized its strategy process. Although many have discussed GE's experiences with this effort, we draw on the following succinct analysis by Christopher Lorenz of the *Financial Times:*

> What G.E. has done is not to dump the discipline or the rigor of strategic planning, but to streamline and de-bureaucratize the process, shifting the main planning responsibility away from the center and out to line management. The aim throughout has been to make G.E.'s strategies more effective, more international and much more responsive to the constant changes in its competitive environment.
>
> . . . .
>
> [The plastics] business still makes a formal strategic plan each year. . . . But there the resemblance with the old process ends. Because of all today's unpredictabilities,

the plan has only a three-year horizon, instead of the previous five. At under 20 pages, it is less than a fifth as large, and much of the material in it is qualitative rather than numerical. . . . Its competitive analysis is far more detailed and more attention is paid to how the plan will be implemented. Updates of the plan, and head office reviews, are arranged and done within weeks, at any time of the year; previously the planning process took a full seven months, from January to July, before the ritual head office review procedure. Head office reviews these days include all Hiner's [head of GE's plastics business] peers—the heads of GE's other businesses—in order to encourage cross-unit co-ordination.

. . . .

A prime example of the new process of "strategic thinking" in practice, says Hiner, is the speed with which plastics—in common with other G.E. businesses—has forged a spate of strategic alliances around the world. One joint venture . . . was born over lunch in 1985 and quickly spurred a set of further collaboration with the same company. . . . "Under the old process, I just don't think it would have happened—there'd have been fixed goals and checkpoints," says Hiner. "By the time the proposal had got through the process, someone else would have done the deals ahead of us."[31]

GE's experience points to the need for a periodic cleansing of the strategy process. Top management should signal through its own actions that the primary aim of the strategy process is to help managers "think harder (and smarter)." The process has periodically to be unclogged of its accumulated rituals. On occasion, fresh thinking may be possible only by conducting a "ceremonial funeral" for an old ritual, such as the symbolic dismantling by Jack Welch of GE's planning department and its planning rituals.[32] Incidentally, Welch's predecessor, Reginald Jones, had to engage in a similar revitalization of the strategy process when he took charge of GE. Fighting entropy in the strategy process is a constant challenge for top management.

SUMMARY

In this chapter, we discussed six critical areas in which top management must support the strategy process: infusing the process with a clear vision, ensuring value creation for the firm's stockholders and managing the satisfaction of other stakeholders, nurturing strategic thinking within the firm, encouraging organizational learning, promoting intrafirm cooperation, and periodically revitalizing the process. We did not discuss, however, the specific roles that top management plays in a firm's strategic planning; monitoring, control, and learning; and incentives and staffing systems. These will have to be tailored to suit the context of a firm. We devote our attention to these tailored roles in the following chapters.

NOTES

1. See G. Hamel and C. K. Prahalad, "Strategic Intent," *Harvard Business Review* (May–June 1989): 63–76.

2. J. Carlzon, *Moments of Truth* (New York: Harper and Row, 1987).

3. Hamel and Prahalad, "Strategic Intent."

4. S. P. Sherman, "Inside the Mind of Jack Welch," *Fortune* 119 (March 27, 1989): 38–50.

5. P. A. Wack, "Learning to Design Planning Scenarios: The Experience of Royal Dutch Shell," unpublished manuscript (Boston: Harvard Business School, 1984).

6. M. C. Jensen, "Eclipse of the Public Corporation," *Harvard Business Review* (Sept.–Oct. 1989): 61–74.

7. This view has been well articulated in A. Rappaport, "Selecting Strategies That Create Shareholder Value," *Harvard Business Review* 59 (May–June 1981): 139–149.

8. See B. S. Chakravarthy and H. Singh, "Value-Based Planning: Applications and Limitations" in *Advances in Strategic Management,* vol. 6, ed. R. Lamb and P. Shrivastava (Greenwich, CT: JAI Press, 1990): 169–181.

9. See the following: M. S. Salter and W. A. Weinhold, *Diversification Through Acquisitions* (New York: Free Press, 1979); and Chakravarthy and Singh, "Value-Based Planning."

10. This definition is from R. E. Freeman, *Strategic Management: A Stakeholder Approach* (Marshfield, MA: Pitman, 1984).

11. See B. S. Chakravarthy, "Measuring Strategic Performance," *Strategic Management Journal* 7 (1986): 437–458.

12. This discussion is based on Freeman, *Strategic Management,* 126–176.

13. See F. Sturdivant, "Executives and Activists: A Test of Stakeholder Management," *California Management Review* 22 (1979): 53–59.

14. See R. W. Ackerman, "How Companies Respond to Social Demands," *Harvard Business Review* 51 (July–Aug. 1973): 88–98.

15. A. Bhambri and J. L. Wilson, "The IBM Corporation: The Bubble Memory Incident" in R. F. Vancil, *Implementing Strategy* (Boston: Harvard Business School, 1982), 51–56.

16. See the following: R. A. Cosier and J. C. Aplin, "A Critical View of Dialectic Inquiry As a Tool in Strategic Planning," *Strategic Management Journal* 1 (1980): 343–356; and D. M. Schweiger and P. A. Finger, "The Comparative Effectiveness of Dialectic Inquiry and Devil's Advocacy: The Impact of Task Biases on Previous Research Findings," *Strategic Management Journal* 5 (1984): 335–350.

17. For an elaboration of this approach, see the following: R. O. Mason and I. D. Mitroff, *Challenging Strategic Planning Assumptions* (New York: John Wiley, 1981).

18. The problems of groupthink and escalating commitment have been well articulated in the following: J. L. Janus, *Victims of Groupthink: Psychological Studies of Foreign Policy Decisions and Fiascoes* (Boston: Houghton Mifflin, 1972); and B. M. Staw and J. Ross, "Knowing When to Pull the Plug," *Harvard Business Review* 65 (Mar.–Apr. 1987): 68–74.

19. See "Competitive Benchmarking: What It Is and What It Can Do for You" (Xerox Corporation, 1987).

20. For example, see the following for an extensive discussion of the important links between information technology and the strategy process: J. F. Rockart, *Executive Support Systems* (Homewood, IL: Dow Jones Irwin, 1988); C. Wiseman, *Strategic Information Systems* (Homewood, IL: Dow Jones Irwin, 1988); F. W. McFarlen and J. L. McKenney, *Corporate Information Systems Management* (Homewood, IL: Richard D. Irwin, 1983); and H. L. Poppel and B. Goldstein, *Information Technology* (New York: McGraw-Hill, 1987).

21. See J. F. Rockart and M. S. Scott Morton, "Implications of Changes in Information Technology for Corporate Strategy," *Interfaces* 14 (1984): 84–95.

22. For an elaboration of this point, see the following: R. M. Cyert and J. G. March, *A Behavioral Theory of the Firm* (Englewood Cliffs, NJ: Prentice-Hall, 1963); and H. A. Simon, *Administrative Behavior* (New York: Free Press, 1945).

23. This is the characteristic of a single-loop learning firm, which is described in the following: C. Argyris, "The Double-Loop Learning in Organizations," *Harvard Business Review* 55 (Sept.–Oct. 1977): 115–125.

24. See W. R. Ashby, *An Introduction to Cybernetics* (London: University Paperbacks, 1971).

25. See P. R. Lawrence and D. Dyer, *Renewing American Industry* (New York: Free Press, 1983).

26. See the following: R. H. Miles, "Learning from Diversifying," in *Coffin Nails and Corporate Strategies* (Englewood Cliffs, NJ: Prentice-Hall, 1982), 154–196; and R. Normann, *Management for Growth* (New York: Wiley-Interscience, 1977).

27. This view is advocated by P. C. Haspeslagh and D. B. Jemison, *Managing Acquisitions: Creating Value Through Strategic Renewal* (New York: Free Press, in press).

28. Jensen, "Eclipse of the Public Corporation."

29. P. C. Browne, "General Electric Company: Background Note on Management Systems: 1981," in R. F. Vancil, *Implementing Strategy* (Boston: Harvard Business School, 1982), 77–94.

30. R. Lorange and R. T. Nelson, "How to Recognize and Avoid Organizational Decline," *Sloan Management Review* 28 (Spring 1987): 41–49.

31. Christopher Lorenz, "Why Strategy Has Been Put in the Hands of Line Managers," *Financial Times* (May 18, 1988): 20.

32. McCaskey refers to these ceremonies as "little dying." See M. B. McCaskey, *The Executive Challenge: Managing Change and Ambiguity* (Marshfield, MA: Pitman, 1982). The term suggests that what are being buried are the former rituals of strategic planning and not strategic planning per se.

REFERENCES

Bourgeois, L. J., and D. R. Brodwin, "Strategic Implementation: Five Approaches to an Elusive Phenomenon," *Strategic Management Journal* 5 (1984): 241–264.

Bower, J. L., and T. M. Hout, "Fast-Cycle Capability for Competitive Power," *Harvard Business Review* (Nov.–Dec. 1988): 110–119.

Chakravarthy, B. S., and S. Kwun, "The Strategy-Making Process: An Organizational Learning Perspective" (Working paper, University of Minnesota, 1989).

Chakravarthy, B. S., W. Loomis, and J. Vrabel, "Dexter Corporation's Value-Based Strategic Planning System," *The Planning Review* 16 (Jan.–Feb. 1988): 34–41.

Hitt, M. A., and R. D. Ireland, "Corporate Distinctive Competence, Strategy Industry and Performance," *Strategic Management Journal* 6 (July–Sept. 1985): 273–294.

Lorange, P., "New Strategic Challenges for the Materials-Oriented Firm," in *Materials Futures: Strategies and Opportunities,* eds. B. Pipes and D. Arpelian (Pittsburgh: Material Research Society, 1988), 139–146.

Rockart, J. F., "Chief Executives Define Their Own Data Needs," *Harvard Business Review* 57 (Mar.–Apr. 1979): 81–92.

Wack, P., "Scenarios: Uncharted Waters Ahead," *Harvard Business Review* 63 (Sept.–Oct. 1985): 72–89.

Scandinavian Airlines System

When the Scandinavian Airlines System (SAS) Group's financial results for the fiscal year 1986–1987 were released, it marked the trinational transport group's sixth straight profitable year and their best year ever with a net operating income of 1.6 billion Swedish kronor (SEK), or 0.25 billion U.S. dollars, on revenues of 23.9 billion SEK, or 3.7 billion U.S. dollars. This was a huge improvement over the situation in 1981, when losses mounted and the airline rapidly lost market share. A summary of the company's financial results for 1977–1978 and 1986–1987, along with relevant exchange rates, is shown in Exhibit 1.

Much of the credit for the company's dramatic turnaround was ascribed to Jan Carlzon, who succeeded Carl-Olov Munkberg as President and CEO in 1981 and quickly initiated a number of major changes in the airline and its associated companies. He reoriented SAS toward the business travel market and gave top priority to customer service. This involved a complete reorganization of the company and a major decentralization of responsibility. As a result, SAS became the leading carrier of full-fare traffic in Europe. Carlzon joined SAS as Executive Vice President in 1980, after serving as president of Linjeflyg, the Swedish domestic airline. Previously he was Managing Director of the SAS tour subsidiary, Vingresor.

Despite these dramatic successes, the company still faced considerable threats, and many analysts questioned if it could survive as a viable competitor in the increasingly global and competitive airline industry. Its population base of only 17 million spread out over a large area was too small by itself to support a comprehensive international traffic system. In addition, its geographic location at the periphery of

Europe was a disadvantage when compared to Western Europe's densely populated areas.

The most pressing problem was the airline's operating costs, which were among the highest in the industry (Exhibit 2). It was estimated that labor charges accounted for 35 percent of SAS's total costs, compared with only 25 percent for the major U.S. carriers since deregulation and 18 percent for the large Asian airlines. The evolution of the U.S. "megacarriers" was a major concern as they eyed Europe as an area for continued expansion.

The senior managers of the company were fully aware of these challenges. When discussing future developments in the airline industry and SAS's role in particular, Helge Lindberg, the Group Executive Vice President, noted the following:

> I doubt very much that SAS can survive alone as a major intercontinental airline. We need to expand our traffic system in order to compete with major European carriers having much larger population bases, as well as with the major American and Asian carriers who maintain considerably lower operating costs. We need to develop with other partners a global traffic system with daily connections to the important overseas destinations. The nature of our industry is such that if you are not present in the market the day the customers wish to travel, the business is lost. Another priority is to reduce our costs. Our social structure in Scandinavia leaves us with one of the highest personnel costs in the industry, coupled with the fact that increased emphasis on service caused us to lose our traditional budget consciousness over the past few years. A third major issue is to develop a competitive distribution system, a problem we are about to solve in partnership with Air France, Iberia and Lufthansa, with the so-called Amadeus system.

THE TURNAROUND

Sweden, Denmark, and Norway had always shared an interest in creating an ambitious air service, both to link their scattered communities and to ensure a role for Scandinavia among the world's international airlines. They first considered a joint airline in the 1930s, when all three countries wanted to establish a route to America. No firm agreement was reached until 1940, however, when they decided to operate a joint service between New York and Bergen, on Norway's west coast. This plan was unfortunately scuttled by the German invasion three days later.

The 1946 Bermuda conference on international air travel put an end to any hopes of true freedom of the air and served to underline the importance of developing a common airline in order to establish a stronger world presence. The three countries agreed on an ownership structure, and in the summer of 1946, a DC-4 bearing the Scandinavian Airlines System name lifted off from Stockholm bound for Oslo and New York. Sweden controlled three-sevenths of the new airline, and Norway and Denmark controlled two-sevenths each, with ownership split 50/50 between the respective governments and private interests.

SAS gained a strong foothold in the European market—at the expense of the

(*Text continues on page 30*)

Exhibit 1 SAS Group Financial and Operating Results (1977–1987)

Financial Summary—Group	'77/'78	'78/'79	'79/'80	'80/'81	'81/'82	'82/'83	'83/'84	'84/'85	'85/'86	'86/'87
SEK millions										
Operating Revenue	7,050	8,066	9,220	10,172	12,807	15,972	18,005	19,790	21,585	23,870
Operating Expenses	(6,437)	(7,561)	(8,920)	(9,664)	(11,895)	(14,696)	(16,415)	(18,256)	(19,369)	(21,524)
Depreciation	(347)	(360)	(391)	(430)	(474)	(483)	(545)	(574)	(863)	(1,126)
Financial and Extra Items	(140)	(7)	28	(129)	10	(192)	(77)	57	162	443
Net Operating Income	126	148	(63)	(51)	448	601	968	1,017	1,515	1,663
Exchange Rate—SEK/$U.S.	4.60	4.15	4.17	5.61	6.28	7.83	8.70	7.40	6.91	6.40

Revenue by Business Area (%)	'82/'83		'83/'84		'84/'85		'85/'86		'86/'87	
SEK millions										
SAS Airline Consortium	12,600	(79)	14,151	(79)	15,434	(78)	16,495	(76)	17,510	(73)
SAS International Hotels	732	(5)	843	(5)	948	(5)	1,083	(5)	1,230	(5)
SAS Service Partner	1,681	(11)	2,049	(11)	2,393	(12)	2,712	(13)	3,223	(14)
SAS Leisure (Vingresor)	1,311	(8)	1,474	(8)	1,537	(8)	1,897	(9)	2,379	(10)
Other	456	(3)	460	(3)	390	(2)	415	(2)	730	(3)
Group Eliminations	(808)	(−5)	(972)	(−5)	(912)	(−5)	(1,017)	(−5)	(1,202)	(−5)
Total	15,972	(100)	18,005	(100)	19,790	(100)	21,585	(100)	23,870	(100)

Income by Business Area
(%)

SEK millions	'82/'83		'83/'84		'84/'85		'85/'86		'86/'87	
SAS Airline Consortium	461	(77)	729	(75)	811	(80)	1,207	(80)	1,453	(87)
SAS International Hotels	14	(2)	21	(2)	67	(7)	72	(5)	73	(4)
SAS Service Partner	75	(12)	15	(2)	81	(8)	123	(8)	180	(11)
SAS Leisure (Vingresor)	41	(7)	43	(4)	81	(8)	133	(9)	141	(8)
Other	17	(3)	5	(1)	(15)	(–1)	(31)	(–2)	(99)	(–6)
Group Eliminations	(25)	(–4)	(21)	(–2)	(7)	(–1)	(22)	(–1)	(85)	(–5)
Extraordinary Items	18	(3)	176	(18)	–1	(0)	34	(2)	0	(0)
Total	601	(100)	968	(100)	1,017	(100)	1,516	(100)	1,663	(100)

Operating Statistics
SAS Airline

	'77/'78	'78/'79	'79/'80	'80/'81	'81/'82	'82/'83	'83/'84	'84/'85	'85/'86	'86/'87
Cities Served	98	102	103	105	99	93	91	88	89	85
Kilometers Flown (mill)	123	124	120	113	113	120	124	125	136	N/A
Passengers (thou)	7,886	8,669	8,393	8,413	8,861	9,222	10,066	10,735	11,708	N/A
Cabin Load Factor (%)	56.4	59.9	59.4	60.9	63.6	65.5	67.2	67.2	66.2	68.9
Employees	16,010	16,755	17,069	16,425	16,376	17,101	17,710	18,845	19,773	N/A

Source: SAS annual reports.

Exhibit 2   **Comparison of Estimated Airline Operating Costs (in U.S. cents per available tonne-kilometer)**

Airline	1982	1983	1984	1985	1986
Singapore Airlines	36	36	33	32	30
British Caledonian	37	37	29	35	38
United Airlines	39	39	38	44	40
KLM	35	29	26	35	44
Pan American	34	36	38	36	N/A
British Airways	40	38	31	37	44
Delta	42	43	43	45	44
Lufthansa	51	44	40	53	57
Swissair	54	47	41	53	58
Sabena	53	43	44	56	63
SAS	53	53	50	65	76

Source: SAS annual reports.

Germans, who were forbidden from establishing their own airline—and quickly developed a worldwide route network. The airline established numerous firsts in the early years of worldwide air travel, beginning in 1945 with the Swedish parent company ABA, which was the first to re-establish trans-Atlantic service after the war. In 1954, SAS pioneered the Arctic route with a flight from Copenhagen to Los Angeles via Greenland; in 1957, it inaugurated transpolar service to Tokyo, cutting travel time by half. The Scandinavians were the first to operate the French Caravelle, introducing twin-engine jet travel within Europe, and worked with Douglas Aircraft to develop the ultra-long-range DC-8-62, which was capable of flying nonstop to the U.S. West Coast and Southeast Asia. A list of the airline's major milestones is shown in Exhibit 3. SAS often looked for overseas partners and purchased 30 percent of Thai Airways International in 1959. This stake was bought back by the Thai government in 1977, but the two airlines since entered into a cooperative service agreement.

The 1960s and early 1970s were the golden years for the airline. Apart from 1972, when profits shrank to $8 million due to currency fluctuations, the average annual net profits from 1969 to 1975 were between $15 million and $20 million. In the late 1970s, the second oil shock had a severe effect on profits, and the airline sustained considerable losses in 1979–1980 and 1980–1981.

SAS developed close relationships with Swissair and KLM. An agreement between the three airlines (the KSSU agreement) was signed in 1969 with the objective of strengthening technical cooperation and of jointly assessing any new aircraft entering the market. For example, it was agreed that SAS would be responsible for overhauling the Boeing 747 engines of all three airlines, while the other partners performed other joint maintenance activities.

Although the trinational airline generally functioned smoothly, there were

Exhibit 3   SAS Milestones

1946—July 31–August 1
DDL, DNL and SILA found SAS for the operation of intercontinental services to North and South America.

1946—September 17
Route to New York opened.

1946—November 30
Route to South American opened.

1948—April 18
ABA, DDL and DNL form ESAS to coordinate European operations.

1948—July 1
SILA and ABA amalgamated.

1949—October 26
Route to Bangkok opened.

1950—October 1
ABA, DDL and DNL transfer all operations to SAS in accordance with a new Consortium. Agreement dated February 8, 1951, with retroactive effect.

1951—April 18
The Bangkok route is extended to Tokyo.

1951—April 19
Route to Nairobi is inaugurated.

1952—November 19
First transarctic flight by commercial airliner.

1953—January 8
The Nairobi route is extended to Johannesburg

1954—November 15
Polar route to Los Angeles inaugurated.

1956—May 9
Pre-war route to Moscow reopened.

1957—February 24
Inauguration of North Pole short cut to Tokyo.

1957—April 2
SAS participates in formation of Linjeflyg.

1957—April 4
Route opened to Warsaw.

1957—April 16
First flight to Prague.

1958—October 6
Agreement of cooperation signed by SAS and Swissair.

1959—August 24
SAS and Thai Airways Co. establish THAI International.

1960—July 2
Monrovia added to South Atlantic network.

1961—October 1
SAS Catering established as subsidiary.

1962—May 15
Inauguration of all-cargo service to New York.

1963—May 4
Route opened across top of North Norway to Kirkenes.

1963—November 2
First service to Montreal.

1964—April 2
Route to Chicago inaugurated.

1965—April 5
Nonstop service New York–Bergen begun.

1966—September 2
Inauguration of service to Seattle via Polar route.

1967—November 4
Opening of Trans-Asian Express via Tashkent to Bangkok and Singapore.

1968—March 31
Dar-Es-Salaam added to East-African network.

1969—November 1
Route opened to Barbados and Port-of-Spain in West Indies.

1970—February 18
KSSU agreement ratified.

1971—April 3
Trans-Siberian Express to Tokyo inaugurated.

1971—November 1
SAS participates in formation of Danair.

1972—April 5
Route to East Berlin opened.

1972—May 24
New York–Stavanger route opened.

1973—November 4
All-cargo express route opened to Bangkok and Singapore.

1973—November 6
Delhi added to Trans-Orient route.

1975—September 2
Inauguration of Svalbard route, world's northernmost scheduled service.

1976—April 21
Route opened to Lagos.

1977—April 7
Kuwait added to Trans-Orient route.

1977—November 2
Opening of Gothenburg–New York route.

Source: "The SAS Saga" (Anders Buraas, Oslo, 1979)

some problems among the constituent groups, particularly when Denmark joined the EEC in 1973. This underlying rivalry was reflected in Norway by the statement, "SAS is an airline run by the Swedes for the benefit of the Danes," which was in reference to the airline's head office in Stockholm and its main traffic hub at Kastrup airport in Copenhagen. Nonetheless, the larger traffic base and increased bargaining power afforded by the union had helped to make SAS a major world airline.

Problems Facing SAS in 1981

When Jan Carlzon assumed the presidency of SAS in August 1981, he realized that major changes would have to be made to restore the airline and its associated companies to profitability and to meet the growing challenges of an increasingly competitive industry. After 17 profitable years, the SAS Group posted operating losses of 63.1 million SEK and 51.3 million SEK in fiscal years 1979–1980 and 1980–1981, respectively. This dramatic decline gave rise to rumors that the three constituent countries were considering disbanding SAS and running their own separate airlines.

In addition to the problems that beset the industry—the international recession, higher interest rates and fuel costs, overcapacity, and less-regulated competition—specific problems plagued SAS. The airline was losing market share, even in its home territory; its fleet mix and route network did not meet market needs; and its reputation for service and punctuality was deteriorating. For example, on-time performance (defined as the percentage of arrivals within 15 minutes of schedule) slipped from over 90 percent to 85 percent, a major drop by airline standards.

In addition, many regular travelers from Norway and Sweden were increasingly avoiding transitting through Copenhagen's troublesome Kastrup airport—SAS's major hub—in favor of the attractive and efficient terminals at Amsterdam, Frankfurt, and Zurich. Under the umbrella of regulation, bad habits developed within the company's management ranks. Carlzon felt that SAS, like most airlines, had allowed itself to become too enamored with technology—new aircrafts and new engines—often at the cost of meeting the customer's needs. They had become a product-driven airline instead of a service-driven one. A typical example was the acquisition of the state-of-the-art Airbus A300 aircraft in the late 1970s. These larger planes required high load factors to be profitable, and this necessitated lower flight frequencies, which was not in the best interests of customers who needed frequent and flexible flight schedules. In the past, customers were willing to plan their trips according to a particular airline's schedule and even were willing to sacrifice some time to do so, because air travel was still somewhat of a novelty. The market changed, and experienced travelers then chose flights to suit their travel plans. "In the past, we were operating as booking agents and aircraft brokers," said Carlzon. "Now we know, if we want the business we must fight for it like the 'Street fighters' of the rough-and-tumble American domestic market."

New Strategy: The Businessman's Airline

Faced with the situation of a stagnant market, general overcapacity in the industry, and continuing loss of market share to competitors, Carlzon recognized that a new strategy was necessary to turn SAS around. In a similar situation when he was the President of Linjeflyg, Carlzon decided to increase flight frequency and cut fares dramatically in order to improve aircraft utilization and boost load factors. These actions proved to be very successful, and profitability improved substantially. However, the market SAS operated in was quite different from Linjeflyg's market, and it was not clear that a similar strategy could be applied successfully. Another possible option was to initiate a major cost reduction program aimed at obtaining a better margin from a declining revenue base. This strategy would have required significant staff cuts, fleet reduction, and an overall lower level of flight frequency and service.

In the airline industry, the most stable market segment was the full-fare-paying business traveler, who provided the vast majority of revenues. First-class travel within Europe was declining, mainly because businesses could not justify the extra expense, especially during a recession. All the major, scheduled airlines were after the business traveler, and some had created a separate "business" class, which offered many of the amenities of first class and was priced at a 10 percent to 20 percent premium over economy.

SAS chose the strategy of focusing on the business traveler. As described by Helge Lindberg, then the Executive Vice President of Commercial, "although other options were considered, we quickly decided there was no alternative but to go after the business traveler segment with a new product which offered significant advantages over the competition." In the words of Jan Carlzon: "We decided to go after a bigger share of the full-fare-paying pie."

There were a number of risks involved in this strategy. Increasing investment to provide an improved level of service at a time of mounting losses could bankrupt the airline if revenues did not improve sufficiently. On the other hand, if investment was the way to go, perhaps it would be better spent on more-efficient aircraft so as to reduce costs. Another concern was that differentiating the product could alienate the tourist-class passengers, especially among Scandinavian customers, who might resent any increase in passenger "segregation." In spite of these considerable risks, management increased expenditures and staked the future of the airline on its ability to woo the European business traveler away from the competition.

As a result, first class was dropped and EuroClass was introduced to offer more amenities than the competing airlines' business classes but at the old economy fare. (A similar service, First Business Class, was introduced on intercontinental routes, where first class was retained.) Thus any passenger paying full-fare would be entitled to this new service, which included separate check-in, roomier seating, advance seat selection, free drinks, and a better in-flight meal. The other European airlines reacted strongly. Air France saw EuroClass as a serious threat to its own *Classe Affaires,* which cost 20 percent more than economy, and at one point refused to book any EuroClass fares on its reservation system. Other airlines protested to their local government authorities, but the new fare structures were allowed to remain. SAS backed up the new service with the largest media advertising campaign ever launched by the airline. Typical of the aggressive advertising copy that was used in this campaign is the following excerpt from an SAS advertisement that appeared in *Advertising Age:*

> Of the eight major airlines competing in Sweden for European traffic, five do not give you separate check-in and seating, separate cabin or free drinks. Of the three remaining airlines, two do not give you extra room and larger seats. Only one airline in Europe has EuroClass which gives you more service and comfort for the economy fare.

In conjunction with the new EuroClass services, a drive was launched to improve flight schedules and punctuality. The aircraft fleet mix was modified in order to meet the demands of increased flight frequency. The recently acquired high-capacity Airbus aircraft were withdrawn from service and leased to SAS's Scanair charter subsidiary because they were not suitable for the frequent, nonstop flights that the new schedule demanded. For the same reason, some Boeing 747s were replaced by McDonnell Douglas DC-10s, and the older DC-9s were refurbished instead of being replaced because they were the right size for the new service levels.

On certain short distance routes, such as Copenhagen to Hamburg, a new EuroLink concept was introduced. This involved substituting 40 passenger Fokker F-27s for 110 passenger DC-9s and doubling flight frequencies to provide an attractive schedule. In short, the previous high-fixed-cost, high-capacity fleet was changing into a lower-fixed-cost, high-frequency one. This evolution of the SAS fleet is shown in Exhibit 4.

Every effort was made to differentiate the business traveler product as much as possible from the lower-priced fares. In this respect, Scanorama lounges were introduced at many of the airports served by SAS in an effort to improve service further. These lounges were for the exclusive use of the full-fare-paying passengers and offered telephones and telex machines and a relaxing environment. A joint agreement with the Danish Civil Aviation Authority was reached to invest in refurbishing Kastrup airport to bring it up to competitive standards. The objective was to make Kastrup Europe's best airport by the end of the decade.

The introduction of these new products and their related services represented a change in the overall philosophy of SAS. All the tasks and functions within the organization were examined. If the business traveler benefitted from a particular service or function, it was maintained or enhanced; otherwise, it was cut back or dropped altogether. Managers were urged to look on expenses as resources—to cut those that did not contribute to revenue, but not to hesitate in raising those that did. Administrative costs were slashed 25 percent, but at the same time an extra 120 million SEK was invested on new services, facilities, aircraft interiors, and other projects that affected the passengers directly. As a result, annual operating costs

Exhibit 4 **Evolution of SAS's Fleet**

Aircraft Type in Service[1]	Seat Cap.	'77/'78	'78/'79	'79/'80	'80/'81	'81/'82	'82/'83	'83/'84	'84/'85	'85/'86	'86/'87
Boeing 747	405	3	4	4	5	5	3	5	5	2	0
Airbus Industries A300	242	0	0	2	4	1	1	0	0	0	0
McDonnell-Douglas DC-10-30	230	5	5	5	5	5	5	6	8	9	11
McDonnell-Douglas DC-8-62	N/A	5	5	2	3	3	3	3	3	3	0
DC-8-63	170	5	3	4	2	2	2	2	2	2	0
McDonnell-Douglas DC-9-21	75	9	9	9	9	9	9	9	9	9	9
DC-9-33	(freight)	2	2	2	2	2	2	2	2	2	2
DC-9-41	110/122	45	49	49	49	49	49	49	49	49	49
DC-9-81	133	0	0	0	0	0	0	0	0	6	8
DC-9-82	156	0	0	0	0	0	0	0	0	6	8
DC-9-83	133	0	0	0	0	0	0	0	0	0	4
Fokker F-27	40	0	0	0	0	0	0	4	6	9	9
Total		74	77	77	79	76	74	80	84	97	100

[1]Aircraft owned or leased by SAS that were leased to other operators are not included in this table.

Source: SAS annual reports.

were increased by 55 million SEK at a time of deep deficits and continuing losses. Furthermore, these additional investments for improved service delayed the acquisition of new, more-efficient aircraft to replace the aging DC-9 fleet.

The results of this new strategy were dramatic. Full-fare-paying passenger traffic rose over 8 percent in the first year, and profits rose to 448 million SEK for the fiscal year 1981–1982. In punctuality, SAS improved on-time performance to 93 percent, which was a record in Europe. The share of full-fare-paying passengers rose consistently, and by 1986 it had risen to 60 percent, giving SAS the highest proportion of any airline in Europe. Accompanying this change in passenger mix were impressive profit gains. In 1986, SAS turned in the third-best profit performance among the world's major airlines with a net operating profit of 1.5 billion SEK. A comparison of financial and operating results of major world airlines is shown in Exhibit 5.

Corporate Cultural Revolution

Due in part to the protected, stable growth environment, the SAS organization was not ready to meet new competitive challenges without a major restructuring. Previously the reference point had been fixed assets and technology, with emphasis on return on investment, centralized control, and orders from top management. Across-the-board cost cutting was the usual approach to improve profits and to adapt to changing market conditions. The customer interface was neglected. A senior manager of the company said the following:

> In those days, many employees felt that passengers were a disturbing element they had to contend with, rather than the ones who were in fact paying their salary. Taking control of a situation, and bypassing the regulations in order to please a customer were not the things to do in SAS.

Thus personal initiative was discouraged, and adherence to the company policy manuals was the norm. A large corporate staff was needed to run this bureaucracy, with layers of middle management to follow up directives from the top. Throughout the organization, the morale of employees was low, and the level of cooperation, such as between ground staff and the air crews, was not always the best. "There was a feeling of helplessness, and a fear for the future of the company," remarked an SAS pilot when he was asked to comment on the situation prevailing prior to 1981.

A transformation "from bureaucrats to businessmen" was essential, and an emphasis on the customer was needed. A major reorientation was contemplated by Carlzon's predecessor, Munkberg, but it was felt that the implementation of a new organization would be more effective under a new CEO. "New brooms sweep clean," remarked Carlzon when relating his decision to replace or relocate 13 of the 14 executives in the SAS management team. Helge Lindberg, the sole survivor in the top management team, was put in charge of the day-to-day running of the airline. Lindberg's extensive knowledge and experience were valued by Carlzon,

---

Exhibit 5   **Comparison of Major World Airlines' Statistics (1986)**

Passengers	(in thousands)	R.P.K.s	(in hundred thousands)
1. Aeroflot	115,727	1. Aeroflot	188,056
2. United	50,690	2. United	95,569
3. American	45,983	3. American	78,499
4. Eastern	42,546	4. Eastern	56,164
5. Delta	41,062	5. Delta	50,480
6. TWA	24,636	6. TWA	48,100
7. All Nippon	24,503	7. Northwest	46,346
8. Piedmont	22,800	8. British Airways	41,405
9. US Air	21,725	9. Japan Air Lines	38,903
10. Continental	20,409	10. Pan American	34,844
22. SAS	11,700	30. (est) SAS	12,471

Fleet Size	(no. of aircraft)	Employees	
1. Aeroflot	2,682	1. Aeroflot	500,000
2. United	368	2. American	51,661
3. American	338	3. United	49,800
4. Northwest	311	4. Eastern	43,685
5. Eastern	289	5. Federal Express[1]	43,300
6. Delta	253	6. Delta	38,901
7. Continental	246	7. British Airways	37,810
8. CAAC (China)	241	8. Air France	35,269
9. TWA	167	9. Lufthansa	34,905
10. Republic	165	10. Northwest	33,250
18. SAS	106	22. SAS	19,773

Operational Revenue	(in hundred thousands, U.S. dollars)	Operational Profit	(in hundred thousands, U.S. dollars)
1. United	6,688	1. American	392
2. American	5,857	2. Federal Express[1]	365
3. Air France	4,747	3. SAS	260
4. Japan Air	4,578	4. Delta	225
5. Eastern	4,522	5. Cathay Pacific	206
6. Delta	4,496	6. Swissair	200
7. Northwest	3,598	7. Northwest	167
8. TWA	3,181	8. USAir	164
9. Federal Express[1]	2,940	9. Continental	143
10. Pan American	2,580	10. KLM	131
11. SAS	2,387		

[1]Freight only.

Source: Air Transport World (June 1987).

who saw Lindberg as a "bridge between old and new" and a valuable asset now that the time for change had arrived.

In the past, SAS focused on instructions, thereby limiting potential contributions from the employees. A key element of the cultural revolution under Carlzon was a new emphasis on information instead of instructions. The practical implications of this were that any employee in the front line (that is, in the SAS/customer interface) should have the decision-making power necessary to do, within reasonable limits, whatever that person felt appropriate to please the customer. Each "moment of truth," when the customer encountered the service staff, would be used to its full potential in order to encourage repeat business. "Throw out the manuals and use your heads instead!" was the message from Lindberg. The underlying assumptions, made explicit throughout the organization, were that an individual with information could not avoid assuming responsibility and that hidden resources were released when an individual was free to assume responsibility instead of being restricted by instructions.

Some of the tools used by Carlzon in the reorganization were personal letters and several red booklets ("Carlzon's Little Red Books") distributed to all employees. In these booklets, the company's situation and its goals were presented in very simple language, using cartoonlike drawings to emphasize their importance. Some employees found this form of communication too simple, but the overall response was very positive. In his first year, Carlzon spent approximately half of his time traveling, meeting with SAS employees all over the world. This made it very clear to everyone that management was deeply committed to turning things around, and he helped to implement the changes quickly.

Education was considered necessary to reap the full benefits of the new organization. Both managers and front-line staff were sent to seminars. The courses for the front-line personnel were referred to by many as the "learn-to-smile seminars," but the real benefits probably resulted more from the participants' perception that the company cared about its employees than from the actual content of the courses.

Certain problems were encountered in the process of change. Confusion and frustration were the typical reactions of many middle managers when they suddenly found themselves bypassed by the front line on the one hand and by the top management on the other. "You can't please everyone, and some people will have to be sacrificed," said an SAS manager when he was asked to comment on this problem. The cross-training of employees to perform several tasks was attempted but met with resistance from the unions. An example was the "turnaround" check—a visual check of the aircraft performed between each flight. This could be done by the pilots, but the mechanics' union insisted on this task being done by their people, resulting in higher operating costs.

Another problem was that the first reorientation had short-term goals, and when these goals were achieved, the early momentum diminished. By 1984, SAS received the "Airline of the Year" award from *Air Transport World* magazine, and its financial situation improved dramatically. These factors led to a feeling of contentment, so people started to fall back into old habits. Demands for salary increases were again raised. Some people thought that SAS was now out of danger and wanted to harvest the fruits of hard work. Small "pyramids" started to crop up in the organization, and it became evident that the problems in the middle management had not been solved. "The new culture was taking roots, but we had problems keeping up the motivation," noted Lindberg.

Consequently a second wave of change was launched. New goals with a much longer time horizon were outlined. Management wanted to prepare the company for the coming liberalization in the airline industry and to ensure a level of profitability sufficient to meet upcoming fleet replacement needs. The ultimate goal was for SAS to be the most efficient airline in Europe by 1990.

THE SECOND WAVE

SAS wanted to integrate the various elements of the travel package offered to the business traveler—to develop a full-service product for the full-fare-paying passenger. In the words of Lindberg, "We wanted to be a full-service, door-to-door travel service company. We aimed to offer a unique product which we could control from A to Z." To meet this objective, the SAS service chain concept was established by creating a distribution system and network of services that met the needs of the business travelers, from the time they ordered their tickets to the time they got back home. This meant that the development of a hotel network, reservation system, and credit card operation were decisive for the company's future.

SAS International Hotels

In 1983, SAS International Hotels (SIH) became a separate division within the SAS Group. A new concept, the SAS Destination Service—"ticket, transport and hotel package"—was introduced in September 1985. SAS market research indicated that ground transportation and hotel reservations ranked high among the needs of business travelers. Indeed surveys also indicated that more than 50 percent of the Scandinavian business travelers had no prior knowledge of the hotels into which they had been booked and thus would appreciate the standards and facilities guaranteed by the SAS Destination Service. The hotels in which guaranteed reservations could be made under this scheme totaled 80, and the chain, already one of the biggest in the world, was marketed as SAS Business Hotels. With this new service, passengers were able to order airline tickets, ground transportation, and confirmed hotel reservations with one telephone call.

At each SAS destination where public transport from the airport to the city center was time consuming or complicated, a door-to-door limousine service was made available at reasonable prices to full-fare-paying passengers. A helicopter shuttle service was introduced for travelers transfering between New York's Kennedy and LaGuardia airports. Many of the hotels featured SAS Airline Check-in. This meant that passengers could check their luggage and obtain boarding passes before leaving the hotel in the morning and then go directly to the gate at the airport for afternoon or evening departures. With the creation of the SAS Destination Service, a complete door-to-door transport service was offered, and it reflected SAS's conviction that, to a large extent, the battle for full-fare-paying passengers would be won on the ground. The total product had to be seen as an integrated chain of services for the business travel market, including reservations, airport limousines, EuroClass, hotels, car rentals, airline check-in at the hotel, hotel check-in at the airport, airport lounges, and the SAS 24-hour telephone hotline.

SAS Reservation System

SAS was facing a rising number of reservation transactions: one million in 1980 and two million in 1983. This demand created the need for an integrated information system and a network able to accept higher access without increasing the response time. To respond to this need, the company introduced a new reservation system in 1984. Developed at a cost of over 250 million SEK, the new system had around the world more than 13,000 terminals that were connected with SAS's centralized computing center. The company believed that innovative and aggressive applications of computerized information and communication technology would decide which airlines would survive. The strategy was to ensure that SAS products found the shortest and least expensive access to the market, either directly or via travel agencies. Management believed that the company had to retain independence from credit card companies and the huge distribution systems of the major U.S. airlines. By creating its own information and communication system to assure continued direct access to markets, SAS would have control of the complete purchase process.

The controversy over ticket distribution increased in Europe, and European carriers maneuvered to protect their national markets. The threat of competition from the U.S. systems and the danger of losing control of the distribution process forced Europe's major airlines to improve and update their computer reservation systems (CRS). A summary of the major American CRS systems can be found in Exhibit 6. In 1987, SAS joined a CRS study group formed by Air France, Lufthansa, and Iberia. Later that year, the group announced its intention to develop one of the world's largest and most complete reservation and distribution systems. The system, known as AMADEUS, was expected to provide travel agencies with product and service information; reservation facilities for a world-wide array of airlines, hotels, car rentals, trains, and ferries; and ticketing and fare-quoting systems. Representing a total investment of $270 million, the system was scheduled to be operational in mid-1989 and was expected to handle 150 million annual booking transactions. Finnair (Finland), Braathens S.A.F.E. (Norway), and Air Inter and UTA (France) joined the AMADEUS group by the end of 1987. A competing system, known as GALILEO, also was announced in 1987 grouping, among others, British Airways, KLM, Swissair, Alitalia, and Austrian Airlines.

Exhibit 6 **Selected Operating Data for U.S. CRS Systems**

	Sabre (American)	Apollo (United)	SystemOne (Texas Air)	Pars (TWA/NWA)	Datas II (Delta)
Terminals					
USA	54,800	40,688	21,450	17,907	9,600
abroad	316	330	100	352	300
Subscriber locations	13,018	8,944	6,350	4,816	3,100
Percent total agency sales processed, Jan—June 1986[1]	43	30.1	8.5	8.5	4.1
Percent US RPMs of airlines, Jan–May 1987	14.136	17.124	19.212	17.766	12.317
1986 revenues[2]	$336 mn	$318 mn	—	—	—
1986 profits	$142 mn	—	—	—	—
Airline booking fees					
basic	$1.75	$1.85	$1.75	$1.75	$1.50
direct access	$2.00	$1.85	$2.00	$2.00	$1.75
Direct access airlines as of July 1987	13	30	20	13	5
Current strengths	Size; depth of data; most advanced technically	Size; depth of data	Aggressiveness	International pricing; large number installed in corporations; flexibility	

[1]United States only. Sabre estimate.

[2]American is the only airline reporting publicly. Apollo estimate as published previously in the *Travel and Tourism Analyst* and not disputed by the company. A dash indicates that information is not available.

Source: Travel and Tourism Analyst (July 1987).

Credit Cards

In 1986, through the acquisition of Diners Club Nordic, SAS took over franchise rights in the Nordic countries for the Diners Club card, which had 150,000 cardholders in Scandinavia, Finland, and Iceland. The annual sale of hotels and transport services was a multibillion Kronor business in Scandinavia. SAS alone sold 11 billion SEK worth of airline tickets in Scandinavia during its 1984–1985 fiscal year. Credit card purchases accounted for 13 percent of these sales, and the share was steadily rising. The credit card acquisition, a practical tool for the business traveler, was seen as an important element in SAS's distribution strategy.

SAS Service Partner

SAS Service Partner (SSP), an SAS subsidiary in the catering business, was expanded from 12 international airline flight kitchens to an enterprise with more than 7,000 employees in over 100 locations. The subsidiary operated in 13 countries, from the United States to Japan, delivering 18 million airline meals a year. SSP was made up of a group of independent companies in airline catering and the international restaurant business. In 1984, SSP catered to more than 100 airlines, operated flight kitchens for several others, and ran airport restaurants in all three Scandinavian countries as well as in England and Ireland. It had a separate unit for its Saudi Arabian business, which was expected to have possibilities for growth in the Middle and Far East. In the early 1980s, Chicago was chosen as the entry point in a planned expansion among U.S. airports. Despite the cyclical nature of the airline business, the subsidiary remained consistently profitable. SAS believed that more and more airlines would concentrate on operating aircrafts and leave service industry tasks, such as catering, to specialist companies. British Airways was an example because it handed over its short- and medium-haul catering at London's Heathrow airport to SSP.

Other Related Activities

SAS began to offer a dedicated service to U.S. magazine publishers wishing to distribute their products in Europe. The airline offered a fast freight and delivery service at a reasonable price through a single distribution system. Management believed this to be a growing market. This new activity allowed otherwise unused cargo capacity to be put to productive use.

The role of Vingresor, an SAS subsidiary since 1971 and Sweden's largest tour operator, also was expanded considerably. All-inclusive tours on charter flights from Sweden and Norway remained the basic service offered. Additional service products, such as Vingresor's resorts with hotels in Europe and Africa, as well as a travel program including the Vingresor family concept, were developed.

New Group Structure

In March 1986, SAS was reorganized into five Independent Business Units: the airline, SAS Service Partner, SAS International Hotels, SAS Leisure (Vingresor), and SAS Distribution (Exhibit 7). The rationale was that each of these businesses faced very different strategic demands, and therefore each was required to have its own management team to allow for aggressive business development in an increasingly competitive climate. The same philosophy was pushed further down the line— for example, the new organization restructured the airline's route sectors into separate business units functioning as independent profit centers. The SAS Group management—consisting of the Chief Executive Officer, three Executive Officers, and three Executive Vice Presidents representing Denmark, Norway, and Sweden— was expected to focus primarily on overall development of the SAS Group's business areas.

SAS planned to introduce the new organization as early as 1984, but Carlzon felt that the time was not right because the airline was involved in a public debate on air safety and there were problems with various trade union groups. "Now, I fear we might have waited too long. It has become clear that the two jobs cannot be combined. The burdens of the day-to-day operation of the airline and work on the future development of it and other business units are simply too heavy," he commented in 1986.

FACING THE FUTURE

Looking ahead to the turn of the century, the management of SAS was concerned about the future of the company. The globalization trend in the airline industry was gaining momentum, as exemplified by the actions of such giants as British Airways (BA) and American Airlines (AA). BA had made it clear that it did not intend to stop growing after its acquisition of British Caledonian and the so-called "marketing merger" with United Airlines, in which the two carriers agreed to coordinate flight schedules and marketing programs, offer joint fares, and share terminals in four U.S. cities. AA was moving into Europe after recently closing a leasing deal covering 40 new wide-body aircraft. "Globalization is inevitable" commented Carlzon. "Nobody will fly European unless we have a shake-out and become more efficient." This underlined the threat of being relegated to a regional carrier, and SAS's need to unite with other airlines to create a Pan-European system.

Aircraft replacement was another threat to SAS. The average age of its 60-strong DC-9 fleet (exclusive of the newer MD-80s) was 25 years, and an upcoming EEC directive on noise levels could, if put into effect in 1992, ground 30 aircraft. The required investment in new aircraft was estimated at 40 billion SEK over the next decade, which translated into one new plane per month from 1988 until the year 2000. This process of replacement started with the purchase of nine Boeing 767s for trans-Atlantic traffic. To be able to finance these projects, the airline had to

Exhibit 7 **SAS Group Structure**

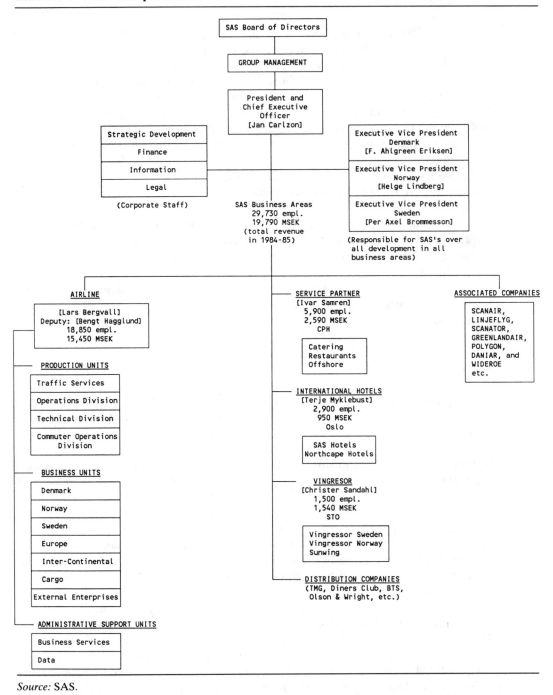

Source: SAS.

attain a gross profit level of 13 percent (before depreciation), compared to its level of 11 percent in 1986. This increase was difficult to achieve in an increasingly competitive environment and one in which SAS had a cost disadvantage with respect to other airlines.

Partnerships or mergers with other airlines was clearly an attractive option, but the company was frustrated in its attempts to develop such relationships. In spring 1987, SAS entered into negotiations with Sabena of Belgium with the goal of merging the operations of the two companies. Sabena was 52 percent state-owned, and the Belgian government expressed an interest in selling part of its holding to the private sector. With $3.3 billion in sales, the merged carrier would have been Europe's fourth largest. Sabena Chairman Carlos Van Rafelghem stated that any accord with SAS would involve combining medium- and long-distance networks in a system based on hubs in Copenhagen and Brussels. The negotiations failed, however, mainly on the issue of the degree of integration. SAS wanted all of Sabena's operations, including its hotels and catering, while the Belgian carrier was interested only in merging the airline systems.

In the fall of that same year, SAS launched a bid to acquire a major shareholding in British Caledonian Airways (BCal). SAS was eager to expand its traffic base and gain access to BCal's American, African, and Middle East destinations and to the carrier's Gatwick Airport hub outside London. A battle for control with British Airways ensued, with BA emerging the winner, having paid 250 million pounds, more than double the original bid. A major issue during the takeover battle was the implication of SAS gaining control of a British airline. The question of national control was important because of bilateral agreements. If BCal were deemed to be non-British, the foreign partner in an agreement might revoke the airline's licenses on routes to that country.

By the middle of 1988, it was clear to the corporate management of SAS that although past actions led to a sound base for the future, they were not sufficient by themselves to ensure long-term viability of the company. Within the rapidly changing environment, a new thrust was necessary, and it had to be found without much delay.

The U.S. Nuclear Regulatory Commission

William J. Dircks, the Executive Director for Operations (EDO) of the U.S. Nuclear Regulatory Commission (NRC), reviewed in 1985 the aftermath of his agency's October 1981 decision to "regionalize" its regulatory activities. He began by stating that the decision was merely an extension of earlier decentralization efforts:

> We viewed the initiatives to decentralize NRC operations as an expansion because NRC's inspection and enforcement functions have been largely decentralized for many years. As a result, we had a good deal of experience with this method of management. . . . My point is that we were not venturing into uncharted waters in our efforts to decentralize. We were planning to expand regional operations in a deliberate, phased manner in order to make the best decisions along the way . . . decisions which were based on our best judgment with consideration of needs and views of the public, the regulated industry, and our own people both at the working level and within the NRC management structure.

The regionalization program, however, quickly ran into severe opposition from several of the NRC's internal and external stakeholders, forcing Dircks to compromise aspects of the original program. The pervasiveness and intensity of the opposition took him by surprise:

> We considered regionalization to be a fairly innocuous transitional way to deal with our evolution. It made sense to bring the regional offices increasingly into the decision-making process. We didn't spend too much time thinking about stakeholders and interest groups. Maybe it was a mistake on my part, or maybe it was a mistake on the

part of others who give titles to these things. I didn't like the term regionalization and I didn't particularly care for the term decentralization either. I really didn't see this thing as a program worthy of a title. As soon as it was called 'regionalization,' all of a sudden we found stakeholders developing in all sorts of strange and unusual shapes. I was caught a bit flat-footed. I think we learned a few lessons in management.

This case describes the NRC's regionalization decision, the reactions to the decision, and the compromise program that was agreed to in November 1983.

A BRIEF OVERVIEW

The U.S. Nuclear Regulatory Commission is an independent federal agency responsible for licensing and regulating nuclear facilities and materials and for conducting research in support of this licensing and regulating. The NRC was created by the Energy Reorganization Act of 1974[1] to assume all the licensing and related regulatory functions of the abolished Atomic Energy Commission, and it formally came into existence on January 19, 1975. The NRC's regulatory objective is the protection of public health and safety and the common defense and security of the nation. The Energy Reorganization Act of 1974 (as amended), the Nuclear Non-Proliferation Act of 1978, and the Uranium Mill Tailings Radiation Control Act of 1978 have each given the NRC certain additional responsibilities, including the authority to license nuclear power reactors and waste-storage facilities that may be built for the Department of Energy (DOE). Additionally the NRC is required to comply with the requirements of the National Environmental Policy Act of 1969 (NEPA), which include the preparation of environmental impact statements, to assure that NRC licensing and regulatory activities will be conducted in a manner that will preserve and enhance the environment.

The NRC performs a wide variety of functions, including the following: setting standards and making rules; conducting technical reviews and studies; evaluating operating experience and confirmatory research; conducting public hearings; issuing authorizations, permits, and licenses; inspecting, investigating and enforcing; and issuing licenses for the export of nuclear materials and hardware. By far the most visible of the NRC's activities is the licensing of nuclear power plants. The licensing procedures followed by the Commission at the time of the regionalization decision are summarized in Exhibit 1. At that time, 79 nuclear power plants were licensed to operate, 3 more were licensed for low-power testing, and another 53 (two thirds of which were more than 50 percent complete) were under construction. The remaining licensing activities of the NRC, loosely called "materials licensing," affect licenses covering activities as diverse as the following: the operation of the "fuel-cycle" activities that support nuclear power reactors; the use of low-level-waste burial grounds, industrial radiography, gauging devices, gas chromatography, and well logging; the manufacture of consumer products that contain small amounts of radioactive materials (for example, smoke detectors); and the medical use of radioactive materials in diagnosing and treating patients.

(*Text continues on page 50*)

Exhibit 1   **The Licensing Process**

Obtaining an NRC construction permit—or a limited work authorization, pending a decision on issuance of a construction permit—is the first objective of a utility or other company seeking to operate a nuclear power reactor or other nuclear facility under NRC license. The process is set in motion with the filing and acceptance of the application, generally comprising ten or more large volumes of material covering both safety and environmental factors, in accordance with NRC requirements and guidance. The second phase consists of safety, environmental, safeguards and antitrust reviews undertaken by the NRC staff. Third, a safety review is conducted by the independent Advisory Committee on Reactor Safeguards (ACRS); this review is required by law. Fourth, a mandatory public hearing is conducted by a three-member Atomic Safety and Licensing Board (ASLB), which then makes an initial decision as to whether the permit should be granted. This decision is subject to appeal to an Atomic Safety and Licensing Appeal Board (ASLAB) and could ultimately go to the Commissioners for final NRC decision. The law provides for appeal beyond the Commission in the Federal courts.

As soon as an initial application is accepted, or "docketed," by the NRC, a notice of that fact is published in the *Federal Register,* and copies of the application are furnished to appropriate State and local authorities and to a local public document room (LPDR) established in the vicinity of the proposed site, as well as to the NRC-PDR in Washington, D.C. At the same time, a notice of a public hearing is published in the *Federal Register* and local newspapers which provides 30 days for members of the public to petition to intervene in the

proceeding. Such petitions are entertained and adjudicated by the ASLB appointed to the case, with rights of appeal by the petitioner to the ASLAB.

The NRC staff's safety, safeguards, environmental and antitrust reviews proceed in parallel. With the guidance of the Standard Format (Regulatory Guide 1.70), the applicant for a construction permit lays out the proposed nuclear plant design in a Preliminary Safety Analysis Report (PSAR). If and when this report has been made sufficiently complete to warrant review, the application is docketed and NRC staff evaluations begin. Even prior to submission of the report, NRC staff conducts a substantive review and inspection of the applicant's quality assurance program covering design and procurement. The safety review is performed by NRC staff in accordance with the Standard Review Plan for Light-Water-Cooled Reactors, initially published in September 1975 and updated periodically. This plan states the acceptance criteria used in evaluating the various systems, components and structures important to safety and in assessing the proposed site, and it describes the procedures used in performing the safety review.

The NRC staff examines the applicant's PSAR to determine whether the plant design is safe and consistent with NRC rules and regulations; whether valid methods of calculation were employed and accurately carried out; whether the applicant has conducted his analysis and evaluation in sufficient depth and breadth to support staff approval with respect to safety. When the staff is satisfied that the acceptance criteria of the Standard Review Plan have been met by the applicant's preliminary report, a Safety Evaluation Report is prepared by the staff summarizing the results of its review regarding the anticipated effects of the proposed facility on the public health and safety.

Following publication of the staff Safety Evaluation Report, the ACRS completes its review and meets with staff and applicant. The ACRS then prepares a letter report to the Chairman of the NRC presenting the results of its independent evaluation and recommending whether or not a construction permit should be issued. The staff issues a supplement to the Safety Evaluation Report incorporating any changes or actions adopted as a result of ACRS recommendations. A public hearing can then be held, generally in a community near the proposed site, on safety aspects of the licensing decision.

In appropriate cases, NRC may grant a Limited Work Authorization to an applicant in advance of the final decision on the construction permit in order to allow certain work to begin at the site, saving as much as seven months time. The authorization will not be given, however, until NRC staff has completed environmental impact and site suitability reviews and the appointed ASLB has conducted a public hearing on environmental impact and site suitability with a favorable finding. To realize the desired saving of time, the applicant must submit the environmental portion of the application early.

The environmental review begins with a review of the applicant's Environmental Report (ER) for acceptability. Assuming the ER is sufficiently complete to warrant review, it is docketed and an analysis of the consequences to the environment of the construction and operation of the proposed facility at the proposed site is begun. Upon completion of this analysis, a Draft Environmental Statement is published and distributed with specific requests for review and comment by Federal, State and local agen-

cies, other interested parties and members of the public. All of their comments are then taken into account in the preparation of a Final Environmental Statement. Both the draft and the final statements are made available to the public at the time of respective publication. During this same time period NRC is conducting an analysis and preparing a report on site suitability aspects of the proposed licensing action. Upon completion of these activities, a public hearing, with the appointed ASLB presiding, may be conducted on environmental and site suitability aspects of the proposed licensing action (or a single hearing on both safety and environmental matters may be held, if that is indicated).

The antitrust reviews of license applications are carried out by the NRC and the Attorney General in advance of, or currently with, other licensing reviews. If an antitrust hearing is required, it is held separately from those on safety and environmental aspects.

About two or three years before construction of the plant is scheduled to be complete, the applicant files an application for an operating license. A process similar to that for the construction permit is followed. The application is filed, NRC staff and the ACRS review it, a Safety Evaluation Report and an updated Environmental Statement are issued. A public hearing is not mandatory at this stage, but one may be held if requested by affected members of the public or at the initiative of the Commission. Each license for operation of a nuclear reactor contains technical specifications which set forth the particular safety and environmental protection measures to be imposed upon the facility and the conditions that must be met for the facility to operate.

Once licensed, a nuclear facility remains under NRC surveillance and undergoes periodic inspections throughout its operating life. In cases where the NRC finds that substantial, additional protection is necessary for the public health and safety or the common defense and security, the NRC may re-

quire "backfitting" of a licensed plant, that is, the addition, elimination or modification of structures, systems or components of the plant.

Source: U.S. Nuclear Regulatory Commission.

The organization structure used by the NRC in the early 1980s to discharge its responsibilities is shown in Exhibit 2. At the head of the organization was the Commission itself, consisting of five members appointed by the President, with the advice and consent of the Senate, to serve staggered five-year terms. The Commission was in a sense the NRC's board of directors, except that all its members were full-time employees of the NRC. A quorum of three members was required for the transaction of business, and the action of the Commission was determined by a majority vote of the members present. Not more than three members could belong to the same political party. One member of the Commission was designated the Chairman, to serve in that capacity at the pleasure of the President.

Prior to 1980, the action of the full Commission was required on even routine matters. The management difficulty associated with this requirement of collegial action, particularly in emergency situations, was long recognized, but it was made irrefutably clear after the nation's worst commercial power plant accident, at Three Mile Island (TMI) on March 28, 1979. The President's Reorganization Plan No. 1 of 1980 altered the Commission's original management structure by strengthening the authority of the Chairman relative to the other members. The Chairman became the principal executive and the official spokesperson of the Commission.

Reporting to the Chairman were several supporting staff groups: seven offices, two panels, and a committee. One such staff group (whose role was crucial in the regionalization decision) was the Advisory Committee on Reactor Safeguards (ACRS). The ACRS reviewed safety studies and applications for construction permits and facility-operating licenses and made reports on these; advised the Commission with regard to the hazards of proposed or existing safety standards; and reviewed any generic issues or other matters referred to it by the Commission. At the request of the Department of Energy (DOE), the ACRS also reviewed and advised with regard to the hazards of DOE nuclear activities and facilities. The ACRS could on its own initiative also conduct reviews of specific generic matters on safety-related items in nuclear facilities. It also conducted studies of reactor safety research and submitted to Congress an annual report containing the results of such studies.

The Commission's Chief Operating Officer was the Executive Director for Operations (EDO). The EDO held a statutory post and was charged with directing and coordinating the Commission's operational and administrative activities and also with developing policy options for the Commission's consideration. The EDO

Exhibit 2 Organization Structure

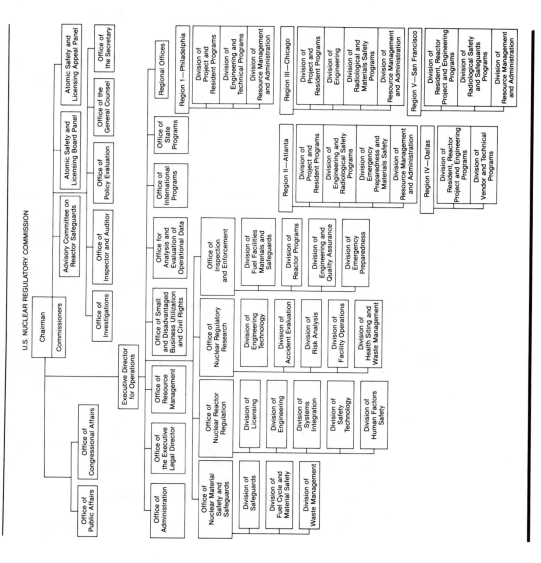

U.S. NUCLEAR REGULATORY COMMISSION

served at the pleasure of, and could be removed by, the Commission. Acting under a delegation of authority from the Commission, the EDO was responsible for the supervision and coordination of policy development and the operational activities of the Office of Nuclear Reactor Regulation (NRR), the Office of Nuclear Material Safety and Safeguards (NMSS), the Office of Nuclear Regulatory Research (RES), the Office of Inspection and Enforcement (IE), and the several staff services that supported these offices.

The EDO was authorized to discharge the licensing, regulatory, and administrative functions of the NRC, including rule making, but the EDO could not promulgate rules involving significant questions of policy or affecting certain parts of the Commission's regulations without advance approval. When doing this, the EDO was governed by the general policies, regulatory decisions, findings, and determinations of the Commission. The EDO presented for resolution all significant questions of policy and, through the Chairman, ensured that the Commission was fully informed about current regulatory developments.

With the exception of a relatively small number of Commission staff offices (such as the Office of Congressional Affairs) and personal assistants to Commissioners, most of the Agency's 3,300 employees reported to and through the EDO. Reporting immediately to the EDO were a number of Office Directors and Regional Administrators.

Three of the offices (and the respective Director positions) were established by statute and charged with specific functions. The Director of Nuclear Reactor Regulation (NRR) was principally responsible for licensing and regulating nuclear power, test, and research reactors. However, at the full-power license stage, the Commission's authorization was necessary for the NRR to issue the license. The Director of Nuclear Material Safety and Safeguards (NMSS) licensed and regulated nuclear facilities other than reactors (for example, uranium mills, fuel-fabrication facilities, and nuclear-waste storage and disposal activities) and safeguarded nuclear facilities and materials. In addition, the NMSS was responsible for licensing the possession and use of most radioactive materials in industry, research, and medicine in the 26 states that had not entered into agreements with the Commission to assume such licensing authority. Finally, the Director of Nuclear Regulatory Research (RES) planned and implemented confirmatory research programs that were deemed necessary for the performance of the Commission's licensing and regulating functions. The fourth major office, not specifically mandated by statute, was the Office of Inspection and Enforcement (IE), which inspected licensees to determine whether their operations were conducted in accordance with NRC regulations and to initiate enforcement action when violations were detected.

Several staff offices also supported the EDO (see Exhibit 2). The Office of the Executive Legal Director (ELD), for example, provided legal support, including representation of the agency staff at hearings for the licensing of nuclear reactors.

The independence, authority, and effectiveness of the EDO increased in the 1980s as a result of action taken in response to several studies—including those done in the aftermath of the accident at Three Mile Island—and in accordance with the President's Reorganization Plan of 1980. Office Directors of NRR, NMSS, and RES, who were previously empowered to report directly to the Commission, began reporting to the EDO.

THE DECISION TO REGIONALIZE

In late 1981, the NRC felt that its role had changed so substantially that it would be appropriate to move certain regulatory activities from the headquarters to the regions. One official of the NRC explained its changing role in the following manner:

> In the early days of commercial nuclear power [1960s and early 1970s] the main regulatory activities were the establishment of safety regulations and guidelines and then the review of plant designs to assure conformance with these regulations and guidelines. For example, in the 6-year span from 1968 through 1974, there were 62 construction permits issued. When NRC came into existence as a separate agency in 1975 there were only 52 plants operating while 156 were under review for either an operating license or a construction permit.
>
> As we look a few years ahead, we see that there will be over one hundred plants licensed to operate, perhaps a couple of dozen plants under review for operating licenses, and very few, if any, applications for construction permits. Thus, the staff time devoted to setting safety guidelines and reviewing designs will decrease relative to the staff time devoted to inspection, enforcement, license amendments and evaluation of operating experience for the operating reactors. It is this evolutionary change in NRC's mission that is the impetus for regionalization.

As later events show, the NRC identified its changing mission quite accurately. The escalating costs of nuclear power plant construction, the low growth in demand for nuclear power, and the public concern over nuclear safety led to the deferral or even the cancellation of plants that were as much as 97 percent complete. Rationalizing these abandonment decisions, Hugh Parris, the Manager of Power at the Tennessee Valley Authority (TVA), made the following observation:

> Some folks might look at abandoned nuclear plants as monuments to mistakes and stupidity. I look at them as monuments to good management.[2]

Escalating costs and tighter regulatory standards forced the construction cost of a nuclear power plant to jump from $200 per kilowatt in 1970 to about $3,000 per kilowatt in 1984. The growing demand for nuclear energy that followed the second oil shock of 1979 began easing because of unexpected improvements in energy conservation and the sustained oil glut. The last straw, of course, was the loss of public confidence in the safety of nuclear power plants. Industry analysts now agree that many nuclear projects had been badly conceived, poorly designed, shoddily constructed, and inadequately controlled. The events at Three Mile Island and a series of other less-serious accidents heightened the public's distrust of the industry. Former NRC Commissioner Victor Gilinsky summarized the public fear this way:

> What shook the public the most was seeing the men in the white lab coats standing around and scratching their heads because they didn't know what to do. The result was that accidents were taken seriously in a way they never had been before.[3]

Although most industry experts admitted that the odds of U.S. utilities shutting down any of the 82 nuclear power plants in operation were rather small, they nevertheless were not betting against the cancellation of plants in various stages of construction around the country. The NRC's mission, as visualized in the early 1980s, was indeed one of license maintenance and not one of license issuance.

Impetus for Regionalization

The regionalization program was enunciated in October 1981 and was expected to improve the NRC's coordination of license maintenance, inspection, and enforcement activities at each facility; to strengthen the NRC's incident response capability; and to bring the NRC nearer to state and local governments and the public.

The changing mission of the NRC provided a rationale for regionalization, but an important question was who within the NRC had championed the regionalization cause. The answer to that question remains somewhat fuzzy. A senior NRC administrator believes that the prime mover was John Ahearne, an NRC Commissioner from 1978 to 1983 and the NRC Chairman for 18 months prior to the 1981 decision to regionalize. Ahearne was very impressed with the decentralized management of the Department of Defense, with which he had many years of association, and he felt strongly that this decentralization could apply to the NRC as well. The background of William Dircks, the acting EDO in 1980 and the EDO since 1981, also may have led to the decision. He came to the NRC from the Environmental Protection Agency (EPA), a decentralized organization. He saw regionalization not as a radical change in nuclear regulation but rather as a new approach in the internal management of the NRC activities:

> I think what we did in this area contributed to better decision-making as far as protecting public health and safety. It got the right people making the correct level of decision and it made those decisions in an effective way. It freed up the major policy-making office to do policy-making and program goal-setting and evaluation, which I think is a headquarters function. It freed up these offices from making day-to-day licensing decisions that can very easily be made at the regional level.

A former employee of the NRC stated that the decision was influenced in part by the Carter administration's drive to bring governmental agencies closer to the public. Oddly enough, the Reagan administration's goal of returning power to the states may have given the regionalization decision sustained momentum.

It was perhaps this combination of a strong administrative rationale, willing bureaucratic support, and a favorable political context that encouraged Nunzio

Palladino, the newly appointed Chairman of the NRC in 1981, to approve the regionalization program and to demand that the reorganization be completed by November 2, 1981, less than a month after he gave his approval. Dircks recently speculated that the new Chairman may have provided a significant stimulus to the regionalization decision:

> He was freshly appointed. He wanted to make a statement as any new head of any agency: "I'm coming in and here are all the new things I'm going to do." One of the things he latched on to was regionalization.

IMPLEMENTING THE REGIONALIZATION DECISION

The decision to regionalize was in a sense the culmination of a great deal of successful experimentation. For several years prior, the NRC had conducted pilot programs to decentralize the regulatory activities on a limited basis. Examples of such programs are resident inspection, selected materials licensing, emergency planning, state liaison, and some reactor operator licensing actions. One of the most successful of these was the resident inspector program. This pilot program showed that by using resident inspectors at each plant, instead of a pool of region-based inspectors, there was an improvement in the effectiveness of inspection and the quality of interaction between the NRC and its licensees at the inspector level. Also, contact between the local public and the resident inspector improved. A two-year pilot program to decentralize selected materials-licensing activities had been conducted in Region III from March 1978 to March 1980. The overall experience of this pilot program was good because it provided better coordination between the materials-licensing staff and the regional inspectors and better services to applicants and licensees.

As a result of these pilot programs and in recognition of the fact that in a license maintenance mode the regions would increasingly become the focus of the NRC's interaction with licensees, the NRC decided that the status of its regional officers also should be upgraded.

To enlarge the role of the five regional offices, the NRC first reorganized the Office of Inspection and Enforcement, transferring its five regional offices from the direct control of the Executive Regional Director to that of the Regional Administrator. It also simultaneously created the position of Deputy Executive Director for Regional Operations and Generic Requirements (DEDROGR). The DEDROGR, in addition to functioning as a Chairman of the Committee to Review Generic Requirements (CRGR), provided support for the EDO's managerial and supervisory tasks.

Early in 1982, the headquarters and regional offices developed planning assumptions and began to identify regulatory activities that could be decentralized. The following criteria were used to identify activities that could be transferred to the regions:

1. The activities should require frequent interactions with licensees or local government representatives.

2. The transfer of the activities should be possible under existing legislation, or the enabling legislation should be easy to enact.
3. The regionalization of the activity should lead to closer coordination and better communication between the licensing and inspection programs.
4. The transferred activity should not require increases in number and expertise of the regional staff that could not be accommodated within the Commission's budget constraint.
5. Sufficient written guidelines must exist or should be easy to develop so that the program could be uniformly implemented in all regions.

After the candidate activities were identified, the NRC prepared a list of activities and estimates of dates by which the activities could be transferred to the regions (Exhibit 3). Even as the task force set up by Dircks was busy detailing the implementation of the regionalization decision, opposition to the idea was building both inside and outside the NRC. Some of the stakeholders openly criticized the decision; others silently dissented.

Employees of the Commission

These civil servants, many with years of service in the federal government, had long had a keen stake in the programmatic directions chosen by the Commission. As a group, they looked forward to and expected the benefits of the lifetime career of federal service promised them at the time of their recruitment. Mindful of a sense of obligation to those long-time employees, the Commission nevertheless had to deal with new skills and some competencies in the existing work force that were no longer needed, at least not in some geographic locations.

Grievance of the Office Directors.   The reorganization of the NRC placed its three Office Directors in an awkward position. As mentioned earlier, the heads of Nuclear Reactor Regulation, Nuclear Material Safety and Safeguards, and Nuclear Regulatory Research were charged by statute with the responsibility for their programs. With the reorganization, however, they had to rely on the Regional Administrators for discharging part of their responsibility.

Although the three Office Directors had been consulted on the reorganization and regionalization plans, they felt that they had no choice but to agree to a difficult arrangement. Regionalization undermined their importance. It did not take away any of their responsibilities, but it did lessen their formal authority.

The Regional Administrators quickly took the position that they reported to only the EDO and did not consider themselves answerable, especially on a day-to-day basis, to the Office Directors, whose statutory mission they were accomplishing. The Office Directors, albeit reluctantly, assumed that this was what the EDO intended. The EDO finally had to tell them the following:

> You [Office Directors] are responsible for these programs whether they are carried out here or in the regions. The regional administrators are your agents. You must see that

they keep you informed of major events and bring you into the decision-making process. You will rate them [at annual performance appraisal time] on their handling of problems. This is not day-to-day supervision, but close communication on big issues, similar to the relationship each of you has with me.

Operating Reactor Project Managers.   The Operating Reactor Project Manager (ORPM) was the common contact point for the licensee and the regulatory staff on licensing issues for an assigned plant. The ORPM was the initiator and motivator for completing licensing activities, both those requested by the licensee and those generated within the NRC. A primary function of the ORPM was coordinating and communicating closely with the technical staff who performed the review. The technical staff relied on the ORPM for plant history and information unique to the plant under review. Because most ORPMs were located within the same building at their Bethesda headquarters, they were available to each other for consultations. In addition, if the issue was a multiplant action (MPA), the ORPM also met with and sought guidance from the lead Project Manager (another ORPM) assigned to the MPA.

The ORPMs typically communicated with licensees only by telephone, speaking with their contact at each licensee's corporate headquarters. The regionalization plan envisaged the decentralization of the ORPMs' functions, moving the Project Managers closer to the plants from their current base in Bethesda. The Project Managers did not see this as a desirable move. Some of their reactions to the proposed regionalization plans were these:

> The management resources to resolve 'crises' have to be at headquarters [HQ]. If the ORPM is at a regional office, he would have to come to HQ to do the job. As the population of plants ages, the tendency is to have more 'crisis' events. This suggests that there will be even more activity at HQ, even if routine reviews are transferred to regional offices.

> Another serious drawback to the proposed regionalization plan is the large exodus of NRC project managers [and licensing assistants] that can be anticipated. Most ORPMs [and LAs] for either personal or financial reasons are not able to relocate to any of the five regions. Involuntary reassignments to a region will result in the resignation of probably at least 90% of the affected personnel within a short time of the reassignment. In my case, I guarantee it.

> The point is that Federal employment is hardly the gravy train it's made out to be, even for existing employees. The NRC, if faced with large-scale defections as a result of involuntary regional assignments, will not be able to recruit talented, capable people to fill the vacated positions. The consequences from both a safety and economic point of view will be enormous.

Driven by personal considerations and motivated by a strong desire to speak out against the safety risks that they perceived in the proposed regionalization, 36

(Text continues on page 61)

Exhibit 3 Headquarters' Functions to Be Decentralized

Function (Headquarters' Office)	FY 1982	FY 1983	FY 1984	FY 1985
1. Operating reactor licensing actions—technical review (NRR)	532, all regions	400, all regions	500, all regions	615, all regions
2. Licensing authority for operating power reactors[1] (NRR)	—	Region IV: 1 reactor	Regions I, II, III: 6 reactors per region; Region IV: 1 reactor	Regions I, II, III: 12 reactors per region; Region IV: 7 reactors; Region V: 6 reactors
3. Licensing authority for TMI-2 cleanup[2] (NRR)	—	—	Region I	Region I
4. Licensing authority for operating non-power reactors (NRR)	—	All nonpower reactors in Regions I, IV, V	All nonpower reactors in all regions	All nonpower reactors in all regions
5. Licensing authority for new and renewal applications for nonpower reactors (NRR)	—	—	All nonpower reactors in Regions I, IV, V	All nonpower reactors in all regions
6. Administer reactor operator license examinations (NRR)	Region III[3]	Region II, III[3]	All regions	All regions
7. Uranium mill tailings (NMSS)[4]	—	Region IV	Region IV	Region IV
8. Authority to issue materials licenses (NMSS)	5 types of high-volume licenses, Regions I, III	5 types of high-volume licenses, all regions	10 types of high-volume licenses, all regions	10 types of high-volume licenses, all regions
9. Issue safeguards license amendments that do not decrease effectiveness for reactors and SNM facilities (NMSS)	—	Regions I, II	All regions	All regions
10. Conduct transportation route surveys and review contingency plans for spent fuel and Category 1 SNM shipments (NMSS)	—	—	Region III	All regions
11. Perform closeout surveys and termination of uranium fuel fabrication licenses (NMSS)	—	All regions	All regions	All regions
12. Maintain oversight of ten CFR 70 licenses for advanced fuel (Pu) plants that have initiated decontamination and decommissioning activities (NMSS)	—	All regions	All regions	All regions

Function	Col 1	Col 2	Col 3	Col 4
13. Issue proposed civil penalties[5] (IE)	All regions	All regions	All regions	All regions
14. Issue orders and make ten CFR 2.206 decisions consistent with the transfer of licensing and enforcement authority from IE, NRR, and NMSS (IE, NRR, and NMSS)	—	Regions I, IV, V	All regions	All regions
15. Conduct special licensing activities for operating reactors after emergency preparedness appraisal and reports (IE)	—	All regions	All regions	All regions
16. Observe and appraise the annual emergency preparedness exercises for operating reactors (IE)	All regions[6]	All regions	All regions	All regions
17. Provide legal assistance consistent with the transfer of functions to review severity of level III violations, proposed civil penalties and orders, 2.206 decisions, material licenses, mill tailings licenses, and reactor licensing (ELD)	All regions	All regions	All regions	All regions
18. Provide state agreement officer (SP)	Regions II, IV	Regions I, II, IV, V	Regions I, II, IV, V	Regions I, II, IV, V
19. Continue state liaison function	All regions	All regions	All regions	All regions
20. Perform license-fee billings for materials licensing and inspection activities (ADM)	—	Regions I, III	All regions	All regions
21. Perform budget formulation/execution and management information reporting activities	All regions	All regions	All regions	All regions
22. Perform various administrative support services	—	All regions	All regions	All regions

[1] The NRR will retain licensing authority for certain types of operating power reactor licensing actions (for example, pressurized thermal shock and steam generator inspection and repair). The NRR will identify and maintain a current list of these items.

[2] The transfer of this function remains uncertain until the licensee funding sources are confirmed and the major core removal activities begin.

[3] The NRR will provide for contract examiner assistance.

[4] To be implemented in accordance with Dircks' August 2, 1982, memorandum on establishing the Denver field office.

[5] With IE concurrence.

[6] With IE assistance.

Exhibit 4

UNITED STATES
NUCLEAR REGULATORY COMMISSION
WASHINGTON, D.C. 20555

DATE: March 14, 1983

MEMORANDUM FOR: Chairman Palladino
                        Commissioner Gilinsky
                        Commissioner Ahearne
                        Commissioner Roberts
                        Commissioner Asselstine

FROM: Operating Reactors Project Managers
                        and Licensing Assistants, Undersigned

SUBJECT: CONCERNS REGARDING REGIONALIZATION OF
                        THE OPERATING REACTORS' PROJECT MANAGE-
                        MENT FUNCTION

We are concerned about the proposed regionalization of the project management function. As experienced Operating Reactor Project Managers and Licensing Assistants, we believe that our concerns should be brought to your attention. We believe that regionalizing the project management function would reduce the agency's effectiveness in performing its regulatory function, and could ultimately result in a reduction in overall plant safety.

The project management function is not performed in a vacuum. Rather, a key element in the management of operating reactor licensing activities is the ready access the project manager has to the centralized body of technical expertise now located in Bethesda. This access is personal, timely, and encourages helpful dialogue between the project manager and the technical review staff. Moving the project management function to the regions would severely impede the project manager's access to that expertise. This would significantly impair the effectiveness of the project manager and could have an adverse effect on plant safety due to poor communications, misunderstandings, or untimely responses.

One benefit perceived by proponents of the proposed regionalization program is the increase in effectiveness of the project manager because of his proximity to the plant. This perception is based upon a misunderstanding of how the project management function operates. Whether conducted in Bethesda or in a regional office, the project manager works most closely with the various technical review branches and with the licensees' licensing personnel. In matters where plant-specific information or expertise is required, the project manager consults also with the NRC resident inspector, who is relied upon for first-hand knowledge of plant conditions. Contact with the licensee and with the resident inspector is primarily by telephone; if a site visit is required by either the project manager or the reviewer, it can be initiated equally as well from Bethesda as from a regional office. Thus, the perceived benefit of proximity to the plant for the project manager in order to conduct his work is not well-founded.

This discussion simply illustrates some of the concerns we have regarding this proposed program. We believe that our concerns are substantial. We would welcome the opportunity to meet with you to discuss them.

---

of the 60 Project Managers, in an unprecedented move, sent a letter of protest to the Commission (Exhibit 4).

In retrospect, William Dircks conjectured that the fears of the Project Managers were largely misplaced. Although the regionalization program did propose the transfer of project management positions to the regions, there was no intent at any time to transfer Project Managers forcibly to the regions. The staffing of the regions would have been brought up to planned levels through the transfer of vacancies and the voluntary transfer of personnel from headquarters.

> First of all, I don't think we were talking about massive numbers of personnel. In the nuclear reactor regulation area we were planning to transfer over a period of time something like one hundred positions. We have a seven percent turnover rate in the commission, anyway, so what we were trying to do was to move the vacancy slots out to the regions and let them hire out there as opposed to moving large numbers of people involuntarily out to these regional offices.
>
> While some of our employees saw themselves being moved out of their homes in Bethesda, Maryland and moved to ungodly places like Chicago, San Francisco, Atlanta or Dallas or Philadelphia, we also had a relatively large number of people wanting to move from the Washington, D.C. area to other areas of the country. Some regions were naturally more popular than others. San Francisco, for example, used up all of its available slots fairly rapidly.
>
> Moreover, most of the commission's personnel growth since 1979 has been in inspectors, who went to the regions anyway. That is a totally decentralized program. So we did not face massive dislocation because of regionalization as alleged. That is why I was greatly surprised by the huge furor we had about this thing.

Guy Cunningham, the Executive Legal Director of the NRC, added this:

> We don't need any more, for example, people who can perform a seismic review of the design of a nuclear power plant. We are no longer reviewing designs. Moreover, the seismic reviewer we have doesn't make a very good piping inspector. So we have relied on attrition. We haven't had layoffs here to hire new kinds of skills. The regionalization program essentially sought to hire the new personnel in the regions instead of at the headquarters.

As for the issue of safety, Dircks pointed out that adequate controls to supervise the regional effort were in place. He believed that with better communication, the grievances of the Project Managers could have been addressed.

Concerns of the ACRS

As mentioned earlier, the Advisory Committee on Reactor Safeguards (ACRS) is a statutory committee (of 15 scientists and engineers) that advises the Commission on the safety aspects of proposed and existing nuclear facilities and the adequacy of proposed reactor safety standards. The Committee was very powerful through the mid-1970s, until the NRC was created. In the 1980s it was still a prestigious body of elite scientists whose advice to the Commission carried a weight disproportionate to its formal authority.

The ACRS had serious concerns about the impact that decentralization might have on the safety of nuclear facilities. In a letter dated April 19, 1983, the acting chairman of the ACRS stated this:

> If there is one among us who fully supports the present program and pace for regionalization, he has not made himself known. Our concerns are several, but all have to do with the potential negative impact on reactor safety.

The Committee suggested that decentralization be stopped or deferred until its impact on safety was clearly understood or that it proceed with caution with regard to safety-related matters.

In a letter to the Chairman of the NRC, the acting Chairman of the ACRS stated the following:

> We are concerned about whether it is possible to form six adequately staffed multidisciplinary organizations (Headquarters and the Regional Offices) with the current NRC staffing and resource limitations. The regulation of the nuclear industry calls for the consideration of complex systems and their integration, which requires the application of many diverse disciplines. Interactions among the needed disciplines are essential, and are facilitated when the people involved have easy access to each other. We are concerned that regionalization will make this access more difficult.
>
> The potential for confusion as to where the ultimate authority of the Staff lies [with the Regional Administrators or with Headquarters] will be increased by regionalization. We believe that a structured appeal process will be needed with provisions for protection against possible retaliation by Regional authorities who might be sensitive to appeals over their heads.
>
> As decisions are made in the Regions, it will be unavoidable that differences in interpretation and implementation of regulations will occur. This lack of uniformity could have significant safety implications.
>
> The benefits of shared operating experience will be lost unless effective communication channels are provided among the Regional Offices, and between the Regions and NRC Headquarters. There are already communication problems among the separate offices at NRC Headquarters, and these will certainly not be relieved by regionalization.
>
> Although it is proposed that issues with generic implications will be handled at

NRC Headquarters, the decisions on which issues fall into this category will be made in the Regional Offices. We are concerned that the relatively small technical staffs at the Regional Offices will not have sufficient experience or expertise to make appropriate decisions on these issues.

The ACRS drew parallels between the NRC's efforts at decentralization and the FAA's efforts. The Acting Chairman of ACRS pointed this out to the Commission:

> The adhoc National Academy of Sciences' review of the Federal Aviation Administration [FAA] in the aftermath of the Chicago DC-10 accident [aviation's Three Mile Island] strongly criticized the regionalization of the FAA. . . . While there are differences in the two cases, the many similarities make the Academy group's conclusions difficult to ignore.

When discussing the adverse reaction of the ACRS, Dircks conceded this:

> I underestimated the reaction that this whole thing [regionalization] was going to get. When the ACRS entered the picture suddenly, it flabbergasted me, but I guess I should be accustomed to some of these strange entities walking on center stage once in a while. They had a set of concerns I think we dealt with. Here again, I believe fundamentally we had a defensible plan but did not identify all the relevant stakeholders in time and communicate our plan to them. It is possible that the ACRS seized the regionalization issue to ventilate their own grievances about their diminishing influence on the management of nuclear energy.

The Commissioners of the NRC

The Kemeny Commission, which President Carter created to look into the Three Mile Island accident, was critical of the fact that the NRC Commissioners had lost touch with the nuclear regulatory process. Its report charged the following:

> We found serious managerial problems within the organization. These problems start at the very top. It is not clear to us what the precise role of the five NRC commissioners is, and we have evidence that they themselves are not clear on what their role should be. The huge bureaucracy under the Commissioners is highly compartmentalized with insufficient communication among the major offices.

The Commissioners felt frustrated that the President's Reorganization Plan of 1980, which was proposed in response to the TMI accident, further distanced the Commissioners from the NRC's operations. The reorganization gave more powers to the Chairman and the EDO of the Commission. Regarding this, Dircks indicated that the Commissioners were naturally suspicious of the regionalization decision, which seemingly took the NRC's operations farther from their scrutiny:

> I think there were some Commissioners who said, "Hey! Wait a minute, now, this business of regionalization, is there something behind this that would take even more control away from us and delegate it to the Executive Director and to the regional administrators? We are losing control of this agency." All of a sudden they got agitated and they started working another road of opposition.

Exhibit 5

May 12, 1983
NS-EPR-2766

Mr. Samuel J. Chilk, Secretary
U. S. Nuclear Regulatory Commission
Washington, D. C. 20555

Attn: Docketing and Service Branch

Dear Mr. Chilk:

This letter is in response to the Nuclear Regulatory Commission's request for comments related to the Policy Statement on Regionalization, 48 Fed. Reg. 12619, March 25, 1983. Westinghouse Electric Corporation welcomes the opportunity to respond to the Commission's request and offers the following comments:

In general, Westinghouse believes that further NRC regionalization should be approached with caution. Our primary concern is whether NRC will be able to perform technical reviews and interpret and apply regulatory requirements in a uniform and consistent manner if its licensing activities become decentralized to the regional level. We see the potential for conflicting staff positions being applied from region to region. The Standard Review Plan (SRP) is an attempt to define acceptance criteria, but in some cases they have been inconsistently applied from branch to branch, and especially when reviews were decentralized to national laboratory contract personnel.

Westinghouse is also concerned that the experience base built up over the years with headquarters personnel may be lost due to regionalization. Efficiency in the licensing process depends on maintaining the closure of items resolved in earlier proceedings, especially when standard plants or generic issues are involved. This is possible with the current NRC organization due to the physical proximity of the headquarters technical staff and the project management function, which permits free communication between and within each function. We are concerned that regionalization may cause some of these issues to be re-opened for no valid technical reason. Our concern is again based on our experiences with the NRC's use of national laboratory reviews—a form of decentralized headquarters review.

We also see a potential problem with respect to the handling of generic issues, which surface as a result of occurrences in operating plants and plants under construction. With the proposed regionalization program, it is not clear to us as to how the NRC will be able to recognize occurrences in different regions as a generic issue. It also appears that coordination of a particular generic issue will entail unnecessary duplication of effort between the regions and NRC headquarters. It is also unclear how the lead responsibility for a particular issue will be identified. It could be any of the regions dealing with the issue or the region with responsibility for the associated vendor or NRC headquarters.

As a final comment, we do see the potential for regionalization confusing the review process by introducing another level of review. If appeals and conflicts on technical matters have to be resolved at the headquarters level, regionalization simply adds additional parties to the proceedings, making resolution more time-consuming.

Westinghouse feels that these comments on the proposed NRC regionalization plan merit your consideration. We would be pleased to discuss these items further with you if you so desire.

Very truly yours,
E. P. Rahe, Jr., Manager
Nuclear Safety Department

The Regulated Nuclear Industry

Historically the Atomic Energy Commission was the nuclear industry's champion. However, since the creation of the NRC and especially after the 1979 Three Mile Island accident, the industry and the NRC assumed increasingly adversarial roles. The Commission sought to impose an ever-increasing number of additional safety requirements on a reluctant industry. The proposed assignment of certain specific licensing responsibilities to the regions was welcomed by only a few. The majority feared that dealing with five different regulatory bodies could lead to divergent and inconsistent policies. A letter from Westinghouse that was typical of the industry's fears is presented in Exhibit 5. Dircks recalled the industry's reactions to the regionalization plan:

> They were a mixed bag. Some of them said they didn't want this to happen to them because we were going to throw them off to the untender mercies of the regional administrators scattered around the country, and they had built up all these nice relationships with our people in Washington, D.C. We were accused of dealing them a different deck. They didn't particularly care for that, and we had to fend off the argument.
>
> We should not be regulating only in an adversarial way, but to do otherwise will be interpreted as being in league with them. I never realized the depth of suspicion that lurks around the nuclear question. There is a continuous search for conspiracy, for hidden motives.

The industry was distrustful of the NRC's motives and was quick to blame the Commission for many of the industry's ills, but other critics of the Commission believed that, if anything, the NRC had been too soft on the industry. Victor Gilinsky, a Commissioner of the NRC until June 1984, believed that the Commission staff was afraid of being blamed for holding up projects. So instead of taking tough action, they nibbled at companies with a succession of minor punitive measures.

> It often turns out that nibbling which in the short run seems kinder, is in the long run the least beneficial for the company. . . . It's like dealing with your children— sometimes you have to put your foot down.[4]

Dircks commented: "It is damned if you do and damned if you don't."

Members of the Public

The Commission holds legislative-type hearings in connection with major rule making. Members of the public may participate in Commission rule making by submitting written comments that must be addressed before final action is taken. In major licensing actions, they may participate *as full parties* in contested hearings (similar to court proceedings), which may last for months or even years (see Exhibit 1 for details). Those who do not wish to intervene formally as parties may make informal statements of their position—called limited-appearance statements—at licensing hearings generally held in the vicinity of the proposed nuclear plant. Public comment is sought in connection with all substantive rule makings and on all drafts of environmental impact statements prepared by the NRC.

The Three Mile Island accident and the ensuing enhanced awareness of nuclear hazards contributed to an increase in the number of members of the public who regularly participated in NRC proceedings. The NRC's draft policy statement on regionalization received several oral comments and 66 written comments.

About half of the commenters favored regionalization, while the remainder expressed concern or opposed regionalization. The two areas of particular concern to the public were the delegation of operating power reactor licensing to the regions and the delegation of nonpower reactor licensing to the regions. These two actions were perceived as detrimental to public safety. There was broad approval, however, for the rest of the NRC's proposals.

The Executive Branch

The Executive Branch of the federal government is an important stakeholder in two respects. Despite the NRC's independence, the President clearly expects the Commission to be sympathetic to and act in accordance with his programs, at least whenever that can be done without compromising safety or due process. The most direct means of exerting influence is by the use of the power to appoint the NRC Chairman (a power exercised by President Carter to demote the previously designated Chairman after the Three Mile Island accident). Less direct but with far greater impact is the Executive Branch's role in the budget process. The NRC submits its budget requests not to Congress but to the Office of Management and Budget (OMB), which in turn incorporates the NRC budget in the President's budget with such amendments as it sees fit. Although the OMB's reductions and amendments can be restored by Congress, the OMB has significant influence over the NRC's budget-making process. The OMB's impact on the staffing levels at the NRC illustrates this office's power.

The OMB was neutral to the administrative streamlining implied by the regionalization proposal, but it was very strict in implementing President Reagan's plan for reducing the number of federal employees. The NRC's personnel request for fiscal year 1984 was reduced, for example, by 65. An additional problem for the NRC was the federal government's switch to a "full-time equivalency" (FTE) personnel accounting system.[5] Before 1981, federal agencies had a great deal of flexibility in budget and personnel practices. An absolute personnel ceiling was set by the OMB, but compliance was checked only once during the fiscal year, usually on the last day. This meant that it was possible for a federal agency to operate at an unauthorized personnel level for most of the year, without incurring any penalty, as long as the agency got under the ceiling on the day of reckoning. The switch to a FTE personnel accounting system, together with the OMB's pressure to reduce NRC manpower, posed problems for the implementation of the regionalization plan.

Congress

As an independent regulatory agency, the NRC must be responsive to legislative oversight. The NRC is dependent on Congress for its appropriations and is expressly responsible for keeping that body fully and currently informed. The Committee on Interior and Insular Affairs, the Committee on Energy and Commerce in the House of Representatives, and the Committee on Environment and Public Works in the Senate were the three important oversight committees with interest and jurisdiction on the regionalization decision. The doubts expressed by the ACRS, the NRC's own project managers, and industry representatives made Congress seriously question the justification for the regionalization decision. One congressional aide, who then worked on the House Interior and Insular Committee, recalled the following:

> We had several concerns on the proposed regionalization program. There was some evidence, for example, that regional responsibility for operator licensing [Exhibit 3, item 6] may have problems. Incidents of cheating and alleged cheating on reactor operator exams seemed to be on the upswing (e.g., Three Mile Island #1 and Grand Gulf #1).
>
> Moreover, the proposed transfer of licensing authority for operating power reactors to the regions [see Exhibit 3, item 2] had no precedent. To cite the Fort St. Vrain reactor as a prototype of this decision was wrong. Fort St. Vrain was a one-of-a-kind high-temperature gas-cooled reactor. It made sense to concentrate NRC's knowledgeable HTGR staff near the Ft. St. Vrain reactor. However, this situation was not similar

to the boiling water reactor containment experts, the Mark III technical specification experts, or the Babcock & Wilcox experts within NRC who have a national responsibility because those types of plants are located throughout the U.S.

On Capitol Hill we heard reports that NRC had only 4 project managers who were expert in Babcock & Wilcox nuclear steam supply systems. The argument was made that dismantling this group and sending each B&W expert to different regional offices would inhibit their ability to caucus and compare notes as technical issues arose. Also, we questioned whether sending a technical expert to King of Prussia, Pennsylvania, would really get that person closer to Maine Yankee, Vermont Yankee, Seabrook or Shoreham than they would be by staying in Washington, D.C.

In its final days, the 98th Congress placed a moratorium on regionalization. The following is the relevant section of the Authorization Act (Section 106 of S-291, NRC FY 84/85):

Sec. 106: (a) No funds authorized to be appropriated under this Act may be used to carry out any policy or program for the decentralization or regionalization of any Nuclear Regulatory Commission authorities regarding commercial nuclear powerplant licensing until sixty legislative days after the date on which the Commission submits to the Congress a report evaluating the effect of such policy or program on nuclear reactor safety: Provided, however, that the prohibition contained in this subsection shall not apply to any personnel assigned to the field, or to activities in which they were engaged, on or before September 22, 1983. The report shall include—

1. A detailed description of the authorities to be transferred, the reason for such transfer, and an assessment of the effect of such transfer on nuclear reactor safety;
2. An analysis of all comments submitted to the Commission regarding the effect on nuclear reactor safety which would result from carrying out the policy or program proposed by the Commission; and
3. An evaluation of the results, including the advantages and disadvantages, of the pilot program conducted under subsection b.

(b) Notwithstanding the prohibition contained in subsection (a), the Commission is authorized to conduct a pilot program for the purpose of evaluating the concept of delegating authority to regional offices for issuance of specific types of operating reactor licensing actions and for the purpose of addressing the issues identified in paragraphs (a)(1)–(3) of this section.

THE COMPROMISE PLAN

In response to the reactions of the NRC's stakeholders to the proposed regionalization, the EDO prepared in November 1983 a new policy statement that was approved with modification by the Commission in January 1984. Exhibit 6 shows the revised plan. The following major changes were approved:

1. Nonpower reactor licensing activities would not be decentralized but rather would remain in the Office of Nuclear Reactor Regulation (NRR).
2. License fee management would not be decentralized.

3. Licensing authority for operating power reactors and the NRR project managers would not be transferred to the regions, but limited licensing authority and the project manager for Fort St. Vrain would remain in Region IV.
4. A pilot program would be launched. The program would use the unique skills of each region and decentralize the limited technical review responsibility for operating reactor licenses without restructuring the project management function.

The major concession was the abandonment of the plan to delegate to the regions the licensing authority for operating power reactors. In the 1981 proposal, Fort St. Vrain was to be the prototype. The licensing authority for 48 other reactors was to be delegated to the 5 regions by 1985. Widespread opposition to the idea made the NRC drop this important part of its reorganization plan. Items 2, 3, 4, 5, 14, and 20 also were dropped from the 1981 proposal (see Exhibit 3). Items 2 and 14 refer to operating reactor licensing activities, items 4 and 5 pertain to nonpower reactor licensing, and item 20 refers to the licensing fee management activity.

As a result of the compromise plan, the NRC program offices continued to perform regulatory functions that required a qualified technical staff in the headquarters—such as high-level-waste repository systems licensing and all safety, environmental, and antitrust reviews of applications for reactor Construction Permits (CP), Operating Licenses (OL), and Standard Plants design approval. The NRC headquarters offices continued to be responsible for resolving Unresolved Safety Issues (USIs), risk and reliability assessments, and the systematic assessments of reactor operating experience.

The approval of new regulatory requirements and the modification of existing requirements remained the responsibility of the headquarters offices. Relative to licensing actions associated with operating reactors, the NRC headquarters issued all license amendments and retained the Project Manager position, except for Fort St. Vrain, where the Project Manager position and limited authority to issue license amendments were transferred to Region IV. In addition, the headquarters offices were responsible for implementing certain generic licensing actions (for example, requirements associated with pressurized thermal shock and steam generator tube integrity) on all reactors to which they apply. Licensing activities for nonpower test, research, and training reactors continued to be retained by the NRR.

Furthermore, the plan also included the transfer of technical review actions for operating reactor licenses. During fiscal year 1984, the technical review of up to 500 operating power reactor licensing actions was scheduled to be done in the regions. A two-year pilot program, limited to two operating power reactors in each of three regions, was proposed to test the method of selecting licensing actions for technical review in the regions. The regions were expected to perform technical review and safety evaluation for these actions. The Office of Nuclear Reactor Regulation was given the authority to select the technical reviews to be sent to the regions, to retain licensing authority, and to issue all license amendments and

Exhibit 6 **Headquarters' Functions to Be Decentralized**

Function (Headquarters' Office)	FY 1982	FY 1983	FY 1984	FY 1985
1. Operating reactor licensing actions—technical review (NRR)	532, all regions	100, all regions	500,[2] all regions	615,[2] all regions
2. Licensing authority for operating power reactors[1] (NRR)	—	Region IV: 1 reactor	Region IV: 1 reactor	Region IV: 1 reactor
3. Administer reactor operator license examinations[3] (NRR)	Region III	Region I, II, III	All regions	All regions
4. Uranium mill tailings (NMSS)[4]	—	Region IV	Region IV	Region IV
5. Authority to issue materials license (NMSS)	5 types of high-volume licenses, Region I, III	5 types of high-volume licenses, all regions	10 types of high-volume licenses, all regions	10 types of high-volume licenses, all regions
6. Issue safeguards license amendments that do not decrease effectiveness for reactors and SNM facilities (NMSS)	—	Regions I, II	All regions	All regions
7. Conduct transportation route surveys and review contingency plans for spent fuel and Category 1 SNM shipments (NMSS)	—	—	Region III	All regions
8. Perform closeout surveys and terminations of uranium fuel-fabrication licenses (NMSS)	—	All regions	All regions	All regions
9. Maintain oversight of ten CFR 70 licenses for advanced fuel (Pu) plants that have initiated decontamination and decommissioning activities (NMSS)	—	All regions	All regions	All regions
10. Issue proposed civil penalties[5] (IE)	All regions	All regions	All regions	All regions
11. Issue orders and make ten CFR 2.206 decisions consistent with the transfer of licensing and enforcement authority from IE, NRR, and NMSS (IE, NRR, and NMSS)	—	Region IV	Region IV	Region IV

12. Review license amendments of emergency plans for operating reactors	—	All regions	All regions	All regions
13. Observe and appraise the annual emergency preparedness exercises for operating reactors (IE)	All regions[6]	All regions	All regions	All regions
14. Provide legal assistance consistent with the transfer of functions to review severity of level III violations, proposed civil penalties and orders, 2.206 decisions, material licenses, and mill tailings licenses (ELD)	All regions	All regions	All regions	All regions
15. Provide state agreement officer (SP)	Regions II, IV	Regions I, II, IV, V	Regions I, II, IV, V	Regions I, II, IV, V
16. Continue state liaison functions	All regions	All regions	All regions	All regions
17. Performance budget formulation/execution and management information reporting activities	All regions	All regions	All regions	All regions
18. Perform various administrative support services	—	All regions	All regions	All regions

[1]The NRR will retain licensing authority for certain types of operating power reactor licensing actions (for example, pressurized thermal shock and steam generator inspection and repair). The NRR will identify and maintain a current list of these items.

[2]Includes licensing action technical review as part of the NRR pilot program at two reactors in each of three regions.

[3]The NRR will provide for contract examiner assistance.

[4]Implemented in accordance with Dircks' August 2, 1982, memorandum establishing the Denver field office.

[5]With IE concurrence.

[6]With IE assistance.

Safety Evaluation Reports for the reactors in the pilot program. The licensing actions transferred as part of this pilot program were expected to comprise a portion of the 500 licensing actions transferred during fiscal year 1984.

Response to the Plan

The revised proposal was clearly more palatable to the Director of the NRR, most of whose authority was restored. The proposed pilot program strengthened the Director's control over the regional administrators. It is not surprising that the proposal met with resistance from the regions. Thomas Murley, the Regional Administrator for Region I, wrote the following to the Director of the NRR in September 1983:

> The original plan for decentralizing operating reactor licensing functions had as its goal the transferring of substantial licensing authority for operating reactors from NRR to the regions. With this clear-cut goal in mind, the plan contemplated a phased approach of assigning licensing review actions followed by partial licensing authority for a few plants in each region. Fort St. Vrain was to be the prototype for this phased process.
>
> The proposed pilot program would assign operating reactor licensing review tasks to the regions, thereby using the technical resources of the regions as an extension of the NRR staff. But why are we doing this?
>
> Your proposal states that the intent of the pilot program is to demonstrate the use of regional technical resources in conducting license reviews. If this is in fact the goal of the pilot program, I don't think we need go any further since that goal has already been demonstrated, in my judgment.

The ACRS, on the other hand, felt strongly that the proposed pilot program was a necessary step.

> The Committee is still concerned that the regionalization of operating reactor licensing activities could have a detrimental effect on reactor safety. The approach that is currently being recommended by NRR is a significant improvement. . . .
>
> It is possible that the proposed pilot program, which we hope would be administered so as to be reversible if unsuccessful, could identify ways to resolve our concerns. If such a pilot program is undertaken, the ACRS would like an opportunity to comment on the issues that are identified for resolution by the Regional Offices.

The pilot program proposal was accepted by the Commission over the objections of some of the regions. Tom Murley reminisced:

> The Regional Administrators are very weak stakeholders. I am not in a position to fight. Being in the regions, we are outside the corridors of power in Washington.

Although the compromise proposal was approved by a majority vote of the Commission, Commissioner Gilinsky seemed to feel that regionalization had gone as far as it should. It was time to "declare a victory" and put an end to all further experimentation with the idea. In his dissenting remarks, Gilinsky stated this:

> Although I certainly preferred having a pilot program to having all project managers summarily transferred to the regions, I do not, in fact, see any value to this program

[further pilot programs for decentralizing operating reactor licensing]. It is an example of fixing something that isn't broken. The present system does not work badly. The new system even as a pilot program, involves complicated procedures for deciding which licensing actions will be transferred, which will be kept, who will review the decisions made in the regions, and so on. What is the problem for which this is the solution? The goals for regionalization, except for this program, have been accomplished. We should let the dust settle on the whole program and give the Regional Administrators time to adjust to their additional responsibilities. We do not have a single region where the time and effort spent on this program could not be better spent on inspection, operator training and other vital issues. No one supports the regionalization of reactor licensing—not the industry, not the licensing staff, not the Congress, not the ACRS. So why are we doing this?

ADMINISTRATIVE CONTROLS

The NRC's administrative systems changed with decentralization. Although the responsibility for licensing programs was not transferred, the authority to implement certain licensing activities was delegated to the Regional Administrators.

The Commission, through the EDO, intended to ensure consistency in regional operations through the following mechanisms:

1. Quarterly management meetings between the EDO, the Office Directors, and the Regional Administrators
2. Frequent meetings of the Regional Division Directors, the Branch Chief, and the working-level personnel with counterpart headquarters staff on a variety of issues
3. Weekly conference calls between the DEDROGR, the Office Directors, and the Regional Administrators
4. Development of Commission policies and procedures, and with the Commission's guidance, formulation of operating plans for each region

If decisions at the regional level appeared to be inconsistent in the application of regulatory requirements, licensees could appeal to the Office Directors, the EDO, or the Commission.

An audit program also was being developed to measure the success of the pilot program for the transfer of technical review actions to the regions. The quantitative criteria examined included the time to complete reviews, the number of review hours expended, the inventory reduction per fiscal year, and the number of appeals. The qualitative criteria included the uniformity of program application and results among the regions, the enhanced incident response capability, the quality of work products, and the efficiency of interoffice communications. These criteria were to be used to judge the effect of regional technical reviews on safety. The Commission planned to review the results of the pilot program at the end of two years.

POSTSCRIPT

Although the Commission and Congress found satisfaction in the manner in which the regionalization decision was resolved, Dircks wondered what lessons all those concerned had learned. In particular, he questioned the role of strategic planning within his agency when it operated in such a fish-bowl environment:

> We have a policy programming guidance document that is developed by the Commission every year. We use that to set our goals and give us performance objectives, and we then translate those goals into operating plans. Then we delegate the responsibility for those plans to the various directors. We evaluate each director on performance against his goals. Then we hold our breaths and pray that we don't have a major incident out there that will change everything around on us. We hope we don't have an unforetold incident like the Byron licensing decision where we have to go back and retrace our steps and find out who did what to whom and when and defend ourselves along those lines. I think you have to keep your balance and be quick on your feet in this agency. It requires quick adjustment. It is not very satisfying, though, because you can't set a target goal and rationally hope to achieve it.

Tom Murley, a Regional Administrator, shared Dircks' frustration.

> We are very much a reactive agency, and in the field I notice that even more. It is almost like we are just fighting fires every day. A strategic plan to me is what we are going to do two weeks from now. We do marshall our resources, we plan a year ahead, but I don't kid myself that that is actually what we will be doing next year. We find plants that have problems we didn't know about and we suddenly have to adjust our resources to fix that. There can be an incident or an accident in Texas that will change our priorities totally. I think all that we can do now is to set goals for the next six months and allocate resources to reach those goals. But we must assume that there will be fire drills all through the year.

NOTES

1. All the other functions of the Atomic Energy Commission, which was abolished by the Act, were transferred to the Energy Research and Development Administration (ERDA), which was the second entity created by the Act. Subsequently the ERDA also was abolished, and its functions were transferred to the Department of Energy (DOE) as a result of the Department of Energy Reorganization Act of 1977.

2. J. Branegan and J. Madeleine Nash, "Pulling the Nuclear Plug," *Time* (Feb. 13, 1984): 41.

3. Ibid., 36.

4. G. Brooks, "James Keppler, Chief of NRC in Midwest, Is Beset by Problems," *Wall Street Journal* (Aug. 28, 1984): 1. Reprinted by permission of *Wall Street Journal*, © 1984 Dow Jones & Company, Inc. All Rights Reserved Worldwide.

5. FTE is the cumulative number of employee days used by an agency divided by the standard number of days worked by an average employee.

Infotron Systems Corporation

INTRODUCTION

In October 1987, Dr. James C. Castle took over as the President and Chief Executive Officer (CEO) of Infotron Systems Corporation, an $83-million-in-sales-per-year electronics specialty products corporation that is based in Cherry Hill, New Jersey. The former President, James C. Hahn, stayed on as the Vice Chairman of the Board. Hahn's departure, largely by his own choice, was due to his beliefs that seven years as the CEO of a fast-growing, high-technology company should be enough and that his entrepreneurial style might no longer be the perfect response to the firm's present needs. He perceived a need to shift toward a more professional management approach. Finally, circumstances in Hahn's personal life, including the death of his wife, prompted him to seek this change. An extensive search for a new CEO, therefore, was initiated in April 1987. Exhibit 1 provides brief biographical sketches of Hahn and Castle.

During his first weeks in office, Dr. Castle assessed Infotron's situation and formulated a list of issues that he considered to be critical. These issues, as he saw them by the end of 1987, are reported at the conclusion of this case. Castle did realize, however, that he would need to orchestrate a turnaround of the company's immediate performance because of an anticipated flattening out of the firm's anticipated profits for 1987 and also to strengthen the longer-term strategic direction that the firm would be following. This would all occur in the face of an intense competitive climate, rapid technological change, and pressure for results from the financial market.

This case describes Infotron's situation at the time Dr. Castle took over as the

---

Exhibit 1   **Biographies of the Principal Infotron Executives**

James C. Hahn (born 1942), a founder of Infotron and its Vice Chairman, had previously been President and Chief Executive Officer from March 1980 until September 1987 and a Director since 1968. From 1968 to March 1980, he served as the company's Vice President of Engineering. Hahn is known to have a strong track record in the development of new products and is widely credited with being instrumental in positioning Infotron in the marketplace with successful, new, high-technology products at the right time. He is seen by many as a classic entrepreneur.

Dr. James C. Castle (born 1935) has had varied experiences in senior management positions in several firms, most recently (1984–1987) as President of TBG Information Systems, Inc., the Thyssen Bornemisza Group. Previously he had been Executive Vice President with Memorex (1982–1984) and Vice President of Operations in the Small Systems and Terminal Division at Honeywell Corporation (1980–1982) and had served in various management positions with General Electric and Honeywell (1966–1982). He received his Ph.D. in Computer and Information Sciences from the University of Pennsylvania in 1966, his M.S.E.E. from Penn in 1963, and his B.S. from West Point in 1958. Although considered by many to be a highly proficient professional manager who emphasizes management processes, he also sought to keep in close contact with his people and their problems.

President and CEO as well as the firm's approaches to strategic management and efforts to strengthen its direction while working out its short-term problems. The case first describes the rapidly growing information communications industry segment in which Infotron participates, then discusses the specific scope of businesses that Infotron undertakes within this industry, and then focuses on Infotron's specific competitive challenges. Particular cost-cutting programs and Infotron's approach to strategic planning also are discussed. Dr. Castle's tentative assessment regarding potential actions that might be taken under his leadership concludes the case. Exhibit 2 provides an organization chart for Infotron at the time of the management transition. Exhibit 3 gives Infotron's abbreviated financial statements through 1987.

RECENT HISTORY

During 1986, Hahn anticipated a somewhat smaller percentage sales increase than was previously envisioned in budgets and plans. Further, the company's product lines had not gained anticipated ground relative to the competition, and the company had not made major new product announcements. In addition, the competitive pressure on Infotron's data-switching and multiplexing products was becoming stronger. Hahn blamed these setbacks on the following:

- Sales were generally weaker than expected, especially in the so-called InfoStream product line. Point-to-point statistical multiplexers and so-
(Text continues on page 80)

Exhibit 2   Organization Chart (mid-1987)

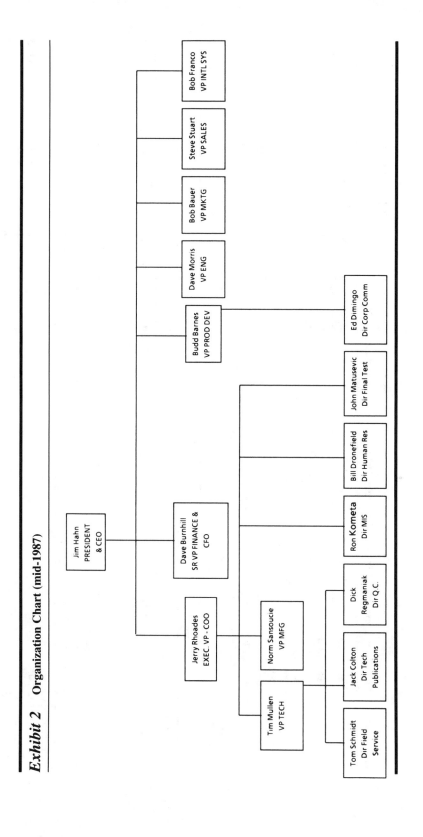

Exhibit 3 **Five-Year Summary of Selected Financial Data and Revenue and Expense Items**

($000 omitted except per share amounts.)

Five-Year Financial Summary	1987	1986	1985	1984	1983
			For the Years Ended December 31,		
Revenues	$83,305	$81,049	$72,199	$70,851	$51,239
Costs and Expenses					
Cost of revenues	40,285	40,609	32,424	30,663	23,348
Engineering and product development expenses	11,648	9,768	8,027	6,355	4,371
Selling, general and administrative expenses	32,493	33,467	27,537	23,672	15,495
	84,426	83,844	67,988	60,690	43,214
Income (Loss) from Operations	(1,121)	(2,795)	4,211	10,161	8,025
Other Income (Expense)	(9,283)	(1,708)	239	728	748
Income (Loss) before Income Taxes	(10,404)	(4,503)	4,450	10,889	8,773
Provision for (Benefit from) Income Taxes	517	(2,168)	747	2,767	2,543
Net Income (Loss)	$(10,921)	$(2,335)	$ 3,703	$ 8,122	$ 6,230
Earnings (Loss) per[1] Share	$ (2.15)	$ (.45)	$ .72	$ 1.59	$ 1.31
Common and Common Equivalent Shares	5,068	5,142	5,151	5,100	4,765
Year-End Statistics					
Working capital	$ 23,205	$21,259	$34,127	$38,955	$38,883
Total assets	84,353	92,210	85,434	64,967	57,106
Long-term debt	—	291	403	688	114
Stockholders' equity	51,128	59,955	61,959	57,749	49,059
Number of employees	927	1,068	1,021	959	724

[1] No cash dividends have been paid during the five-year period ended December 31, 1987.

| | Percentage of Revenues | | | Year-to-Year Change | |
| | For the Years Ended December 31, | | | 1987 vs. 1986 | 1986 vs. 1985 |
	1987	1986	1985		
Revenues (%)	100	100	100	3	12
Costs and Expenses					
Cost of revenues	48	50	45	(1)	25
Engineering and product development expenses	14	12	11	19	22
Selling, general and administrative expenses	39	41	38	(3)	22
	101	103	94	1	23
Income (Loss) from Operations	(1)	(3)	6	60	(166)
Other Income (Expense)	(11)	(3)	—²	(444)	(814)
Income (Loss) before Income Taxes	(12)	(6)	6	(131)	(201)
Provision for (Benefit from) Income Taxes	1	(3)	1	124	(390)
Net Income (Loss)	(13)%	(3)%	5%	(366)	(163)

²Not significant.

Source: Company annual report, 1987.

called low-end T-1 multiplexers represented specific problems. Lower revenue levels at first were not offset by lower costs.
- A cost reduction program had been instituted and was expected to contribute to better 1987 earnings. However, significant costs of implementing this
program were incurred in 1986.

Hahn expected to see the firm's performance for 1987 strengthen. As one
indication of this, he cited the international area, where 1986 sales were $13 mil-
lion, up from 1985's $6 million, and were expected to be $25 million in 1987. In
general, Hahn reconfirmed his commitment to a strategically driven approach to
Infotron's recovery. The challenge, as he saw it, would be to stick to a direction with
high long-term strategic viability and not to get bogged down in short-term fire
fighting without an underlying basic direction.

Above all, Hahn felt that it was necessary to redirect a team of senior executives who would pull together in a unified sense, counteracting what he saw as a
tendency for some of the senior managers to be preoccupied with their own agendas
and projects. He was prepared to take reorganization steps, if necessary, to achieve
this. However, he did not feel comfortable in bringing his senior managers together.
He hoped that the new CEO would shape the potential realignment of Infotron's
management team and structure.

THE INFORMATION COMMUNICATIONS INDUSTRY

The growth pattern in the information communications industry did not continue in
1986–1987 at its customary high pace. There was evidence that the maturing data
communications segment was behind this industry slowdown. However, the business community seemed to be more aware of its significant reliance on information
communications technology for establishing competitive advantage. Because integrated service networks provided end-to-end digital capability through the use of
high-speed fiber optics, communications bandwidth became a more readily available commodity. Probably the most dramatic change in the technology of communications networking was the speed with which information can be transmitted. The
transmission capacity will in all likelihood continue to increase greatly, while line
costs might remain more or less the same or even decrease. The probable result will
be expanding communications networks that might provide an impetus for business
growth in many industries.

A number of additional environmental forces shaped the development of new
products within Infotron. The advancements in desktop computers, in terms of their
power and ability to implement broader sets of applications, created needs among
the users for more communication, in turn creating needs for more elaborate networks. New technological breakthroughs for high-speed networking capabilities further accentuated the shift toward the development of local area networks and the
interlinking of several of these. Previously networks were seen as peripheral nodes

interlinked with central processors into a "star pattern with a clear center." The new shape of the networks was, in contrast, a set of nodes directly interlinked without a central processor. This provided an important opportunity for building T-1-type equipment for high speeds, allowing transmittal through such emerging networks.

This growing importance of a manageable communications network seemed, in general, to influence the user's approach to selecting equipment and vendors. More than ever, primary users' concerns emphasized quality and reliability. These concerns became even more critical as development moved manufacturers into even higher-speed, higher-capacity, *digital* networks. Another emerging concern was the *total* system performance of an integrated communications network, including voice and data transport. Complete network management and control also were part of this.

Recently AT&T made available to the commercial market a special communications link previously used exclusively by the Bell companies. This was the so-called T-1, which can carry huge amounts of information per second and handle a continually shifting load of data, voice, facsimile, and video signals. A T-1 channel might cost about three times as much as the more traditional lines, but it had 24 times the capacity. Because it transmitted both data and voice, the T-1 gave the user a more flexible general-purpose network that was also economical. The number of T-1 circuits was projected to increase significantly due to the rapidly increasing communications requirements of most corporations.

High-speed T-1 links also meant that one needed equipment for controlling such a high-speed flow of data, sending it along the best path within the network and making sure it got where it was going efficiently and cost effectively. This was a major source and a significant new business opportunity for Infotron as well as for several of its major competitors. The key was to be able to provide to the customer a portfolio of products that provided a clear benefit relative to the costs for the customer.

To fulfill customers' needs, however, Infotron had to be increasingly sensitive to the users' own strategic applications, and had to provide quality systems engineering and responsive, dependable field service support. This shift toward addressing how to assist the customer, through better understanding of the customer's critical success factors, in all likelihood will involve an upgrading of the sales efforts, with critical contacts with the customer being made at a higher organizational level. These contacts more often will take the form of "how can we assist you" versus being a matter of haggling on selling price. Developing the marketing side of the organization's revenue-generating capabilities will supplant a more classical transaction-oriented selling approach. Further, after a customer has been captured, the emphasis will be expected to shift more toward follow-up services.

INFOTRON'S BUSINESS SCOPE

Infotron designed, manufactured, marketed, and serviced a wide range of equipment for both private and public data communication network uses. Its principal products included data multiplexers, modems, "intelligent" switching systems, network concentrators, and network management systems.

In 1985, Infotron introduced an advanced voice-and-data T-1 (high-speed) multiplexer. Infotron's products were designed to be compatible with each other based on a network architecture intended to provide an efficient total solution. Its capabilities extended beyond its equipment, however. All products and systems were backed by a comprehensive service-and-support program, covering the various facets of developing, installing, and maintaining a communications network. Teams of people worked together to serve customers both before and after the sale. This advanced multiplexer was designed to have several feature advantages over many early T-1 product entries.

A systems engineering staff was the customer's major technical contact. Field systems engineers developed solutions to communications problems and worked with customers to figure out new networks or to integrate equipment into existing ones. Turnkey systems engineers helped to make Infotron a more valuable total data communications source for planning, design, project management, and installation. Field service professionals provided repairs, making use of Infotron's computerized Trouble Reporting Action Center to answer questions and solve problems. This group also served as a "clearing hub" for field engineering support, keeping complete records of all the service actions and tracking performance.

Competitive Challenges

Competition in the data communications equipment industry was intense. The company's principal competitors in the multiplexer market included Codex Corporation (a subsidiary of Motorola); Timeplex, Inc.; Micom Systems, Inc.; General DataComm Industries; and Digital Communication Associates.

Competition in the U.S. network concentrator marketplace was felt particularly from Codex Corporation and Digital Communications Associates, Inc. Competition in the European, and lately the U.S., marketplace was felt from CASE (Computer and Systems Engineering Ltd.).

"Intelligent" switch competition came from Micom Systems, Inc.; Gandalf Technologies, Inc.; Develcon Electronics, Inc.; and, to a lesser extent, from voice/data PBX products—such as those manufactured by Rolm Corporation, Northern Telecom, Intecom Corporation, and Mitel Corporation.

Local area network products—such as those manufactured by Xerox Corporation; Wang Laboratories, Inc.; and UngermannBass, Inc.—were yet another source of competition. Finally, the company's network systems competed with public data networks and networks provided by mainframe manufacturers.

In addition, Infotron's management believed that a number of new competitors might enter Infotron's markets. A company named Network Equipment Technologies (NET) had recently done so with what looked to be a very powerful product. Many of Infotron's competitors had more extensive manufacturing and marketing capabilities, as well as greater financial, technological, and personnel resources.

Prospective customer purchasing decisions in the data communications equipment market were influenced by such factors as sales coverage, product quality and reliability, service quality, and price. Infotron's management believed that the company was competitive in each of these respects and was benefiting in particular from what its executives believed to be a built-up reputation in terms of both a high level of engineering, quality, and dependability and the product's ease of maintenance and repair.

Infotron had many competitors including a wide range of firms that traditionally had not been active in the Infotron marketplace. This marketplace was undergoing a period of rapid and substantial change, with virtually no major players left unscathed. The forces of change were many, including the rapid emergence of some significant new markets, such as local area networks and T-1-based products; aggressive competition from traditional suppliers; telecommunications deregulation beginning in many other countries in the world; major new suppliers, including IBM; fundamentally new technologies; and the radical new distribution channels coming into existence primarily as a result of the divestiture of AT&T.

INFOTRON'S POSITIONS

In response to the above competitive challenges, Infotron began pursuing more aggressively a variety of new market segments and became a more marketing-driven company. Such an evolution would typically be difficult for any organization with a history of succeeding primarily through engineering excellence. There might be, for instance, a bit of "arrogance" in Infotron's engineering and marketing organizations. In a dynamic marketplace such as Infotron's, there was little room for blinders. A healthy respect for all competitors was vital.

One of the major strategic moves Infotron contemplated was whether and when to move into the market for supplying more powerful software to support emerging network applications. Such a move, however, might exert considerable pressure on the culture of the organization, since Infotron traditionally had been a supplier of hardware, such as multiplexers and switches and not software.

Infotron's management felt that the company would have to leverage its greatest strengths when implementing such a strategic move. This would mean activating its internal professional staff and technical expertise to build on its marketplace presence, its customer base, and its generally favorable image. Infotron, indeed, enjoyed a reputation as a supplier of top-quality products that performed reliably and met the central real needs of its customers. However, the company did not seem to have as strong an image for being innovative and nimble, that is, a leading-edge company that consistently was the first to market new products. The new T-1 market, for example, began to materialize without Infotron's involvement as the driving force or even as an early participant. Further evidence of this was the significant revenues that other companies—such as NET, Timeplex, and General Datacom—had carved out of the T-1 marketplace.

Thus, there was reason to believe that considerable business had been lost to competition in the T-1 market and in the open transport area. The T-1 marketplace was already a $100-million-a-year business, but Infotron did not seem to be getting any measurable piece of that business. The apparent dilemma was that the most important new segment on which Infotron might concentrate was exactly this T-1 multiplexing, switching, and networking equipment market.

Reviewing Infotron's competitive position in light of both the competitive challenges in the industry and Infotron's business portfolio, Infotron's top management found two major sets of issues:

1. The breadth of Infotron's product line: Was it too broad and insufficiently focused?
2. The timing issue regarding the T-1 multiplexers: Had Infotron "missed the boat" by entering too late?

Regarding the potential lack of focus of the overall business portfolio, the company felt that, with the expected industry slow down, it would be hard to support a broad range of products. The observer could see that several competitors had shown success by focusing themselves on particular niches. For instance, it might be hard to maintain sufficient technical and selling support to move a broad, full-fledged line of products, with these expenses easily getting out of hand. The added needs for specialized software was another disincentive.

A choice to narrow down a product line, on the other hand, would not necessarily be very easy. The emphasis on making the right choices would be critical. In this context, it was pointed out that the market seemed to appreciate more and more the suppliers who could provide a "one-stop supplier service approach," that is, to give the customer the whole spectrum of products he or she would need for networking applications. Both compatibility and complete networking features were seen to be critical, thus making it difficult to pare down the product line too much.

The Vice President of Marketing reflected on the necessity to pay strong attention to the signals from the marketplace when it came to focusing the product line. Perhaps a more "reactive" strategy would be appropriate. In contrast, a more proactive strategy with a broad set of new, untried, sophisticated products might require excessive planning and preparation and would be too hard to manage. The difficulties in planning such a line from scratch would include the challenge of carving out the specific developmental programs and of committing a wide array of resources. A more incremental approach—learning from and reacting to signals from the environment, customers, and competitors—might be more viable.

The timing of new products was seen to be critical by all of the senior executives. To misjudge a major new product opportunity would be costly. Several senior managers felt that they might have misjudged the T-1 product line and that Infotron was therefore significantly behind its competitors in this area.

Several of Infotron's top executives asked themselves whether misjudging the T-1 timing decision could have been avoided. Some felt that they were dealing with a "Catch-22" situation—the very breadth of Infotron's product line would draw the company's resources in many directions at once, making it more difficult to put sufficient resources behind one area, particularly when it came to a new start-up such as the T-1 line. To focus most of the company's resources behind the T-1 line—as, for instance, one of its competitors, Timeplex, seemingly had been able to do—might be difficult.

By spreading Infotron's resources over several product lines and perhaps perceiving the new opportunity too late, top management concluded that the initial T-1 market had been missed. This was further aggravated by the fact that the initial coverage of the T-1 market was through licensed products. Subsequently this product had to be abandoned because it did not conform to the industry standard. Even though the licensing agreement would have put Infotron in the position of eventually owning the technology, this was of little help, given inaccurate judgments in the past regarding how key industry standards would evolve. When more than a year later the decision was made to enter with the company's own products, the licensing arrangement was terminated, leading to a virtual absence of the product and thereby a setback in penetrating the T-1 market for more than a year. Infotron's initial product for the T-1 niche, which came out in 1985, was not sophisticated enough. As of 1987, however, the company had readied a new line of multiplexers based on its proven switching product line and with functional capabilities that were at par with, and in some cases even better than, those of its competitors.

Reflecting on his experience with the T-1 business, Hahn felt that a high-technology company must manage its development resources very tightly. Because Infotron was a public company, it would have to show a profit and return on investment at a level high enough to attract capital from the stock market and also maintain a high development effort. It would be a true challenge to be able to set aside resources for development at the same magnitude, say, as a newly started company that bases its activities on venture capital solely for the first few years. Again, it would be essential to manage very tightly and not spread the company's resources too thinly. Hahn felt that a relatively small, publicly traded high-technology company might easily fall "between the chairs"—the recent venture capital startups and the very large public companies. On the one hand, small, specialized, startup venture companies would be able to draw on private venture funds, as noted, and would not typically be subject to the same immediate performance requirements called for by the stock market. On the other hand, the large, well-established public firms would still have strong financial reserves to spearhead aggressive technological development. Infotron's management felt that it was in an "in-between" situation.

In light of these factors, Hahn believed that it was critical to focus the company's business activities even further. Accordingly he initiated a process of eliminating the less profitable products as much even though he realized that he was creating a short-term problem in the marketplace. He felt that it was critical to focus on products that he knew would "sell" and that might have relatively limited developmental costs.

Hahn had felt that even though the company entered the T-1 market relatively late, Infotron might capitalize on its strong reputation and customer following. It would be an advantage, too, to come out with the very latest generation of products, thereby allowing the company to leap ahead of its competitors on the feature dimension. The major challenge for Hahn was therefore to develop products that would build more directly on past experience on a more focused basis. This would incrementally draw on relatively known features and technologies as well as be based more explicitly on customer demand. Such a maintenance of focus was seen as particularly critical because of the high costs of new product development.

Organization

A number of organizational issues emerged over the last few years, affecting the way Infotron's strategy evolved. As of 1987, marketing, engineering, and sales, reported directly to the President, Hahn. Several executives commented that they saw as key Hahn's "feel" for what would be right from the dual technical and commercial points of view. Several years earlier, Hahn had delegated marketing and engineering to the Executive Vice President and Chief Operating Officer. In retrospect, he felt that this might have led to a fragmented organization. He now saw that having sales, engineering, and marketing together was a major vehicle for focusing the implementation of the firm's strategies. The then organizational structure also had led to Hahn's frequent involvement in the resolution of conflicts between the three functions.

Significant in this respect, too, was the merging of engineering and marketing into one organization. Even though no one had acknowledged any friction as a result of this, the subresponsibilities of the engineering versus marketing parts were never really clarified. The primary challenge in the marketing area was to bring more of a business orientation, overcoming a past weakness of emphasizing technical features rather than customer's business needs.

Another important issue was to strengthen and motivate the sales force further. For a long period, the Infotron sales force had been accustomed to having the best products, but this was no longer the case from the point of view of the customers and the marketplace.

A final issue was a situation that had developed three years earlier, when three senior executives left the company in an attempt to set up a competing organization. These abrupt departures led to a number of temporary setbacks, including the cancellation of a public issue that had been planned. In addition, Infotron was left for more than a year without a Vice President of Engineering, and its marketing and engineering talents were spread dangerously thin.

EMPHASIS ON COST CUTTING AND MANAGEMENT CONTROL

The drop in revenue growth, coupled with continued increases in costs and dramatically reduced financial results, had put a great deal of pressure on Infotron to reduce costs. Accordingly the so-called "performance-plus" cost-cutting program was launched and was followed up by a more formal control system. More accurate allocations were made in the budgeting process when it came to charging for such services as MIS, training, travel, and telephone. Company officials attempted to clarify where the costs actually came from and what their actual cost levels were as well as who was accountable for the various costs.

The "performance-plus" sought to cut dramatically overhead costs and direct costs, thereby lowering the break-even point. As noted, the immediate reason for this cost cutting was the drop in the growth rate in sales and revenue while the expense levels continued to rise; the cost levels would have to be reduced to be consistent with lower revenue levels. The Executive Vice President was charged with the responsibility of reducing overhead costs by $6.3 million. As of January 1987, Infotron already spent $4.5 million less in overhead. The Executive Vice President commented that, to some extent, the Infotron organization might have gotten "a little fat" over the years.

The cost-reduction program was highly participative with approximately 60 members involved. Forty-two so-called operating unit teams were formulated, each to study how to execute its particular operation more efficiently. One result of the process was that approximately 50 people including several managers were laid off. The effect on morale did not appear to be too severe; there seemed to be relatively widespread recognition that these layoffs were necessary to improve the company's profitability and competitiveness. That the company did not pursue an across the board formula for cost cutting was also viewed positively. Follow-up of the program was also carefully monitored in terms of dates, milestones, interim results, and so forth, and overall substantial and sustainable savings were anticipated.

However, Hahn and others stated that in the future revenues would have to be increased in order to maintain satisfactory profitability. If not, Infotron would have to go back and cut even more to scale the internal activity level down to a realistic scope. Again, it was deemed particularly critical to motivate and stimulate the sales organization to go after the new markets. The dual challenge was to cut costs but still do a good job of pushing the new products in the marketplace.

In addition to the reduced overhead costs, a number of steps were taken to cut costs in the manufacturing process. Direct labor was reduced 25 to 30 percent through the use of quality circles and just-in-time inventory management. Work-in-progress was scaled back, and the assembly flow was simplified significantly. More fully automated circuit boards were integrated into the designs.

The "performance-plus" cost-cutting program was painful but necessary. It took a longer time to carry out the cost cutting than was anticipated. By necessity a highly participative process—emphasizing not only where to make cuts but also how to make cuts so that they would be less disruptive—this program had the unintended negative side effect of drawing the executive's attention away from critical external activities, such as sales. The effort was simply all-absorbing—a painful experience for many executives and employees, particularly for those who had been with the company for a long time. In hindsight, top management might possibly have reacted faster and trimmed the costs earlier; however, the sales and marketing organization had come up with optimistic sales forecasts two years in a row, and top management had probably allowed itself to be "led down the primrose path" by believing in these optimistic forecasts with little reservation.

In retrospect, Hahn felt that the cost-cutting program was only half-way beneficial to Infotron. Although the program had been effective in identifying waste and in pointing out what had to be done, it did not help generate viable strategic directions for the corporation. Thus, Hahn felt that the cost-cutting program did not bring the management team together in a unified sense due in part to a lack of a shared strategic direction and in part to the individual characteristics of the managers involved. Many managers did not seem to emphasize the team dimension.

THE STRATEGIC PLANNING PROCESS

Infotron's strategic planning process, based on a conceptual scheme provided by the American Management Association (AMA), began in 1982. It went through its first phase until the end of 1984, at which time it was disrupted by two significant events. The first of these was the already noted departures of several Vice Presidents and the eight-member planning committee. In addition, the Planning Director, supplied by the AMA, was in the process of separating from his organization. As a result, Infotron postponed planning activities from the latter part of 1984 until early 1985. After intense discussions with its new AMA Planning Director, Infotron decided that it should, in effect, restart its planning process by reviewing and restating its objectives as a company. The heavy emphasis on planning as a team effort remained.

The planning framework proposed by the AMA consisted of these three basic steps:

1. *Where Are We?* This analysis began by defining the company's business and then establishing its position in the market. Historical performance also was stated to help determine where the company should be. The current business state was then viewed in relation to the external environment, and the company's own position was examined relative to such factors as economic conditions, political and business trends, technical developments, and competitors' positions. Also, the emerging current business state was compared with the company's internal capabilities. This took into consideration a listing of the firm's strengths and weaknesses, including its organization and management style.
2. *Where Do We Want To Go?* The next section of the process attempted to establish the company's mission or philosophy and how this would relate to the picture established under the first phase. Objectives were established at this point. Infotron's revenue and profit targets were set.
3. *How Do We Get There?* Here Infotron defined its basic strategic moves as

well as how it intended to develop action plans that would be oriented toward reaching its established objectives.

Hahn and the other members of management had felt that this planning process appeared to be well-suited for Infotron's needs, given the ɪapid changes that typically take place in the industry. The company therefore decided to hold planning sessions at least three times a year, in hopes that this more frequent schedule might help keep Infotron's shorter-term activities better in line with a longer-range plan.

Central to the strategic planning activities were the two- to three-day strategic planning sessions attended by the top management planning team three times a year away from the corporate office. Generally the same agenda was followed at each meeting—namely to go through the various steps in the planning process. Each section of the plan was revisited and "updated" in light of new information and added experience, leading to a continuing set of changes.

The internal analysis started out by assessing the various strengths of the company and determining how to capitalize on each one specifically. The analysis tended to become more complicated over time, however. The numbers of strengths were specified more clearly in the later versions of the planning efforts, and these were accompanied by more detailed statements regarding how to capitalize on the strengths. It was felt that the initial analyses of strengths and how to capitalize on them had been too general and thus not all that useful. Typically these analyses concerned such factors as aspects of the firm's reputation and its customer base; how to build on the technology and product base; how to develop a further momentum based on sales and service organization, including being more user-friendly; and how to maintain better flexibility vis-à-vis the environment.

The internal analysis of weaknesses became more specific over time. Each piece of this analysis was followed by a detailed assessment of the necessary corrective actions. The weaknesses dealt with in the latest planning report concerned how to deal with inadequate product life-cycle management, how to develop a better line of products, and how to strengthen the marketing capabilities and bolster the management capabilities in total. Also, this analysis looked at how to find a general, unified product strategy. A final dimension was concerned with how to improve intermanagement communication and cooperation between the various functions within the firm.

The external analysis had to do with assessing major changes in the environment of anticipated importance to Infotron's strategy and then specifying on what critical assumptions these changes were based.

A number of external factors dealt with the changes in business climate and the communication industry's life cycle, the entry of certain competitors, the introduction of new products, the changes in the regulatory climate, labor force issues, and technological developments in a broader sense within the telecommunications business.

The financial objectives then were reviewed in light of the perceived external and internal changes. These objectives concerned expected revenues as they would change over the next three years, accompanied by expected changes in profits after tax as well as expected assessment of the percentage of profits after tax. The assessments were then broken down for each of the five business units that the company recognized in its planning efforts: International Sales Organization, United States; District Sales Organization, United States; the United Kingdom; Canada; and other international.

Specific strategies were detailed for each of the business units. Typically these strategies had to do with how to penetrate the markets, what potential acquisition steps the company might contemplate, the new product development program, and how to strengthen Infotron's exposure to prospective customers.

Hahn felt that when the planning process started about seven years earlier, the approach had been based on the various functions in the company and did not have a total business focus. Nevertheless, this process was beneficial to Infotron's top management because they learned much about how the company actually operated. Above all, the company's officers better understood how to make a sale, what type of production planning needed to be done, and so forth. The company became more explicit regarding what it was doing and also became clearer about where it had been and where it was going.

Planning during the first years took place during a period of very strong market growth—a rate of 50 to 75 percent per year. The main challenge had been to stay on track; to manage growth and to identify limiting factors with personnel being particularly critical. In this context, where the emphasis was to stay on top of the growth, a functionally oriented planning process might indeed have been appropriate. There was no real need for a more business-oriented adaptive set of concerns because of the particular strength of the market.

The leveling off of the market in the latter part of 1984 led, in turn, to a major transition in how the company was run and how the planning process was executed. First, as noted above, more emphasis was placed on operational control, so as to take initial steps to reduce costs in the face of a flattening out of growth. Second, key challenges for adaptation were identified. However, many felt that focus on effective implementation was still lacking. In this context, Mr. Hahn commented the following at the end of 1986:

> When it came to the T-1 multiplexing market, we definitely identified these new niches. We had also laid out the strategy for how to get in. What was lacking, however, was our ability to implement. There was no real plan for executing the penetration of this niche. We had control problems in not monitoring the implementation on a thorough enough basis. Partly we made marketing decisions which were ill conceived in retrospect. This had to do with relying on licensed products in the beginning before we had our own products in the market. I, myself, made a mistake by getting away from the new business development too much. There was no one who was watching the new business development and the future hard enough.
>
> It seemed clear in retrospect that we did not utilize strategic planning as effectively as we could have during this period. The timing of the change in the planning process

was not good. Above all, the problem with the old process was that it did not bring enough of the general strategies back into daily action. In the old way of planning, we monitored key result areas and came up with actual performance measures versus goals. It turned out however that these measures were too broad, they did not fit the speed of change within our business. The measures did not focus enough on changes in key growth areas and changes in customer satisfaction. Thus, our planning approach was too "sluggish" for the rapidly changing technological environment/customer mobility that we were faced with. The new planning approach with its action plans that are thoroughly overhauled three times per year is much more responsive. In this respect, it fits the kind of business we are in.

It is clear to me that we are not utilizing strategic planning enough, though. When it comes to control and follow up, I am perhaps not strong enough as a CEO. I need to spend more time on implementation in the sense of ensuring that things happen. I have had a tendency to give direction in the past without enough emphasis on monitoring and following up. Another need is to strengthen the further coordination downward in the organization. Presently planning is too much of a top management activity only.

The Executive Vice President and Chief Operating Officer also commented on why planning did not work when it came to the new T-1 business opportunity:

We recognized the T-1 market and its growth potential. We did think, however, that demand would be more of a one-shot nature, focused largely around the large multinational corporations only, and that this market would then level off. We were wrong on that assumption. A second problem was that we did not sufficiently emphasize the need to carry out the delivery of networks. Our approach was too simple, not emphasizing the entire networking package. A small company, General Data Comm, was the first successful penetrator of the T-1 market. Then came Timeplex with a better product and took marketshare away from General Data Comm.

David Barnhill, the Vice President of Finance, felt that several major lessons could be learned from the strategic management approach over the few years. When it came to the strategic product choice direction, basic mistakes were made, such as being slow to recognize the T-1 segment, particularly in underestimating how large this segment would be. The licensing of Datatel's product had served as an initial sleeping position, delaying Infotron's development of its own T-1 product line. It was ironic that the Datatel Corporation was formed by a group of executives who left Infotron in 1980. Barnhill also noticed how hard it is to phase out a licensed product in order to enter with your own product. The line gap in the marketplace, without any product at all, is hard to cope with.

A second aspect of the learning experience was that new products must have very strong support. The management of Timeplex was impressive because it was able to throw all of its support behind its T-1 line. Relative to this, it might seem as if Infotron was too weak in its marketing. It did not see the T-1 as a real opportunity and did little about the slowdown in the company's growth. In many ways, Infotron was still managed as a small, entrepreneurial company, relying to a great extent on Jim Hahn, its guiding light for many years. It had taken years for Infotron to recognize that it could not rely on the heavy growth and that it had to start managing in a tighter manner based on less growth in the marketplace. The implementation side of the planning process was particularly weak.

In retrospect, Hahn felt that the AMA-based strategic planning approach might have been too modest in demanding that management time and energy be put into the development of strategic plans. Maybe a much "stronger dose" would have been required. No doubt, Hahn felt, the planning sessions helped the organization to understand its business better. What might have been lacking, however, was the emergence of a strong focus on the interpersonal relations among senior executives regarding what should be addressed and achieved. Instead, the strategic planning process seemed to allow executives to emphasize their own agendas broadly—sufficient emphasis on clear priorities did not seem to be coming out of the process. Hahn also felt that his own entrepreneurial style might have contributed to this. He had some doubts regarding the extent to which the management team actually wanted to live by the strategic planning process.

DR. CASTLE REFLECTS ON THE SITUATION

Dr. Castle gradually got a clearer idea of what might become the key issues on his agenda as Infotron's CEO. He listed on his yellow pad the following eight potentially important issues:

1. *The Organizational Structure.* Castle asked himself several questions: Would the organizational structure be appropriate in terms of providing clear responsibilities, clear expectations, and accountability for individual executives? He also suspected that it might be too deep and too fat. Further, was there an appropriate delineation regarding the division of labor among the various functions? In short, was the organizational structure such that it would create sufficient focus around the key strategies? Were the senior management members the right ones to manage the company in the next phase?

2. *Strategic Planning.* Were the strategic plans, as they then existed, sufficient in terms of charting where the firm should go? Castle was unsure about this, as well as about whether the plans merely represented aggregations of medium- to long-term wish lists from individual organizational members. Further, could the process of developing strategic plans be strengthened? Was the amount of involvement by senior executives sufficient? Should greater emphasis be put on the critical analysis of competitors and customers? Did the company provide proper focus of effort and also exclude areas that the company should discontinue?

3. *The Board of Directors.* Although Castle felt very comfortable with the members of the board, he asked himself whether there might possibly be too little representation of technical background and large company operations among the members. Perhaps the board's experience base could be shifted somewhat.

4. *The Product Line.* Castle was concerned that Infotron had missed out on a critical product lineup when it came to the introduction of the T-1 equipment. He

felt that it was critical to firm up the present line of products in order to better serve the firm in its nearer-term competitive actions. How, specifically, though, might such an upgrading be accomplished? In the longer run, a new generation of products might have to be developed. Castle asked himself how to articulate the longer-term new product development efforts.

5. *International.* In 1986, 17 percent of Infotron's revenue came from outside the United States. Castle expected nearly 30 percent to come from non-U.S. revenue sources in 1987. For 1988, he hoped to see a 50–50 split between U.S. and off-shore revenues. The major foreign emphasis thus far had been primarily in Europe. Castle asked himself about the appropriateness of such an international strategic emphasis. He wanted the firm eventually to have bases in Europe and the Fast East as well as in the United States, with approximately one third of Infotron's revenue coming from each area. Was this realistic and appropriate? When it came to the international strategy, the product lineup revamping, and the new product development strategy, Castle realized that a careful prioritization would be needed. In fact, Infotron might have to cut back on the sum total of what it was doing presently in order to emphasize only the truly critical product developments and market developments. But which were the critical choices? How should these choices be made? Strategic alliances might be used to a larger extent, Castle felt, for extending the product line further as well as for entering particular foreign markets where Infotron would not have sufficient resource bases.

6. *The Control Process.* Castle asked himself whether the management control process seemed to be sufficient for his purposes. He seemed satisfied with the processes in place, but he stated that better control approach would have to be developed for managing the company, particularly for the anticipated non-U.S. activities and joint ventures. Over time, he was looking for greater emphasis in the control processes for pinpointing major trends, for providing snapshot pictures of the Infotron business portfolio.

7. *Human Resource Management.* What were the major human resource management challenges? Should and could the marketing emphasis within the firm be upgraded? What about the necessity for developing a more systematic recruitment and development approach for human resources? Castle was not sure how much immediate emphasis would have to be placed on issues such as these. Over the long term, however, he had no doubt that they would be critical.

8. *Incentives.* Castle felt that incentives should be focused where they really mattered, say, by involving senior management in a management-by-objectives approach. However, should the number of executives involved be few or remain relatively large? Should the sales force be remunerated based on a more aggressive pay-for-performance basis? Should those not "making it" be encouraged to leave?

After his first few weeks on the job, Castle was more optimistic that Infotron would have a strong future. There would certainly be ample challenges ahead because there were many areas that needed development. However, the strong technological base, a core of human skills and knowhow, and a loyal group of customers with positive perceptions—coupled with a strong financial equity position—did give him a great deal of encouragement for tackling these challenges.

When reviewing the list of potential challenges, Castle was struck by the fact that management process and systems considerations directly or indirectly predominated. Reflecting on his previous experiences with other firms, he realized, however, that it would be critical to "professionalize without bureaucratizing." He felt strongly that the development of a rigid set of procedures should be avoided by all means. He also felt that he had to move quickly.

Chapter 3

THE STRATEGIC PLANNING SYSTEM

We described in Chapter 1 some of the key elements in the design of a firm's strategy process. In this chapter, we discuss how the strategic planning system can be tailored to suit the different business contexts that a firm may face.

We use the term *strategy process* to mean an entire configuration of planning; monitoring, control and learning; incentives; and staffing systems. Unless the planning system is suitably aligned with these other support systems, it will not be very effective. We focus in this chapter on the planning system and postpone a detailed discussion of the other systems to Chapters 4 and 5.

This chapter is organized into three sections. The first section provides a framework for classifying the context of a business unit. The next section describes the strategic challenge in the four distinct business contexts that are identified in the first section. The final section discusses how the planning system can be tailored to meet these challenges.

CLASSIFYING BUSINESS CONTEXTS

The context of a business has been classified in the literature in a number of ways. Some of the more popular approaches are described in the Appendix at the end of this book.

One of the earliest classification schemes was proposed by Bruce Henderson[1] and his colleagues at the Boston Consulting Group (BCG) (see Figure A-2 in the Appendix). They suggested that the context of a business unit can be defined in terms of the attractiveness of its industry segment (as measured by the segment's growth rate) and by the unit's strengths in that segment (as measured by the business unit's relative market share). Popularly called the growth-share matrix, this classification scheme was improved on later (see Figures A-3 and A-4 in the Appendix) by General Electric and other consulting firms, such as McKinsey and

Arthur D. Little.[2] Although these later schemes added more measures to the two dimensions of the growth-share matrix, they were in essence similar to the BCG matrix. Business strategy is determined in all of these matrices by the position of a business unit in the classification matrix.

A more recent approach, proposed by Michael Porter,[3] challenges the determinism implicit in the above classification schemes. It suggests that within any industry environment, a business unit has several strategic alternatives ranging in competitive scope from broad to narrow and in emphasis from cost leadership to differentiation. For example, in a mature and highly competitive industry such as metal containers, the Crown Cork and Seal Company[4] was able to find an attractive niche by choosing to serve select customers who were more interested in quality products, excellent technical support, and quick delivery of smaller lot size orders rather than in lower price. The company, contrary to conventional wisdom in that industry, chose to produce only steel cans (not aluminum cans). Even though its market share was low, it was the most profitable firm in its industry.

As in the Crown Cork and Seal example, a creative business manager can unearth attractive opportunities even in mature and declining industries. Therefore it is not industry structure alone that should define the environment of a business unit. In addition, the strategy intended for that business unit must also be considered (see Figure 3-1).

The environmental complexity associated with a business unit is a function of both the heterogeneity and the unpredictability of the stakeholders who confront it in its chosen niche. The stakeholders of a business include its competitors, suppliers, customers, various regulatory bodies, and host communities.[5] The more numerous the stakeholders that a business unit must deal with and the less transparent their agendas, the more complex is the environment that the business unit faces. Additionally if either the constellation of stakeholders or their agendas keep changing frequently, it becomes difficult for a business unit manager to predict the opportunities and threats in his or her chosen environment with any certainty.

Because industry niche is a matter of choice, why would a manager choose to operate in a niche associated with high environmental complexity? A primary reason for this choice is the future financial payoffs that the business unit manager sees in this niche. It is important to note that environmental complexity is as *perceived* by the manager of a business unit. This perception is a function of both the objective characteristics of the niche in which a business unit chooses to operate and the lack of familiarity of its managers with that niche. Therefore, any exploration beyond the niche in which a business unit currently operates can potentially increase environmental complexity, especially if the exploration is in unrelated products and markets.

Just as the environment of a business unit cannot be defined without an understanding of the business unit's strategy, similarly the resources available to a business unit cannot be evaluated without considering its strategy. For example, large-scale operational and logistical capacity may be critical to a business unit that seeks to be a cost leader; other competencies, such as technological know-how, reputation, and brand name, may be more important to a business unit that aims at being a differentiated player.

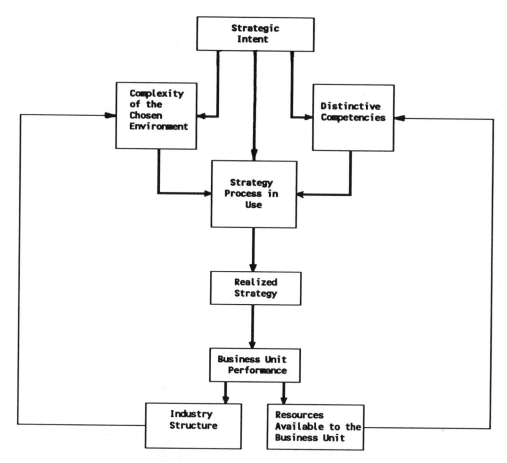

Figure 3-1   Context, Strategy, and Process

Distinctive competencies refer to the resources, which are not easily tradable, imitable, or substitutable, that a business unit has in support of its strategy. The more distinctive competencies that a business unit has, the better able it is to defend its strategy from existing and potential competitors.[6] Both tangible and intangible resources can contribute to its distinctive competence.[7] The former includes material reserves and operational and logistical capacities; the latter includes technical and managerial know-how, motivation and commitment of employees, and the firm's reputation. Depending on the strategy with which the business unit chooses to compete, one of these sets of resources may lead to distinctive competencies for the business unit. As we noted earlier, if the business unit seeks to compete in the low-cost segment, it needs relatively more of the tangible resources; if it wants to be a specialized competitor, it may require relatively more of the intangible resources.

We define the context of a business unit in terms of the two dimensions that were discussed above: the environmental complexity associated with its *chosen* industry niche and its distinctive competencies in that niche (Figure 3-1). The former is determined both by the structure of the industry to which a business unit belongs and by the strategy the unit intends to pursue within that industry; the latter refers to the business unit's resources and their uniqueness given the business unit's strategic intent. The framework proposed here is very different from the growth-share matrix and its successors. First, it explicitly recognizes the role of strategic intent in shaping the environmental context of a business unit. Second, it suggests that the competitive position of a business unit in its chosen environment should not be measured by its past performance, for example, its market share. Rather, it should be measured by the number of distinct competencies that it has to compete in its chosen niche.

As we discussed in Chapter 2, strategic intent is a concise description of the direction in which an organizational unit should head in order to survive and prosper. There can be disagreements between top management, divisional managers, and business unit managers on what the appropriate strategic intent should be for a given business unit. These disagreements have to be resolved in the objectives-setting step of the strategy process. Figure 3-1 describes the shared strategic intent that results from the negotiations across organizational levels in the first step of the strategy process. Although a business unit's context is influenced by both the structure of the industry in which it participates and the resources that are available to it, its context is not *determined* by either of these conditions. As noted earlier, strategic intent challenges the business unit to overcome the structural handicaps of its industry and to reconfigure the available resources to yield distinctive competencies.

Strategic intent, however, has to be translated into a set of meaningful strategies, and these strategies have to be implemented efficiently. The intended strategy of a business unit can be realized only if the strategy process used by the business unit is supportive in both the strategy making and implementation steps. The primary focus of this chapter is to provide a framework for designing such a tailor-made process. It is important to note here that the strategy process is concerned not only with implementation but also with the elaboration of the business unit's strategic intent into action plans and budgets.

We must also point out that the context of a business unit remains invariant only in the medium term. In the long run, its context can alter due to changes in the resources available to the business unit and in the structure of the industry in which it participates (see Figure 3-1). In fact, sustained superior performance can itself be a destabilizing force because of its direct impact on the resources of the business unit and its indirect effects on the structure of its industry. These influences in turn can lead to a reassessment of the business unit's strategic intent and a redesign of its strategy process.

The classification grid proposed in Figure 3-2 defines four business contexts. The demarcation between the four contexts is intentionally drawn with wavy lines to show that the definition of a business context is influenced significantly by managerial perceptions. The contexts are labeled by the primary strategic challenge faced in each: Pioneer, Expand, Reorient, and Dominate. Each of these labels has

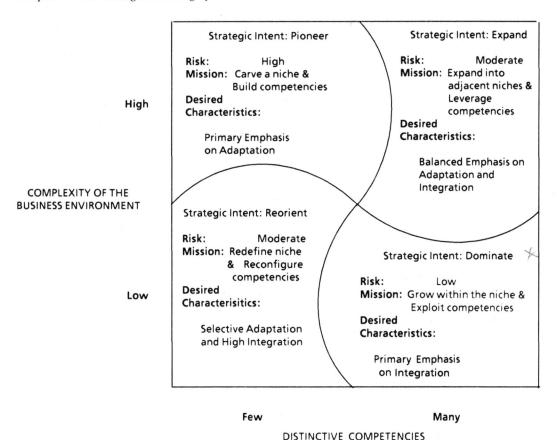

Figure 3-2   **Desired Planning System Characteristics under Different Business Contexts**

a positive ring to it—implying that no matter what the context, a business unit has the potential for self-renewal. In this respect, Figure 3-2 is very different from the traditional business strategy matrices (see Figures A-2, A-3, and A-4 in the Appendix at the end of the book for illustrations of these matrices).

STRATEGIC CHALLENGES IN THE FOUR BUSINESS CONTEXTS

Pioneer

The most risky of the four contexts is Pioneer, a business context defined by high environmental complexity and few distinctive competencies. The environmental flux can present the business unit with attractive opportunities, but it typically does not have the resources to exploit many of them. The primary planning challenge in this context is for the business unit manager to carve a niche in which the unit can thrive despite its limited resources. Because of the riskiness of the context, top management may wish to limit the size of the investment placed at risk. If the exploration is unsuccessful within those limits, the business unit may have to exit from such a business context. The other major emphasis in this business context should be on building competencies. Even a failed exploration offers the potential to help the firm build a new competency.

Expand

In contrast with the Pioneer business context, the Expand business context is typically less risky. Even though the environmental complexity continues to be high, the business unit manager should have little difficulty in identifying a viable niche because of the business unit's many distinctive competencies. The primary challenge for the manager in this context is to expand the business unit's position in adjacent business niches by leveraging its competencies in its core niche.

Reorient

In a Reorient business context, environmental complexity is low. The stakeholders for the business unit are well identified, and their actions are predictable. But the business unit's relatively small number of distinctive competencies prevents its manager from exploiting this knowledge. The challenge for a business unit manager in such a context is to reorient the business by participating in only the more simple subsegments of its industry niche. The business unit manager should also attempt to reconfigure the business unit's competencies, strengthening those that are relevant to the more focused strategy that is necessary in this context.

Dominate

The Dominate business context is the least risky of the four contexts described in Figure 3-2. The business unit experiences an environment of low complexity and enjoys many distinctive competencies in it. It has a well-protected niche and experiences stable relationships with its stakeholders in a slowly changing environment. The primary endeavor of the manager in such a context should be to exploit opportunities so that the business unit dominates the chosen niche by growing aggressively and profitably.

During its evolution a business unit can experience several of the strategic challenges described above. For example, Komatsu—the Japanese earth-moving equipment manufacturer—has passed through the Reorient, Dominate, and Expand business contexts in its quest to become a dominant global competitor.[8] In the

1960s the company focused on its home market and on smaller machines, while it tried to upgrade its product and process technologies and improve its quality. Its strategic intent in that era was clearly Reorient in the face of strong international competition from Caterpillar in its home market. Having successfully built its competencies in the technology and quality areas, Komatsu then chose to exploit these competencies in the 1970s in markets that were relatively simple, as in Eastern Europe and in the Third World countries. Its strategic intent in that era was Dominate. But once these niches began to become saturated, the company enhanced its competencies further in new product development and entered the more complex European and North American markets in the late 1970s. Its strategic intent had changed to Expand. One can see this evolution as prototypical of any business unit that is engaged in self-renewal, calling for alternate phases of competency building, niche domination, and niche expansion. The strategy process appropriate to each of these phases is distinct. Failure to provide the necessary process support can abort business self-renewal.

DESIGNING THE STRATEGIC PLANNING SYSTEM

The Critical Design Elements

The strategic planning system desired in each of the four contexts varies in its relative emphasis on adaptation and integration. An adaptive planning system is designed to assist the business unit discover and consolidate new niches in its chosen environment. The emphasis is on improving the effectiveness of a business unit through product/market innovation. An integrative planning system, on the other hand, is designed to assist the business unit defend its chosen niche and exploit efficiently the opportunities available in that niche. The emphasis is more on process innovation.

The relative emphasis on adaptation or integration in a business unit can be altered by manipulating four key elements in its strategic planning system: (1) the nature of goal setting, (2) the time-spending patterns in planning, (3) the relative importance of the strategic budget to the business unit, and (4) the linkage between the financial plan and the budgets. The role of the four elements (Figure 3-3) can be best understood by referring to the conceptual framework (see Figure 1-4) that was introduced in Chapter 1.

Direction of Goal Setting. In Chapter 1, we discussed that in the first step of the strategy process, top management interacts with divisional and business unit managers to finalize the corporate objectives and to translate these into goals and strategies at their levels. We pointed out in that discussion that the nature of the interactions between these various levels of managers can vary from firm to firm. We describe here two distinct types of interactions and discuss their implications for the orientation of a planning system.

	Orientation	
Design Element	**Integration**	**Adaptation**
1. Nature of goal setting	Top-down	Participative and iterative
2. Time-spending patterns in planning	More time spent on budgeting	More time spent on objectives setting and strategic programming
3. Relative importance of budgets	Operating budget more important	Strategic budget more important
4. Linkage between the financial plan and budgets	Very tight	Relatively loose

Figure 3-3   **Designing the Strategic Planning System for Integration or Adaptation**

In certain business units, as for example those in a Dominate business context, the goals proposed by top management are not really open to extensive discussion. The meetings between top management and the business unit managers are primarily meant for communicating these goals. Such a planning system is more integrative in its orientation. The premise behind top management's behavior is that no major changes are necessary in the business unit's strategic thrust. Discussions with business unit managers on their goals are brief because past performance data are available to judge how reasonable the imposed goals are.

By contrast, goal setting has to be much more participative and iterative for an adaptive planning orientation. A top-down goal-setting process is not conducive to some business units, as for example those in a Pioneer business context, that are expected to search for new business opportunities. The managers of these business units must be able to renegotiate at various steps of the strategic planning system the goals that they commit to top management in the objectives-setting step. Denying them the opportunity to do so will force them to set very conservative goals.

It would clearly be desirable to have a participative and iterative goal-setting process in all contexts. Rich interactions between top management and business unit managers in the objectives-setting step are vital to any business unit. However, one of the scarcest resources in large corporations is top management time. Top management must at a *minimum* ensure that the goal-setting process is participative and iterative in those business contexts where it wishes to encourage adaptation.

Time-Spending Patterns in Planning.   There are three steps in the strategic planning system: objectives setting, strategic programming, and budgeting. The goals and business strategies agreed to in the first step get detailed into cross-functional programs in the next step and are finally translated into budgets in the budgeting step. Depending on the planning orientation it wishes to provide, top management may choose to allocate its scarce time in one of two distinct patterns: a back-end emphasis or a front-end emphasis.

In some business contexts, top management may choose to have short objectives-setting and strategic programming steps with limited interactions and spend most of its time with a business unit in the budgeting step. This back-end emphasis in planning is not conducive to adaptation but can support integration. Here again, the premise underlying top management's behavior is that the basic strategic thrust of the business unit does not require major change. Although the business unit may need a few new strategic programs, its main focus is on the efficient implementation of a well-understood strategy. How a business unit details the agreed-on strategy in its operating budgets is, therefore, critical. The back-end emphasis of top management is aimed at helping business units with this challenge.

If, however, top management wishes to provide an adaptive orientation to the planning system, it must shift its emphasis to the front-end of the planning system. The objectives-setting and strategic programming steps would take longer in order to accommodate the large number of interactions and iterations that may be necessary before a new strategic thrust can be shaped for a business unit. Top management involvement throughout this lengthy process is critical for adaptation.

The Relative Importance of the Strategic Budget. In the budgeting step of the strategy process, both the strategic budget and the operating budget of a business unit are finalized. The operating budget, as defined in this book, refers to the budget through which capital investments and expenses required to sustain the current strategic momentum of a business unit are allocated. The strategic budget, on the other hand, is used to allocate the capital investments and expenses required for strategic leap—that is, either to engineer major restructuring of an existing business or to pursue a new business opportunity. It is important to note that the two budgets proposed here are quite different from the capital and expense budgets that are typically assigned to business units (Figure 3-4).

The capital budget allocates capital resources, and the expense budget provides for human resources, research and development (R&D), and business intelligence gathering expenses. All of these resources—that is, capital investment, working capital, human resources, and technological and business know-how—are required both to sustain current strategic momentum and to accomplish strategic

	Classification Proposed Here	
Commonly Used Classification	**Strategic Budget**	**Operating Budget**
Capital Budget (fixed assets, working capital)	Investments that appear on the balance sheet	
Expense Budget (human resources, R&D, business intelligence)	Investments that do not appear on the balance sheet	Expenses

Figure 3-4   **A Typology of Budgets**

leap.[9] Therefore—unless these resources are clearly earmarked in an operating and strategic budget, respectively—there is the real danger that resources allocated for engineering strategic leap may get diverted to sustaining strategic momentum. Or, alternatively, where the business unit is judged on its return on investment, these resources may not be expended as planned due to fear of increasing investment without a corresponding return in the short run. Moreover, a firm's control and incentive systems may encourage such a bias by primarily monitoring and rewarding short-term performance.

Some companies, such as Texas Instruments, have indeed followed the approach recommended here, with a clear distinction between the strategic and the operating budgets. Although it is preferable to have distinct operating and strategic budgets, it is not a must. What is required at a minimum is a careful accounting of investments and expenses under these two budget categories. In the Vick International Division of Richardson-Merrell (see Case 4), for example, resources required to pursue new strategies were allocated to a country budget along with the resources required to sustain the momentum of existing strategies. However, the resources expended on each strategy were meticulously tracked through distinct work programs. As long as the monitoring process ensures that resources are expended only on the purposes for which they were budgeted, the absence of a separate operating budget and strategic budget is not a handicap.

It is obvious that in an adaptive planning system, the strategic budget of a business unit will be considerably more important than its operating budget. The bulk of the resources demanded by the business unit are for either carving a new business niche or building distinctive competencies. In an integrative planning system, the operating budget is likely to be more important. Even though the business unit may continue to be the recipient of some funds through the strategic budget, these will be small when compared to the size of its operating budget.

Linkage Between the Financial Plan and the Budgets. The fourth design element refers to the tightness of the linkage between the long-term financial plan as formulated in the strategic programming step and the budgets as approved in the budgeting step. As we noted in Chapter 1, a long-term financial plan is prepared for each business unit at the end of the strategic programming cycle. This plan includes both the investments and the expenses associated with new strategic programs (see Figure 1-5), as well as those required for ongoing operations. A long-term capital expenditure and profit plan for the business unit is approved by top management at the end of the strategic programming step, and the strategic and operating budgets proposed in the budgeting step should normally correspond to this plan. When the correspondence is exact, the linkage between the financial plan and the budgets is said to be tight.

However, in the case of a business unit that is developing a new strategic thrust, the planning process cannot artificially be frozen at the end of the programming step. Major environmental changes could have occurred during the three- or four-month lag between the two steps. The business unit may have to revise its strategic programs and the associated financial plan. These revisions may often be reflected directly in the strategic and operating budgets proposed by a business unit. The budgets will therefore be at variance from the financial plan that was submitted during the strategic programming step. Unless this "loose linkage" is tolerated by top management, strategic thinking will freeze in a business unit once its financial plan is approved. Such an orientation is not very conducive to adaptation.

The tightness of the linkage between the long-term financial plan and a business unit's budgets can be measured along two key dimensions: content linkage and timing linkage.[10] Content linkage refers to the commonality between a business unit's long-term financial plan and its budgets on format and content and the precision with which the numbers are presented. The larger the commonality that is insisted on, the tighter the linkage. Timing linkage is tight if the budgets are prepared prior to the financial plan. In such a system planning can be reduced to a mere extrapolation of the budgets.

Tailoring the Planning System

In the previous section, we identified four distinct business contexts. Of these, the Pioneer business context needed a predominantly adaptive orientation, and the Dominate business context needed a predominantly integrative orientation. The two ideal types of system configurations described in Figure 3-3 are tailor-made for these two contexts. We will first describe the strategy process appropriate to the Pioneer and Dominate business contexts before addressing the needs of the other two contexts.

Pioneer.   Given the high environmental complexity of this business unit, the strategic planning system in use should encourage participative goal setting. Top management may not understand the business context sufficiently well to set credible goals in a top-down fashion. Also, the objectives-setting and strategic programming steps should receive relatively more of top management's attention than the budgeting step does. As we noted earlier, the primary challenge for this business unit is to discover defensible niches. The budgeting step is meaningful only so far as the resource limit for such exploration is specified in the strategic budget.

The linkage between the long-term financial plan and the budgets should deliberately be kept loose, so as not to force the business unit manager to implement plans that can rapidly become obsolete.

Dominate.   In contrast with the adaptive strategic planning system described above, an integrative strategic planning system is required in a Dominate business context. As we described earlier, this business context is characterized by low environmental complexity and many distinctive competencies. The business environment is highly predictable, and the few surprises that it may offer can easily be handled by the business unit, given its many distinctive competencies. The goal setting in such a context can be top-down. First, top management has adequate data on the business unit's past performance and a good forecast of its future environment to set goals in a top-down fashion. Second, and most important, by setting difficult but achievable profit goals, top management can induce business unit managers to search for new ways of exploiting their favorable industry niche.

The emphasis in the strategy process must also shift to the budgeting step. Exploiting current opportunities is the key challenge in this context. Although objectives setting and strategic programming are still important, they do not need to be as long drawn as in the Pioneer business context. This is not to suggest that a business unit in a Dominate business context has no room for innovation but to acknowledge that such innovation will be focused on process efficiencies rather than on new products or services. The link between the business unit's long-term financial plan and its budgets can be tight, as changes in the business unit's environment can be forecast in the strategic programming step with some accuracy.

Expand.   In this business context, the business unit has to be simultaneously adaptive and integrative—it needs a system that is a hybrid of the two systems described above.

Given the high environmental complexity, as in a Pioneer context, goal setting in this context should be participative. Top management must also spend more time with this business unit in the objectives-setting and strategic programming steps. In addition (as in a Dominate context), the budgeting step is very important in this context. Because the business unit has a strong position in its industry niche, it should be encouraged to set a challenging operating budget. However (unlike the situation in a Dominate context), the business unit manager should be allowed to renegotiate his or her strategic budget if the manager can show that it is necessitated by changes in the business environment that are outside his control and could not have been foreseen.

The link between the financial plan and the operating budget has to be tight if the business unit is to be encouraged to start earning returns on its investments. However, the link with the strategic budget may have to be loose. Both the plan and the strategic budget should be revised periodically if the environmental assumptions made by the business unit in the strategy-making process are subsequently falsified.

Reorient.   This is a difficult business context to manage because it calls for either a dramatic turnaround or a divestiture.[11] There are two distinct processes that must be employed here: (1) Identify products in which the business does not have and cannot build many distinctive competencies and divest these as quickly as possible for the best salvage price; (2) target not only products that have a higher-than-average growth potential for the industry but also ones in which the business can build distinctive competencies.[12] The strategic planning system is thus differentiated within this business context to suit the mission assigned to each product line.

The product lines that are targeted for divestment in a Reorient business clearly require an integrative focus, until they are sold. This will help improve the contributions from these product lines. The other product lines may require more of an adaptive focus, as the business unit tries to reposition itself in their markets.

SUMMARY

In this chapter we provided a framework for classifying a business context. The two dimensions of the framework are the complexity of the business unit's chosen industry niche and the business unit's distinctive competencies in that niche. In a clear departure from the popular classification schemes in use, our framework recognizes that the environmental complexity and the distinctive competencies of a business unit can be measured only with reference to its strategic intent. Classifying a business context should not therefore be a mechanical exercise but an important decision process in and of itself. The industry structure in which the business unit participates and its resources do affect its context, but strategic choice can mediate their influence (see Figure 3-1).

Depending on the positioning of a business unit within the two-dimensional grid that is proposed, its context can be described as Pioneer, Expand, Reorient, or Dominate. These labels are chosen to indicate the primary challenge of the business unit in each of these contexts. The contexts vary in their risk and in the adaptation and/or integration orientation that they demand of the strategic planning system.

We then discussed four key elements of the strategic planning system: the direction of goal setting, the time-spending patterns in planning, the relative importance of the strategic budget, and the linkage between the financial plan and the budgets. We also examined how these elements can be configured to meet the needs of each of the four business contexts. The proposed framework assumes close alignment among the systems used in a business unit: planning; monitoring, control, and learning; incentives; and staffing. We have more to say on this alignment in the next two chapters.

Before we leave this chapter we must make two other important points. The first is to highlight the important role that a strategic planning system plays in the strategy process. As we noted earlier, both the popular business press and academia have been unduly harsh on strategic planning systems. Implicit in their criticism is the assumption that a strategic planning system cannot but be *integrative* in its orientation. We suggest that the orientation of a strategic planning system is a matter of design, and it can show several different orientations along the integration-adaptation spectrum. If planning systems have indeed failed, it is because managers have failed to retailor them. Second, the chapter questions the popular advocacy for an *adaptive* orientation in all business settings.[13] It suggests that there is nothing inherently virtuous about an adaptive orientation; in fact, such an orientation may even be dysfunctional in a Reorient or Dominate business context. What is important for the effective management of a business unit is to ensure congruence between its context and its strategic planning system. The framework provided in this chapter is a useful template for checking this congruence.

NOTES

1. See B. D. Henderson, *Henderson on Corporate Strategy* (Cambridge, MA: Abt Books, 1979).

2. For a description of these approaches, see A. C. Hax and N. S. Majluf, *Strategic Management: An Integrative Perspective* (Englewood Cliffs, NJ: Prentice Hall, 1984).

3. See M. E. Porter, *Competitive Strategy* (New York: Free Press, 1980).

4. See R. Hamermesh, K. D. Gordon and J. P. Reed, "Crown Cork and Seal Company, Inc.," Harvard Business School case 9-378-024 (Boston, MA: Harvard Graduate School of Business Administration, 1977).

5. For an extensive discussion of stakeholder analysis in strategic management, see R. E. Freeman, *Strategic Management: A Stakeholder Approach* (Marshfield, MA: Pitman, 1984).

6. For an elaborate scheme for evaluating the competitive position of a business unit, see the following: Porter, *Competitive Strategy,* 47–74.

7. For a framework, see B. S. Chakravarthy, "Human Resource Management and Strategic Change: Challenges in Two Deregulated Industries," in *Strategic Human Resources Planning Applications,* ed. R. J. Niehaus (New York: Plenum, 1987), 17–27.

8. For a more detailed description, see C. A. Bartlett and U. S. Rangan, "Komatsu Limited," Harvard Business School case 9-385-277 (Boston, MA: Harvard Graduate School of Business Administration, 1985).

9. For a more detailed discussion, see P. Lorange, M. F. Scott Morton, and S. Ghoshal, *Strategic Control* (St. Paul, MN: West Publishing, 1986).

10. For a detailed discussion, see J. Shank et al., "Balance Creativity and Practicality in Formal Planning," *Harvard Business Review* (Jan.–Feb. 1973): 87–95.

11. For a useful framework for managing this context, see Porter, *Competitive Strategy,* 254–274.

12. For the need for selective adaptation and integration in any successful turnaround strategy, see the following: R. G. Hamermesh et al., "Strategies for Low Market Share Businesses," *Harvard Business Review* 56 (May–June 1978): 95–102; and C. Y. Woo and A. C. Cooper, "The Surprising Case for Low Market Share," *Harvard Business Review* 60 (Nov.–Dec. 1982): 106–113.

13. The following are the more vocal supporters of a universal tilt toward adaptation: T. J. Peters and R. H. Waterman, *In Search of Excellence* (New York: Harper and Row, 1982); and G. Pinchott III, *Intrapreneuring* (New York: Harper and Row, 1985).

REFERENCES

Armstrong, J. S., "The Value of Formal Planning for Strategic Decisions: Review of Empirical Research," *Strategic Management Journal* 3 (1982): 197–211.

Burgelman, R. A., "A Process Model of Internal Corporate Venturing in the Diversified Major Firm," *Administrative Science Quarterly* 28 (1983): 223–244.

Camillus, J., and J. H. Grant, "Operational Planning: The Integration of Programming and Budgeting," *The Academy of Management Review* 5 (July 1980): 369–380.

Caves, R. E., "Industrial Organization, Corporate Strategy and Structure," in *Competitive Strategic Management,* ed. R. B. Lamb (Englewood Cliffs, NJ: Prentice Hall, 1984), 134–170.

———, and M. E. Porter, "Market Structure, Oligopoly, and the Stability of Market Shares," *Journal of Industrial Economics* 26 (1978): 285–308.

———, "From Entry Barriers to Mobility Barriers: Conjectural Decisions and Contrived

Deterrence to New Competition," *Quarterly Journal of Economics* 91 (May 1977): 241–262.

Charan, R., "How to Strengthen Your Strategy Review Process," *Journal of Business Strategy* 3 (Winter 1982): 50–60.

Day, G. S., "Diagnosing the Product Portfolio," *Journal of Marketing* 41 (Apr. 1977): 29–38.

Demsetz, H., "Information and Efficiency: Another Viewpoint," *Journal of Law and Economics* 12 (Apr. 1969): 1–22.

Freeman, J., and M. T. Hannan, "Niche Width and the Dynamics of Organizational Populations," *American Journal of Sociology* 88 (1983): 1116–1145.

Hall, W. K., "Survival Strategies in a Hostile Environment," *Harvard Business Review* 58 (Sept.–Oct. 1980): 75–85.

————, "SBUs: Hot New Topic in the Management of Diversification," *Business Horizons* 21 (Feb. 1978): 17–25.

Hambrick, D. C., and I. C. Macmillan, "The Product Portfolio and Man's Best Friend," *California Management Review* XXV (Fall 1982): 84–95.

Hamermesh, R. G., and S. B. Silk, "How to Compete in Stagnant Industries," *Harvard Business Review* 57 (Sept.–Oct. 1979): 161–168.

Hannan, M. T., and J. H. Freeman, "The Population Ecology of Organizations," *American Journal of Sociology* 82 (1977): 929–964.

Hayes, R. H., and S. C. Wheelwright, "The Dynamics of Process Products Life Cycles," *Harvard Business Review* 57 (Mar.–Apr. 1979): 127–135.

————, "Link Manufacturing Process and Product Life-Cycle," *Harvard Business Review* 57 (Jan.–Feb. 1979): 133–140.

Hrebiniak, L., and W. Joyce, "The Strategic Importance of Managing Myopia," *Sloan Management Review* 28 (Fall 1986): 5–14.

King, P., "Is the Emphasis of Capital Budgeting Theory Misplaced?" *Journal of Business and Finance Accounting* 2 (1975): 69–82.

Lindblom, C. E., "The Science of 'Muddling Through,' " *Public Administration Review* (Spring 1959): 79–88.

Lindsay, W. M., and L. W. Rue, "Impact of the Organization Environment on the Long-range Planning Process: A Contingency View," *Academy of Management Journal* 23 (1980): 385–404.

Macmillan, I. C., "Seizing Competitive Initiative," *Journal of Business Strategy* 2 (Spring 1982): 13–57.

Mintzberg, H., and J. A. Waters, "Tracking Strategy in an Entrepreneurial Firm," *Academy of Management Journal* 25 (1982): 465–499.

Mintzberg, H., D. Raisinghani, and A. Theoret, "The Structure of 'Unstructured' Decision Processes," *Administrative Science Quarterly* 21 (June 1976): 246–275.

Moore, W. L., and M. L. Tushman, "Managing Innovation over the Product Life-Cycle," in *Readings in the Management of Innovation,* ed. M. L. Tushman and W. L. Moore (Boston: Pitman, 1982), 131–150.

Normann, R., "Organizational Innovativeness: Product Variation and Reorientation," *Administrative Science Quarterly* (1971): 203–215.

Ramanujam, V., and N. Venkatraman, "Planning System Characteristics and Planning Effectiveness," *Strategic Management Journal* 8 (1987): 453–468.

Rothschild, W. E., "How to Ensure the Continued Growth of Strategic Planning," in *Competitive Strategic Management,* ed. R. B. Lamb (Englewood Cliffs, NJ: Prentice Hall, 1984), 195–208.

Utterback, J. M., and W. J. Abernathy, "A Dynamic Model of Process and Product Innovation," *Omega* 3 (Dec. 1975): 639–656.

Van de Ven, A. H., "Central Problems in the Management of Innovation," *Management Science* 32 (May 1986): 590–607.

Vancil, R. F., and P. Lorange, "Strategic Planning in Diversified Companies," *Harvard Business Review* 53 (Jan.–Feb. 1975): 81–90.

Woo, C. Y., and A. C. Cooper, "The Surprising Case for Low Market Share," *Harvard Business Review* 60 (Nov.–Dec. 1982): 106–113.

Chapter 4

THE MONITORING, CONTROL, AND LEARNING SYSTEM

In this chapter, we examine how to design a monitoring, control, and learning system for a business unit and discuss the system's links with the strategic planning system. Monitoring and control are required to ensure that strategies are implemented as planned, and learning is required to validate and change from time to time the assumptions on which these strategies are based. This validation is especially important when the business unit either faces high environmental complexity or has few distinctive competencies. Business strategy may have to be modified several times or even abandoned during its implementation in such contexts. The system discussed in this chapter is concerned with both the successful implementation of chosen strategies and the timely reformulation of these strategies for their sustained relevance in a complex environment.

The structure proposed for the monitoring, control, and learning system (Figure 4-1) mirrors the structure for strategic planning that we described in Chapter 3. The major elements of the system are its links with the business unit's budgets, strategic programs, and objectives. The link with operating budgets is an important and obvious element of the control structure. Monitoring operating budgets, reporting variances, and ensuring corrective actions are aspects of the operating control system that are widely understood and hence not elaborated here.[1] However, it is pertinent to note that the failure of a business unit to meet its strategic budget may not always be due to inefficient implementation. It can also be caused by ineffective strategic programs or irrelevant objectives. And yet conventional control systems typically fail to question the premises on which the strategic budget under implementation is based.[2]

Furthermore, even where this is such a questioning, strategic programs and objectives are re-examined only when there is a negative variance from the strategic budget. But a business unit can show excellent performance when compared to its strategic budget and yet have ineffective strategic programs that do not capture all the opportunities that are available to it. The validation of strategic programs and objec-

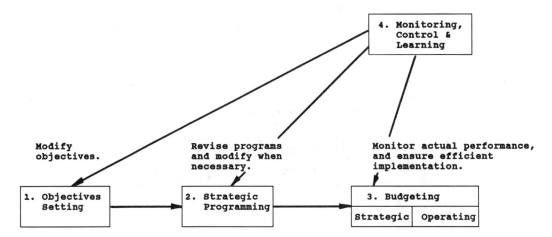

Figure 4-1   Monitoring, Control, and Learning

tives must therefore be an exercise that is carried out independent of the performance of a business unit against its strategic budget. In other words, the links in Figure 4-1 are important control elements for all businesses, even though (as we argue later) the relative emphasis on the three links can vary with the business context.

The chapter is organized into two sections. The first section discusses the role of monitoring and control in strategy implementation. We extend the conventional view of control, as pertaining to operating budgets, to include the control of strategic budgets as well. We call this expanded control system the strategic control system. The second section discusses how the strategic control system can be further modified to ensure the relevance of a business unit's strategic programs and objectives in different settings. We call this more comprehensive system the monitoring, control, and learning system.

STRATEGY IMPLEMENTATION

In Chapter 1, we showed how a strategy must be broken down into strategic programs and strategic and operating budgets to ensure its successful implementation. Figure 4-2 captures the essence of the proposed system for controlling strategy implementation in the illustrative case of a beer company.[3] The company seeks to be a Pioneer in the light beer business while Dominating its niche in the dark beer business. Each of these strategies requires the support of strategic programs, which in turn cut across several functions.

Light beer is a new business for the company. The successful implementation of the company's strategy for this business calls for three strategic programs: (1) the formulation of a new beer (which involves the brewing and beer-marketing functions), (2) the development of an appropriate package (which involves the market-

Functional Departments

Strategic Programs	Brewing (A)	Package Manufacturing (B)	Bottling (C)	Marketing (D)	Distribution (E)	Program Budgets
I. Light Beer **Strategic intent: Pioneer**						
1. Formulate new beer	*					Σ_1
2. Develop new packaging	*	*	*	*		Σ_2 — Σ_{I}
3. Launch product	*	*	*	*	*	Σ_3
II. Dark Beer **Strategic intent: Dominate**						
4. Develop new segment		*		*	*	Σ_4 — Σ_{II}
Functional Budgets	$\overline{\Sigma_A}$	$\overline{\Sigma_B}$	$\overline{\Sigma_C}$	$\overline{\Sigma_D}$	$\overline{\Sigma_E}$	

Figure 4-2 **Controlling Strategy Implementation**

Note: An asterisk (*) indicates the functional departments that are involved with a program.

ing, brewing, bottling, and package-manufacturing functions), and (3) the actual launch (which involves all of the above functions in addition to the distribution function). By contrast, the development of another market segment for dark beer requires only one strategic program that involves a fewer number of functions.

Also, although it may be possible to implement the strategy for dark beer in a single budget year, the programs that support the light beer strategy may require multiple budget years for implementation. The data in Figure 4-2 refer to only one of these budget years.

It should be clear from Figure 4-2 that both functional (Σ_A–Σ_E) and program budgets (Σ_1–Σ_4) must be monitored in order to ensure the successful implementation of a strategy. In practice, however, neither of these budgets is the basis for monitoring and control. Program budgets are typically rolled into business unit budgets, and business units are evaluated in turn as profit or investment centers. For example, in Figure 4-2, both the light beer and the dark beer business units will typically be judged from year to year based on their profitability.[4]

However, the above approach is valid only in the case of businesses where the investments and the expenses made in a budget year are expected to yield results in the same year. The investments and expenses incurred in the dark beer business unit (Σ_{II}) are of this type. On the other hand, in the case of the light beer business unit, the resources are expended through the strategic budget (Σ_I) in anticipation of positive returns in future budget years. Consequently the profitability in any given year for such a business may be a poor measure of its performance. Instead, monitoring investments and expenses by individual functions and programs is a superior method of assessing performance against a strategic budget.

The strategic budget allocates four important types of resources: (1) investments in fixed assets, (2) investments in working capital, (3) expenditures on human resources, and (4) expenditures on R&D and market research that enhance a firm's knowledge base. Each item of investment or expenditure must be monitored to ensure that it does not exceed its spending limits. But it is possible to stay within the aggregate spending limits for a business unit while being overbudget or underbudget on approved strategic programs. Resource expenditures must therefore be monitored by individual programs. But even this would not provide any information on the quality of the implementation effort.

The quality of effort can be assessed only by monitoring both the physical progress on the functional activities planned during the budget period and the timeliness of such a progress. Approaches such as PERT (Program Evaluation and Review Technique) and CPM (Critical Path Method) used in project management can be invaluable in this regard.[5] The budgeted activities must be carefully broken down into a set of subactivities, each spanning well-defined milestones in the associated strategic program. By monitoring whether and when each milestone is reached, the quality of effort expended against a strategic budget can be assessed with reasonable accuracy.

The above discussion would suggest that controlling strategy implementation has to go beyond conventional responsibility center accounting and include the measurement of physical progress as well. This is not a novel suggestion,[6] and in fact many companies use such a mixed approach. But what is lacking in many instances is the realization that strategies can be implemented as planned only in a few business contexts. There are situations where a strategy may have to be modified or even abandoned. In other words, rather than ensure the unerring implementation of a strategic plan that may have become flawed, the business unit manager must ensure that corporate resources are directed at all times only to *relevant* strategic plans.

STRATEGY VALIDATION

In the previous chapter, we saw that the context of a business unit is defined by the complexity of the industry niche in which it chooses to operate and its own distinctive competencies within that niche. Assumptions relating to environmental complexity fall into three categories.[7] The first refers to assumptions about the stakes and power of stakeholders in the chosen niche. Prominent in the second category are assumptions about likely changes in the industry structure. The final category consists of assumptions about the broad sociopolitical and macroeconomic context within which all businesses in the industry have to operate. Assumptions about a firm's distinctive competencies relate primarily to the uniqueness of the firm's resources and how easily these resources can be imitated or substituted.[8]

These assumptions are sometimes unfortunately forgotten because of the false sense of precision that a plan can provide. An obvious prerequisite for effective monitoring of the plan is that all critical assumptions made in choosing objectives, strategic programs, and budgets are explicitly stated in the planning process.

The process of monitoring the above assumptions and validating the strategies on which these assumptions are based will vary with the business context (Figure 4-3).[9]

Pioneer

In a Pioneer business context a formal monitoring of the business environment may not be very cost effective because of the complexity of the environment. Top management may have to rely instead on the shared perceptions of the business environment that are held by managers based on their day-to-day contacts with the business's stakeholders. Although frequent and open discussions with the business unit manager in the objectives-setting and strategic programming steps can help top management make some judgments about the validity of the chosen strategy, the strategy can be truly validated only by its eventual success. However, given the high risk associated with this context, it is prudent practice to prespecify the maximum resources that a firm is willing to gamble on such a business. When these are expended, serious consideration should be given to exiting this business context.

The control system recommended for this business context is called Go–No Go. It encourages top management to "go" with the business until the prespecified

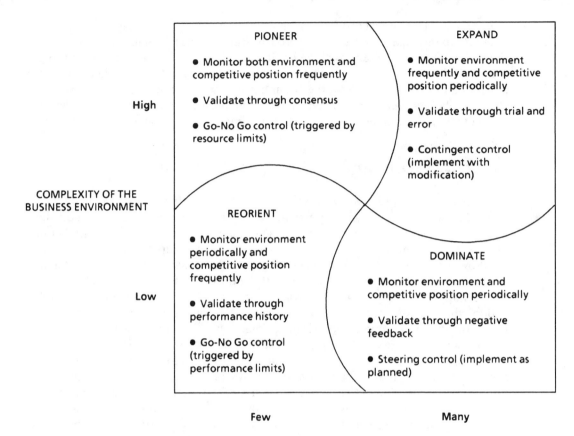

Figure 4-3 Monitoring, Control, and Learning in Different Business Contexts

resource limits are reached. If either a viable niche or a distinctive competency has not been built by then, the decision changes to "no go." Establishing the limit on the resources that can be spent on pioneering depends on the financial well-being of the firm and the importance it attaches to the business unit in question. In this mode of strategic control, the business unit is monitored primarily on its strategic budget. Consequently the emphasis is more on measuring effort and resource commitment than on profit output.

Expand

If the business context is one of Expand, the business unit has multiple distinctive competencies to probe its environment in a proactive fashion. The business unit manager can establish contingency plans and select the winning plan through trial and error. This is indeed a difficult validation process to use, because failed trials are more likely to be interpreted as flawed implementation than as experiments designed to decipher the business environment. The frequent monitoring of the business unit's environment and its competitive position can help top management interpret the business unit's performance better. As noted in Chapter 3, this is done by spending more time with the business unit in the objectives-setting and strategic programming steps of the strategy process.

In general, the strategic control system used in an Expand context emphasizes performance against both the strategic budget and the operating budget. However, it allows for changes in the strategic budgets (and the strategic programs on which they are based) if the environment so dictates. It is therefore called contingent control. The emphasis is not on having the business unit manager make the right assumptions about a business unit's environment during the planning process, but rather on expecting him or her to make the appropriate modifications to the plan during its implementation.

Reorient

In a Reorient business context the business environment is often not very complex and can therefore be interpreted with reasonable accuracy even through periodic monitoring. However, given its few distinctive competencies, the business unit may be unable to cope with even minor surprises that the environment may have to offer. Its competitive position must be monitored frequently. Although the business unit should be judged more by its ability to implement its strategic budget (given its attempts to build new competencies), the consistent failure of the business unit to meet its operating budget is a danger signal. Steadily increasing variances between the budgeted and the actual operating performance may suggest that the business unit is unable to exploit its growing competencies, so the business may have to be divested. At any given point in time, the business unit manager may optimistically believe that the desired turnaround is at hand. A prudent approach to control is therefore for top management to negotiate in *advance* performance thresholds with the business unit manager below which reorientation is unlikely. When these limits are reached divesting the business unit must be seriously considered.

Dominate

Finally, in a Dominate business context, the primary challenge is one of strategy implementation, even though it may be prudent to monitor periodically the assumptions around which the business strategy was shaped. The validation of these assumptions is possible by investigating variances in performance from a business unit's budgets. The normal expectation in this context is that the manager can eventually steer the business unit to the output targets promised in his or her budgets. This control system is called steering control. However, in the exceptional case where variances in the realized output appear to question the validity of the strategic programs chosen by the business unit managers, the periodic monitoring of assumptions can be very helpful in revising these programs.

SUMMARY

In this chapter, we proposed two complementary aspects of control: successful implementation of chosen strategies and the strategies' timely reformulation for sustained relevance to a complex environment. We suggested that implementation is helped by separating the operating budget from the strategic budget. Without such a separation, resources earmarked to support strategic programs with future payoffs can easily get diverted to existing operations, or else these resources may never be expended for fear of hurting the business unit's short-term profit performance. We further suggested that strategic budgets must be monitored not only for resource allocation as planned but also for achieving commensurate physical progress and for timeliness of such a progress.

Strategy can be implemented as planned only in a Dominate business context. When a business unit is faced with the three other generic contexts of Pioneer, Expand, and Reorient, it has to validate frequently the assumptions on which its strategy is based. It may have to modify its strategy, as is frequently seen in the Expand context, or even abandon it, particularly in the Pioneer or Reorient context. The failure to recognize the differences in the control process required by the four contexts can lead to dysfunctional behaviors in the business units. For example, there may be a preponderant tendency to use steering control in all business contexts because of the mistaken belief that successful strategy implementation is merely a matter of applying the right managerial skills and initiative in response to budgetary variances. What this chapter suggests is that imposing such a monolithic control system can lead to missed opportunities in a Pioneer context, to understatement of the true potential of a business in an Expand context, and to exaggerated claims of business potential in a Reorient context. To avoid such dysfunctional behaviors, we suggested four distinct approaches to control, each complementing a corresponding planning orientation that was proposed in the previous chapter.

NOTES

1. For an excellent discussion of the conventional budgetary control process, see R. A. Anthony and J. Dearden, *Management Control Systems* (Homewood, IL: Richard D. Irwin, 1980).

2. The conventional control system has single-loop features. The control system proposed here continuously questions the premises underlying a strategy; it has more of the double-loop features. See C. Argyris, "Double-Loop Learning in Organizations," *Harvard Business Review* 55 (Sept.–Oct. 1977): 115–125.

3. For a detailed description of this case study, see P. Lorange, "Implementing Strategic Planning: An Approach by Two Philippine Companies," *Wharton Annual* 8 (1983): 165–176.

4. Some recent approaches for measuring profitability look beyond the current year's performance. For example, see A. Rappaport, *Creating Shareholder Value* (New York: Free Press, 1986).

5. For an overview of project management techniques, see D. I. Cleland and W. R. King, *Systems Analysis and Project Management* (New York: McGraw-Hill, 1968).

6. For example, see W. H. Newman, *Constructive Control* (Englewood Cliffs, NJ: Prentice-Hall, 1975).

7. This is based on M. E. Porter, *Competitive Strategy* (New York: Free Press, 1980).

8. See I. Dierickx and K. Cool, "Asset Stock Accumulation and Sustainability of Competitive Advantage," *Management Science* 35 (Dec. 1989): 1504–1510.

9. This is adapted from R. L. Daft and K. E. Weick, "Toward a Model of Organizations as Interpretation Systems," *Academy of Management Review* 9 (1984): 284–295.

REFERENCES

Ansoff, H. I., "Managing Strategic Surprise by Response to Weak Signals," *California Management Review* 18 (Winter 1975): 21–33.

Cohen, K. J., and R. M. Cyert, "Strategy: Formulation, Implementation, and Monitoring," *The Journal of Business* 46 (1973): 349–367.

Eisenhardt, K. M., "Control: Organizational and Economic Aproaches," *Management Science* 31 (1985): 134–149.

Hitt, M. A., and R. D. Ireland, "Corporate Distinctive Competence, Strategy, Industry and Performance," *Strategic Management Journal* 6 (July–Sept. 1985): 273–294.

Lorange, P., "Strategic Control: Some Issues in Making It Operationally More Useful," in *Competitive Strategic Management,* ed. R. B. Lamb (Englewood Cliffs, NJ: Prentice Hall, 1984), 247–271.

Merchant, K. A., "The Control Function of Management," *Sloan Management Review* 23 (Summer 1982): 43–56.

Ouchi, W. G., "Markets, Bureaucracies and Clans," *Administrative Science Quarterly* 25 (March 1980): 129–141.

Quinn, J. B., "Managing Strategies Incrementally," in *Competitive Strategic Management,* ed. R. B. Lamb (Englewood Cliffs, NJ: Prentice Hall, 1984), 35–61.

Vancil, R. F., "What Kind of Management Control Do You Need?" *Harvard Business Review* 51 (Mar.–Apr. 1973): 75–86.

———, "Better Management of Corporate Development," *Harvard Business Review* 50 (Sept.–Oct. 1972): 53–62.

Wack, P., "Scenarios: Uncharted Waters Ahead," *Harvard Business Review* 5 (Sept.–Oct. 1985): 72–89.

Willis, R. E., *A Guide to Forecasting for Planners and Managers* (Englewood Cliffs, NJ: Prentice Hall, 1987).

Chapter 5

THE INCENTIVES AND STAFFING SYSTEMS

As we noted in the Introduction, a dual set of problems that top management faces when dealing with a business unit manager are goal incongruence and information asymmetry.[1] Goal incongruence arises when individual business unit managers, acting in their self-interest, pursue goals that are different from those desired by top management. Information asymmetry refers to a situation in which, by virtue of their experience and proximity to their local environments, business unit managers possess relevant information that top management does not.

The major focus of the previous two chapters was to minimize both goal incongruence and information asymmetry through well-designed strategic planning and monitoring, control, and learning systems. However, these systems may be unable in a large diversified firm to neutralize fully the goal incongruence and information asymmetry that may exist between its top management and its business unit managers. Top management has limited time in which it must influence the goals of a business unit manager, and it has limited cognitive abilities to absorb all of the information pertaining to a business unit.[2] It must therefore complement the use of planning and monitoring, control, and learning systems with the use of incentives and staffing systems.

This chapter focuses on the complementary role that incentives and staffing can play in the strategy process. Incentives are inducements that bring about desired changes in managerial behavior. Staffing refers to the appointment of managers to a business unit through either recruitment or internal transfer.

This chapter is divided into three sections. The first section explores the roles of incentives and staffing under different levels of information asymmetry and goal incongruence. The second section discusses how an incentives system can be designed to suit the context of a business unit. The third section addresses the issue of staffing for different business contexts.

THE ROLE OF THE INCENTIVES AND STAFFING SYSTEMS

In Figure 5-1, we assume that a well-designed planning and control process would always neutralize some of the goal incongruence and information asymmetry that exists between top management and business unit managers. We deal here with the residuals. We have depicted this in Figure 5-1 by suggesting that high information asymmetry and/or goal incongruence should not normally exist for any business unit if it is managed by well-tailored strategic planning and monitoring, control, and learning systems.

The residual information asymmetry is likely to be moderate if the complexity of the industry environment in which a business unit competes is high. The more complex the business environment, the higher is the probability that a business unit manager is better informed about the business environment than top management.

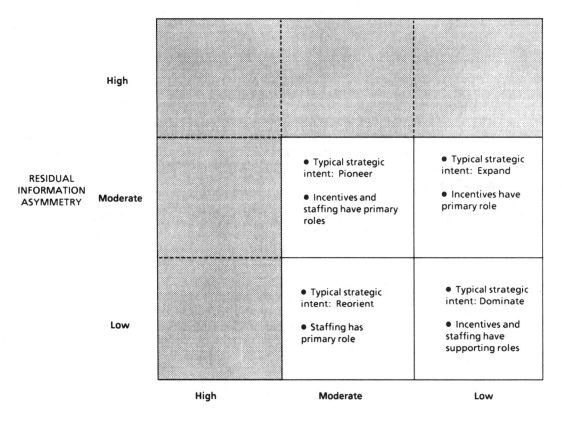

Figure 5-1   **The Role of Incentives and Staffing in Different Business Contexts**

This is especially likely when there are a large number of complex businesses in the firm's portfolio. The business manager is in closer touch with his or her environment and monitors it continuously, but top management must comprehend it through infrequent and secondary information.

Similarly the residual goal incongruence is likely to be moderate when the business unit has few distinctive competencies. Business unit managers may be more inclined then to seek pioneering explorations or risky reorientations to rejuvenate their businesses. Top management, on the other hand, may be in favor of more modest goals for such business units, given the other opportunities that the firm may have. Moreover, although "No Go" or divestment is always a serious option pursued by top management for business units with few distinctive competencies, this cannot be an attractive option for managers responsible for those business units.

The four quadrants in Figure 5-1 therefore correspond approximately with the four business contexts discussed in the previous two chapters.

An incentives system can be very helpful in dealing with the problem of residual information asymmetry, provided that it is well tailored to the business context. However, for reasons of equity there is a tendency among firms to use a standard incentives system throughout. Moreover, the typical incentives system in use seems geared toward improving employee satisfaction and organizational efficiency,[3] rather than toward ensuring the continued relevance of the firm's strategies. As we see in the next section, a well-tailored incentives system can minimize information asymmetry by encouraging the business unit manager to share all relevant information on a business unit with his or her superiors, even if this may lead to the modification (or even the abandonment) of the strategy pursued by the business unit.

But incentives systems can modify a manager's behavior only within his or her "zone of acceptance".[4] The zone of acceptance defines an area in which a business unit manager is willing to suppress his or her own goals in favor of the superior's goals. There can still be lingering goal incongruence, which can be resolved only by replacing the business unit manager.

Figure 5-1 suggests that the relative importance of staffing and incentives varies across the four business contexts. When goal incongruence is the major problem, as often is found in Pioneer and Reorient business contexts, proper staffing is important. On the other hand, if information asymmetry is the major problem, a well-designed incentives system can help, as can be the case in a Pioneer or Expand business context. When the planning and control systems have neutralized most of the goal incongruence and information asymmetry in a business context, as is the case in a Dominate context, staffing and incentives have only a supporting role. In other words, staffing and incentives are more important design elements when a business unit is required to validate its strategy than when it is merely required to implement that strategy efficiently. Despite this, it is more common to find incentives systems used primarily to promote efficient strategy implementation.

TAILORING THE INCENTIVES SYSTEM

Types of Incentives

We previously defined an incentive as any inducement that brings about a desired change in managerial behavior. However, what is perceived as an inducement can vary from one individual to another and from one culture to another. In many U.S. companies, for example, salary increases, performance bonuses, promotions, and stock options are common inducements. In some countries of Europe, because of either heavy personal taxation or governmental regulation, monetary rewards are not very potent inducements. In Japan, additional job responsibility can be a more powerful incentive than either promotion or salary increase.[5] It is therefore impossible to specify what inducements are appropriate in different business contexts. The country's context may be an important determinant of the type of incentives that has the highest potency. Moreover, the type of inducements offered must be tailored to the needs of the recipient manager. Finally, although incentives aimed at individuals may be appropriate in some settings, they may have to be complemented by group incentives in other contexts.

Because of the above, we avoid a detailed discussion of what types of incentives are appropriate in various business contexts. However, we must point out that incentives need not be only rewards; they can also be nonpunishments. Particularly in the Pioneer and Reorient business contexts, forgiving negative variances against budgets can be a powerful incentive.

Performance Criteria

Figure 5-2 lists the important performance criteria on which incentives should be based in the four distinct business contexts that were discussed in the earlier chapters.

Pioneer. If the business context is one of Pioneer, more attention is required in the front end of the strategic planning system, that is, during the objectives-setting and the strategic programming steps. Because of the various uncertainties associated with such a business, it is unreasonable to expect that the operating budget will be met with any consistency. Consequently the control emphasis has to be primarily on the strategic budget. Even here the chosen strategy may have to be modified or even abandoned during implementation.

It therefore follows that the incentives for such a business must be based primarily on the quality of the pioneering effort. Performance against milestones in the strategic budget is one measure of this quality. Moreover, incentives must also be based on the contributions by a manager toward ensuring the relevance of the chosen strategy. The business unit manager must have the incentive to recommend major changes in the strategy or even abandonment if the resources risked on the strategy exceed prudent limits. The primary incentive in such a context is not

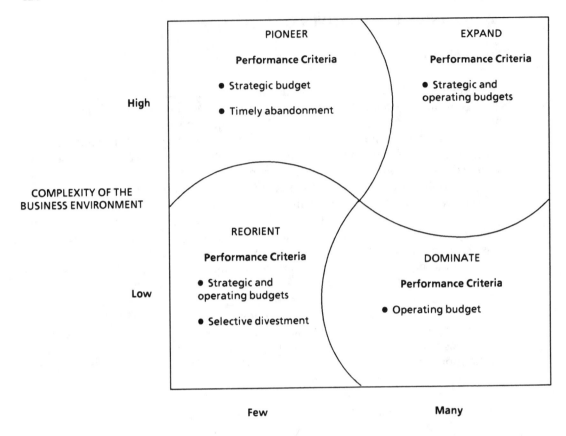

Figure 5-2   **Incentive Systems for Different Business Contexts**

reward, but the absence of punishment. The manager's job must be guaranteed, and every effort must be made to redeploy the employees and assets associated with this business to other businesses. In addition, the manager must be rewarded for the quality of his or her effort in implementing the strategic budget. Moreover, should the business succeed, the manager should be able to share in its profits.

Expand.   If the business context is one of Expand, where both integration and adaptation needs are high, it is very important to base incentives on performance relative to both the strategic budget and the operating budget (see the discussion in Chapter 4). Incentives for performance against the strategic budget should be based primarily on meeting agreed-on milestones and on taking the necessary actions to modify business strategy as needed (triggered by shifts in key assumptions around strategic programs and/or objectives). However, incentives for performance against the operating budget can be based on exceeding predetermined profit targets.

Reorient.   Reorient is another business context in which managers may have to be rewarded for their performances against both their strategic and operating budgets.[6] After all, managers should be rewarded for performance against their missions and not by the nature of the missions that they are assigned. If the manager of a Reorient business chooses to abandon investment in a project because of adverse environmental signals (No Go signals), the incentives system should be "forgiving" of this manager's failure to meet budgeted profit commitments. Given that the business unit has few distinctive competencies, it may not be always possible for its manager to adjust to changing environmental conditions, and forcing a manager to do so will only encourage deceit.[7] Instead, by rewarding "honest failures," top management can probably limit the firm's financial loss.

Dominate.   Finally, providing incentives for performance against the operating budget is quite appropriate if the business context is one of Dominate. As we discussed in Chapter 4, the appropriate mode of control for such a business is steering control. The manager should be able to steer the performance of such a business to meet the budgeted profit targets.

Despite the obvious appeal of the simple scheme laid out here, there is a tendency among firms to use uniform criteria, such as profitability, to determine incentives in all business contexts. The presumed advantage of such a practice is the objectivity with which incentives can be awarded. However, because variances in profitability can be measured more accurately does not make it a relevant criterion for all business contexts. Managers faced with a Pioneer or Expand business context may compromise growth in their chase after profitability, and, as mentioned earlier, managers in a Reorient business may be forced to exaggerate the profit potential of their business in order to look respectable in such a profit-driven culture. In short, unless incentives are tailored to suit the context of a business, they can become counterproductive. This challenge is illustrated well in the Becton Dickinson study (see Case 7). The company's incentive system was based primarily on profitability, thus handicapping business units such as Instruments and Reagents, which were assigned a Pioneer/Expand mission.

STAFFING THE BUSINESS UNIT

The staffing system is responsible for the assignment of managerial personnel throughout the firm. Aligning this system to the other systems—planning; monitoring, control, and learning; and incentives—is critical to the success of the firm's strategy implementation and reformulation efforts.[8] If the requisite managerial profile is unavailable within the firm, then recruitment from outside becomes an important activity. Besides internal assignment and external recruitment, the firm should anticipate managerial requirements in advance and meet them through suitable training and development activities. Assigning, recruiting, training, and developing managers are all important concerns of Human Resource Management (HRM).[9] However, in this chapter we focus on only the staffing system and defer a discussion of training and development to Chapter 9.

Managerial Profile and the Business Context

The managerial profile best suited to the business contexts described earlier can be defined along two dimensions: experience and personality (Figure 5-3). Managers with prior experience in operations or financial management, for example, may be suited for business units in need of an integrative orientation, and managers with a background in marketing or research and development may be suited to business

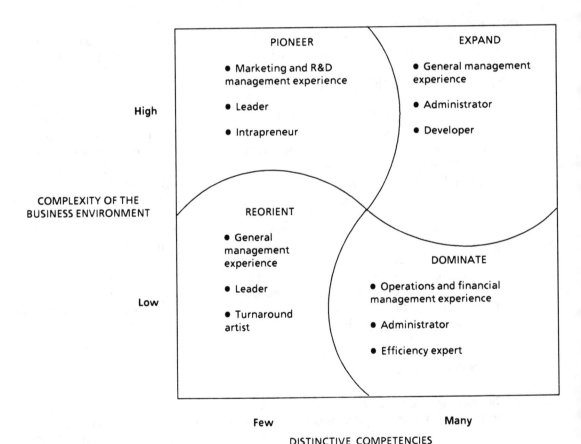

Figure 5-3   **Staffing for Different Business Contexts**

units in need of adaptation.[10] When a business unit needs both integration and adaptation simultaneously, the business unit manager should preferably have had prior general management experience. Thus Expand and Reorient are two business contexts that need well-rounded managerial experience.[11]

The personality of a business unit manager is defined by a host of factors, including management style and self-image. The dichotomy between an administrator and a leader is a useful one for distinguishing management style.[12] The administrator will tend to move a business unit along established tracks, but a leader can energize or transform the business unit to move down new tracks. A leader develops a vision of what the business unit can be, mobilizes its members to accept and work toward achieving the new vision, and implements the needed changes to effect a permanent transformation. It would be desirable to have a leader in every business context, but it is especially important in a Pioneer context where a new niche is sought and in a Reorient context where modifying the existing niche is a priority.

The self-image of a manager is another critical determinant of his or her personality. A manager sees himself or herself to be an expert at some managerial tasks more than others.[13] For purposes of our discussion, we consider four types of expertise: the intrapreneur, the developer, the turnaround artist, and the efficiency expert. The intrapreneur[14] is a manager who believes that he or she can successfully initiate new ventures even when working within a bureaucratic organization. Such a self-image is ideally suited to a Pioneer context. The developer is a manager who believes that he or she can grow a venture to its full-profit potential and so is best suited for an Expand context. The Reorient context needs a manager who believes that he or she can turn most bad businesses around. Finally, the Dominate context needs a manager who prides in being an efficiency expert. The intrapreneurs and the turnaround artists are usually leaders; the developer and the efficiency expert can be administrators.

To the extent top management can match managerial experience and personality to the context of a business unit, it will help enhance the performance of that business unit.[15] As we noted earlier, staffing is an especially critical activity if the business context is one of Pioneer or Reorient (see Figure 5-1).

Planner Profile and the Business Context

The key staff support for a business unit is provided by the business planner. The skills of a business planner can be broadly classified as analytical or administrative. The former refers to the abilities of a planner to forecast the business environment, analyze the competitive forces, generate and evaluate strategic alternatives; the latter refers to the planner's abilities to ensure the participation of key managers in the business unit's planning process and to assist the business unit manager in preparing and defending the business plan. Analytical skills are likely to be honed through staff assignments, and administrative skills are likely to be honed through line assignments.

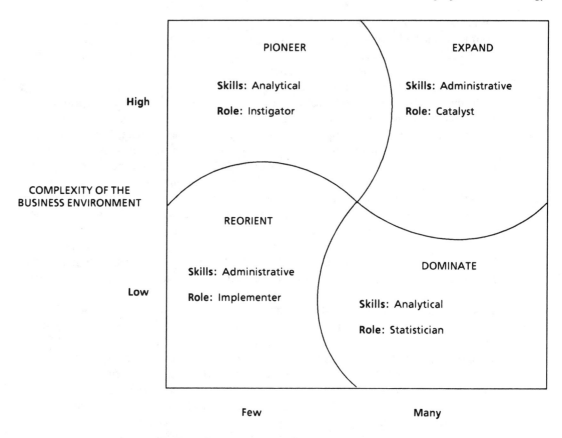

DISTINCTIVE COMPETENCIES

Figure 5-4   **Profile of a Business Planner for Different Business Contexts**

Four distinct roles can be envisaged for the business planner,[16] each appropriate to a particular business context (Figure 5-4).

When the business context is one of Pioneer, we recommend the appointment of an intrapreneurial business unit manager. A planner who can be an instigator would be an ideal complement for such a manager. An instigator helps the business unit manager make strategic choices by questioning the assumptions behind the available alternatives.[17] The role requires superior analytical skills. It would help the planning process if the planner is not perceived as a rival decision maker but rather as a supporting partner. If the planner's past experience is predominantly in staff functions, he or she can readily project such an image.

When the business context is one of Expand, the appropriate role of the planner is that of a catalyst. The planner's primary role, unlike that of an instigator, is to manage the participation of managers in the planning process. His or her role is not to shape the content of the strategies that are chosen because the business unit already has a well-defined strategy and a critical mass of managers who can ensure its validity. This business context requires a simultaneous adaptive and integrative orientation. The business unit manager thus needs help to ensure that the planning process is tailored appropriately to suit the different missions assigned to product lines within the business unit and that there is proper synchronization between the strategic, operating, and functional budgets for the different product lines. The primary skills required of the planner are not analytical but administrative.

When the business context is one of Reorient, the planner's role is that of an implementer. The business unit manager in such a context often has to make several unpleasant decisions on divestments and product line pruning as part of his or her turnaround effort. It is the job of the planner to help plan and implement these decisions. Clearly administrative skills are important in such an assignment.

Finally, when the business context is one of Dominate, a high-powered planner is not really needed. If one has to be hired, his or her role will be that of a statistician, helping the manager analyze budget proposals and identify additional areas for improving efficiency. The skills required of the planner are primarily analytical although not as sophisticated as the ones required in a Pioneer business context.

SUMMARY

Depending on the context of a business unit, the problems of goal incongruence and information asymmetry can be quite severe. The relative importance of staffing and incentives varies correspondingly. In this chapter, we provided a framework for tailoring an incentives system to suit a business unit and for staffing it with a suitable manager. We suggested that the fairness of an incentives system should be judged primarily by its relevance to the business context to which it is applied and not by its reliance on objective measures of performance. Effort, for example, may have to be evaluated subjectively, and yet rewarding managers for effort is important in some business contexts.

We also highlighted the differences in the managerial profiles that are required by the four business contexts. A versatile business unit manager may be able to meet more than one of these profiles. Training and job rotation can help in this regard. We address that aspect of human resources management in Chapter 9.

NOTES

1. See M. Jensen and W. Meckling, "Theory of the Firm: Managerial Behavior, Agency Costs, and Ownership Future," *Journal of Financial Economics* 3 (1976): 305–360.
2. See the following: G. Donaldson and J. W. Lorsch, *Decision Making at the Top* (New

York: Basic Books, 1983); J. P. Kotter, *The General Managers* (New York: Free Press, 1982); and H. Mintzberg, *The Nature of Management Work* (New York: Harper and Row, 1973).

3. See E. E. Lawler, *Pay and Organizational Effectiveness: A Psychological View* (New York: McGraw-Hill, 1971).

4. For a discussion of the zone of acceptance, see H. Simon, *Administrative Behavior* (New York: Free Press, 1945).

5. For an elaborate description of the incentive system used in Japanese companies, see M. Fruin, *Cooperative Structures, Competitive Strategies: The Japanese Enterprise System* (London: Oxford University Press, in press).

6. See D. C. Hambrick and I. C. MacMillan, "The Product Portfolio and Man's Best Friend," *California Management Review* 25 (Fall 1982): 84–95.

7. See R. G. Hamermesh, "Responding to Divisional Profit Crises," *Harvard Business Review* 55 (Mar.–Apr. 1977): 124–130.

8. For discussion, see M. Beer et al., *Managing Human Assets* (New York: Free Press, 1984).

9. See M. M. Tichy, C. J. Fombrun, and M. A. De Vanna, "Strategic Human Resource Management," *Sloan Management Review* 23 (Winter 1982): 47–62.

10. For an elaboration of this position, see A. K. Gupta, "Matching Managers to Strategies: Point and Counterpoint," *Human Resource Management* 25 (Summer 1986): 215–234.

11. This argument has been made by Hambrick and MacMillan, "The Product Portfolio."

12. The following have noted the differences between a leader and a manager: H. Levinson and S. Rosenthal, *CEO: Corporate Leadership in Action* (New York: Basic Books, 1984); N. M. Tichy and D. O. Ulrich, "The Leadership Challenge: A Call for the Transformational Leader," *Sloan Management Review* (Fall 1984): 59–68; and A. J. Zaleznik, "Managers and Leaders: Are They Different?" *Harvard Business Review* 55 (May–June 1977): 67–80. We have relabeled managers as administrators to avoid confusion with our use of the term *manager* as any head of a business unit.

13. See J. P. Kotter, *The General Managers* (New York: Free Press, 1982).

14. For a rich description of an entrepreneur, see G. Pinchott III, *Intrapreneuring* (New York: Harper and Row, 1985).

15. For some empirical support for this widely claimed relationship, see A. K. Gupta and V. Govindarajan, "Business Unit Strategy, Managerial Characteristics, and Business Unit Effectiveness at Strategy Implementation," *Academy of Management Journal* 27 (1984): 25–41.

16. This classification is adapted from the one proposed in P. Lorange, *Corporate Planning: The Executive Viewpoint* (Englewood Cliffs, NJ: Prentice-Hall, 1980).

17. For a discussion of how this dialectic should proceed, see J. R. Emshoff and I. I. Mitrof, "On Strategic Assumption-Making: A Dialectical Approach to Policy and Planning," *Academy of Management Review* 4 (Jan. 1979): 1–12.

REFERENCES

Chakravarthy, B. S., and E. Zajac, "Tailoring Incentive Systems to a Strategic Context," *Planning Review* 12 (Nov. 1984): 30–35.

Lorange, P., and D. C. Murphy, "Strategy and Human Resources: Concepts and Practice," *Human Resources Management* 22 (Spring–Summer 1983): 111–133.

Lyles, M. A., and R. T. Lenz, "Managing the Planning Process: A Field Study of the Human Side of Planning," *Strategic Management Journal* 3 (Apr.–June 1982): 105–118.

Rhenman, E., "The Hemispheres of the Brain Have Minds of Their Own," *New York Times* (Jan. 25, 1976): E8.

Winter, S. G., "Knowledge and Competence as Strategic Assets," in *The Competitive Challenge: Strategies for Industrial Innovation and Renewal,* ed. D. J. Teece (Cambridge, MA: Ballinger, 1987), 159–184.

Zaleznik, A., "Managers and Leader: Are They Different?" *Harvard Business Review* 55 (May–June 1977): 67–78.

Vick International Division: Tom McGuire

Sitting at breakfast, Tom McGuire was going over in his mind the key issues that were likely to come up during the day. The sun was just beginning to peek through the branches of the fir trees beyond the parking lot of the Rye Town Hilton. Across the top of the menu propped in the holder at the next table was the date: Thursday, August 10, 1978.

Throughout the week, management personnel from headquarters and field offices of Vick International, Latin America/Far East Division (LA/FE), had been attending the mid-August quarterly review meeting. As division president, McGuire had scheduled for that day individual agreement sessions with six of his overseas directors. There would be much ground to cover. It was essential that the important questions not be lost in a myriad of details. Tom also wanted to be sure that he assumed the appropriate role with regard to each critical issue, and that he was clear in his mind on the roles of others.

Of particular concern was a program in Mexico to develop and launch Alpha, a new nutritional product. Several other policy questions of greater moment would be dealt with in the next 18 hours. Among them were the approach to be taken on a partial divestment of equity in Indonesia, the approval of capital financing for two product introductions in Australia, and a move to broaden the division's product line in a dynamic Japanese market. But the Alpha situation required special attention because it touched upon the way in which the division's formal management system was working.

"It's ironic," McGuire mused. "Our management system calls for the explicit

Copyright © 1978 by the President and Fellows of Harvard College
Harvard Business School case 9–179–068

This case was prepared by Paul C. Browne, Research Assistant, under the supervision of Professor Richard F. Vancil, and with the cooperation of Vick International, Latin America/Far East, and its president, Thomas M. McGuire. It is intended for use as the basis for class discussion rather than to illustrate either effective or ineffective handling of an administrative situation. Reprinted by permission of the Harvard Business School.

assignment of work roles to the various managers within the division who must contribute to the attainment of a certain objective. Yet, with regard to Alpha, there seems to be some misunderstanding about who is responsible for each role, and what that means in terms of managing the project."

BACKGROUND

McGuire had been president of Vick International, Latin America/Far East, since 1969. A native of New York, he had studied chemistry at Notre Dame before working for Union Carbide. In 1956, at 29, he joined Richardson-Merrell, Inc., a diversified company engaged in the development, manufacturing, and marketing of proprietary medicines and toiletries, ethical pharmaceuticals, veterinary products, laboratory and diagnostic chemicals and equipment, and plastic packaging. (See *Exhibit 1* for RMI's organization chart.)

McGuire: As one of RMI's nine operating divisions, we are given considerable independence in running our business, so long as we contribute to the company's goals of stable growth, improving profitability, and product excellence. Richardson-Merrell's original business, starting in 1905, was built around Vick's VapoRub and subsequently other proprietary drugs in the cold remedy area. But in order to achieve more stability and growth the company began to diversify in the 1930s. As a result, a number of other products have been added to RMI's lines, but the Vick divisions, which handle proprietary health and personal care products, continue to be the mainstay of the business [see *Exhibit 2*].

When I became division general manager in 1969, Vick International, LA/FE, was having difficulty sustaining adequate growth and profitability. During the previous two years we had missed our budgets by wide margins. My initial analysis of the situation was that the division had an inadequate budget system, ineffective tracking and control mechanisms, and a lack of action-oriented reporting. So we instituted a budget manual, undertook improvements in the data base for planning, initiated a program to improve communications, and overhauled our reporting system. As a result, it was extremely frustrating when we didn't make our budgets the next two years either.

I had not experienced this type of failure before, and it led me to a far-ranging examination of what the division's business was and how we went about accomplishing it. Dick Waters, my executive vice president, had expressed his concern. I told him I would like to initiate some fundamental changes. He promised me his support and wished me success. The pressure to deliver was now really on my back.

Our business strategy was based on running with products already developed by other divisions within the company. In essence, it was an extension of

Exhibit 1   Richardson-Merrell, Inc., Organization Chart

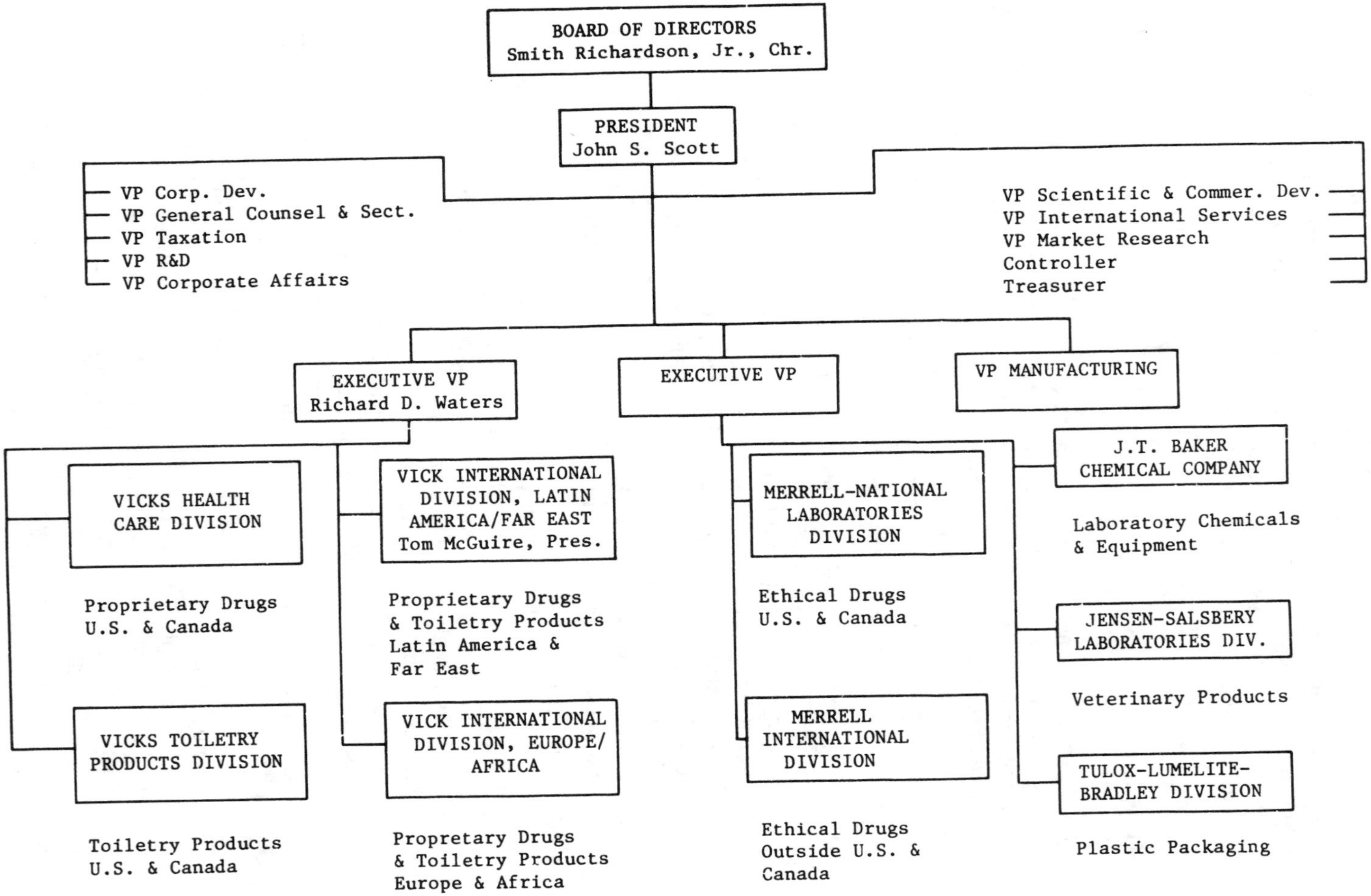

BOARD OF DIRECTORS
Smith Richardson, Jr., Chr.

PRESIDENT
John S. Scott

VP Corp. Dev.
VP General Counsel & Sect.
VP Taxation
VP R&D
VP Corporate Affairs

VP Scientific & Commer. Dev.
VP International Services
VP Market Research
Controller
Treasurer

VP MANUFACTURING

J.T. BAKER CHEMICAL COMPANY

Laboratory Chemicals & Equipment

JENSEN-SALSBERY LABORATORIES DIV.

Veterinary Products

TULOX-LUMELITE-BRADLEY DIVISION

Plastic Packaging

EXECUTIVE VP

MERRELL-NATIONAL LABORATORIES DIVISION

Ethical Drugs U.S. & Canada

MERRELL INTERNATIONAL DIVISION

Ethical Drugs Outside U.S. & Canada

EXECUTIVE VP
Richard D. Waters

VICK INTERNATIONAL DIVISION, LATIN AMERICA/FAR EAST
Tom McGuire, Pres.

Proprietary Drugs & Toiletry Products Latin America & Far East

VICK INTERNATIONAL DIVISION, EUROPE/AFRICA

Proprietary Drugs & Toiletry Products Europe & Africa

VICKS HEALTH CARE DIVISION

Proprietary Drugs U.S. & Canada

VICKS TOILETRY PRODUCTS DIVISION

Toiletry Products U.S. & Canada

Reproduction of original company document

134

Exhibit 2 Selected Financial Data

Richardson-Merrell, Inc.

Category	Year Ending June 30,					
	1973	1974	1975	1976	1977	1978
Net sales ($ thousands)						
Total	505,384	576,441	658,691	745,877	836,004	944,961
Consumer products only	274,453	313,601	364,972	439,304	507,967	605,942
Consumer products sold abroad only	132,363	166,855	207,227	241,842	271,344	na
Percent of contribution to income[a]						
Consumer products	57.5	55.9	58.4	70.1	71.5	79.9
Ethical products	35.7	35.5	33.2	25.3	26.0	18.7
Other products	6.8	8.6	8.4	4.6	2.5	1.4

Vick International, LA/FE

Category	Year Ending June 30,											
	1967	1968	1969	1970	1971	1972	1973	1974	1975	1976	1977	1978
Net sales ($ millions)	32	38	35	41	45	50	57	63	86	106	112	136
Controllable marketing expense as percent of sales	13.6	12.7	14.2	14.2	14.9	15.4	15.7	16.1	13.1	14.9	15.5	17.6
Operating profit as percent of sales	13.6	9.0	9.6	12.6	7.3	9.1	9.4	10.5	12.1	14.6	16.7	15.1
ROAE	na	na	na	na	na	na	13.5	15.4	18.5	24.2	28.5	27.3

[a] Income before taxes and allocation of central administrative expense

Source: Company annual reports and division financial records.

our highly successful export business of the forties and fifties, but it no longer fit the requirements of our expanding and changing markets. During the sixties we had set up manufacturing and distribution operations in a large number of countries, and as a result the management emphasis had been on sales generation to cover the rather substantial overhead.

My challenge was to refocus the division's resources and energies into more productive and successful patterns. I became convinced that we should stop running and pushing products in favor of returning to a more comprehensive marketing stance. We had to put major emphasis on analyzing consumer needs, to identify or develop products to satisfy those needs. We had to improve communications to the consumer that the product was available and superior in meeting his needs. Measurement of our success would then shift from sales volume shipped to distributors and focus on consumer awareness and retail take-off.

I also decided the division should concentrate on fewer products with higher profitability potential and higher volume potential across the countries. This meant encouraging our overseas operating units to reduce the number of low-volume and low-margin items in their product line, to shift away from price-controlled categories, and to consider introducing products that were highly successful in other markets. It has become something of a slogan that "we can't afford one-market products or one-product markets." This required that we become proficient in the transfer of strategy and expertise among the markets.

To bring about these changes, we had to introduce significant improvements in our organization and management practices. This message emerged clearly from a division management conference which I convened in November of 1971 to look at our organizational problems. The following summary of that session was presented some time back at a meeting in which we shared some of our experiences with a sister division:

THE 1971–72 SITUATION AS DEFINED BY MANAGERS

Managers were by no means unanimous in their views, but some of the feelings that were most often put forward can be summarized as follows:

1. Managers were influenced too much by immediate circumstances or events.

    Managing consisted of disposing of one crisis quickly enough to be ready for the next.

2. Almost without exception managers brought out one topic which they felt was of prime importance to them: "Making this year's budget."

    Managers expected their budgets to be revised in detail arbitrarily at headquarters.

Managers felt they were judged only on whether or not the current year's budget was achieved in their markets.

3. Corporate and division objectives were known to have been stated for sales and profit growth. However, this was not the starting point for planning or budgeting within the markets.

4. The overall feeling about "knowing where they were going" was that immediate problems did not allow time to worry to any great extent about the *long-term* future.

5. They believed that as long as everyone carried on as they had been doing, there was no reason for any serious doubts about the *short-term* future.

6. Headquarters staff (division and corporate) was essentially "reaching over the shoulder" of both line management and functional counterparts in markets—emphasis was on audit ("police") and problem-solving ("intervention") activities, self-generated, or on behalf of corporate or division management.

Clearly, we needed to delegate more responsibility for key managerial decisions, especially in marketing, to our operating units, but we lacked the focus, discipline, and procedural mechanisms to assure that such delegation would produce positive results.

John Steiger joined the division as finance director shortly thereafter and went to work on improving and systematizing our financial reporting and planning practices. Even before that, I had started working on ways to bring more rigor and discipline to our marketing activities in line with the new view of our business strategy. I set up the headquarters marketing departments to help me manage this new approach. The essence of the approach is reflected in a memo I issued in 1976 which formalized a classification of our products into three categories, each of which we had found to require different management approaches. The first, which we call development products, are those that are not currently being sold in commercial volume in any of our markets but promise to be winners. The main job of the HQ marketing directors is to assure that enough of these products are successfully introduced and spread throughout the division to provide us growth in future years. In the jargon of our management system, the development product program is "prime moved" by our HQ marketing directors.

Commercial products are those currently marketed successfully in several regions. They provide the bulk of our current business, but we have to watch their product life cycle and be especially wary of declining profitability in price-controlled markets under the pressure of cost inflation. Our HQ staff plays only a supporting role in the management of these products, with the Prime Movers being in the overseas operating units.

Nondivisional products are those associated with only one market, with unknown or no potential for expansion to others (our insecticide line in Aus-

Exhibit 3 Division Organization Structure

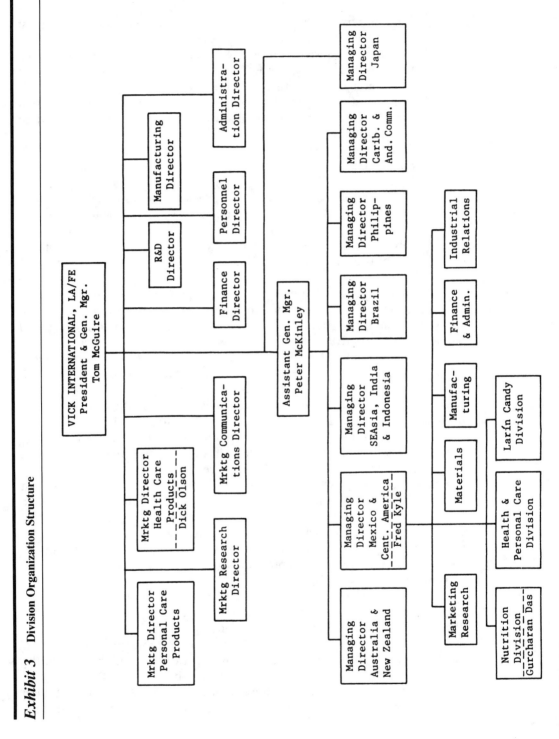

tralia is a good example). We want our people overseas who handle these products to make them fully self-supportive while meeting our policies and standards. If they can't, we must divest the products. Generally they cannot rely on division resources, and support for these products that they themselves provide must not divert their own resources or attention from the expansion of profitable commercial products and the introduction of promising development products.

Given the diversity of our markets and of the local personnel working in each of them [see *Exhibit 3* for LA/FE organization chart], as well as the inherent difficulties in obtaining timely information flows that would allow markets to learn from each other and HQ staff to provide adequate support, we have developed a set of elaborate, formalized, and rather standardized management procedures. Through them we have been trying to professionalize our management and clarify the relationship between the various country operations and the headquarters' departments.

VICK INTERNATIONAL, LA/FE's CP-R MANAGEMENT SYSTEM

Vick International, LA/FE employed an extensive formalized system of planning and control to direct and coordinate its widely scattered operating units. The system, known affectionately as CP-R (continuous planning and review), was not put in place all at once. McGuire built up the division's management capacity piece by piece over a period of several years. He moved management personnel around to make better use of talent. He brought in additional help, especially in the marketing management area. He worked closely with his headquarters staff to develop an all-encompassing marketing methodology which could be applied consistently throughout the division and serve as a link for coordination with other functions. He worked individually with each manager reporting directly to him to develop a mutual understanding about the nature of managers' responsibilities. He knew that as the division grew, effective delegation of decision making to the appropriate levels would be indispensable. To assist in making this possible and to improve coordination, he established a work role assignment process. And to energize the division, he instituted a series of periodic management meetings tied to a detailed planning and review system that looked backward twelve months and forward three years, with a complete update every quarter.

Over the years, the division gained substantial experience with the various components of this process. Eventually, much of it became formalized in a series of manuals: the Product Marketing Guides, the Manager's Guides, and the Planning and Review Guide.

McGuire: The key to our management process is its thoroughness, combined with its flexibility. Take the Marketing Guides, for example. For each of our major products we develop a guide which includes eight separate documents. The first two, the Product Profile Statement (PMG-1) and the Product Marketing Policy (PMG-2), are developed by one of the marketing directors and his staff at division headquarters as a standardized blueprint for the product across the division. They serve as a basis for planning the expansion or introduction of the product in a market.

The Product Data Book (PMG-3) and Product Marketing Assessment Statement (PMG-4) are developed by each regional or country unit handling or interested in introducing the product, to assess its appropriateness and potential in the local market. The regional market managing director is assigned the Approver role for the PMG-3, but because of its strategic importance, the PMG-4 is approved by the division president. The assessment in these two documents includes the discussion of reasons for deviations from the policies or standards set for the products in PMGs 1 and 2, if any are deemed necessary.

The remaining PMG documents, covering specific aspects of marketing, advertising, promotion, and sales and distribution strategy in a given market, are put together to refine the assessment of the feasibility of the product in that market, and then to serve as the basis for the management of the product once it is introduced.

The elaboration of each PMG document must be preceded by extensive research work. This might involve analysis of market conditions, product development, consumer attitude surveys, packaging design and testing, and so forth. Once the PMG package has been completed for a given product in a given market, however, all the pertinent results of this work are brought together in one place and are available for assessment and reference by managers throughout the division.

As one of our product managers at HQ, who has had substantial field experience, likes to say, "The PMG system doesn't let you take anything for granted. We are forced to go through all the steps and as a result we don't make those mistakes that used to slip by when we tried to finesse a difficult part of the marketing planning process." But at the same time, each overseas operating unit is free to adapt the product policy to its own circumstances, giving us substantial built-in flexibility. And each exception to standard practice is thus made explicit.

The marketing management process is embedded within a wider planning and review process, through which we obtain agreement on business financial objectives and functional operational objectives for each regional or country market, and between those markets and the division headquarters. These objectives in turn are tied to explicitly formulated strategic objectives for each unit and the division as a whole.

The process also provides procedures for the continuing review, analysis, testing, and reporting of performance and progress toward achieving division and market objectives and standards. We have found it necessary to break with RMI's traditional annual planning and budgeting cycle. It isn't dynamic enough for our markets, nor does it take a systematic enough look at the prospects for three, four, and five years out. So we have opted for our own system which calls for quarterly updates and includes the prior year, the current year, and the next three years. [See *Exhibit 4* for graphic representation of the CP-R planning cycle.]

Once operational objectives are set, we use succinct but explicit Work Programs following a standard format. These serve to draw together from all involved parts of the organization the information required so that we can view each program as a whole. This lets us test and evaluate the risk/cost/benefit relationship of the operational objective and the Work Program for its achievement. We can also assure efficient use and timing of resources, and identify conflicts between the demands of various Work Programs for limited resources.

The Work Programs, of course, quickly multiply. They can cover objectives related to development products and commercial products within various markets. They can touch on issues of personnel development, improving inventory management, building new facilities, managing an acquisition or divestment, and so on and so forth. The roles our managers are called upon to play will vary from one Work Program to another. As a result, we have found it indispensable to devise a mechanism for keeping our wires untangled. We assign all concerned parties a specific role in each Work Program, Action Plan, or other formal CP-R scheduling document. The four roles are: Approver, Prime Mover, Concurrer, and Contributor. The terms are all positive by design. We want to get things done, not get them hung up.

The Prime Mover, as the name implies, is the manager with the action. Quite frequently he will be at a third or fourth level in our hierarchy. This allows us to get around the rigidity of a chain of command and recognize the important and indispensable contribution to be made by those who actually push the work to its completion.

The Approver is a higher level manager than the Prime Mover—frequently, but not always, his immediate superior. His job is to assure that the measures taken by the Prime Mover are in line with division policies and overall objectives. And especially in the case of relatively inexperienced Prime Movers, the Approver will take care to see that serious mistakes which might damage the division or the subordinate's career are avoided.

Concurrers, of which there can be more than one on any given job, supply technical or specialized judgment to the Prime Mover. Their agreement is necessary prior to the implementation of any decision involving their area of expertise, although unresolvable disagreements can be referred to higher management. This perhaps is the one area where we still have to learn to do the job better. There is at times a tendency for Concurrers to behave as vetoers rather than positive collaborators. But by making the roles explicit,

Exhibit 4   **CP-R Planning Cycle**

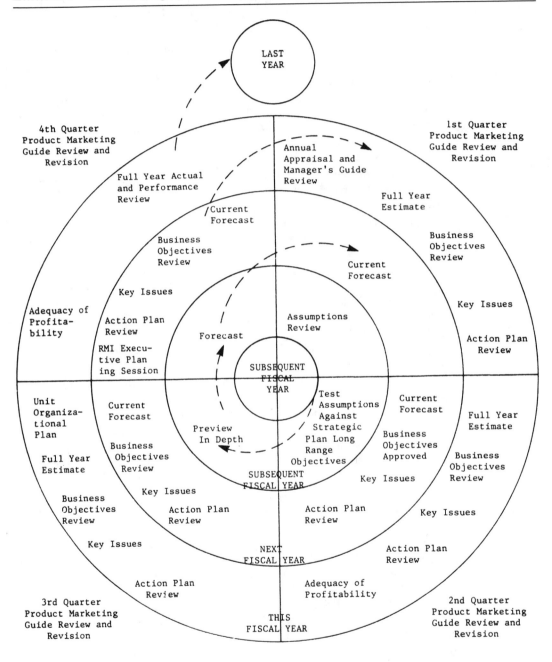

we find that such behavior becomes visible and can be dealt with. [*Exhibit 5* presents the definitions of the work roles as they are set forth in the CP-R Manual.]

I personally find the work role assignment process very valuable. By nature I am inclined to get involved in the details of every task. But now that the roles are formally specified, it has become commonplace for some of my directors to remind me to stay off their turf when I start getting too involved. There are days when I will be with one of them in two successive meetings in which our formally assigned roles change. It really helps us change gears.

Dick Olson also found the CP-R management system of much help. As marketing director for Health Care Products, he had several hats to wear and many markets to work with. Olson had been with RMI for 15 years since receiving his MBA from Cornell. Most of his career so far had been within the marketing function with the Vicks domestic Health Care Division. He had been in his present job for the last three years.

Olson: I have enjoyed this job very much. While some people might find it difficult to move from the less formally structured management process in a domestic division to LA/FE with its CP-R system, I have found it invigorating. Tom is a great guy to work for. He is bright, competent, and has a very professional approach to management. He has involved me deeply in the development and refinement of the division's marketing management approach and the techniques and procedures needed to carry it out. These are brought together in the PMG process.

Working with Tom on the elaboration of my Manager's Guide has made it possible to see where I can concentrate my efforts most productively for the division. It also has helped me see where my actions and those of my department affect the outcomes of other units and in what ways we are dependent on them. [*Exhibit 6* shows one page from Olson's Manager's Guide.]

As I see it, I have three main responsibilities. First, as part of Tom's management team, I help him as he feels the need on a broad set of general issues along with the other division headquarters directors. Then, more specifically, I assist him in the development of the marketing function throughout the division in the Health Care area.

Second, I am responsible for the adequate functioning of the division's activities aimed at business development in the health care field, including, more recently, nutritional products. My staff and I look for new ideas or products both from our people abroad and from outside the division or even outside the company. We undertake projects on our own to translate some of these ideas into physical products backed by a marketing strategy and marketing materials that can be tested in a trial market. Then we get the cooperation of one of our overseas units to test and launch it.

For example, just over a year ago the Australian Board of Health relaxed limitations on the advertisement of liquid cold remedies. Australia saw

Exhibit 5 **Work Role Definitions**

Approver:

The individual delegated the authority and responsibility by a higher management level to make the management decision to undertake, regulate or terminate an activity at any phase and to accept or reject recommendation for further action.

The Approver assures adherence to policies and procedures. He approves or rejects requests for exceptions to policy, or endorses them for referral to higher authority if the exception is beyond his approval scope.

Consistent with Delegation of Authority, the Approver retains responsibility for performance and designates Concurrers.

Prime Mover:

The individual responsible to the Approver and delegated authority by the Approver for the management coordination and follow through of all phases of the activity, from planning through implementation to evaluation of results. The Prime Mover makes recommendations for further action to the Approver and recommends Concurrers and selects Contributors.

The Prime Mover is responsible to the Approver for adherence to policies and procedures and for prompt identification and justification of exceptions to policy.

Concurrer:

Responsible to the Approver for providing to the Prime Mover judgment on the validity of those aspects of the activity within the scope of his expertise, and for contributing to the timely completion and quality of the activity. There can be more than one Concurrer.

Discusses with the Prime Mover areas of disagreement to reach a mutually acceptable agreement. If agreement cannot be reached between the Prime Mover and Concurrer, they jointly discuss with the Approver, who makes the decision or establishes the basis for resolution. If disagreement continues between the Concurrer and the Approver (and Prime Mover) on matters of technical expertise or exceptions to policy within the scope of the Concurrer's expertise, either the Approver or the Concurrer may refer the matter to higher management authority.

It is the responsibility of each manager and supervisor to exercise his own initiative in assuming the role of Concurrer for a particular work activity that involves his expertise. If not nominated, he should approach the Prime Mover and secure both the Approver's and Prime Mover's agreement to his involvement as Concurrer.

Contributor:

Responsible to the Prime Mover for providing resources on aspects of the activity required or requested by the Prime Mover. There normally will be more than one Contributor. Contributors do not take part in the decision process.

Each manager and supervisor who, because of his expertise or resources, recognizes himself as a Contributor to a particular work activity must also exercise initiative in assuming this work role. If not designated he should approach the Prime Mover and secure the Prime Mover's agreement to his involvement as Contributor.

144

Exhibit 6   **Excerpt from Olson's Manager's Guide**

Key Result Area: Tomorrow's Products	<u>KEY TASK #1</u> Position: Div. Marketing Dir. Page: Date: Revised: December 6, 1976

<u>KEY TASK #1</u>

As Prime Mover to ensure that sufficient viable ideas for
<u>Development Products</u> are being identified and acted upon at
least to meet future Division growth needs.

<u>STANDARDS OF PERFORMANCE</u>

a. When there is an approved plan, consistent with Division
objectives and strategy, for Long-Term Business development of the field of activity, including product development, acquisition and licensing.

b. When there is an ongoing program to track and screen,
against Division criteria and objectives for the category,
new product activity within the Vick Divisions.

c. When, there is an ongoing program to test objectives and
screenining criteria and to identify or generate ideas
for prospective Development Products.

d. When all ideas which pass the screening against Divisional
criteria are promptly referred to R&D for exploratory
feasibility.

e. When 80% of the recommendations of the Active Development
Slate are approved and allocated the necessary resources
on the basis of reasonable or supportable quantified
statements of costs and potential benefits/risks.

f. When the marketing checkpoints included in assigned
Active Development Projects are adequate to validate
continuance, to select an alternative course or to
terminate, and when appropriate action is taken when
each checkpoint is reached.

g. When no assigned Active Development Project is significantly delayed, has its cost increased, or fails because
of inadequate or delayed marketing information or because or failure to provide, promptly, requested and
agreed upon HQ Marketing support or resources.

h. When, at all times, there is at least one Development
Product of the assigned category on the Active Development Slate (or under negotiation for license/acquisition
<u>and</u> at least one other undergoing testing (including
Test Marketing) each with a first sustaining year national
contribution <u>total</u> for <u>major</u> markets in excess of $1 million,
at a Contribution ratio, growth rate, investment level and
ROAE equal to or better than criteria for the category:
and whose resource requirements are within the capabilities
of the Division and the major markets.

<u>EVIDENCE OF ACHIEVEMENT</u>

a. GM Approval of HQ Marketing Preview in
Depth (PID) for the category

b. Individual Performance Reviews against
Action Plans
Minutes of Meetings within the Program

c. Individual Performance Reviews against
Action Plans
Minutes of Meetings within the Program

d. R&D Approved Projects

e. GM Approvals of not less than 80% of
submitted Project Guides

f. GM Approval of Action Plan
Individual Per. rmance Reviews against
Action Plans

g. Individual Performance Reviews against
Action Plans

h. Project Guides and Action Plans

Reproduction of original company document

this as an opportunity for itself, and we saw it as a good opportunity for the division, especially as we had indications that similar policy changes were in the making in some other countries in our half of the world. At division headquarters we pooled information worldwide on RMI's capabilities in this area. Working with our Australian marketing staff, we did some consumer survey work. Out of this we concluded that NyQuil, which was being sold successfully in the U.S. and Europe, had promising potential. We then drew up a plan that would allow us to launch the product successfully in Australia within nine months. Members of my department and I, as well as other HQ staff members, traveled to Sydney several times during the subsequent months working very closely with, and providing assistance to, our local people out there. It required a concentrated joint effort, but we were successful in launching the product, which we call MediNite in that market, within the time period specified. We beat the competition into the market by several weeks. We used the PMG process very successfully as an aid in getting all the pieces together, and the CP-R process helped get all the actors collaborating in a timely fashion. Manufacturing and marketing MediNite in Australia is now primarily the responsibility of our people out there, although in our third role as a resource department on marketing we will continue to be available to assist our people in Australia if and when they need it.

Back to the issue of business development: when our overseas units have a substantial nondivision business segment which warrants product development as part of its long-term strategy, we allow them to develop such products within our policies, procedures, and standards, and try to support them in every way we can. The PMG system provides us with regular feedback reports, and through it we are assured that a thorough review is made of all aspects of the product which could make it successful or cause it to flounder. Several of our units, especially Australia, Mexico, and India, are strong in new product development, but they still each have some shortcomings. We try to capitalize on their strengths by letting them take a lot of initiative and operate quite independently, while we remain available to help whenever it's needed.

This job allows me to act both as a marketing staff director and as an operating director for the new product development program. This is challenging and personally satisfying. I know that my counterpart for Personal Care Products feels the same way. It is what attracted him to come to RMI. It would be nearly impossible to carry out this dual role without the work role assignment approach of the CP-R system. Since it started being used regularly in the division, the amount of wasted time and effort has dropped considerably. Delays in communication between the field and headquarters have also been reduced substantially.

Fred Kyle, managing director in Mexico since 1974, while committed to the CP-R system, was less enthusiastic about it. Of his 20 years with RMI, he had spent about half in manufacturing and marketing management, first with Vicks domestic and then with International. For the last 10 years, he had held various field management positions in Latin America.

Kyle: CP-R certainly has a lot going for it, but it does cause us some problems. The quarterly management review meetings are tremendously helpful. We get a lot of problems resolved, and are able to adjust our objectives often enough to keep an even keel in a very volatile political and economic environment. But there is an overload of paper work. My financial director has to keep records for me under the CP-R system, but since we also service the Mexican office of Merrell International, he has to follow a different setup for them.

And then there is the language barrier. Most of our Mexican management people have a working knowledge of English, but we conduct our business in Spanish and as a result they find it hard to tune in to the CP-R system, which is all in English. Some of the terminology can't even be translated. Then of course there is a cultural barrier in almost all LA/FE overseas locations. Some are not comfortable with such explicitly assigned responsibilities, with everyone's performance open to the general view, especially if they are accustomed to use a more personalized form of supervision.

We are trying to apply the CP-R system to our operations, but so far it has been more difficult than we anticipated. However, I feel it will be worth all the effort.

Some of our managers feel CP-R is really an extension of Tom McGuire, that he makes it work by pure willpower, and they're sure we are all the better for it. The division's performance certainly has improved. In part it's a big advantage, but in part it may be a drawback that Tom knows so much about our market and our operations. He has a tendency to get too involved from time to time in the details of running our business. Maybe Mexico is a special case. He spent 18 months here in 1964–1965 as director.

CORPORATE/DIVISION RELATIONS

Although RMI went public in 1925, the Richardson family maintained a strong ownership position and an active role in the company's corporate management. Smith Richardson, Jr., chairman of the board since 1961, had previously been a vice president, administrative vice president, and president (1957–1961). The company had a long tradition of hiring top-of-the-class graduates from leading colleges and moving them through a management career ladder, starting in field sales, thus "developing our own managers." Vice chairman Robert Marschalk, who was president from 1961 to 1975, and John Scott, president since 1975, both had followed this path.

Top management, therefore, had a strategy of monitoring the growth and development of its young managers carefully, placing them in key positions as they showed an ability to handle the challenges at that level, giving them basic guidance as to overall corporate objectives, and allowing them substantial freedom to manage their own shops. As Dick Waters, executive vice president for the Vick divisions, put it: "The most important part of my job is on the people side. The better the people, the less I have to be involved in day-to-day operations."

Corporate officers had an open door policy toward key operating managers and expected them to bring up any problems or opportunities that required attention at any time. They also traveled and visited field operations from time to time, with particular interest in staying in touch with management personnel at various levels. John Scott made it a habit to have lunch once or twice a month with junior managers from various divisions at the RMI headquarters.

Formal reviews of divisional plans and performance were limited to the following three areas:

1. Previews-in-Depth (PIDs) of a particular business or market, initiated by the Operating Committee (president, executive vice presidents, vice president for manufacturing services, and controller). Such a planning exercise would look at all facets of that part of the business going out three to five years into the future.
2. The Step Planning Process, designed to spread planning and budgeting activities out over the year. For Step 1, in late January, the divisions would highlight for top management the key problems and opportunities for the coming fiscal year. Step 2, around March, involved the presentation of recommended plans of action in light of the discussions during Step 1. In May, Step 3 was undertaken, involving the presentation, analysis, and approval of an annual operating plan and budget for the upcoming fiscal year. This was known as the executive budget session. The key parameters set at this time were sales projections, profit targets, and plans for controllable marketing expenses. Capital investment requirements would also be discussed, if relevant. Approval for particular investment projects, however, was normally handled on a case-by-case basis throughout the year, with final approval frequently following a review by the board of directors. Step 4 involved a less formal monitoring of performance against budget.

   Although corporate management indicated an openness to alternative approaches to formal planning and reporting procedures between the Operating Committee and the divisions, only Vick LA/FE had introduced innovations, all based on the functioning of the CP-R system. Prior to each quarterly review meeting and drawing on the preparation for it, Vick LA/FE submitted a planning and review book to top management which encompassed a rolling four-quarter plan, spanning two fiscal years. Waters and other corporate officers had an open invitation to attend the quarterly meetings. The preparation prior to the fourth quarter meeting also served as the basis for the submission of the division's executive budget proposal for the upcoming fiscal year.
3. The management personnel appraisal and promotion process. This was a regular, yearly process whereby each manager evaluated his direct reports

and discussed with his personnel their strengths and weaknesses. Relevant information was then passed up to successive levels of management along with recommendations for training, promotions, salary increases, and participation in the incentive compensation plan, which consisted of both a cash bonus and a stock option plan based on corporate and division profit performance. Salary, promotion, and incentive recommendations were reviewed by committees at the division level (with participation by the executive vice president) and corporate level, depending on the manager's rank. The recommendations of the division general manager and the executive vice president carried a lot of weight.

PROJECT ALPHA

Mexico was the largest operating entity within LA/FE, and had concentrated traditionally on proprietary drugs. In 1964 it entered the nutrition field with the acquisition of ChocoMilk, a well-established brand of powdered milk supplement with an existing distribution network. Consisting mainly of powdered milk, chocolate, and sugar, ChocoMilk provided nutritional reinforcement as well as flavoring. It took several years to modernize the production facilities, improve the formula to suit changing tastes and meet several competitive entries, and develop the management capacity to deal with this new market. One of the main stumbling blocks was the absence of a reliable source of supply for high quality chocolate that would make it possible to upgrade the product. This was achieved in 1966 with the acquisition of the Larín Candy Company, one of Vick's major chocolate suppliers. Now local management faced a new set of challenges. Not only did it have to proceed with the upgrading and expansion of ChocoMilk, but it also had to learn to manage the specialty candy business into which it had entered. It took several more years for both tasks to be accomplished.

When Fred Kyle became managing director in Mexico in 1974, one of his early concerns was to strengthen the ChocoMilk segment of the business. It seemed risky to have such an important segment relying on only one product which already dominated its market with a 50% market share, and which was under considerable competitive pressure. Secondly, the traditional proprietary drug business continued to be price controlled, offering negative prospects for improved profitability. Additional entries into the nutrition field appeared to be worth serious consideration.

After consultation with division headquarters, Kyle commissioned a study of potential entries for the Mexican nutritional product market. The study was carried out by the marketing research department in Mexico with assistance from a New York consulting firm in 1975–1976. The study took an exhaustive look at food items sold in grocery stores in Mexico, the United States, and Canada, to identify categories of consumer needs for which solutions were sought through processed foods sold in food stores. Then surveys were carried out with panels of Mexican housewives to learn their underlying concerns regarding each class of needs. Out of this emerged a slate of product concepts for development and testing. These were screened for feasibility as products for Vick Mexico.

At a divisional management meeting in August of 1976, the results of the study were presented along with a final slate of potential new products for development and market testing. The slate was approved, as was an overall new product development program. A target was set to test market at least one new product from the slate each year. Product Alpha was the first new item on the slate.

Gurcharan Das was assigned in October of 1976 to become director of Vick Mexico's newly established Nutrition Division, responsible for the ongoing Choco-Milk business and the new nutritional product development program. He already had a track record of successful development and introduction of new products with Vick International's Indian subsidiary.

A philosophy major at Harvard College, Das had decided after graduation to look for opportunities in business management that would allow him to return to India, use his creative energies, and still have time for personal development as a thinker and writer. He found the opportunity with RMI, which he joined in 1963. In 1976, Das was offered the choice of joining the division's Health Care Products marketing department to work on new product development, or to take the job in Mexico.

Das: I decided to go to Mexico because I wanted to be close to the market, where the action is. I wanted to have responsibility for all the facets of product development, testing, and launching. I like to have control over my piece of the business and to be judged by the results I achieve. It allows me to exercise my creative energies. I guess I have an entrepreneurial spirit.

Alpha was Das's first challenge in this new position. The product was aimed at a felt need of the Mexican mother for a quick, easy, yet nourishing beverage for use on hectic school days. Over the next 18 months Das worked intensively with a technical group in the ChocoMilk plant to develop a suitable product. He also enlisted the help of the marketing research department to carry out extensive product concept research with potential users. During this period there was little interaction with headquarters staff other than routine communication of progress and occasional inputs from the division research and development director on issues of product quality.

No formal Work Program was drawn up. Nonetheless, Vick Mexico did have extensive internal plans and schedules including a PERT-type plan for Alpha. Since it was a totally new product with which the HQ staff had no familiarity, there were no PMG-1 and PMG-2. Kyle and Das considered Alpha a nondivisional product like ChocoMilk, for which they were responsible.

In January of 1978, Das contracted with a Mexico City advertising agency to start developing material for use in the first market tests later that year. He had another contractor develop an innovative container for Alpha.

With the time approaching to make initial commitments for market testing, it was necessary to obtain overall division management approval of the project's current status and direction. A meeting for this purpose was planned for early May. In preparation for this meeting, the PMGs 3, 4, 5, 6, 7, and 8 were completed in late April and sent to headquarters personnel for their review.

By separating the PMG into various documents, the CP-R system made it possible to assign different work roles to various individuals for each piece. While PMGs 1 and 2 were primarily the work of headquarters staff, the remaining parts required substantial collaboration between headquarters and field. The Approver role for the PMG-3 was assigned to the regional managing director, with the Prime Mover, Concurrers, and Contributors coming from the local staff. The PMGs 4 and 5, which were key strategy documents, required the approval of the division president and the concurrence of several headquarters directors, as well as overseas unit functional managers. PMGs 6, 7, and 8, which usually were prepared after 4 and 5 had been approved, usually could be approved by the division assistant general manager with concurrence only from the headquarters director with specific functional expertise in each case.

With the Alpha PMG, however, because all six parts arrived at the same time, the package was reviewed as a unit by all the potential Concurrers and Approvers. Dick Olson, as Prime Mover for the overall Development Product program, became the focal point for the review at HQ.

In studying the PMG documents on Product Alpha, Olson was surprised to see it classified as a nondivisional product. Nonetheless he felt that an excellent job had been done in the area of product concept research, product development in the lab, and assessment of market potential. Reactions from other headquarters departments were similarly supportive, with a few technical suggestions for improvement. The material on marketing strategy and advertising, however, was very spotty and failed to take full advantage of the marketing research.

During the next several weeks Das made three trips to division headquarters in the hope of getting the necessary approvals to proceed with a test market launch of Alpha. After the first meeting in May, Tom McGuire approved the Alpha program and the PMG-4 in principle. It was agreed that Mexico would undertake several technical improvements having to do with packaging, labeling, and product quality, as well as obtain some additional information on potential users. McGuire also asked Das to review PMGs 5 through 8 with Olson after the meeting, since extensive comment had been made about their adequacy. At this point a Work Program was prepared (see *Exhibit 7*).

For the first time, Das became aware that an MC-1 (a CP-R document designed to provide an advertising agency with guidance for developing advertising material) would be required, and that for Development Products the MC-1 had to be approved by the division president and concurred with by Assistant General Manager Peter McKinley, Dick Olson, and the marketing communications director.

In June, Das returned with a draft MC-1 and a package of advertising material which he wished to use in the test launch. He needed various concurrences and approval from headquarters management in order to proceed. Dick Olson and the marketing communications director had previously reviewed the material and made

Exhibit 7 **Alpha Work Program**

OBJECTIVE/STANDARD: Test Market and evaluate Alfa leading to a decision to introduce nationally.

MAJOR STEPS	PERSON OR UNIT	OUTPUTS	START DATE	END DATE	•	COMMENTS
1. Wilton approval of project	GCD	1. Minutes of May 8 meeting		05/78	*	1. Completed.
2. Order packaging molds, raw and packaging materials.	RB	2a. Approval of preliminary molds.	R7/78	R9/78	*	2. A. Tassin will be required to approve preliminary molds.
		b. Receipt of all materials necessary for initial production	R8/78	R10/78		
3. Obtain advertising approval.	GCD AQ	3. Approved commercials for air.	R6/78	R2/79	*	
		a) MC-1 approval		R7/78		
		b) Storyboard approval		R8/78		
		c) Pretesting/SSA		R10/78		
		d) Approval to produce		R10/78		
4. Manufacturing booklet	SH/ WRG	4. Red Book issued	R8/78	R9/78	*	4. W.R. Gillap to issue.
5. Product ready	AFS	5. Pipeline stock plus first 2 mos. expected consumer takeoff of finished stock in warehouse	Rt-135	Rt-15	*	5. Contingent on approval of MO-2 (test market proposal) or separate approval to buy material and packaging inventories.
6. Production of marketing communication materials	GCD	6. Commercials in can	Rt-75	Rt-15	*	
		Promotion/display materials in warehouse	Rt-60	Rt-15		
		Media space booked	Rt-30	Rt-30		
		Sales force briefing/training	Rt-5	Rt-1		
7. Test market distribution	GCD	7. Pipeline horizontal and vertical distribution objectives and promotion/display objectives achieved or surpassed	Rt	Rt+21 Rt+56	*	(Note: In the date columns O stands for original and R stands for revised)
8. Month x evaluation of test market	GCD	8. Implement month x reaction program	O 1/w R 1/x	O 30/w R 30/x	*	GCD = Das
						RB = Mexico Materials Mgr.
						AQ = Mexico Nutritional Dn. Prod. Mgr.
9. Month y evaluation of test market	GCD FWK	9. Month y reaction program. Order balance of equipment.	O 1/x R 1/y	O 30/x R 30/y	*	WRG = Division Manuf. Director
						APS = Mexico Manuf. Director
10. Month z evaluation of test market	GCD FWK	10. TMM approval to go national, expand text market, or recycle.	O 1/y R 1/z	O 30/y R 30/z	*	HB = Mexico Nutritional Dir. Sales Mgr.
						t = Test market starting date - disguised for competitive reasons

CORP/COUNTRY	WORK PROGRAM	PRIME MOVER	BUSINESS SEGMENT OR DEPARTMENT		DATE INITIATED	5/78	PAGE
		GCDas			LAST REVISION	8/78	CFR WP
MEXICO		APPROVER FWKyle	NUTRITIONAL	ALFA PROJECT			

March 78

(In preparation for mid-Aug. Inventory Review Meeting.)

some suggestions for improvement. When Das met with Tom McGuire for approval, he found that Tom thought basic changes in the market positioning of Alpha, implicit in the advertising copy, would be necessary. He suggested that Das return to Mexico and revise the PMG-5, PMG-6, and MC-1, in line with their discussion. He should then submit the MC-1 to headquarters for approval which, Tom promised, would be forthcoming within 48 hours. To assure a quick turnaround, he delegated the Approver role jointly to McKinley and Olson.

Das was crushed. He told McGuire that he felt let down by the whole system. How could it be that after getting professional inputs from the agency in Mexico, approval in principle of the PMG, and comments about the advertising copy from headquarters staff which had been incorporated into the material, a major flaw should come out in a meeting with the division president? And with every passing day the project was falling further behind schedule.

Upon returning to Mexico, Das revised the MC-1 and sent it to division HQ in early July. A week later he received a request from Olson to come to the United States for a meeting to get the MC-1 approved. In late July that meeting took place. The PMG-5, PMG-6, and MC-1 were jointly rewritten. Then all Concurrers and the Approvers initialed the MC-1 document. Das returned to Mexico to have the agency prepare storyboards for TV ads. He had instructions to return to headquarters with these for approval in late August.

Prior to his departure for the mid-August quarterly review meeting, Fred Kyle, who had been away for six weeks at a management education program, had a long discussion with Gurcharan about the Alpha project.

Kyle: Gurcharan was very unhappy. He had worked for a year and a half getting Alpha off the ground. He had been successful in getting our Mexican R&D, marketing research, manufacturing, and other staff departments involved and excited. They were all committed to a tightly programmed project schedule and had produced truly innovative top quality results. We were convinced that we had identified a project with very significant potential.

After moving along so well, however, we are now running into trouble. While the difficulties focus on Alpha, it is really the entire nutritional new product program that is at stake. The establishment of such a program had been attempted without success ever since the acquisition of ChocoMilk in 1964. I had taken a different approach from my predecessors and, after four years of work with the entire Mexican organization and with the full knowledge of division management, appeared to be achieving results.

To succeed, however, our people need to be free to take risks, to move quickly, to be entrepreneurial, and to feel that they will be judged on their results. The way the CP-R process is being applied is making this extremely difficult.

I hope at the quarterly meeting we can work out some way of maintaining our present momentum and of providing the freedom and flexibility we need to ensure the continued progress of our whole nutritional new product program.

Texas Instruments Incorporated: MODPLAN

By April 1979, Texas Instrument's (TI) computer-based financial planning and control system, "model planning" (MODPLAN for short), was being used throughout TI's worldwide operations. In fact, the sustained 100 percent annual growth in the use of MODPLAN was beginning to cause longer response times[1] for its users. When describing the problem in April 1979, Fred Teter, the Manager of MODPLAN, said the following:

> Up until 1976, most MODPLAN usage was at the division or product line level and models were mostly financial in nature. In 1977 and 1978, MODPLAN usage was extended to the cost-center level. This year we are beginning to use MODPLAN more in modeling operations at product levels, such as in unit costing. Users are beginning to use MODPLAN to develop specific product profit plans (at the lowest levels) to be used in their financial consolidations. In turn these new applications have really put pressure on the system for added flexibility and reduced cycle time for modeling definition, model changes, and improved response times to "what if" inquiries.[2]
>
> The financial "Blue Book"[3] consolidation part of MODPLAN has now decreased from probably 80 percent of the usage in 1974 and 1975 to about 2 percent today. There is still a tendency at TI to think of MODPLAN as a Blue Book system. It really isn't; it has gone far beyond that.

When describing MODPLAN's rapid growth, Teter continued with this:

> You can look at what has been happening to MODPLAN by looking at its growth. For example, the number of data bases have grown from 31 at the end of 1976 to 62 in

Copyright © 1979 by William R. Boulton and Charles W. Kight

This case was abridged and revised by Professor Balaji S. Chakravarthy, University of Minnesota, from the TI MODPLAN (A) and (B) cases written by Professor William R. Boulton, University of Georgia, and Charles W. Kight, Division Manager in Information Systems and Services, Texas Instruments. The case is intended for use as the basis for class discussion rather than to illustrate either effective or ineffective handling of an administrative situation. Reprinted with the permission of the authors and the North American Case Research Association.

April, 1979. The number of arrays used have grown from nearly 6,000 in 1976 to over 28,000 in April. Our inquiry usage, which is on-line, has gone up from almost one million in 1976 to over 3 million in 1978, and nearly 1.4 million through April 1979. We had 1,620 terminals authorized for MODPLAN usage in April, up from 349 in 1976.

Charles Kight, the Division Manager within TI's information systems and services group, commented this on MODPLAN's growth:

> To understand the explosive growth of MODPLAN, you have to understand that technology is the driving force. The question is, why couldn't we have done MODPLAN even earlier? Well, for one thing, we didn't have the worldwide computer network to be able to do it nor did we have the required software or organizational expertise in the user's camp. Technology causes changes. There is now an opportunity to take advantage of TI's new 990 minicomputer.

BACKGROUND ON TI'S PLANNING PROCESS

The planning process at Texas Instruments was at the core of its system of management. Planning was a nearly continuous process that integrated near-term actions and constraints on profitability and resources with the company's long-range plans and corporate objectives.

There were "four loops" through which TI's planning process was administered (Exhibit 1). The first loop—the long-range planning loop—focused on TI's direction for the next ten years and the strategies for getting there. The second loop—intermediate-range planning—concentrated on planning for facilities, manufacturing equipment, and major production cost reductions for the next three years. In this second loop, the current year plus one was the critical time horizon because the strategic plan, intermediate plan, and rolling plan were reconciled in this loop. The third loop—the rolling plan—was a quarterly update that occurred in January, April, July, and October of each year. Rolling plans included a full set of profit and loss and resources objectives, or indices, along with the most current thinking as to volume levels and changing business conditions. The fourth loop was for monthly forecasting. In the first month of each quarter, the product customer centers (PCCs) prepared their forecasts for three months into the future. In the second month of a quarter, the forecasts were for five months; in the third month, the forecasts were for four months. This final loop was used to monitor and control variances from performance indices. The performance indices were developed from a set of key indices such as net sales billed (NSB), growth rate, gross profit margin (GPM) percent, strategic investment (OST) percent, organization profit percent, and return on assets (ROA). These indices also were referred to as "models" for an organization.

When relating TI's models to the planning system in 1977, Mark Shephard, the Chairman and Chief Executive Officer, commented the following:

> We have what we call the "basic model." This is a model of key indices which together express the standard of achievable performance against which the performance of an

Exhibit 1   Four Cycles of Planning

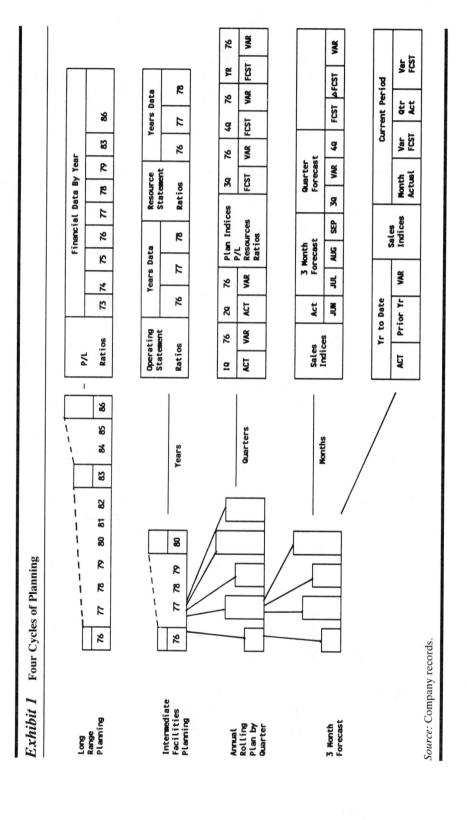

Source: Company records.

organization will be measured. It is a stretch, but not an impossibility. We then also end up with "models of the year" in the intermediate plan. These models don't necessarily equal the basic model. The basic model itself is not fixed in concrete, and can vary a great deal over time. One of the dangers in modeling is that people begin regarding them as more than benchmarks. When you begin thinking of them as the gospel which can never be changed, you have problems. They have to be very living things.

The rolling plan which is developed near year-end, and comes into print in January, is called the "bench-mark plan" from which our bench mark indices are established. Those indices are what we hold our managers' noses to the grindstone on for the rest of the year. We don't let them informally change each quarter as we produce these rolling plans. If they want to make a change, they have to come and negotiate it with me.

The ideal that we can strive for, though will never reach, is to understand our businesses well enough so that we can model them. We should be able to understand our business structure, the interrelationships between the different businesses, and different parts of the same business, so that you can pick a billings number and have the computer tell you what you should have in every department. You have to be careful not to be a slave to that and must be able to recognize and investigate anomalies which may come out of such models.

The kind of measure which we use in these models includes the output, what we call "net sales billed" or what some people call sales. We define a "sale" as an "order" which creates backlog. Our "net sales billed" are actual "shipments" of product to the customer. From net sales billed, we subtract manufacturing costs to get gross product margin. From this margin, we deduct operating expenses called D&A (distribution and allocated) expenses which leaves a sum that can either be invested in profits or in future OST[4] expenditures.

In the models, we have numbers which describe what percentage OST should be of net sales billed. This percentage includes some subjective inputs and some pseudo-mathematical derivations, but it varies a great deal from business to business. It becomes a function of the technical sophistication of your business, of your competition, and of the product life cycle. OST represents a much higher percentage of billings for products with short life cycles. If you have a life cycle of 40 years, it takes much less input each year to stay abreast or ahead than it does if you have a product life cycle of three years.

When discussing the early development of TI's models, Shephard continued with this:

We're not as sophisticated as we would like to be with models, but we are making progress. What we try to do with this is to get our managers to look very hard at the structure of their business, rather than having them feel virtuous because they have pushed a pencil a lot. Pencil pushing is easy for the computer. MODPLAN does this for us.

I believe we're about half way, within a ten-year cycle, of getting models to do everything that they ought to be able to do for us, and in getting managers to accept them. The more "administrative" managers don't particularly like the idea of models, because models do automatically what they have been doing most of their lives. The innovators and entrepreneurs like models, because models give them more time to spend on things they're interested in.

MODPLAN AT TEXAS INSTRUMENTS

MODPLAN was a management data-base system for collecting, consolidating, and reporting of numerical information. MODPLAN was developed to help TI managers, planners, and analysts do their jobs easier and better. Specifically, it provided a tool that allowed computer power to be applied to the tasks of collection, manipulation, analysis, and reporting of any numerical data that could be arranged by time periods—such as was commonly done in forecasting, planning, budgeting, reporting, and controlling activities. To understand MODPLAN's success at TI, it is necessary to understand the basic capabilities of the system. Most users of MODPLAN stored historical data and forecasts within their data bases. These were specified as dollars, people, units, sites, or any other logical quantity that could be tracked by time periods. Each MODPLAN data base was three-dimensional with data items called line items, time periods, and organizations called "entities."

Each data base had separate definitions for their line items—such as net sales billed, total people, direct material cost, and manufacturing overhead—but these definitions did not necessarily coincide with the names used in other data bases. Time periods could be specified in months, quarters, or years. In order to save storage space and thus reduce the cost of operation, the MODPLAN system differentiated between calculated lines and noncalculated lines and stored only those lines that could not be calculated from other lines.

Exhibit 2 shows a sample report of time period comparisons for 55 line items. Lines such as percent GPM (line 13) to sales, percent OST expense (line 22) to sales, and net fixed asset as a percent of sales (line 38) were calculated within MODPLAN. The drudgery associated with calculations, consolidation, and clerical work in the financial and operating data was greatly reduced by MODPLAN. "What if" questions were rapidly answered during the development of forecasts and plans. MODPLAN therefore performed the functions of collecting, calculating, consolidating, storing, and retrieving data in a very rapid and cost-effective manner.

The various MODPLAN capabilities were offered to TI managers through over 1,600 on-line inquiry terminals plus batch (card deck) production terminals. This allowed user flexibility around the world.

When describing the motivation for the increased usage currently being experienced by MODPLAN, Teter explained the following:

> MODPLAN started as a financial forecasting system for corporate control. Eventually, as more people gained exposure, they began using it for their own operations. As the costs have been significantly reduced, from 5 to 13 percent per year, it became easier to use; people began to increase their use of it in tracking their operations. That was coupled with management's need for better information on how the businesses were doing.
>
> As businesses grew, it took more and more clerks to do the work and leverage of the system became quite high. People began moving to MODPLAN as a way to trim down the number of people that they had to hire for tracking their businesses. Furthermore, through MODPLAN managers could track their businesses using the same

system as that used by the corporation. Because of these obvious benefits, we have never had to actively go out to sell managers on using the MODPLAN system for their operations. We've had a constant backlog of requests.

Corporate Consolidations

As previously mentioned, the original use of MODPLAN was for the corporate "Blue Book" financial consolidations. Each month, TI's actual results for the current month and forecasts through year end were updated worldwide. In addition, the year plus one results were forecasted each quarter, and the long-range plan for year plus ten was forecasted annually.

When describing the impact that MODPLAN had on TI's financial consolidation, Den Hiser, the Corporate Operations Controller, observed the following:

> I can't say enough good things about MODPLAN. It has made control a lot more fun. In the last four years we've reduced the time it takes to consolidate by two days. Without MODPLAN, we couldn't hire enough people to do the job we do. A report that used to take us two hours to prepare now takes 10 minutes. As a result, we can recycle consolidations two or three times which means we have half a day to QC the numbers before we send them to top management.

> I have only added one person in corporate financial analysis in the last six years. We reduced our staff by two when MODPLAN came in, so we have one less than in 1972. Our work load has gone up six times as sales and complexity have tripled since 1972. Even more important for a multi-national company is the use of standard definitions. Now people really understand the definitions.

Other Uses of MODPLAN

TI's International Semiconductor Trade Organization (ISTO) was one of MODPLAN's major users. Karl Kehler, the Profitability Manager for ISTO, explained his use of MODPLAN:

> I manage the intercompany transfer prices so that each corporate entity, or off-shore plant, is able to achieve the level of profit before tax (PBT) that we set as a goal. I couldn't do this without MODPLAN. In fact, I probably do as much work myself using MODPLAN as three or four professionals could do without MODPLAN. It gives you a lot of leverage.

Another major user of MODPLAN was TI's Consumer Electronic Products (CEP) group, which included calculators and watches. Raj Seekri, the Manager of Product Planning, said this about the development of CEP's MODPLAN data bases:

> When I started the product data base with MODPLAN, I used only data bases for calculators, watches and personal computers. As we grew, we put personal computers and calculators into a second data base. Now, with the addition of home computers, we have started a third product data base with personal and home computers.

Exhibit 2 Sample "Blue Book" Report—Monthly Comparison

	"Security Label" Dummy Entity			December 1976	"Security Label" John Doe				
	Operating Unit 12345678 Year to Date				Responsibility				
					Current Period Comparison				
	Actual	Last Year	Variance	Description	Month Actual	Variance FCST	QTR ACT/FCET	Variance PFST/FCST	Variance ORP
1	62202	7051	55151	NSE-TOTAL	150	-56	12146	-56	-138
2	60306	3694	56612	BACKLOG-TOTAL	60306	102	60306	102	429
3	12772	6521	6251	BILLABLE ACT	1983	-310	3208	-376	-848
4	5550	6984	-1394	MSB-TOTAL	1406	-158	1591	-158	-567
5	3725	1610	-1665	DIRECT LABOR	394	46	1247	46	-40
6	4103	1644	-2455	DIRECT NATL	1099	-560	2418	-560	-759
7	3026	1417	-1609	MFG OVERHEAD	396	51	1079	51	135
8				OTH OVERHEAD					
9				COST ADJ-NET					
10	4	-7	-11	OTH MFG COST	4	-6	4	-4	-4
11	-5851	409	6260	INV REDUCTION	-675	484	-2940	484	903
12	1033	1911	-878	GPM%	188	-141	-217	-141	-332
13	18.5	27.4	-8.9	GPM% NSB	13.4	-7.6	-13.6	-9.3	-18.9
14	681	606	-75	OPER A	53	3	172	3	1
15	701	628	-73	OPER D + A	55	3	178	3	1
16	12.9	5.0	-3.5	OPER D + A% HSB	3.9	-.2	11.2	-.9	-2.9
17	67.9	32.9	-35.0	OPER D + A% GPM	29.3	-11.7	-82.0	-156.2	237.7
18				DIV OTH I/E					
19	332	1283	-951	OPER PROFIT	133	-138	-345	-138	-331
20	5.9	18.4	-12.5	OPER DFT% NSB	9.5	-7.8	-24.8	-10.1	-21.8
21	137	135	-2	DST D + A	15		37		10
22	2.5	1.9	-.8	DST D + A% NSB	1.1	-.1	2.3	-.2	-.1
23	838	763	-75	D + A O DOIE	70	3	215	3	11
24	81.1	39.9	-41.2	D + A EDOIE% GPM	37.2	-15.0	-99.1	-187.7	245.6

25	DEPT EXPENSE	157	157	157	17		43		10
26	ORGAN PROFIT	195	1148	-953	118	-138	-432	-138	-321
27	ORG PFT% NSB	3.5	16.4	-12.4	8.4	-8.0	-27.2	-10.4	-22.1
28	ORG PFT ROA	-14.4	-115.5	101.1	-237.0	-999.9	217.8	-22.2	430.9
29	CASH & OTHER	179	156	17	179	16	179	16	57
30	RECEIVABLES	-2505	-3202	-700	-2502	1527	-2502	1527	2322
31	REC/MIL NSB	-153	-700	-547	-153	83	-153	83	141
32	INV—NET	6857	1002	-5855	6857	-484	6857	-484	-903
33	INV/MIL NSB	1077	207	-870	1077	-166	1077	-166	-387
34	UNLIQ PRG PAY	-5461	-554	4902	-5461	786	-5461	786	996
35	UPP/MIL NSB	-858	-115	743	-858	190	-858	190	341
36	NFA-FACIL DST	772	220	-552	772	-24	772	-24	-5
37	TOTAL NFA	772	519	-253	772	-24	772	-24	-5
38	TOT NFA/N NSB	121	107	-14	121	-14	121	-14	-32
39	ASSETS EQP	-155	-2044	-1889	-155	1821	-155	1821	2467
40	ASTS/NNSB EQP	-24	-422	-398	-24	262	-24	262	292
41	AVG ASSETS	-1352	0994	358	-598	911	-794	304	1002
42	ORG CASH FLOW	-1782	2272	-4054	-820	1745	-1477	1745	2290
43	QP EXPEND TOT								
44	DEPR EXP TOT								
45	CAP AUTH TOT								
46	DIR EX PED ID	53	50	-3	53	1	53	1	7
47	DIR NE PED ID	24	20	-4	24	-2	24	-	-1
48	IND EX PED ID								
49	IND NE PED ID								
50	TOTAL FEC EDP	77	70	-7	77	-1	77	-1	6
51	TOTAL AVG PED	74	66	-8	76		73		3
52	BILL ACT/APER	172304	98554	73750	313105	-51345	174982	-20845	-37559
53	ORG PFT/A PER	2631	17350	-14714	18632	-22057	-23564	-7491	-17747
54	TOTAL PAYROLL								
55	A IND/DIR PER	.007	.007	-.007	.007		.009		-.005

Source: Company records.

We use a fourth data base for people and expenses because we have to track all our customer marketing expenses. A fifth data base helps our market analysis people look at the total availability of the market (TAM) for North America, Japan, Middle East, etc. and track our penetration in units and dollars.

We also have to track sales by each salesman by each product because he is paid a bonus if he reaches his forecast. As MODPLAN capabilities increase, we can do all these calculations with MODPLAN.

Explaining how MODPLAN was used in CEP, Seekri continued:

MODPLAN is used to calculate our month-to-date sales and to compare our projections to forecast. We have a forecast system to calculate net sales and units for each product model or series. We then look at sales month-to-date and compare our forecast to actual every week. We follow this closely because units don't always get shipped to the market as quickly as forecasted. At our weekly operating reviews, we look at our revised projection. At the end of the month, we then show our variance to forecast and explain the reasons for each variance.

We use all three arrays in our forecast cycle. We get a rough forecast from the field which is reviewed by the area managers each month. They look at the highest NSB we can support with our production capacity and put that in array one. We then start making changes by analyzing each region's forecast and enter that in array two. We then review the forecast with our assistant vice president and he may make additional changes in array two. We then go to the plants and review array two and make changes in array three. If I had additional arrays, I could use them to store historical data from obsolete models.

When discussing some of the strengths and weaknesses in MODPLAN, Seekri explained:

MODPLAN is most helpful in forecasting. We used to do the forecasts manually. We now change our forecasts about 20 times during the two or three days of our current forecast cycle. With MODPLAN we can change the numbers and reconsolidate within five minutes while everyone is still in the conference room.

MODPLAN has also allowed us to add entities. First we were only tracking products at the area level. We have since moved to regional and are planning to go to salesmen levels with about 70 salesmen.

The only problem is that we are limited to 175 prime lines and 512 calculated lines. With only 175 prime lines and each product taking a line for net sales and net units, we can only have 87 products in a data base. When you count design changes and the need for historical data, we are too restricted.

MANAGING MODPLAN

Fred Teter, the MODPLAN Manager, reported to Ron Green, who was in charge of corporate systems within the Information Systems and Services (IS&S) organization (Exhibit 3). Corporate systems included the "general accounting systems," such as the general ledger, accounts payable, accounts receivable, and tax-treasury

---

Exhibit 3   **Information Systems and Services Organization**

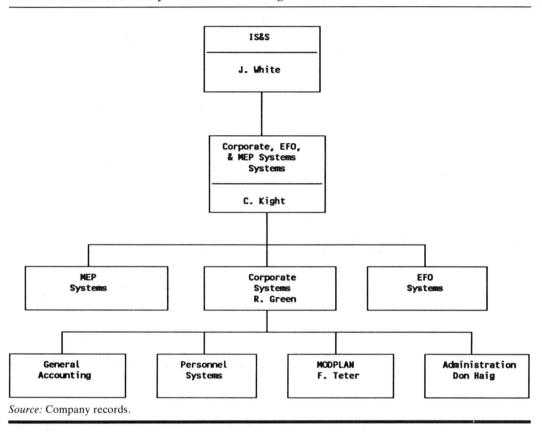

Source: Company records.

---

systems; the "personnel systems," such as payroll, personnel file management, benefits, and personnel reporting; and "financial planning systems." Each of these systems was set up as a product line with its own cost center within IS&S.

The basic concept used to manage TI's systems was considered rather unique. Charles Kight said the following:

> Industry wide, there are several aspects of systems management that are getting increased attention. Everyone is spending money on systems, but feeling that they have not received appropriate value for their investment. Still the budget for systems keeps going up. It's probably one of the real growth sectors in business today—just look at IBM's growth. It's not uncommon for corporations to now spend between a half of a percent and two percent of their sales for data processing. Therefore it's probably one of the biggest functional growth areas in the U.S. Yet there are few approaches you can use to make sure you're getting the kind of performance you want. One of the things

we have done at TI is to create pseudo-profit centers for systems. This is a common approach for products, but seldom used for systems.

We treat systems as a business and have subdivided systems into major product lines. Financial systems, personnel systems, and general accounting systems are product lines. We treat each of these as businesses and have quantitative measures of their performance. For example, we look at the "fan out" of new capabilities—the percent penetration of available market. We take a product line like our capital asset system and unit price it. We may charge five cents per asset to users around the world plus an adjustment where legal requirements demand different depreciation or currency fluctuation tracking. So the user pays five cents per asset and is sheltered from technical problems and development costs. Each year of operation lets us bring this system down a learning curve and allows us to charge users only for services rendered. That means that the system's budget has to have a certain amount of scrap in it just like in manufacturing. It then becomes possible to consolidate these systems, compare them, and provide tracking and motivational force for productivity improvements.

We decided to treat planning systems as a profit center and apply the learning curve in the systems area to get costs down. We did that because we felt "planning systems" would give us the highest leverage on payback to TI. This would then provide the resources to invest in other systems so you could grow the product line. The idea of having a "cash cow" in the system area is kind of unique, but is one more step towards treating systems as a business. Now we can take funds from our cash cows and invest in shooting stars.

We chose "general accounting" as the second product line because we had over 40 corporate entities which were subdivided into operational entities. Since these corporate entities all needed their own payroll system, planning system, general ledger, etc., we couldn't do what we wanted in terms of management reporting if each system were unique. We then set a goal to get general accounting to be common throughout the company as soon as our planning system was up. We then started improving product cost accounting when the other two were working well.

A good example of self-funding is when we took revenues from the financial planning product line (MODPLAN) and invested it in the general ledger system—our "shooting star." For general ledger, we reduced prices for on-line journal entries so that people could do their operational statistical reporting as well as statutory reporting using the system. Reduced prices resulted in rapid growth in usage and revenues. Fixed costs were spread over larger volumes and efficiency improved. Once this happens, you have another cash cow.

Kight and Green also were concerned with systems performance. Kight continued:

In managing systems, we start off with three priorities. The first concern is that the system works, that it works right, is reliable and available. Secondly, we are concerned about the system's performance, how fast the function can be carried out and at what cost. Our third priority is developing new capabilities.

To track the implementation of these priorities, we have measures of these concerns. Under availability, we have green and yellow charts for all our systems for "on-time delivery" of reports, "response-time" on inquiries, unit cost reductions, etc.;

green is good, yellow is acceptable but not good, and black is bad. We have numerous quantitative measures that we hold the product line manager responsible for.

Once we begin measuring quantitative factors, such as the amount of paper per user, we begin to identify areas for making improvements. The only way we really make a breakthrough is by analyzing what is happening quantitatively. If we don't measure something, then we can't know for sure that we are making progress. It is therefore the development of performance measures that is key to achieving the productivity that we need and the culture that we want to foster in this operation.

Don Haig, the Corporate Systems Administrator, said the following about how MODPLAN was reviewed (Exhibit 4) as a profit center:

> We show our unit price revenue, which comes from selling inquiries on-line. Operating revenue comes from user organizations who want us to do special work for them. Costs are then broken into sustaining costs related to production, and expenditures for new developments. Since MODPLAN is self-sufficient, we aren't spending OST funds on it. Instead, MODPLAN shows expenses for corporate systems projects which is funding cost reductions elsewhere. So we spent $95,000 out of revenues of $2.1 million to reduce costs in other product lines.
>
> If you subtract our people related expenses of $219,000, production costs of $1.2 million for keeping the system going and updated, and $139,000 for sustaining the system, it still leaves $363,000 in profit margin. At the IS&S division level, profits and losses balance out.
>
> We also have the new general ledger system which has now reached $780,000 in revenues. With costs of almost $900,000 we have a loss of $104,000. We fund it with $73,200 coming from other MODPLAN products and with $31,000 from corporate level OST funds. This loss is acceptable in a new system which is in the process of being fanned out. In 1980, with full utilization and cost reduction, we plan to break even on this system.

DISTRIBUTED MODPLAN: A FURTHER IMPROVEMENT

In an effort to improve direct productivity further, TI planned to introduce by 1979 a new "distributed MODPLAN" (MODPLAN 990) for use on their new TI 990 minicomputer. Distributed MODPLAN was one of the first application systems that was universally distributed and used across TI worldwide. The major thrust of this program, according to Mr. Kight, was the following:

> To locate the computer near the users with resulting improved cycle time, cost and reliability. Lower level data bases such as cost center data bases, will be located in the plant where the work is done. Only summary results communicated to corporate consolidation data bases will run on the central computer.

Distributed MODPLAN was developed to allow users to make their own changes in line items of data bases much faster than they could in the central MODPLAN. With the flexibility that the distributed MODPLAN offered, Kight believed that the number of data bases could increase to around 500 in five years. In

Exhibit 4 **MODPLAN Financial Review**

MODPLAN	1Q79	2Q79	3Q79	4Q79	YR79	1Q80	2Q80	3Q80	4Q80	YR80
Unit Price Rev	503	486	532	571	2,092	542	570	598	628	2,338
Operating	25	7	1		33	4				4
Corp Sys Proj	−20	−17	−27	−31	−95	−25	−25	−25	−25	−100
Total Funding	508	476	506	540	2,030	521	545	573	603	2,242
Sust:S&W Peo	52	46	60	61	219	77	77	78	78	310
CIC Prod	311	279	286	310	1,186	310	325	341	358	1,334
CIC Sust	40	37	31	31	139	45	45	45	45	180
Other	53	13	28	29	123	36	36	36	36	144
Sus Total	456	375	405	431	1,667	468	483	500	517	1,968
OST:S&W Peo										
CIC Cost										
Other										
Total										
Total Cost	456	375	405	431	1,667	468	483	500	517	1,968
Production Net	52	101	101	109	363	53	62	73	86	274
Int Price Sup	−61	−89	−64	−44						
GPM	−9	12	37	65	105	53	62	73	86	274

Source: Company records.

166

eight years, the data bases might reach 2,000 and could even reach 5,000 to 10,000 in the very long run. Of course, the hardware capabilities were expected to improve, too.

Advantages of Distributed MODPLAN over MODPLAN

Kight described two major advantages that distributed MODPLAN offered:

> With distributed computing, you can reduce response times even with a less powerful computer. We trade off job complexity and extensiveness with response time to decide whether to use the central or distributed computer. While MODPLAN is still a fantastic bargain (at a 20 to 30 second response time, at the 90th percentile) to make "what if" inquiries; it can do it in 5 seconds and at a lower cost through new technology we would get new growth. Now if we also develop new software, eliminating the middle man so that users can do their own modeling, there should be another spurt in usage.
>
> In addition to doing current jobs better, we can also do new jobs with distributed MODPLAN. Right now we have modeling with an emphasis on understanding the structure of the business. We would like to have a few key parameters for generating plans, but it gets very complicated once you go into specific operations. For example, in our production model, we have real world constraints like the capacity of the machinery in the plant, the capacity of the people, etc. Well, you program all these equations once, but you can't keep them current. We would like to provide the user the ability to change his own equation. I think this will cause an explosive growth in MODPLAN usage.

Distributed MODPLAN offered users the opportunity to change line items, time periods, and entities by themselves with much faster cycle time. Another advantage was that distributed MODPLAN had a formatted screen that eliminated the need for users to know key words in order to use the system. Finally the system was expected to result in cost advantages. Distributed MODPLAN was expected to be 20 percent cheaper for the average user. For bigger users, the purchase of a 990 and the MODPLAN software was expected to result in larger savings.

Green explained that as a consequence of distributed MODPLAN, mapping capabilities would evolve over time. Mapping refers to moving information between different data bases. The ultimate goal for distributed MODPLAN was to communicate between data bases in the network with minimum user inconvenience.

Kight's Concerns

Despite MODPLAN's impressive advantages, an issue that occupied management's mind was the level of investment that TI should commit to the distributed MODPLAN system. In January 1979 an OST funding of $120,000 was approved for distributed MODPLAN. And yet, Kight pointed out the following:

> We're bucking the momentum of a very successful central system which has not yet begun to reach its potential in terms of areas used or depth of penetration in those areas where it is used. The first large installations, if done very well, with quantified benefits

and strong user champions, can start the momentum for distributed MODPLAN. But the user may not be sufficiently convinced of the payback from distributed MODPLAN to be willing to bet his scarce investment dollars. We may have to prompt initial usage through support from corporate OST funds.

NOTES

1. Response time for an on-line inquiry is defined as the elapsed time between pressing the Enter button and receiving a response.

2. At TI, a separate data base was used for each model or its definition.

3. The corporate financial Blue Book was a summary of TI's budgets and forecasts for all the corporate entities and major profit centers. MODPLAN was originally used only to track monthly results against the budget and to update forecasts.

4. OST refers to TI's long-range strategic planning system, which specifies objectives, strategies, and tactics.

Becton Dickinson and Company (Part 1)

In November 1976, Wesley J. Howe, the President of Becton Dickinson and Company, and Marvin Asnes, the Executive Vice President, were concerned about the company's ability to continue its historic rate of 15 percent compounded annual growth in earnings per share (EPS). Continuing this rate of growth in EPS was the company's fundamental financial objective and a cardinal element of its corporate strategy. In fiscal year 1976, however, EPS had grown only 13 percent.

Over the past twelve months, the company had performed an exhaustive analysis of its operating units that revealed two striking facts about the company's portfolio of businesses. First, 69 percent of sales came from strategic business units (SBUs) in mature or aging industries; only 31 percent came from SBUs in growth industries; and sales of SBUs in embryonic industries were so small that they disappeared in the rounding. Second, 48 percent of sales came from SBUs with competitive positions that offered little strategic flexibility beyond the growth stage of their industry. Having seen their corporate sales thus dissected, Becton Dickinson's officers concluded that within a few years their objective of 15 percent compounded annual growth in earnings per share might slip out of reach. They concluded further that in their quarterly quest for earnings growth, they had unconsciously selected an overly mature portfolio capable of producing current profits but incapable of sustaining growth in the future. The company had become "short-run overachievers," said Mr. Howe. The dilemma he and his fellow officers now faced was to ensure growth for the future without sacrificing it in the present.

BECTON DICKINSON'S OPERATIONS

Corporate Strategy

Becton Dickinson defined itself as "a diversified multinational health care growth company" and considered each element of that description an important part of its identity. The company's financial performance from 1967 to 1976 is shown in Exhibit 1.

Diversified.   The company was made up of 42 SBUs spread among 19 divisions and linked in a highly decentralized organization. The purposes of this diversification were to avoid the risk of relying on one product and to allow steady growth. By the early 1970s, as a result of its diversification, the company, in Mr. Howe's words, "looked a little bit like a holding company."

Multinational.   In 1976, the International Group accounted for $122 million of the company's $509 million in sales, or nearly 25 percent. Although the U.S. health care industry continued to grow rapidly, Becton Dickinson believed that the largest growth in demand for health care and health care products would be abroad, particularly in developing nations.

Health Care.   Nearly all of Becton Dickinson's products were for health care markets—primarily hospitals and laboratory equipment and supplies. The leading products are shown in Exhibit 2. The company was best known for its needle, syringe, and thermometer products, but it did in fact market a wide range of sterile, disposable products and some other devices, such as kidney dialysis machines.

Growth.   Over the last decade, Becton Dickinson had averaged 12 percent in compound annual growth in earnings per share. Since 1971, its average had exceeded its goal of 15 percent, a rate of growth significantly faster than the growth rate of the health care industry as a whole. Howe stated the following:

> Growth is the essence of our management strategy. It allows us to continue to make careful contributions to our society. It provides opportunities to our people. But EPS growth is the most essential element of our growth strategy. EPS growth keeps the capital markets open to us. EPS growth brings rewards to our shareholders.

THE HEALTH CARE EQUIPMENT AND SUPPLY INDUSTRY

The health care equipment and supply industry, in which Becton Dickinson competed (with the exception of the Industrial Safety Group), was made up of over 2,000 companies.

In 1974, the industry's average return on sales (after tax) was 6 percent,

Exhibit 1 Ten-Year Financial Review

	1976	1975	1974	1973	1972	1971	1970	1969	1968	1967
Net Sales	$506,990	$456,039	$408,254	$340,253	$289,221	$260,965	$245,022	$221,052	$189,237	$170,543
Gross Profit	224,354	197,337	172,183	146,761	125,495	111,643	105,362	98,464	81,596	73,122
Interest Expense	6,867	7,747	5,700	4,898	4,614	4,380	3,821	2,274	1,504	1,405
Income Before Income Taxes	72,966	59,990	52,190	47,500	38,577	33,339	35,057	33,812	27,565	23,923
Income Taxes	32,308	26,228	23,641	23,026	17,762	16,086	16,958	17,008	13,278	11,388
Net Income	40,658	33,762	28,549	24,474	20,815	17,253	18,099	16,804	14,287	12,535
Earnings Per Share	$ 2.20	$ 1.94	$ 1.69	$ 1.45	$ 1.24	$ 1.03	$ 1.08	$ 1.00	$ .86	$ .77
Dividends Per Share	50¢	40¢	38¾¢	35¢	30¢	30¢	30¢	32½¢	20¢	20¢
Shares Outstanding	18,515,856	17,438,230	16,916,739	16,893,106	16,830,932	16,810,945	16,785,754	16,729,935	16,644,785	16,300,449
Cash and Short-Term Investments	$105,565	$ 87,057	$ 16,722	$ 59,028	$ 73,058	$ 66,075	$ 57,466	$ 26,760	$ 43,681	$ 24,714
Current Assets	322,962	293,144	223,955	214,763	195,211	178,810	164,745	121,567	117,455	91,195
Current Liabilities	69,938	63,365	60,591	54,422	32,975	33,368	26,203	25,065	24,989	24,610
Current Ratio	4.6	4.6	3.7	3.9	5.9	5.4	6.3	4.8	4.7	3.7
Property, Plant, and Equipment	148,125	144,387	125,212	102,514	88,795	85,151	78,640	68,452	54,296	45,096
Total Assets	486,601	450,536	361,430	331,816	292,198	271,978	250,729	196,929	179,048	143,705
Long-term Debt	80,894	84,196	77,176	76,464	81,100	78,463	79,969	41,849	42,732	19,479
Shareholders' Equity	320,183	287,628	200,695	186,558	165,732	149,249	136,137	122,922	110,776	98,991
Book Value Per Share	$ 17.26	$ 15.56	$ 12.34	$ 11.03	$ 9.83	$ 8.87	$ 8.10	$ 7.33	$ 6.64	$ 5.97
Pretax Income as a Percent of Sales	14.3%	13.2%	12.8%	14.0%	13.3%	12.8%	14.3%	15.1%	14.6%	14.0%
Net Income as a Percent of Sales	8.0%	7.4%	7.0%	7.2%	7.2%	6.6%	7.4%	7.5%	7.5%	7.4%
Return on Equity	13.4%	13.6%	14.4%	13.9%	13.2%	12.1%	14.0%	14.4%	13.6%	14.4%
Return on Assets	8.7%	8.3%	8.2%	7.8%	7.4%	6.6%	6.1%	8.9%	8.9%	9.6%
Depreciation and Amortization	$ 16,170	$ 13,905	$ 11,742	$ 10,250	$ 8,682	$ 8,159	$ 7,132	$ 5,993	$ 5,125	$ 4,474
Capital Expenditures	21,923	34,943	36,501	25,123	14,423	16,644	17,591	20,953	13,919	12,402
Research and Development Expense	20,087	17,849	15,749	12,844	11,546	11,809	11,499	10,434	9,521	7,146
Number of Employees	16,800	15,300	17,400	16,400	14,100	13,300	13,300	13,700	11,800	11,700
Number of Shareholders	13,208	15,784	14,469	15,232	14,466	14,363	12,808	12,124	10,570	10,632

Source: 1976 Becton Dickinson Annual Report.

Exhibit 2   Becton Dickinson's Product Line

Medical Group (42 percent of 1976 sales)

Needles, syringes, and other hypodermic equipment
Thermometers and thermometry systems
Suctioning and respiratory care equipment
Vacutainer blood-collecting products
Bard-Parker surgical blades
Ace elastic bandages
Electrodyne electronic patient monitoring equipment
Vivacell kidney dialyzer

Laboratory Group (20 percent of 1976 sales)

Plastic and glass labware (plates, tubes, and so on)
Plated culture media
Centrifuges and other laboratory instruments
Blood analyzers
Radioimmunoassay tests
Plasma reagent tests

Industrial Safety Group (14 percent of 1976 sales)

Industrial gloves
Safety instruments
Nuclear safety equipment
Acoustic emission equipment
Electronic keyboards
Industrial testing systems
Contract packaging

International Group (24 percent of 1976 sales)

This group produced or sold products from the domestic Medical and Laboratory
Group—mostly sterile disposables, thermometers, and basic laboratory equipment and
   supplies.

---

compared to 10.5 percent for drug manufacturers and 5.3 percent for all industrials. The average annual growth rate had been 12 percent; analysts expected 10 percent growth through the 1980s.

Equipment and supply manufacturers' products ranged from adhesive bandages selling for a fraction of a cent to computerized axial tomography (CAT) scanners selling for $400,000 or more.

These products were sold to many different segments of the health care market: consumers (as in the case of such products as bandages, thermometers, needles, and crutches), individual physicians, group clinics, hospitals, and private laboratories. In the largest market—hospitals—each department (surgery, radiology, and so on) and each laboratory (clinical, pathology, and so on) constituted a separate market.

BECTON DICKINSON'S STRATEGIC PLANNING SYSTEM

Evolution of the Present System

When Howe and Asnes took the reins of Becton Dickinson in 1972, they began immediately to search for a management system that would serve the company as it continued to grow larger and more diverse. "Although both Marvin and I spent most of our careers in components of the company," Howe explained, "we were concerned about the lack of concept and system to deal with the complexity of managing the company as a whole." In 1973, they installed a formal planning system based on the management-by-objectives (MBO) method. This system employed five-year divisional plans as the central tools for planning and control.

Although the new system gave Becton Dickinson greater flexibility and firmer control of operations than it had before, the company nonetheless suffered a number of problems in 1973, 1974, and 1975 as the economy bounced across its washboard of inflation and recession. The most serious problem was controlling the capital budget. Inflation had made the capital requirements of the divisions heavier, and the division presidents, responding to a corporate call for new ventures to fuel long-run growth, had independently embarked on projects that raised the company's capital needs to an unsupportable level. Howe and Asnes rejected the 1975 capital budget, and at a meeting of the division managers early in 1975, corporate executives lectured on the need to restrain capital expenditures. The cutbacks were executed successfully, but they proved to be unnecessarily severe, due partly to improvements in the economy. These cutbacks left the company with what one executive called "an embarrassing oversupply of cash."

In these fluctuations of the company's fortunes, Howe and Asnes saw the need for a better management system than the one they had installed. Their management-by-objective system, they believed, did not allow adequate control over the company's strategic direction. Mr. Asnes explained the following:

> The MBO system proved to be a very effective method for getting things done—for insuring that all levels of the organization were focused on achieving the same objectives. The problem, however, was in the O's—the objectives.

Under the MBO system, Becton Dickinson found that duplicating the corporate financial objectives became the objective of most division managers. Howe called this "the infamous 15 percent solution." The managers of profitable, established businesses tried to create new businesses to bring up their growth rates. The managers of new ventures, on the other hand, pushed their units into profitability too soon, thereby sacrificing long-term competitive position. The managers of both kinds of units were failing to focus on their strengths, and the corporation as a whole suffered from what the executives called "corporate sprawl."

The company also found that it was suboptimizing its allocations of resources because much of the allocation process was decentralized. Wealthy divisions had money to put wherever they wanted, whereas poorer divisions were unable to fund projects whose success might be more important to the corporation. So long as they produced their assigned profits, the division managers could allocate resources pretty much as they chose.

Both problems were deepened because the company had no method for discriminating among the different kinds of units or among the various projects of a unit. Becton Dickinson's criteria for measuring performance—ROI, discounted cash flow, and so on—were all financial criteria that failed to measure the strategic progress of a unit. When corporate earnings fell temporarily, cutbacks were made across the board. As a result, important projects that could ill afford any cutback were trimmed as closely as inconsequential projects. Mr. Howe said the following:

> We were not exactly wandering alone in the wilderness. I suppose you might say that we were undergoing the experience of many other diversified multinational companies—within and without the health care field—because we had the same set of problems that we hear other people have.

Together, Becton Dickinson's executives made a list of requirements for the kind of strategic planning system that the company needed in order to solve the problems it faced under the MBO system. Asnes summarized these requirements:

> First, we had to have a common language to facilitate communication from bottom to top of the organization. Accounting concepts were incomplete for describing our businesses' strategic oppportunities.
>
> Second, we needed an improved planning structure that would serve the operational needs of the divisions at the same time that it allowed coordination of the whole corporate portfolio.
>
> Third, as part of the common language, we needed a conceptual scheme for formulating appropriate business strategies at the operating level and for seeing the financial implications of those strategies.
>
> The fourth requirement was a system for allocating resources among all of the strategic opportunities, while allowing corporate management to control the timing of profits and cash flows.
>
> The fifth, and final, requirement was that we be able to monitor our strategic performance in terms of relative competitive position, not just measure our financial performance for an accounting period.

Arthur D. Little's SBU system

To meet these requirements, Becton Dickinson turned to Arthur D. Little, Inc. (ADL), a firm of management consultants who built a strategic planning and management system around several now-familiar marketing concepts. These concepts were segmentation, the product life cycle, and competitive position. Segmentation suggested that a company should be divided into strategic business units (SBUs) according to the industry segments they competed in. Each division of Becton Dickinson manufactured a variety of products for markets at various stages of development, rates of growth, and levels of profitability. Thus, identical objectives and strategies for those products, merely because they were in the same division, would not allow the company to maximize the potential of each of its diverse businesses.

ADL extended the product life-cycle concept to encompass the evolution of a whole industry and its market. The consultants argued that a view broader than that of a single product was required to formulate a strategy for an SBU. Similarly the concept of competitive position was broader than market share—although market share was an important element of the concept.

ADL incorporated these extended concepts into a system for managing diversified corporations that set five sequential tasks:

1. Defining SBUs
2. Classifying SBUs
3. Developing strategies
4. Establishing priorities within the portfolio
5. Achieving objectives

Tasks 1 through 3 belonged to the divisions or to the SBUs once they had been identified. They represented an alteration in nature, but not in spirit, of Becton Dickinson's existing, bottoms-up planning system. Task 4 belonged exclusively to the corporate executives. Task 5 belonged to the corporate executives because it involved establishing incentive, measurement, and control systems and also to the SBUs because it involved performance.

Tasks 1 through 3, on which the ADL system focused, were accomplished in two-day "profiling sessions" held at each division and attended by the division president, all first-line functional managers, and usually several managers below the first line. Rank was dismissed as much as possible, and the profiling sessions were conducted by a knowledgeable outsider. Ray Gilmartin, the ADL consultant who led Becton Dickinson's early profiling sessions and later joined the company as a Vice President, stated the following:

> The purpose of the profiling session is to gather the information that exists in an SBU and organize it so that it is useful for formulating strategies. The SBU's managers, rather than a consultant's industry expert, are the data source; and the managers are the master strategists, not the consultant. Profiling is really a sort of anticonsulting. It recognizes that nobody knows more about a business than the people who run it.

The first part of each profiling session was given over to building a data base, which the session leader usually wrote down on presentation sheets spread around the meeting room. The data base included vital statistics on the division's businesses and information about competitors, customers, and so on—anything that was needed to perform the session's three tasks. Once the data base was established, the profiling group moved in turn to each of their three tasks—defining SBUs, classifying them, and developing broad strategies for each. As they performed these tasks, the profiling group was guided by ADL's four axioms of strategic planning:

> (1) Planning is a process based on data; (2) strategic business units can be identified within a corporation; (3) strategy is more condition-driven than ambition-driven; (4) there is a finite set of available strategies from which a business chooses those it will pursue.

Task 1: Defining SBUs.   Becton Dickinson's management described a strategic business unit as "a natural business . . . comprised of a group of products which serve common markets, contend with the same competitors, and are linked together so that strategies cannot be formulated for any of the products without impact on the others." To distinguish among their businesses and to define the SBUs that made up their division, the profiling group used a set of clues provided by ADL. For example, how do price, quality, or style changes in one of the unit's products affect other products and product lines inside and outside the unit? To what distinct sets of customers does the unit sell? What distinct sets of competitors does it have? The experience of the consultant who led the profiling session was particularly important at this step, for none of the clues was conclusive by itself. Generally the examination of customers and competitors proved to be most important to defining SBUs. The acid test, if a division's SBUs proved hard to delineate, was whether a portion of the business could be divested or liquidated without altering the division's competitive situation; if it could, that portion was a distinct SBU.

Task 2: Classifying SBUs.   The purpose of the classification process, in the words of one divisional executive, was "to do a careful examination of the environment and a careful self-examination, then hook the two together." The final step of the classification process was to place the SBU into 1 of 24 cells of a matrix charting competitive position and industry maturity (see Exhibit 3).

Maturity was assessed at the level of the industry or market being served by the SBU. Within each SBU's industry were usually a number of related products, each having its own life cycle. For example, the thermometry equipment industry in the United States was rated a mature industry, but the mercury glass thermometer was in the declining stage of its product life cycle. Some thermometry products were in the early stages of their product life cycles.

An industry's maturity was determined by the maturity of the function it performed or the customer's need it served—by the emergence, satisfaction, and dissipation of the generic function or need filled by the set of products produced to serve that need. To determine maturity, Becton Dickinson executives looked carefully at the industry's growth rate over time. Other indicators were the age of products in the SBU's industry, the industry potential, the behavior of product lines within the industry, the number of competitors and the distribution of their market shares, the ease of entry, the customer loyalty, and the role of technology (see

---

Exhibit 3   **Classifying SBUs**

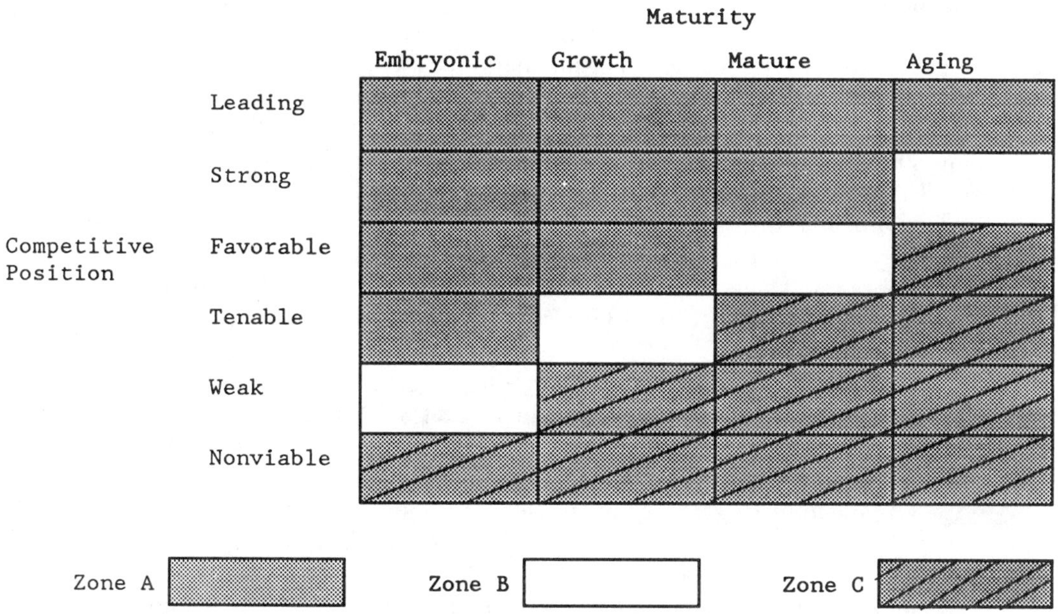

Maturity

| | Embryonic | Growth | Mature | Aging |

Competitive
Position:
Leading, Strong, Favorable, Tenable, Weak, Nonviable

Zone A   Zone B   Zone C

Source: Arthur D. Little, Inc.

Exhibit 4). Becton Dickinson's experience was that, in the health care field, the embryonic stage of an industry's development usually lasted seven to eight years; the growth stage lasted around twelve years; and the mature and aging stages lasted much longer.

Competitive position was a qualitative assessment of an SBU's standing in its market relative to its competitors. To assign a ranking of competitive position, the profilers studied a wide range of factors: market share over time; shares of appropriate segments; relative breadth of product line; degree of customer concentration; technological strength compared to competitors; value of brand name or corporate name in the market; strength in the channels of distribution; degree of integration; quality of production facilities and nearness to capacity; and cost position compared to competitors.

The rankings of competitive position ranged from leading to nonviable:

Leading: Controls behavior of other competitors. (Example: De Beers in diamonds.)

Strong: Able to take independent stance. (Example: General Motors [GM] in automobiles.)

Exhibit 4   **Guide for Assessing Industry Maturity**

Definitions

Embryonic industries usually experience rapid sales growth, frequent changes in technology, and fragmented, shifting market shares. The cash deployment to these businesses is often high relative to sales, as investment is made in market development, facilities, and technology. These businesses are generally not profitable, but investment is usually warranted in anticipation of gaining position in a developing market.

Growth industries are generally characterized by a rapid expansion of sales as the market develops. Customers, shares, and technology are better known than in the embryonic stage, and entry into the industry can be more difficult. Growth businesses are usually capital borrowers from the corporation, producing low to good earnings.

In *mature industries,* the competitors, technology, and customers are all known, and there is little volatility in market shares. The growth rate of these industries is usually about equal to the GNP. Businesses in these industries tend to provide cash for the corporation through high earnings.

Aging industries are characterized by falling demand for the product and limited growth potential. The number of competitors is shrinking and survivors gain market share through attrition. Product lines have little variety. Little, if any, investment is made in research and development or plant and equipment, even though the aging business typically generates extremely high earnings.

EXAMPLES OF U.S. INDUSTRY MATURITY

Embryonic	Growth	Mature	Aging
• Home Computers		Steel •	Railcars •
	• Home Smoke Alarms		Men's • Hats
• Solar Energy Services		Golf • Equipment	
	• Sporting Goods		Baseball • Equipment
Paddle • Tennis		Roller Skates	

Note: In work with clients, the company used a matrix charting in detail the normal changes over the life cycle in such attributes of an industry as growth rate, potential size, breadth of product lines, number of competitors, distribution of market share, customer loyalty, nature of technology, and ease of entry. The company provided these summary definitions to exemplify the methods of analysis they use to determine industry maturity.

Source: Arthur D. Little, Inc.

Favorable: Has a strength that is selectively exploitable. (Example: Wendy's in fast food.)

Tenable: Exists at the sufferance of the leading company. (Example: Johnson and Laughlin [J&L] in steel.)

Weak: Currently performs unsatisfactorily but has opportunity for improvement. (Example: A&P in retail groceries.)

Nonviable: Currently performs unsatisfactorily but does not have opportunity for improvement.

In this ranking system, a leading competitor truly dominated its industry. An industry could have only one company with a leading position, and not every industry had a company with that strong a position.

Task 3: Developing Strategies.   The third task of the profiling group was to develop broad strategies for the SBUs. The profiling group was responsible for identifying natural strategies for its SBUs and for identifying workable unnatural strategies. Natural strategies were those that were appropriate to the maturity of the SBU's industry and the competitive strength of the SBU; workable unnatural strategies were those that could be adopted by the SBU if the natural strategy should prove impossible for the corporation to fund or antithetical to corporate goals.

To aid in the development of strategies, Becton Dickinson divided the Competitive Position/Industry Maturity Matrix into three zones—A, B, and C. Those SBUs falling into zone A cells could be expected to have a fairly wide range of successful strategies from which to choose. SBUs in zone C would generally have few, if any, from which to choose. In most cases, their choices would be to withdraw to a market niche or to leave the market. SBUs in the B zone might have an adequate range of options for the present, but unless they strengthened their competitive position the natural maturation of their industry would carry them into the C zone, restrict their options, and probably dampen their financial performance in the later phases of the industry's life.

According to the theory followed by Arthur D. Little and Becton Dickinson, the financial characteristics of an industry should be expected to follow a predictable pattern. Sales should grow during the embryonic and growth stages, peak during the mature stage, and decline thereafter. The industry should begin to show profits late in the embryonic stage or early in the growth stage. And the industry's funds flow should become positive late in the growth stage.

This normal pattern of financial characteristics, in conjunction with the varying degrees of strategic flexibility belonging to different positions in the Competitive Position/Industry Maturity Matrix, suggested that certain generic strategies were appropriate to certain positions in the matrix and inappropriate to others. Backward integration, for example, could be expected to have a higher value in the mature phase than in earlier or later phases, and a higher value for stronger than for weaker competitors. As they selected strategies for their SBUs, the profiling groups worked from a menu of 25 generic strategies, such as "backward integration,"

Exhibit 5 Tools for Selecting Strategies

Generic Strategies

Arthur D. Little identified 25 generic strategies and for each identified the action to be taken, the probable consequences, the normal requirements, and the usual level of risk. Example:

Strategy: Backward Integration.

Action to be taken: to incorporate within the business organization functions, operations, or products that were previously external and that served to supply and support existing business operations.

Probable consequences: reduced unit costs; secured supplies; somewhat increased profit margins; increased product line and sales volume if other than an entirely captive source; may inhibit responsiveness to the marketplace because of a commitment to particular new materials, components, or manufacturing process.

Requires: considerable capital investment.

Risk: moderate.

Natural Periods of Execution

Each generic strategy was associated with a period in the industry's life cycle during which its use was most appropriate. For purposes of illustration, ADL combined their 25 strategies into five groups of strategies, each with a common strategic focus:

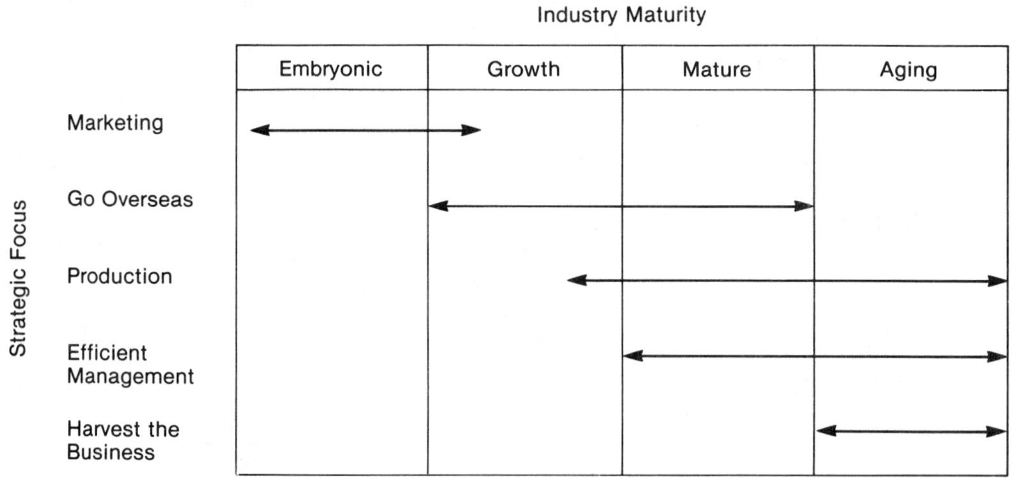

Industry Maturity

Strategic Focus	Embryonic	Growth	Mature	Aging
Marketing	◄——————————►			
Go Overseas		◄——————————►		
Production			◄——————————————►	
Efficient Management			◄————————►	
Harvest the Business				◄————►

Performance Measures

Arthur D. Little had developed a set of more than 50 performance measures by which to monitor the progress of the 25 generic strategies. The following matrix shows the expected trends for seven of these measures during the execution of typical strategies within each of the five illustrative strategy groups. Arrows indicate the direction of the trend. Crosses indicate that a performance measure needed to be watched carefully even though the direction of change could be predicted only in the specific case.

Strategic Focus	Performance Measures						
	Sales	Cost of Goods Sold	Margin	Sales/ Administrative Expenses	Profit	Fixed Asset Investment	Return on Assets
1. Marketing	↑	X	X	↑	X		X
2. Go Overseas	↑		X	↑	X	X	X
3. Production		↓	↑	↓	↑	↑	X
4. Efficient Management		↓	↑	↓	↑		↑
5. Harvest the Business	↓			↓	↑	↓	↑

Source: Arthur D. Little, Inc.

"distribution rationalization," and "excess capacity." Gilmartin emphasized that the process of selecting strategies was in no way mechanistic.

> We don't use this system as a black box to spew out strategies. Rather, we use it as a tool for finding the best strategies to follow. An SBU's location in the matrix limits and clarifies the generic strategic options available to it.

Exhibit 5 gives further information about the selection of generic strategies.

The 25 generic strategies of the ADL system could be used for three broad kinds of strategic moves: build, maintain, and retrench. Becton Dickinson did not find these three strategic categories, which are common to a number of planning systems, adequate for describing the full range of roles an SBU might take. Dr. Wilson Nolen, Vice President, explained in the following manner:

> Consider the maintenance role. It implies staying where you are—holding your market share and improving your cost structure, but making no major investment in the business and taking no aggressive competitive action. But we believe that it is respectable to invest in maturity and that it is sometimes necessary for a mature business to take aggressive action. The crucial factor, if you want to hold the position you have won, is to maintain the competitive *distance* between you and your nearest competitor. When that distance narrows, you lose competitive strength and you lose the benefit of your position—even if your market share doesn't fall. And it may be necessary to take aggressive action to prevent this.

Thus, Becton Dickinson identified two maintenance roles: maintain aggressively and maintain selectively. Similarly it identified three building roles and two retrenching roles. Its full array of strategic roles was as follows:

1. *Build aggressively.* Appropriate for moving up in competitive rank early in the industry's life or for increasing competitive distance for an SBU that already has a leading position.
2. *Build gradually.* Strategic actions to continue the momentum of an aggressive move.
3. *Build selectively.* To establish a strong position in a subsector of the industry, or to exploit the weakness of a particular competitor.
4. *Maintain aggressively.* Aggressive action to maintain competitive distance or to resist attacks by competitors on an SBU with a leading or strong position.
5. *Maintain selectively.* Actions to increase short-term profitability at the expense of market position.
6. *Prove viability.*
7. *Divest or liquidate.*

Tasks 4 and 5: Establishing Priorities Within the Portfolio and Achieving Objectives.   These tasks could begin only after the corporation had been divided into SBUs, all the SBUs had been profiled, and the appropriate strategic role had been assigned to each. Arthur D. Little, Inc., did not prescribe a method for undertaking these tasks, as it did for Tasks 1, 2, and 3. Although the corporate executives at Becton Dickinson had given considerable thought to methods that might work, they had not yet settled on a system for executing Tasks 4 and 5. Instead they chose to wait until Tasks 1–3 had been completed for all the SBUs.

THE PRINCETON MEETING

By the end of October 1976, profiles had been completed for all of the company's SBUs. In the first week of November, Becton Dickinson's Management Committee (board members, corporate officers, and group presidents) adjourned to Princeton, New Jersey, for a three-and-one-half-day discussion of corporate strategy in light of the recent SBU analysis.

The Princeton meeting began with an examination of the corporate portfolio. Exhibit 6 portrays the distribution of the company's SBUs as it was revealed by the past year's profiling sessions. The number in each cell represents the percentage of total corporate sales generated by SBUs falling into that cell.

Becton Dickinson's officers were troubled by what they saw. They concluded that in order to continue meeting their goal of 15 percent compound annual growth in earnings per share in the future, they needed to lift the center of gravity of the portfolio up in competitive position and to the left in stage of maturity.

Exhibit 6 Becton Dickinson's Corporate Portfolio, 1976

Competitive Position	Maturity: Embryonic	Growth	Mature	Aging	
Leading	0	8	16	0	24%
Strong	0	5	23	0	28%
Favorable	0	15	21	2	38%
Tenable	0	1	2	0	3%
Weak	0	2	4	0	6%
Nonviable	0	0	0	1	1%
	0%	31%	66%	3%	100%

Zone A Zone B Zone C

Source: Company records.

Lifting the Portfolio

At first blush, the 1976 shortfall in earnings growth had seemed a minor fluctuation around the 15 percent trend Becton Dickinson was on. Seeing how heavily the portfolio was weighted with mature and aging SBUs, however, made the company's executives worry that the trend had started to deflect downward. "We had been pushing hard for a long time to meet our 15 percent goal in the short term," Howe said. "Now we had to ask, could we also do it in the long term? And the tougher question was, could we do both at once?"

Becton Dickinson's management recognized that they had three tools for lifting their portfolio up and to the left. The first was to acquire businesses with leading competitive positions in embryonic or growth industries. Although Becton Dickinson looked at several acquisition candidates a week, the company believed that it could not rely on acquisitions alone to strike the desired balance in its portfolio. A second tool would be to change the composition of the portfolio from within—by generating new products and new SBUs from existing SBUs. How to do this had been an important issue to the company for several years and had been the subject of the 1974 meeting of corporate officers and division presidents.

The third tool for moving the portfolio would be to change role assignments for SBUs presently in the portfolio. Nolen explained how this tool would work:

> To give an example, you can tell a tenable SBU in a growth industry—which presumably is generating steady profits although its net funds flow is still negative—to stop making money and seek a strong or leading competitive position. If it succeeds in the maneuver, you have raised the average point for your whole portfolio; perhaps you've even moved an increment to the left if, in the process, your SBU has identified new products or new markets for itself. Moreover, you've guaranteed a stronger financial performance for the SBU, and the company, as the SBU drifts naturally to the right in the future: you've paid now to fly later. But there's a limit to what you can do with role assignments. Consider a weak SBU in a mature or aging industry. Very likely its profitability is disappointing. Moving it to the left is impossible. Moving it up to a strong or leading position, even if possible, would be prohibitively expensive. You simply can't milk a steer.

The task facing Becton Dickinson was to develop a strategy for lifting the portfolio to ensure long-term growth but without endangering short-term growth. In a sense this task posed a dilemma, as Dr. Nolen explained:

> Each strategic move to shift the portfolio up or left has its price. In each case we must choose: do we fly now and pay later, or do we pay now and fly later? But, of course, we want to do both. Looking at our portfolio, you can see that we're in something of a box. We want to increase the number and size of our growth business, and we want to keep increasing our profits. But increasing growth, reason tells us, decreases profits, and increasing profits decreases growth. The lid on the box is that your existing portfolio always, inexorably, moves to the right, taking you out of growth and, eventually, when the businesses have aged enough, out of profits too.

As Becton Dickinson selected among its tools for lifting the portfolio and decided on the proper tradeoffs between long-term and short-term opportunities for growth, it also had to manage a less quantifiable problem: This problem was how to change the corporate culture to allow a renewal strategy to succeed. Howe said the following after the Princeton meeting:

> A big worry on my mind was that all the divisions had taken the corporation's 15 percent as *their* target. For some of the divisions that wasn't entirely inappropriate, though it probably wasn't good. But apply that target to each SBU and you're in trouble. So how do you get the notion that everybody has to meet 15 percent out of their heads? How do you get the divisions to stop formulating unnatural strategies?

Becton Dickinson and Company (Part 2): The Clay Adams Division

In 1978, Frank Iris, the President of Becton Dickinson's Laboratory Group, had to decide whether to reorganize the Clay Adams Division, one of his group's seven divisions. Clay Adams' largest SBU, Labware, had a "maintain selectively" strategic role. Clay Adams' second-largest SBU, Instruments and Reagents, had a "build aggressively" role. Iris worried that the division could not pursue two contradictory strategic roles simultaneously.

One possible solution was to transfer the Labware SBU to the Falcon Division, also in Iris's Laboratory Group, because Falcon had a somewhat similar strategic role. This idea would enable each division to focus on implementing one role. On the other hand, there were important organizational, systems, personnel, and financial considerations in such a transfer. These could outweigh any benefits from greater divisional focus. Furthermore, Iris could trust that Ed Rapoza, the President of Clay Adams and a manager in whom he had the highest confidence, would find a way to grow the Instrument and Reagent SBU at the same time that he managed Clay Adams' "maintain" SBUs.

THE LABORATORY GROUP

Becton Dickinson's Laboratory Group was one of the world's largest suppliers of instruments, reagents, services, and supplies to clinical laboratories. Seven divisions and ten SBUs made up this group, which had sales of $141 million in 1977 and an annual growth rate of 13 percent over the last five years.

Iris, who was responsible for directing and controlling the operations of his divisions and for harmonizing corporate and divisional planning, reported to the Executive Vice President, Marvin Asnes. Each division president in the group was responsible for the division's organization, general management, and planning and reported directly to Iris (see Exhibit 1).

THE CLAY ADAMS DIVISION

Clay Adams, of Parsippany, New Jersey, had been a major supplier of laboratory products for nearly 60 years and a wholly owned subsidiary of Becton Dickinson since 1964. In all, Clay Adams had five SBUs by the end of fiscal year 1977.

See Exhibit 2 for the positions that the SBUs commanded in the Competitive Position/Industry Maturity Matrix; their strategic roles also are shown. Note that Instruments and Reagents SBU occupied more than one cell. This was because the SBU competed in three market segments. The High End (large laboratories requiring highly automated instruments) Hematology segment was mature, and the SBU held a tenable position. The Low End (medium and small laboratories) Hematology segment was growth, and the SBU's position was favorable. The Low End Chemistry segment was mature, and the SBU held a favorable position. The SBU did not compete in the High End Chemistry segment.

Each SBU's sales, income, and assets (in thousands) for 1973 and 1977 and goals for 1982 are shown below:

	1973			1977			1982		
	Sales	**Net Income**	**Total Assets**	**Sales**	**Net Income**	**Total Assets**	**Sales**	**Net Income**	**Total Assets**
Labware	$8,331	$934	$4,160	$11,520	$1,242	$4,940	$13,892	$1,460	$5,704
Centrifuges	3,166	126	1,870	4,449	355	3,790	5,206	509	3,354
Instruments and Reagents	2,321	(300)	2,046	6,709	(237)	4,726	21,294	1,715	10,741
Other	5,512	795	3,045	5,092	807	3,374	4,530	813	3,139
Princeton Biomedix	—	—	—	918	(100)	655	3,025	187	1,765
Unassigned Assets	—	—	661	—	—	1,739	—	—	2,657
Total	$19,330	$1,555	$11,782	$28,688	$2,067	$19,224	$47,947	$4,684	$27,360

Implementation Actions

The Labware SBU intended to implement its "maintain selectively" role by making product line extensions in its better lines while discontinuing low-volume and low-profit products, reducing the size of the sales force but increasing end-user marketing, and raising prices.

Exhibit 1 **Laboratory Group Organization**

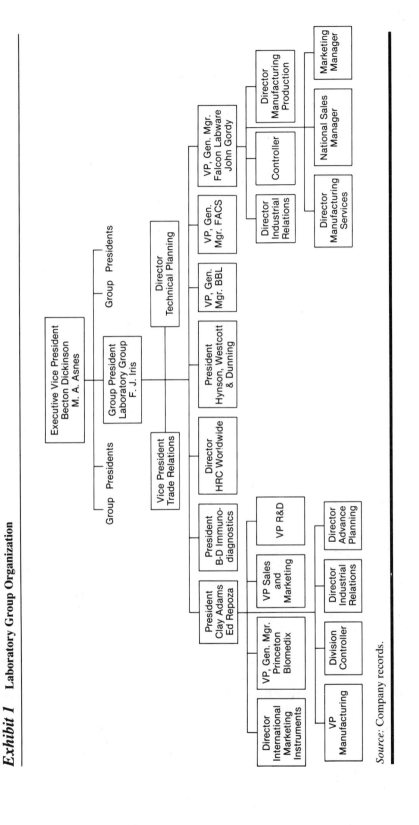

Source: Company records.

Exhibit 2   The Clay Adams Portfolio of Businesses

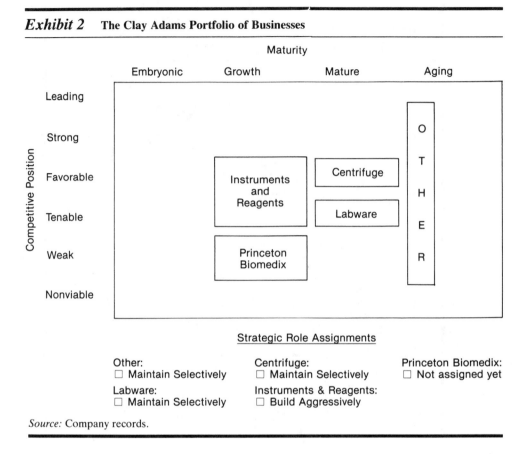

Maturity

Strategic Role Assignments

Other:
☐ Maintain Selectively

Labware:
☐ Maintain Selectively

Centrifuge:
☐ Maintain Selectively

Instruments & Reagents:
☐ Build Aggressively

Princeton Biomedix:
☐ Not assigned yet

Source: Company records.

The Instruments and Reagents SBU intended to implement its "build aggressively" role by adding products, increasing the number of sales representatives, and stepping up its own customer service function (a service that was presently performed by Honeywell) in both High End and Low End Hematology segments and introducing product improvements in Low End Chemistry as necessary to maintain market share.

By and large, Ed Rapoza thought that the strategic roles, 1982 goals, and implementation actions for each SBU were appropriate and feasible. He was particularly enthusiastic about the Instruments and Reagents SBU because, as Vice President of R and D before taking over the Clay Adams Division, he had developed the technology. Furthermore, he believed that in order for Clay Adams to grow in the future, it had to invest heavily in embryonic and growth markets.

THE FALCON DIVISION

The Falcon Division, located in Oxnard, California, made seven different lines of disposable plastic labware and was regarded as one SBU.

Becton Dickinson ranked Falcon as a strong competitor in a mature industry. The division's assigned strategic role was to "maintain aggressively," which it intended to execute by improving its technological efficiency and its manufacturing methods and functions, by integrating forward (in the sense of handling more sales directly), and by introducing several new products. It anticipated sales growth averaging 11 percent annually, as shown below (figures in millions):

	1977 (actual)			1982	
Sales	Net Income (AT)	Total Assets	Sales	Net Income (AT)	Total Assets
$18.3	$1.6	$13.5	$30.9	$4.3	$22.8

Until October 1977, Falcon had been a SBU in the BioQuest Division, when that division split into BBL Microbiological Systems and Falcon. John Gordy, the President of Falcon, came from Clay Adams in July 1977 to establish Falcon as a separate division. He explained that the following needed to be done at Falcon:

> Before the BioQuest split, Falcon was no more than a plant functioning through quasicentralized purchasing, sales, and marketing. First, I had to establish a full organization—marketing, sales, R&D, finance, and industrial relations—so that Falcon could operate as a separate division. Second, I had to coordinate the details of the switchover. Third, I had to learn what was wrong in manufacturing and turn the problem around. I set out to meet everyone in the plant, got to know them individually, and learned their individual problems. And if there's one single reason that things are going well at Falcon today, that's it—we're doing our human resources work better.

Iris expected improvements at BBL because the management there was freed to focus its efforts on that single business. But he was surprised to see benefits to Falcon, too: Sales were 16 percent above the previous year's level; a 17 percent negative manufacturing variance was now below 1 percent; ROS and ROA were rising; and as a competitor liquidated its labware business, Falcon was gathering the lion's share of its orders.

IRIS'S DECISION

Iris had already made one organizational change in the Laboratory Group, splitting the BioQuest Division into two divisions, BBL and Falcon. If he transferred Clay

Exhibit 3   **Reorganizing the Laboratory Group**

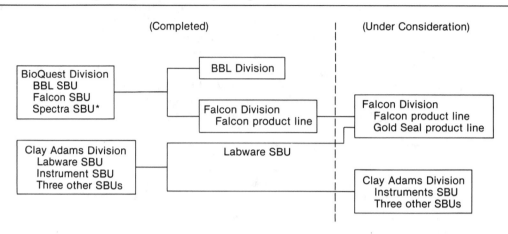

Note: The Spectra SBU, 10 percent of BioQuest's sales, went to another division at the time that BBL and Falcon were formed.

Adams Labware to Falcon, the effect would be as though two divisions had each spun off a portion of its business to create a third division, as shown in Exhibit 3.

If the proposed reorganization took place, the largest change would be in the sales forces. Falcon's force would begin selling the Labware line in addition to the Falcon line. Some of Clay Adams' Labware salespeople would move to Falcon, others would move to other Clay Adams product lines, and still others would lose their jobs. The Labware line would continue to be manufactured in the Clay Adams plants where it was now made, but warehousing and shipping changes would be necessary because Clay Adams would be manufacturing to Falcon's inventory. Financially all of Labware's identifiable assets, liabilities, revenues, and costs would transfer to Falcon.

Arguments for Reorganizing

The Need for Focus.   Iris did not consider Clay Adams a troubled division, and he was not dissatisfied with the division's performance under Ed Rapoza. On the other hand, the strategic role assignment to "build aggressively" the competitive position of the Instrument SBU was a demanding one, and the division showed signs of its difficulty.

One such sign was a failure to meet budgets for net income. The shortfalls were generally not large, and they were always readily explained: Budgeting for a growth business such as instruments could never be as exact as for a mature business such as labware; if essential programs turned out to cost more than expected, or if unanticipated expenditures become necessary on short notice, they could not be trimmed or postponed without risking the very development of the business. Even though the shortfalls were explicable, their consequences were serious. First, divisional executives lost a portion of their bonuses for every increment that net income fell below budget. Second, a heavy emphasis on profitability was so ingrained in Becton Dickinson's corporate culture that the reputations of the division and its executives were endangered by the consistent shortfalls. Because a number of corporate executives had served in Clay Adams—including Howe, Asnes, and Iris—the division was a particularly visible one.

A second sign was the difficulty Clay Adams had in developing a sales force for the instrument business. "They've had a hard time moving from dealer sales to direct sales," Iris said. "They've had to rely on another company for their repair service. And at each juncture they've needed more of a sales force than they've had."

In the next year, Rapoza's assignment for the instrument business would become significantly more complex. First, he would be introducing new instruments in a new segment, High End Hematology. To do so, he was establishing a new sales force while trying to keep the divisional selling expense at its historic rate of 13 percent of sales. Second, he would have new responsibility for building the fluorescent-activated cell sorter business and for coordinating European sales of his own and all other Laboratory Group instruments. Finally, he would be integrating into the division Princeton Biomedix, Clay Adams' recent acquisition.

As the assignment to build instruments became more demanding, a number of executives worried that the inherent conflict between a "build" assignment for instruments and a "maintain" assignment for labware and Clay's other businesses would become even more difficult to manage. John Gordy, who had served as Clay's Director of Sales before taking over Falcon, spoke about this conflict:

> The two businesses require different investment modes, different financial objectives, and different compensation. Melding these differences for growth and mature businesses is impossible. And here, too, personalities are probably the most important thing. The two situations require different personalities. Or maybe the same manager could do both jobs, but not at the same time. Both the instrument business and labware business would benefit from focused management.

Results of the Profiling Sessions. Becton Dickinson's 1976 profiling sessions had revealed a large difference between Clay Adams' labware and instrument businesses and also a close similarity between Clay Adams' Labware SBU and Falcon Labware. To define SBUs, Becton Dickinson found, the most important considerations by far were competitors, customers, and distribution channels. Clay Adams' two most important competitors in the instrument and reagent business were Coulter and Technicon, both instrument manufacturers; in the labware business, the competitors were Corning and Kimble, who were also Falcon's leading competitors. Clay Adams sold its instruments and reagents exclusively to customers in the health care industry—hospital labs, private labs, and physicians. Although Clay Adams' Labware SBU and Falcon sold much of their labware to customers in this industry, they also sold to government labs, industrial labs, original equipment manufacturers, and educational labs. The sales methods and distribution channels of the three businesses suggested splitting the labware business from Clay Adams and adding it to Falcon. The two labware businesses relied primarily on dealers, whereas instruments required more direct selling, could not be sold through labware dealers, and needed strong technical and service support for the sales force. As Clay Adams built the instrument business, it found it necessary to establish a separate sales force for the purpose.

Benefits to Labware.   A decision to remove the Labware business from Clay Adams, Iris emphasized, would not be a punishment for mismanaging it. "Eventually," he said, "you would expect Ed's focus on instruments to hurt the Labware business, but we have no sign that that's happened yet." Nonetheless, he was confident that the Labware SBU would be managed well as part of Falcon.

Iris's Philosophy of Management.   A strong impetus for reorganizing Clay Adams, Iris said, was his own philosophy of management:

> I prefer to run small, decentralized businesses. My experience has been that large, centralized businesses—and even large, decentralized ones—don't work well. Communication becomes too complicated. Response is too slow.

Indeed, Iris's philosophy had been the primary motivation for his earlier reorganization of BioQuest into Falcon and BBL. As for the question of reorganizing Clay Adams, Iris said that the results of the profiling sessions were a more central part of his analysis than they had been in the question of splitting up BioQuest. But his desire to decentralize, to simplify lines of responsibility, and to put like with like as a way of sharpening managerial focus on strategic tasks was a major influence on his thinking about Clay Adams.

Arguments Against Reorganizing

Problems for Clay Adams.   By moving the Labware SBU to Falcon, Iris hoped to free the division to focus on its Instrument and Reagent SBU and thus to improve the performance of that SBU. Iris's greatest concern was that the damage caused by the reorganization might prove greater than the benefits of improved focus. At the very least, the loss of the Labware SBU would force Clay Adams to endure a difficult transition; at the worst, it might force rending changes in personnel and in managerial methods from which Clay Adams would not easily or quickly recover. Iris and Rapoza expected to encounter problems in the plant, in the sales force, and among the managerial cadre.

Iris named two problems for the production force. First, even though Clay Adams would continue to produce glass labware after Falcon took over sales, the reorganization would require laying off a number of employees, chiefly warehouse and shipping workers. Rapoza believed that he could hold the number laid off to eight or nine by keeping extra employees in anticipation of increased instrument and reagent production. But even this number of lost jobs would be a serious matter to the employees. Second, there would be a large change in job mix as Clay Adams' focus moved from labware to instruments. Instrument production required vocational skills for which the prevailing wage was higher than for jobs in labware production. Rapoza already faced the beginning of this problem. Older, experienced employees, often people with a strong loyalty to the company, found it hard to see young, inexperienced employees come in at higher wages. The proposed reorganization would not only accelerate the change in job mix but also would deepen Rapoza's problem. As labware production workers saw the division give their business away, they would likely feel the same isolation and alienation that Falcon employees had felt under BioQuest.

Problems in the sales force, Iris said, would be caused by realignment of positions in the force and by relocation of labware salespeople. He expected morale and salary problems as people moved laterally in the reorganization, and he anticipated a relocation from New Jersey to California to be difficult, even repugnant, for many of the salespeople. To illustrate the problems that would arise, he gave this hypothetical example:

> Consider an imaginary labware salesman whose skill is understanding medical supply dealers, who has been with the company ten years, who has developed strong relations with his dealers, and who—because he is good at selling labware to dealers—consistently earns bonuses among the highest paid by the division. For personal reasons he can't move, but he has no interest in instruments and no understanding of them or how to sell them to labs and physicians. You have a choice. If you move him to centrifuges or educational supplies, in the first place you may not need him and, second, you've stolen his ten years worth of contacts from him. You've turned him from a top notch salesman into a mediocre salesman who will earn only medium bonuses. On the other hand, if you move him to instruments you turn him into a rotten salesman who you'll probably have to fire.

Rapoza said the following about the third area of problems, the management group:

> In the past we've had a solidly profitable division. We've mirrored pretty well the company's profit level, with 7–8% net income each year, and our managers are oriented to making money. If you take Labware out of Clay Adams, you change the nature of our division and our goals radically. Profit won't be our goal for a number of years. People with a profit mind-set who are thrown into an unprofitable situation—a situation where they're actually asked to lose money—are going to be very uncomfortable. We'll have a long, hard struggle to get away from thinking in terms of 7–8% earnings.

As he made his decision about reorganizing, Iris kept in mind that the greatest difficulties of the reorganization would fall to Ed Rapoza to solve:

> The tough job will be Ed's job of selling the reorganization within Clay. First, his organization is where the problems of the change will be felt strongest. Second, the

farther down the organization you go, the more the employees' loyalty and concern are for Clay Adams and for their own jobs; and the less they are loyal to or concerned about the Laboratory Group, Becton Dickinson, or some new abracadabra of a planning theory from headquarters in Paramus.

Rapoza agreed that the problems of managing this change might be severe.

I will have a lot of unhappy people, and a hard job working with them. In addition, I have a lot of people here who are not made up to operate in the build aggressively mode that Clay will enter if we focus on instruments. Their comfort indexes will go way down the minute they hear about the reorganization. Either they'll have to change or I'll have to change people.

Problems for Falcon.   Falcon also faced several potential problems as a result of the reorganization. First, even though both companies made labware and the two labware units appeared to be a single SBU in the profiling sessions, Falcon's and Clay Adams' product lines and distribution networks differed significantly. Falcon made only plastic ware, and Clay Adams made only glassware. The only product they shared was nonvolumetric, nonprecision pipettes, which were 25 percent of Clay's labware sales and 22 percent of Falcon's. In addition to these differences in product line, Clay Adams and Falcon used different distribution networks. The top four distributors were the same for both, and 60 percent or more of their combined volume went through shared dealers; but Clay Adams' network was much larger and included many small dealers; whereas Falcon, which relied on large dealers, had little experience with small dealers. Iris did not know how serious a problem these differences would cause if he combined the two labware businesses.

Second, Iris was uncertain about the effect of combining SBUs with different competitive positions. Falcon's position was rated as strong; although Clay Adams had originally rated its Labware SBU as strong, in subsequent re-evaluations, it had lowered this rating to favorable and then to tenable. Iris did not know whether combining the two SBUs would create one strong SBU or would create one tenable—or maybe favorable—SBU. Would the strong pull up the weak, or vice versa? Yet another possibility was that the tenable and strong SBUs would not mix, that Falcon and Clay Adams Labware would remain two distinct SBUs even though they were joined administratively and would require two distinct strategies.

Gordy's opinion was that, under ideal circumstances, the two SBUs would mix without trouble and that Falcon, the stronger SBU, would pull up Labware, the tenable one.

Actually, I don't think of Labware as only a tenable SBU. Given its manufacturing capability and Becton Dickinson's marketing strength, it's inherently a favorable SBU at the very least. I'd call it a 'neglected favorable,' and combined with Falcon I'd expect it to have a favorable position, particularly if it rides along with Falcon's international growth.

At the same time, Gordy was not certain whether the Falcon Division, which was only six months old, presently had the organizational resources to improve Clay Adams' Labware SBU without hurting Falcon's own business. This raised a third problem that the reorganization might cause, which Gordy explained as the following:

> In the past I've been uncertain whether to call Falcon's position favorable or strong; but I would say it is now a full strong, and it is moving toward a dominant position. The risk is that the Labware SBU will hurt it from a timing standpoint. Falcon's sales are growing rapidly, and our sales people are heavily loaded. Adding the Labware SBU might overload them, hurt Falcon's sales growth, and prevent Falcon from reaching a dominant position. In addition, we're working to develop computerized MIS and MCS systems for Falcon. Our divisional organization is entirely new, since this was only a plant until last October. The computer system is new, too, and so far it's only marginally adequate. As our own sales grow we're having to rely too much on expensive manual backups. If we add the Labware SBU, we'll have to go heavily to manual systems and I'm afraid our development of the computer systems will be retarded seriously.

Risks to Ed Rapoza.   The riskiness of Ed Rapoza's position if the reorganization proceeded was a subject of much discussion among the corporate executives, some of whom doubted that he truly supported the change and others of whom believed that his position after the reorganization would be disastrous if the corporation's commitment to changing key elements of its culture waned. Rapoza himself was ambivalent about the proposed change. Intellectually he supported the move, but emotionally he hesitated.

> I have a technical background; I'm very analytical and logical. I don't say this to brag or anything. I'm describing myself. I believe something if it makes sense intellectually and if it tests out empirically against reality. Intellectually, I'm entirely comfortable about the reorganization. I recommend it. Emotionally, I feel very different, and I have to repress a lot. If the reorganization goes through, as I believe it should, I'll be a long way out on a limb. I won't have any security blanket.

After discussing the reorganization with Rapoza, Frank Iris made these comments about Rapoza's personal position:

> The reorganization can hurt Ed personally. The reason is that bonuses are based on divisional net income compared to plan. Currently, the Labware SBU is Ed's largest and it's his biggest contributor to the division's net income. After Labware is gone, Instruments will be the largest SBU, and the division's total net income will be much smaller. Because of its strategic role, you can expect Instruments to show variance from plan. It's bound to happen. Assume the division's actual net income falls $200,000 short of planned net income because of the Instrument SBU. It makes a big difference to Ed's bonus whether you measure that $200,000 shortfall against a planned net income of $2 million for the division, or against a planned net income of $200,000 for the division.

Mr. Iris said this in conclusion:

> The most insidious thing is not what can happen to his bonus, but the idea that the more profitable you are the more important you are. Ed will be doing an important job

for the company. But if he doesn't show large profits, will he get the respect and recognition he deserves?

Another corporate officer discussed this question of what he called, alluding to Freud, "profit envy":

> The belief that profits equal power and importance is a very significant part of our corporate culture, and has been for a long while. I have two concerns about a manager taking Ed's position. First, will his effort be discounted because it can't be measured in current profitability? Second, will the pressure of the corporate culture—of profit envy, if you will—cause him to push too soon and too hard for profitability, rather than to seek sales growth and to strengthen his competitive position as he should?

A change in the company's compensation scheme, this executive said, would be the start of a solution, but a full solution would come only with a major shift in corporate culture to recognize the importance of growth projects, however unprofitable their beginnings.

Rapoza said the following from the division presidents' point of view about the problems caused by Becton Dickinson's compensation scheme:

> It's been two years or more since Becton Dickinson began pushing for new products. At the outset the division presidents were enthusiastic and a number of us put growth projects high among our priorities. We had a lot of optimism at first, but that quickly turned to frustration, for the people who were pushing new products wound up being penalized for doing it by the compensation scheme. The SBU system offers a solution, for it offers a way of seeing the difference between old and new businesses. But nothing is solved yet. There is still a lot of frustration. As for myself, I have a lot of tolerance and some faith. So far the two have got me through, but the situation will have to change or they'll wear thin.

Managerial and Management Systems Congruency

In recent months, the corporate executives had been turning to the question of how to implement strategies once they had been selected. A concept that they were finding particularly useful for attacking implementational problems was congruency.

At the heart of Arthur D. Little's planning methodology was a conviction that the environment, strategy, structure, managers, and performance of a business unit needed to be congruent with one another. If an embryonic business were to succeed, it could not afford a rigid, unadaptable manager with a passion for order and details. Such a manager would be better suited to a mature or aging business. Similarly the planning procedures, organization, communication methods, and control measures would be different for an embryonic and a mature business. "Form must follow function," as one Becton Dickinson executive put it, "whether in a chair and table, in a building, or in management." The factors that were considered when assessing congruency are shown in Exhibit 4.

Exhibit 4 **Management Characteristics by Stage of Industry Maturity**

Management Activity or Function	Embryonic Industry	Growth Industry	Mature Industry	Aging Industry
Managerial role	Entrepreneur	Sophisticated market manager	Critical administrator	"Opportunistic milker"
Planning time frame	Long enough to draw tentative life cycle (10)	Long-range investment payout (7)	Intermediate (3)	Short-range (1)
Planning content	By product/customer	By product and program	By product/market/function	By plant
Planning style	Flexible	Less flexible	Fixed	Fixed
Organization structure	Free-form or task force	Semi-permanent task force, product or market division	Business division plus task force for renewal	Pared-down division
Managerial compensation	High variable/low fixed, fluctuating with performance	Balanced variable and fixed, individual and group rewards	Low variable/high fixed group rewards	Fixed only
Policies	Few	More	Many	Many
Procedures	None	Few	Many	Many
Communication system	Informal/tailor-made	Formal/tailor-made	Formal/uniform	Little or none, by direction
Managerial style	Participation	Leadership	Guidance/loyalty	Loyalty
Content of reporting system	Qualitative, marketing, unwritten	Qualitative and quantitative, early warning system, all functions	Quantitative, written, production oriented	Numerical, oriented to written balance sheet
Measures used	Few fixed	Multiple/adjustable	Multiple/adjustable	Few/fixed
Frequency of measuring	Often	Relatively often	Traditionally periodic	Less often
Detail of measurement	Less	More	Great	Less
Corporate departmental emphasis	Market research; new product development	Operations research; organization development	Value analysis; Data processing; Taxes and Insurance	Purchasing

Source: Arthur D. Little, Inc.

At first, Becton Dickinson executives paid little attention to the idea of management congruency. They were more concerned with finding strategies appropriate to the SBUs' maturities and competitive positions. As the company's use of the system evolved, however, a number of executives turned their attention to the idea of management congruency. In the view of Jack Howe, the President and CEO, and of several other corporate executives, congruency between management methods and the SBU's position in the Competitive Position/Industry Maturity Matrix was fully as important as the fit between strategy and position in the matrix. Because Becton Dickinson's product line had become mature, these executives reasoned, its management systems had become mature; to succeed at regenerating its product line, the company would also have to regenerate its management systems.

Applying the Concept of Congruency. The device that Becton Dickinson used as a summary tool for examining congruency was an industry life-cycle curve on which were plotted industry maturity, financial performance, strategies, and management system for the SBU under examination (see Exhibit 5). The SBU for which all of these factors were congruent (indicated by diamonds) could be expected to better realize its full potential throughout the life cycle than the SBU for which these factors were incongruent (indicated by squares). Exhibit 6 shows congruency analyses following this method for the Falcon Division, the Clay Adams Instrument and Reagent SBU, and the Clay Adams Labware SBU.

Gordy explained Falcon ratings on the basis that his division competed in a mature industry with a "growth" management system. Because the division was new, it had not had time to develop fully such elements of a mature management system as a fully computerized information and control system.

At Clay Adams, Rapoza ranked his management system as mature, which was congruent with the majority of the industries in which his Labware, Centrifuge, and other SBUs competed. The mature management system was incongruent,

Exhibit 5 **Congruency Analyses**

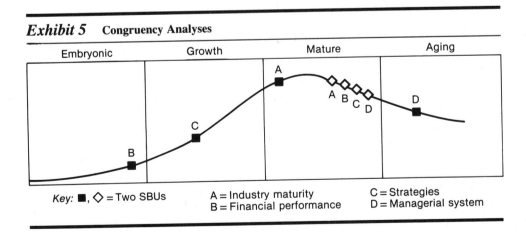

| Embryonic | Growth | Mature | Aging |

Key: ■, ◇ = Two SBUs   A = Industry maturity   C = Strategies
                                           B = Financial performance   D = Managerial system

Exhibit 6

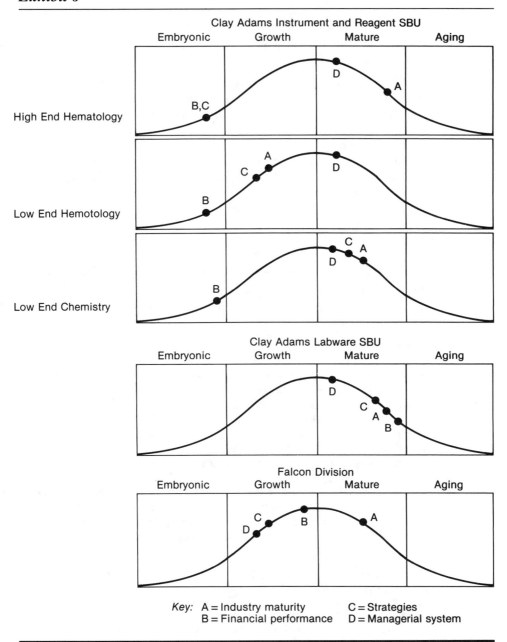

Clay Adams Instrument and Reagent SBU

High End Hematology

Low End Hemotology

Low End Chemistry

Clay Adams Labware SBU

Falcon Division

Key: A = Industry maturity   C = Strategies
B = Financial performance   D = Managerial system

however, with competition in his Instrument SBU's growth industry. This incongruity, Rapoza said, posed this potential difficulty:

> The most glaring area of incongruity is the sales force management. The instrument business requires aggressive sales management people. If the reorganization goes through and the Instrument SBU becomes Clay's biggest SBU, then either my present sales managers will have to change their attitudes or I'll be forced to change people.

The idea of congruency between manager and strategy was simply that a manager should be suited to his or her task—by temperament, experience, and skill—if the task were to be performed well. As Iris applied this concept to the reorganization of Clay Adams, he asked himself two questions. First, did the strategic role assignments in question, the "build aggressively" assignment of the Instrument and Reagents SBU and the "maintain assignment" of Clay Adams Labware SBU and Falcon, require different managers to execute them? Second, which manager, Rapoza or Gordy, was better suited to which assignment? Exhibits 7 and 8 show Rapoza's and Gordy's résumés.

Corporate Considerations

Corporate executives with whom Iris had discussed the reorganization of Clay Adams raised three issues that were especially important for the whole company: the effect of the reorganization on managers outside the Laboratory Group; the locus of portfolio management in the corporation; and the role of the division in the company's organization. One corporate executive discussed the first issue:

> My question is whether you reduce the incentive to manage when managers see that a successful business can be taken away from them. This issue came up as a theoretical question during the BioQuest split. It wasn't a real issue then because the managers of BioQuest's main business—now BBL Microbiology—considered Falcon an unimportant sideline, almost a nuisance. With Clay Adams, though, we're talking about spinning off a major, very profitable part of the division. How will a division president somewhere else in the company react when he sees this? Will he say, 'Why bother to make this profitable if they'll just take it away from me?'
>
> A second unfavorable reaction that's possible is simply anxiety: will they do to me what they're doing to Ed Rapoza? Anxiety about change can constrict the flow of information through a company and distort the information that does flow. We can't afford that at Becton Dickinson. As we install the SBU system and try to make it work well, we need a free, clear flow of the best possible information. So I worry that other managers will think Ed is being screwed, become anxious, and throw up defenses.

This executive also commented on the second issue—the locus of portfolio management in Becton Dickinson:

> Dividing BioQuest and, if they decide to do it, dividing Clay Adams changes the location of the Laboratory Group's portfolio. Previously it has been managed at the divisional level, with supervision at the corporate level. Now it will be managed at the corporate

(Text continues on page 203)

Exhibit 7   **Ed Rapoza's Résumé**

Experience

July 1973–present	President, Clay Adams Division, Becton Dickinson. General management of company. Developed instrumentation business.
July 1971–July '73	Vice President, Research and Development, Clay Adams Division. Added new products in established lines. Developed chemistry and hematology instruments.
July 1968–July '71	Director, Research and Development, Clay Adams Division. Enlarged development capability to include chemistry, engineering, product management. Developed chemistry and cell-counting instruments.
May 1967–July '68	Manager, Product Development, Clay Adams Division. Reorganized R&D group, developed laboratory products.
Oct. 1966–May '67	Chief Engineer, Clay Adams Division. Designed new centrifuge, developed new engineering group.
Mar. 1963–Oct. '66	Program Manager of Kearfott Products Division, Singer Company, Clifton, N.J. Designed and built electro-mechanical actuators for space and earth environment. (Patent applied for.) Placed twelve actuators on moon, on lunar orbiter. Proposal development to potential customers.
Apr. 1962–Mar. '63	Senior Engineer, ITT-Avionics Laboratory, Nutley, N.J. Associate systems management on Tacan Simulator.
June 1958–Apr. '62	Mechanical Engineer, RCA Aerospace Communications & Controls, Camden, N.J. Designed tape transport system (patent awarded); design responsibility for airborne equipment; system integration.

Education

1958–1960	University of Pennsylvania. MS in Mechanical Engineering.
1954–1958	Stevens Institute of Technology. BS in Mechanical Engineering.

Activities

Board of Trustees, High Crest Community Club.
Vice President, Industrial Section, Parsippany Chamber of Commerce.
Management Seminars.

Personal

Age 42.
Married, four children.

Exhibit 8   John Gordy's Résumé

Experience

July 1977–present   President, Falcon Division, Becton Dickinson. Successfully reorganized Falcon from a plant operation as part of the BioQuest Division to an independent division, with full sales, marketing, and operational responsibility. Profit and loss responsibility. Increased sales, reduced negative manufacturing variances; raised ROA and ROS.

Feb. 1976–July '77   Director of Sales and Technical Service, Clay Adams Division, Becton Dickinson. Responsible for $35 million of sales. Responsible for marketing and strategies for three SBU sections and one non-SBU section, including Labware and Instrument and Reagent SBUs. Responsible for all technical service and warranty service for all instrumentation manufactured by the division.

Aug. 1974–Feb. '76   Director of Marketing, Clay Adams Division. Responsible for market and product segmentation, market research and analysis, new product development, and product extensions for three SBU sections and one non-SBU section. Responsible for divisional forecasting, business planning, and annual planning. Gross profit responsibility for new product introduction and selling mix.

Feb. 1974–Aug. '74   Senior Industrial Relations Representative and Marketing Consultant to Becton Dickinson (corporate headquarters). Corporate labor relations, evaluations and negotiations. Marketing, sales and advertising consultant to the consumer products division.

Aug. 1969–Feb. '74   President and Chairman of the Board, Visual Sounds, Inc., Upper Saddle River, N.J. Managed all business activities concerning company's two facets—production of medically-oriented cassettes, films, slides, and booklet presentations, and manufacture of audio cassette tape and 8-track cartridge sound tape. Managed all sales, marketing, and operational matters, including import and export business by letters of credit. Sales, $5 million; 150 employees.

Dec. 1968–Dec. '69   Independent Manufacturers' Representative for Rip the Rep, Inc., Southfield, Michigan. Represented manufacturers' products in U.S. and Canada to the big four automobile manufacturers. Product categories: aluminum extrusion; screw machine parts; injection molded plastic parts; molded rubber parts. Increased net sales from $250,000 to $3 million in one year.

Sept. 1962–Dec. '68   Assistant to the Director of Advertising and Sales Promotion, Autolite Division, Ford Motor Company. Market research, product segmentation and analysis; market segmentation and analysis. Research and development of media advertising and print for radio and TV. Assisted in the production of national TV and radio advertising, and promotional film presentations.

	Designed, implemented, and tracked divisional sales and promotional campaigns.
Jan. 1960–June '61	Second Lieutenant, U.S. Army Reserve, Ft. Benning, Georgia. Platoon officer.
Apr. 1958–May '59	Assistant Coach, University of Nebraska. Coached offensive line for football team.
1957–1968 (except '58)	Offensive guard, Detroit Lions, National Football League. Active player, team captain, and Player Representative to the NFL Players Association.

Education

1953–1957	University of Tennessee. B.A. in Education.
	Wharton School, Executive Education Program in Matrix Management.
	IBM Executive Management Program, Systems Development.

Activities

Jogging, golfing, tennis, sailing.

Personal

Age 43.
Married, four children.

---

level. My belief is that portfolio management is a corporate function, not a divisional function. As a general statement, if you install portfolio management in the division, you divide focus. The result is old, steady businesses that become shells because they are neglected and new ventures that don't take off because they are underfunded.

I recognize the argument against this position, however. It concerns career development. If the company removes portfolio management responsibility from the divisions, then managers who are promoted to the corporate level will arrive with no experience at managing portfolios. That might in fact hurt the corporation, although the increased number of general management opportunities that the SBU system brings can be expected to aid the development of managers in the company.

The question of where portfolios should be managed was part of a larger question about the role of divisions in Becton Dickinson. This question pointed directly to the discontinuity between the company's divisional organization and its new SBU planning system. Six divisions, for example, produced one kind or another of hypodermic equipment. Profiling sessions for these six units indicated that they were one worldwide SBU and thus that one strategy should be developed for the whole hypodermic business, not six strategies for its six geographic and administrative pieces. Did this mean that the various hypodermic businesses should be removed from the six managements that now ran them and formed into one division under one management?

The executives at Becton Dickinson identified four broad answers to the question of what a division should be. First, divisions should be the basic strategic, organizational, and reporting unit of the company. This was the role they had before the introduction of SBU planning. Second, they should be the basic organizational and reporting units, while the SBUs were the basic strategic units. This was the role they had taken after the introduction of SBU planning. (As a variation on this role, strategic planning *and* reporting could be done by SBUs, while the division remained the basic organizational and administrative unit.) Third, the SBU should be made the basic organizational unit of the company, in effect turning each SBU into a division. This was the option Iris had chosen when he reorganized BioQuest into BBL and Falcon. Fourth, divisions should be organized around key SBUs, so that no division had two key SBUs but any division might have several ancillary SBUs, either linked or unlinked to its key SBU by technology, markets, or functional interdependence. This was the role Iris would be choosing for the division if he proceeded with the reorganization of Clay Adams.

In their discussion of this question, the executives at Becton Dickinson were far from unanimous about the relation between SBUs and divisions. Many agreed with the consultants from Arthur D. Little, who said that spillage of SBUs across organizational lines was common in the companies they had profiled. Discontinuities between strategic units and administrative units, they believed, neither should prohibit the development of coordinated SBU strategies nor should require reorganization to align administrative units with strategic units. The SBU could be used as the basic unit for formulating strategy, while the division remained the basic unit for such functions as reporting and control. Nonetheless, soon after the SBU planning system had been introduced in 1976, operating managers in Becton Dickinson's divisions and a number of corporate executives began to discuss the possibility that the company should reorganize around its SBUs.

By his decision about Clay Adams, Iris would be casting a vote on the question of what role the division should have, and he would be setting up the Laboratory Group as a test case. He also would be testing the meaning and implications of two concepts that were finding an important place in the corporate lexicon, "focus" and "congruency." Granting that an increased focus on instruments would improve the prospects of that business, was reorganization the best way to achieve focus? Was focus possible without congruency of management and mission? Since Clay Adams' management system was incongruent with the Instrument SBU's strategic role, would that incongruity prevent management from focusing more on the SBU even after reorganization? Should the division therefore bring its management system into congruity with its strategic role before Iris attempted to gain focus by reorganizing? If the division brought its management system into congruity with the Instrument SBU's strategic role, would reorganization even be necessary?

Iris summarized his options thus:

> What I'm trying to figure out is what will be the best for the Laboratory Group as a whole and, particularly, what will be the best for the instrument business. We've talked it over as well as we can, so now it's time to act—either move Labware out of Clay Adams, leave it there temporarily and make plans to move it later, or leave it there for good.

Chapter 6

MANAGING MULTINATIONAL STRATEGY

In Part II, we discussed how the strategy process can be tailored to suit the context of a business unit. Each of these contexts—Pioneer, Expand, Reorient, and Dominate—varies in the complexity of the chosen business environment and the distinctive competencies that the firm has for competing in that environment. The former is determined by the heterogeneity and unpredictability of the stakeholders that a business unit confronts in its chosen niche. In a multinational corporation (MNC), this niche is defined both by the product/market positioning of the business unit and by the unit's country mix. Environmental complexity is therefore determined not only by the configuration of competitive forces that a business unit confronts in its chosen niche but also by the political forces that it is subjected to in the countries in which it operates.[1] Similarly the distinctive competencies of a business unit, its unique resources to compete in a chosen environment, must be expanded to include the goodwill it enjoys in its host countries, the know-how it has for dealing with the business environment in these countries, and the sensitivity it has to different national cultures.[2]

The context of a business unit can thus vary from country to country for the same family of products. The top management of a MNC can deal with this diversity in one of two distinct ways: global integration or national responsiveness. In a global integration orientation, top management seeks to exploit synergies in a business unit's worldwide operations. These synergies can be in economies of scale, as in a global cost leadership strategy, or in economies of scope, as in a global differentiation strategy. In either case, top management first seeks to build a global business architecture and then to adapt that architecture to suit each national market. The individual needs of a country are clearly secondary in this orientation. If necessary, the MNC would rather exit a country rather than compromise its business architecture. National responsiveness, on the other hand, is an orientation where the fit of a business strategy to the local context is of primary concern to top management. The product offerings may not be standardized across countries, but top management is willing to accept the resulting inefficiencies.

Building congruence between the desired strategic orientation and the roles assigned to product and country managers in the strategy process is an important responsibility of top management. This has been accomplished in the past primarily through organizational design. Business units that need a national responsiveness orientation are organized geographically. Country managers report to top management through the area organization. Product expertise is provided as staff support either directly in each country or through dotted-line relationships with product experts at the area or corporate headquarters. Business units that need a global integration orientation are organized by product groups. In each country, there are product representatives who report directly to the product managers at the corporate headquarters. These representatives have a dotted-line reporting relationship with their respective country managers.

The simple structural solution described above is not adequate because of the new competitive and political pressures that confront a MNC. The two ideal types of global integration and national responsiveness are increasingly giving way to a more balanced orientation in many business contexts, even as MNCs try to improve their efficiency through better global integration and local appeal through keener national responsiveness.

This chapter is divided into three sections. In the first section, we discuss the two strategic orientations, global integration and national responsiveness, in some detail. In the second section, we discuss the growing need for a simultaneous focus on global integration and national responsiveness in many multinational business contexts. In the third section, we propose a strategy process for providing such a balanced focus.

GLOBAL INTEGRATION AND NATIONAL RESPONSIVENESS

Determining whether a business unit needs a global integration or a national responsiveness orientation depends in part on the proportion of value that is added in the different activities of its value chain (see Figure A-6 in the Appendix).[3] The value chain of a business includes both direct value-creating activities—such as operations, inbound and outbound logistics, marketing, and sales and service—as well as support activities—such as administration, procurement, and research and development. The value added by one of these activities is measured by the investments and expenses associated with it, relative to other activities in the value chain. Depending on whether the business unit seeks to add most of its value upstream or downstream, the strategic orientation appropriate to it can vary.[4]

A global integration orientation is especially appropriate when the value added by the business is predominantly in upstream activities—such as operations and logistics—or in support activities—such as research and development. On the other hand, a national responsiveness orientation is the appropriate one if the value added by the business is predominantly in downstream activities such as marketing, sales, and service.

In such capital-intensive industries as automobiles, motorcycles, chemicals, steel, and heavy electrical systems, where significant value is typically added in upstream and support activities of the business unit's value chain (that is, in manufacturing, logistics, and R&D), many MNCs have found global integration to be the desired strategic orientation. Tailoring or replicating these activities to suit the needs of each international market can be very expensive. The aim therefore is to arrive at a standard global product specification that will be acceptable to most international customers, with minor modifications to suit local demands.

In service industries, such as insurance, or in consumer products industries, such as toiletries, where a substantial proportion of the value is typically added in downstream activities (that is, marketing, sales and service), national responsiveness has been the preferred orientation. Here the rationale appears to be that significant differences in consumer tastes, buying power, and marketing infrastructure across countries requires a more country-specific strategy. Besides, given the relatively smaller proportion of value that is added upstream, tailoring or even duplicating these upstream activities to suit a national market is usually inexpensive.

But, as we noted in Chapter 3, it is not the industry but rather the industry segment in which a business unit chooses to operate that will dictate whether a national responsiveness or global integration is the appropriate strategic orientation for it. Thus, for example, even in a capital-intensive industry such as chemicals, a business unit could add more value downstream by becoming a formulator and marketeer of specialty chemicals. Such a business unit will be competitive only if it is nationally responsive. Alternatively, even in a service industry such as insurance, a business unit may choose to offer only a few standard services, for example, marine insurance. The desired emphasis in this business is in the upstream and support elements of its value chain, such as actuarial and logistical activities.

FORCES OF CHANGE

Two forces push MNCs toward a balanced orientation to both national responsiveness and global integration in many business contexts. The first is the growing pressure on MNCs to become more efficient at exploiting all the available synergies in their worldwide operations.[5] The other is the pressure requiring MNCs to be more responsive to the needs of the governments and consumers in host countries.[6] Imperial Chemical Industries (ICI), for example, has reorganized itself recently into six global divisions. However, only half of ICI's divisions are headquartered in the home territory, the United Kingdom. The others are based in the United States (two) and in Belgium (one). The divisions are headquartered in the country that is the most appropriate, given the focus of that worldwide business.[7] Even smaller MNCs, as we saw in the Infotron study (see Case 3), seem to be moving toward global product divisions with worldwide responsibilities for strategy formulation and implementation and yet at the same time seem to be attempting to be more responsive to the needs of their host countries. This coordination is being facilitated by the international communications revolution—integrated transmission of voice, data, and video signals worldwide is already a reality.[8]

Toward Global Integration

The move toward global integration is being helped by the continuing homogenization of product needs among consumers in various countries.[9] Cheaper and more reliable transportation and the emergence of global buyers and suppliers (with global brands) have also contributed to this trend.[10] The lowering of customs barriers and the adoption of common standards for products within trade blocks, such as the European Economic Community, have been two other important contributors to the homogenization of product needs.

With increased globalization, a relatively small number of firms compete against one another in many international markets.[11] Even in businesses where value is predominantly added in downstream activities, MNCs have to consider opportunities for global integration in order to be competitive. For example, we see in Procter & Gamble (see Case 9) a consumer-oriented firm with traditionally heavy emphasis on national responsiveness that is attempting to create "Eurobrands." National responsiveness has to be coupled with efficient exploitation of intrafirm synergies.

A consequence of the trend toward globalization is that shifts in customer attitudes anywhere in the world can reshape a business.[12] For instance, the development of new health foods based on biotechnology in Japan can in turn have significant impacts on U.S. and European consumers. Many MNCs have systems for gathering global intelligence on changing consumer preferences. Such data are often systematically collected and analyzed on a country-by-country basis. However, a country manager is too close to his or her data to be able to see patterns across several regions. It should be the responsibility of product managers to elicit this data and to help identify emerging global trends.

Also, technological breakthroughs can take place in many parts of the world, and this trend toward a dispersed pattern of innovations is likely to accelerate. The challenge for a MNC is to be able to scan new technological developments on a worldwide basis. One way of achieving this would be to create, through its national subsidiaries, an international alliance of universities and research laboratories.

Toward National Responsiveness

The political forces that shape the business strategies of a MNC can be understood in terms of the bargaining power of the firm relative to its host governments and other key stakeholders.[13]

The bargaining power of the host governments derives from the size and the attractiveness of the national markets that they represent and their ability to regulate access to these markets. In addition to their role as regulators, host governments also can engage in other relationships with a MNC: for example, as a co-negotiator along with unions in labor disputes, as an architect of national standards, as a provider of financing, as a supplier where public utilities and/or raw material industries may be state owned, as a competitor through its public sector corporations, or even as a distributor where channels are state owned. The host governments can use all of these roles to influence the orientation of a MNC operating on their soil.

The bargaining power of the MNC is based on four sources: proprietary technology, worldwide market share (economies of scale), brand strength (economies of scope), and product differentiation.

In situations where the MNC is a technology or market leader, the host government has relatively little power to oppose global integration. Boeing and IBM, for example, have used their enormous technology and market power to resist pressures from host governments to compromise their orientation toward global integration.[14] On the other hand, in situations where the power balance is skewed in the favor of the host government, the strategic orientation of the business unit has to be more nationally responsive. An example would be the pressures that Honeywell experienced to conform to the wishes of the French government in its computer business.[15]

It must be noted, however, that the locus of relative power can easily shift back to the host government if there are other eager competitors who are willing to collaborate with it. In fact, as in the case of Honeywell in France, the host government can provide suitable incentives to attract or support a "weaker" MNC. This can mean at least a temporary loss of market share for the industry leader. The rise of the Société Airbus can also be seen in this light as an effort by several European governments to counteract in part the strong dominance of Boeing in the civilian aircraft industry. Similar examples of how power can shift away from a dominant MNC can be seen in other industries, such as telecommunications, defense, and power systems. Consequently the global integration approach must always be tempered with some sensitivity to the needs of the host country.

Besides host governments, a MNC may also be pressured by other powerful stakeholders—such as its own home government, powerful global suppliers, or customers—and international labor unions to redirect its foreign direct investment to countries that may otherwise not be ideal for achieving global integration. As a result, even Toyota, which is an upstream value adder, has been forced to locate some of its manufacturing activities in the United States and in Europe; it has to learn to be nationally responsive without seriously compromising its past strengths in global integration.

TOWARD A BALANCED ORIENTATION

Toward Regional Integration

Figure 6-1 is a simple framework for describing the pressures faced by a multinational business. Cell 1 describes a business context where the business unit adds

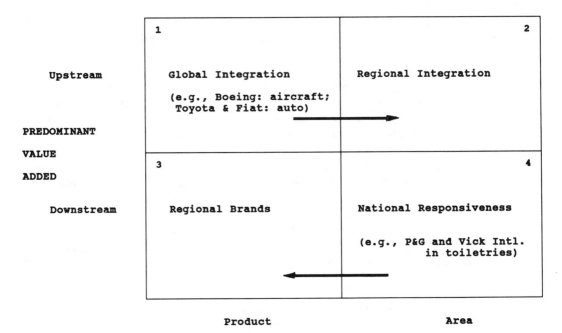

LOCUS OF RELATIVE POWER WITHIN THE
BUSINESS UNIT

Figure 6-1   **The Need for a Balanced Orientation**

most of its value upstream and is organized in a product divisional structure. Boeing's aircraft business and Toyota's and Fiat's automobile businesses would fit this context. These companies had adopted a global integration orientation, with a view to economize their efforts on research, design, engineering, manufacturing, and testing. But, because of growing competitive and political pressures, the orientation of these firms has become more responsive to their host countries. This is depicted in the figure as a transition to cell 2. This cell is regional integration. Although the MNC is not as monolithic in its strategic orientation as it is in cell 1, it still seeks to cluster countries into a small number of regions, within each of which it can strive for integration.

Fiat, for instance, has had to complement its global emphasis in basic research, development, and manufacturing and assembly process technologies with smaller and more flexible manufacturing and assembly plants worldwide. These distributed manufacturing and assembly capabilities allow Fiat to tailor its cars to the tastes of various regions of the world without unduly compromising efficiency.[16] Similarly Boeing has decided to develop its new commercial aircraft with heavy Japanese participation—in recognition of the growing importance of the Japanese market to the company. It may also have to consider relocating some of its upstream activities to Europe, if the threat from Airbus becomes more serious. Incidentally Airbus is a good example of how a global competitive threat can emerge from what started primarily as a political response from some customer countries.

Toyota's automobile business illustrates a transition to cell 2 because of mounting political pressures. In the face of growing demands by host governments for local manufacture, the company has retreated from global integration to regional integration. It is attempting to replicate on a smaller scale in Europe and the United States the intricate operational and logistical strengths that it has built so successfully in Japan.

In all of the above examples, a global integration orientation has had to give way to a more-limited regional integration orientation (cell 2 in Figure 6-1). Unlike global integration, the more-balanced orientation allows for a tailored response to the competitive and political pressures in a region. At the same time, unlike a national responsiveness orientation, regional integration allows for better exploitation of company-wide synergies.

Toward Regional Brands

Cell 4 in Figure 6-1 describes a business context where the business unit adds most of its value downstream and is organized in an area divisional structure. The toiletries business of Procter & Gamble (see Case 9) and Vick International Division (see Case 4), for example, had adopted a national responsiveness orientation, tailoring their products to the tastes and packaging, advertising, and distribution needs of the various national markets that they served.

In both of these companies, the need to improve efficiency and the desire to leverage product innovations beyond the country of origin led them to a regional brand strategy. The Procter & Gamble case study describes the endeavors of the company to build Eurobrand, and the Vick International case study describes the LAFE division's decision to focus its product developmental efforts on only projects with a division-wide payoff. Cell 3 describes a business context where the MNC seeks to pursue such a regional brand strategy.

Organizational Structure and Process

The transitions from global integration (cell 1) to regional integration (cell 2) or from national responsiveness (cell 4) to regional brands (cell 3) have in turn forced companies to abandon the simple distinction between product and area organizations and adopt complex administrative arrangements.[17] Regional management positions are created within a product divisional organization and these regional managers are placed on par with the product managers at the business unit's headquarters. Conversely brand management positions are created within an area divisional organization, and these regional brand managers are placed on par with country managers at the regional headquarters. A business unit seeking a balanced orientation, as de-

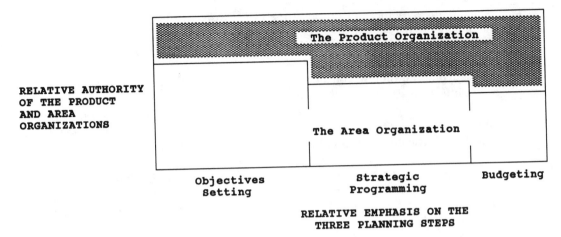

RELATIVE AUTHORITY OF THE PRODUCT AND AREA ORGANIZATIONS

The Product Organization

The Area Organization

Objectives
Setting

Strategic
Programming

Budgeting

RELATIVE EMPHASIS ON THE THREE PLANNING STEPS

Figure 6-2   **Tailoring the Strategy Process: The Illustrative Case of Regional Integration in a Pioneer Business Context**

scribed in cells 2 or 3, is typically organized in a matrix-type structure, with product and geographical areas being the two sides of the matrix.[18]

By managing the locus of power between the two sides of the matrix, top management can change the orientation of the business unit.[19] If, for example, top management wants to promote regional integration in a globally integrated firm, it should enhance the relative authority of the regional managers in the objectives-setting step of the strategy process. Conversely to provide a regional brand orientation in a national responsive firm, top management should shift relative authority to the product side of the matrix.

It is important to recognize that the varying roles of area and product managers have to be overlaid on the tailor-made process that was suggested in Chapter 3 to suit the context of a business unit. This superimposition is represented pictorially in Figure 6-2.

The figure refers to the tailor-made process in the case of a business transitioning to regional integration in a Pioneer business context. As is appropriate to its Pioneer context, the emphasis in strategy making for this business unit is more on the first two steps of objectives setting and strategic programming than on the third step of budgeting. In addition, the process must have other supporting features as described in Part II. However, because of the business unit's desired orientation of regional integration, the regional managers in the area side of the matrix take a slightly more dominant role in the objectives-setting and strategic programming steps than its product managers do.

Conversely when the desired transition is to a regional brand, as in the Vick International Division (see Case 4), the product side of the matrix must have relatively more power. Tom McGuire, the president of the Latin American and Far East (LAFE) division, wanted the basic strategy to be formed by product managers at the regional headquarters (as detailed in their PMG 1 and 2 documents). Thereafter, country managers would have a chance to tailor this basic strategy to their national contexts in their PMG 3 and 4 proposals.

Although the strong side of the matrix defines the strategic orientation of the business unit, the implementation of the chosen strategy is the joint responsibility of both sides of the matrix.[20] This means that both the area and the product sides must contribute equally in the budgeting step of the strategy process (see Figure 6-2).

Organizational Predisposition

A major hurdle in building the required cooperation between the product and the area sides of the business matrix is the organizational predisposition of the firm. Predisposition is shaped by a number of factors, including the firm's history; the past administrative practices; the culture, myths, and folklore that have endured in the organization; and the national culture of its home country. Predisposition can be classified under three broad categories:[21]

1. *Ethnocentrism.* This is a predisposition where all strategic decisions are guided by the values and interests of managers in the home country. Such a firm may find it difficult to get the full cooperation of its country managers, who perceive themselves as second-class citizens of the corporation with little corporate mobility outside their own countries.
2. *Polycentrism.* This is a predisposition where strategic decisions are primarily tailored to suit the parochial needs of the various countries in which the MNC competes, often at the cost of intrafirm synergies. Country managers tend to guard their individual fiefdoms fiercely.
3. *Regiocentrism.* This is a predisposition that falls between the extremes of ethnocentrism and polycentrism. It does not presume a monolithic world view, but it also does not seek to focus on fine-grained differences between individual nations. It focuses instead on differences across regions and commonalities within them. This is the predisposition that is best suited to a balanced strategic orientation (cells 2 and 3 in Figure 6-1).

The steps that are needed to build a regiocentric predisposition include the following:

1. The creation of a corporate and a regional management cadre representing managers from all nations in which the firm competes.
2. The use of a single corporate language throughout the firm—or, if that is not possible, limiting the languages used within the firm to a few regional languages.
3. Recruitment and training of executives to ensure that they are not only technically skilled but also well versed in the languages, politics, and the cultures of several countries that are of interest to the MNC.

4. Planned rotation of executives to ensure a balanced perspective in decision making at corporate, regional, and country levels.
5. Willingness to locate activities throughout the world, including manufacturing plants, administrative offices, research and development facilities, and training centers.

SUMMARY

In this chapter, we examined the special challenges for managing a multinational business. By managing the locus of authority for strategy making between product managers and area managers, top management can influence the orientation of a business unit toward either global integration or national responsiveness. Growing competitiveness and political pressures, however, call for a better balance between these two orientations. The product/area matrix organization can help bring about such a balance, provided that the two sides of the matrix can be made to function as partners. The firm needs a regiocentric predisposition to support such a partnership.

NOTES

1. See Y. Doz, *Strategic Management in Multinational Companies* (Oxford: Pergamon Press, 1986).
2. See the following: A. Laurent, "The Cross-Cultural Puzzle of International Human Resource Management," *Human Resource Management* 25 (Spring 1986): 91–102; and G. Hofstede, "The Cultural Relativity of Organizational Practices and Theories," *Journal of International Business Studies* (Fall 1983): 75–90.
3. For an elaboration of the value chain concept, see M. Porter, *Competitive Advantage* (New York: Free Press, 1985), 33–52.
4. M. E. Porter, *The Competitive Advantage of Nations* (New York: Free Press, 1990.)
5. See C. K. Prahalad and G. Hamel, "The Core Competence of the Corporation," *Harvard Business Review* 90 (Jan.–Feb. 1990): 79–93.
6. See Doz, *Strategic Management.*
7. P. Lorange and G. Probst, "Effective Strategic Planning Processes in the Multinational Corporation," in *Managing the Global Firm,* C. Bartlett, Y. Doz, and G. Hedlund, eds. (London: Routledge, 1989), 146–163.
8. Porter, *The Competitive Advantage of Nations.*
9. T. Levitt, "The Globalization of Markets," *Harvard Business Review* 61 (May–June 1983): 92–102.
10. Porter, *The Competitive Advantage of Nations.*
11. Ibid.
12. P. Lorange, "Challenges to Strategic Planning Processes in Multinational Corporation," in *International Strategic Management,* A. R. Negandhi and A. Savara, eds. (Lexington, MA: D. C. Heath, 1989), 107–125.
13. C. K. Prahalad and Y. Doz, *The Multinational Mission: Balancing Local Demands and Global Vision* (New York: Free Press, 1987).
14. Y. Doz, *Strategic Management.*

15. Ibid.

16. C. Romiti, *Questi Anni Alla Fiat* (Milan: Rizzoli Libri, 1988).

17. See C. Bartlett and S. Ghoshal, *Managing Across Borders: The Transnational Solution* (Cambridge, MA: Harvard University, 1989).

18. Ibid.

19. S. Chakravarthy and H. V. Perlmutter, "Strategic Planning for a Global Business," *Columbia Journal of World Business* 20 (Summer 1985): 3–10.

20. P. Lorange, "A Framework for Strategic Planning in Multinational Corporations," *Long Range Planning* 9 (June 1976): 30–37.

21. D. Heenan and H. V. Perlmutter, *Multinational Organizational Development* (Reading, MA: Addison-Wesley, 1979).

REFERENCES

Chandler, A. D., "The Evolution of Modern Global Competition," in *Competition in Global Industries,* ed. M. E. Porter (Boston: Harvard Business School Press, 1986), 405–448.

Fouraker, L. E., and J. M. Stopford, "Organizational Structure and Multinational Strategy," *Administrative Science Quarterly* 13 (1968): 47–64.

Hamel, G., and C. K. Prahalad, "Do You Really Have a Global Strategy?" *Harvard Business Review* (July–August 1985): 139–148.

Jacque, L. L., and P. Lorange, "International Control Systems for Hyperinflationary Subsidiaries: A Variance Smoothing Model," *Journal of International Business Strategies* (1984).

Porter, M. E., "Changing Patterns of International Competition," in *The Competitive Challenge: Strategies for Industrial Innovation and Renewal,* ed. J. D. Teece (Cambridge, MA: Ballinger, 1987), 27–58.

Chapter 7

MANAGING STRATEGIC ALLIANCES

Strategic alliances have recently grown in popularity, especially among multinational corporations.[1] A wide range of cooperative arrangements is covered by the term *strategic alliance,* including franchising and contract- and asset-based joint ventures. Some of these are based on formal contracts, while others are not; some are limited to a specific project, while others are more enduring. A number of potential benefits have been attributed to these cooperative arrangements, including access to new markets, access to know-how and contacts, and risk reduction.[2] For firms that do not have many of the distinctive competencies that are required to compete successfully in their chosen business niche, a strategic alliance can strengthen or diversify their competencies. It can also reduce the lead time and resources that are required to build these competencies.

We focus our attention in this chapter on a specific type of strategic alliance: long-term joint ventures that are established through formal contracts. We describe three important aspects of the strategy process required to manage such an alliance:

1. The delineation of the strategic rationale(s) for a joint venture, and the reconciliation of it with the business objectives of the two parents.
2. The step-wise process of forming a joint venture.
3. The process of managing a joint venture.

We recognize that the strategy process described here for a long-term joint venture may not be directly applicable to other types of strategic alliances, such as licensing or franchising arrangements and project-based joint ventures. However, it is beyond the scope of this chapter to address each alliance separately. We hope that the reader is able to extend the framework provided here to other types of strategic alliances.

THE RATIONALES FOR A STRATEGIC ALLIANCE

Figure 7-1 portrays the value chains of the business units of two prospective partners. There are three basic types of strategic alliances that are possible between the
two firms, each with a distinct rationale.[3] When describing these rationales, we
relate our discussion to Figure 3-2 in Chapter 3 in order to point out the distinct
strategy processes that are required by different types of alliances.

The first type of strategic alliance, Type 1, seeks to combine the upstream
know-how of one business with the downstream strengths of the prospective ally.
The benefit of such an alliance would be to gain insight and access to the partner's
technological and manufacturing know-how or to benefit from the partner's established position in the marketplace.

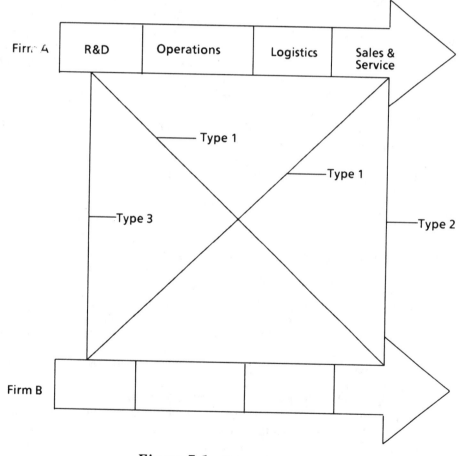

Figure 7-1   **Types of Alliances**

Typically a Type 1 strategic alliance is associated with a Pioneer or Reorient business context. The two parties may either seek to go after a new business niche or reorient themselves in a difficult business context by pooling their diverse competencies. The strategic intent for a Type 1 alliance is risk sharing and resource conservation. Depending on the business context prompting this type of alliance, the planning orientation within it will be one of either adaptation, as in a Pioneer context, or selective adaptation, as in a Reorient context. Many MNCs use a Type 1 alliance to explore a new national market. The long-standing alliance between Xerox and Fuji started out this way. Another example of a Type 1 alliance used in a Reorient context would be that attempted by Dunlop and Pirelli in the tire industry. The marketing capabilities of the former were intended to complement the operations and R&D capabilities of the latter, and the alliance was designed to shore up the sagging competitive positions of both firms.

The second type of strategic alliance, Type 2, combines the downstream activities of the two cooperating firms. It may call for the merging of their product lines and sales/service channels. The alliance may thus be able to offer a broader product line and provide systemic solutions to customers of both parents. This is especially important when the firms operate in a business environment with high complexity. The consolidation of customers and the strengthening of market share may help the joint venture reduce the heterogeneity of its stakeholders and assess their expectations with better certainty.

An example of this type of alliance is that between Chrysler and Alfa Romeo involving the distribution of the latter's top-of-the-line cars through select Chrysler dealers. Because the primary motivation behind this type of an alliance is not to diversify competencies but rather to manage environmental uncertainty through the pooling of similar competencies, this is especially appropriate in an Expand business context.

In a Type 3 strategic alliance, the operational capabilities of the two partners are combined to exploit economies of scale. A Type 3 alliance also may seek to combine the research and development capabilities of the two prospective partners.[4] Important complementary technologies are made available to the cooperating firms through such an alliance. A good example of this type of alliance is the one attempted by GTE and United Telecom in the U.S. long-distance telecommunications market. Their joint venture was intended to exploit economies of scope in their technological capabilities. Another example is the alliance between General Motors and Toyota in their NUMMI venture. The cooperating parties in a Type 3 alliance seek primarily to consolidate and deepen their strengths in a well-established niche. This type of alliance is popular in a Dominate business context.

Although for purposes of illustration each of the three types of alliances has been discussed as a pure form, in reality there can be multiple motives. Moreover, as some[5] have argued, an important motive for a cooperative arrangement may be neither the pooling of competencies nor the reduction of environmental complexity, but rather the transfer of competencies. This is especially a problem in a Type 3 alliance, where the cooperating firms have the base from which they can quickly absorb the other's know-how. If the benefits from the alliance are perceived to be unequal, with one partner standing to lose its unique know-how to the other, adequate safeguards will have to be negotiated during the alliance formation process.

THE PROCESS OF ALLIANCE FORMATION

There are four critical activities in the formation of a joint venture (see Figure 7-2): (1) ensuring that the venture has the support of key stakeholders, (2) sharing the overriding premises for cooperation with one's partner and articulating the win/win benefits from the joint venture, (3) selling the joint venture to key members at all levels of the participating organizations, and (4) specifying strategic plans and implementation responsibilities within the joint venture.[6] The first two activities constitute the preliminary, or "dating," phase of venture formation, and the latter two activities belong to the negotiation phase.

The first activity in the dating phase is to ensure that the prospective partners will be mutually acceptable to the firm's key stakeholders. The senior managers of the cooperating firms are clearly important stakeholders. Good personal chemistry between these senior managers is a precondition for a successful joint venture. It is equally important that the owners of the two firms also see the alliance in a positive

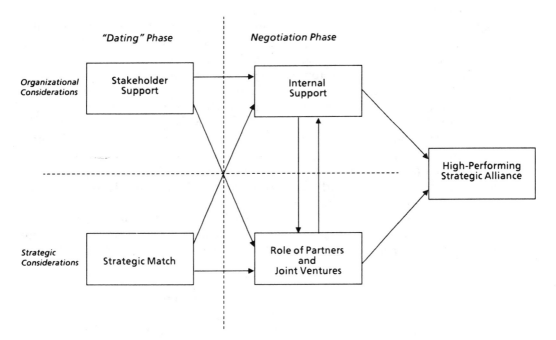

Figure 7-2   **A Conceptual Framework for the Strategic Alliance Formation Process**

light. The preferences of the major stockholders of both parents must be assessed early in the dating phase to avoid expensive cancellations later on.

The second activity in the dating phase calls for an analysis of the strategic fit between the prospective partners. The purpose of this exercise is to ensure that a clear win/win prospect exists for *both* partners. The overall strategy of the joint venture—including the products that will be sold, target markets, target customers, modes of competing, and key competitors—must be broadly assessed up front. It is important that the partners agree on a common strategic thrust for the joint venture. For example, in a recent joint venture between a U.S. chemicals company and a Japanese partner, it was never made clear what role the joint venture would play in exports to other East Asian and Southeast Asian countries. The U.S. parent had other joint venture partners in neighboring countries, and the resulting confusion in the marketplace caused it to abandon its Japanese joint venture. This type of a problem is especially likely when either of the two partners seeks different types of alliances or, even worse, when one partner unilaterally assumes a dominant role in the partnership, ignoring the strategic interests of the other.

The basic outcomes of the dating phase should be the following: (1) an agreement on how the partners can complement each other, (2) an understanding of how the joint venture supports the business strategies of the cooperating firms, and (3) how each of these business strategies fit within the corporate portfolio strategies of the partners.

The third phase in the strategic alliance formation process is the full-scale negotiation phase. There are two activities that are associated with this phase—testing the internal support for the joint venture at various levels in both firms and delineating a preliminary business plan for the joint venture.

It is important that the top management teams of the cooperating firms inform key members of their organizations about the prospective joint venture early, even though no agreement may have been reached. Several of these key managers should be drawn into the task forces charged with analyzing the proposed joint venture. This early buy-in and the establishment of multiple points of contact between the cooperating firms are important to the eventual success of a joint venture.[7] Also, it is desirable that managers who are likely to be assigned to the joint venture be identified early and allowed to participate in the delineation of the joint venture's management routines.

The fourth activity in Figure 7-2 is the delineation of the roles of the partners in the joint venture. The partners should discuss as part of this activity how the joint venture will be managed and controlled between them, including the following issues:

1. The exact ownership structure of the joint venture.
2. The legal liabilities of the partners.
3. The staffing of the joint venture.
4. The physical location of the venture.
5. The financial obligations of the partners.

Although the four activities are necessary in all three types of strategic alliances, their relative importance varies with each type.

Type 1 Strategic Alliance

In the previous section, we discussed that in this type of an alliance, the cooperating firms seek to diversify and complement their competencies, so as to establish a balanced capability in all activities of a business unit's value chain. Finding such a strategic match is not easy. A Type 1 alliance typically needs a long dating phase, when several possible "suitors" may have to be "dated," before the partners can be convinced of the appropriateness of the alliance from a strategic and an organizational point of view.

The negotiation phase is also likely to be long, since the two partners would be intricately tied operationally. The independent functional departments of the two firms will have to be coordinated very closely if their complementary competencies have to be leveraged effectively. Specifying the role of each partner inside and outside the joint venture and mobilizing internal support within the cooperating organizations to subscribe to this specification can be time consuming.

Paradoxically the typical business context in which such an alliance is to be found—that is, Pioneer or Reorient—does not allow for an extended dating or negotiating phase. Potential partners faced with these contexts also seek urgent actions. Alliances out of desperation are therefore not uncommon, and their subsequent failure is also not very surprising.

Type 2 Strategic Alliance

In this alliance, the two partners seek to supplement their competencies in sales and service. Because of their many similarities, the partners are likely to know each other and can therefore establish a strategic match and stakeholder support in a relatively short dating phase. The negotiation phase can also be short since the primary purpose of this type of alliance is to rationalize the product offerings and sales logistics of the two partners. It does not call for the sharing of competencies that would be otherwise difficult to imitate, as in the case of a Type 3 alliance.

Type 3 Strategic Alliance

The alliance formation process for this type is similar to the one discussed for Type 2. However, the negotiation phase may have to be long. Both partners would want to protect their R&D and operational competencies from being absorbed by the other. Since they are similarly endowed, they have the basis on which to learn the other's competencies. Crafting contracts that provide acceptable safeguards to the two partners and yet allow for the pooling of their competencies can be time consuming. Building internal support for the joint venture within the two cooperating firms can also be a slow process. For example, when

Rolm and IBM attempted this type of an alliance, seeking to supplement the telecommunications know-how of the former with the computers know-how of the latter, the mistrust between the employees of the two firms did not allow for the desired pooling of their competencies. Eventually the two partners had to resort to a full-fledged merger.

MANAGING A STRATEGIC ALLIANCE

Once a strategic alliance is established, the process of managing it depends on the type of alliance that it represents (see Figure 7-3). As we discussed in the previous section, the mission of a strategic alliance differs with each type of alliance. In a Type 1 alliance, the joint venture has a clear business mission: either to pioneer a new business niche or to strengthen an existing niche. In a Type 2 alliance and Type 3 alliance, the joint venture is not a stand-alone business unit but rather a shared functional department. Consequently it has no business goals of its own. Its role is primarily to provide the needed functional support.

The strategy process used by the two parents must first be synchronized: Their objectives-setting, strategic programming, and strategic budgeting steps must take place in a common time frame.

In a Type 1 alliance, given the centrality of the joint venture to the business interests of the cooperating firms, it must be heavily involved in all the steps of the strategy-making process used by the two parents. The joint venture is viewed as a business unit belonging to both parents. Therefore, apart from the interactions between the parents and the management team of the joint venture, there is also a need for the two parents themselves to interact closely when defining the goals for the joint venture and when approving its strategic programs and budgets. A convenient administrative arrangement for doing this would be to establish for the joint venture a separate management board representing both partners. Over time, as the trust between the partners grows, this management board will become increasingly autonomous from the two parents, except on broad policy matters.

In a Type 2 alliance or Type 3 alliance, by contrast, the joint venture is viewed as a shared strategic program and not as a shared business unit. Consequently the joint venture is brought into the strategy process of the two parents only in the strategic programming and strategic budgeting steps. However, in a Type 2 strategic alliance, it may be useful to invite the management team of the joint venture to participate in the objectives-setting step of the two parents. Because the aim of this alliance is to manage environmental complexity, any assumptions made about it by the parents should be verified with the joint venture.

The basis of judging the joint venture's performance follows from the above description. In a Type 1 alliance, it is judged as a business unit by yardsticks that are appropriate to its context (see Part II for a discussion). In a Type 2 alliance or Type 3 alliance, it is judged more as a strategic program contributing to the goals of its parents.

Strategy Process	Strategic Alliance			
	Type 1		**Type 2**	**Type 3**
1 Shared intent	Pioneer new business. Pool complementary competencies.	Reorient and explore alternate niches. Pool complementary competencies.	Support business expansion by the parents. Provide economies of scope.	Support business domination by the parents. Provide economies of scale.
2 Involvement of the j.v. in the strategy-making process of the parents:				
• Objectives setting	Heavy	Heavy	Moderate	—
• Strategic programming	Heavy	Heavy	Heavy	Heavy
• Budgeting	Heavy	Heavy	Heavy	Heavy
3 Basis of judging the j.v.'s performance	Stand-alone business unit; strategic intent: Pioneer	Stand-alone business unit; strategic intent: Reorient	As a strategic program contributing to the business goals of the parents	As a strategic program contributing to the business goals of the parents

Figure 7-3   The Strategy Process for Managing a Joint Venture

SUMMARY

In this chapter, we extended the framework developed in Part II to the management of strategic alliances. We described three generic types of joint ventures: Type 1, between firms seeking to complement their competencies in upstream or downstream activities of their business units' value chain; Type 2, between firms seeking to supplement their strengths in sales and service capabilities; and Type 3, between firms seeking to deepen their upstream strengths in R&D and operations. The process through which each of these alliances should be formed varies, and we discussed how such a tailoring can be done. We also suggested how different types of joint ventures should be managed after they have been established. Although we recognize that this short chapter cannot do justice to the vast domain of strategic alliances, we wanted to demonstrate here that the framework developed in Part II can be adapted to the special context of a strategic alliance.

NOTES

1. F. Contractor and P. Lorange, eds., *Cooperative Strategies in International Business* (Lexington, MA: Lexington Books, 1988).
2. P. Lorange, "Creating Win-Win Strategies for Joint Ventures," *The CTC Reporter,* Center for Transnational Corporations, United Nations, New York, 1990.
3. Ibid.
4. L. Hakansson and P. Lorange, "R&D-Based Cooperative Ventures," in L. Mattsson and G. Stymne (eds.), *Corporate and Industry Strategies for Europe,* in press.
5. C. K. Prahalad and Y. Doz, "Collaborate with Your Competitors and Win," *Harvard Business Review* 67 (Jan.–Feb. 1989): 133.
6. P. Lorange and J. Roos, *Strategic Alliances: Formation, Implementation, Evolution* Cambridge, MA: Basil Blackwell, in press); and J. Roos, "The Cooperative Venture Formation Process: Characteristics and Impact on Performance" (Doctoral dissertation, Institute of International Business, Stockholm School of Economics in Stockholm, Sweden, 1989).
7. P. Lorange, "Cooperative Strategies: Some Experiences of U.S. Corporations," in *Advances in Strategic Management,* vol. 6 (Greenwich, CT: JAI Press, 1990), 1–29.

REFERENCES

Perlmutter, H. V., "Building the Symbiotic Societal Enterprise," *World Futures* 19 (1984): 271–284.

———, and E. Trist, "Paradigms for Societal Transition," *Human Relations* 39 (Jan. 1986): 1–27.

Pfeffer, J., and P. Nowak, "Joint Ventures and Interorganizational Interdependence," *Administrative Science Quarterly* 21 (1976): 398–414.

Porter, M. E., and M. B. Fuller, "Coalitions and Global Strategy," in *Competition in Global Industries,* ed. M. E. Porter (Boston: Harvard Business School Press, 1986), 315–343.

Teece, D. J., "Profiting from Technological Innovation: Implications for Integration, Collaboration, Licensing, and Public Policy," in *The Competitive Challenge: Strategies for*

Industrial Innovation and Renewal, ed. D. J. Teece (Cambridge, MA: Ballinger, 1987), 185–220.

———, "Transactions Cost Economics and the Multinational Enterprise," *Journal of Economic Behavior and Organization* 7 (Mar. 1986): 21–45.

Elkem

The Elkem Group was a worldwide market leader in the ferroalloys industry and one of Norway's largest industrial companies, with 1984 revenues of 7.8 billion Norwegian Kroner[1] (NOK) ($1.02 billion) and 10,000 employees. The firm had approximately 30 production units worldwide; in addition, it had cooperative agreements and strategic alliances to secure vital raw materials and obtain market positions in various international markets. Exhibit 1 shows Elkem's organization chart.

During the 1970s, Elkem underwent a period of rapid expansion, but the worldwide recession of the late 1970s and early 1980s plunged the firm into its first financial losses. This led to a major retrenchment and revamping of the business portfolio. See Exhibit 2 for the profit contributions by each business division and Exhibit 3 for the company's consolidated balance sheet.

As Kaspar Kielland, the Chief Executive Officer of Elkem, reviewed these environmental shifts in early 1985, he enumerated the following goals:

> Our number one corporate goal today is to improve the financial position of the firm. That is an overriding corporate goal, and is brought into all strategic discussions we have. Second, we want to improve our breakeven point. Our third overall goal is to become less vulnerable to cyclicality, building on our position as a dominant ferroalloys producer to help stabilize prices. And our fourth dimension is the development of managers who will be internationally oriented, and who can cope with the problems we will face in the future.

Exhibit 1   **Elkem's Organization Chart**

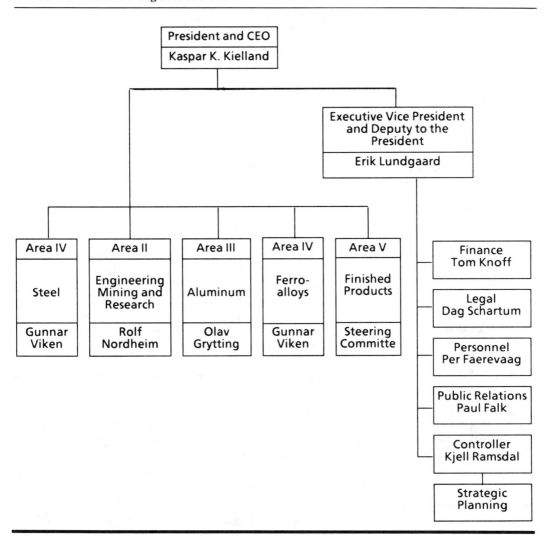

A BRIEF HISTORY

In 1904, Sam Eyde, a Norwegian industrial pioneer, founded Elkem to utilize hydroelectric power for industrial purposes. Elkem originally was a research and development company, and its core business was developing and marketing technology, primarily for the aluminum and smelting industries. Elkem became a major

Exhibit 2 **Sales and Financial Results by Division (in NOK million)**

Gross Sales	1984	1983	1982	1981	1980
Ferroalloys	4,317	2,748	2,224	1,670	975
Aluminum	1,401	1,112	784	862	755
Steel	1,069	1,117	1,174	1,201	1,356
Engineering	318	280	237	243	157
Mining	162	219	230	240	272
Allied products	553	623	705	653	442
Microsilica	40	18	10	5	3
Total	7,860	6,117	5,364	4,874	3,960

Income Before Extra-ordinary Items	1984	1983	1982	1981	1980
Ferroalloys	328	95	(143)	(44)	47
Aluminum	238	115	(52)	4	160
Steel	(35)	1	(74)	(68)	(36)
Engineering	2	3	6	(24)	(23)
Mining	7	(8)	(26)	(31)	(3)
Allied products	37	14	37	(11)	5
Microsilica	(72)	(52)	(72)	(17)	—
Oil	21	(9)	21	6	5
Total	526	159	(311)	(185)	155

supplier of furnaces and other production equipment. It soon established a reputation for its furnace design, engineering, and technology. One of its key innovations was the Soederberg continuous electrode, created in 1917 and still used in many smelting furnaces. In 1917, Elkem acquired its first ferroalloys production facility, Fiskaa Verk in southern Norway, and this facility served as a pilot plant for developing and testing processes and techniques. Elkem gradually expanded into the production of metals and alloys, mining, and finished products, growing at a slow, steady pace and selling primarily to the Norwegian market until the 1950s.

During the 1950s and 1960s, the pace of growth quickened, as Elkem added capacity and became one of Norway's largest industrial concerns. Although its businesses were subject to cyclical swings, its income growth was steady, and the company was able to utilize its strong financial resources to fund this growth internally.

During the next two decades, the company diversified and expanded primarily in Norway, where it acquired or built a number of ferroalloys plants and became involved in aluminum smelting, mining, and manufacturing finished products. A particularly important development was the cooperation, which began in the early 1960s, between Elkem and Alcoa, the leading producer of aluminum in the United States. Elkem and Alcoa were co-owners (55 percent and 45 percent, respectively)

Exhibit 3   **Consolidated Balance Sheets (in NOK million)**

	1980	1981	1982	1983	1984
Fixed assets					
Tangible assets	1,861	2,406	2,366	2,221	3,096
Investment	212	202	199	203	369
	2,073	2,608	2,565	2,424	3,465
Long-term debtors	173	208	250	351	230
Current assets					
Stocks and work in progress	1,040	1,605	1,475	1,361	2,308
Debtors	892	1,207	1,039	1,394	1,656
Cash	129	244	195	317	575
	2,061	3,056	2,709	3,072	4,539
Current liabilities					
Creditors	888	1,218	1,319	1,533	2,992
Bank overdrafts	242	403	446	299	492
	1,130	1,621	1,765	1,832	2,484
Net current assets	931	1,435	944	1,240	2,055
Long-term liabilities	1,379	2,435	2,410	2,511	3,463
Minority interests	1	21	1	2	220
Conditional tax free funds	856	881	717	729	1,037
Net assets	941	926	631	773	1,030
Shareholders' equity					
Share capital	385	480	495	493	595
Reserves	556	446	136	280	435
	941	926	631	773	1,030

of two aluminum smelters in Norway, and Elkem also had a 25 percent interest in Alcoa's two aluminum-fabricating plants in Wales and the Netherlands.

Another major event in Elkem's Norwegian expansion occurred in 1972, when Elkem merged with Christiania Spigerverk, a steel and ferroalloys producer. This merger made Elkem Norway's largest ferroalloys producer. During the 1970s, Elkem also acquired two mini–steel mills in the United Kingdom, entered a joint venture for ferrosilicon production in Iceland, and entered into negotiations with Union Carbide to purchase its U.S. ferroalloys division.

By the late 1970s, Elkem had become much more international in scope, with

Exhibit 4   **Sales by Markets (1979–1983)**

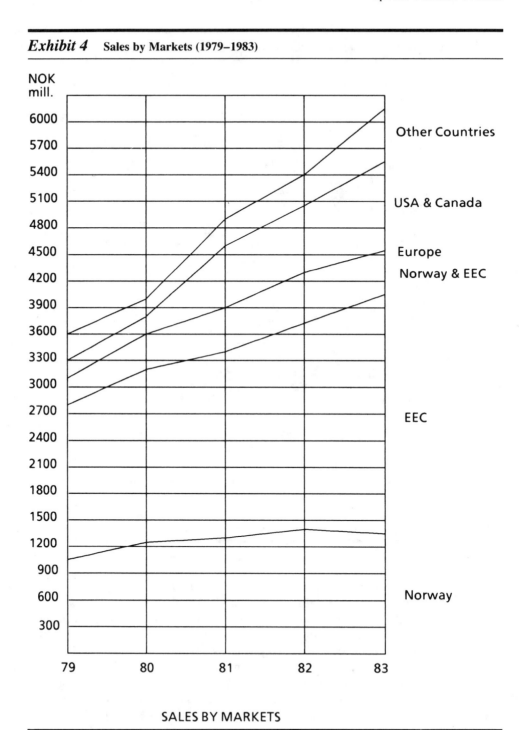

NOK
mill.

6000 — Other Countries

5700

5400

5100 — USA & Canada

4800

4500 — Europe
        Norway & EEC
4200

3900

3600

3300

3000

2700 — EEC

2400

2100

1800

1500

1200

900

600 — Norway

300

79   80   81   82   83

SALES BY MARKETS

Exhibit 5   **Earnings per Share (1972–1983)**

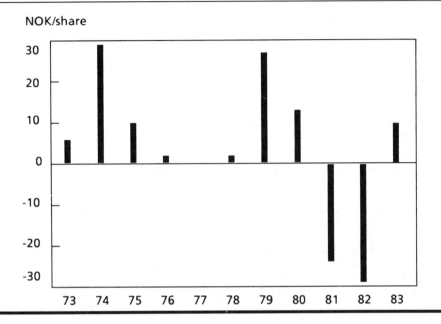

NOK/share

72 percent of its 1979 sales occurring outside Norway. See Exhibit 4 for Elkem's sales by markets. This same decade saw the world economy become subject to much wider cyclical swings than it had in the preceding twenty years, and these swings led to volatility in many of Elkem's key product/markets and weakened the company's financial stability. These swings were reflected in Elkem's earnings per share during the period (Exhibit 5).

The early 1980s were a period of dramatic structural change for Elkem. The years 1981 and 1982 were marked by major economic upheaval. At this time, a major portfolio reorganization and consolidation was undertaken. Elkem reduced ownership of, sold, or closed over 30 projects and businesses, cutting employment by 30 percent and eliminating $10 million in annual losses and $30 million in annual costs. Selected acquisitions were made, the foremost being the acquisition of Union Carbide's ferroalloys division and research facility in the United States, with options to buy the Canadian ferroalloys division. This option was exercised in July 1984. Exhibit 6 is a listing of the major portfolio changes from 1980 to 1983.

Kielland said the following about the rationale behind these steps in restructuring Elkem's portfolio:

> We had believed, as many companies did, that we could go into virtually anything and make money. I think we came to realize that you have to structure your company around a few basic ideas. The basic ideas we structured around are:

Exhibit 6   **Portfolio Changes (1980–1983)**

Several strategic decisions were taken after 1980 to change Elkem's structure. The most important decisons were the following:

Increased Activities

Bought Union Carbide's ferroalloys activities including the research facility at Niagara Falls	(1981)
Established Elkem Chemicals (development and marketing of microsilica technology)	(1982)
Bought 6 percent interest in Comilog, a manganese ore producer	(1983)
Bought 50 percent of the Tana quartz mine	(1983)

Reduced or Redirected Involvements

Withdrew from Fesil, a marketing organization for ferroalloys	(1980)
Reduced ownership in Norsk Glassfiber (fiberglass) from 60 percent to 30 percent	(1980)
Sold share in A/S Saga Petrokjemi & Co.	(1980)
Ceased production of iron ore concentrates at the Roedsand Mines	(1981)
Ceased pig-iron production at Bremanger	(1982)
Nordic cooperation on nuts-and-bolt production. The Elkem unit, Fonas, is transferred to Bulten AB, in which Elkem has an ownership share	(1982)
Sold TrioVing to Waertsila OY	(1983)
Mining rights at Sulitjelma Gruber A/A transferred back to the State	(1983)
Nordic cooperation on steel wire rope production. Elkem's unit Staal og Tau merged with the units of Norsk Jernverk and Gunnebo AB.	(1983)

- a superior technology or know-how;
- a solid base for critical raw materials;
- a dominant market position, either geographically or in market niches;
- strong management praxis.

By 1983, the changes began to yield positive results. Elkem had a larger earnings base, an increased base in electrical power, an increased metallurgical competence, and a stronger international position. These factors, coupled with an improved world economy, contributed to Elkem's improved financial results. Elkem was again posting a profit, and a stock offering made in December 1983 was oversubscribed.

ELKEM'S ENERGY BASE

Throughout Elkem's history, its energy base had been a critical resource. Kielland said this about its importance:

> All the production in which we're engaged is based on one major factor. In fact, if you were to ask me what the driving force is in our company, I would give only one: Our

Exhibit 7   **Elkem's Energy Base**

Operation	Total Power Requirement (GWb)	Captive Power	Long-term Contracts
Aluminum plants, Norway	3,200	0	3,200
Ferroalloy plants, Norway	3,800	2,050	1,500
Ferroalloy plants, U.S.	2,650	2,000	650
Ferroalloy plants, Iceland	480	0	480
Steel and other activities, Norway	330	0	330

ability to convert electrical energy to metallurgical products. All other things we have done have been based on that ability. All our products are based on a high use of energy. It's our number one resource.

Elkem obtained most of the electrical power for its production facilities from either its own hydroelectric plants ("captive power") or from long-term contracts at favorable rates. The captive plants, especially, were of immense importance to the firm, both as a guaranteed source of energy and as a valuable resource in themselves. Elkem's energy sources and the relative advantage Elkem enjoyed in energy costs are illustrated in Exhibit 7.

As noted, Elkem was primarily a producer of ferroalloys, aluminum, and steel, and it continues to develop and market metallurgical technology. The Elkem Group in 1984 was organized into five business areas: ferroalloys; aluminum; steel; finished products; and engineering, mining, and research (see Exhibit 1). Of these areas, ferroalloys and aluminum produced the greatest cumulative contribution to total income during the ten-year period from 1973 to 1982. See Exhibit 8 for the cumulative ten-year results by division.

ELKEM'S MAJOR BUSINESS AREAS

Ferroalloys

Since its acquisition of the ferroalloys division of Union Carbide in 1981, Elkem had become the world's largest producer of ferroalloys, with a worldwide market share of between 10 percent and 25 percent for major product groups. What also was significant in this regard was the fact that the next-largest competitor in each of its major products segments was represented by a different firm. Elkem had a particu-

Exhibit 8   **Cumulative Net Income by Division (1973–1982)**

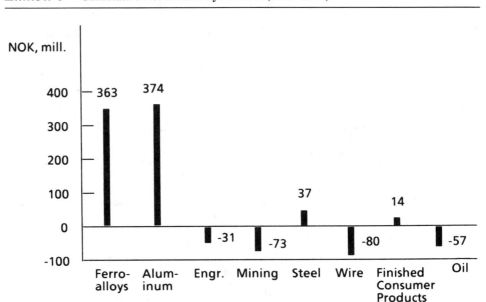

larly strong position in two of the world's largest markets, Europe and North America, and had a significant entry into the third largest market, Japan.

Elkem's competitive energy base was a key to its success. Also helping Elkem to attain dominance was the integration of production, marketing, and technology. For example, its engineering division installed between 50 percent and 60 percent of the world's ferroalloys electric smelting furnaces. Elkem utilized this customer base in its sales of electrode paste, an important consumable in such furnaces. Elkem was the world market leader in electrode paste.

The acquisition of Union Carbide's ferroalloys business changed and increased Elkem's emphasis on ferroalloys dramatically. The production capacity changes are summarized in Table 1.

The worldwide ferroalloys business was organized into two divisions. The first was the Ferroalloys Divisions, headquartered in Oslo, Norway (wholly owned), with business responsibility for all of the world except North America. The second was Elkem Metals Company (EMC), headquartered in Pittsburgh, Pennsylvania (49 percent Elkem ownership[2]), with business responsibility for North America.

Elkem also owned 45 percent of a modern ferroalloys plant in Iceland, the output of which was marketed by Elkem. Even though Elkem did not have majority ownership in the Icelandic operations, its management agreements give it a substantial say in the choice of strategy.

Table 1   **Elkem's Production Capacity of Major Ferroalloys Product Groups**

	Production Capacity (thousand tons)	
	Before 1981	After 1981
Ferrosilicon	165	350
Silicon metal	55	130
Manganese alloys	160	590
Other ferroalloys	0	125
Calcium carbide	0	110

The ferroalloys group's main products with their served markets are shown in Table 2.

Ferroalloys were used primarily as additives in metallurgical industries. The primary users were steel producers and foundries (75 percent of world demand), and the aluminum and chemical industries accounted for most of the remainder. Elkem's product range was dominated by standard, commoditylike products. Elkem sought to upgrade a significant part of its production to specialty products in order to increase margins and stabilize demand.

The demand for ferroalloys was affected by basic steel production, which had shrunk significantly in North America and Europe from a decade earlier. However, ferroalloys were used extensively in specialty steel products, and these products were enjoying relatively greater usage. Industrial trends pointed to fewer, more concentrated ferroalloys-manufacturing units, which would face increasing competition from new government-subsidized manufacturing units from developing countries. The ferrosilicon market bottomed out in 1982. The fall to this low point was due to overcapacity and declining levels of steel production. In 1983, prices increased 20 to 30 percent and demand grew again, although slowly.

The company produced a wide range of silicon metal grades. The majority of Elkem's silicon metal was sold to the aluminum industry, where it was used as an alloying agent, while 30 percent was sold to the chemical industry, where it was the basis of silicone rubber compounds and other silicone products. A growing market for silicon was the data-processing industry. Silicon was the basic material in the

Table 2   **Major Product Types, Raw Materials Inputs, and Markets**

Product	Main Raw Material	Main Market (industries)
Silicon metal	Quartz	Chemicals and aluminum
Ferrosilicon	Quartz	Steel and foundry
Manganese alloys	Manganese ore	Steel and foundry

manufacture of silicon chips and other electronics components. Elkem estimated that it currently supplied approximately 50 percent of the silicon used in silicon chips in the Western world, and the demand for silicon was expected to grow. New applications were expected to create additional demand. Elkem allocated substantial resources to maintain a strong economic and technological position in the market. Silicon production was energy intensive, so Elkem concentrated its production primarily in Norway to utilize its captive power base there.

Elkem discussed joint ventures with producers of silicon metal in certain developing countries, such as Brazil. Its advanced technology and global marketing network complemented the natural resources (hydroelectric power, pure quartz, and other raw materials) of these countries.

The manganese alloy market had been subject to large overcapacity and price pressure. Another important factor in this business was to secure an assured supply of ore at competitive prices. To assure ore supplies and prices, Elkem acquired 6 percent of Comilog, a mining corporation that produced its ore in Gabon. This company was also owned by the government of Gabon, French interests, and U.S. Steel. This cooperative agreement reduced dependency on manganese ore from South Africa, the major supplier.

Ferroalloys production caused potential environmental pollution problems. This led to increased costs due to pollution-control requirements. These filtration technologies in turn created new opportunities—microsilica, a byproduct of cleaning gases from furnaces, turned out to have substantial potential economic value as an additive raw material for other industries. Elkem devoted substantial resources to developing this product and new applications for its use.

In summary, Elkem felt that it had the following major competitive strengths in the ferroalloys business area.

Energy. As noted, nearly all of Elkem's power requirements were provided either by its own power stations or through long-term contracts on competitive terms. In the United States, Elkem was the only producer of ferroalloys with its own power stations.

Raw Materials. The Norwegian plants obtained the high-quality quartz needed to produce silicon from a quartz mine in Spain, in which Elkem had an indirect 16.5 percent interest, and through the ownership of three quartzite quarries in Norway. Manganese ore was partly secured through Comilog.

Technology. Elkem's engineering, mining, and research resources helped maintain Elkem's technological leadership in engineering design, product development, and process control.

Marketing. Elkem had a worldwide marketing network with sales offices in 8 countries and some 37 agents in 27 other countries.

Table 3   **Overall Consumptions, Elkem's Sales, and Market Shares**

	Estimated Western World Consumption (in thousands of tons)	Elkem Sales (in thousands of tons)	Elkem's Sales as a Percentage of Western World Consumption	Largest Competitor's Market Share (%)
Silicon	415	105	25	10
Ferrosilicon	1,900	250	13	6
Ferromanganese	2,400	187	8	10
Silicomanganese	1,100	201	18	15
Refined manganese alloys	445	119	27	10
Electrode paste	430	120	28	8

These figures were estimates prepared by Elkem, based on latest available published statistics, in most cases for 1983.

There were a relatively small number of globally significant competitors in the ferroalloys industry. A major competitor was a French multinational corporation, Pechiney, which had a capacity slightly less than Elkem's but was known for its emphasis on the upper end of the market, its high quality, and its sophisticated product development. Another large competitor was a sales cartel of Norwegian ferroalloys producers, K/S Fesil. This consortium consisted of a handful of producers who had a joint sales and marketing effort. They played quite an active role in the world market and were known for their aggressive pricing policy.

Elkem's market share in the different products had grown over the years. Table 3 illustrates Elkem's position in the silicon, ferroalloys, and electrode paste markets in 1984.

Even though many Elkem managers felt that the strategic direction of the firm was satisfactory, many others were concerned that shared critical strategic challenges remained unresolved in the ferroalloys division. The changes in the ferroalloys industry had been dramatic, revealing the following issues for Elkem:

1. Recessionary trends in several of Elkem's key markets. There were questions whether demand growth would ever return to the historical high or whether Elkem would be faced with a dramatic "maturing" of its business.
2. Changing conditions in the steel industry, the primary user sector of ferroalloys. These included the following:
   a. Reduced demand due to economic conditions
   b. Reduced demand due to substitution from other product in key industries—for example, aluminum and plastics in the automotive industry
   c. Shift in steel production from Elkem's traditional markets in the Western World and Japan to Third World countries
   d. Shifts in steel production processes, toward minimills, requiring less ferroalloys

3. Changes within the ferroalloys industry. These included the following:
   a. Overcapacity in major product categories, especially ferrosilicon and manganese alloys
   b. Migration of production to Third World countries
   c. Depressed prices for ferroalloys, caused in part by subsidized new production capacity that was coming from Third World countries

Although the Union Carbide acquisition gave Elkem a dominant position in ferroalloys, problems in the industry made it a difficult challenge to capitalize on the advantages that such a position would normally confer. With any such acquisition, it was often a major undertaking both to integrate the acquisition into the present organization and to take advantage of the synergistic effects of such a large merger. This integrating effort was even more difficult due to its occurrence at a time when Elkem was (1) posting significant operating losses amidst heavy downward pressure on its stock price; (2) undergoing extensive portfolio shifts in several sectors; (3) facing severe adverse market conditions in several business groups; and (4) instituting cost-cutting and rationalization measures in several areas.

Aluminum

Elkem, in a joint venture with Alcoa, produced primary aluminum at two smelters in Norway, and it had a 25 percent interest in two aluminum-fabricating plants in Wales and the Netherlands.

The Elkem/Alcoa cooperation in Norway was organized as a general partnership called Mosal Aluminum, A/S & Co. Elkem was the managing partner and majority owner (55 percent) of Mosal—which owns Mosjoen Aluminiumverk, with an annual production capacity of 90,000 tons, and Lista Aluminiumverk, with an annual production capacity of 80,000 tons. As managing partner, Elkem was responsible for the operation of the two smelters and for the marketing and sale of the metal produced. The plants in Wales and the Netherlands fabricated part of the primary aluminum from Norway into extrusions and rolled sheet products. It provided a stable outlet for almost half the annual output of the smelters. The remainder was sold to other fabricators, mainly in Europe.

The production of aluminum was particularly energy intensive. Of the major aluminum-producing countries, only Canada had lower electrical power costs than Norway. Elkem obtained the power to operate the smelters on favorable long-term contracts with the Norwegian State power authority. These contracts, which with one small exception ran through 2006, secured virtually all the smelters' energy requirements at low power costs. These arrangements provided the firm with exceptional security of supply compared with that of many of its foreign competitors. The cooperation with Alcoa ensured that Elkem would rely on Alcoa for a stable supply of alumina, which is the most important raw material in aluminum production. In addition, this cooperation gave each partner access to the other's technology.

An extensive five-year modernization program was initiated for Mosjoen, the older of the two smelters. The modernization was budgeted to cost approximately 1,200 million NOK, with Elkem's share of the costs amounting to 660 million NOK. Production would be gradually increased, and the improvements were designed to reduce energy consumption, increase productivity, and enable a higher-quality metal to be produced.

It was an important part of the strategy of the aluminum division to maximize the value added to the metal. Most of the aluminum produced by Mosal was in the form of extrusion billets and rolling slabs produced to customer specifications regarding dimension and alloy; these had higher added value and commanded a premium above the ingot price.

The aluminum market experienced a period of weak prices and demand in 1981 and 1982, but it strengthened in 1983 as the world economy picked up. However, aluminum prices, formerly influenced by producers, were increasingly established on the London Metal Exchange, and therefore they were more subject to outside factors and increased volatility. This had accelerated the strategy of maximizing value added through the production of semifinished and finished products.

Steel

In the steel sector, Elkem operated three steel minimills—one each in Oslo, Manchester, and Liverpool. The economies of these minimills differed from those of the large, integrated steel mills because the minimills were more flexible and were located close to their served markets. Elkem's units were relatively efficient; substantial rationalizations undertaken in the early 1980s made the steel area profitable as of 1983.

The product spectrum was relatively simple, consisting of billet, wire rod, and reinforcement bar, primarily for the local construction industry. All three steel works used similar raw materials, scrap metals, and electrical furnace production equipment.

Elkem agreed to sell its steel-making business in Norway to Norsk Jernverk A/S, the Norwegian state-owned steel company. Under this agreement, Elkem received payments of 270 million NOK and a 20 percent interest in Norsk Jernverk A/S; this interest will be carried in Elkem's balance sheet at a nominal value.

In May 1985, Elkem sold its interests in the Manchester and Liverpool steel-producing operations to Allied Steel and Wire (Holdings) Limited, a U.K. company. As a consequence, Elkem received a 3.5 percent interest in Allied Steel and Wire and also a cash compensation of 3.7 million British pounds.

Finished Products

The finished products sector consisted of a number of wholly owned, majority-owned, and minority-owned holdings in various finished products–manufacturing companies. One manufactured aluminum, tin, and plastic packaging and had achieved a significant increase in export sales over the past five years. Another was a leading manufacturer of hand tools for gardening, farming, and the construction industry in Scandinavia. Still another operation manufactured winches and tire chains for the European forest industry. A 50-percent-owned company produced mineral wool and polystyrene insulation.

Until 1983, the steel and finished products sectors were run as one group. However, this structure did not sufficiently reflect the rather substantial differences in the two sectors. Elkem's core businesses were in process industries, while finished goods were unit parts businesses and so required greater market orientation and different management approaches. Therefore, a reorganization in 1984 established the finished products sector as a wholly owned subsidiary of Elkem, with its own Board of Directors and an independent management structure. The subsidiary was given considerable autonomy so that it could cultivate an approach to its businesses that better reflected its particular competitive realities.

Engineering, Mining, and Research

Elkem's engineering division, through its advanced smelting furnace designs and process control techniques, paved the way for the company's initial international expansion. The division worked in close cooperation with the ferroalloys operations, and the resulting combination of technical skills and practical experience established Elkem as a world leader in metallurgical technology and production equipment for the smelting industry. In addition to designing, constructing, and installing smelting furnaces and plants, Elkem provided on-site training of personnel and assisted during the startup phase. Among its largest customers were producers in India and Brazil, where Elkem had played a major role in the establishment of metallurgical industries.

The mining division operations were severely curtailed by the closing of mines and the reversion of other mining rights to the state. The remaining mining activities centered on industrial minerals. Elkem's sole remaining mine was Norsk Nefelin in Norway; it produced nepheline syenite, a mineral used in the manufacture of glass, porcelain, and ceramic products.

Elkem's research and development activities were primarily concentrated on the silicon and ferroalloys sector. Its comprehensive research program helped establish the firm in its leading position in the international ferroalloys industry.

The firm's strong technological position was above all the result of the close cooperation between three groups of constituents within Elkem, the company's research centers in Norway and the United States, its engineering division, and its ferroalloys plants. The plants drew on the metallurgical expertise of the engineering division and the research centers, while the engineering division's design work was supported by the operating experience at the plants and the experimental work at the research centers.

STRATEGIC PLANNING

Elkem had a long tradition of commitments to formalized approaches to the development of its strategies. In the mid-1960s, a detailed five-year long-range planning approach was implemented, with heavy emphasis on financial projections. This approach was inspired by guidelines developed by the Stanford Research Institute. In 1978, when Kielland became the Executive Vice President and President Designate, he initiated a review of the long-range planning effort based on a commonly felt need that the process had become too much of a financial extrapolation and failed to reflect strategic issues sufficiently.

Kielland felt that:

> Planning had become too much of a numbers game. It was a projection of numbers, very little else—ten year forecasts. It was amazing to see what kind of capability the company would have in year ten. And of course it never came true; not even in the next year. And the whole organization got very frustrated by that kind of exercise, which was very time-consuming and academic.

In 1979, a revised planning approach was launched, spearheaded by Kielland. This approach was based on the delineation of the firm's business activities into freestanding product/market entities, so-called Strategic Business Units (SBUs), which then became the basis for the development of the strategic plans. Each Strategic Business Unit was charged with developing a competitive strategy, based on the attractiveness of its business segment and on the competitive strength that the Elkem organization would have in this business segment. Teams of executives from the relevant areas of Elkem's organization, primarily line executives who were involved in running each particular business, were put in charge of developing these plans. The plans were carefully scrutinized by Kielland and other top managers. Extensive interaction between the business level and the corporate level resulted.

The initial efforts to introduce the system were stimulated by means of a number of two-day workshops, with an outside process consultant in charge. Each workshop was typically attended by 20 to 25 executives. More than 100 executives attended the workshops. The basic approach at these workshops was to introduce the strategic planning concepts to the participants in a practical, hands-on way. The workshop facilitator would typically start out by introducing a number of planning concepts, such as how to assess the attractiveness of the business and how to assess one's own competitive strength. The workshop participants would then be broken into small groups of five to six members. Each group's members would be asked to assess the business attractiveness and competitive strength of the particular business entity they were most familiar with. A number of written questions were provided to facilitate this. After completing this, each work team would present an analysis in a plenary session, which also became the basis for discussion and gave the workshop leader the opportunity to underscore certain more-general issues, problems, and approaches. In this manner, the entire strategic planning process would be stimulated in the course of two days, taking the participants through an objective setting stage, a strategic implementation stage, and finally a monitoring stage.

The typical result of these workshops was a strongly shared belief that strategic planning would be useful for the managers themselves. It also provided a "head start" learning experience, which basically followed a format similar to the workshop outline, so that subsequently it would be easier for the managers to develop their own plans.

The actual planning was guided by a calendar that set out the time for the submission for various parts of the plan. This calendar also gave the dates for review and feedback meetings. A brief "planning manual" also was developed, which gave various formats for submission of plans, a set of definitions, some background readings, and so forth. This manual was in looseleaf form and was deliberately kept thin and flexible. Exhibit 9 is a copy of a typical planning calendar. Strategic planning at Elkem, in the words of the firm's planning manual, was intended to be ". . . a daily working habit, and not just a job that has to be done once a year."

Although planning at Elkem was formal, it was not intended to be rigid—it was the *process* of planning that the firm stressed. Elkem's aims in planning were many. One basic goal was to develop a coordinated, multilevel common understanding of the positions and direction of the overall corporation, the divisions, the subsidiaries, the companies, and the SBUs. The process was intended to be proactive, to involve a conscious process of choice by paying continuous attention to projects necessary for the future and to be highly sensitive to the basic conditions that influence success. The process also was intended to be deliberately cross-functional, to tie programs in all sections of the firm as closely as possible to the

---

Exhibit 9   Time Schedule (1982)

Strategic Planning

Strategic plans, Part I	March 26, 1982
Reassessing strategic position, strategic direction, subgoals	
Preliminary feedback from corporate management	April 1982
Discussions according to needs	
Strategic plans, Part II	June 4, 1982
Strategic programs	
Divisional memo	July 2, 1982
Important strategy issues	
Eventual discussions with corporate management	June/August 1982
General feedback for corporate management	Late August 1982
Specific feedback for each SBU family	September 1982
Investment frames, detailing strategic direction	
Budgets	October/November 1982

chosen direction. Through continual monitoring, the process was meant to help the company to be more flexible in reacting to changes. Kielland said the following:

> I don't think it is any good to have any strategic planning unless you are able to develop the strategic plan into strategic decisions. Strategic management—that's what you strive for.

The first planning cycle was finished in December 1979. The present system reflects an extension of this approach.

Planning Roles

Planning at Elkem began at the corporate level, where the overall direction for the firm was set and the major portfolio decisions were made. Top management provided the "frame" for the planning process by suggesting overall broad directions for the firm. In 1984, Elkem's main overall corporate strategies were the following:

1. Make the most of the advantage gained by the firm's strong energy base.
2. Achieve and maintain dominance in ferroalloys.
3. Exploit potential synergies among related activities in the firm.

In addition to stating these broadly stated guidelines, the corporate level provided financial targets for ROA and cash flow levels.

The corporate level grouped SBUs into "business families" for portfolio planning, review, and monitoring purposes. Top management's intention was to review and approve the initial goals set by the families, review and approve the programs developed to meet those goals, approve the budgets, monitor the critical success factors, and evaluate the performance of the plan developed by the business management teams.

At least in concept, there was heavy involvement at the corporate level. However, it was the divisional/subsidiary company/SBU levels that shouldered the basic responsibility for developing the plans. The stages in the planning process conducted at this level are summarized in Exhibit 10. The stages were sequential and conformed to a timetable set by the corporate level, but in actual practice the managers worked on several stages simultaneously.

At the divisional level, the most important strategic issues were delineated in order to give more specific guidance to the business managers. This level helped identify SBUs and conditionally approved plans and budgets before submission to the corporate level. Each division was expected to monitor actual performance continually with regard to changes in strategic position, resource use, and progress toward "milestones" and budgetary results.

The basic unit of responsibility for analysis and program development was, however, the SBU manager. He or she was expected to update and analyze the SBU's progress continually while being tuned to changes in the business environment. The manager was accountable both for the monitoring of plan progress and for the quality of plan preparation.

Exhibit 10   Stages in the Strategic Planning Process

SBU Delineation	Strategic Positioning	Strategic Direction	Specification of Subgoals	Strategic Programs	Budgets	Follow-up/ Control
Definition of strategic business units	Analysis of external factors such as market attractiveness and internal factors such as own competitive strength	• Grow, hold position harvest, withdraw, explore • Critical success factors • Risk, alternative strategic directions		Delineation of goal-oriented action programs	Numbers delineation of plans over a 3 year period	Follow-up of: • Critical success factors • Key strategic programs • Budgets

SBU Delineation

The SBUs at Elkem were expected to be self-supporting, viable business units with a unique mission. They could be composed of one or more Product/Market Segments (PMS). Proper delineation of the SBUs, an ongoing process, was considered crucial. A PMS might be designated as a SBU if the manager felt that it had growth potential large enough to warrant special attention. Each SBU was expected to have a SBU manager, who was often supported by a cross-functional team to help with the planning. The formal organizational structure could in some cases be different than the SBU delineation, or the organization could be changed to correspond to the SBU. What was crucial was that the SBU would be market oriented in order to maintain emphasis on market-driven issues as opposed to internal organizational efficiency needs.

Individual SBUs were grouped into "families" for corporate review and portfolio-planning needs. Exhibit 11 gives a delineation of these SBU families.

Analysis of Strategic Position

The analysis of strategic position was conducted primarily at the SBU level. The SBU managers were expected to evaluate market attractiveness as well as their own competitiveness by focusing on the customer and relevant environmental trends, opportunities, and threats. The financial-monitoring system had been modified to provide information for each SBU family.

Strategic Direction

Based on the strategic position analysis, the SBU manager was expected to recommend a basic direction for the SBU—from "grow" to "withdraw." As part of this, the manager identified critical success factors for the chosen strategy, along with suggestions for monitoring these factors. In conjunction with the setting of the basic direction, subgoals were set for how the direction was to be achieved in the market. Subgoals could be, for example, product/market penetration, geographical expansion to achieve particular target growth rates, and target market shares. It was only after the market strategy was developed that additional further subgoals were derived for production, R&D, and so on. Those SBUs that found themselves in particularly volatile markets were expected to develop scenarios or alternative goals and directions and specified the "triggers" that would indicate the need to use one or the other of the alternatives.

Strategic Programs

After the foregoing stages were approved at the divisional and corporate levels, the SBU managers developed strategic programs. These programs were the actual projects that allowed the SBU to reach its subgoals. The programs were based on

Exhibit 11 **Subfamilies in Elkem (1981)**

	Division
Area 1	
1. Steel and reinforcement	Steel
2. Rods	Rods
3. Fasteners	
4. Packing	
5. Chains and winches	Finished Goods I
6. Plastic coating	
7. Consumer products	
8. Isolation	Finished Goods II
9. Locks and fitting	
10. Skates and leisure products	
11. Transportation equipment and services	
Area II	
12. Mining, minerals	Mining
13. Mining, sulfurs	
14. Iron	
15. Engineering	Engineering
16. Trading	
Area III	
17. Aluminum	Aluminum
Area IV	
18. Ferroalloys	Ferroalloys
19. Silicon	
20. Carbon products	
21. Mineral fillers	
Petroleum	
22. Petroleum activities	

the critical success factors delineated during the strategic position and strategic direction stages for each program. The manager specified a time schedule; who would be responsible for each task; which resources—human, financial, or technical—would be needed; which profitability measures would be applied; and which critical factors had to be monitored to indicate whether a program needed to be modified.

Strategic Budgeting

Strategic budgets were prepared on a three-year basis. Costs (and profits where they were possible to estimate) associated with strategic programs were distinguished from normal operating costs. These budgets had to be approved by both the divisional and the corporate levels.

Budgeting was considered an essential part of the planning process. Kielland emphasized the following:

> This is the critical part. If you sit down and discuss strategic plans which are not in the budgets, they live a life by themselves. But by putting them into the budget, they become part of the decision system.

Monitoring

Each organizational level played a role in the monitoring process. At the corporate level, the larger strategic programs that were of a particularly high overall priority were monitored with respect to critical success factors, resource use, and progress. The monitoring occurred formally through the formal plan review meetings and informally through ad hoc discussions. Kielland met weekly with the business area heads and the heads of various functional departments to discuss strategic issues. Each month, special meetings were held with each of the areas. In this way, monitoring occurred on a continual basis.

At the business area, divisional, and SBU levels, continual monitoring also occurred by watching critical success factors, updating the strategic position analysis, and evaluating plan progress. Functional areas also were responsible for monitoring resource use associated with strategic programs.

Evaluation

Evaluation was considered to be an integral part of the planning process at Elkem. It occurred in two ways:

1. SBU managers used "checkpoints for self-control," whereby each manager critically examined his or her own analyses, programs, and results.
2. The corporate level gave feedback on the quality of the plans.

This process was not tied specifically into the compensation system. Strategic planning was considered to be part of a manager's responsibility; incentives were not related to the achievement of plan goals on a short-run basis. In the long run, however, they were considered to be part and parcel of a manager's overall performance and promotability.

THE STRATEGIC PLANNING DEPARTMENT

The corporate planning department played an important role as a catalyst to make the planning process function. The department was deliberately kept small—one person and a secretary. This person reported to the Vice President and Controller.

The manager of strategic planning had several functions. First, he or she was expected to manage the strategic planning process. This included scheduling the planning review meetings, making sure that plans were submitted on time, and making sure that the various background materials were made available to all parties concerned. Second, he or she was in charge of managing the formal part of the planning process. This included developing standardized formats, suggesting changes in these formats, and making the planning approach more comprehensive. Third, he or she was to assist the strategic business units with their own planning efforts. This included contacting the SBU managers with suggestions, responding to questions, and being a discussion partner with the various managers. Fourth, he or she was to work closely with top management, helping them and making preparations for their reviews and feedback on business plans.

It was Kielland's intention to select the planning managers from among fast rising line executives in order to give them extensive exposure to corporate-level strategic issues, from which they could then benefit in line positions later on. Kielland did not envision the strategic planning position as permanent, and he did not envision a large corporate planning staff.

Experiences with the Strategic Planning Process

The experiences that various members of the Elkem organization had with the strategic planning process were generally positive, even though some members had reservations that merited further analysis and discussion.

Kielland's major praise of the strategic planning process was that it provided focus and a coherent overview of the corporation and its various business activities. For the first time, Kielland felt that he was on top of the basic strategic developments in every part of the company. He was, however, concerned that the preparation of strategic plans at the business level might become too much of a routine. The members of his organization should be able to evolve in sophistication to "strategic management" from "strategic planning." Kielland was not sure whether the present planning process had not become overly bureaucratic.

The Vice President of Strategic Planning felt that it was hard for top management to analyze all the various planning inputs that were generated from the various SBUs. Further, the massive inflow of bottom-up inputs made it hard for top management to provide meaningful feedback. In order to make it easier for the top management group to understand the overall portfolio impact of the various business plan inputs, he created a one-page summary document for each SBU, analyzing and critiquing the plan in question and suggesting feedback issues and questions that top management could raise (Exhibit 12). This process was seen as highly useful by Kielland and his colleagues. A number of executives at the business level did, however, feel that this analytical step had become a "filter" that took away much of the flavor of their strategies.

One concern that was shared by several of the senior executives within the ferroalloys group had to do with difficulties in providing business unit strategies

Exhibit 12   **Strategic Planning Summary**

SBU	SBU Family	Division	Date	Sign

Products/Services	
1. Direct customers/needs	2. Indirect customers/and-use
3. Competitors	4. Strategic Position
5. Matrix	6. Strategic Direction
7. Critical success/actors	8. Subgoals
9. Strategic programs	10. Comments

Estimates		yr-2	yr-1	this year	yr-1	yr-2
Marketvolum	Own sale (mil. loc. curr.)					
Marketsales	Cash flow					
Marketshare of sales	Cash contribution					

that would better fit together in an overall group strategy. These executives felt that many of the strategies were too narrow in focus to be able to penetrate opportunities for creating economies between them when it came to sharing manufacturing, research and development, and distribution. Also, they felt that opportunities to coordinate strategies in the marketplace might be missed or not analyzed and understood.

Some executives at the business level felt that the format of their strategic plan was becoming increasingly restrictive. They felt that it became a more or less repetitive exercise to "fill out" the plans the second or third time around. The first year's experience in putting together a strategic plan was seen as a highly rewarding activity. Several complained, however, that this type of positive experience declined over time. Still there remained a widespread support for strategic planning throughout the organization.

Strategic Challenges to the Firm

Reviewing the strategic events of the last few years, the executives concluded that Elkem as a corporation and several of its key businesses and markets had undergone profound changes.

Strategically many challenges faced Elkem, and these were especially far-reaching in the ferroalloys group. However, almost all the product areas shared at least some of ferroalloys' characteristics of severe downward price pressures, shifts in the competitive structure of their industries, reliance on the competitive strengths of a low-cost energy base, and low raw materials costs.

As Elkem faced the future, several areas required careful scrutiny. Some of these areas were the following:

Product/Market Policies.   How could the executives gauge the future impact on Elkem of the changes that had been taking place in key user industries? Also, what might be the effects of the geographical shift in production? User segments with higher growth rates, less price sensitivity, and greater needs for specialty products or know-how should be watched especially closely.

Production Policies.   Trends in production, cost, efficiencies, optimal facility size(s) and location(s), raw materials costs and sources, technological innovations, and energy consumption were all factors that might potentially be critical. Were current policies and strategies toward the key factors of production receiving optimal attention? Was the firm truly realizing the economies of scale, or were there in fact diseconomies due to suboptimal plant locations or other factors? Was the product mix optimal to meet market needs and to maximize profits? What were the political risks in sourcing raw materials?

Competitive Analysis.   How could the executives keep up to date in the analysis of competition, especially in the current environment of price and cost cutting, overcapacity, new entrants, and plant closures? What changes were competitors likely to make? What countermeasures were possible?

Increasing Capacity for Innovation.   What was the role of the potential threats and opportunities deriving not from within the industry but from changes generated by new technology in other areas? In this respect, was the R&D effort sufficiently well planned and implemented to aid short-term product development and to develop new products and applications for the long term? How were the research facilities in Norway and the United States to be integrated into these efforts? Four major developmental projects were being pursued in particular. How much sense did each of these make?

Ultra-Pure Silicon Metal.   Elkem was developing a special process for producing silicon of a very high purity for specialized applications, such as solar cells and advanced ceramic products. As a related move, Elkem acquired a 10 percent interest in a U.S.-based company—Ceramatec, Inc.—which was engaged in research and development as well as small-scale production of various high-purity ceramic products, including components for the automobile and electronics industries.

Microsilica.   Microsilica as a byproduct from the ferroalloys production was the minute set of particles of silicon dioxide that were collected by the gas-cleaning filters on furnaces producing ferrosilicon. Other substances were subsequently added to the microsilica to produce a range of additives with special properties. Microsilica additives could, for example, improve the strength and durability of concrete, permit asbestos fibers used in certain cements to be replaced by nontoxic but equally effective materials, or improve the mechanical properties of various polymers and refractory materials.

To date, Elkem has invested approximately 150 million NOK in research and development. In 1984, the first year in which microsilica products were actively marketed, a turnover of 40 million NOK was achieved. This turnover had produced a significant loss (see Exhibit 2). Further significant investment would be required. Still, there seemed to be an optimistic consensus among the corporate executives that this activity had substantial growth potential.

Offshore Engineering.   Elkem had considerable experience in engineering and project management. This had been extended into the offshore sector through the activities of Elkem Offshore. In line with this, Elkem acquired a 12.5 percent interest in Norwegian Petroleum Consultants A.S. (NPC), one of Norway's largest offshore engineering consultancy companies. Elkem was currently negotiating to increase its interest in NPC up to 50 percent.

High-Purity Quartz.   Elkem and A/S Norcem, another leading Norwegian industrial conglomerate, successfully developed a novel purification process to produce high-purity quartz specially adapted for use in fiber optics, semiconductor manufacturing, and other high-technology applications. For this purpose, they established a joint company, Minnor A/S, that was to mine deposits of quartz with special properties permitting the production of this high-purity quartz. Minnor A/S constructed in Norway a new plant that commenced production in 1986.

A STRATEGIC DECISION

During late fall 1985, an unexpected opportunity arose for Elkem to make an acquisition in the Norwegian ferroalloys industry. Elkem was given the opportunity to purchase a ferroalloys company, Orkla metals, for 60 million NOK and also take over the responsibility of serving 250 million NOK of long-term debt. This company was 50 percent owned by the Orkla Corporation and 50 percent owned by a U.K.-based firm, Associated Metals (AMMC). This ferroalloys plant produced about 55,000 tons per year and had a capacity of about 60,000 tons per year. It was quite modern, having started production in 1964. However, its hydroelectric power base was expensive but it was not able to draw on its own wholly owned hydroelectric power plant. Elkem had to respond quickly to this offer.

Elkem simultaneously got the opportunity to purchase 51 percent of the shares of another Norwegian producer of ferroalloys, A/S Bjoelvefossen. This company manufactured 55,000 tons of ferrosilicon alloys. It had an old plant but was fully modernized and enjoyed cheap electric costs because it had its own hydroelectric power plant. Elkem also had to respond relatively promptly to this opportunity, which involved a purchase price of approximately 120 million NOK for the 51 percent share.

It was not clear whether Elkem would benefit from going ahead with these two purchases, or whether it should attempt to pursue both or only one. A number of arguments were made in favor of making the purchases. The strongest among these was the argument that the acquisitions might lead to a further restructuring of the European ferroalloys industry and allow for a significant lessening of the competitive climate between Elkem and the other Norwegian ferroalloys producers, which were organized in a sales cartel, Fesil. The departure of two strong producers from this cartel significantly reduced its volume base and thus its ability to impact prices. In line with this argument, several executives also pointed out that since Elkem's core business was indeed ferroalloys, it would make particularly strong sense to increase market shares further when possible.

Several reservations were raised regarding whether it would be wise to make these acquisitions. It was pointed out that since the present ferroalloys price level seemed to be on the peak side of the typical business cycle and thus could be expected to go down, it might not make much sense to purchase new capacity just before an expected downturn. This would make it difficult to have the new acquisition generate sufficient return to pay for itself. It would also probably impact the purchase price for the acquisitions. In short, why buy expensively when the market was just near its peak?

Another objection was raised, this one on a more basic issue. It was pointed out that Elkem's present portfolio was heavily committed to relatively mature and cyclical industries—ferroalloys and aluminum in particular. As such, it would be strategically important to search for a "third strategic leg," that is, to build a new substantive business either from internal efforts or from acquisitions (or through a combination of these two means) so that a third, more growth-oriented and unrelated business could be established. This might create a better balance in Elkem's portfolio and help generate a more stable stream of earnings over the years. It was hoped that this might also provide a way to lift the firm's image vis-à-vis the stock market. With the two acquisitions proposals at hand, Elkem could certainly not pursue such a portfolio diversification strategy; on the contrary, each would make the perceived imbalances in the portfolio even worse.

Kielland knew that a decision would have to be made soon. At the same time, he asked himself whether the strategic planning process in its present form and with its current formats was able to provide sufficiently effective support to cope with emerging strategic issues such as these. Another question facing upper management then was what improvements and modifications might be made in the strategic planning process to allow Elkem to adapt to its changing environment.

NOTES

1. In March 1984, one Norwegian Kroner equaled $0.132 in U.S. dollars.
2. In June 1984, Elkem's ownership share was increased to 67 percent. In 1985, its ownership share was increased to 100 percent.

Procter & Gamble Europe: The Vizir Launch

There were three critical decisions facing Procter & Gamble's (P&G) senior management in June 1981 as they reviewed the German test market results for Vizir, the new heavy-duty liquid (HDL) detergent.

- Should they follow the recommendation of Wolfgang Berndt and his German team and authorize a national launch on the basis of four months of test results? Or should they wait until final test market results were in, or perhaps even rethink their entire HDL product strategy?
- If and when the decision was taken to launch Vizir, to what extent could this be considered a European rather than just a German product? If a coordinated European rollout was planned, to what degree should the company standardize its product formulation, packaging, advertising, and promotion?
- Finally, what organizational implications would these decisions have? For example, to what extent should individual country subsidiary managers retain the responsibility to decide when and how this new product would be introduced in their national market?

PROCTER & GAMBLE: COMPANY BACKGROUND

To understand anything in P&G, one had to appreciate the company's strong and long-established culture that was reflected in the corporate values, policies, and practices. The following paragraphs outline how the company saw itself in each of these areas.

Corporate Values

Established in 1837 by two men of strong religious faith and moral conviction, P&G soon had developed an explicit set of corporate standards and values. From their earliest contact, prospective employees were told of P&G's firm belief that the interests of the company were inseparable from those of its employees. Over the years, this broad philosophy had been translated into a variety of widely shared management norms such as the following:

- P&G should hire only good people of high character;
- P&G must treat them as individuals with individual talents and life goals;
- P&G should provide a work environment that encourages and rewards individual achievement.

The shared beliefs soon became part of the company's formal management systems. General managers would tell you they were evaluated on their achievements in three areas: volume, profit, and people. P&G also tried to attract people willing to spend their entire career with the company. Promotions were made from within, and top management was chosen from career P&G people rather than from outside the company.

Management Policies

Over its almost 150-year history, P&G has also accumulated a broad base of industry experience and business knowledge. Within the company, this accumulated knowledge was seen as an important asset and a great deal of it had been formalized and institutionalized as management principles and policies. In the words of Chairman Ed Harness, "Though our greatest asset is our people, it is the consistency of principle and policy which gives us direction."

It was in the marketing area that these operating principles and management policies were the most strategically important for a company with reputation as a premier consumer marketer. One of the most basic policies was that P&G's products should provide "superior total value" and should meet "basic consumer needs." This resulted in a strong commitment to research to create products that were demonstrably better than the competition in blind tests. (In the words of one manager, "Before you can launch a new brand, you must have a win in a white box.")

Furthermore, P&G believed strongly in the value of market research. In a business where poorly conceived new product launches could be very expensive and sometimes not very successful, continuous and detailed market research was seen as insurance against major mistakes. Chairman Ed Harness had described their market research objectives as being "to spot a new trend early, then lead it."

For similar reasons, P&G also believed in extensive product and market testing before making major brand decisions. Having spotted a trend through market research, the company typically spent two or three years testing the product and the marketing strategy it had developed before committing to a full-scale launch. One paper goods competitor said of them: "P&G tests and tests and tests. They leave no stone unturned, no variable untested. You can see them coming for months and years, but you know when they get there, it is time for you to move."

Finally, P&G believed that through continual product development and close tracking of consumer needs and preferences, brands could be managed so that they remained healthy and profitable in the long term. Their rejection of the conventional product life cycle mentality was demonstrated by the fact that Ivory Soap was over 100 years old, Crisco shortening was more than 70, and Tide detergent more than 35, yet each was still a leader in its field.

Organization Practices

In addition to strong corporate values and clear management principles, the P&G culture was characterized by well-established organization practices and processes. Its internal operations had been described as thorough, creative, and aggressive by some, and as slow, risk-averse, and rigid by others. There was probably an element of truth in both descriptions.

Perhaps the most widely known of P&G's organizational characteristics was its legendary brand manager structure. Created in 1931, the brand management system was designed to provide each brand with management focus, expertise, and drive at a low level in the organization. By legitimizing and even reinforcing the internal competition that had existed since Camay Soap was launched in competition with Ivory in 1923, the brand manager system tended to restrict lateral communication. This resulted in a norm among P&G managers that information was shared on a "need to know" basis only.

While the brand manager system may have impaired lateral communication, vertical communication within P&G was strong and well established. Proposals on most key issues were normally generated at the lower levels of management, with analysis and recommendations working their way up the organization for concurrence and approval. In P&G, top management was intimately involved in most large decisions (e.g., all new brand launches, capital appropriations in excess of $100,000, and personnel appointment and promotion decisions three levels down). Although the approval system could be slow and at times bureaucratic (one manager claimed that a label change on Head and Shoulders shampoo had required 55 signatures) it was designed to minimize risk in the very risky and expensive consumer marketing business. Once a project was approved, it would have the company's full commitment. As one manager said, "Once they sign off [on the new brand launch], they will bet the farm."

A third characteristic of the P&G management process was that proposals were committed to paper, usually in the form of one- or two-page memos. The purpose was

to encourage thoroughness and careful analysis on the part of the proposal origina-
tors, and objectivity and rationality on the part of the managers who reviewed the
document. Written documents could also flow more easily through the organization,
building support or eliciting comments and suggestions.

P&G INTERNATIONAL: EUROPEAN OPERATIONS

Expansion Principles

Although P&G had acquired a small English soap company in 1926, it was not
until the postwar years that the company built a substantial European presence. In
1954 a French detergent company was acquired; two years later, a Belgian plant
was opened; and by the end of the decade P&G had established operations in
Holland and Italy. A Swiss subsidiary served as a worldwide export center. In the
1960s, subsidiaries were opened in Germany, Austria, Greece, Spain, and the
Scandinavian countries. The European Technical Center (ETC) was established in
Brussels in 1963, to provide R&D facilities and a small regional management
team.

By 1981 Europe represented about 15 percent of P&G's $11 billion worldwide
sales, with almost all of that substantial volume having been built in the previous
two and a half decades! The German and U.K. subsidiaries were the largest, each
representing about one-fifth of the company's European sales. France and Italy
together accounted for another 30 percent, and Belgium, Holland, Spain, Austria,
and Switzerland together made up the balance.

As international operations grew, questions arose as to how the new foreign
subsidiaries should be managed. As early as 1955, Walter Lingle, P&G's Overseas
V.P., laid down some important principles that guided the company's subsequent
development abroad. Recognizing that consumer needs and preferences differed by
country, Lingle emphasized the importance of acquiring the same intensive knowledge of local consumers as was required in the U.S. Lingle said: "Washing habits . . . vary widely from country to country. We must tailor products to meet
consumer demands in each nation. We cannot simply sell products with U.S. formulas. They won't work—they won't be accepted."

But Lingle insisted that the management policies and practices that had
proven so successful for P&G in the U.S. would be equally successful overseas. He
said: "The best way to succeed in other countries is to build in each one as exact a
replica of the U.S. Procter & Gamble organization as it is possible to create."

European Industry and Competitive Structure

From their earliest exposure to the European market for laundry detergents, U.S.
managers realized how important the first of these principles would be. Washing
habits and market structures not only differed from the familiar U.S. situation, but

also varied from one country to the next within Europe. Among the more obvious differences in laundry characteristics were the following:

- Typical washing temperatures were much higher in Europe, and the "boil wash" (over 60°C) was the norm in most countries. However, lower washing temperatures were commonplace in some countries where washing machines did not heat water (e.g., U.K.) or where hand washing was still an important segment (e.g., Spain, Italy).

- European washing machines were normally front loading with a horizontal rotating drum—very different from the U.S. norm of an agitator action in a top loaded machine. The European machine also had a smaller water capacity (3–5 gallons versus 12–14 gallons in the U.S.) and used a much longer cycle (90–120 minutes versus 20–30 minutes for U.S.).

- Europeans used more cottons and less synthetics than Americans, and tended to wear clothes longer between washes. Average washing frequency was 2–3 times per week versus 4–5 times in the U.S. Despite the lower penetration of washing machines, much higher detergent doseage per load resulted in the total European laundry detergent consumption being about 30 percent above the U.S. total.

Market structures and conditions were also quite different from the U.S., and also varied widely within Europe, as illustrated by the following examples:

- In Germany, concentration ratios among grocery retailers were among the highest in the world. The five largest chains (including co-ops and associations) accounted for 65 percent of the retail volume, compared with about 15 percent in the U.S. In contrast, in Italy, the independent corner store was still very important, and hypermarkets had not made major inroads.

- Unlimited access to television similar to the U.S. was available only in the U.K. (and even there was much more expensive). In Holland, each brand was allowed only 46 minutes of TV commercial time per annum; in Germany and Italy, companies had to apply for blocks of TV time once a year. Allocated slots were very limited.

- National legislation greatly affected product and market strategies. Legislation in Finland and Holland limited phosphate levels in detergent; German laws made coupons, refunds and premium offers all but impossible; elsewhere local laws regulated package weight, labeling, and trade discounts.

The competitive environment was also different from P&G's accustomed market leadership position in the U.S. In Europe, P&G shared the first tier position with two European companies, Unilever and Henkel. By the early 1970s each company claimed between 20 percent and 25 percent of the European laundry detergent market. P&G's old domestic market rival, Colgate, had a 10 percent share and was in a second tier. At a third level were several national competitors. Henkel was present in most European markets but strongest in Germany, its home market; Unilever was also very international, dominating in Holland and U.K.;

Colgate's presence in Europe was spottier, but it had built up a very strong position in France. National companies typically were strong at the lower priced end of their local markets.

Each company had its own competitive characteristics. Unilever had long been a sleeping giant, but was becoming much more aggressive by the mid-1970s. Henkel was a strong competitor and could be relied on to defend its home market position tenaciously. Colgate was trying to elbow its way in, and tended to be more impulsive and take bigger risks, often launching new products with only minimal testing. As a result, P&G's market share varied by national market.

Laundry Detergent Market ($ million)

	Total Market	P&G Share
Germany	950	200
U.K.	660	220
France	750	160
Italy	650	140
Spain	470	90
Total Europe	3,750	950

By the mid-1970s, the rapid growth of the previous two decades dropped to a standstill. Not only did the oil crisis add dramatically to costs, but almost simultaneously, washing machines approached the 85 percent penetration rate many regarded as saturation point. In the late 1970s, volume was growing at 2 percent per annum. As market growth slowed, competitive pressures increased.

P&G Europe's Strategy and Organization

These differences in consumer habits, market conditions, and competitive environment led to the development of strong national subsidiaries with the responsibility for developing products and marketing programs to match the local environment. Each subsidiary was a miniature Procter & Gamble, with its own brand management structure, its own product development capability, its own advertising agencies, and typically, its own manufacturing capability. The subsidiary general manager was responsible for the growth of the business and the organization. (See Exhibit 1.)

Most subsidiaries faced a major task of establishing P&G in the basic detergent and soap business in their national market. The general manager typically tried to select the best volume and profit opportunity from the more than 200 products in the company's portfolio. The general manager of the Italian subsidiary described the choices he faced when he took over in 1974:

> Given the limits of P&G Italy's existing brands [a laundry detergent, a bar soap, and a recently acquired coffee business], we had to build our volume and profit, and broaden our base. The choices we had were almost limitless. Pampers had been very successful in Germany and Belgium, but Italy couldn't afford such an expensive launch; Motiv, a

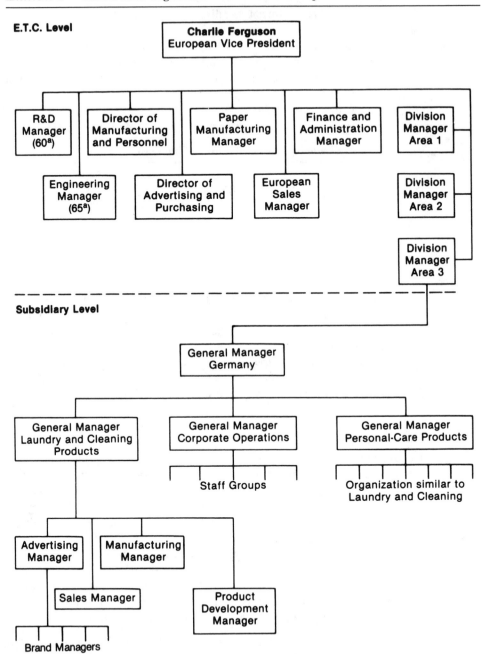

Exhibit 1   **Abbreviated Organization Chart: P&G Europe**

aNumber of managerial and technical/professional staff. (Total number of managerial/technical/professional staff at ETC was 175.)

new dishwashing liquid, was being launched in France and Germany, but we were unconvinced of its potential here; Mr. Propre [Mr. Clean in the United States] was successful in three European countries, but competition in Italy was strong; finally we decided to launch Monsavon, the French bar soap. It represented an affordable new product launch in a traditionally good profit line.

Each of the country general managers reported to Tom Bower, an Englishman who had headed up P&G's European operations since 1961. Bower had a reputation as an entrepreneur and an excellent motivator. He believed that by selecting creative and entrepreneurial country general managers and giving them the freedom to run their business, results would follow. The strategy had been most successful for P&G, and sales and profits had grown rapidly throughout the '60s and into the early '70s. Growth had been aided by P&G's entry into new national markets and new product categories, and by the rapid growth of the core detergent business with the penetration of washing machines into European homes.

Tom Bower made sure that his small headquarters staff understood that they were not to interfere unduly in subsidiary decisions. Primarily, it was the subsidiary general manager's responsibility to call on ETC if there was a problem.

When Tom Bower retired in 1975, his successor, Ed Artzt, was faced with a situation quite different from the one that existed in the 1950s and '60s. As growth slowed, competition intensified, prices weakened, and profits dipped. Artzt felt that if profit and sales growth were to be rekindled, the diverse country operations would have to be better coordinated.

Over the next five years, under his leadership, the role of ETC took on new importance. (Exhibit 1 shows an abbreviated organization chart.) If increased competition was leading to declining margins, more emphasis must be placed on controlling costs, and Artzt moved to strengthen the ETC finance manager's role. The finance manager described the problems:

> Largely because of duplication of marketing and administrative groups in each subsidiary, our overhead expense per unit was 50% higher than in the U.S. parent. We needed to get it under control. Our problem was that we couldn't get meaningful or comparable costs by subsidiary. Our introduction of better cost and reporting systems helped put pressure on subsidiaries to control their costs. It had a very beneficial effect.

Artzt was also concerned about the slowing of innovation in P&G Europe, and felt that part of the sales and profit problem was due to the fact that too few new products were being developed, and those that were, were not being introduced in a coordinated manner. Under the strong leadership of Wahib Zaki, Artzt's new R&D manager, ETC's role in product development took a dramatic shift.

Previously each subsidiary was responsible for initiating its own local product development. These groups drew on the company's basic technology from the U.S., as modified by ETC. The R&D group in a subsidiary the size of France was around 30, while Germany's technical staff was perhaps twice that large. Responding to its own local market, the subsidiary defined and developed products with the appropriate characteristics, perhaps calling on ETC for specialized technical support or backup. There was no requirement for a subsidiary to use standard formulations or technology. As a result, Ariel detergent had nine different formulas Europe-wide, having been positioned diversely as a low- and a high-suds powder, and for low- and high-temperature usage, depending on the country.

The problem with developing products in this way, concluded Zaki, was that there was insufficient focus, prioritization, or strategic direction for the work. As a result, the strong technical capabilities housed in the European Technical Centers as well as in the United States were not being fully or effectively utilized. Furthermore, their efforts were not being appreciated by local country management who tended to view the Technical Center as a high cost, perfectionist group that did not respond rapidly enough to market needs.

Zaki aimed to change this by having ETC take a stronger leadership role in R&D and by assuming responsibility for coordinating the new product development efforts among the subsidiaries. He felt the time had come where this was possible. His analysis indicated that habit differences between countries were narrowing and no longer justified product differences of the type that then existed from one country to another. He felt the need to establish priorities, to coordinate efforts and, to the extent possible, to standardize products Europe-wide. To achieve these goals he needed the involvement and cooperation of the subsidiaries.

In 1977, Zaki reorganized European R&D, creating European Technical Teams to work on products and technologies that had Europe-wide importance. In his vision, European products would be superior to existing local national products, but without compromising performance or increasing cost. The objective was to focus the resources of the total European R&D community around key brands and to define a long-term European approach to product development.

As roles became clearer, the ETC technical groups were seen as being the developers of new technologies ("putting the molecules together" as one described it), while the subsidiaries took responsibility for testing and refining the products in the field. After a couple of painful years, the new process seemed to be working. "Lead countries" were named for each of the key products thereby giving more local subsidiary responsibility and ownership for the development process, and also to ensure ongoing coordination among subsidiaries. Transfer of technical staff between ETC and subsidiaries further encouraged the interdependence and cooperation.

An experimental attempt at "Europeanization" in marketing, however, had been less successful. In a break from the philosophy of product adaptation, a group of managers in Cincinnati had concluded that "a baby is a baby" worldwide, and that the laborious market-by-market evaluations necessary for cleaning products would not be needed for disposable diapers. In line with this decision, it was decided to gain experience by managing key elements of Pampers (such as product and copy strategy) on a Europe-wide basis. A senior manager was transferred from the German subsidiary where Pampers had been launched in 1973 to ETC where he was given responsibility for leading key activities on Pampers in all subsidiaries.

The brand promotion manager responsible for Pampers in France at the time recalled the experiment:

> As soon as it was known I would be principally working with the European Pampers manager in ETC and not the subsidiary GM, my local support dried up. I couldn't get a brand manager or even an assistant to work with me. The French subsidiary manager was preoccupied with the Motiv [dishwashing liquid] launch, and was trying to regain leadership with Ariel [laundry powder]. The Pampers situation was a disaster. Eventually Pampers was given back to the subsidiaries—it was the only way to get their support.

This experience conveyed a very important lesson to P&G's top management. It appeared that while coordination and planning could be effectively centralized and implemented on a European basis, the day-to-day management of the business had to continue to be executed at the local subsidiary level.

In 1980, Ed Artzt was transferred back to Cincinnati as executive vice president of P&G, and Charlie Ferguson was named Group V.P., Europe. Ferguson had a reputation as an energetic, creative, and intelligent manager who got things done. Impressed by the effectiveness of the European approach to technical development, Ferguson was convinced that a similar approach could succeed in product marketing.

With the encouragement and support of his boss, Ed Artzt, who remained a strong advocate of Europeanization, Charlie Ferguson began to test the feasibility for developing Europe-wide brand and marketing strategies. In pursuing the Euro-brand concept, as it was becoming known, Artzt and Ferguson saw Vizir, the new heavy duty liquid being prepared for launch in Germany, as being a good test case.

THE VIZIR PROJECT

Product Development

Following Lever's succcess in the U.S. with a product called Wisk, in 1974 P&G launched Era as their entrant into the fast-growing heavy-duty liquid (HDL) detergent segment. As a late entrant, however, they were unable to match Wisk's dominant share. P&G managers watching developments from Europe realized that if the HDL product concept was transferable to their market, the first company to stake out the territory would have a major advantage. The success of liquids in other product categories (e.g., household cleansers), the trend towards low temperature washes, and the availability of liquid product plant capacity, all provided additional incentives to proceed with the project.

ETC initiated its HDL project in late 1974, and as a first step tested the U.S. product Era against European powders in a small-scale test panel. Given the differences in laundry habits on either side of the Atlantic, it was not surprising that Era was evaluated poorly. The problems reported by the panel related not only to the product's washing performance (e.g., whitening ability, suds level) but also to its form. European washing machines were built with drawers that allowed different powdered products (pretreatment, main wash detergent, fabric softener) to be activated at different times in the typical 90-minute cycle. To win acceptance of a laundry liquid would be difficult. First consumers would have to be convinced that this product would achieve similar results; then their established usage behaviors would have to be changed.

Undeterred, a group at ETC began to work on a HDL product that would be more suited to European laundry practices. It was with high hopes and considerable corporate visibility that the modified European HDL product was placed in six full-scale blind tests in Germany, France, and U.K. The results were disastrous in all tests. Given the high level of internal expectations that had been created, many P&G insiders felt that the product was dead since it would be impossible to rebuild internal support and credibility.

However, the scientists at ETC were convinced that they should be able to capitalize on the intrinsic ability of a liquid detergent to incorporate three times the level of surfactants compared to a powder. (The surfactant was the critical ingredient that removes greasy stains). The challenge was to compensate for the shortcomings of the HDL that offset this important advantage. Unlike U.S. products, European powdered detergents normally contained enzymes (to break down proteins) and bleach (to oxidize stains) in addition to builders (to prevent redisposition of dirt), phosphates (to soften water), and surfactants. Unfortunately, it was not then possible to incorporate enzymes and bleach in a liquid detergent, and it was this limited capability that was behind the new product's blind test failure in Europe.

The challenge of overcoming these deficiencies excited P&G's scientists at ETC and in the U.S. Eventually they were able to patent a method to give enzymes stability in liquid form. Soon afterwards, a bleach substitute that was effective at lower temperatures was developed. The product modifications showed in improving consumer blind test results. In late 1976, the new HDL product won a blind test against the leading French powder, Ariel; the following year it won against Persil, the German market leader.

Although the project was still on shaky ground within P&G, the successes resulted in the establishment of a HDL brand group in Germany. The group reported to Germany's newly appointed Advertising Manager for laundry and cleaning products, Wolfgang Berndt, a 34-year-old Austrian who was recognized as one of the promising young managers in Europe. He had started his career ten years earlier in the company's Austrian subsidiary, and after gaining training and experience in brand management in Austria, U.K., and Germany, had spent two years in Cincinnati as a Brand Manager in the parent company's Toilet Goods Division. He returned to Europe in 1973 as Brand Promotion Manager in P&G Italy, before transferring to Germany a year later. He was appointed Advertising Manager in 1977, and having been in this new position only a few months, Berndt was keen to ensure he gave appropriate attention to this important but delicate new HDL responsibility.

In early 1977, Colgate began test marketing Axion, a HDL formula that was similar to its U.S. product, Dynamo. Axion showed excellent initial results, gaining almost 4 percent share in three months. However, sales declined from this peak and within 18 months Colgate closed down the test market and withdrew Axion.

Meanwhile, P&G's research team had developed three important additional breakthroughs: a fatty acid that provided similar water-softening performance to phosphate, a suds suppressant so the product would function in European drum washing machines, and a patented washing machine anticorrosion ingredient. By 1979, European development efforts had shifted to product aesthetics, and the search began for perfumes compatible with the newly formulated *HDL-Formula SB* as it was known.

Meanwhile, during this period Henkel had been working to reformulate their leading powder and relaunched it as New Persil. Blind tests against New Persil in early 1980 were a breakeven. Finally, in October 1980 with a new fragrance, Procter's Formula SB won a blind test against New Persil by 53 to 47. The product's superiority was confirmed in subsequent tests against the main competitive powders in France (58 to 42 win for Formula SB) and in the U.K. (61 to 39 win).

Now, Berndt and his German brand group were ready to recommend a full-scale test market. During the previous 18 months they had cleared the proposed brand name (Vizir), appointed an advertising agency (Grey), designed packaging (bottles and labels), and collected and analyzed the masses of consumer and market data that were necessary to justify any new product launched in P&G. Management up to the highest level was interested and involved. Although an initial capital approval had been received for $350,000 to buy molds and raw materials, the test market plan for Berlin was expected to involve a further investment of $1.5 million plus $750,000 for original advertising production and research. A national launch would involve an additional $1.5 million in capital investment and $16 million in marketing costs and would pay out in about 3 years if the product could gain a 4 percent market share. A Europe-wide launch would be 5 or 6 times that amount.

While Berndt and his team had decided to proceed with the test market, a great deal of uncertainty still surrounded Vizir. There were some in the company questioning whether it made sense to launch this product at all in Germany, particularly with the proposed marketing positioning and copy strategy. Others were less concerned about the German launch but were strongly opposed to the suggestion that Vizir be made a Eurobrand and launched in all key European markets.

Vizir Launch Decision

One issue that had resulted in some major concern in P&G's senior management related to Vizir's positioning in the detergent market. Its strength was that it gave superior cleaning performance on greasy stains at low temperatures, and (following the product improvements) matched powder performance on enzymatic stains and whiteness. The problem was that P&G's Ariel, the leading low-temperature laundry powder in Germany, made similar performance claims, and it was feared that

Vizir would cannibalize its sales. So close were their selling propositions that two separate agencies operating independently produced almost identical commercials for Vizir and Ariel in early 1981 (Exhibit 2).

The German brand group argued that Vizir had to be positioned in this way, since this was the promise that had resulted in high trials during the Axion test. To position it as a pretreatment product would severely limit its sales potential, while to emphasize peripheral benefits like fabric care or softness would not have broad appeal. They argued that it had to be seen as a mainwash product with superior cleaning performance at lower temperatures.

Another concern being expressed by some managers was that P&G was creating a product segment that could result in new competitive entries and price erosion in the stagnant heavy duty detergent market. Liquids were much easier to make than powders and required a much smaller capital investment. ("For powders, you need a detergent tower—liquids can be made in a bath tub," according to one manager.) Although P&G had patented many of its technological breakthroughs, they were a less effective barrier to entry than might be expected. One product development manager explained:

> Our work on Vizir was very creative, but not a very effective barrier to competition. Often it's like trying to patent a recipe for an apple pie. We can specify ingredients and compositions in an ideal range or a preferred range, but competitors can copy the broad concepts and work around the patented ranges. And, believe me, they are all monitoring our patents! Even if they don't (or can't) copy our innovations, there are other ways to solve the problems. If enzymes are unstable in liquid form, you could solve that by dumping in lots of enzymes so that enough will still be active by the estimated usage date.

If capital costs were low, and products could be imitated (at least partially), the concern was that new entrants could open up a market for "white labels" (generic products). Without the product or the market development costs of P&G they probably could undercut their prices. The Germans' proposed pricing strategy had been to price at an equivalent "cost-per-job" as the leading powders. This pricing strategy resulted in a slightly higher gross profit margin for Vizir compared to powders. The pricing decision was justified on two grounds: a premium price was required to be consistent with the product's premium image, and also to avoid overall profit erosion, assuming that Vizir would cannibalize some sales of the company's low temperature laundry detergent brands.

At this time P&G was a strong number 2 in the German detergent market—the largest in Europe. Henkel's leading brand, Persil, was positioned as an all-temperature all-purpose powder, and held a 17 percent share.[1] P&G's entrant into the all-temperature segment was Dash, and this brand had 5½ percent share. However, the company's low-temperature brand, Ariel, had a share of 11 percent and was a leader in this fast-growing segment, far ahead of Lever's Omo (4½ percent) and Henkel's new entrant, Mustang (2½ percent).

The final argument of the opponents was that even ignoring these risks there

---

Exhibit 2   Comparative Scripts: Vizir and Ariel Commercials

Vizir ("Peter's Pants")	*Ariel* ("Helen Hedy")
(Woman in laundry examining newly washed pants on her son)	(Woman in laundry holding up daughter's blouse)

Announcer: Hey, Peter's things look pretty nice.

Woman: Thanks.

Announcer: Too bad they're not completely clean.

Woman: What?

Announcer: There's still oily dirt from his bicycle.

Woman: I can't boil modern fabrics. And without boiling they don't get cleaner.

Announcer: Oh yes! Here is Vizir, the new liquid detergent Vizir, the liquid powder that gets things cleaner. Without boiling!

Woman: Bicycle oil will come out? Without boiling?

Announcer: Yes, one cap of Vizir in the main wash—and on tough soil pour a little Vizir on directly. Then wash. Let's test Vizir against boilwash powder. These make-up stains were washed in powder at 60°—not clean. On top we put this unwashed dirty towel, then pour on Vizir. Vizir's liquid power penetrates the soil and dissolves it, as well as the stain that boilwash powder left behind.

Woman: Incredible. The bicycle oil—gone! Without boiling. Through and through cleaner.

Announcer: Vizir—liquid power to get things cleaner.

Announcer: Looks beautifully clean again, doesn't it?

Helen: Yes, sure.

Announcer: Also close up?

Helen: Well, no. When you really look up close—that's gravy. A stain like that never comes out completely.

Announcer: Why is that?

Helen: Because you just can't boil these modern things. I can't get Barbel's blouse really clean without boiling.

Announcer: Then use Ariel. It can clean without boiling.

Helen: Without boiling? Even these stains? That I want to see.

Announcer: THE TEST: With prewash and mainwash at low temperature we are washing stubborn stains like egg and gravy. The towel on the right had Ariel's cleaning power.

Helen: Hey, it's really true. The gravy on Barbel's blouse is completely gone. Even against the light—deep down clean. All this without boiling.

Announcer: Ariel—without boiling, still clean!

were serious doubts that this represented a real market opportunity. P&G's marketing of its HDL in the U.S. had not been an outstanding success. Furthermore Colgate's experience with their European test market had been very disappointing.

In early 1981, Wolfgang Berndt's attention was drawn to an interesting article that concluded that it would be difficult for a liquid to compete in the European heavy duty detergent field. The paper, presented to an industry association congress in September 1980 by Henkel's director of product development and two other scientists, concluded that heavy duty liquids would continue to expand their penetration of the U.S. market, due to the less demanding comparison standard of American powder detergents, and also to the compatibility of HDLs with American washing practices. In Europe, by contrast, the paper claimed that liquids would likely remain specialty products with small market share (1 percent compared to 20 percent in the U.S.). This limited HDL market potential was due to the superiority of European powder detergents, and the different European washing habits (higher temperatures, washing machine characteristics, etc.).

While managers in Brussels and Cincinnati were wrestling with these difficult strategic issues, Wolfgang Berndt was becoming increasingly nervous. He and his Vizir brand group were excited by the product and committed to its success. Initial test market readings from Berlin were encouraging (see Exhibit 3) but they were certain that Henkel was following Vizir's performance in Berlin as closely as they were. The product had now been in development and testing for seven years, and the German group felt sure that Henkel knew their intentions and would counterattack swiftly and strongly to protect their dominant position in their home market. By the early summer, rumors were beginning to spread in the trade that Henkel was planning a major new product. Henkel salesmen had been recalled from vacation and retailers were being sounded out for support on promotional programs.

On three separate occasions Wolfgang or a member of his group presented their analysis of the test market and their concerns about a preemptive strike; but on each occasion it was decided to delay a national launch. Senior management on both sides of the Atlantic explained it was just too risky to invest in a major launch on the basis of 3 or 4 months of test results. Experience had shown that a 1-year reading was necessary to give a good basis for such an important decision.

Eurobrand Decision

Another critical issue to be decided concerned the scope of the product launch. Within P&G's European organization, the budding Eurobrand concept, whereby there would be much greater coordination of marketing strategies of brands in Europe, was extremely controversial. Some thought it might conflict with the existing philosophy that gave country subsidiary managers the freedom to decide what products were most likely to succeed in their local market, in what form, and when.

The primary argument advanced by Artzt and Ferguson and other managers with similar views was that the time was now ripe for a common European laundry detergent. While widely differing washing practices between countries had justi-

Exhibit 3   **Selected Test Market Results: Vizir Berlin Test Market**

A. Total Shipments and Share

Month	Shipments: MSU (Volume Index)		Share (%)	
	Actual	**Target**	**Actual**	**Target**
February	4.6	1.8		
March	5.2	2.5	2.2	1.8
April	9.6	4.5	5.2	2.7
May	3.1	3.1	3.4	3.4

B. Consumer Research Results

Use and Awareness (at 3 months; 293 responses)			Attitude Data (at 3 months; including free-sample-only users)		
	Vizir	**Mustang[1]**		**Vizir**	**Mustang[1]**
Ever used (%)[2]	28	22	Unduplicated comments on:		
Past 4 weeks	15	9	whiteness, brightness, cleaning or stain removal	65/11[3]	58/8[3]
			cleaning or stain removal	49/8	52/4
Ever purchased[2]	13	15	cleaning	12/2	17/NA
Past 4 weeks	8	6	stain removal	37/6	35/NA
Twice or more	4	NA	odor	30/4	15/3
Brand on hand	15	11	effect on clothes	7/—	13/6
Large sizes	3	5	form (liquid)	23/11	NA
Advertising awareness	47	89			
Brand awareness	68	95			

[1]Mustang was a recently launched Henkel low-temperature powder on which comparable consumer data was available. It was judged to have been only moderately successful, capturing 2½ percent market share compared to Ariel's 11 percent share as low-temperature segment leader.

[2]Difference between use and purchase data due to introductory free sample program.

[3]Number of unduplicated comments, favorable/unfavorable about the product in user interviews. (E.g., Among Vizir users interviewed, 65 commented favorably about whiteness, brightness, cleaning or stain removal, while 11 commented negatively about one or more of those attributes.)

fied, up until now, national products tailored to local habits, market data indicated a converging trend in consumer laundry habits (see Exhibit 4).

Others were quick to point out that despite the trends there were still huge differences in washing habits that were much more important than the similarities at this stage. For example, Spain and Italy still had a large handwash segment; in U.K. and Belgium top-loading washers were still important; and in Southern Europe, natural fiber clothing still predominated. Besides, the raw statistical trends could be misleading. Despite the trend to lower temperature washing, even in Germany over 80 percent of housewives still used the boilwash (over 60°C) for some loads. In general, they regarded the boilwash as the standard by which they judged washing cleanliness.

Some subsidiary managers also emphasized that the differences went well beyond customer preferences. Their individual market structures would prevent any uniform marketing strategy from succeeding. They cited data on differences in television cost and access, national legislation on product characteristics and promotion tool usage, differences in distribution structure and competitive behavior. All these structural factors would impede standardization of brands and marketing strategies Europe-wide.

The second point Artzt and Ferguson raised was that greater coordination was needed to protect subsidiaries' profit opportunities. (However, they emphasized that subsidiary managers should retain ultimate profit responsibility and a leadership or concurrence role in all decisions affecting their operations.)

Increasingly, competitors had been able to imitate P&G's new and innovative products and marketing strategies, and preempt them in national markets where the local subsidiary was constrained by budget, organization, or simple poor judgment from developing the new product category or market segment. For example, Pampers had been introduced in Germany in 1973, but was not launched in France until 1978. Meanwhile in 1976, Colgate had launched a product called Calline (a literal French translation of Pampers) with similar package color, product position, and marketing strategy, and had taken market leadership. Late introduction also cost Pampers' market leadership in Italy. The product was just being introduced in the U.K. in 1981. An equally striking example was provided by Lenor, a product similar to Downy in the U.S. This new brand was launched in 1963 in Germany, creating a new fabric softener product category. It quickly became an outstanding market success. Nineteen years later, Lenor made its debut in France as the number three entrant in the fabric softener category, and consequently faced a much more difficult marketing task.

Artzt and Ferguson were determined to prevent recurrences of such instances. Particularly for new brands, they wanted to ensure that product development and introduction was coordinated to ensure a consistent Europe-wide approach, and furthermore, that marketing strategies were thought through from a European perspective. This meant thoroughly analyzing the possibility of simultaneous or closely sequenced European product introductions.

At the country level, many were quick to point out that since the company

Exhibit 4 Selected Market Research Data

A. Selected Washing Practices

	Germany		U.K.		France		Italy		Spain	
	1973	1978	1973	1978	1973	1978	1973	1978	1973	1978
Washing Machine Penetration										
Households with drum machines (%)	76	83	10	26	59	70	70	79	24	50
Washing Temperature										
To 60° (including handwash)	51	67	71	82	48	68	31	49	63	85
Over 60°	49	33	29	18	52	32	69	51	37	15
Fabric Softener Use										
Loads with fabric softener (%)	68	69	36	47	52	57	21	35	18	37

B. Selected Consumer Attitude Data (German Survey Only)

	Grease Based	Bleach Sensitive	Enzyme Sensitive
Laundry Cleaning Problems (% respondents claim)[1]			
Most frequent stains (%)	61	53	34
Desired improvement (%)	65	57	33
in washes to 60°	78	53	25
in washes above 60°	7	36	65

[1]Do not add to 100 percent because multiple responses allowed.

271

wanted to keep the subsidiary as a profit center, the concept was not feasible. To establish a new brand, and particularly to create a new product category like disposable diapers was an incredibly expensive and often highly risky proposition. Many country general managers questioned whether they should gamble their subsidiary's profitability on costly, risky new launches, especially if they were not at all convinced their local market was mature enough to accept it. In many cases they had not yet completed the task of building a sound base in heavy and light duty detergents, and personal products. They felt that their organization should not be diverted from this important task.

The third set of arguments put forward by the advocates of the Eurobrand concept related to economics. They cited numerous examples: the fact that there were nine different Dash formulas in Europe; Mr. Clean (known as Mr. Propre, Meister Proper, etc.) was sold in nine different sizes Europe-wide. To go to a single formula, standard size packs and multilingual labels could save the company millions of dollars in mold costs, line downtime for changeovers, sourcing flexibility, reduced inventory levels, etc.

Other managers pointed out that the savings could easily be offset by the problems standardization would lead to. The following represent some of the comments made at a country general managers' meeting at which Charlie Ferguson raised the Eurobrand issue for discussion:

> We have to listen to the consumer. In blind tests in my market that perfume cannot even achieve breakeven.
>
> The whole detergent market is in 2-kilo packs in Holland. To go to a European standard of 3-kg and 5-kg sizes would be a disaster for us.
>
> We have low phosphate laws in Italy that constrain our product formula. And we just don't have hypermarkets like France and Germany where you can drop off pallet loads.

One general manager put it most forcefully in a memo he wrote to ETC management:

> There is no such thing as a Eurocustomer so it makes no sense to talk about Eurobrands. We have an English housewife whose needs are different from a German hausfrau. If we move to a system that allows us to blur our thinking we will have big problems.
>
> Product standardization sets up pressures to try to meet everybody's needs (in which case you build a Rolls Royce that nobody can afford) and countervailing pressures to find the lowest common denominator product (in which case you make a product that satisfies nobody and which cannot compete in any market). These pressures probably result in the foul middle compromise that is so often the outcome of committee decision.

Organization Decision

The strategic questions of whether to launch Vizir, and if so on what scale, also raised some difficult questions about the existing organization structure and internal decision-making processes. If product market decisions were to be taken more in relation to Europe-wide strategic assessments and less in response to locally perceived opportunities, what implications did that have for the traditional role and responsibility of the country general manager? And if the Eurobrand concept was accepted, what organizational means were necessary to coordinate activities among the various country subsidiaries?

By the time Charlie Ferguson became vice president of P&G Europe, the nontechnical staff in ETC had grown substantially from the 20 or so people that used to work with Tom Bower in the early 1970s. Ferguson was convinced that his predecessor, Ed Artzt, had been moving in the right direction in trying to inject a Europe-wide perspective to decisions, and in aiming to coordinate more activities among subsidiaries. He wanted to reinforce the organizational shift by changing the responsibilities of the three geographic division managers reporting to him.

In addition to their existing responsibilities for several subsidiaries, Ferguson gave each of these managers Europe-wide responsibility for one or more lines of business. For example, the division manager responsible for the U.K., French, Belgian, and Dutch subsidiaries was also given responsibility for packaged soaps and detergents Europe-wide. Although these roles were clearly coordinative in nature, the status and experience of these managers meant that their advice and recommendations would carry a good deal of weight, particularly on strategic and product planning issues.

Following this change, for the first time clear Euro-wide objectives and priorities could be sent by line of business, product group, or brand. Not surprisingly, some country subsidiary managers wondered whether their authority and autonomy were being eroded. Partly to deal with this problem, and partly because the division managers had neither the time nor the resources to adequately manage their product responsibilities, Ferguson created a new organizational forum he termed the Euro Brand Team.

Borrowing from the successful technical team concept, each key brand would have a team with a "lead country." Typically the country subsidiary with the most resources, the leading market positions or the most commitment for a product would be given the lead role so it could spread its knowledge, expertise and commitment. The charter of the lead country would be to coordinate the analysis of opportunities for the standardization of the product, its promotion and packaging. It would also be asked to facilitate the simplification of the brand's management by coordinating activities and eliminating needless duplication between subsidiaries.

The main forum for achieving this responsibility would be the Euro Brand Team meetings. It was envisioned that various managers from the regional office and the subsidiaries would be invited to these meetings. From ETC, the appropriate European division manager and European functional managers (e.g., technical, manufacturing, purchasing, advertising, etc.) would be invited. Advertising and brand managers from all countries selling the product would also be invited. It was proposed that the meeting be chaired by the brand manager from the lead country. Thus, a typical team might have more than twenty invited participants.

At the subsidiary level, the proposal received mixed reviews. Some saw the teams as a good way to have increased local management participation in Eurobrand decisions. These individuals saw the European technical teams as evidence such an approach could work, and felt it represented a far better solution than having such decisions shaped largely by an enlarged staff group at ETC. Another group saw the Euro Brand Teams as a further risk to the autonomy of the country manager. Some also saw it as a threat to intersubsidiary relations rather than an aid. One general manager from a smaller country subsidiary explained:

> When a big, resource-rich subsidiary like Germany is anointed with the title of Lead Country, as it probably will be for a large number of brands, I am concerned that they will use their position and expertise to dominate the teams. The rich will become more powerful, and the small subs will wither. I believe this concept will generate further hostility between subsidiaries. Pricing and volume are the only tools we have left. The general manager's role will be compromised if these are dissipated in team discussions.

Another concern was that team meetings would not be an effective decision-making forum. With individual subsidiaries still responsible for and measured on their local profitability, it was felt that participants would go in with strongly held parochial views that they would not be willing to compromise. Some claimed that because the teams' roles and responsibilities were not clear it would become another time-consuming block to decision making rather than a means to achieve progress on Eurobrands. A subsidiary general manager commented:

> The agenda for the Euro Brands Teams is huge, but its responsibilities and powers are unclear. For such a huge and emotionally charged task, it is unrealistic to expect the "brand manager of the day" to run things. The teams will bog down and decisions will take forever. How many of these meetings can we attend without tying up our top management? Our system is all checks and no balances. We are reinforcing an organization in which no one can say yes—they can only veto. With all the controls on approvals, we've lost the knack to experiment.

At least one manager at ETC voiced his frustration directly: "If we were serious (about standardization), we would stop paying lip service, and tell everyone 'Like it or not, we're going to do it.' "

Charlie Ferguson remained convinced that the concept made sense, and felt that *if* Vizir was to be launched and *if* it was to be considered a Eurobrand, it might provide a good early test for Euro Brand Teams.

NOTE

1. These share data are related to the total detergent market (including dishwashing liquid). The heavy-duty segment (i.e., laundry detergent) represented about two-thirds of this total.

FiatGeotech and Hitachi

Fiat S.p.A. of Turin, Italy, with 1989 sales of more than $40 billion, was one of Europe's leading industrial groups. One of its wholly owned divisions, Fiat-Geotech, produced and marketed tractors, combine harvesters, and harvesting equipment under the Fiatagri brand, as well as bulldozers, loaders, excavators, and other construction equipment under the FiatGeotech brand. In 1989 net consolidated revenues of FiatGeotech were $2.3 billion, with the Farm Equipment Division generating $1.5 billion and the Construction Machinery Division $795 million in revenue, respectively. In 1989 Construction Machinery Division subsidiaries sold 7,800 units (up 7 percent from 1988). FiatGeotech's market share, on a global basis, rose from 6 percent to 7 percent, passing 8.5 percent to 11 percent in Europe.

After a peak in the late 1970s, the global structure of the earth-moving machinery (EMM) industry changed dramatically in the early 1980s. The general recession in the Western countries, the large debts of Third World countries, and the crisis in the oil-producing countries resulted in a significant decrease in public works investments and large construction. The core business shifted toward maintenance, services, and city works, away from major greenfield construction activities. The crisis also shifted the relative importance of various product lines of EMMs toward smaller and lighter machines.

With a mature industry, with strong global competitors such as Caterpillar and Komatsu, with strongly competitive markets characterized by overcapacity and low margins, FiatGeotech reexamined its strategy. Could it realistically continue to pursue its own full line EMM strategy, or would this be prohibitive in terms of the resources that were required? The outcome of these deliberations was the pursuance of a cooperative strategy. At the same time, Hitachi Construction Machinery Company (HCM) was actively searching for joint venture partners in Europe in anticipation of increasing European protectionism and to further increase its market share. In January 1987, the two firms established a joint venture in Italy, Fiat-Hitachi Excavator, S.p.A., to manufacture and market hydraulic excavators.

The present case provides a brief historical description of the earth-moving machinery industry and its globalization. Then follows a discussion of FiatGeotech and its relatively weak competitive situation in the early 1980s. The case then discusses how the company came to pursue a cooperative strategy and delineates FiatGeotech and Hitachi's approach to forming such a joint venture. Finally, the joint venture's operations during its early stages are discussed.

EVOLUTION OF THE EARTH-MOVING MACHINERY INDUSTRY

The EMM industry in Europe took off in the late 1940s. The main product then was an adapted agricultural tractor, and the markets were national. Based on the band wagon concept, the first dozers and crawler loaders were introduced. In general, the machines had relatively weak engines, only 40 to 50 horsepower. The machines were typically sold and distributed through the same marketing channels as agricultural tractors. Caterpillar arrived in Europe with the U.S. Army, and another strong U.S. manufacturer, Allis Chalmers, was similarly establishing a presence. At that time, Fiat had only an agricultural tractor division, where simple EMMs were manufactured.

During the 1950s, the EMMs were still derived from the agricultural tractor, but the number of models had increased. The postwar reconstruction of Italy resulted in a strong domestic demand, and Fiat produced approximately 2,000 units per year. Fiat introduced the 60/C, FL/6, and AD/7 models and began to market its product in other European countries. At that time, the European market was still frequented by some international competition, including the major U.S. suppliers, but no Japanese companies were present.

In the 1960s, product development took off in earnest, and EMMs no longer displayed many similarities to the agricultural tractor. The distribution channels were also changing; new dealers were appointed, and new assembly branches opened in France and Germany. The international competition was increasing. Fiat's presence in Europe also grew, with an annual production of approximately 8,000 units. In 1964, Fiat acquired 60 percent of a smaller Italian manufacturer of excavators.

In the 1970s, the world market for EMMs reached its highest level. In 1979, a total of 198,000 units was produced, across many product lines. Of this number, Fiat produced some 10,000 units. The production know-how was mainly American, particularly with respect to larger machines, such as dozers and wheel loaders. In the mid-1970s, however, the two Japanese firms Komatsu and Hitachi also aggressively started to manufacture dozers and excavators. The degree of internationalization further increased, and global marketing became a must for all EMM manufacturers. As a consequence of the pressure to be present in the U.S. market, Fiat formed a Chicago-based joint venture with Allis Chalmers in 1974. The purpose was mainly to develop and manufacture larger EMMs. Fiat was to own 74 percent and Allis Chalmers 26 percent of the joint venture. Through the joint venture, Fiat was able to complement its product lines with wheel loaders, large dozers, scrapers, and graders. Hence, Fiat could now offer a reasonably full line of EMMs. But severe demand turndowns in the markets served by the joint venture, coupled with a number of unexpected management problems, led to disappointing performance for the joint venture. Considerable effort to improve the performance failed, and in 1985 Fiat had to acquire Allis Chalmers' share of the joint venture as part of a general salvaging effort. This led to a restructuring and scaling down of the latter firm's activities.

CHANGES IN THE COMPETITIVE SITUATION

In the early 1980s, the EMM industry became even more fiercely competitive. Demand declined rapidly, reaching a low in 1983. The main reasons for this industry-wide recession were:

- The general recession in the Western countries
- The debt crisis in the Third World
- The slow-down crisis in the oil-producing countries as a result of depressed oil prices

In general, the recession had two major effects on the EMM industry. First, there was a dramatic worldwide decrease in public works investments and large greenfield construction projects, and this in turn resulted in a significant drop in large contractors' demand for EMMs, particularly for heavy equipment. The global production of EMMs decreased from roughly 200,000 units in 1979 to less than 150,000 units in 1983—a decrease of more than 25 percent. Even though production increased somewhat after 1983, the high levels of sales from the late 1970s did not return until 1988. It should be noted, however (see Exhibit 1), that the main markets did not all decline or recover at the same rate.

In addition, not only were fewer EMMs needed, but these were also typically smaller and consequently represented less value per unit. One result of this new situation was that many EMM manufacturers left the industry: Massey Ferguson withdrew in 1981, IBH in 1984, and International Harvester in 1985. The recession also changed the relative importance and size of the product lines in the industry. As can be seen from Exhibit 2, excavators and backhoe loaders—typically smaller vehicles—became relatively more important. Hence, the excavators and backhoe loaders gradually became the two most important product lines in the industry, while bulldozers and crawler loaders lost ground. The volume of wheel loaders

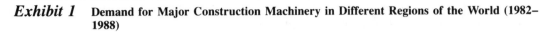

Exhibit 1   **Demand for Major Construction Machinery in Different Regions of the World (1982–1988)**

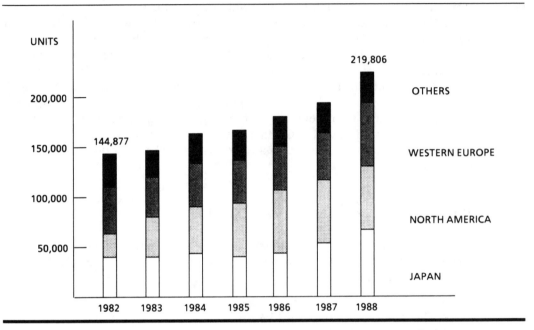

remained approximately the same. The composition of demand by products did differ among the major geographic areas, as can be seen from Exhibit 3. These differences reflect underlying differences in infrastructure, the construction industry's structure and practices, and economic climates.

GLOBALIZATION OF THE EMM INDUSTRY

In the early 1980s, the EMM industry accelerated in its evolution to become even more global. There were at least four reasons for this. First, the industry had become more capital intensive and less labor intensive—the result, primarily, of the need for increasingly sophisticated robotization. Consequently the industry developed a greater need for capital. Second, the level of technical development was accelerating quickly. Companies had to increase their R&D spending significantly in order to keep even with the competition. Third, it became increasingly necessary to offer a full line of EMMs. Customers often purchased several types of EMMs; therefore, it was preferable that all equipment be supplied by one manufacturer, through one distributor, with a standardized service function and after-market sup-

Exhibit 2   **Worldwide Demand for Major Construction Machinery (1982–1988)**

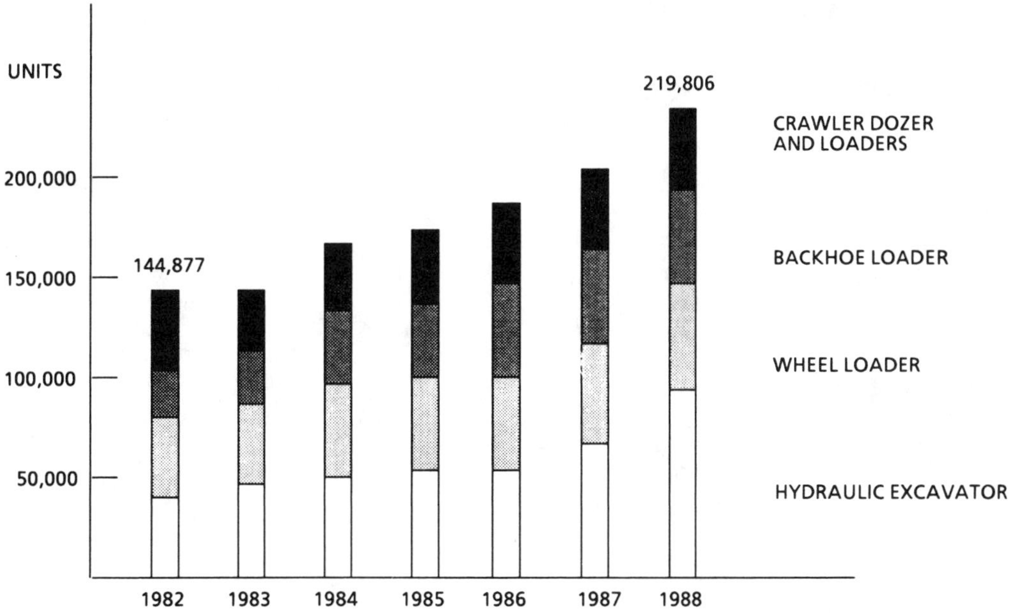

UNITS

219,806

CRAWLER DOZER
AND LOADERS

200,000

BACKHOE LOADER

144,877

150,000

100,000

WHEEL LOADER

50,000

HYDRAULIC EXCAVATOR

1982   1983   1984   1985   1986   1987   1988

port. Finally, there was no longer much difference among EMMs offered in various parts of the world; the product had become global, and global scale and scope advantages were increasingly needed to succeed.

Over time, it became obvious that companies needed to be present in all three major trading blocks in order to survive. For marketing purposes, one of the key issues was to be recognized as a "local" company in each of these markets. Of all the players in the industry, only Caterpillar had fully succeeded in gaining this image.

Caterpillar, the major global company in the industry, was the major actor in the U.S. and European markets and was also present in Japan through a joint venture with Mitsubishi. The second largest manufacturer, Komatsu, was also global and had manufacturing facilities in Europe and the United States in addition to its home base.

Exhibit 4 provides a list of the major EMM manufacturers and their involvement in the four major product-line categories. As can be seen, the major companies had developed a number of collaborative arrangements in order to offer fuller product lines within affordable resource limits. Excluding the Caterpillar-Mitsubishi joint venture, Fiat ranked third in the world among EMM manufacturers. The sales

Exhibit 3   **Demand by Products and Areas (1988)**

Hydraulic Excavator (Over 6 Tons)

Wheel Loader

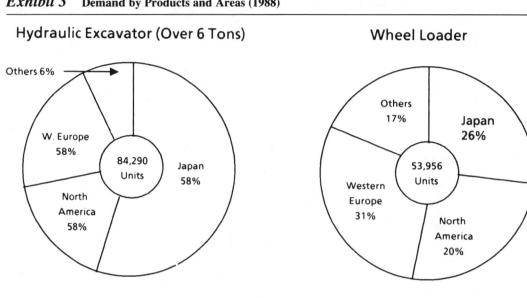

Backhoe Loader

Bulldozer

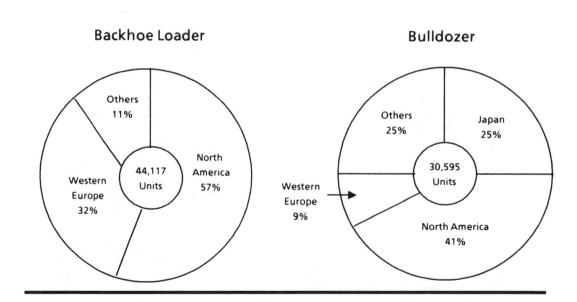

Exhibit 4   **Product Development Strategies of Major Manufacturers (1988)**

	Construction Machinery Sales (Billion Yen)	Bulldozers	Hydraulic Excavators	Wheel Loaders	Dump Trucks	Remarks
Caterpillar	1,070	Own development	Collaboration with Mitsubishi	Own development	Own development	Worldwide full-line manufacturer
Komatsu	450	Own development	Own development	Own development	Own development	Worldwide full-line manufacturer; collaboration with Dresser
Shin Caterpillar Mitsubishi	290	Own development	Own development	Own development	Own development	Subsidiary of Caterpillar and Mitsubishi; Heavy Industries
Fiat	285 (Agricultural machinery included)	Own development	Collaboration with Hitachi	Own development	—	Worldwide full-line manufacturer
Case	250	Own development	Invest in Poclain	Own development	—	Worldwide full-line manufacturer
Hitachi Construction Machinery	220	—	Own development	Joint development with John Deere and Furukawa	—	Promoting sales mainly with hydraulic excavators
John Deere	450	Own development	Collaboration with Hitachi	Joint development with Hitachi and Furukawa	—	Sales of full-line products mainly in North America
VME	450	—	Invest in Ackerman	Volvo Clark	Volvo Eucrid	Worldwide full-line manufacturer

Note: Exchange rate: $1.00 = 130 yen.

volumes for each producer indicate clearly, however, that after the "big two" there were a number of much smaller producers, each likely to struggle to provide a full product line globally.

The relative leadership position and degree of dominance differed among the firms on major product categories. Caterpillar, for instance, had always been an undisputed leader in the bulldozer segment but had been relatively weaker in hydraulic excavators. Until 1975, the technological leadership in excavators had been European, with Poclain and Liebher being the leading companies. But while the European market declined in the late 1970s, the Japanese market increased significantly. The Japanese manufacturers of hydraulic excavators, dominated by Hitachi Construction Machinery and Mitsubishi, had started with technical licenses from European companies in the 1960s. Over time, the technological edge shifted toward these Japanese companies.

Alliances were formed among partners from all three major trading blocks. The cooperative agreement between Caterpillar and Mitsubishi, the entrance of Komatsu on the European market, and the increasing presence of Hitachi in Europe made the future situation of a firm such as FiatGeotech very delicate.

FIATGEOTECH'S POSITION

The competitive situation of FiatGeotech was that of a "not quite global," medium-size, full-line manufacturer with a strong base in the domestic Italian market. Due to the fact that the company offered a full line of products, its position was also relatively strong in some international markets, notably in several European countries and in Brazil. Its manufacturing plants for EMMs were located in Italy, Brazil, the United Kingdom, and the United States—the latter a consequence of the joint venture with Allis Chalmers in 1974.

By the mid 1980s, FiatGeotech had significantly restructured its manufacturing activities in the United Kingdom and in the United States, as well as in the production units in Italy. Plants were consolidated, modernized, or closed down. The product lines were also modernized and simplified. Certain models were phased out.

In the excavator segment, FiatGeotech was a medium-sized European manufacturer with an annual production of some 1,000 excavators. Its competitive position in the Italian home market had traditionally been strong but was perceived as weakening, and it was relatively weaker in most of the other European markets. Even though the excavators had the reputation of relatively good quality, the line did not have sufficient technical sophistication to compete effectively with the other leading EMM manufacturers, such as Caterpillar and Komatsu. The company had problems in living up to the need for accelerated technical development; it had estimated that it could develop only one new model per year. The technological gap between FiatGeotech's excavators and those of the major competitors was thus rapidly widening. Further, one core component of the strategically critical and sophisticated hydraulic system was not manufactured within the Fiat Group but had to be purchased from competitors. Only Caterpillar, Hitachi, and Komatsu manufactured their own hydraulic systems. This gave them distinct advantages in quality and cost. It should be noted that FiatGeotech never had taken an interest in manufacturing such hydraulic systems, because of its recognition of its size limitation.

It was becoming increasingly difficult to find the internal resources within FiatGeotech to compete with the emerging strong competitors and strategic alliances. This led the company's management team to consider seeking a strategic alliance themselves. Many agonizing discussions were needed to reach this stage, given the negative experience the group had had in its joint venture with Allis Chalmers. There were three main reasons that made FiatGeotech's management conclude that the company would either have to withdraw from the hydraulic excavator segment of the EMM industry or upgrade its lines through a cooperative strategy:

1. The requirements to be global in this industry
2. The costs of the necessary technical improvements of the products
3. The emerging cooperative tendencies among the other main actors

A JOINT VENTURE WITH HITACHI CONSTRUCTION MACHINERY (HCM)

In April 1986, a delegation from the Sumitomo Group visited FiatGeotech. Prior to this meeting, Fiat's vice-chairman, Dr. U. Agnelli, had contacts with the chairman of the Sumitomo Group. During this visit, executives from both companies discussed FiatGeotech's problems and possibilities, including the desire to find a joint venture partner. These discussions were relatively detailed.

At that time, HCM produced annually some 15,000 hydraulic excavators. These were generally sophisticated with very advanced technology. Because of its advanced technical know-how and experience, HCM's overall competitive position in the domestic Japanese market was very strong. As already noted from Exhibit 3, the Japanese market in this EMM segment was much larger than both the European and the American markets together. It was dominated by HCM, Komatsu, and Mitsubishi. HCM exported some 1,000 excavators per year to Europe—a number approximately equal to FiatGeotech's total European sales.

Several reasons, however, made HCM interested in considering a cooperative strategy. The company ultimately wanted to offer a full line of EMMs. There was also a strong wish to increase its global market shares for its existing excavator products. This was seen as increasingly difficult, not only because of the emergence of the European Economic Community, but also because of increasing European protectionism in the form of anti-dumping tariffs of 12 to 32 percent on Japanese goods in the excavator segment. In conclusion, the company decided to search for a joint venture between FiatGeotech and HCM's partner in Europe. Initial discussions with VME (Volvo/Clark) did not materialize in any cooperative agreement, however.

During May and June 1986, Sumitomo discussed the possibilities of a joint venture between FiatGeotech and HCM. In July 1986, FiatGeotech's top management went to Japan and was introduced to HCM by Sumitomo, and a letter of intent was signed between the parties. Dr. P. Sighicelli, who subsequently became president of the joint venture, remembered that Sumitomo took an active role as catalyst in the negotiations and thereby helped the parties overcome initial difficulties. This was seen as particularly helpful given the fact that the parties had virtually no in-depth experience with each other. HCM's management team, in particular, had come to put a lot of emphasis on knowing its partner and developing deep two-way trust. Its long-term cooperation with John Deere had contributed to this attitude.

At the time, FiatGeotech had contemplated building on its own a new manufacturing plant for excavators. HCM did not have a plant in Europe. It became obvious that, through a joint venture, the parties could share in risks, investments, and future development.

The joint venture, Fiat-Hitachi Excavator S.p.A., was established in November 1986, with a new plant in San Mauro outside Turino. Ultimately, the plans were to manufacture between 2,500 and 3,000 units of 12-to-45-ton hydraulic excavators for the European market, the Mediterranean basin, and some African countries. The excavators were to be marketed through an integrated sales organization under FiatGeotech control. In principle, both parent companies were to withdraw as separate players from these markets. They were to jointly meet the competition through the joint venture.

FiatGeotech owned 51 percent and had four board members; Hitachi had a 44 percent ownership share with two board members; and Sumitomo, a 5 percent share with one board member. The staffing of the joint venture was almost exclusively Italian. In addition to the president, Dr. Sighicelli, Mr. K. Ogimoto from HCM served as the executive vice president, with responsibility for technology. From seven to ten additional executives were assigned to the joint venture from HCM at different times, all functioning as technological advisors. Sumitomo was responsible for importation of key components from HCM to Italy. Exhibit 5 provides a summary of the joint venture's activities.

Based on its initial performance, the joint venture turned out, by most measures, to be a success. The San Mauro plant was set up in a way similar to a typical Hitachi plant, and high quality levels—at par with Japanese standards—were achieved for the products. The productivity levels were also at par with Japanese standards. A key reason for this was the extensive investment in state-of-the-art robotics.

Both parties felt that the joint venture contract would have to be of long duration for such a strategic alliance to work. Both parties recognized that they contributed important complementary inputs to the joint venture, thereby justifying the division of benefits. HCM continued to provide the most advanced technol-

Exhibit 5   **Hitachi's Joint Ventures in Construction Machinery**

	Deere-Hitachi Construction Machinery Corporation		Fiat-Hitachi Excavators S.p.A.		
Business	Production and sale of hydraulic excavators		Production and sale of hydraulic excavators		
Company Foundation	May 1988		November 1986		
	Billion Yen		Billion Lira		
Scale of business	1989	1991	1988	1989	1991
Sales	35.5*	41.7*	163	224	321
Production Units per year	208	3,400	1,462	1,943	2,600
	*Includes both imported machines and local production				
Sales Territories	North, Central, and South America		All European, Mediterranean countries and Africa		
Capital and Shares	Capital:	30.8 million dollars (4.3 billion yen)	Capital: 73.8 lira		
	Shares:	Deere 50% Hitachi 50%	Shares: Fiat 51% Hitachi 49%		
Employees	140		775		

ogy, enabling the joint venture to produce competitive and reliable machines. FiatGeotech, on the other hand, was responsible for marketing, including after-sales service and spare parts supply as well as the overall management of the joint venture. A potential problem, the integration of dealers in Europe, was resolved in an amicable way. The basic principle was to make use of both dealership organizations wherever these were complementing each other, and to choose the strongest dealer where there would be duplication. The costs of dealer integration were shared in proportion to the capital contributions to the joint venture.

The marketplace responded very favorably to the new product. Demand was so strong that the plant's capacity had to be subsequently increased.

COOPERATION BETWEEN HCM AND DEERE

In May 1988, HCM and Deere signed a joint venture agreement to produce hydraulic excavators in North America. Hitachi had been the original equipment manufacturer/supplier for Deere for many years, and the two organizations thus knew each

Exhibit 6   **Joint Ventures in the EMM Industry: FiatGeotech, Hitachi, and John Deere**

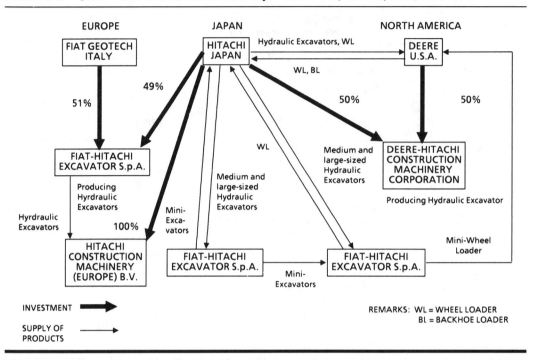

other well. It was therefore felt that as the culmination of a long cooperation, the two parties should enter into this more binding joint venture agreement. The particulars regarding the Deere-Hitachi joint venture are shown in Exhibit 5. HCM executives reflected on the fact that this joint venture with Deere had been quite easy for them, given their long-term relationship with Deere. In contrast, they felt that the joint venture with FiatGeotech, where the parties did not know each other for any length of time beforehand, had been a tougher choice to make. Despite this obstacle, however, HCM executives felt that the FiatGeotech joint venture had developed extremely well.

With the joint ventures with Deere and FiatGeotech, HCM had indeed developed a global network of cooperation. This is delineated in Exhibit 6.

A further development in this pattern of global cooperation was an agreement signed in November 1989 between Deere and FiatGeotech to develop a backhoe loader based on joint research. Another agreement between FiatGeotech and Deere called for the development of new medium-sized track-type loaders and bulldozers. Overall, the various joint ventures signaled the emergence of a more integrated pattern of global cooperation between the three players, not only within the hydraulic excavator segment but within the EMM industry as a whole.

Chapter *8*

BALANCING NEW BUSINESS DEVELOPMENT AND PROFITABILITY

The emphasis thus far has been on managing business strategy. Although the strategic intent in each business context is to facilitate business renewal, the contributions of a business to the firm's short-term profitability can vary depending on its context. Thus, for example, a business unit faced with a Pioneer business context may show poor profit performance in the short run even though it may generate for the firm an attractive growth opportunity in the long run. Similarly, a business unit attempting to build its distinctive competencies—as in a Reorient business context—may not be able to show good profit performance in the short run. Even a business unit endowed with many distinctive competencies, such as one facing an Expand business context, may show erratic profit performance because of the complexity of the industry niche in which it chooses to operate. Only a business unit operating in the Dominate business context can show a consistent profit performance. Why then should a firm seek to operate in the other three contexts? Necessity is one reason: the firm may not have distinctive competencies in all of the businesses in which it participates. Moreover, it is only by venturing into new (and often more complex) environments that the firm can establish growth options for the future. The long-term survival of the firm calls for a delicate balance between generating short-term profits and developing new business opportunities for the future.[1]

In this chapter, we examine how a portfolio of business units can be managed for both new business opportunities and profitability in a multibusiness firm. In particular, we examine how the responsibility for portfolio balance is shared between top management and divisional managers in such a firm.

This chapter is divided into two sections. We first describe the four basic options that are available to a multibusiness firm for balancing new business development and profitability. We then examine the corporate contexts to which each of these options is best suited.

THE BASIC OPTIONS

The four basic options[2] that are available may be distinguished along two major dimensions (Figure 8-1): the organization level(s) at which new business development and profitability are balanced within the firm and the primary mode it uses for generating new business opportunities.

Central Planning

Under this option, the firm's corporate or top management and its planning staff assume primary responsibility for new business development. Acquisitions and mergers are often the preferred route for generating new business opportunities. In other words, future growth options are acquired and not nurtured from within. The emphasis in the divisions is primarily on short-term profitability and on maintaining the current growth momentum. Central planning is generally used by firms that have limited opportunities for diversification in their existing businesses and therefore seek to diversify into businesses unrelated to their current product, market, or technology domains.

The approach used by Harold Geneen to manage ITT in the 1960s (see Case 11) is a good example of the central planning option. Top management at ITT carried the primary responsibility for balancing new business development and profitability. Geneen was helped in this effort by a large staff of product line managers, each of whom monitored a portion of the firm's business portfolio. New business development was mostly fueled by acquisitions planned and executed by ITT's corporate staff. Profitability was the major responsibility of divisional managers, each of whom was assigned a demanding profit budget. ITT's control and incentives systems ensured that these profit budgets were met or exceeded.

Central planning can be very effective in the hands of a strong and brilliant CEO, as was the case at ITT under Geneen, but it does have definite drawbacks. In this option, divisions are run as efficiently as possible, so as to provide predictable cash surpluses for the top management's use in its acquisition attempts. Consequently it is possible for growth opportunities at the division level to be overlooked. Moreover, managers running these divisions can become easily disenchanted with their limited role in new business development. Managerial turnover is a serious problem in this option, as was indeed the case at ITT. The success of this option also hinges on such outside factors as the general health of the stock market, the cost of acquisitions, and the societal acceptance of acquisitions and divestitures.

Corporate Portfolio Management

In contrast to divisions under the central planning option, divisions under this approach selectively enjoy greater autonomy to develop new businesses.

Even though individual divisions may contribute differently to the overall profitability or future growth goals of the firm, in the aggregate they should provide

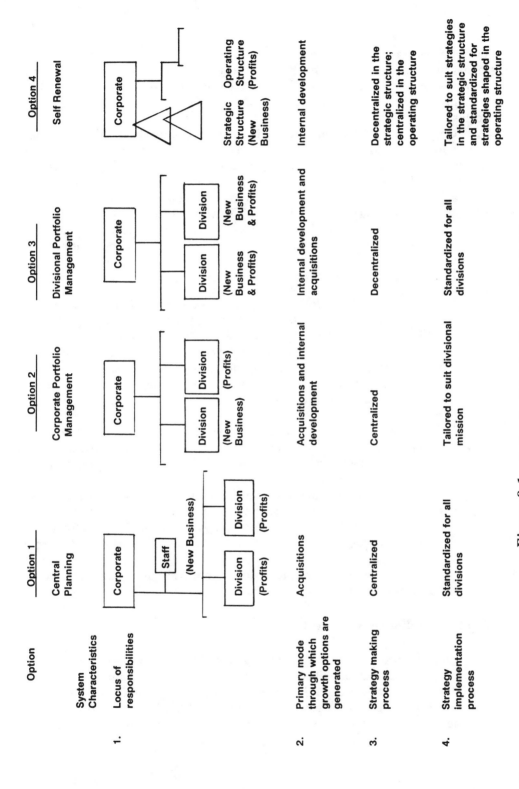

System Characteristics	Option 1 Central Planning	Option 2 Corporate Portfolio Management	Option 3 Divisional Portfolio Management	Option 4 Self Renewal
1. Locus of responsibilities	Corporate — Staff — Division (Profits), Division (Profits) (New Business)	Corporate — Division (New Business), Division (Profits)	Corporate — Division (New Business & Profits), Division (New Business & Profits)	Corporate — Strategic Structure (New Business) / Operating Structure (Profits)
2. Primary mode through which growth options are generated	Acquisitions	Acquisitions and internal development	Internal development and acquisitions	Internal development
3. Strategy making process	Centralized	Centralized	Decentralized	Decentralized in the strategic structure; centralized in the operating structure
4. Strategy implementation process	Standardized for all divisions	Tailored to suit divisional mission	Standardized for all divisions	Tailored to suit strategies in the strategic structure and standardized for strategies shaped in the operating structure

Figure 8-1 Options for Balancing Growth and Profitability

289

the firm with a balanced approach toward both. It is the responsibility of top management to audit the firm's business portfolio periodically and to initiate actions that will ensure its balance over the long run. Such an audit may provide the stimulus for initiating new ventures in some of the divisions or for making new acquisitions.

Corporate portfolio management is a popular approach among multibusiness firms.[3] Becton Dickinson and Company (see Case 6) is but one example of firms that use such an approach. At Becton Dickinson, some divisions were expected to develop new businesses aggressively and others were required to focus primarily on profitability. By clustering business units into divisions with distinct missions, it becomes relatively easy to tailor the firm's strategy process to the divisional context. Thus a division assigned a profitability mission may experience integrative planning, while another given the mission of new business development may have adaptive planning.

Despite its popularity, this approach has limitations that must temper its use:

1. *Static Design.* A portfolio configuration is but a snapshot in time. Business units evolve in their contexts, and so must their missions. It is therefore difficult to sustain the integrity of a division's mission because it is made up of several business unit missions. If the homogeneity of business missions is accomplished through top management fiat, the firm runs the risk of either missing growth opportunities in a division managed for profitability or wasting resources on futile ventures in a division managed for new business development.

2. *Labeling.* It is very difficult to avoid the typecasting of divisional managers in this approach. The administrative mission assigned to a divisional manager is often confused with his or her role in the company. For example, a divisional manager who is assigned a profitability mission may find it difficult to move on to a division assigned a mission of new business development. Managerial turnover can be a problem in this option as well.

3. *Scarce Opportunities for Development.* A related limitation of corporate portfolio management is the scarce opportunities that it provides for the development of general managers. The exposure to a limited range of business missions can contribute to a myopic view of strategy in the various business units and divisions of the firm.

Divisional Portfolio Management

This is similar to corporate portfolio management because it seeks to balance future growth options and profitability by balancing the mix of businesses in a firm's portfolio. There is one major difference—the portfolio is balanced primarily at the division level. Moreover, the emphasis is typically placed in this approach on internally generated growth options. Consequently the new businesses that are pursued are variations of the products, markets, and technologies allied to the current operations of the firm.

Examples of firms that have used divisional portfolio management are Dexter Corporation (see Case 13) and Richardson-Merrell (see Case 4). In the 1970s, both of these firms encouraged their divisions to manage their own portfolios of businesses, with very little cross-subsidization across the divisions. The role of top management was to audit periodically the divisional portfolio and to assist the divisions with any acquisitions that were needed to balance their portfolios. In Richardson-Merrell, this was done both through the formal strategic planning process and through what the firm called Previews in Depth (PID). In the Dexter Corporation, a variety of analytical tools were used by top management to evaluate and guide strategy formulation at the division level. However, divisional managers, such as Tom McGuire in Richardson-Merrell (see Case 4) and Jim Mayerhofer in the Dexter Corporation (see Case 14), had a great deal of autonomy to structure their own business portfolios.

The obvious advantages of this approach are (1) low corporate overhead, (2) no problems of cross-subsidization among divisions, (3) "a hell of a lot more interesting life" for people in the division, (4) better decisions because they are made closer to the marketplace, and (5) better leveraging of divisional competencies. However, divisional portfolio management has the drawbacks of not encouraging interdivisional cooperation and of limiting the size and risk of the new business options pursued by the firm because of the smaller pool of resources that is available at the divisional level.

Self-renewal

This option has been used in recent years by a few high-technology companies. Firms that use this option are linked in a matrixlike fashion by both a strategic and an operating structure, the former encouraging new business development and the latter ensuring profitability (Figure 8-2).

The strategic structure is used to manage new strategic initiatives for existing businesses as well as to seek new business opportunities that build on the firm's core competencies. The strategic structure, however, is not a permanent structure. The more-permanent operating structure deals with the implementation of strategies. The link between the strategic and the operating structures is through the assignment of roles in the strategic structure to managers from the various operating divisions of the firm. They are tied (through the strategic structure) into several temporary task forces or think tanks, each of which is responsible for developing new business options for the firm.

We might have a hierarchy of ad hoc task forces, as indicated on the left side of Figure 8-2, where each serves particular entities within the formal operating structure. Three such task forces are shown in Figure 8-2 for purposes of illustration. It is important to note that the composition of the task force can ignore the

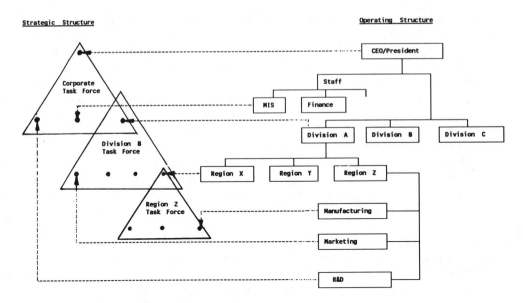

Figure 8-2   **The Dual-Structure Organization**

operating hierarchy. In the illustration, a task force for division B can be headed by the manager of division A, and likewise a task force for region Z can be headed by a manager from region X. Also, various staff managers and functional managers can cut across hierarchical lines and participate in a corporate-level task force, as is the case with the corporate MIS manager and the R&D manager for division A in the example shown in Figure 8-2. Membership in the various task forces of the strategic structure is determined purely by the expertise that a manager can contribute and not by his or her position in the operating structure. However, because the strategies formulated in the strategic structure are often implemented through the operating structure, it is prudent practice to include in the strategy task forces managers who may be critical to the successful implementation of the proposed strategy. Occasionally the new business proposals shaped through the strategic structure may require the establishment of new operating divisions.

As should be clear from the above discussion, the strategic structure is primarily meant for idea generation and exploration of new business opportunities. Although a separate strategic budget is available for these activities, it can be expended only through the operating structure. In other words, the strategic structure has no assets or manpower of its own and so must borrow both of these from the operating structure. Consequently many divisional and business unit managers wear two hats in a dual-structure organization, one representing their role in the strategic structure and the other representing their responsibilities in the operating structure.

In Texas Instruments, for example, nearly all the divisional managers had twin responsibilities, one for short-term profits through the firm's operating budget and the other for new business development through its strategic budget.[4] Although the ultimate balancing of new business development and profitability for the firm was done by top management, through its allocation of resources to the firm's strategic and operating budgets, respectively, divisional managers were encouraged to seek funding from both budgets and to emphasize both new business development and profitability in their business families.

The dual structure is difficult to administer. Accounting for the twin roles of managers can be a headache. Operating managers may not always be released for assignments in the strategic structure unless the operating head sees direct benefits to her division. A corporate dual structure can therefore work only when the organizational structure forces interdivisional dependencies, as in the case of Texas Instruments. Moreover, the structure should be backed by a supporting strategy process. In Texas Instruments, there were two distinct systems of planning, control, and incentives to support the dual structure. Since it is difficult to establish such an elaborate process to cover the entire firm, the self-renewal option is often used at the divisional level.

A CONTINGENCY FRAMEWORK

In the previous section, we described four different options that are available for balancing new business development and profitability within multibusiness firms. In this section, we present a contingency framework for deciding which of the four options is best suited to the strategic context of a firm.

Strategic Context

It is difficult to capture in a simple framework the corporate strategic context of a multibusiness firm. We have chosen two dimensions to describe this context: portfolio pressure and financial pressure.

Portfolio Pressure.   This is a measure of the quality of the firm's business portfolio. When the portfolio offers very few opportunities for future growth, the firm's portfolio pressure is said to be high. Growth is important for two reasons: managing the firm's cash flows and ensuring the cooperation of all of the firm's stakeholders.

As businesses in the firm's portfolio mature, they may not have many profitable reinvestment opportunities that can generate a net positive cash flow for the firm. Theoretically these "free cash flows" should be returned to the firm's stockholders.[5] But top management is typically reluctant to do so.[6] If, however, the firm continues to generate attractive investment opportunities in other businesses in its portfolio, the "free cash flows" from one set of businesses can be used to fund growth in others. The availability of new business opportunities provides a justification for top management to retain the firm's cash flows. The value of these new business options may not be fully appreciated by the firm's stockholders, but they do not have all of the information that top management has to evaluate these options. If the past track record of top management in new business development has been good, the firm's stockholders are likely to support the retention and reinvestment of a firm's earnings.[7]

Although from a stockholder's standpoint any investment in a new business is justified only if it is projected to yield a return in excess of the cost of capital used to fund it, new business development can be an important goal in and of itself for other stakeholders. Diversification can mean, for example, job security and career advancement opportunities for the firm's employees. It can facilitate greater vendor and customer loyalty and stronger support from the host community. Investments in the satisfaction of these stakeholders can also be in the stockholder's long-term interests.[8] At any rate, top management may seek to emphasize new business development when it believes that it is vital for maintaining the continued cooperation of the firm's key stakeholders.

Financial Pressure. This varies inversely with a firm's ability to satisfy its stockholders. Stockholders are not impressed with diversity or growth but by a firm's ability to implement its chosen business strategies efficiently so as to yield a financial return commensurate with the investment risks in these businesses.[9] A firm can therefore experience high financial pressure even when its portfolio pressure is low and vice-versa.

Depending on the portfolio and financial pressures experienced by the firm, one of the four options discussed in the prior section will be suitable (Figure 8-3). The cells in Figure 8-3 are separated by wavy lines to point out that the cell boundaries are based on the perceptions of these pressures by top management. The dissatisfaction of a firm's stockholders can be measured more objectively, but the dissatisfaction of other stakeholders or the portfolio pressure experienced by a firm is largely a matter of top management judgment. As we discussed in Chapter 2, top management uses its corporate vision not only to provide direction to the firm's businesses but also to stretch the organization toward superior performance. By its statement of the portfolio and financial pressures faced by the firm, top management defines these stretch goals for the organization.

Tailoring the Strategy Process

In our discussion in Part II, we assumed for ease of exposition that business strategies are shaped exclusively by top management. In reality, they are shaped jointly by top management and the divisional managers to whom the business units report. When top management delegates business strategy management to divisional managers, we call the process decentralized. By contrast, when it retains its direct influence over the firm's business strategies, we call the process centralized. We pointed out in Chapter 1 that top management has the opportunity both through

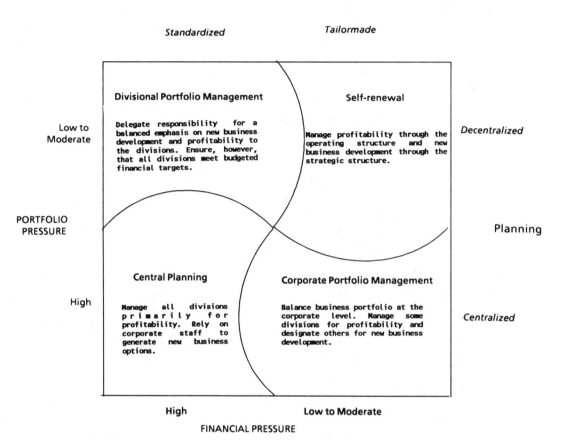

Control and Incentives

Standardized   *Tailormade*

Divisional Portfolio Management

Delegate responsibility   for   a
balanced emphasis on new business
development and profitability to
the divisions. Ensure, however,
that all divisions meet budgeted
financial targets.

Low to
Moderate

Self-renewal

Manage profitability through the
operating   structure   and   new
business development through the
strategic structure.

Decentralized

PORTFOLIO
PRESSURE

Planning

Central Planning

Manage   all   divisions
p r i m a r i l y   f o r
profitability.   Rely   on
corporate   staff   to
generate   new   business
options.

High

Corporate Portfolio Management

Balance business portfolio at the
corporate   level.   Manage   some
divisions for profitability and
designate others for new business
development.

Centralized

High   **Low to Moderate**
FINANCIAL PRESSURE

Figure 8-3   **Corporate Context and the Choice of a Strategy Process**

formal and informal interactions in the strategy process to influence business strategies. In a decentralized process, top management limits most of its interactions to
the firm's divisional managers and lets the divisional managers deal with the business managers.

The other important consideration in tailormaking is the degree of standardization in the control and incentives systems used across a firm's divisions. When
the systems used are identical across all the divisions, we call the process standardized; when they are designed to suit the mission assigned to a division, we call it
tailor-made.

Central Planning.   When top management senses that both the portfolio and
the financial pressures faced by the firm are high, it is essentially faced with a major

turnaround situation. The central planning option discussed in the previous section can be very helpful both in a symbolic and in a substantive sense. By involving itself with all business strategy decisions, top management can signal to the financial community that it is in charge. This may be of immense symbolic value in and of itself. Also, by managing all divisions for short-term profitability, top management can at least improve the efficiency with which business strategies are implemented in the firm, even though some of the business strategies may themselves be questionable. Furthermore, by taking direct responsibility for pruning the business portfolio, top management can help alleviate the firm's financial pressure. Although top management may lack the resources to fix immediately any imbalances in the firm's portfolio, acquisitions may help to solve the problem. Select acquisitions can bring the needed balance to the firm's portfolio more quickly than internal development can.

Corporate Portfolio Management.   If the context of a firm changes to one where at least the financial pressure drops to low or moderate levels while the portfolio pressure continues to be high, the firm can use the corporate portfolio management option and look internally for some of its new business options. It now has the slack resources to sponsor internal ventures. In fact, top management may choose to create a few divisions expressly for pursuing new business opportunities while continuing to manage others for profitability. However, because of the high portfolio pressure experienced by the firm, top management's direct involvement with business strategy decisions is a must. Portfolio balancing decisions are made at the corporate level for the same reason. Acquisitions continue to be an important alternative for correcting portfolio imbalances.

The control and incentives systems are, however, tailor-made to correspond to the mission assigned to the various divisions. Thus a division assigned a profitability mission may experience steering control, and a division assigned a business development mission may experience a contingent or Go–No Go control. The manager of the former division may be rewarded for his or her performance against the operating budget, but the manager of the latter division may be rewarded for performance against both the operating and strategic budgets (see Chapters 4 and 5).

Divisional Portfolio Management.   If the context of the firm is one where portfolio pressure is not high but financial pressure is, the firm can use the divisional portfolio management option. The business portfolio of the firm is healthy in such a context, with opportunities for growth in every division. Internal development is therefore a strong possibility. Also, if the firm organizes its divisions around related businesses, it makes available additional opportunities for growth through related diversification. The strategy process is decentralized, and the divisions have considerable authority in shaping the strategies of business units within their division. Divisional managers have a great deal of autonomy in this option to structure their own business portfolios, but they must live with a standardized control and incentives systems that measures them primarily on their profit performance.

Meeting agreed-on financial targets is an important measure of the divisional manager's performance. Top management can manipulate the slack allowed to a divisional manager by the profit targets that it sets. The financial pressure experienced by the firm is clearly an important determinant of the amount of slack that is allowed. Under conditions of high financial pressure, top management may allow the divisional manager very little slack, thus forcing him or her to forego some new business options. Corporate-level acquisitions are used to provide the portfolio balance in such a setting.

Self-renewal.   Only when the context of a firm is one of low to moderate financial and portfolio pressures can it benefit from a self-renewal process. The process relies primarily on internal business development to generate future growth options. The business portfolio of the firm must be of good quality. Also, because internal development takes time, the financial pressures on the firm must be low to moderate. Some researchers have argued that self-renewal is best encouraged when the contextual pressures are moderate.[10] When the pressures are high, internal development takes a back seat—as we saw in the case of the other three options. When these pressures are low, there is no incentive in the process to explore for new business opportunities.[11] Top management can, of course, magnify a division's contextual pressures by raising the division's performance standards.

The strategy process used in this option is different in the two structures. In the operating structure, the process is centralized. Top management gets involved with every business unit, typically in the back end of the planning process to ensure efficient implementation of the chosen strategies. The control and incentives systems are standardized and driven primarily by operating performance. By contrast, the process is more decentralized in the strategic structure. The heads of the various task forces are expected to develop detailed strategies without the close supervision of top management. The control and incentives systems are tailor-made to suit the mission of individual task forces.

SUMMARY

The four basic options presented in Figure 8-1 strive to alleviate the financial and portfolio pressures faced by a firm. If both pressures are high, the primary concern of top management should be to ease the firm's financial pressure. A central planning approach is appropriate for this purpose. When either portfolio or financial pressure is not high, top management can shift its attention to both portfolio balance and financial performance. Corporate and divisional portfolio management are the two choices in these contexts. When neither pressure is high, the self-renewal option becomes feasible.

NOTES

1. For a discussion of the need to balance these two elements and a third element called member involvement, see P. R. Lawrence and D. Dyer, *Renewing American Industry* (New York: Free Press, 1983).

2. The typology proposed here is based on that found in the following: B. S. Chakravarthy and P. Lorange, "Managing Strategic Adaptation: Options in Administrative Systems Design," *Interfaces* 14 (Jan.–Feb. 1984): 34–36; and B. S. Chakravarthy, "Management Systems for Innovation and Productivity," *European Journal of Operations Research* 47 (July 1990): 203–213.

3. For survey results that support this claim, see P. Haspeslagh, "Portfolio Planning: Uses and Limits," *Harvard Business Review* 60 (Jan.–Feb. 1982): 58–73.

4. See R. F. Vancil, "Texas Instruments Incorporated: Management Systems in 1972," Harvard Business School case 9-172-054 (Boston: Harvard Graduate School of Business Administration, 1972).

5. See M. C. Jensen, "Eclipse of the Public Corporation," *Harvard Business Review* 67 (Sept.–Oct. 1989): 61–74.

6. Ibid.

7. Several scholars have argued against business portfolio diversification for shareholder value creation. For a review of the literature, see M. S. Salter and W. A. Weinhold, *Diversification through Acquisition* (New York: Free Press, 1979). Unless top management has an established track record of prudent diversification, the stock market may not view the retention of earnings with favor.

8. For empirical evidence to support the claim that well-managed firms do have a balanced approach to profitability and long-term growth, see B. S. Chakravarthy, "Measuring Strategic Performance," *Strategic Management Journal* 7 (1986): 437–458.

9. This view is representative of modern finance theory. For example, see S. C. Myers, "Finance Theory and Financial Strategy," *Interfaces* 14 (Jan.–Feb. 1984): 126–137.

10. See Lawrence and Dyer, *Renewing American Industry*. These authors suggest that self-renewal—or readaptation, as they call it—is best nourished when both efficiency and effectiveness are moderate.

11. The need for external pressure or internal simulated crisis to encourage self-renewal is documented in A. H. Van de Ven, H. L. Angle, and M. S. Poole, *Research on the Management of Innovation: The Minnesota Studies* (New York: Harper and Row, 1989).

REFERENCES

Abernathy, W. J., and J. M. Utterback, "Patterns of Industrial Innovation," *Technology Review* 80 (June–July 1978): 40–47.

Burgleman, R. A., "A Model of the Interaction of Strategic Behavior, Corporate Context, and the Concept of Strategy," *Academy of Management Review* 8 (Jan. 1983): 61–70.

Cardozo, R., and D. Smith, "Applying Financial Portfolio Theory to Product Portfolio Decisions: An Empirical Study," *Journal of Marketing* 47 (1983): 110–119.

Chakravarthy, B. S., "Human Resource Management and Strategic Change: Challenges in Two Deregulated Industries," in *Strategic Human Resource Planning Applications,* ed. R. J. Niehaus (New York: Plenum, 1987), 17–28.

———, "On Tailoring a Strategic Planning System to Its Context: Some Empirical Evidence," *Strategic Management Journal* 8 (1987): 517–534.

———, "Beyond Portfolio Planning," *The Wharton Annual* (1984): 159–164.

————, "Adaptation: A Promising Metaphor for Strategic Management," *Academy of Management Review* 7 (Jan. 1982): 35–44.

————, and P. Lorange, "Strategic Adaptation in Multibusiness Firms" (Discussion paper 119, The Strategic Management Research Center, University of Minnesota, 1989).

Clark, K. B., "The Interaction of Design Hierarchies and Market Concepts in Technological Evolution," *Research Policy* 14 (1985): 235–251.

Colvin, G., "The DeGeneening of ITT," *Fortune* 105 (Jan. 11, 1982): 34–39.

Davis, S. M., and P. R. Lawrence, "Problems of Matrix Organizations," *Harvard Business Review* 56 (May–June 1978): 131–142.

Geneen, H. S., "The Strategy of Diversification," in *Competitive Strategic Management,* ed. R. B. Lamb (Englewood Cliffs, NJ: Prentice Hall, 1984), 395–414.

Goggin, W., "How the Multi-Dimensional Structure Works at Dow-Corning," *Harvard Business Review* 52 (Jan.–Feb. 1974): 54–65.

Guth, W. D., and I. C. MacMillan, "Strategy Implementation versus Middle Management Self-Interest," *Strategic Management Journal* 7 (1985): 313–327.

Haggerty, P. E., "The Corporation and Innovation," *Strategic Management Journal* 2 (Apr.–June 1981): 97–118.

Hayes, R. H., "The Real Story on Group Executives," *Directors and Boards* 5 (Fall 1980): 11–16.

Hirsch, P. M., "Organizational Effectiveness and the Institutional Environment," *Administrative Science Quarterly* 20 (1975): 327–344.

Lewis, W. W., "The CEO and Corporate Strategy in the Eighties: Back to Basics," *Interfaces* 14 (Jan.–Feb. 1984): 3–9.

Lorsch, J. W., and S. A. Allen, *Managing Diversity and Interdependence* (Boston: Harvard Business School, 1973).

Miles, R. E., and C. C. Snow, "Fit, Failure and the Hall of Fame," *California Management Review* 26 (Spring 1984): 10–28.

Prahalad, C. K., and R. A. Bettis, "The Dominant Logic: A New Linkage Between Diversity and Performance," *Strategic Management Journal* 7 (Nov.–Dec. 1986): 485–502.

Singh, H., "Corporate Acquisitions and Economic Performance" (Ph.D. thesis, University, 1984).

Utal, B., "Texas Instruments," *Fortune* 106 (Aug. 9, 1982): 40–45.

Chapter 9

ADAPTING TO CONTEXTUAL CHANGES

For the ease of exposition, we assumed in the previous chapter that the context of a firm is static. But in reality the firm's context can change due to several internal and external forces (Figure 9-1). The very performance of a firm is an important change force. The four process options that we discussed in the previous chapter, if they are successful, will alter the portfolio and the financial pressures faced by the firm.

Another important force is change in top management's strategic intent. As we noted in our discussions in Chapter 8, portfolio and financial pressures are influenced in part by how top management views a firm's performance. Thus, for example, when Jack Welch became the CEO of General Electric in 1981, he brought a new vision that revealed the need for change in the company's business portfolio.[1]

Structural modifications to the industries in which the firm competes are a third important force of change.[2] An industry can mature with time, limiting the growth opportunities that are available in it. The world auto industry, for example, is projected by most forecasters to grow at only a modest rate of 2 percent per year, with the bulk of the growth opportunities concentrated in the difficult markets of the developing world. Also, the attractive niches in which a firm operates can come in for severe competitive attack. Several leading Western firms in the automobile, motorcycle, consumer electronics, earth-moving equipment, musical instruments, and semiconductor industries have learned this the hard way in the past two decades. Moreover, the suppliers or customers to a firm's business units can themselves become powerful threats to its profitability; or new technologies and substitutes can make the distinctive competencies of a firm obsolete. The firm's portfolio and financial pressures can intensify as a result of any of the above structural changes in its industry environments.

Finally, the growing power of a firm's stakeholders is another important force of change. We discussed in Chapter 6 the increasing sophistication with which host governments influence the strategies and profitability of the multinational corpora-

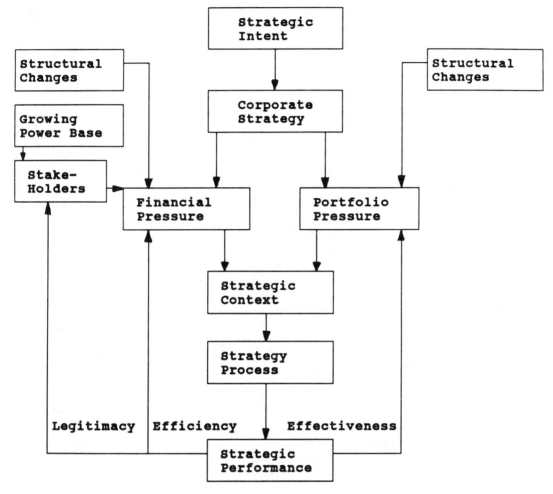

Figure 9-1   **External and Internal Change Forces**

tions (MNCs) that operate on their soils. Consumers, environmentalists, and labor are examples of other stakeholders who have been able to build very effective global coalitions to promote their causes. The additional costs that the firm may have to incur in order to be legitimate in the eyes of these increasingly powerful stakeholders can add to its financial pressure.

All of the above influences on a firm's portfolio and financial pressures have the effect of changing a firm's strategic context. The strategy process used by the firm must therefore be continuously modified to deal with its changing context. We describe in this chapter some of the important inertial forces that inhibit such an adaptation. We also offer some suggestions for designing a more-resilient strategy process.

CHALLENGES IN ADAPTING TO A CHANGING CONTEXT

Reactive Changes

A well-adapted firm must show sustained legitimacy, effectiveness, and efficiency over time.[3] Legitimacy describes a firm's right to persist with its chosen mode of operations (external legitimacy) and the degree of commitment its members have to its mission and strategies (internal legitimacy).[4] Legitimacy is a primary performance criterion that all firms must meet in order to survive. In addition, a well-adapted firm is judged by how effective and efficient it is. Effectiveness is a measure of the growth opportunities that are available to a firm in its chosen industry niches; mounting portfolio pressure is a sign of diminishing effectiveness. Efficiency refers to the amount of surplus contributions that a firm is able to generate through its chosen strategies, over the inducements that it has to provide its stakeholders for implementing those strategies;[5] increasing financial pressure is an indication of declining efficiency.

Figure 9-2 maps a set of transitions labeled as R (for reaction) that are triggered by the failure of a strategy process to maintain the firm's strategic performance. Transitions shown by the dark arrows R_{21}, R_{31}, R_{32}, R_{42}, and R_{43} are of this type. For example, the transition made by Becton Dickinson in the late 1970s (see Case 6) was an R_{32}-type transition from divisional to corporate portfolio management in response to mounting portfolio pressure. Similarly the transition made by Texas Instruments in the 1980s (see Case 15) from a self-renewal process to a divisional portfolio management process in response to mounting financial pressures was a R_{43}-type transition. The failure to make these transitions can further aggravate the firm's portfolio and financial pressures.

Proactive Changes

By helping top management alleviate the firm's portfolio and financial pressures, the four options described in the previous chapter help improve the firm's effectiveness and efficiency. However, they have different abilities to maintain the balance between legitimacy, effectiveness, and efficiency over time.

Central Planning: The Temporary Balance. The central planning option can help a firm improve its efficiency and effectiveness. However, the balance it provides is temporary. Even as the performance of the firm starts to improve, it creates new expectations among the firm's divisional and business-unit managers. Having had no major responsibility for business development in the turnaround years, they begin to seek a more active role once the financial pressure eases. Failure to

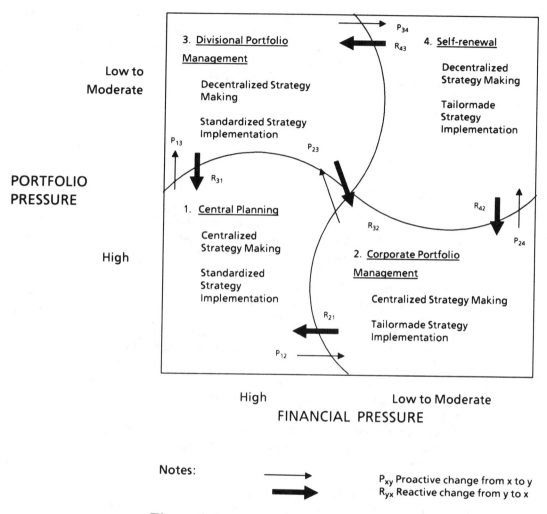

Figure 9-2   **Changing the Strategy Process**

accommodate their demands can lead to loss of motivation and managerial turn-over. Witness, for example, the high managerial turnover at ITT under Geneen (Case 11) once he had reduced the firm's portfolio and financial pressures. Internal legitimacy of the firm starts to drop in the central planning option even as the firm's effectiveness and efficiency start to improve.

Moreover, as noted in the previous chapter, the success of this option is predicated on the firm's ability to find attractive acquisition targets. In recent years it has been very difficult to find undervalued acquisition targets, and the bidding war that typically ensues erodes any value that the acquisition may have for the acquiring firm.[6] Any improvements in effectiveness from an acquisition must, therefore, be traded off against the associated pressures that it places on a firm's efficiency. A related issue is the social costs of potential disruptions to the firm's host communities because of its acquisitions, mergers, and divestitures. The external legitimacy of the firm may also come under attack.

Developing new businesses only through acquisition is, therefore, not a viable strategy in the long run for a multibusiness firm. Even as central planning begins to relieve the firm's portfolio and financial pressures, the firm must begin to focus on profitable renewal opportunities afforded by its current businesses, instead of letting them decay in the hope of future replacements.[7] Although the profitable extension of the life of a product or the rejuvenation of a maturing business may not always be possible, managers must consistently be encouraged to seek such opportunities.[8]

Corporate Portfolio Management: The Fragile Balance. The corporate portfolio management option has many of the same problems as central planning. Its reliance on acquisitions to relieve the firm's portfolio pressure may have only a short-term effect. However, the predominant reliance on acquisitions in the central planning option is moderated in corporate portfolio management by a selective emphasis in some of the firm's divisions on internal business development. But managers who are assigned to divisions run primarily for their profitability may feel frustrated with this arrangement, since it denies them the opportunity that is available to some of their colleagues to develop new businesses. This selective opportunity for new business development can breed a caste system within the firm, with managers assigned a profitability mission being perceived as less creative than those assigned a business development mission. The internal legitimacy of the firm can be hurt as a consequence.

Moreover, corporate portfolio management is not very conducive to the exploitation of cross-business and cross-divisional synergies. The efficiency of the firm can also suffer in the long run.

Divisional Portfolio Management: The Stable Balance. The divisional portfolio management option is relatively more stable than the prior two options because it attempts to balance new business development and profitability simultaneously in all divisions. The primary emphasis is on the continuous internal development of new business ideas. This heavy reliance on internal development encourages the divisions to build on their strengths. Even if some of their new business ideas fail, the resource base on which they were developed can be easily redeployed to other business opportunities within the division. Consequently, the efficiency of the firm is protected even as it explores ways of improving its effectiveness.

Also, by providing divisional managers the autonomy to shape the strategies for businesses within their portfolios, divisional portfolio management builds greater internal commitment to the firm's goals and strategies. This, together with the fact that all divisional managers have the opportunity to pursue new business and profitability goals, enables the firm to maintain its internal legitimacy on a sustained basis.

The one serious deficiency with this option is that the resource allocation decisions made within individual divisions can be suboptimal, since they ignore the opportunities in other divisions. This in turn can lead over time to a poorly balanced corporate portfolio, as was the case in Becton Dickinson (Case 6).

Self-renewal: The Ultra-Stable Balance.   This provides the most robust performance balance of the four options.[9] In the self-renewal option, efficiency is maintained through the operating structure and effectiveness through the strategic structure. The operating structure is profitability oriented, whereas the strategic structure is more oriented to new business development. The two structures are intertwined, allowing for the lateral transfer of slack from the operating to the strategic structure.

Internal legitimacy is always high in the self-renewal option because it does not typecast managers. Regardless of their roles in the operating structure of the firm, managers can participate in the search for new business opportunities through their roles in the firm's strategic structure. Also, through their participation in both the operating and strategic structures of the firm, managers at all levels are keenly aware of the scale and scope economies that can be exploited in the firm. This awareness helps sustain the efficiency of the firm. Finally, by a continuous and broad-based search for new business opportunities, this option maintains the effectiveness of the firm.

A Process Hierarchy.   As the above discussion would suggest, central planning and corporate portfolio management help *improve* the firm's effectiveness and efficiency. However, only the divisional portfolio management and self-renewal processes help the firm *maintain* its external and internal legitimacies at a moderate to high level. The transitions labeled P (for proaction) in Figure 9-2 and shown by the light arrows P_{12}, P_{13}, P_{23}, P_{24}, and P_{34} represent transitions to a balanced process (Figure 9-3).

INERTIAL FORCES

There are two important inertial forces (Figure 9-4)—organizational inertia and congruence with top management style—that make both the reactive and the proactive transitions that were described above difficult.

Organizational Inertia

In the previous chapter, we discussed that the organizational structure associated with central planning, corporate portfolio management, and divisional portfolio

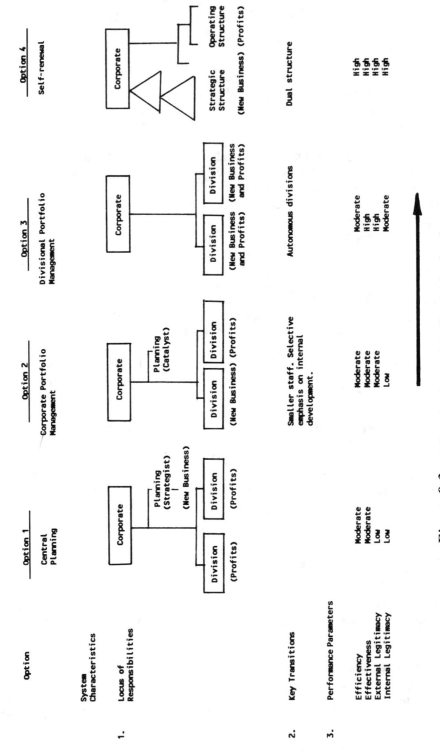

Figure 9-3 A Stepwise Approach to Overcoming Inertia

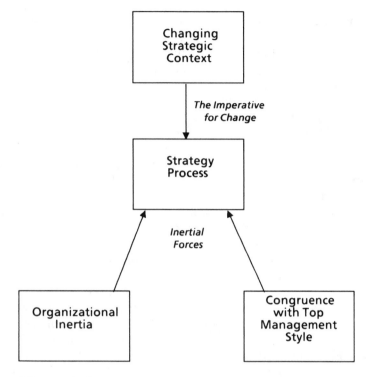

Figure 9-4   **The Dynamics of Adapting the Strategy Process**

management is a divisional structure and that the self-renewal process uses a dual-structure organization (see Figure 8-1). The transition from a dual-structure organization to a divisional structure is difficult.

The dual-structure organization offers a great deal of flexibility to the firm's managers. As we described in Figure 8-2, the strategic structure houses teams of managers who are drawn from different divisions, regions, businesses, and functional departments of the company. A transition of the R_{43} type restricts the interactions between a firm's managers to only their operating divisions.

A transition of the R_{42} or R_{32} type is even more restrictive. A corporate portfolio management process segregates the responsibilities for new business development and profitability, so a division typically will be assigned only one of these challenges. In a self-renewal process or in a divisional portfolio management process, the divisional manager is used to managing his business portfolio for both new business development and profitability.

The transitions to central planning, that is, R_{31} and R_{21}, will be even less welcome because of its single-minded pursuit of profitability in all of the firm's divisions. By contrast, in a divisional or corporate portfolio management process, at least some business unit managers are encouraged to develop new business ventures. Transitions away from such a process of bottom-up idea generation will be resisted by the organization.

In general, the transitions that imply a centralized strategy-making process and a standardized strategy implementation process will be resisted by line managers because these abridge the autonomy of divisions to pursue both new business development and profitability.

It is pertinent to note, however, that even as the authority of divisional managers gets abridged in the strategy process with the above transitions, the role of the planning department can grow in importance.

In firms that use the self-renewal option, such as Texas Instruments, the corporate planning staff is usually very small. The analytical support at Texas Instruments was provided by a computer software called MODPLAN (see Case 5). Similarly in Dexter Corporation (see Case 13)—a company that used divisional portfolio management—the Senior Vice President for Corporate Development had only a very small planning staff. The responsibility for strategic planning in these two options is typically delegated to the divisions, which have their own planning support to discharge this responsibility.

By contrast, corporate planners play an important role in the corporate portfolio management option, taking responsibility for auditing the firm's portfolio and making acquisitions and mergers. But they are not the firm's strategists. That responsibility still rests with the divisions, although under stricter corporate guidelines. For example, the role of the Vice President of Planning in Becton Dickinson (see Case 6)—a company that used the corporate portfolio management option— was more of a catalyst.

Of the four options described in Figure 9-3, the corporate planning department is the most powerful in a central planning process. The corporate planning department manages all of the firm's new business development activities, primarily through acquisitions and mergers. As was true with ITT under Geneen (see Case 11), in a central planning company corporate planners have an important role in shaping the firm's strategies.

The proactive transitions (the P transitions in Figure 9-2) require a shift in the locus of relative power away from the corporate planning executives to the operating managers of the firm. As desirable as these transitions are, a potential source of resistance can be the firm's corporate planners, who are ironically the ones also responsible for modifying a firm's strategy process to suit its changing needs.

Congruence with Top Management Style

Administering each of the four options discussed earlier requires a very different management style.

In a central planning process, the Chief Executive Officer of the firm assumes a significant role in shaping the firm's corporate and business strategies, albeit with the help of a powerful corporate planning staff. By contrast, in the two portfolio management processes, the CEO does not seek to make all strategic decisions but rather to manage the premises around which these decisions are made. If analytical brilliance is important to strategy making in central planning, portfolio management calls for superior administrative skills. The CEO has to shape the agenda of the firm through the planning system and to ensure its implementation by mobilizing the necessary support network through the other steps in the strategy process.[10]

The CEO managing a self-renewal process faces the added challenge of motivating his or her managers to produce two very different behaviors concurrently: a profit orientation in the operating structure and a business development orientation in the strategic structure. Balancing the locus of power between the strategic and the operating structures is a key skill for managing this process. It also requires the establishment of an organizational culture where constructive conflict is encouraged. Companies such as Texas Instruments and IBM[11] have carefully nurtured this culture over the years. Given the rich links between operating managers and SBU managers in the dual structure, conflicts will emerge. Business missions, program priorities, and resource budgets can all be bones of contention. Top management must encourage the airing of all such contentions and, if necessary, play the court of last resort.

Although CEOs are expected to be versatile in their skills, they tend to see themselves more expert at certain tasks.[12] There is a tendency therefore for the incumbent CEO to retain a strategy process that is best suited to his or her management style and skills, even if that process is inappropriate to the changed context of the firm. Occasionally the strategy process can be changed only with a change in the CEO.

TOWARD A SELF-ADAPTING ORGANIZATION[13]

The discussion in the previous section suggests that attempting to continuously align the strategy process of a firm to its changing context can be futile, because of the variety of external and internal change forces at work and the inertias within the firm. One alternative would be to wait until the strategic performance of the firm falls to a crisis threshold and then revive performance, probably through a central planning process.[14] Another would be to design the organization for better resilience.[15] In this section, we briefly outline some important elements of such a self-adapting organization.

Building Around Core Competencies

The basic organizational unit for strategic planning is the Strategic Business Unit (SBU), but this is too narrow in scope. As we noted earlier, products can become obsolete, the technologies used in their manufacture can change radically, or the market segments in which they compete can get saturated. But if the basic organizational unit for planning is defined in terms of the fundamental customer satisfaction that the organizational unit provides, the unit can experience a prolonged if not infinite life cycle.[16] Thus a company such as Canon finds it more useful to think in terms of the imaging needs of its business and residential customers as opposed to their demand for cameras and photocopiers.[17]

Furthermore, it is useful to examine what distinctive competencies the firm has to serve the customer needs that it has identified. A Strategic Business Family (SBF) is a collection of related business units that share common distinctive competencies. Operationally each business family can be a division. For example, it may be appropriate to cluster plain-paper copiers and videotape recorders in the same division, image processing, if the firm expects to derive its competitive advantage in both of these businesses through its superior components: image sensors, memories, and microprocessors.[18] In a similar manner, if control of the same distribution channel is crucial to the success of the toothpaste, soap, and shampoo businesses, they can be combined into a common toiletries division. Each division will be charged with the responsibility of nourishing certain unique competencies, which will benefit all the business units in its family.

In order to exploit both economies of scale and economies of scope that each SBF can provide, the division should use the dual structure. Unlike the self-renewal process, this proposal restricts the use of the dual structure to only business families. The transience of the strategic structure in which most SBU managers will be housed is in itself a deterrent against rigid mind sets. As we noted earlier, the strategic structure is temporary so that it can be reshaped to suit new environmental realities. The exchange of ideas across SBUs, especially for exploiting their shared competencies, broadens the vision of SBU managers. Rotating them through other SBUs within the division also is made easier by such familiarity.

In concept, such a structure should help a division balance its growth and profitability on a continuous basis. Divisional management can cope with adverse changes to the divisional context merely by shifting the relative importance of the strategic and operating structures. For example, if portfolio pressure becomes high, divisional management can increase the slack transferred to the strategic structure and signal its importance by skewing rewards to activities performed in that structure. Conversely if financial pressure becomes severe, divisional management can cut back on the funding given to the strategic structure and also skew the rewards more towards performance in the operating structure. Although such shifts are not trivial, at least the process can handle contextual changes without major internal disruptions.

Another feature of the proposed configuration is that the divisional manager will enjoy far greater autonomy in establishing missions for each SBU and allocating resources to it. Although the overall allocation of resources to each SBF will be based on the SBF's position in the corporate portfolio, the further allocation of an SBF's resources among its SBUs would be left to the discretion of the divisional manager (provided that the division meets its overall goals and stays within the resources allocated to it). The intent is to move away from formula-driven planning and to use more of the divisional managers' judgment on the soundness and ingenuity of the business plans that are proposed to them. However, the use of portfolio planning at the corporate management level would ensure that resources are directed toward SBFs that present the best investment opportunities in the aggregate.

The real challenge at the corporate level would be to move the resources from one type of distinctive competency to another type because allocating resources to an SBF is synonymous with supporting the competencies around which it is organized.

Nurturing and Developing Human Resources

In our discussion on staffing in Chapter 5, we limited our attention to the assignment of managers, ignoring the predicament of finding business unit managers unsuited to their changed mission or finding a serious shortfall in the managers needed to fulfill the chosen mission. One way of handling these would be to terminate unsuitable managers and to hire outside people with the needed skills. Such an approach to Human Resources Management (HRM) is called the market approach.[19] Managers are seen as transient subcontractors in this approach. Although it may work in some contexts, the market approach may not be looked on favorably by several of the firm's stakeholders, notably its employees, host community, and governmental agencies. Moreover, there is the real danger in such an approach of losing the commitment of a firm's managers to its mission. We propose a broader approach to HRM that helps sustain both the internal and the external legitimacies of the firm.

The proposal envisages the full participation of the corporate human resources manager in the objectives-setting step. This person's role—like that of his or her counterpart, the firm's chief financial officer—is to evaluate all major trends in the environment that may affect the supply of human resources to the firm. Forecasted changes in external factor markets, shifts in public policy that have a bearing on personnel matters, changing societal values, and anticipated competition for human resources are some of the demographic, political, social, and economic trends that the corporate human resource manager must track routinely in order to decide whether the goals chosen in the objectives-setting step can be supported by the human resources available to the firm.

In the strategic programming cycle, each business provides a detailed action plan for meeting its chosen goals. As we discussed in Chapter 5, the successful implementation of a chosen strategy requires a matched managerial orientation. It should be possible to compare the mix of managerial orientations demanded by the proposed programs with that available to arrive at a human resources gap. Once a firm's human resources gap is determined, the proportions that should be met through outside recruiting and internal transfers can be estimated. If internal transfers are to be a meaningful option, the firm should ensure that its business managers are provided with opportunities for job rotation and training.

In our discussions in Chapter 5, we noted that a manager was assigned to a business based on his or her experience and personality. This does not mean, however, that a typical manager is not versatile in his or her administrative skills. The personality of managers may be different at entry, but a well-designed program of job rotation, training, and development together with a suitable reward system and a supportive culture can enrich the administrative repertoire of most managers. In conjunction with the divisional human resources managers, the corporate human resources manager must therefore come up with a series of strategic programs for recruitment, career development, employee training, job rotation, and outplacement aimed at eliminating the human resources gap.

However, it is rare for a firm to develop new skills ahead of their requirement (through either new hires or retraining). Staffing budgets are typically tied to a business plan and consequently are forced to lag behind strategic decisions. But just as a central R&D budget is necessary to fund projects that no business unit will sponsor, a central human resources budget must be provided to nurture critical human resources skills not linked to a specific business plan. Divisional managers can be apportioned some of these funds through their strategic budgets, primarily to do the necessary recruiting or to provide the needed induction or training. In addition, we suggest that the corporate human resources manager control two other strategic budgets, one for employee development through job rotation and the other for outplacement services; the former is meant to subsidize divisions that may take an "on-the-job" trainee as a supernumerary, and the latter is designed to help those managers who cannot be retrained.

Planning Top Management Succession

The most potent force for changing a firm's strategy process is its CEO. As we noted in the previous section, the strategy process in use tends to conform to the style of the incumbent CEO. We see this, for example, at ITT (see Case 11). Long after the firm's portfolio and financial pressures were relieved, ITT still used a central planning process to accommodate the style of the firm's then CEO, Harold Geneen. Only under a new CEO, Rand Araskog, could the strategy process be changed.[20] Similarly we see in the Alfa-Laval study (see Case 16) how the firm continued to use a divisional portfolio management process, despite mounting portfolio pressure. The process could not be changed until Harry Faulkner took charge of the company in 1980. The most dramatic example of a new CEO's strong influence in changing the strategy process is, of course, that of Jack Welch at General Electric.[21] In Chapter 2, we used a report from Christopher Lorenz of the *Financial Times*[22] to summarize the dramatic changes that Welch has made at General Electric in a few short years. What is even more remarkable about that example is that his predecessor, Reginald Jones, hand-picked Welch despite the major differences in their experiences and personalities. In Jones' view, the decade of the 1980s and beyond needed the kind of leadership that only Welch could provide to General Electric.[23] Ensuring the resilience of the strategy process requires, above all, such far-sighted top management succession planning.[24]

SUMMARY

In this chapter, we suggested that the four strategy processes of central planning, corporate portfolio management, divisional portfolio management, and self-renewal differ in their ability to provide a dynamic balance between the three performance measures of legitimacy, effectiveness, and efficiency. However, the proactive transition to the best balanced self-renewal process is not easy. The organizational inertia of the firm and its top management style may inhibit the firm from moving up this hierarchy (see Figure 9-4). These very same inertial forces can also make it difficult for the firm to change its strategy process in reaction to mounting portfolio and/or financial pressures.

Appointing a CEO whose style is congruent with the desired strategy process is the obvious first step in bringing about change. Succession planning is a critical activity in this regard. The firm should also begin to build more resilience to change by reorganizing around core competencies and helping managers become more versatile.

NOTES

1. See F. J. Aguilar, *General Managers in Action* (New York: Oxford University Press, 1988): 67–79.
2. See M. E. Porter, *Competitive Strategy* (New York: Free Press, 1980).
3. See B. S. Chakravarthy, "Measuring Strategic Performance," *Strategic Management Journal* 7 (1986): 437–458.
4. See M. L. Tushman and E. Romanelli, "Organizational Evolution: A Metamorphosis Model of Convergence and Reorientation," in *Research in Organizational Behavior,* eds. B. M. Staw and L. L. Cummings (Greenwich, CT: JAI Press, 1985), 171–222.
5. This definition is from C. I. Barnard, *The Functions of the Executive* (Cambridge, MA: Harvard University Press, 1973), 55–59.
6. See H. Singh, "Corporate Acquisitions and Economic Performance" (Ph.D. thesis, University of Michigan, 1984).
7. See R. T. Pascale, "Our Curious Addiction to Corporate Grand Strategy," *Fortune* (Jan. 25, 1982): 115–116.
8. See D. C. Hambrick and I. C. Macmillan, "The Product Portfolio and Man's Best Friend," *California Management Review* XXV (Fall 1982): 84–95.
9. Its robustness parallels that of the system described in B. L. T. Hedberg, P. C. Nystrom, and W. H. Starbuck, "Camping On Seesaws: Prescriptions for a Self-designing Organization," *Administrative Science Quarterly* 21 (1976): 41–65.
10. See J. P. Kotter, *The General Managers* (New York: Free Press, 1982).
11. R. F. Vancil, *Implementing Strategy: The Role of Top Management* (Boston: Harvard Business School, 1982), 37–56.
12. See Kotter, *The General Managers.*
13. This section has been adapted from B. S. Chakravarthy, "Strategic Self-renewal: A Planning Framework for Today," *Academy of Management Review* 9 (July 1984): 536–547.
14. For example, this view is advocated in D. Miller and P. H. Friesen, *Organizations: A Quantum Review* (Englewood Cliffs, NJ: Prentice Hall, 1984).
15. See Hedberg, Nystrom, and Starbuck, "Camping on Seesaws."

16. T. Levitt, "Marketing Myopia," *Harvard Business Review* 53 (Sept.–Oct. 1975): 26–37.

17. See Y. Ishikura, "Canon, Inc.: Worldwide Copier Strategy," Harvard Business School case 9-384-151 (Boston: Harvard Graduate School of Business Administration, 1983).

18. See K. Ohmae, *The Mind of the Strategist* (New York: McGraw-Hill, 1982).

19. See M. Beer et al., *Managing Human Assets* (New York: Free Press, 1984).

20. For a description of the problems of the transition at ITT, see Case 11.

21. For a description of the changes that were made under Welch, see "General Electric: 1984," in F. J. Aguilar, *General Managers in Action* (New York: Oxford University Press, 1988), 284–308.

22. See C. Lorenz, "Why Strategy Has Been Put in the Hands of Line Managers," *Financial Times* (May 18, 1988): 20.

23. This is based on the videotape "General Electric Company: Management Succession" from the Wharton School at the University of Pennsylvania.

24. R. F. Vancil, *Passing the Baton* (Boston: Harvard Business School, 1988).

REFERENCES

Bettis, R. A., and W. K. Hall, "The Business Portfolio Approach—Where It Falls Down in Practice," *Long Range Planning* 16 (April 1983): 95–104.

Chakravarthy, B. S., "Strategic Self-renewal: A Planning Framework for Today," *Academy of Management Review* 9 (July 1984): 536–547.

———, and P. Lorange, "Vers un Système de Gestion Autoadaptif," *Revue Internationale de Gestion* 14 (Sept. 1989): 61–75.

Clark, K., "Investment in New Technology and Competitive Advantage," in *The Competitive Challenge: Strategies for Industrial Innovation and Renewal,* ed. D. J. Teece (Cambridge, MA: Ballinger, 1987), 59–82.

Hambrick, D. C., and P. A. Mason, "Upper Echelons: The Organization as a Reflection of its Top Managers," *Academy of Management Review* 9 (1984): 193–206.

Hedberg, B. L. T., P. C. Nystrom, and W. H. Starbuck, "Camping on Seesaws: Prescriptions for a Self-designing Organization," *Administrative Science Quarterly* 21 (1976): 41–65.

Miller, D., and P. H. Friesen, "Momentum and Revolution in Organizational Adaptation," *Academy of Management Journal* 23 (1980): 591–614.

Moore, W. L., and M. L. Tushman, "Managing Innovation over the Product Life-Cycle," in *Readings in the Management of Innovation,* ed. M. L. Tushman and W. L. Moore (Boston: Pitman, 1982), 131–150.

Normann, R., "Organizational Innovativeness: Product Variation and Reorientation," *Administrative Science Quarterly* 16 (1971): 203–215.

Sherman, S. P., "Inside the Mind of Jack Welch," *Fortune* (Mar. 27, 1989): 38–50.

Starbuck, W. H., "Information Systems for Organizations in the Future," in *Information Systems and Organizational Structure,* ed. E. Grochla and N. Szyperski (New York: de Gruyter, 1975), 217–229.

Wheelwright, S. C., "Restoring Competitiveness in U.S. Manufacturing," in *The Competitive Challenge: Strategies for Industrial Innovation and Renewal,* ed. D. J. Teece (Cambridge, MA: Ballinger, 1987), 83–100.

The ITT Corporation

The legendary Harold Geneen, the Chief Executive Officer of ITT for nearly two decades, stepped down in January 1978 and handed over the reins of the company to Lyman Hamilton. Geneen, formerly of Raytheon, joined ITT in 1959 as President, Chief Executive Officer, and Director. He initiated a strategy of acquisitions that led ITT to two decades of growth and prosperity. This case study, assembled from a variety of public sources, describes the management systems used by ITT in the Geneen era and the decade that followed.

THE GENEEN ERA

Growth Through Acquisitions

When Geneen was hired for the top spot at ITT, nearly all of the company's operations were overseas, and many governments—especially those in Latin America—were becoming hostile to foreign companies. To counteract these potential threats abroad, Geneen first sought to develop the U.S. operations of ITT. "ITT became international by coming back to the U.S.," he liked to say when speaking of his first strategic decision. This task was made difficult by AT&T, which had a near monopoly in the U.S. telecommunications market.

ITT came very close to merging in 1960 with United Telephone of Kansas City, then the third-largest telephone company in the United States. There was strong support for that merger from ITT's operating executives, but Geneen actually felt a sense of relief when negotiations with United Telephone broke down. He

Copyright 1986 by Balaji S. Chakravarthy, The Carlson School of Management, University of Minnesota

This case was written from published sources by Celia S. Kapsomera, Research Assistant, under the direction of Associate Professor Balaji S. Chakravarthy. It is intended for use as the basis for class discussion rather than to illustrate either effective or ineffective handling of an administrative situation.

Exhibit 1 Principal Product Groups in the Geneen Era (1972)

	Sales and Revenues, 1972 (million dollars)		Income[1], 1972 (million dollars)	
Manufacturing				
Telecommunications Equipment	$1,909	22%	$111	23%
Industrial Products	1,562	18	61	13
Automotive and Consumer Products	1,008	12	43	9
Natural Resources	355	4	38	8
Defense and Space Programs	469	6	11	2
	5,303	62	264	55
Consumer and Business Services				
Food Processing and Services	1,013	12	6	1
Consumer Services	602	7	13	3
Telecommunication Operations	186	2	26	6
Business and Financial Services	413	5	28	6
Hartford Fire	—	—	126	26
	2,214	26	199	42
Divestible Operations (all or part of earnings may be replaced by reinvestment of proceeds)				
Under Consent Decrees	1,040	12	14	3
	$8,557	100%	$477	100%

[1]Excludes gain on divestments under consent decrees of $6.7 million, or $.05 per common share.

Source: Annual report, ITT Corporation, 1972.

did not relish the thought of ITT's becoming a telephone utility, with the associated high investment cost, frozen asset base, and regulated returns. Instead, Geneen recommended to his board that ITT diversify from telecommunications into other industries that were more open and less prone to economic cycles. He believed that the service sector offered an especially attractive opportunity for ITT.

Geneen was convinced that internal diversification into unrelated businesses rarely worked. Thus, if a "reasonably sized company" in a wholly new field became available at a bargain price, he was interested in gaining a toehold. He started in 1960 with the acquisition of the Aetna Finance Corporation. In 1965, he acquired Avis, followed by Sheraton, Levitt, Canteen, Continental Baking, and Hartford Fire Insurance. Exhibit 1 shows the diversity of ITT's product groups by 1972. During the Geneen era, ITT acquired over 275 firms and paid, according to the House Antitrust Subcommittee, excessive premiums for some. The House Subcommittee cited as examples ITT's payment of $60 million above Levitt's net worth of

$32 million and $133 million over Sheraton's net worth of $60 million.[1] Geneen defended these high premiums, arguing that they were needed to keep the sellers happy and ensure their continued cooperation after their companies were acquired. Moreover, he felt that despite the high prices he paid for some of his acquisitions they were always excellent values for ITT's stockholders, resulting in a capital appreciation of $8 billion (by his own estimate) at the time of his retirement in 1977.

A challenging task for Geneen was to assimilate the acquired companies into the corporate fold, helping them make the transition from being a subsidiary to being an integrated division of ITT. But not all the companies found it easy to join ITT and adopt its practices. The transition for Sheraton Corporation was, for example, a painful one. Sheraton's operating managers reacted very negatively to ITT's system of reports, review, and task forces.[2]

The acquisitions in the North American service sector in turn became the anchor for Geneen's strategy for expanding foreign operations. The fact that Europe was ITT's traditional stomping ground did not guarantee, however, automatic successes for ITT's American businesses that sought diversification in Europe. ITT-Avis, for example, was a failure for the first two years of its move into the European market. Yet ITT did have a significant advantage over other American firms in Europe because it knew how to deal with foreign governments and in foreign currencies. In addition, Brussels-based ITT-Europe helped the parent company coordinate its European subsidiaries.

Strategic Planning and Control[3]

Geneen delegated the responsibility for managing ITT's diverse businesses (over 200 at one time) to the business unit managers. Each business unit was organized within product groups (numbering ten at their peak). The product groups in turn were organized into two sectors: Manufacturing and Consumer and Business Services (see Exhibit 1). Manufacturing included Telecommunications Equipment, Industrial Products, Automotive and Consumer Products, Natural Resources, and Defense and Space Programs; Consumer and Business Services included Food Processing and Services, Consumer Services, Telecommunications Operations, Business and Financial Services, and Hartford Fire Insurance.

The Business Plan.   Geneen introduced and established a very detailed central planning and control system to manage the diverse businesses in ITT's portfolio. The heart of ITT's reporting and control system was the business plan, an extremely comprehensive document that was prepared annually by each business unit. The business plan was the primary standard for evaluating the performance of the business unit managers, and top management did everything possible to give authority to the plan.

The planning cycle began in January, when the business units received from the corporate headquarters tentative objectives for the next five years. The product line managers assisted corporate management in setting these tentative objectives, which covered the following five key performance parameters: sales, net income, total assets, total employees, and capital expenditures. In formal meetings that were held from January through April, the business units were given the opportunity to negotiate their objectives with regional and corporate headquarters. The purpose of these negotiations was to resolve all the differences between the business unit managers and the product-line managers or other headquarters personnel. After a final review, the approval of the negotiated objectives was given by the corporate headquarters in May.

Using the approved objectives as guidelines, the business units prepared their business plans in June and July. Each business plan was expected to contain detailed explanations on how the business unit sought to achieve its objectives over the next two years. It also required a less-detailed forecast for the fifth year onward.

Each business plan began with a one-page financial and operating summary that contained comparative data for the preceding year (actual data), the current year (budget), the next year (forecast), two years hence (forecast), and five years hence (forecast). Anticipated changes in net income for the current year and for each of the next two years were explained. These condensed summary reports were followed by a complete set of financial statements—income statement, balance sheet, and a statement of cash flow—for the current year and for each of the next two years. Each major item on these financial statements was then analyzed in detail in separate reports. The business plan continued with a description of the major management actions planned for the next two years and an estimate of the favorable or unfavorable effect each action would have on total sales, net income, and total assets.

Within each business unit, each functional area—marketing, manufacturing, research and development, financial control, and personnel and employee relations—presented its own separate plans. These functional plans began with a statement of the function's mission, an analysis of its present problems and opportunities, and a statement of the specific actions it intended to take in the next two years.

The final portion of the business plan was a series of comparative financial statements that depicted the estimated item-by-item effect if sales fell below forecast or increased above forecast. For each sales scenario chosen, the costs were divided into three categories: fixed costs, unavoidable variable costs, and management discretionary costs. The business unit managers described the specific actions that they would take to control employment, total assets, and capital expenditures in case of a reduction in sales and indicated when these actions would be put into effect.

Each completed business plan was submitted to ITT's headquarters by mid-summer. In early fall, meetings were attended by senior corporate and regional executives and by the general managers and functional managers of many of the business units. Geneen viewed these meetings as an important forum for the business unit managers to share their experiences in resolving common problems. It was not uncommon for a business unit to be asked to revise its business plan based on ideas presented in the review meeting.

Each approved business plan became the foundation of the budget for the following year, which was submitted by mid-November. The budget was essentially the same as the business plan, except that the various dollar amounts that were presented in the business plan on an annual basis were broken down by months. Minor changes between the overall key results forecast in the business plan and those reflected in greater detail in the budget were not permitted. Requests for major changes had to be submitted to top management no later than mid-October.

Control Reports.   Every business unit had to submit periodic reports according to a fixed calendar. The reporting system was essentially the same for all units, and identical forms and chart of accounts were used by all units regardless of their size.

A report that was a particular favorite of Geneen's was the monthly management report, which each ITT business manager throughout the corporation sent to world headquarters in New York detailing all the facts affecting the performance of his or her unit. Each report contained financial analyses of sales, profits, return on investment, and virtually every other measurement used in business—often running to twenty single-spaced typewritten pages. This report was very important because it described existing and potential problems, which Geneen called "red-flag" items, to explain how the problems arose and to propose solutions. All these monthly reports were mimeographed, collated, bound into sets, and then airmailed to the 50 top ITT executives around the world. They met with Geneen in New York ten times a year to discuss these reports.

General Management Meeting.   An important feature of Geneen's management system was the monthly general management meeting. The preparation for these meetings was an important activity for ITT business unit managers worldwide. They knew that Geneen could single their business out for detailed scrutiny in front of their peers. Moreover, they also were expected to provide constructive solutions to the problems faced by other business units. Because there was so much ground to cover, the meetings often lasted for several days and ran late into the night. One estimate of the time spent in meetings at ITT was at least 50 meeting days a year. Not only were these meetings long, but also the pace was grueling and the demands on perfection were stringent.

The tight scrutiny of the business plan was made possible by a huge central staff, numbering at one time about 400 administrative, technical, and financial experts. These staff experts acted as the "eyes and ears of Geneen" and were free to examine the operations of a business unit and to delve into books any time they thought it was necessary. Line managers worked with the unsettling knowledge that they were being constantly scrutinized by teams at headquarters. The consequent fish-bowl environment in which the unit managers operated was one of the pressures singled out by critics of the Geneen system. In response to this criticism, Geneen once said the following:

I delegate, but I don't abdicate. I want to know what's going on. I don't want some proud guy to get into his own Vietnam and then suddenly hand me his resignation. Hell, his resignation can't bring back the $10 million he'd lose.[4]

Management Style

Geneen had a rather unusual management style. He was an afternoon, evening, and night person. The executives at ITT headquarters recall his arriving for work as late as noon, staying until 8 P.M. or later, and telephoning their homes at midnight or after. Of course, they had to adjust their schedules accordingly.

Geneen chaired marathon meetings that would start at 9:30 A.M. and continue until 11:15 P.M. Some of the executives who left the company cited the frenetic pace that Geneen imposed as a serious reason for their resignation. One of his managers complained thus:

> I can work as hard as he can, but I have a family and Hal has none. He goes too far—drives people to the wall. Then, suddenly, no matter how much he pays them, the money becomes unimportant.[5]

But most who knew Geneen agreed that it was results, and not the feeling of power, that he was after. No one could claim that Geneen, who relished 16-hour days and absorbed thousands of details about ITT's businesses, expected more of his team than he did of himself. "If I had enough arms and legs and time," he once said, "I would do it all myself." Because he could not quite achieve that feat, he evolved a management system that responded as much as any organization could to the boss's relentless urge for constant improvement.

For those who could respond effectively to his stringent demands and endure the long hours and the grueling pace, Geneen supplied top pay, sizable bonuses tied directly to performance, and plenty of excitement. Many executives had admiringly admitted that their top boss knew how to get the most and the best out of them. A former McKinsey consultant who joined the organization commented on his experience at ITT: "Geneen got a lot out of me, but I got a lot out of Geneen. No one else could have given me the job he did at that age without any line experience."[6]

Geneen's energy and enthusiasm were so contagious that he drove his managers to do their absolute best. It was expected that some would not stand the pressure and would leave, but the high turnover did not hurt ITT. Talented managers were hired as replacements or came with the acquired companies. ITT's high turnover meant that those who stayed had plenty of opportunities to move up.

Although the middle management turnover did not hurt ITT financially, Geneen tried to stop it by raising salaries and changing the company's stock-option plan. He also toned down the pressure that he put on his managers. He continued to criticize them in front of their colleagues, but he avoided shouting at them. He acknowledged this effort in the following manner:

> I don't think anyone could have gone through the experience of the last nine years and not changed. Now we're much more diplomatic. When a guy is in trouble, we don't say he's stupid—we try and see how we can help him.[7]

Geneen clearly had a strong orientation for short-term results. He was a dedicated advocate of the importance of quarterly figures, and he did not consider this a short-sighted approach to the future. He explained his reasoning in his book, *Managing:*

> What do you do if your company or your division or your department has not made its quota for the quarter? First of all you locate the problem. Then you find the cause. Then you fix it. That is why we had the comptrollers of every ITT company sending us in headquarters the figures of their companies every week. Less than satisfactory results showed up in those reports very clearly. That's why our line managers "red-flagged" their major problems for immediate attention. That's why we held monthly managers' meetings. We wanted to pinpoint the causes of the problems and find the best possible solutions as quickly as possible.[8]

He also stressed the importance of the proper use of numbers.

> You don't want them [managers] to manage the numbers—pushing sales or receivables from one quarter to another. That is like treating the thermometer instead of the patient.[9]

In his opinion, the difference between well-managed companies and not-so-well managed companies is the degree of attention they pay to numbers, the temperature chart of their business.[10]

Geneen believed that a manager should do whatever he or she could in order to achieve a certain result. He exemplified this with a three-word credo: "Management must manage." This meant "that we would do everything we had to that was honest and legal to bring in the results we desired." His critics, however, linked this management philosophy of "get-it-done-I-don't-care-how" of "the Geneen machine" with several scandals that subsequently tarnished the company's image in the business community and with the general public.[11]

Geneen believed that in order to make "winning" business decisions, namely those that the decision maker believes are a little better than anyone else's, one must base them on what he called "unshakable facts." "I don't believe a man before I believe his facts," he used to say. One method that he proposed to get these facts was to maintain open communications in the organization, insisting on face-to-face communication. Geneen firmly believed that it was not enough for a CEO to see the figures; "he must also see the expression of the man who presents them, and how he presents them."[12]

His strong and extensive financial background was apparent in the way he managed. He knew everything about measures of financial performance but had no experience in operations. One particularly critical analyst said the following:

> Harold Geneen was an absolute disaster as an operating manager. You have only to look at the record—he could acquire companies but not manage them. And his further failing was that he couldn't recognize this.[13]

Yet the financial performance of ITT under Geneen's leadership (Exhibit 2) was matched by very few companies of his era.

Exhibit 2 ITT Corporation and Subsidiaries Consolidated Selected Operating Data,[1] 1959–1977 (million dollars except per share figure)

	1977	1975	1973	1971	1969	1967	1965	1963	1961	1959
Sales and revenues	13,145	11,368	10,183	7,346	5,475	2,761	1,783	1,414	931	766
Income before extraordinary items[2]	562	398	521	407	234	119	76	52	36	29
Earnings per share	4.14	3.20	4.22	3.45	2.90	2.27	1.79	1.35	1.09	.95
Dividends declared per common share	1.82	1.54	1.32	1.16	0.98	0.78	0.62	1.00	1.00	1.00
R&D expenditures	608	483	400	288	236	210	182	170	131	N.A.
Gross plant additions	815	540	852	654	513	238	146	123	105	84
Depreciation	369	298	292	231	190	116	64	39	31	27
Return on stockholders' equity (%)	11.5	9.5	13.6	13.3	11.8	11.7	10.8	9.1	8.0	7.0

[1] As reported in the ITT annual reports for the respective years, except earnings per share amounts that have been adjusted for 2-for-1 stock split effective January 16, 1968.

[2] Extraordinary (losses) gains were $(12) million in 1977, $(70) million in 1971, $3.5 million in 1967, and $7.6 million in 1961.

Source: ITT Corporation annual reports.

THE POST-GENEEN ERA

After nearly two decades at the helm of ITT, Harold Geneen stepped down in 1977 as its Chairman and CEO. The widely publicized investigations of the company by government agencies and ITT's relatively poor performance in the mid-1970s were rumored to be the prime motivations for his resignation. Geneen, then in his sixty-eighth year, stayed on as the Chairman of ITT's board of directors. Lyman Hamilton assumed the post of CEO in January 1978.

ITT under Lyman Hamilton

Hamilton, formerly of the World Bank, joined ITT in 1962 to start the ITT Credit Corporation. He rose rapidly within the finance function to become a corporate director by 1974. But it was only in 1976, with his move to the six-member office of the President, that Hamilton became a serious contender for ITT's top job.[14] He was elected President and Chief Operating Officer in 1977, before becoming CEO in 1978.

A New Strategy.   When Lyman Hamilton assumed leadership of ITT, he began to divest weak subsidiaries and attempted to build the more profitable ones. The divestiture program was obviously a point of disagreement with Geneen. Hamilton also sought to compensate for flat earnings in the telecommunications and insurance businesses by expanding into potential growth areas such as consumer appliances and pulp and making acquisitions in the emerging field of "information delivery," which sought to connect telecommunications with computers. The office equipment business was another area in which Hamilton felt that ITT had to make entry.

Hamilton also changed the company's preoccupation with earnings per share. This ratio has been criticized as a measure of profitability because it is divorced from the amount of assets or capital required to generate a firm's earnings. Hamilton redefined the company's goals in terms of return on equity (ROE). ITT's return on equity during the last three years of Geneen's tenure ranged from 9.5 percent to 11.5 percent when the median ROE for the Fortune 500 companies was 13.3 percent. Hamilton's goal of achieving a 15 percent ROE was one of the driving forces behind his divestitures program. Although the ROE improved to 12.4 percent in the first year, it dropped dramatically to 6.8 percent in Hamilton's second year as a CEO (Exhibit 3). However, the poor ROE was in part due to debt reduction and foreign exchange losses.

Reorganization.   Hamilton saw his role as that of a "fine-tuner" and a consolidator. Seeking to help ITT grow internally through the product lines it already owned, he reorganized its more than 1,000 product lines into 5 fairly homogeneous business groups—Telecommunications and Electronics, Engineered Products, Consumer Products and Services, Natural Resources, and Insurance and Finance (Ex-

Exhibit 3   Selected Operating Data, 1978–1984 (million dollars except per share figures)

	1984	1983	1982	1981	1980	1979	1978
Sales and revenues	12,701	14,155	15,958	17,306	18,530	17,197	15,261
Income before extra-ordinary items[1]	448	675	703	695	894	381	662
Earning per share	2.97	4.50	4.75	4.70	6.12	2.65	4.66
Dividends declared per common share	1.88	2.76	2.70	2.62	2.45	2.25	2.05
R&D expenditures	974	1,024	1,080	1,099	1,116	959	799
Gross plant additions	786	823	920	1,020	1,131	1,049	941
Depreciation	489	553	540	532	520	472	439
Return on stockhold-ers' equity (%)	7.4	11.1	11.5	11.1	15	6.8	12.4

[1]Extraordinary (losses) gains were $(18) million in 1981.

Source: ITT Corporation annual reports.

hibit 4). He instituted the office of the Chief Executive, which was comprised of himself and three Executive Vice Presidents. Each of the five businesses reported to him through a member of this office.

Another change initiated by Hamilton was a restructuring of the management meetings. He cut the monthly meetings from three days to one, renamed them Corporate Management Meetings, and reduced the number of people required to attend. However, he instituted a half-day Management Sector Meeting, at which executives from each business group conferred. The combined effect of the changes was to reduce the time that operating managers spent at headquarters from three days to a maximum of one and one-half day each month. Hamilton also cut ITT's corporate staff, delegating more authority to his line managers.

A New Management Style.   Hamilton's style was also very different from that of Geneen's.[15] Unlike his predecessor, he was able to combine unflappable smoothness with genuine friendliness. Although he was a hard worker, he was not a workaholic. "I look forward to weekends and vacations, and I'm not impressed with someone who says he doesn't take vacations," he used to say. His preference for early-morning work was another point of difference from his predecessor. His associates saw him as warm, egalitarian, considerate, humane, and thoughtful. It is acknowledged, however, that few acquaintances inside and outside ITT knew him well because he never got very intimate with people.

Hamilton's Departure.   Hamilton had been CEO for a mere 18 months when, on the morning of July 11, 1979, the board asked Hamilton to submit his resignation because of "policy differences." Rand Araskog became ITT's new

CEO. Araskog, a West Point graduate, was an Executive Vice President at the time of his promotion. He joined the corporation in 1966 and had extensive experience in operations.

ITT Under Rand Araskog

Araskog essentially followed Hamilton's strategy and refined it further with his own initiatives. Despite his reservations, Geneen left Araskog free to pursue his plans and eventually retired from ITT's board in 1983.

Changes in Strategy.   Araskog felt that ITT's environment had changed significantly since the Geneen era. Interest rates, for example, had jumped to 20 percent by 1980. Araskog sought to reduce the company's debt ratio from its high of 50 percent to an ambitious low of 30 percent. The ratio of debt to total capitalization was lowered by 1984 to 37.4 percent, the lowest for the company in over two decades. However, Araskog also simultaneously sought a 15 percent return on equity.

Continuing the divestiture of unprofitable operations initiated by his predecessor, Araskog sold 63 companies beginning in 1979. In 1983, he reorganized the five business groups that Hamilton had instituted into four management corporations, in order to take advantage of either market or technological synergies. The new management corporations were the following: Telecommunication, Industrial Technology, Diversified Services, and Natural Resources (Exhibit 5). He also established the Telecommunication and Electronics Advisory Board with the mandate of coordinating and integrating the various research and development efforts throughout the corporation and of gathering market intelligence.

Araskog pinned the company's future on U.S. telecommunications and automated office equipment markets. ITT's announced strategy of investing in telecommunications, using other businesses as a source of cash, is exemplified by an interesting planning detail. The annual budget for the telecommunications division was due one month before the budgets for the rest of the company. This gave corporate management the opportunity to determine the level of cash required by telecommunications and to pare other budgets accordingly.

Critics of Araskog's plan pointed out that the U.S. telecommunications market was an unfamiliar arena for ITT. The competition in it was fierce, and the customers were very demanding. ITT had to spend, for example, $300 million over two years to adapt its European telephone-switching technology to the U.S. market. The company lacked trained staff to market its telecommunications equipment. The U.S. market differed from other ITT markets because individual telephone-operating companies and private businesses were direct customers for telecommunications and office automation products—unlike in Europe, where large government-controlled phone-and-telecommunication companies made all the critical buying decisions. Whereas selling in Europe required political savvy and

(*Text continues on page 329*)

Exhibit 4 Business Groups in the Hamilton Administration (in millions of dollars)

	Sales and Revenues		Operating income		Identifiable Assets	
	1979	1978	1979	1978	1979	1978
Telecommunications and electronics						
Telecommunications equipment	$ 5,342	$ 4,721	$ 392	$ 451	$ 4,408	$ 3,916
Telecommunications operations	292	265	91	90	530	474
Defense and avionics systems	673	654	45	30	338	327
	6,307	5,640	528	571	5,276	4,717
Engineered products						
Automotive products	1,711	1,541	140	178	1,023	911
Industrial products	2,961	2,527	221	170	1,807	1,652
Components and semiconductors	1,160	910	106	81	804	676
	5,832	4,978	467	429	3,634	3,239
Consumer products and services						
Food products	1,743	1,702	48	55	472	531
Consumer appliances	878	922	(14)	12	574	597
Hotels and other	1,109	976	99	82	929	901
	3,730	3,600	133	149	1,975	2,029

Natural resources					
Timber and earth	1,088	872	147	54	1,394	1,515
Energy	240	171	26	16	351	333
	1,328	1,043	173	70	1,745	1,848
Unallocated	—	—	(98)	(107)	2,461	2,202
	17,197	15,261	1,203	1,112	15,091	14,035
Less investment in insurance and finance Subsidiaries included in Unallocated	—	—	—	—	(2,235)	(1,990)
Insurance and finance					
Casualty and Life Insurance	4,281	3,761	297	259	10,008	8,612
Finance	518	377	107	90	3,314	2,685
	4,799	4,138	404	349	13,322	11,297
Total	$21,996	$19,399	$1,607	$1,461	$26,178	$23,342

Intersegment Sales—Sales for 1979 and 1978 of the Components and Semiconductors segment exclude intersegment sales of $148 and $165, respectively, which are priced on an arms-length basis and eliminated in consolidation. Intersegment sales in all other groups are not material.

Sales to foreign governments—Sales to various foreign governments, primarily of telecommunications equipment aggregated $2,560 and $2,384 in 1979 and 1978, respectively.

Net income and net assets—U.S. operations accounted for approximately 66 percent and 62 percent of 1979 and 1978 income, respectively. Before the writeoff of a Canadian pulp mill in 1979, net assets employed in the United States amounted to $3,753 and $3,438 at December 31, 1979 and 1978, respectively.

Source: ITT Corporation annual reports.

Exhibit 5 **Management Corporations in 1984 under the Araskog Administration (in millions of dollars)**

	Sales and Revenue	Operating Income	Identifiable Assets
Telecommunications			
Telecommunications equipment	$ 4,381	$ 178	$ 3,652
Defense and space	1,213	56	482
	5,594	234	4,134
Industrial technology			
Automotive	1,645	130	883
Connectors, components, and semiconductors	879	98	583
Industrial products	1,813	136	1,065
	4,337	364	2,531
Diversified services			
Communications operations and Information services	874	58	902
Hotels and community development	626	36	872
Insurance operations	5,724	(149)	14,167
Financial services	1,128	217	6,595
	8,352	162	22,536
Natural resources	1,002	80	1,617
Total segments	19,285	840	30,818
Unallocated	—	(102)	313
	19,285	738	31,131
Dispositions	268	(10)	83
Net assets of discontinued bakery and energy operations	—	—	127
Total	$19,553	$ 728	$31,341

Business segment presentations have been modified to reflect activities of the asset redeployment program. Dispositions include other major units sold, partially divested or closed.

Intersegment sales—Sales for 1984 of the Connectors, Components, and Semiconductors segment excluded intersegment sales of $121, on an arm's-length basis and eliminated in consolidation. Other intersegment sales are not material.

Sales to foreign government—Sales to various governments primarily of telecommunications equipment, aggregated $1,687 in 1984.

Net income and net assets—U.S. operations were 53 percent of 1984 income, excluding the gain on the sale of ITT / Continental Baking Company in 1984. Net assets employed in United States amounted to 73 percent as of December 31, 1984.

the ability to impress key bureaucrats, selling in the United States required technical expertise and the ability to make spot decisions in the field.

In the office equipment market, the main attraction for ITT was the private branch exchange, the PBX switchboard that could route phone traffic around an office building and connect a building to the outside phone network. ITT's sole product in this market was 3100 PBX, which appealed only to small customers—a segment about one-fourth the size of the total PBX market in the United States. The company intended to upgrade the 3100 PBX to have data capability for transmitting digital bits of computer traffic around an office. The expectation was that the purchase of a 3100 PBX would induce customers to buy ITT's computer terminals, printers, and Xtra personal computer. However, the company had serious problems in marketing these products.[16]

ITT also found it difficult to penetrate the business-user market for personal computers, which was dominated by IBM. Its first IBM-compatible machine, the Xtra, was late and met with significant price competition. But Araskog was determined to stick with it and make it central to ITT's office equipment-marketing strategy.

The Planning System.   In January of each year, the presidents of ITT's four management corporations issued strategic directions to the field. In February and March, the unit's preliminary plans were reviewed in the field by the senior group personnel; in April, the plans were submitted to the management corporations. The business unit managers had to ensure in their plans that there was proper balance between long- and short-term performance and that R&D spending was well justified. In early May, the four management corporations submitted to corporate management their own plans, which were reviewed later that month. The budget guidelines were issued in mid-July. The budgets of the four management corporations were due by the end of November. After a corporate review in December, the budgets were returned to the management corporation for incorporating changes. The final budgets were approved by the end of the year.

Araskog modified Geneen's emphasis on short-term results, giving projects time to prove themselves. The two-year strategic plan was therefore deleted from the planning process. Disruptions in profits also were tolerated when necessary. He sought to delegate more authority to the business units and to instill an entrepreneurial spirit in the organization by returning decision-making power to the line managers and to the heads of ITT's large European subsidiaries. His attempt to move ITT from an exclusively top-down, centralized organization to a more-decentralized entity resulted in tensions between the old, but not totally abolished, top-down planning system (with its detailed controls) and the new bottom-up process. Executives familiar with both the Geneen and the Araskog systems complained that although the five-year document asked managers to set specific milestones, there was little impetus now to develop a specific business plan that detailed how the strategic direction identified in the five-year plan would be implemented in the next 18 to 24 months.

The decentralization did not, however, affect ITT's unique financial control organization. The controller of each business group still reported to both the President of the group and the corporate Controller.

A New Style.   Araskog was a conservative CEO. He set about reversing the adverse publicity that ITT received in the late 1970s by setting high ethical standards for ITT managers.

But the task of turning the company around proved to be more difficult. A former ITT executive who had worked closely with him felt that "Araskog has little tolerance for bad news, and he's been getting a lot of that lately. Because of his reactions, a number of executives are beginning to fear him."[17]

NOTES

1. See "ITT Takes the Profit Path to Europe," *Business Week* (May, 9, 1970): 60–62.

2. "ITT: The View from Inside," *Business Week* (Nov. 3, 1973): 42–63.

3. This section relies on the following sources: "How One Man Can Move a Corporate Mountain," *Fortune* 74 (July 1, 1966): 80–83; "The Financial Key at ITT," *Duns Review* 96 (Dec. 1970): 24; "How ITT Tightens Its Spreading Net," *Business Week* (June 24, 1967): 58–62; H. Geneen and A. Moscow, *Managing* (Garden City, NY: Doubleday, 1984), 181–196; and conversations with ITT executives.

4. "They Call It 'Geneen U'!" *Forbes* 101 (May 1, 1968): 27–30.

5. Ibid.

6. Ibid.

7. Ibid.

8. Geneen and Moscow, *Managing,* 113, 114.

9. Ibid., 184.

10. Ibid., 182.

11. P. S. Meyer, "ITT Chief Hamilton to Shed Parts of 'Geneen Machine,' " *Wall Street Journal* (Oct. 11, 1978): 1. Reprinted by permission of *Wall Street Journal,* © 1978 Dow Jones & Company, Inc. All Rights Reserved Worldwide.

12. Copyright © 1973 by Anthony Sampson. From the book *The Sovereign State of ITT.* Originally published by Stein & Day, Inc., reprinted with permission of Scarborough House/Publishers.

13. G. Colvin, "The De-Geneening of ITT," *Fortune* 105 (Jan. 11, 1982): 34.

14. Meyer, "ITT Chief," 16.

15. J. Connelly, "Lyman Hamilton: ITT's Mr. Outside," *Institutional Investor* 10 (Nov. 1976): 43.

16. "ITT's Big Gamble," *Business Week* (Oct. 22, 1984): 115.

17. M. Langley, "ITT Chief Emphasizes Harmony, Confidence and Playing by the Rules," *Wall Street Journal* (Sept. 13, 1984): 1. Reprinted by permission of *Wall Street Journal,* © 1984 Dow Jones & Company, Inc. All Rights Reserved Worldwide.

Norton Company: Strategic Planning for Diversified Business Operations

Subject to the business-cycle swings of the capital goods industry, Norton Company experienced the usual drop in sales during the economic downturn of 1975. What was unusual for Norton was its ability on this occasion to sustain profits compared to the customary plunge in earnings whenever the economy dipped. Robert Cushman, President and Chief Executive Officer of Norton Company, saw this performance as evidence of the growing effectiveness of Norton's strategic planning.

As of 1976, five years' efforts had gone into developing planning activities that specifically could help top management shape strategies for the firm's diversified business operations. Mr. Cushman was pleased with the results of these efforts:

> Our strategic planning has made a tremendous difference in the way the company is now managed. It gives us a much-needed handle to evaluate strategies for each of our many businesses.

One of the difficult strategic planning decisions faced by top management in 1976 concerned a re-evaluation of the long-term strategy for the coated abrasives business operations in the U.S. This situation is described following a general explanation of the strategic planning process at Norton Company and how it came to be.

THE COMPANY

Norton Company, headquartered in Worcester, Massachusetts, was a multinational industrial manufacturer with 85 plant locations in 21 countries. The firm employed almost 19,000 persons.

Copyright © 1976 by the President and Fellows of Harvard College
Harvard Business School case 9-377-044

This case was prepared by Professor Francis Aguilar with the assistance of Norton Company as the basis for class discussion rather than to illustrate either effective or ineffective handling of an administrative situation. Reprinted by permission of the Harvard Business School.

Exhibit 1 Five-Year Financial Summary (in millions of dollars)

	1971	1972	1973	1974	1975
Net sales	346	374	475	558	548
Net income[1]	11.4	14.5	25.4	21.6	20.9
Net income, excluding effect of foreign currency exchange rate changes[1]	10.3	15.0	21.3	25.1	24.8
By line of business:					
Abrasives					
Sales (%)	70	75	75	75	73
Net income (%)	85	87	89	76	70
Diversified products					
Sales (%)	30	25	25	25	27
Net income (%)	15	13	11	24	30
By subsidiaries outside the USA:					
Sales (%)	41	41	42	45	49
Net income (%)	39	33	56	56	40
Working capital	148	151	155	159	200
Total debt	69	65	66	102	112
Shareholders' equity	211	218	232	244	255
Operating and financial ratios					
Net income as percentage of sales	3.3	3.9	5.3	3.9	3.8
Net income as percentage of equity	5.4	6.7	10.9	8.8	8.2
Current ratio	3.7	3.6	2.9	2.3	3.3
Percentage total debt to equity	33	30	29	42	44
Per share statistics[2]					
Net income	2.12	2.70	4.70	4.02	3.85
Net income, excluding effect of foreign currency exchange rate changes[1]	1.92	2.80	3.94	4.68	4.57
Dividends	1.50	1.50	1.50	1.575	1.70
Stock price (NYSE)	27–37	32–39	23–26	19–29	21–29

[1]Exchange gains and losses resulting from the translation of foreign currency financial statements were included for the first time in the 1975 annual report in determining net income in accordance with a new procedure recommended by the Financial Accounting Standards Board (FASB). The net income results excluding foreign currency effects conform to prior reporting practices at Norton and generally throughout industry.

[2]The average number of shares of common stock outstanding varied between 5.37 and 5.67 million during this period.

Source: Annual reports and *Moody's Industrial Manual* (1975).

As the world's largest abrasives manufacturer, Norton produced both abrasive grain raw materials and finished products. The latter included such items as sandpaper and grinding wheels. The company also produced a wide range of other industrial products including: industrial ceramics, sealants, catalyst carriers and tower packings for the chemical process industries, engineered plastic components, tubing and related products for medical applications and for food processing, and industrial safety products. In 1975, these other products accounted for about 27 percent of the reported total sales of $548 million.[1] Exhibit 1 contains a five-year summary of financial results.

Organization

Norton Company was organized into "low-growth" and "high-growth" product groups. This organizational structure reflected two basic corporate objectives. The first was to remain the worldwide leader in abrasives. The second was to improve profitability through "a limited number of diversified product lines and without conglomeration."[2]

When introducing this structure in 1971, Cushman had remarked:

> As you look at Norton Company you see two major areas of business: our traditional abrasives products, which are good cash generators but have low growth, and our newer nonabrasive lines, which need cash but have a high growth potential. We need a different type of manager to run each business.[3]

Harry Duane, age 45, headed the abrasives group. His job was characterized as that of "running a large, cyclical-prone, slow-growth business with stiff competition in many different markets." Successful performance in this business was said to depend on careful cost control, keeping products up to date, and holding established markets. Duane had had experience in the abrasives business abroad as well as in the U.S. since joining Norton in 1957.

Donald R. Melville, age 50, headed Norton's diversified products business group. He had joined the company in 1967 as Vice President of Marketing after having served in various marketing capacities with Continental Can Company, Scott Paper Company, and Dunlop Tire & Rubber. As reported in *Business Week:*

> Melville's management style relies on creating an entrepreneurial atmosphere. . . . "In the case of abrasives," says Melville, "you compensate your people on the basis of whether or not they make that month's budget. In diversified products, you don't care as much about a month's budget—you try to double your sales in twelve months."

The 1976 company organization structure in shown in Exhibit 2.

Concepts for Strategic Planning

In 1967, as Executive Vice President in charge of company-wide operations, Cushman faced the problem of assessing the role each of some 75 product lines

Exhibit 2 **Partial Organization Chart (June 1976)**

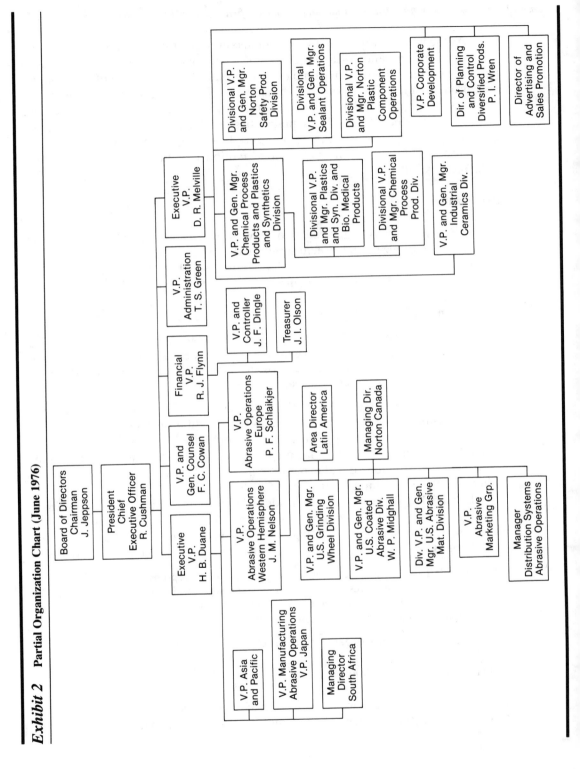

was to play in Norton's future. The conventional corporate long-range planning then in use at Norton was found wanting for this task. Mr. Cushman consequently began to search for more appropriate ways to plan multibusiness operations. He later remarked:

> During the early 60's, Peter Drucker, widely known spokesman, critic, and analyst to business began to describe business in terms of certain variables which seemed to determine a company's future. But it was Fred Borch, Marketing Vice President of the highly diversified General Electric, who in 1960 asked the key question and then assigned two members of his staff, Jack McKitterick and Dr. Sidney Schoeffler, to find the answer. "Why is it," he said, "that through the years some of our businesses fail while others succeed. There must be certain decisions, strategies, or factors which lead to certain results. With hundreds of products ranging from electric pencil sharpeners to diesel engines and nuclear plants, it is difficult to do an effective job of planning. It is, in fact, impossible for management to have direct, personal feeling and knowledge about so many business environments. We need better guidelines."

In 1967, Dr. Schoeffler was invited to Norton to describe the results of G.E.'s "profitability optimization" study. Based on sophisticated multiple regression analyses covering ten years' experience for 150 product lines at General Electric, Dr. Schoeffler had been able to identify some 37 factors which accounted for more than 80 percent of the variations in profit results. The findings showed how profitability varied with respect to such factors as market share, market growth rate, and the level of investments required. The findings also showed how profitability varied with respect to policies on such matters as research and development as a per cent of sales, marketing expenditures, product quality, and pricing.[4] Mr. Cushman was struck with the relevance and concreteness of the resulting guidelines.

In his search for better guidelines, Mr. Cushman also became interested in the work of Bruce Henderson, founder and president of the Boston Consulting Group. Based on the premise that costs decreased with experience in a predictable manner, Henderson held that the firm with the greatest volume should have the lowest costs for a given product line. Market share served as a measure of relative volume for planning purposes.

The cash flows associated with growth and mature industries constituted a second element of Henderson's approach. Product lines with leading market shares in mature industries were generators of surplus cash; those in growth industries represented the potential cash generators for future years. For diversified business operations, Henderson urged that attention be given in strategic planning to the creation of a portfolio in which some product lines could generate sufficient cash throw-off to nourish the development and growth of other product lines in growing markets. Appendix A describes these ideas in some detail.

Strategic Planning at Norton

The basic building block for planning continued to be the strategy analysis for individual product lines. This analysis considered a wide range of business factors, such as competitive conditions, technology, and future trends, and concluded with a proposed course of action over time. Each strategy was prepared by the manager holding profit responsibility for the product line and was evaluated by group and corporate line management. The customary analysis and review of strategy was extended to include two additional tests based on the somewhat related sets of concepts described above.

One of these additional tests concerned the intrinsic profit potential for a business. Based on experiential data for a wide range of businesses (such as had been generated for General Electric), Norton was able to ascertain a measure of the profit level appropriate for a business as it existed. It was also able to ascertain the extent to which profits and cash flows might be increased under alternate strategies. These financial norms helped management to evaluate how well a business was being run and how much additional potential it had. Appendix B describes the kind of information available to Norton for this purpose.

A business strategy was also evaluated in the context of total corporate cash flows. The strategy had to conform to the overall availabilities of or needs for cash. For this purpose, market share performance served as a major controlling device. In broad terms, businesses were assigned the task of building, holding or harvesting market share. "Building strategies" were based on active efforts to increase market share by means of new product introductions, added marketing programs, etc. Such strategies customarily called for cash inputs. "Holding strategies" were aimed at maintaining the existing level of market share. Net cash flows might be negative for rapidly growing markets and positive for slowly growing markets. "Harvesting strategies" sought to achieve earnings and cash flows by permitting market share to decline.

In line with this approach, Norton's operations had been divided into some 60 businesses whose characteristics were sufficiently different to warrant the development of individual business strategies. These subdivisions were known as substrategic business units. Combinations of these substrategic business units were grouped into about 30 strategic business units for purposes of top management review.

Strategy Guidance Committee

In April 1972, Cushman formed a top-management committee to assist in the evaluation of these business strategies. As Cushman later reported to the Norton Board:

> The function of the Strategy Guidance Committee is to review at appropriate levels the strategy of each business unit, to make certain it does fit corporate objectives, and to monitor how effectively its strategy is being carried out. It provides the executive, regional, and division manager an opportunity for an "outside" peer group to examine and advise.
>
> The committee totals twelve. The President, the Executive Vice President, the Regional Vice Presidents, the Financial Vice President, the Controller, the Vice Presi-

dent of Corporate Development and Graham Wren as Secretary. Depending on the circumstances, business units are reviewed on a 2-year cycle. Well documented strategies along standard lines are sent to members for review before meetings.

Each strategic business unit was responsible for preparing a strategy book for review. Copies of this book were distributed to members of the Strategy Guidance Committee at least one week prior to the scheduled review. To focus attention on the critical issues, Cushman had set the following groundrules for the review session:

> No formal presentation is required at the meeting because each committee member is expected to have thoroughly studied the strategy book.
>
> Discussion during the meeting will generally center around these questions:
>
> 1. Questions of facts, trends, and assumptions as presented in the strategy book.
> 2. Questions as to the appropriateness of the mission of the business in terms of Build, Maintain or Harvest.
> 3. Questions as to the appropriateness of the strategy in the context of the facts and mission.
> 4. Questions suggested by PIMS analysis.[5]
> 5. How does the business unit and its strategy fit and relate to similar businesses within Norton (e.g., coated abrasives Europe vs. coated abrasives worldwide)?
> 6. How does the business unit and its strategy fit within the corporate portfolio and strategy?

Involvement of Line Managers

The involvement of key line managers in the Strategy Guidance Committee and the methodology used in generating the strategy books gave a distinct line orientation to planning at Norton. Management for each business unit had to take a position concerning its mission, strengths and weaknesses, likely competitive developments, trends, and finally its strategy. The analysis and recommendations had to stand the test of critical evaluation by an experienced and involved top management.

Although Cushman was pleased with the planning tools Norton had developed, he felt that the deep involvement of line managers in both the formulation and review of strategies served to prevent a mechanical or otherwise undue reliance on the planning tools themselves. He believed it highly desirable that an operating manager's "gut feel" remain an important input to strategic planning.

Other Elements Related to Strategic Planning

In 1976 detailed cash flow models which could be used to support and extend the analysis described above were being completed. Several Norton managers remarked that these models would contribute importantly to the strategic planning efforts.

Also, Norton's incentive system was designed to motivate managers in carrying out their assigned strategic moves—whether to build, maintain, or harvest their business. Cushman reported the use of over 50 different custom-tailored plans for this purpose.

Finally, Cushman's deep-seated involvement in the strategic planning process and the respect he commanded from other senior-level managers at Norton undoubtedly influenced this process in major ways.

COATED ABRASIVES—DOMESTIC[6]

One of the difficult cases for consideration by the Strategy Guidance Committee in 1976 concerned a re-evaluation of the strategy to be followed for the U.S. coated abrasives business. Coated Abrasives Domestic (CAD), one of Norton's larger operating divisions, had had a recent history of declining market share and profitability.

In 1974, Norton management had decided to stem further loss of market share by a major restructuring of the CAD division. During the ensuing two years, market share and profitability continued to decline. These unfavorable results raised important questions about the merits of the earlier decision. The case for holding market share (the current strategy) was further challenged by the recommendation resulting from the PIMS regression analysis. The PIMS report had concluded that the CAD business should be moderately harvested (market share permitted to decline) for its cash throw-off.

The remainder of this case presents excerpts from information presented to the Strategy Guidance Committee or otherwise known by its members concerning CAD.

The Abrasives Market

Abrasive finished products were generally classified as bonded or coated. Bonded abrasives were basic tools used in almost every industry where shaping, cutting, or finishing of materials was required. Some of the major uses were in foundries and steel mills for rough grinding of castings and surface conditioning of steels and alloys; in metal fabrication for such products as automobiles and household appliances; in tool and die shops; in the manufacture of bearings; and in the paper and pulp industry. Norton produced more than 250,000 types and sizes of grinding wheels and other bonded abrasive products.

Coated abrasives (popularly referred to as sandpaper) were widely used throughout the metalworking and woodworking industries, in tanneries and in service industries such as floor surfacing and automobile refinishing. Norton produced more than 38,000 different items in the form of sheets, belts, rolls, discs, and specialties. The most common form of coated abrasives was the endless belt, some major applications of which included the grinding and finishing of automobiles and appliance parts, the precision grinding and polishing of stainless and alloy steel, and the sanding of furniture, plywood, and particleboard.

The overlap of customers' requirements for bonded and coated abrasives varied from industry to industry. For example, the woodworking industry used coated abrasives almost exclusively. In contrast, the auto industry purchased large

Market Share Strategy	Sales ($ mill.)	Abrasive Operations	Diversified Products
Build	96	In the actual presentation, each strategic business	
Build/maintain	135	was listed under its appropriate category. For ex-	
Maintain	257	ample, CAD and 15 other business units were	
Maintain/harvest	60	listed in the abrasives column for the maintain	
Harvest	0	strategy.	
Total	548	400	148

Figure 1   **Summary of Market Share Strategies for the Norton Portfolio of Business**

quantities of both bonded abrasives (e.g., for grinding engine parts) and coated abrasives (e.g., for finishing bodies). Industrial distributors, which accounted for a large portion of Norton's abrasive sales, usually carried both bonded and coated abrasive products. Both Norton and Carborundum offered full lines of bonded and coated abrasive products; 3M competed only in coated abrasives.

In management's opinion, the principal factors which contributed to a favorable market position in this industry included quality and reliability of product, completeness of product line, nonpatented technological "know-how," substantial capital investment, length of experience in the business, familiarity and reputation of name, strength of marketing network, technical service, delivery reliability, and price. In 1975, no single customer, including the United States Government, accounted for as much as 5 percent of Norton's net sales.

CAD in the Corporate Context

As was customary, the meeting of the Strategy Guidance Committee to review the CAD strategy was opened by Mr. Graham Wren, secretary of the committee, with a short presentation showing where the product line in question fit in the Norton portfolio of businesses. The first chart he presented contained an overview of the market share strategies for 31 strategic business units, as summarized in Figure 1.

Separate charts showed the ranking of all business units with respect to return on net assets (RONA), return on sales (ROS), and asset turnover ratio for 1974, 1975, and the average for the two years. CAD placed in the rankings as follows:

Coated Abrasives Domestic

	Rank Among 31	Value for CAD 1974/75 Avg.	Norton Avg., Operations
RONA	27	6.0	10
ROS	26	3.5	6
Asset turnover	23	1.7	1.9

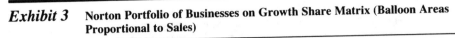

Exhibit 3   **Norton Portfolio of Businesses on Growth Share Matrix (Balloon Areas Proportional to Sales)**

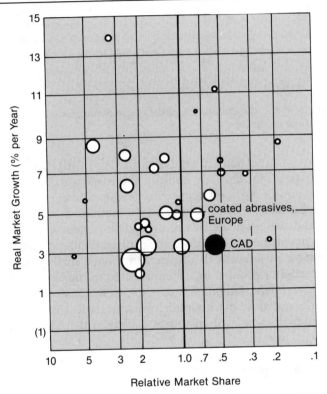

A growth share matrix showed CAD to lie well in the undesirable low-growth/ smaller-than-competitor quadrant (see Exhibit 3). As explained in Appendix A, a product experiencing both low growth and low market share (relative to the industry leader) would likely be a net user of cash with little promise for future pay-off.

Finally, the committee's cash generation vs. market share corporate test was applied to the CAD proposed strategy. As shown in Figure 2, the combination of maintaining market share at its present level and generating cash was acceptable.

CAD STRATEGY PLAN

Paul Midghall, Vice President and General Manager for Norton's U.S. Coated Abrasives Division, was the principal architect of the strategic plan to maintain market share. His reasoning as laid out in the 1976 strategy book for CAD began with a statement of the division's role and strategy:

	Market Share Strategy		
Cash Generation	**Build**	**Maintain**	**Harvest**
Uses cash	A/?	U	U
Provides own cash	A/?	U	U
Disengages cash	A	A*	A

A = The combination is an acceptable strategy.

? = The combination is a questionable strategy.

U = The combination is an unacceptable strategy.

*Given CAD's strategy of maintain market share, it should disengage cash.

Figure 2   The Cash Generation/Market Share Strategy Test

Mission—Cash Generation

Norton's long-term objective is to allocate resources to high growth opportunities while maintaining total world abrasives leadership. CAD's role within that corporate objective is: to be a long term cash generator; to act as the technical focal point for coated abrasives operations worldwide.

Strategy—Restructure and Maintain

To meet that objective, CAD has in the last two years radically restructured its operations. Its strategy now is to complete the restructuring, to consolidate the organization into a confident, coherent team, and to pursue market segmentation based on the strengths which have emerged from restructuring. To understand how this strategy evolved, one must turn to CAD's history.

The strategy report went on to identify the reasons for the earlier deterioration of market share and profitability. These included:

1. Inadequate reinvestment in the basic coated abrasives business in favor of investments which attempted to build allied businesses;[7]
2. High wage rates and fringe benefits coupled with low productivity and poor work conditions;
3. High overheads;
4. Premium pricing without compensating benefits to the customer;
5. A labor strike in 1966.

Serious attempts to reverse the negative trends for CAD had proved unsuccessful, and in late 1973, management decided a major change had to be made to the business. The current strategy report reviewed the alternative strategies that had been considered earlier:

By late 1973, CAD's condition demanded positive action; share had dropped to 26 percent and RONA to 7.5 percent. A fundamental change had to occur. The principal options were:

1. Sell, liquidate, or harvest. These alternatives were eliminated because: (a) a viable coated abrasives business was deemed important to worldwide coated abrasives business; (b) a viable coated abrasives business was judged important to U.S. bonded abrasives business.
2. Attempt to regain lost share and with it volume to cover fixed expenses. In a mature industry, with the major competitors financially secure and firmly entrenched, such a strategy was judged too expensive.
3. Greater price realization. We already maintained a high overall price level, and 3M was the price leader in the industry. In later 1974, Norton tried to lead prices up dramatically to restore profitability but the rest of the industry did not follow.

Alternative—Comprehensive Cost Reduction

A new cost structure was the only reasonable choice for a radical change. We had to scale down to a cost level consistent with our volume and our position in the industry.

In 1974, a decision to restructure the CAD business by making major cost reductions was made by Norton's Executive Committee and approved by its Board of Directors. This move was intended to make CAD more competitive so that it could prevent further erosion of its market share.

Restructuring

The strategy review of 1974 had identified many areas for cost reduction. These touched on almost every segment of operations and included: moving labor-intensive manufacturing operations from New York to Texas; combining the coated abrasives sales force with that for bonded abrasives (e.g., grinding wheels); and reducing fixed assets. The product line was also to be reduced. Earlier about 4,000 product items out of some 20,000 (that is, 20 percent) had accounted for 87 percent of sales.

During the two-year period 1974–1975, over $2 million had been invested to implement the restructuring. The changes were eventually expected to result in over $9 million annual direct recurring savings, raising RONA by about 8 percentage points to a total of 14 percent.[8] The number of employees for CAD had declined from 2,000 to 1,300 by 1976.

CAD's Future Environment

The U.S. coated abrasives industry was expected to experience low growth and gradual changes as a rule. The strategy book forecasted long-term growth at 2.5 percent per annum. Industrial markets, which constituted 75 percent of Norton's CAD business, were to grow even more slowly. Because of the depressed level of business operations in early 1976, annual growth for industrial markets was forecast to spurt to about 7 percent until 1980.[9]

Product technology was expected to change slowly, but in important ways. The strategy book noted:

> The advent of Norzon grain, new resin bonds, and synthetic backings illustrates the fact that although coated abrasives may be a mature product, it is not a commodity product. Technological evolution is slow but continuous, and a competitor who fails to keep abreast cannot survive.

	1975 Sales ($ Million)	Total Market Share	
		1975	1973
3M	99	34%	32%
Norton	76	26%	27%
Carborundum	40	14%	15%
Armak	23	8%	8%
Other U.S.	35	12%	12%
Foreign	21	7%	7%
Total industry	294	100%	100%

Market segment	Metal-Working[1]	Wood-Working	General Trade[2]
Market potential, 1975 ($ million)	130	36	81
Estimated market share, 1975			
3M	30%	27%	65%
Norton	29%	26%	20%
Carborundum	22%	10%	11%

[1]Includes primary metals, fabricated metals, and transportation equipment (autos, aircraft) industries.
[2]Includes hardware retail and automobile finishing businesses.

Figure 3   U.S. Coated Abrasives Market Share Estimates

While product development exhibits highly visible evolution, process development is inconspicuous. No major changes have occurred, or are expected, in manufacturing technology.

Capacity in all segments of manufacturing will be adequate to fill demand well into the 1980's.

The U.S. coated abrasive market was said to have "healthy, strong, rational competition." With the exception of 3M, the return of most competitors was thought to be below the U.S. industrial average. Figure 3 shows sales and market shares for the principal competitors.

CAD Strategy for 1976

The proposed strategy for CAD contained two principal elements. One element was a continuation of the restructuring and cost cutting that had begun in 1974. CAD management estimated that about 75 percent of this program had been put into effect and that two more years would be required to complete the steps underway.

The second element of the strategy was to focus on those market segments where Norton had competitive advantage. Detailed share/growth balloon charts, such as shown in Exhibit 4, were used to identify specific sectors for attention.

To foster product innovation, the 1976 plan had introduced a recommenda-

Exhibit 4   CAD Growth Share Matrices (Balloon Areas Proportional to Norton's Sales)

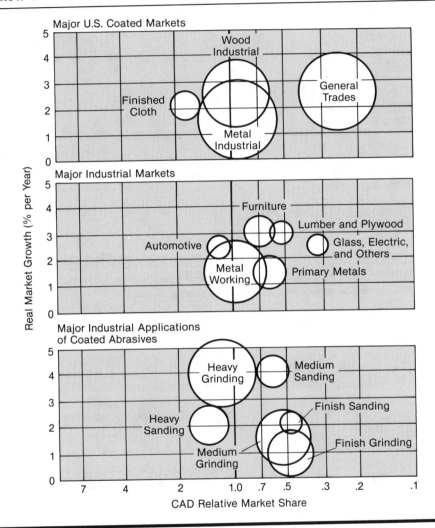

tion to expand R&D efforts. Twenty-two men had been assigned to CAD product development in 1975.

These strategic moves were predicted to produce favorable results. The CAD report identified the unit's future strengths to include: variable costs to be among the lowest in the industry; distribution channel relations to be among the best, especially with the close tie between coated and bonded abrasives; and a technological edge on new products (e.g., Norzon). The ultimate result, the report forecasted, was the generation of more than $7 million cash during 1977–1980. Excerpts from the summary of financial results are shown in Figure 4.

	Actual					Expected[1]				
	1971	1972	1973	1974	1975	1976	1977	1978	1979	1980
a. Market share (%)	29	28	27	26	25.5	26	27	27.5	27.5	27.5
b. Net sales (index)	77	90	107	120	100	108	128	150	160	180
c. Net income (index)	215	220	310	230	100	140	480	760	810	950
d. Percentage return on sales ($\frac{£}{\$}$)	4.4	3.9	4.6	3.0	1.6	2.0	6.0	8.0	8.0	8.0
e. Percentage RONA	8	8	7.5	7	5	4.5	8	13	13	13
f. Funds generated ($ million)						(4.7)	0.5	2.5	3.4	1.3

[1]7 percent inflation per annum assumed.

Figure 4   Summary of Financial Results (Numbers Disguised)

345

The PIMS Report[10]

The PIMS analysis for CAD had resulted in a recommendation at variance with that made by Mr. Midghall. A summary of these findings was included in the Strategy Book submitted to the Strategy Guidance Committee. The remainder of this section presents excerpts from the PIMS analysis:

> The 1975 PAR report[11] indicates that the Coated U.S. business is a below average business in a weak strategic position with a *pre-tax* PAR-ROI of 12.0%. The business' operating performance has been very close to PAR with a 1973–75 average *pre-tax* actual ROI of 12.2%.
>
> The major factors impacting on PAR-ROI and their individual impacts are listed below.[12]

Major Negative Factors	*Major Positive Factors*
(1.5) Marketing only Expense/Sales	1.8 Sales Direct to End Users
(1.7) Capacity Utilization	
(4.1) Effective Use of Investments	

> During the three-year period, the *marketing less sales force expenses/sales* ratio averaged 6% compared to the 4.1% PIMS average. PIMS findings acknowledge that high marketing expenses hurt profitability when relative product quality is low; i.e. it doesn't pay to market heavily a product with equivalent or inferior product quality. The average relative product quality for the business over the three years was estimated as follows: 10% superior, 75% equivalent, and 15% inferior.
>
> For the Coated-U.S. business, the positive impact indicates that selling through distributors instead of direct should lower customer service costs.
>
> Whether the Coated-U.S. business objective is to optimize cash flow or ROI over the long-term, the Strategy Sensitivity Report (SSR) suggests a *moderate harvest* strategy. The SSR is based upon how other participating businesses with similar business characteristics have acted to achieve their objectives.
>
> The SSR suggests that the following strategy should be pursued to optimize either cash flow or ROI over the long-term.
>
> 1. *Prices*—Prices relative to competition should be maintained.
> 2. *Working Capital/Sales*—The SSR suggests that this ratio be lowered significantly to about 25% primarily through reduced inventory levels.
> 3. *Vertical Integration*—Over the long term, the degree of vertical integration should be reduced.
> 4. *Fixed Capital*—Don't add large segments of capacity, and maintain capacity utilization at the 80% level.
> 5. *R&D Marketing Expenses*—The SSR recommends that R&D expenditures should be reduced; and consequently, the relative product quality remains inferior. Also, the products should be marketed less energetically during the implementation phase.
>
> The result from this strategy is (1) a gradual loss of market share from 26% to 21%; (2) an average ROI of 24% vs. the current PAR-ROI of 12%; and (3) a ten-year discounted cash flow value of $2.33 million.

A study was undertaken to compare the PAR-ROI of this business in its steady-state environment (after the recommended strategy has been implemented—1978–80) with the 1973–75 PAR-ROI. The results indicate that the strategy is successful in moving this business into a much better strategic position. The pre-tax PAR-ROI increases from 12% to 24%.

The major factors that had a significant impact on the improved PAR-ROI are *Relative Pay Scale* and *Use of Investments*. These two factors account for a majority of the 12 percentage point increase in PAR-ROI.

The general message from the SSR for the *re-structured* Coated U.S. business is the same as for the *current* business, i.e. if the objective is to manage the business for cash flow or ROI, a *moderate harvest strategy* is recommended by PIMS.

Management Considerations

Norton's top managers recognized how difficult it was for them to remain objective when deciding the fate of a core part of the company's traditional business. As Mr. John Nelson, Vice President, Abrasive Operations, Western Hemisphere, remarked:

> There is no question that this decision has been an emotional one for me and probably for others, as well. It would be difficult to turn our backs on CAD. Yet, if the business cannot produce the target return on net assets, I think we are prepared to take the appropriate actions.
>
> I do not think that we are likely to close shop on U.S. coated abrasives. It is too important to other parts of our business to go that far. For example, coated abrasives strengthens our sales of bonded abrasives and is a plus to our distribution system in the U.S. It also provides us with a bigger base for R&D on coated abrasives. This benefits our overseas coated abrasive operations. Nonetheless, whether to stay with our earlier decision to maintain market share or to harvest the business was and still is very much at issue.

Both Mr. Duane and Mr. Nelson remarked that the choice of strategy in 1973–1974 had been predicated on the belief that the industry could support a profitable number 2 and that Norton could play that role with its existing market share. The continued loss of market share was a cause of concern to them and to other members of the Strategy Guidance Committee. As noted in the minutes for the CAD review session of June 7, 1976:

> In the shorter term period of late 1973 to the first quarter of 1976, CAD market share dropped from 27% to 25%. Some of this drop was due to intentional deemphasis of the general trades segment. However, there was also an unintentional loss in the industrial segment. The key question is whether this short-term market share decline in the industrial area can be stopped and reversed.

The PIMS recommendations for an alternate strategy also served to raise questions about the soundness of the present approach. One Norton executive put in context the relative impact of PIMS with the following observation: "We are still learning how to use PIMS. At present, we consider it a useful input, among many, to our thinking. We would not reverse divisional management's position on the basis of PIMS alone."

Mr. Donald Melville, Executive Vice President, Diversified Products, made the following comment about the CAD issue:

> You have to consider the dynamics of Norton's situation in 1976. We have done a lot to restructure the company, and the results in 1975—a bad recession year for abrasives—show our progress. But we are not yet in a position where we can harvest a major segment of our abrasives business, because that is the major guts of our company.
>
> By the early 80's our restructuring should be complete, and we will not be so dependent on abrasives. If we were faced with the decision in say 1982, instead of 1976, we could and probably should be willing to harvest CAD. In the meantime, we might as well repair CAD, because if we succeed, then we won't have to harvest it in the 80's. And if we fail, we will have lost very little.

A relative newcomer to the top management ranks at Norton, Mr. Richard Flynn, Financial Vice President, made the following comments about Norton's approach to strategic planning:[13]

> However the Strategy Guidance Committee finally decides on this matter, I think they are at least addressing the right issues, and that itself is something.
>
> The wide use of profit centers in large U.S. corporations has often led to bad analysis when different products were lumped together. Corporate-wide planning did not help the situation. Looking at a single product line family, as we are doing for U.S. coated abrasives, gives management much more meaningful data to work with.
>
> The other thing I like about Norton's strategic planning is that we are doing it repeatedly during the year. This means that we are always called on to think strategy. Looking at different businesses at different times enables us to take on different perspectives to our strategic thinking. This sometimes helps us to gain new insights for other businesses.
>
> All in all, the strategic planning sessions have been very effective in helping top management to think about and to deal with business strategies.

Appendix A ———————————————————————————
THE EXPERIENCE CURVE AND GROWTH SHARE MATRIX[14]

> Costs of value added decline approximately 20 to 30 percent in real terms each time accumulated experience is doubled.

This relationship, derived by the Boston Consulting Group from the study of many industries and labeled the Experience Curve[15], provided the basis for an approach to strategic planning for multiproduct companies.

THE EXPERIENCE CURVE

The experience curve reflected actual, constant-money cash flows as opposed to costs from normal accrual accounting. The relationship, plotted on logarithmic coordinates, appeared as shown in Figure A-1. Such cost declines, however, would not occur automatically. They required good management and appropriate added investment.

The decline in costs was thought to be the result of some combination of learning, specialization, improved methods, and increased scale. BCG pointed out the empirical nature of the relationship:

> The experience curve cost effects are an observable fact. They can be confirmed by observation. . . . Understanding of the underlying causes of the experience curve is still imperfect. The effect itself is beyond question. It is so universal that its absence is almost a warning of mismanagement or misunderstanding. Yet the basic mechanism that produces the experience curve effect is still to be adequately explained. (The same thing is true of gravitation.) . . . The principal problems encountered in application are those of defining cost elements and in defining the measuring unit of experience.

The experience curves for two distinctly different industries are shown in Figures A-2 and A-3. Average price was used to reflect costs in these instances.

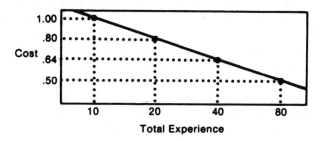

Figure A-1   **The Experience Curve**

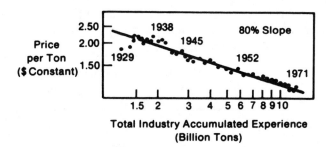

Source: U.S. Bureau of Mines

Figure A-2   **The Experience Curve for Crushed and Broken Limestone**

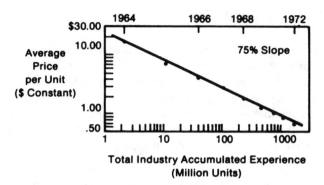

Total Industry Accumulated Experience
(Million Units)

Source: Published Data of Electronics Industry Association

Figure A-3   The Experience Curve for Integrated Circuits

INDIVIDUAL FIRM EXPERIENCES

According to BCG, the experience curve cost decline for a specific product pertained to individual firms as well as to an industry as a whole. This premise led to an important strategic implication: for a specific product, the firm with the largest volume output should have important cost advantages over its competitors.

Market share proved to be a useful measure for relative volume and has become commonly employed for this purpose. For example, assume firm A is largest in its industry with twice the market share of firm B, its closest competitor. Then, following the 20 percent cost decline rule, A's costs of overhead and value added by manufacturing and marketing should be only about 80 percent of B's similar costs. Relative costs of value added as a function of relative market share are shown in Figure A-4.

The relative advantage for total costs would normally be lower than indicated above. Both A and B were likely to share in any cost savings (in constant dollar terms) resulting from supplies, raw materials and equipment going down their own experience curves during the same time period. According to BCG, a two to one difference in market share would normally be expected to result in a five to ten percent difference in total costs.

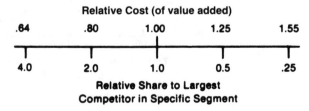

Figure A-4   Relative Cost of Value Added as a Function of Relative
Market Share

GROWTH SHARE MATRIX

BCG focused on corporate cash flows as a critical dimension for strategic planning. Cost reductions associated with the experience curve represented a source or generator of cash for a firm. In contrast, investments associated with growth and expansion represented a use of cash. These two major factors influencing net cash flows were put together in the form of a matrix to highlight the characteristic cash flows for each combination of growth and market share. As shown in Figure A-5 the upper righthand quadrant would contain businesses with a relatively low market share and consequently a relatively low cash inflow. These businesses would also be experiencing relatively rapid growth and a relatively high cash outflow.

BCG had the following to say about the cash flow implications for businesses falling in each of the four quadrants in the matrix:

> Stars are in the upper left quadrant. They grow rapidly and therefore they use large amounts of cash. However, since they are leaders, they also generate large amounts of cash. Normally, such products are about in balance in net cash flow. Over time all growth slows. Therefore, stars eventually become cash cows if they hold their market share. If they fail to hold market share, they become dogs.
>
> Cash cows are in the lower-left quadrant. Growth is slow and therefore cash use is low. However, market share is high and therefore comparative cash generation is also high. Cash cows pay the dividends, pay the interest on debt and cover the corporate overhead.
>
> Dogs are in the lower-right quadrant. Both growth and share are low. Dogs often report a profit even though they are net cash users. They are essentially worthless. They are cash traps.
>
> Question marks are the real cash traps and the real gambles. They are in the upper-right quadrant. Their cash needs are great because of their growth. Yet, their cash generation is very low because their market share is low.
>
> Left alone question marks are sure losers. They can require years of heavy cash

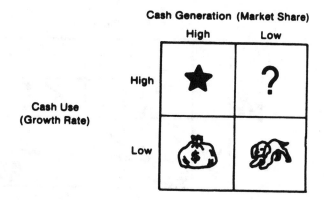

Figure A-5   Growth-Share Matrix

investment. Yet, if they do not develop a leading market position before the growth slows, they become just big dogs.

Yet question marks are difficult to convert into stars. Increase in market share compounds cash needs. The cost of acquiring market share doubly compounds cash needs. Question marks are sometimes big winners if backed to the limit. But most question marks are big losers.

IMPLICATIONS FOR STRATEGY

The growth-share matrix was viewed as particularly useful in dealing with multiple business operations. The concept of a portfolio of businesses was employed to plan corporate cash flows over time.

> When the portfolio of businesses is introduced, it is by no means clear that all businesses should grow—even if they have the financial capacity to do so. Rather, all corporate assets should be viewed in terms of a balance between growth and liquidity, or cash generation versus cash use, with growth as a resultant. Viewed in this sense, every business within a corporation has a purpose, and that purpose is to generate cash or generate growth. Any business that does not fit this criterion is subject to divestment, and, in fact, should be divested.

The matrix, restated, then is shown in Figure A-6. The solid arrows indicate the movements of cash, with the broken lines indicating the desired movement of businesses over time.[16]

A growth-share matrix for a company with multiple business operations is shown in Figure A-7. The size of each balloon is proportional to the sales volume of the product.

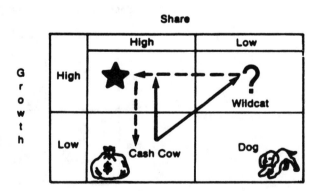

Figure A-6   **Movement of Businesses and Cash**

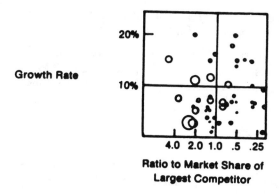

Growth Rate

Figure A-7   A Typical Successful Diversified Company

Appendix B
PROFIT IMPACT REGRESSION ANALYSIS

The Strategic Planning Institute was created in 1975 as a nonprofit, autonomous corporation to develop and to propagate a statistical approach to profit planning started in 1960 at General Electric.[17] Known as the PIMS Program (Profit Impact of Market Strategies), this approach employed a detailed multiple regression analysis of the profit experiences for many businesses. The resulting data were then processed to provide answers to the following questions based on the experiences of other businesses operating under similar conditions:

(a) What profit rate is "normal" for a given business, considering its particular market, competitive position, technology, cost structure, etc.?

(b) If the business continues on its *current track,* what will its future operating results be?

(c) What *strategic changes* in the business have promise of improving these results?

(d) Given a *specific* contemplated future strategy for the business, how will profitability or cash flow change, short-term and long-term?

The analysis to provide answers to these questions rested on the following premise:

> . . . that the profitability of a business is largely determined by *general* factors: growth rate of the market, market share of the business, the joint share of the company's three largest competitors, the degree of vertical integration, the working capital requirements per dollar of sales, the plant and equipment requirements per dollar of sales, relative product quality, and the like. Businesses with similar such characteristics tend to have similar profitability, regardless of differences in the name of the industry.

Businesses differing in these characteristics have different profitability, regardless of similarity in the name of the industry.[18]

In 1976, several major reports were employed to analyze the profit performance for a specific business.[19] These included "Par" reports, Strategy Sensitivity reports, Optimum Strategy reports, and Cross Tables.

"PAR" REPORT

The "Par" report specified the return on investment that was normal (or "par") for the business, given the characteristics of its market, competition, position, technology, and cost structure. It reported whether this business was the kind that normally earned 3 percent on investment or 30 percent, judging by the experiences of *other* businesses with *similar* characteristics. Also, it identified the major strengths and weaknesses of the particular business that accounted for the high or low "par" when compared to all businesses in the PIMS data base.[20]

Table 1 was employed to position a specific company business against the par.[21] The par reflected the pre-tax ROI that would be expected for the business unit in

Table 1 PIMS "PAR" Return on Investment (PRE-TAX) 1972–74

"PAR" Return on Investment is an Estimate of the Pre-Tax Return on Investment (ROI) that in 1972–74 was Normal for Businesses Facing Market and Industry Conditions Equivalent to Those of Your Business and Occupying a Similar Market Position.

For Business NO. 12345, Pre-Tax
"PAR" ROI   34.0%
ACTUAL ROI   39.5%

```
            60   I--------------------I----------I--------------------I
     HIGH        I                    I          I                    I
            50   I                    I          I                    I
                 I                    I          I                    I
            40   I                    I          I                    I
                 I                    I          I *                  I
            30   I                    I          I                    I
                 I  -   -   -   -  -  I  -   -   I -   -   -   -   -   I
 PAR ROI    20   I                    I          I                    I
                 I  -   -   -   -  -  I  -   -   I -   -   -   -   -   I
            10   I                    I          I                    I
                 I                    I          I                    I
             0   I                    I          I                    I
                 I                    I          I                    I
           -10   I                    I          I                    I
     LOW         I                    I          I                    I
           -20   I--------------------I----------I--------------------I
                -20                  -4          4                    20
                    BELOW PAR           NEAR PAR      ABOVE PAR

                            DEVIATION FROM
                               PAR ROI
```

Table 2   **PIMS Impact on "PAR" ROI of the Factors by Category**

"PAR" ROI Equals the Sum of the Total Impact and the Average ROI of All Businesses in the PIMS Data Base.

Category	Impact on "PAR" ROI (Pre-tax) (%)
Attractiveness of business environment	0.6
Strength of your competitive position	1.9
Differentiation of competitive position	4.1
Effectiveness of use of investment	4.5
Discretionary budget allocation	5.4
Company factors	0.2
Change/action factors	0.5
Total impact	17.3
Average ROI, all PIMS businesses	16.7
"PAR" ROI, business 12345	34.0

question (Business "12345"), given its specific characteristics. In this example, Business 12345 should have earned 34.0 percent for the 1972–1974 period. It actually earned 39.5 percent, placing it in the most favorable quadrant of performance—above par in a high return industry.

Table 2 was set out to show the impact of different factors, collected in broad categories, leading to the difference between the par ROI for Business 12345 and that for the average of all businesses in the PIMS data bank. For example, "differentiation of competitive positions" (item 3) was relatively favorable, accounting for a 4.1 percent of the total 17.3 percent that the pre-tax ROI for Business 12345 exceeded "all PIMS businesses."

The broad categories in Table 2 were then broken out in more detail as shown in the example below. (The normal two-page table has been omitted from the case.) According to the data below, Business 12345 product price relative to competitors was such so as to lessen ROI by 1.2 percent compared to all PIMS businesses. The relative pay scale for Business 12345, however, had a 3.9 percent favorable impact on ROI. The combined impact of the five factors totaled the 4.1 percent found in Table 2.

Factors	Impact of Factor on PAR ROI (%)
Differentiation of competitive position	4.1
Price relative to competition	− 1.2
Relative pay scale	3.9
Product quality	1.3
New product sales (% total sales)	− 0.8
Manufacturing costs/sales	0.9

Table 3 **PIMS Strategy Sensitivity Report Summary**

"Most Likely" Environment Key Assumptions: Business 12345

	1975–1978	1978–1984
Industry sales growth rate (%)	7.5	5.6
Annual change in selling price (%)	4.4	5.2
Annual change in wage rates (%)	5.1	
Annual change in material cost (%)	5.1	
Annual change in plant cost (%)	8.0	6.0
Time discount rate (%)	8.0	
Capital charge rate (%)	6.0	
Tax rate (%)	50.0	
Dividend payout rate (%)	0.0	
"Quantum" of additional capacity (%)	2.0	
Targeted capacity utilization (%)	80.0	
Annual depreciation rate (%)	12.0	

Deviations from:	Actual Historical	Assumed Future
PAR ROI	5.5	5.5
DELTA ROI	1.4	0.0

	Market Share				
	Decrease		No Planned Change	Increase	
Summary Results of:	Major	Small		Small	Major
Market share 1979	16.	20.	23.	27.	31.
Net sales billed 1979	1144.	1364.	1603.	1863.	2147.
Net income 1979	91.	103.	126.	151.	182.
Average investment 1979	221.	240.	290.	343.	399.
ROI 1977 (%)	58.	49.	40.	30.	20.
ROI 1979 (%)	41.	43.	43.	44.	45.
ROI 1984 (%)	42.	43.	44.	45.	47.
Discounted net income 10 yr	737.	763.	812.	853.	898.
Discounted cash flow 10 yr	373.	364.	360.	353.	348.
Discounted cash flow + investment 10 yr	236.	245.	260.	271.	284.
Combined income 10 yr	405.	426.	454.	474.	496.
Average net income 3 yr	120.	112.	105.	95.	80.
Discounted cash flow yield rate 10 yr (%)	23.	22.	21.	20.	19.
Average ROI 5 yr (%)	49.	45.	41.	36.	32.
Index of net income change 5 yr (%)	−1.	0.	2.	3.	5.

Incremental return on increased investment for more ambitious strategy:
   Discounted net income (small increase − small decrease) = 90.
   90. / Investment 1979 (small increase − small decrease) = 89.%

STRATEGY SENSITIVITY REPORT

This report indicated the short- and long-term changes in profit likely to occur based on specific strategic moves which might be employed. The output reflected the experiences of other businesses making a similar move, from a similar starting point, in a similar business environment.

The analysis required as input a number of key assumptions concerning the future environment. These are shown at the top of Table 3 for Business 12345. The bottom of Table 3 shows various results for profits and ROI associated with specific decisions concerning market share. For example, discounted net income for a ten year period would increase with market share. The opposite would be true for discounted cash flow in this illustration.

The data for each of the market share strategies was elaborated in a subsequent table. Table 4 shows such data for the strategy of a major increase in market share. Data comparable to that shown in Tables 4 and 5 were also provided for strategic variables other than market share, such as decisions concerning vertical integration and investment intensity. Additional tables could also be prepared which recast the data with selected changes in the original assumptions—for example, higher inflation, a recession, higher interest rates, etc.

OPTIMUM STRATEGY REPORT

This report indicated that combination of several strategic moves that promised to give optimal results for the business, judging by the experiences of other businesses under similar circumstances. Table 5 shows the strategy to be followed in terms of 14 factors in order to maximize discounted cash flow over a ten-year period. Similar tables were prepared to show the strategies to optimize discounted net income for ten years, average ROI for five years, and average net income for three years.

CROSS TABLES

To provide further guidance for changing specific elements of a strategy, data were provided to show the effects on ROI by varying one business factor versus another. Figure B-1 illustrates the cross table for marketing expenditures as a percent of sales versus product quality. Inspection of these data shows that relatively high marketing expenditures were counterproductive when product quality was relatively low (ROI decreased from 15 percent to 3 percent). Cross tables were available for other factor combinations such as:[22]

> R&D costs/sales vs. investment/sales
> Product quality vs. relative market share
> Marketing costs excluding sales force/sales vs. investment/sales
> Inventory/sales vs. fixed capital intensity

Table 4 **PIMS Strategy Sensitivity Report Details: Business 12345**

		Strategy Move: Major Increase in Market Share		
	Recent Position (1972–1974)	During Strategy Implementation (1977)	New Steady-State Position (1979)	New Long-Term Position (1984)
Net sales (current $)	1102.4	1609.3	2146.8	2819.1
Net income	102.6	68.0	181.6	198.2
Average investment	259.5	336.1	399.3	421.1
Net cash flow	43.8	8.5	59.2	94.7
Return on investment	39.5%	20.2%	45.5%	47.1%
Return on sales	9.3%	4.2%	8.5%	7.0%
Factors				
Competitive position:				
Market share	22.3	26.2	30.8	30.8
Relative market share	51.9	64.3	80.5	80.5
Relative price index	3.0	3.0	3.0	3.0
Product quality	60.3	68.9	65.2	65.2
Use of investment:				
Investment/value added	50.8	44.1	40.0	31.9
Investment/sales	23.5	20.9	18.6	14.9
Fixed capital intensity	20.7	17.6	17.4	15.2
Net book/gross book value	55.1	46.3	48.5	31.6
Value added/sales	48.6	48.4	48.6	48.6
Working capital/sales	12.1	12.7	10.1	10.1
Capacity utilization	74.0	79.4	78.6	79.8
Sales/employees	55750.	55517.	57028.	57652.
Budget allocations:				
Marketing expenses/sales	7.8	8.6	7.4	7.4
R & D expenses/sales	2.6	3.7	2.8	2.8
Performance Measures				
Discounted net income 10 yr		898.1		
Discounted cash flow 10 yr		348.2		
Disounted cash flow + investment 10 yr		283.7		
Combined income 10 yr		495.6		
Average net income 3 yr		79.5		
Discounted cash flow yield rate 10 yr (%)		19.2		
Average return on investment 5 yr (%)		32.1		
Index of net income change 5 yr (%)		4.7		

Table 5   **PIMS Strategy Sensitivity Report Details: Business 12345**

Strategy: To Optimize
Discounted Cash Flow 10 yr

	Recent Position (1972–1974)	During Strategy Implementation (1977)	New Steady-State Position (1979)	New Long-Term Position (1984)
Net sales (current $)	1102.4	1142.2	1081.4	1420.0
Net income	102.6	128.4	86.4	108.0
Average investment	259.5	227.5	203.7	247.9
Net cash flow	43.8	74.8	55.1	45.2
Return on investment	39.5%	56.4%	42.4%	43.6%
Return on sales	9.3%	11.2%	8.0%	7.6%
Factors				
Competitive Position:				
Market share	22.3	18.6	15.5	15.5
Relative market share	51.9	41.3	33.2	33.2
Relative price index	3.0	2.9	3.0	3.0
Product quality	60.3	49.0	56.4	56.4
Use of investment:				
Investment/value added	50.8	40.1	35.2	32.6
Investment/sales	23.5	19.9	18.8	17.5
Fixed capital intensity	20.7	16.5	14.3	14.1
Net book/gross book value	55.1	45.6	43.0	34.0
Value added/sales	48.6	52.6	55.7	55.7
Working capital/sales	12.1	12.4	12.7	12.7
Capacity utilization	74.0	80.0	80.0	80.0
Sales/employees	55750.	47536.	44461.	47667.
Budget allocations:				
Marketing expenses/sales	7.8	7.2	8.1	8.1
R & D expenses/sales	2.6	1.6	2.7	2.7

Performance Measures	
Discounted net income 10 yr	725.9
Discounted cash flow 10 yr	377.1
Discounted cash flow + investment 10 yr	232.4
Combined income 10 yr	404.0
Average net income 3 yr	119.8
Discounted cash flow yield rate 10 yr (%)	23.1
Average return on investment 5 yr (%)	48.8
Index of net income change 5 yr (%)	− 1.4

Product Quality	Low	Medium	High
Low	15	15	3
Medium	18	17	14
High	25[a]	26	20

Number in each box is the average pre-tax ROI for all PIMS businesses in that box.
a marks the location of Business 12345.

Figure B-1 Marketing Costs/Sales Revenues

NOTES

1. On September 9, 1976, Norton Company announced an agreement in principle to merge with Christensen, Inc., for stock valued at $100 million. Christensen, with 1975 sales of $118 million and net income of $9.5 million, manufactured diamond-drilling and coring bits for the petroleum and mining industries. Nonabrasive products for Norton and Christensen combined would account for about 40 percent of total sales.

2. The *Norton Company Annual Report* for 1975 also highlighted three other corporate objectives: (1) to maintain responsible corporate citizenship . . . which at times means accepting lower profits; (2) to maintain a superior employee working environment; (3) to enhance the value of Norton stock.

3. *Business Week* (Aug. 7, 1971): 80–82.

4. Examples of profit determinants would include: (1) high marketing expenditures damage profitability when product quality is low; (2) high R&D spending hurts profitability when market share is small but increases ROI when market share is high; (3) high marketing expenditures hurt ROI in investment-intensive businesses. The relationships were quantified as shown in the figure above.

5. The acronym PIMS refers to the regression analysis described in Appendix B.

6. The numbers for the remainder of this case are disguised.

7. According to Duane, coated abrasives and the other allied businesses had been organized in a single profit center at that time. The focus of attention had been on the total unit's overall performance. With the current approach to strategy analysis, each major product line was examined separately.

8. It was estimated that 3M had a RONA of 17 percent to 20 percent in coated abrasives.

9. An investment advisory report issued by Loeb Rhoades some months later (August 1976) had this to say about the future prospects for the industry as a whole (bonded and coated products):

> We have believed for some time that there were fair prospects for higher profitability in abrasives on a secular and not just a cyclical basis, merely because profitability had been poor for a long enough (seven to nine years) time. In a product that is basic to economic activity and that is capital intensive, and where no unusual reason can be discerned for the poor return on investment, such as foreign competition or technological change, etc., a lengthy period of poor profitability generally will lead to changes by industry factors designed to improve returns. . . . At some point supply and demand come into a better balance, which then supports firmer pricing. And in fact . . . pricing had improved significantly since late 1974 despite declining demand in real terms.

10. As a subscriber to the services of the Strategic Planning Institute, Norton received on a regular basis analysis reports for several of its major businesses. These reports were circulated to divisional and corporate managers concerned with the business in question.

11. The PAR report specified the return on investment that was normal for a business, given the characteristics of its market, competition, technology, and cost structure.

12. These figures represent the impact of that factor on PAR-ROI. For example, the higher marketing (excluding sales force) expenses/sales ratio noted in the following paragraph when comparing CAD to all PIMS businesses was said to have the effect of reducing the PAR-ROI by 1.5 percent. In contrast, by selling directly to the end users, PAR-ROI was increased by 1.8 percent compared to all PIMS businesses. See Appendix B for additional explanation of these data.

13. Richard J. Flynn joined Norton Company in January 1984 as Financial Vice President and as a member of the Board of Directors and the Executive Committee. He had been President of the Riley Stoker Corporation, a subsidiary of the Riley Company, manufacturers of steam-generating and fuel-burning equipment. He previously held executive positions with Ling-Temco Vought and Collins Radio.

14. The material in Appendix A was based on information provided in the following brochures published by the Boston Consulting Group: "The Experience Curve—Reviewed" (I to V) and "Growth and Financial Strategies."

15. The name was selected to distinguish overall cost behavior from the the well-known "learning curve" effect for labor costs.

16. The movement of the businesses shown in the diagram cover two distinctly different approaches. One approach is to build a business from the wildcat quadrant (low market share) to a star position (high market share). This is typical of a "follower strategy." The second is to invest cash in research leading to products that will enter the matrix at the upper-left quadrant. This would be an "innovator strategy."

17. The "profitability optimization" study had originated as an internal project of the General Electric Company, where it has been used for over a decade as a tool of corporate- and division-level planning. From 1972 to 1974, the PIMS Program was established as a developmental project at the Harvard Business School so that this study could be extended to a wide variety of businesses.

18. The PIMS Program brochure.

19. SPI provided three broad services to participating companies: (1) reports on the general principles of business strategy disclosed by the analysis of the data base; (2) specific reports on each business the company has contributed to the data base; (3) access to the computer models for strategy planning and simulation.

20. The PIMS data base in 1976 consisted of information on the strategic experiences of over 600 businesses, covering a five-year period.

21. The numbers contained in Tables 1–5 are provided for illustration purposes only. They do not relate to the CAD situation in this case.

22. For further information about the use of cross tables and PIMS in general, see the following: "Impact of Strategic Planning on Profit Performance," *Harvard Business Review* (Mar.–Apr. 1974): 137–145; and "Market Share—A Key to Profitability," *Harvard Business Review* (Jan.–Feb. 1975): 97–106.

Dexter Corporation (Part 1)

On a cold morning in January 1986, Worth Loomis, the President of Dexter Corporation, was lending a helping hand in arranging the conference room at the company's headquarters in Windsor Locks, Connecticut. One by one, the senior managers began arriving for the semiannual management meeting. As the managers assembled around the conference table, Loomis wondered what their reactions would be to the latest semiannual report (Exhibit 1) on the "naïve" value of each Strategic Business Segment (SBS) to the company's shareholders. It was called "naïve" value to show that there were several simplistic assumptions made in its computation. These assumptions are discussed later in the case.

In the past, Dexter had successfully introduced such analytical tools as the Boston Consulting Group's growth-share matrix and the Profit Impact of Marketing Strategies (PIMS) analysis to its planning process. Loomis firmly believed that Dexter should take advantage of the latest advances in planning techniques in order to stay competitive. Value-based planning was one such advance that was aimed at highlighting the interests of the shareholders in all the major strategic decisions made by the firm.

Dexter Corporation first began using a version of value-based planning in 1967 when it went public and subsequently used it for making acquisition and divestiture decisions. With Loomis's enthusiastic support, the use of value-based planning was extended in 1985 to routine strategic decisions within each Strategic Business Segment. SBS managers have since received a semiannual report on their

Copyright © 1987 by Balaji S. Chakravarthy, The Carlson School of Management, University of Minnesota

This case was prepared by Associate Professor Balaji S. Chakravarthy with the research assistance of Bari Abdul and with the cooperation of John Vrabel of Dexter Corporation. It is intended for use as the basis for class discussion rather than to illustrate either effective or ineffective handling of an administrative situation.

estimated contribution to the wealth of Dexter's shareholders. Loomis hoped that this tool would help the market value of the company to correspond more closely to the value of the company's underlying assets, thereby making it unattractive to raiders looking for undervalued companies.

BACKGROUND

Dexter Corporation is the oldest company listed on the New York Stock Exchange. It was founded as a sawmill at Windsor Locks, Connecticut, in 1767. By 1958, Dexter had evolved into a specialty paper products business, but it was still a very small company with a sales turnover of only $9.5 million. In that year, thirty-two-year-old David L. Coffin—a seventh-generation descendant of the founder, Seth Dexter—became the President of the company. He began transforming Dexter into a diversified company.

Coffin initiated a policy of expansion and diversification through acquisitions in high-growth areas. The company's early major acquisitions were Midland Industrial Finishes, Hysol Corporation, Puritan Chemical, Mogul Corporation, and Howe and Bainbridge. Exhibit 2 lists Dexter's acquisitions from 1958 to 1986. By 1986, the company had diversified into more than 3,000 products ranging from inside coatings for beverage cans to adhesives for jet aircraft. Concurrent with this product diversification, the company also underwent geographic diversification. In 1986, Dexter operated over 100 manufacturing, research, or marketing facilities around the world. Dexter's sales turnover had grown to $650 million, placing it among the 500 largest public industrial corporations in the United States. Exhibit 3 is a summary of the company's financial standing from 1982 to 1986.

All of Dexter's acquisitions were friendly. Typically Dexter had a long court-ship with the target prior to acquiring it. Most of the companies were run by strong entrepreneurs, and Coffin wanted the owners to join Dexter and continue to run their companies. Although Coffin realized the importance of continuity of leadership, he sought to develop a professional management cadre that would be capable over time of running these businesses independently.

Worth Loomis joined the company in 1970 as the Vice President of Finance after a career in manufacturing. In 1975, he became Dexter's President. Loomis was a strong supporter of Coffin's strategy of expansion through acquisitions. In addition, he emphasized a conservative and analytical approach to business. He believed that stable and high returns on investment were fundamental elements of the company's mission. Furthermore, despite Dexter's rich diversity of businesses, its top management saw a common strategic thrust to the businesses. Dexter sought for the most part to compete through specialty materials with special applications. Coffin liked to think of the company's mission as that of a creative problem solver.

(*Text continues on page 369*)

Exhibit 1 "Naïve" Value Projection, Half-Yearly Ending December 1985

SBS Name	Div. C* Used (%)	C* (%)	Mkt. Growth Rate (%)	Naïve Value (mil)	Book Value (mil)	Naïve Ratio	12 Mos. Net Sales	12 Mos. Op. Inc. (mil)	12 Mos. ROI (Index)
Chemicals Group									
Hysol	12.0	11.9	11.4			1.0			7
Semiconductor		13.0	16.0			− 2.9			−12
General purpose									
Coating powder		13.0	16.0			1.9			7
Liquids		11.0	8.0			1.0			12
Resists									
Aerospace adh.		11.0	10.0			2.1			13
Engine adh.		13.0	12.0			0.7			5
Release prod.									
Communications									
Midland	12.0	12.1	10.7			1.8			11
Packaging									
Building									
Recreation		11.0	8.0			2.4			14
Wood		11.0	3.0			0.1			−1
Graphic arts		13.0	4.0			1.1			12
Other									
Mogul	11.0	11.3	9.0			4.4			25
Sanitation		12.0	1.0			1.6			17
Other		13.0	12.0			1.9			12
Water/chem. serv.									

Chemicals as sum
Chemicals as sum of divs.
Chemicals consolidated (in Alcar)

Materials Group

C. H. Dexter	11.0				
Food		11.4	6.9	1.0	8
Medical		11.0	6.0	1.6	12
Industrial		12.0	7.5	1.4	10
Other					
Alpha Mercer	11.0	11.7	8.4	2.9	20
Alpha		12.0	11.0	2.8	18
Mercer		11.0	5.0	3.3	24
Howe and Bainbridge	13.0	13.0	5.0	0.3	2
Sailcloth		13.0	5.0	0.3	2
Materials as sum					
Materials as sum of divs.					
Materials consolidated (in Alcar)					
Life Tech. Div.					
LTI Division	11.0	11.7	10.4	0.9	7
Tissue		11.0	11.0	2.1	15
Microbio.		13.0	0.0	− 1.4	−14
BRL		13.0	20.0	1.0	6
LTI as sum					
LTI as sum of divs.					

Note: Numbers are for illustration only.

Source: Company records.

Exhibit 2 **Corporate Development**

Date	Company	Products	Type	Disposition
1958	Standard Insulation	Insulation	A	Divested 1963
1960	Chemical Coatings	Coatings	A	T/U Midland
1962	Lacquer Products	Coatings	A	T/U Midland
1963	Midland Industrial Finishes	Coatings	AC	Core Business
1963	Standard Insulation	Insulation	D	Divested
11/1967	Hysol	Compounds	AC	Core Business
6/1968	Magna Coatings and Chemical	Coatings	A	T/U Midland
11/1968	Hysol Mexico	Compounds	JV	JV Hysol/Indael (49:51%)
9/1969	Hysol Japan	Compounds	JV	JV Hysol (Bought Out 2/81)
10/1969	Shell Chemical	Adhesives	A	T/U Hysol
6/1970	Wornow Process Paint	Inks/resists	A	T/U Hysol
3/1973	Puritan Chemical	Maintenance chemicals	A	Divested 1986
4/1973	Societe Des Vernis Bouvet	Coatings	A	T/U Midland
10/1973	Dexter/Midland Japan	Coatings	JV	JV Midland/Rock Paint (70:30%)
2/1976	Hysol Sterling	Compounds	A	Acquired remaining 50% of JV; absorbed into Dex./Hysol Ltd.
11/1976	Howe & Bainbridge	Sailcloth	AC	Core Business
5/1977	Mogul/GIBCO	Water treatment/Life science	AC	Core Businesses
5/1977	Adhesive Engineering	Adhesives	A	T/U Hysol
8/1977	Microtech Diagnostics	Biotech	A	T/U GIBCO
2/1978	Coast Biologicals	Biotech	JV	JV GIBCO/Courtney/Mauri (45:45:10%)
4/1978	V. S. Supplies	Veterinary	A	T/U GIBCO; divested 8/80 (as Medos)
5/1978	Hunter Chemical	Maintenance chemicals	A	T/U Mogul
5/1978	Lacquer Diluent Francais	Coatings	D	Divest. to M. Bouvet; part of SVB when acquired by Midland
6/1978	DeBeers Laboratories	Coatings	A	T/U Midland
9/1978	Magnachem (Holland, Ger., Belg.)	Water treatment	A	T/U Mogul

Date	Company	Business	Type	Notes
12/1978	Vitarine	Biotech	A	T/U GIBCO
2/1979	SFNT (France)	Nonwovens	A	T/U CHD; divested 1986
5/1979	Ornsteen Chemicals	Adhesives	A	T/U Hysol
7/1979	TRW	Adhesives	A	T/U Hysol (Product Line)
12/1979	ARS Sprague Dowley	Research animals	D	Divested by GIBCO
12/1979	Mogul Ed	Education supplies	D	Divested by Mogul
8/1980	Medos/V. S. Supplies	Veterinary	D	Divested by GIBCO
9/1980	Eurotherm	Water treatment	A	T/U Mogul
10/1980	Midland Mexicana	Coatings	JV	JV Midland/Partners (44:56%)
12/1980	Heun Norwood	Pharmaceuticals	D	Divested by GIBCO
2/1981	Hysol Japan	Compounds	A	Acquired remaining 50% of JV; folded into Toray Hysol JV 2/85
3/1981	FREKOTE	Mold release	A	T/U Hysol
8/1981	Contour Chemical	Mold release	A	T/U Hysol
5/1982	Hysol Canada	Compounds	A	Acquired remaining 50% of JV
9/1982	Mogul Australia	Water treatment	JV	JV Mogul/Maxwell (50:50%)
4/1983	Hysol/Grafil	Carbon fibers	JV	JV Hysol/Courtaulds (50:50%)
4/1983	BRL	Life sciences	A	Merged with GIBCO
8/1983	GIBCO Oriental	Biotech	JV	Marketing JV LTI/Oriental Yeast (59:50%)
9/1983	Life Technologies	Life sciences	Spin-off	GIBCO/BRL = LTI (Dexter 64%); Core Business
10/1983	Midevensa	Coatings	JV	JV Midland/Fiasse (50:50%)
11/1983	Alpha/Mercer	Plastics compounding; Floor accessories	AC	Core Business
12/1983	HEPA(Product)	Filter material	D	Divested by CHD to Lydall (Product line)
6/1984	Sensititre/Unilever	Laboratory instruments	A	T/U LTI (Product line)
7/1984	Whittaker	End sealants	A	T/U Midland (Product line)
9/1984	Am-Met	Metalized film	A	Divested 1986
10/1984	Dexter Miki	Specialty papers	JV	Marketing JV—C. H. Dexter/ Miki (70:30%)
2/1985	Short and Norvill	Sail hardware	A	T/U Howe & Bainbridge
2/1985	Aquabatton	Sail hardware	A	T/U Howe & Bainbridge
2/1985	Toray Hysol	Compounds	JV	Hysol/Toray (50:50%) (Includes Hysol Japan)

(continued)

Exhibit 2 (continued)

Date	Company	Business	Type	Notes
2/1985	Hunter Chemical (Baton Rouge); Hunter Chemical (Houston)	Maintenance chemicals	D	Divested by Mogul to employees (separate transactions)
2/1985	Permag	Magnetic materials	AC	Core Business
4/1985	Sidex	Coatings	JV	JV Midland/SICO–Canada (50:50%)
7/1985	United Veterinary Labs	Animal vaccines	D	Divested by LTI to Harlan Sprague Dawley
8/1985	Invenex Laboratories Div.	Small-volume parenterals	D	Divested by LTI to LyphoMed
8/1985	Evodex	Powder coatings	JV	JV Midland/Evode—UK (75:25%)
1/1986	Mysol Grafil Composite Components	Composites	JV	T/U Hysol Grafl JV
2/1986	Puritan Churchill	Maintenance chemicals	D	Divested to Mogul Australian affiliate
4/1986	SFNT (France)	Nonwovens	D	Divested by CHD to Dalle et Lecompte
5/1986	Am-Met	Metalized film	D	Discontinued operation by CHD; some assets sold to Bollore
6/1986	Magnet Technik (Germany)	Magnetic materials	A	T/U Permag
6/1986	Delta Enterprises	Electronic chemicals	A	T/U Hysol E/C
10/1986	Research Polymers International (RPI)	Plastics compounding	AC	Core Business
11/1986	Sensititre	Automated diagnostic equipment	D	Divested to Radiometer A/S

Core Businesses	8 (Including GIBCO = LTI); (Includes RPI)
Other Acquisitions	32
Joint Ventures	14
Spin-off	1
Divestitures	14 (Hunter Divestitures counted *once*)
Total Transactions	69

Note: A = Acquisition; AC = Acquisition/Core Business; D = Divestiture; JV = Joint Venture; T/U = Tuck-under.

Source: Company records.

ORGANIZATIONAL STRUCTURE

Strategic decisions were made at four levels within Dexter: corporate, group, divisional, and Strategic Business Segments. Exhibit 4 presents the top three decision-making levels in the company as of 1986.

Both Loomis and Coffin believed in decentralized management and in a small corporate staff. Dexter's corporate headquarters had a total of 40 people in 1985, including managers and secretarial staff. Loomis cited three advantages to this approach:

> It keeps corporate overhead to a minimum; it makes life a lot more interesting for the people in the divisions because it allows them to run their own shows; and it produces better decisions because the managers are closer to the sources of facts, particularly the marketplace.

In keeping with Dexter's philosophy of decentralized management, the group level was introduced in 1985. Because of the company's growing diversity, it had become increasingly difficult for Dexter's top management to keep close track of the individual businesses and to provide timely and well-informed advice on their strategies. The group presidents were expected to take on this responsibility for the divisions reporting to them. They also were expected to identify and exploit synergistic links among the businesses in their portfolio. As discussed later in this case, another important motivation to introduce the group level was to plan for Loomis's successor. The two top internal candidates for that job were each assigned a group.

Two operating groups—specialty chemicals and specialty materials—were formed, each of which had four operating divisions. The ninth operating division at Dexter—Life Technologies, Inc.—reported directly to Loomis. The divisions in turn were broken down into 36 Strategic Business Segments. Exhibit 5 presents a list of Dexter's divisions and Strategic Business Segments as of mid-1986.

THE EVOLUTION OF PLANNING

Until the early 1970s, Dexter's planning process was limited to the yearly preparation of divisional five-year sales and profit plans. In 1973, the company faced a severe capital shortage and was unable to fund all of its expansion plans. Dexter's long-term debt grew from $5.1 million in 1968 to $12.7 million in 1973. Working capital requirements increased fourfold during the same period. Dexter's top management retained the Boston Consulting Group to help deal with the capital shortage.

Portfolio Planning

The Boston Consulting Group (BCG) divided the company into 16 Strategic Business Segments (SBSs), and each business was plotted on the BCG growth/share

(*Text continues on page 373*)

Exhibit 3 Five-Year Financial Summary (in thousands of dollars, except per share amounts)

	1986	1985	1984	1983	1982
Operating Results					
Net sales	$650,051	$633,314	$655,264	$582,048	$539,912
Percentage increase (decrease)	3%	(3%)	13%	8%	13%
Gross profit	236,002	222,105	235,840	207,672	191,028
As percentage of sales	36.3%	35.1%	36.0%	35.7%	35.4%
LIFO charge (credit) included in cost of sales	(475)	(678)	2,714	(215)	(721)
Marketing and administrative expenses	142,276	142,260	147,293	133,614	124,782
As percentage of sales	21.9%	22.5%	22.5%	23.0%	23.1%
Research and development expenses	27,583	25,893	24,086	21,286	20,171
As percentage of sales	4.2%	4.1%	3.7%	3.7%	3.7%
Interest expense	12,516	11,911	11,699	8,831	6,329
Income before taxes	56,503	53,762	50,874	49,120	45,614
As percentage of sales	8.7%	8.5%	7.8%	8.4%	8.4%
Tax rate	38.0%	35.3%	32.3%	42.2%	44.6%
Income before minority interests	35,033	34,765	34,420	28,406	25,284
As percentage of sales	5.4%	5.5%	5.3%	4.9%	4.7%
Net income	$ 33,635	$ 28,582	$ 32,830	$ 27,947	$ 25,284
As percentage of sales	5.2%	4.5%	5.0%	4.8%	4.7%
Return on:					
Average shareholders' equity	13.7%	13.0%	16.4%	15.0%	14.4%
Average total capital	12.3%	12.2%	14.7%	13.1%	12.4%
Net income per share	$ 1.35	$ 1.15	$ 1.33	$ 1.13	$ 1.02
Cash dividends declared per share	$ .56⅔	$ .53⅓	$ .50⅔	$ .50	$ .44
Rate of dividend payout	42%	46%	39%	42%	42%

Financial Position

Working capital	$137,980	$129,605	$115,819	$98,378	$116,320
Property, plant and equipment, net	174,644	160,345	161,144	161,273	138,817
Capital expenditures	23,861	26,456	18,628	26,760	29,205
Total assets	565,871	484,567	441,120	422,175	348,306
Long-term debt	112,553	65,310	78,513	69,642	59,469
Deferred taxes and tax credits	32,141	30,827	32,160	36,369	31,590
Shareholders' equity	$258,843	$232,796	$207,048	$192,587	$180,147
Percent debt to capital	30.3%	21.9%	27.5%	26.6%	24.8%
Equity per share at year-end	$ 10.40	$ 9.39	$ 8.35	$ 7.78	$ 7.29

Other Data

Shares outstanding at year-end (in thousands)	24,893	24,800	24,785	24,769	24,726
Average shares outstanding (in thousands)	24,860	24,794	24,774	24,754	24,723
Market price per share—high	$ 23⅜	$ 17⅞	$ 16¾	$ 19⅜	$ 12½
—low	$ 16⅞	$ 12⅜	$ 11⅞	$ 11¼	$ 7¼
—close	$ 22¼	$ 17¼	$ 12⅝	$ 14⅝	$ 11½
Price-earnings ratio range	19–14	15–11	13–9	17–10	12–7
Number of shareholders at year-end	4,500	4,900	4,400	4,200	4,300
Number of employees at year-end	5,500	5,500	6,100	5,800	5,400
Percentage payroll and benefits to sales	24%	25%	25%	26%	25%
Percentage raw material costs to sales	42%	43%	42%	42%	44%

Inflation Adjusted Data

Net sales[1]	$650,051	$645,461	$691,636	$640,522	$613,265
Percentage increase (decrease)	1%	(7%)	8%	4%	(6%)
Cash dividends declared per share[1]	$ .56⅔	$ .54	$ .53	$ .55	$ .50
Market price per share—year-end[2]	$ 22¼	$ 17⅜	$ 13¼	$ 16	$ 13

[1] Stated in average 1986 dollars using the Consumer Price Index.
[2] Stated in year-end 1986 dollars using the Consumer Price Index.
Source: Annual report, Dexter Corporation, 1986.

Exhibit 4 **Organizational Chart**

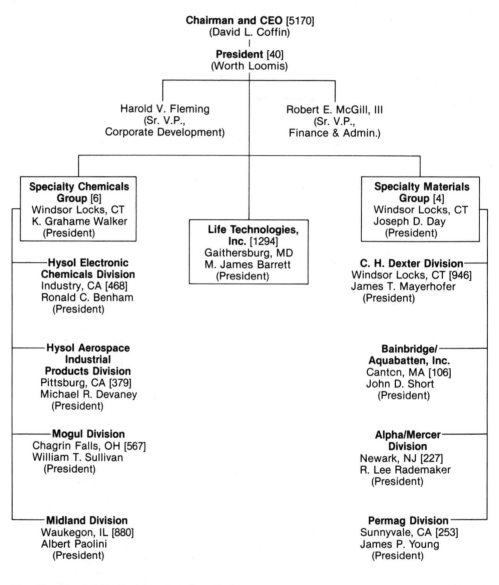

Chairman and CEO [5170]
(David L. Coffin)

President [40]
(Worth Loomis)

Harold V. Fleming
(Sr. V.P.,
Corporate Development)

Robert E. McGill, III
(Sr. V.P.,
Finance & Admin.)

**Specialty Chemicals
Group** [6]
Windsor Locks, CT
K. Grahame Walker
(President)

**Life Technologies,
Inc.** [1294]
Gaithersburg, MD
M. James Barrett
(President)

**Specialty Materials
Group** [4]
Windsor Locks, CT
Joseph D. Day
(President)

**Hysol Electronic
Chemicals Division**
Industry, CA [468]
Ronald C. Benham
(President)

C. H. Dexter Division
Windsor Locks, CT [946]
James T. Mayerhofer
(President)

**Hysol Aerospace
Industrial
Products Division**
Pittsburg, CA [379]
Michael R. Devaney
(President)

**Bainbridge/
Aquabatten, Inc.**
Canton, MA [106]
John D. Short
(President)

Mogul Division
Chagrin Falls, OH [567]
William T. Sullivan
(President)

**Alpha/Mercer
Division**
Newark, NJ [227]
R. Lee Rademaker
(President)

Midland Division
Waukegon, IL [880]
Albert Paolini
(President)

Permag Division
Sunnyvale, CA [253]
James P. Young
(President)

Note: Numbers in [ ] indicate number of employees.
Source: Company records.

Exhibit 5   Strategic Business Segments (1986)

C. H. Dexter Division
1. Infusion materials
2. Casing
3. Sterilization wrap
4. Drape-Pack-Gown
   Other medical
5. Filtration
6. Textile replacement
7. Electronic
   Other industrial

Howe and Bainbridge
8. Sailcloth/hardware
   Other

Alpha/Mercer Division
9. Alpha
10. Mercer

Permag
11. Permanent magnets[1]
12. Ferrites[1]

Hysol Electronic Chemicals Division
13. Semiconductor molding powder
14. Electrical/electronic molding powder
15. Coating powder
16. Formulated liquids
17. Resists and inks

Hysol Aerospace and Industrial Products Division
18. Aerospace adhesives and structural adhesives
19. Engineering adhesives
20. Release products
21. Communications

Midland Division
22. Packaging
23. Coil[1]
24. Industrial—United States[1]
25. Industrial—France[1]
26. Graphic arts
    Other Midland Division

Mogul Division
27. Water treatment—commercial[1]
28. Water treatment—industrial[1]
    Other Mogul

Hysol Grafil
29. Precursor[1]
30. Carbon fiber[1]
31. Composite systems[1]

Life Technologies, Inc.
32. Molecular biology products[1]
33. Cell biology products[1]
34. Media—Dry and prepared[1]
35. Automated microbiology[1]
36. International[1]
    Other LTI[1]

[1]New Segments.
Source: Company records.

matrix. This was the first time that Dexter's divisional managers looked at the businesses independently. Prior to that, long-range plans were made at the divisional level. Based on the position of a SBS on the growth/share matrix, the BCG study identified businesses that should be supported and businesses that should be harvested or divested.

Although Dexter employed the BCG matrix to monitor its portfolio, it did not implement the portfolio planning approach dogmatically. For example, Dexter did not label its businesses as "dogs," "stars," or "cash cows." Loomis believed that this would have led to self-fulfilling behaviors on the part of these SBSs.

The definitions of Strategic Business Segments proposed by BCG were found to be inadequate. Loomis recalled that managers were thoroughly demotivated if they felt that they could not support the logic behind the grouping of products and markets within their SBSs. In 1977, Dexter redefined its SBSs. In addition to including the technical considerations used by BCG (for example, each SBS had to correspond to an unique product market combination), the redefinition also took into account other administrative factors—such as the power and influence of divisional managers, the limits to the managers' span of control, and whether the SBS definitions were meaningful to the managers who worked in the SBSs.

Loomis believed that no division should normally have more than five SBSs because a divisional manager would not be able to provide adequate attention to each business. If any division was dissatisfied with the segments that the corporate staff had defined, its manager was encouraged to discuss the issue with top management and to suggest alternatives. Loomis realized that defining a SBS was as much a political and administrative process as it was an analytical procedure. It was important, however, not to do too much violence to the technical "rules" for defining a strategic business by creating an SBS that did not match marketplace realities or by lumping very dissimilar businesses together.

Dexter also made another basic modification to the portfolio planning approach. Although one of the primary purposes of portfolio planning is to distinguish between those divisions that should be milked for cash and those that would be recipients of cash, Dexter did not differentiate between its divisions regardless of the relative maturity of their portfolios. Each Dexter division was required to maintain a balanced portfolio of businesses, and there was a minimal flow of capital across divisions. Loomis explained the reasons for such a stand:

> We have not often faced the hard issues of funding some businesses and not others. When we have, we said that each division must be a "tub standing on its own bottom." Of course, we have applied some "English" to be sure that no high-potential businesses were shortchanged.
>
> Since each division has had both cash-generating capability and growth opportunities, there has been no real need to move a lot of funds from one division to another. But even if this were not the case, we would be hesitant to do so because of the motivational and political problems of harvesting a whole division.

However, not all of the divisional managers believed that such a compartmental approach to resource allocation was helpful. For example, the Hysol division manager in 1978 pointed to the following experience:

> I would say going back one, two or three years (prior to 1978), that due to the constraints of the profit-sharing and the incentive program for the divisions, we probably underinvested in our two growth businesses: semiconductor molding powder and adhesives, in order to keep a balanced portfolio within the division.
>
> At that time, a division had to earn a pretax ROI of 35 percent in order to qualify for the maximum bonus. This naturally encouraged investments away from growth businesses into those that had high, certain returns in the short run. Dexter has since

changed its incentive system, paying top bonus to a division at different ROIs depending on its mission.

Profit Impact of Marketing Strategies (PIMS)

Dexter introduced the PIMS analysis (see Appendix A at the end of this case) in 1976, and consequently became one of the early subscribers to that analytical planning tool. The PIMS program is a large-scale, continuing empirical enquiry into the interrelationships among a group of factors representing the strategy, competitive position, market environment, and operating results of a business. Unlike the BCG matrix, which was an aid to Dexter's top management in monitoring the company's business portfolio, PIMS was perceived as more useful to SBS managers. It was meant to help these managers make better business strategy decisions by comparing their SBS's performance to that of over 2,000 businesses in the PIMS data bank. Loomis explained his rationale for introducing PIMS thus:

> Portfolio planning tools, such as PIMS and the growth-share matrix, confront business segment managers with information which forces them to think strategically. Without this information, division managers tend to think only about their own business. The portfolio tools force them to think about their business in relation to the marketplace and in relation to other opportunities that the company has.

Because the success of PIMS depended on its implementation at the SBS level, training programs were designed for the company's managers. Over the years, PIMS gained wide acceptance within the company as the managers became more familiar with its working.

Another factor that contributed to the popularity of PIMS was Dexter's incentive system. One manager observed the following:

> We have a strong culture that forces us to meet the profit plan. Since the bonuses are tied to the divisional performance measured in terms of ROI, and PIMS provides an analysis of which factors in a business influence its ROI, PIMS is popular.

The intensity of support for PIMS varied, however, from division to division. One of its proponents noted the following:

> PIMS is beneficial to divisional managers as they can try different strategies; see what other successful companies have done. The model is another way to check out what you think may be the correct strategy to follow.

A detractor observed the following:

> We do all the number crunching and send our data to PIMS and get their recommendations back. But we have no way of vouching for the quality of the data that they use in their analysis, or for verifying the validity of the regression model on which the PIMS recommendations are made. I am not convinced that the historical experiences of other businesses is a valid guide for the future of my business. It can confirm some new strategies, and check some others but at the end of the day we have to make our own decisions. PIMS is a good management tool as long as it doesn't run the business.

Loomis saw these differences of opinion as healthy. He believed that it was important to use a range of analytical techniques to assure that all the important issues were considered. Besides, Dexter's managers had ample opportunities to work with a PIMS consultant for addressing these and other issues.

Formal Planning, Control, and Incentive Systems

In 1977, each SBS at Dexter began preparing a five-year strategic plan. The plan included a fact sheet that defined the market served by the SBS, identified its competitors, and quantified the market's size and the market share of each competitor. A PIMS report for the SBS also was submitted. Finally the plan contained historical and projected financial information on sales growth, gross and net profits margins, and capital expenditures.

Each June, Dexter held a long-range planning meeting that was attended by the division presidents, the corporate officers, and some key staff employees from both the divisions and the corporate area. The focus of these meetings was on discussion of the strategic plans proposed by each division and on such corporate-wide issues as acquisitions opportunities, divestment candidates, and new planning tools. Each division also prepared detailed annual budgets for its SBSs. These budgets were reviewed by the office of Robert McGill, the Senior Vice President of Finance and Administration, before they were approved by Loomis and Coffin.

Capital expansion and other investments were evaluated on a discounted, cash-flow basis, using a hurdle rate that was tied to Dexter's cost of capital. Under Dexter's capital appropriations procedure, projects in excess of $500,000 were submitted for Board approval. Loomis and his subordinates had the authority to approve projects up to $500,000, provided that the annual total for all the projects not taken to the Board did not exceed $2,500,000. Division presidents approved projects up to $25,000, and group presidents approved projects up to $200,000.

The performance of each division was reviewed at the semiannual management committee meetings. The Dexter management committee consisted of all the corporate officers and the division presidents. However, with the introduction of the group level, the major responsibility for SBS strategy was rapidly delegated to the two group presidents. Dexter's top management began concerning itself more with the impact of the two group portfolios on corporate performance. The management committee also discussed such corporate issues as financial performance, acquisitions, new technologies, and growth areas.

It was left to the group presidents to review the performance of their divisions every month. Deviations from the budget were accounted for by the division presidents, and five-quarter rolling forecasts of division sales and contributions were revised and discussed. Because a division could revise its sales and contributions projections every quarter in its five-quarter rolling forecast, it was unusual for a division to have major deviations from its forecast.

Dexter has a profit-sharing program that in some divisions included all the employees—from those on the production floor to those in the corporate office. In such divisions, the divisional profit-sharing pool consisted of 20 percent of the divisional income before interest and tax but after deducting 20 percent (hurdle rate) of the divisional net assets. The bonus payments for divisional personnel came from the division's pool and could not exceed a specified percentage of base salary. The division president determined the criteria on which bonuses would be disbursed to the divisional personnel, subject to approval by the corporate office. Loomis determined the disbursements to the divisional presidents and corporate officers. Typically 45 percent of a division president's bonus was based on divisional performance. The rest was based on the following: individual goals, 25 percent; corporate performance, 20 percent; and subjective criteria used by the president and chairman, 10 percent. Other divisions at the time of their acquisition had satisfactory compensation plans that Dexter chose not to modify. For example, the Mogul Division retained its individual or subunit-based bonus plans.

"Naïve" Valuation System

Despite Dexter's diligent efforts at strategic planning, its stock price remained flat through the early 1980s. By 1985, hostile takeovers and corporate raiders became a major concern for companies whose stock was undervalued. Loomis and Coffin were anxious to ensure that Dexter did not become the target of an unfriendly takeover. Loomis looked to value-based planning (see Appendix B at the end of this case) for restructuring the company's assets and for guiding its future investments.

Value-based planning is anchored in the premise that the purpose of a corporation is to maximize shareholder wealth. It seeks to measure the impact of key strategic decisions on stockholder wealth. A firm is defined as a collection of business investments, and the total value of the firm is the sum of the values of these individual investments. The present value of a project is the sum of its future after-tax income projections, discounted by the average cost of financing it. Subtracting the initial investment in the project from this number gives the Net Present Value (NPV). A project with a high NPV is to be preferred over one with a low or negative NPV.

Dexter's first experience with value-based planning was at the corporate level, where it was used to evaluate potential acquisitions and divestitures and to formulate bidding strategies. By the repeated use of value-based planning in discrete decisions, such as in acquisitions and divestitures, Dexter's corporate officers became very familiar with that technique. A positive experience with the planning tool at the corporate level convinced Loomis of the benefits of extending it for a continuous audit of the firm's business portfolio. This adaptation of value-based planning to the firm's Strategic Business Segments was called the "Naïve" Valuation System.

A basic requirement of the "Naïve" Valuation System was that each business should be treated as if it were a stand-alone company. Dexter was already organized by Strategic Business Segments for the PIMS analysis, and these SBSs became the units of analysis for the "Naïve" Valuation System. To implement the "Naïve" Valuation System successfully on a continuous basis, the financial results of each SBS were required on a monthly or at least a quarterly basis. Dexter had previously reported the divisional performance monthly and the SBS results only annually. In 1980, the company hired consultants to establish an accounting and financial reporting system that could provide monthly profit and loss and balance sheet statements for each SBS. The resulting system was used to monitor the performance of each SBS and later was adapted to estimate each SBS's market value.

Each SBS manager was responsible for providing the projected growth rate for the market segments served by his or her business. This estimate, together with the historical performance of the SBS, was then used by the "Naïve" Valuation System model to structure the future financial statements of the SBS. Exhibit 6

Exhibit 6 **Illustrative Financial Projections for SBS XYZ**

	History 1981	History 1982	History 1983	Projected 1984
Income Statement (% Sales)				
Net sales	100.00	100.00	100.00	100.00
Purchase	50.62	48.30	45.42	45.42
Manufacturing and distribution	12.30	12.37	12.09	12.25
Depreciation	3.83	3.52	4.16	3.84
Gross profit	33.27	35.83	38.35	38.49
Sales force	4.66	3.94	4.29	4.30
Research and development	2.93	2.02	2.65	2.53
Advertising and promotion	0.22	0.28	0.24	0.25
Net operating profit	25.48	29.61	31.18	31.41
Other expense	3.13	3.68	5.31	5.31
Net profit before tax	22.35	25.93	25.88	26.10
Taxes	11.18	12.97	12.94	13.05
Net profit after tax	11.18	12.97	12.94	13.05
Assets (% Sales)				
Operating cash	2.84	2.68	7.32	3.0
Accounts receivable	16.20	16.77	20.13	20.13
Inventory	9.67	15.29	16.56	16.56
Current assets	28.69	34.74	44.00	39.69
Gross plant	69.25	70.13	79.33	79.33
Accumulated debt	(26.25)	(27.95)	(30.55)	(30.55)
Net plant	42.99	42.17	48.77	48.77
Total assets	71.68	76.90	92.77	88.46
Liability and Net Worth (% Sales)				
Current liability	10.68	12.84	18.39	18.40
Net worth	61.00	64.06	74.38	70.06
Total liability and Net worth	71.68	76.90	92.77	88.46

Exhibit 7   **Bond Rating Simulation for SBS XYZ**

Debt/Capital (%)	Bond Rating	
10	3.72	
20	3.33	
30	2.95	← Lowest Rating
40	2.57	over 2.9
50	2.19	

---

provides an illustration of the historical and projected data for SBS XYZ. The projections for 1984 in this example are based on the historical performance from 1981 to 1983.

The next step was to compute the debt-to-capital ratio for each SBS. Exhibit 7 presents the bond-rating simulation model used by Dexter. In the illustration, SBS XYZ needs a minimum bond rating score of 2.9 to earn an A bond rating (the rating preferred by Dexter) in its industry. This translates to a targeted debt to capital ratio of 30 percent for that SBS.

Once the debt and equity proportions of a SBS's investment were known, its cost of capital could be ascertained. The cost of debt was that corresponding to an A-rated bond. Exhibit 8 illustrates the business risk index estimation model used by Dexter to determine the business risk and hence the cost of equity for each SBS. In the example, the standard risk index of 0.64 for the packaging industry is adjusted for risk factors specific to SBS XYZ. The estimates of the SBS's debt capacity and business risk were then utilized to compute a weighted average cost of capital. The cost of capital thus computed was further revised to one of three values—for example, 11 percent, 12 percent, or 13 percent (see Exhibit 1), depending on whether the segment's estimated cost of capital was lower than, equal to, or higher than the corporation's as a whole (12 percent at the time of this calculation).

Using the projected cash flows and the cost of capital, the model then determined the value of the future cash flows of SBS XYZ (Exhibit 9). The output from such a model indicated semiannually whether an SBS had created or destroyed wealth for Dexter's stockholders.

REACTION OF THE MANAGERS TO THE "NAÏVE" VALUATION SYSTEM

Under the "Naïve" Valuation System, the division presidents received a semiannual evaluation of their businesses (see Exhibit 1). Their overall reactions to the "Naïve" Valuation System were positive:

Exhibit 8   **Estimating the Business Risk Index for SBS XYZ**

Industry Number	Industry Segments	(1) Standard Risk Index	(2) Weight	(3) = (1) × (2) Contribution to Risk Index
12	Packaging	0.64	100.0	0.64

Adjustments for:

Number	Risk Factor	(1) Standard Value	(2) Weight	(3) = (1) × (2) Contribution to Risk Index
1	Operating risk	0.80	0.11	0.09
2	Risk in achieving profitable growth	0.29	0.12	0.04
	Profitability	1.05		
	Growth	−0.04		
3	Asset quality	0.24	−0.11	−0.03
	Working capital management	0.03		
	Plant intensity	0.25		
	Plant newness	−0.05		
	Useful plant life	0.14		
4	Size and diversity	−0.18	−0.04	0.01
	Size	−0.45		
	Foreign income	0.27		
	Total adjustment	0.53	0.20	0.11
	Business Risk Index (BRI)			0.75

Exhibit 9   **Free Cash Flow Valuation for SBS XYZ**

Year	(1) Operating Nopat	(2) Operating I	(3) = (1) − (2) Operating FCF	(4) P.V. Factor C* = 13.5%	(5) = (3) × (4) Present Value
1984	$ 6,040	$ 232	$ 5,808	0.9386	$ 5,452
1985	6,629	2,605	4,024	0.8270	3,328
1986	7,279	2,865	4,414	0.7286	3,216
1987	7,993	3,152	4,841	0.6420	3,108
1988	8,778	3,467	5,311	0.5656	3,004
1989 and beyond	9,518	0	9,518	4.1897	39,879
Present Value of Operating FCF					$57,986

They [corporate] have just started the "Naïve" Valuation System. I think in due course it can become a reasonable check on the performance of the division and its subsegments, and provide early warning signals about potential problems.

I believe that in the long run, good performance is rewarded by the stock market. What creates value is not only growth but profit margins. Worth is trying to get that message across.

The manager who had a loss in his division knows it, but what he doesn't know is how much he has dragged Dexter's value down. The results of the model tell him that.

Loomis did not sense any major resistance to the implementation of value-based planning, although he was aware that his managers had not been sufficiently educated on the techniques of the system. In order to rectify this problem, Loomis arranged training programs for his managers with value-based planning consultants. All SBS and divisional managers and financial managers subsequently attended a three-day seminar on the theory and mechanics of value-based planning.

Moreover, due to the semiannual valuation reports, the managers at all levels had become aware of value-based planning. The managers with professional management degrees were especially quick at grasping the working of this new analytical tool. Ironically they were also more skeptical of its relevance, as illustrated by this comment:

I do not find value-based planning very useful. It is important for them [corporate] to understand the value of each business segment and Dexter's worth as a whole. From the viewpoint of a division president or SBS manager, the information would allow us to measure performance in yet another way, but I don't see how we can use that information to make or change any important business decisions. Maybe I need to learn more about this technique before I can appreciate its relevance.

BROADER ISSUES

Since Worth Loomis became President, he had been active in introducing the latest strategic planning tools to Dexter. He believed that these tools helped him understand the company's portfolio better and were instrumental in linking divisional plans with corporate plans. Because of his analytical background, Loomis had kept abreast of the latest planning techniques offered by management consultants and academics. On the other hand, David Coffin, the Chairman of the Board, emphasized entrepreneurship. He urges his managers to "Go to the marketplace. Find out what a customer wants us to develop, and then come back to the lab and invent it." Exhibit 10 provides a brief biographical sketch of Loomis, Coffin, and the two newly appointed group presidents.

The "creative tension" between Loomis's emphasis on analytics and Coffin's drive toward understanding the customer had helped Dexter's managers enjoy the power of analytical models without compromising their entrepreneurial drive. One of them observed:

There is a good balance between Worth, who is numbers oriented and David, who urges us to forget the numbers for a while and think of the marketplace and the customer. Last year, for example, David established a "New Directions" program. We studied the business universe to find out what new product/technologies will emerge in the next ten years and which of these businesses fit our culture of non-consumer products. We also established a program to identify quality companies in growth industries and to establish supplier relationships with them. Some of them are already our customers and we will work closely with them in other areas. We know that this blue skying will eventually lead to sound business propositions that we can defend in front of Worth.

Loomis was, however, planning to retire in two years, and he wanted value-based planning to gain root in Dexter before he stepped down. One of his division managers described how important this was to Dexter:

Loomis is very much into analytics. After his retirement, it is hard to say if the company would continue to use the quantitative goals that it uses now. The financial reporting system may also look very different. Ten years ago there was no corporate financial staff. Dexter could not even close its own books without the help of Coopers and Lybrand. We have come a long way. But I am not sure whether the current enthusiasm for analytical aids to planning would not wane with Worth's retirement.

Loomis also knew that his efforts to implement value-based planning at Dexter would require the support of the incoming President. The two inside contenders were Grahame Walker, the President of the Specialty Chemicals group, and Joseph Day, the President of the Specialty Materials group. Exhibit 10 gives a brief biographical sketch of each contender. Walker, an ex–Royal Navy officer, had joined the company in 1957 and risen to his current position through a series of promotions. Over the years, the company also had recruited managers from Fortune 100 companies. Day was one such manager, having joined Dexter in 1980 from the General Electric Company.

Exhibit 10   **A Profile of the Top Line Managers at the Dexter Corporation**

David L. Coffin
Chairman, Chief Executive Officer, and
Director, The Dexter Corporation

Born in December 1925 in Windsor Locks, Connecticut, David Coffin attended New England and Trinity Colleges. From 1947 on, David held a number of positions in the company before becoming president and CEO in 1958 and chairman in 1975. David serves as director of a number of business and civic organizations: Bank of New England Corporation; Connecticut Bank and Trust Company, N.A.; Connecticut Mutual Life Insurance Company; Hasbro, Inc.; The New England Colleges Fund; The Institute of Living; Mystic Seaport Museum; the Connecticut Historical Society; and the Bushnell Memorial.

Worth Loomis
President and Director, The Dexter Corporation

Born in May 1923 in New York City, Worth Loomis received a Master of Business Administration in International Finance from New York University and a Bachelor of Science in Industrial Engineering from Yale University. Worth joined the company as vice president–finance in 1970 and was elected president in 1975. He currently serves as a director of CIGNA Funds Group, Connecticut Natural Gas Corporation, and Southern New England Telephone Company. Worth is a trustee of Mechanics Savings Bank and a member of the Chemical Bank National Advisory Board.

Joseph C. Day
President, Specialty Materials Group, and
Senior Vice President, The Dexter Corporation

Born in February 1945 in Lowell, Massachusetts, Joe Day received a Bachelor of Science in Plastics Engineering from the Lowell Institute of Technology and completed a series of management training programs with the General Electric Company. Joe joined Dexter in 1980 and was appointed president of the C. H. Dexter Division and corporate vice president in 1983. In January 1985, he was appointed senior vice president of the corporation and president of the newly formed Specialty Materials Group. Joe is on the board of the American Paper Institute and is a member of the executive committee and board of the Association of Nonwoven Manufacturers. In addition, he is president of the Science Museum of Connecticut and serves as a director of the Wiremold Company.

K. Grahame Walker
President, Specialty Chemicals Group, and
Senior Vice President, The Dexter Corporation

Born in June 1937 and educated at Merchant Taylors' School in England, Grahame Walker graduated from the Brittania Royal Naval College at Dartmouth, England, in 1957 and from the Institute of Mechanical Engineers in 1962. Grahame joined Dexter in 1967 as a result of the merger with Hysol, Inc. At that time, he managed Hysol's joint venture operation in the United Kingdom; subsequently he became managing director of The Dexter GmbH in Munich, West Germany, and vice president for European operations until his appointment as president of the Hysol Division and corporate vice president in 1979. Grahame was appointed president of the Specialty Chemicals Group and a senior vice president of the corporation in January 1985. He relocated from the Hysol Division headquarters in Industry, California, to Windsor Locks in April 1985.

Loomis believed that introducing PIMS had been an easier challenge because it was implemented at a time when the corporation was undergoing a cultural change. The entrepreneurial owners who had come with the major acquisitions were retiring, and the professional managers who had 'grown up' with the company were gaining responsibility. At that time, the major challenge facing corporate management was to provide direction to the divisions. PIMS acted as a catalyst in that effort. Loomis was not sure whether a similar opportune moment existed in 1986. He wondered whether one way of grabbing the attention of his managers would be to link their incentive compensation to the creation of shareholder wealth.

Appendix A —————————————————————
A BRIEF DESCRIPTION OF THE PIMS PROGRAM

WHAT IS THE PIMS PROGRAM?

The PIMS Program of the Strategic Planning Institute is a multicompany activity designed to provide an improved and innovative factual base for the business planning efforts of each participant.

Each member company contributes information about its experiences in several different business areas to a combined data base. The PIMS staff analyzes this experience to discover the general "laws" that determine what business strategy, in what kind of competitive environment, produces what profit results. The findings are made available to member companies in a form useful to their business planning.

The intent of the program is to provide business managers and planners with tools and data for answering questions like these:

(a) What profit rate is "normal" for a given business, considering its particular market, competitive position, technology, cost structure, etc?

(b) If the business continues on its current track, what will its future operating results be?

(c) What strategic changes in the business have promise of improving these results?

(d) Given a specific contemplated future strategy for the business, how will profitability or cash flow change, short-term and long-term?

In each case, the answers are derived from an analysis of the experiences of other businesses operating under similar conditions.

This appendix has been excerpted from a brochure on the PIMS Program published by the Strategic Planning Institute, Cambridge, MA 02139. See R. Buzzell and B. Gale, *PIMS Principles* (New York: The Free Press, 1987) for an elaborate discussion of the PIMS program.

HISTORY AND STRUCTURE OF PIMS

The PIMS Program originated as an internal project of the General Electric Company, where it has been used for over a decade as a tool of corporate planning and division-level planning. The basic logic, method of approach, and techniques of application were developed and tested there by a team of people now heavily represented on the PIMS staff.

From 1972 to 1974, the PIMS Program was established as a developmental project at the Harvard Business School, and located at the Marketing Science Institute (a research organization affiliated with HBS). During this phase of its life, PIMS:

- learned to operate on a multicompany basis;
- verified the basic GE research findings on a wider cross-section of businesses, and extended the parameter of strategy exploration;
- developed much of the current computer software package; and
- stimulated interest in the comparative, quantitative analysis of the consequences of business strategy in a large number of companies and academic research centers.

In February 1975, to facilitate the evolution of the program beyond the academic stage to an operating system, PIMS was organized as an autonomous institute, focused explicitly on the analysis of strategic business plans. The Strategic Planning Institute is a non-profit corporation, governed by its member companies, with a charter permitting not only academic research but also application activities of various kinds.

At present over 200 companies participate in PIMS, including:

- About 125 large U.S. corporations, drawn mostly from the top 500 companies on the Fortune list;
- Many medium-sized companies in manufacturing and service businesses;
- A growing group of large European companies.

The PIMS Data Base

The unit of observation in PIMS is a business. Each business is a division, product line, or other profit center within its parent company, selling a distinct set of products and/or services to an identifiable group of customers, in competition with a well-defined set of competitors, and for which meaningful separation can be made of revenues, operating costs, investments and strategic plans.

Currently the data base consists of information on the strategic experiences of over 1,700 businesses, covering a five-year period. The information on each business consists of about 100 items, descriptive of the characteristics of the market environment, the state of competition, the strategy pursued by the business, and the operating results obtained. Each data item has been pretested for significance and relevance to profitability. Table 1 contains an illustrative list of the items of information in the data base.

The PIMS staff has devised a set of standardized forms to be filled out by the participant company for the contribution of its experience records to the computer data bank. The forms are designed to break the required data items into simple elements that can readily be assembled from financial or marketing records, or that can be estimated by someone familiar with the specific business. The time and effort required to complete a set of forms depends on the state of a company's business records. Companies with uniform, well-established accounting systems

Table 1   **Information on Each Business in the PIMS
Data Base (Illustrative List)**

Characteristics of the Business Environment
Long-run growth rate of the market
Short-run growth rate of the market
Rate of inflation of selling price levels
Number and size of customers
Purchase frequency and magnitude

Competitive Position of the Business
Share of the served market
Share relative to largest competitors
Product quality relative to competitors
Prices relative to competitors
Pay scales relative to competitors
Marketing efforts relative to competitors
Pattern of market segmentation
Rate of new product introductions

Structure of the Production Process
Capital intensity (degree of automation, etc.)
Degree of vertical integration
Capacity utilization
Productivity of capital equipment
Productivity of people
Inventory levels

Discretionary Budget Allocation
R&D budgets
Advertising and promotion budgets
Sales force expenditures

Strategic Moves
Patterns of change in the controllable elements above

Operating Results
Profitability results
Cash flow results
Growth results

typically require about two man-days to complete the SPI data forms on one business; other companies require about three man-days.

The Research and Development Program

The research portion of the SPI program consists of a continuing analysis of the experiences reflected in the data base to discover the empirical "law" that determines what strategy, under what conditions, produces what result. The investigators use a variety of analytical tools, the most important being multiple regression analysis.

To date, PIMS has succeeded in identifying 30-odd factors that have a potent and predictable impact on profitability. Taken together, they account for 70 percent to 80 percent of the observed variation in profitability across the businesses in the data base. Most of the factors are listed in Table 1.

These factors are incorporated into a set of profit-predicting and cash flow-predicting models that assign to each factor its proper weight, judging from the experiences reflected in the data base. The models also indicate how the impact of each profit-determining factor is conditioned by other factors. (For example, high plant and equipment per dollar of sales generally reduces return on investment, but this reduction is small in businesses with a strong market share, and large in businesses with a weak market share. Or, high R&D/Sales has a positive impact on earnings in highly integrated businesses, but a negative impact in shallowly integrated businesses.)

The models are designed to aid the assessment of strategic moves. An assumed change in one or several profit-influencing factors can be analyzed to determine the profit and cash consequences both during the time that the move is being executed and after it has been completed.

Feedback to Member Companies

Participating companies receive three kinds of feedback from the Institute:

1. Reports on the general principles of business strategy disclosed by the analysis of the data base;
2. Specific reports on each business the company has contributed to the data base;
3. Access to computer models in which the general strategic principles are incorporated, in a manner useful for strategy planning and simulation; plus instruction and counsel in the interpretation and use of these resources.

The specific reports on an individual business express the net impact of all research findings to date, in the form of (a) evaluative statements about that business, and (b) strategy advice for the business. They are computer-generated reports, using the empirical models mentioned above.

The major specific reports are:

The "Par" Report specifies the return on investment that is normal (or "par") for the business, given the characteristics of its market, competition, position, technology, and cost structure. It reports whether this business is the kind that normally earns, say 3 percent on investment or 30 percent, judging by the experiences of other businesses with similar characteristics. Also, it identifies the major strengths and weaknesses of the business that account for the high or low "par."

The Strategy Analysis Report is a computational pretest of several possible strategic moves in the business. It indicates the normal short- and long-term consequences of each such move, judging by the experience of other businesses making a similar move, from a similar starting point, in a similar business environment. It specifies the profit (or loss) likely to be achieved by such projected changes, along with the associated investment and cash flow. This report is used by (a) upper-level managers and planners, for evidence on potential effects of broad moves in market share, margin, capital intensity, and vertical integration; and (b) by middle-level people, for evidence of the potential effects of specific action in such areas as programs to improve relative product quality, increases in the ratio of marketing expenses to sales, improvements in capacity utilization or employee productivity, or changes in R&D outlays.

The Optimum Strategy Report nominates that combination of several strategic moves that promises to give optimal results for the business, also judging by the experiences of other businesses under similar circumstances. This report offers such an opinion for any of several different measures of profit performance, for example:

discounted cash flow over ten yeàrs;
return on investment for the next five years;
short-term earnings dollars.

The Report on Look-Alikes (ROLA) provides managers with a way to discover effective tactics for accomplishing their strategic objectives (for example, increasing profitability or cash flow, gaining market share, improving productivity or product quality). ROLA retrieves from the data base businesses that are strategically similar to the businesses being analyzed (its "look-alikes") and reports a large number of the strategic and operating characteristics that helped them to attain the specified objective.

If the objective is to increase net cash flow, for example, ROLA first retrieves data on those look-alike businesses that succeeded in increasing their cash flow, and also on those other "look alikes" that did not succeed. Next, the program examines over 200 tactical data elements to discover what the successful businesses did differently from the unsuccessful businesses. Finally, it tests the observed differences in behavior for their statistical significance, to identify the most reliable actions to improve cash flow.

Since the business characteristics used to find "look-alikes" and the business objective can both be specified by the user, ROLA is a very flexible aid to strategic planning.

Major Application of SPI Materials

Member companies use these SPI reports and resources for a considerable range of planning purposes, such as:

- to provide a common language for the discussion of business strategy;
- to generate questions that should be asked about a business;
- to nominate promising future business strategies for detailed exploration;
- to estimate the future consequences of specific strategies;
- to suggest details of strategy execution that usually succeed;
- to screen specific businesses for possible acquisition, disposition, or reorganization;
- to estimate the overall profit levels that constitute normally expected performance for a business with a particular profile of characteristics;
- to identify the strengths of a business on which future strategy can build, or the weaknesses that future strategy should aim to correct;
- to propose a corporate allocation of investment funds to optimize overall corporate performance.

As with other strategic planning tools, Profit Impact of Marketing Strategies should be used as an aid to management judgement and not as a substitute for it. As Dr. Sidney Schoeffler, the originator of PIMS, says, "Don't ignore what the model says, but don't believe what the model says either."

Appendix B
VALUE-BASED PLANNING

Value-based planning focuses on measuring the impact of key strategic decisions on stockholder wealth. In this approach to planning, a firm is defined as a collection of business investments, and the total value of the firm is the sum of (1) the present value of cash flows from these individual investments during the forecast period, (2) the "residual value," or the present value of such investments attributable to the period beyond the forecast period, and (3) cash and marketable securities. The appropriate rate for discounting the company's cash flow stream is the weighted average of the costs of debt and equity capital. The relevant weights attached to debt and equity should be based on their proportions targeted over the long term. The relevant rate for the cost of debt is the long-term rate or yield to maturity, which reflects the rate currently demanded by debtholders. The cost of equity, or the minimum expected return that will induce investors to buy a company's share, is more difficult to measure. It is the sum of the risk-free rate, as reflected in current

See A. Rappaport, *Creating Shareholder Value* (New York: The Free Press, 1986), for a detailed discussion of value-based planning.

yields available in government securities, and an additional return or equity risk premium for investing in the company's more risky shares. Stockholders' wealth is the total value of the firm minus the market value of its debt.

Value-based planning was initially used for discrete decisions such as mergers and acquisitions. It helped assess the value of a target company to the acquirer, by comparing the purchase price to the intrinsic value of the target to the acquirer. The target firm was valued by its future cash flow and also by the potential synergies that could be realized by integrating the target firm with the acquiring firm. Clearly, the premium paid for gaining control of the firm should not exceed the difference between the target's intrinsic value and the market price.

Value-based planning was similarly used for evaluating divestiture decisions. The divesting company compared the purchase price offered with the value to it of the business planned for divestiture.

Based on the success with this approach for discrete decisions like acquisitions, mergers, and divestitures, some companies began using it for routine strategic decisions. Their problem was that the cash flow from incremental business strategies was not always quantifiable. Many investments in new businesses were experimental moves in an emerging market that merely provided the firm with some options for the future. Evaluating these options was difficult. Despite these limitations, the use of value-based planning has spread quite rapidly to business level strategic decisions. The primary contribution of this technique for evaluating such strategies is that risk and return can be explicitly traded off. Riskier businesses are burdened with a higher cost of capital. Businesses that do not earn a return commensurate with their risk should not be funded.

Despite its early promise, implementing value-based planning has been stymied by the fundamental difficulty in accurately projecting cash flows from a business, in correctly estimating its salvage value, and in computing its proper cost of capital. Indeed the bulk of the controversy surrounding its use has centered on debates over these three estimates.

However, companies that currently use value-based planning cite the following advantages:

- It makes managers conscious of their business' impact on the company's stock price,
- It sensitizes them to the risk/return trade-off, and
- It helps in evaluating weaknesses in a company's business portfolio.

Dexter Corporation (Part 2): The C. H. Dexter Division

"If you are an investment intensive, industrial product manufacturer, you are in deep yogurt." With those introductory remarks, Joe Patten, the Senior Vice President of the Strategic Planning Institute (SPI) and PIMS consultant to Dexter, began his presentation to Dexter Corporation's annual Long-Range Planning meeting held in June 1986. Patten went on to elaborate how having high market share and relative product quality were insufficient conditions to solve a SBS's profit problem if it was investment intensive.

The comments seemed addressed particularly to Jim Mayerhofer, the President of Dexter Corporation's C. H. Dexter Division. Mayerhofer's division had seven SBSs (Exhibit 1), most of which were investment intensive and competed in mature industries. With the exception of two new ventures, Battery and Hydraspun, the division's SBSs experienced mature, slow-growth markets. Moreover, they were among the most investment intensive of Dexter Corporation's businesses; for example, their Value Added/Investment ratio (a measure used by SPI to measure investment intensity) was less than 1.01, placing them among the top 40 percent in investment intensity of all businesses in the PIMS data base.[1] In comparison, only one third of the company's other businesses fell in that category.

Joe Patten's research seemed to indicate that it was highly unlikely that an investment-intensive business could sustain its profitability in the long run. In fact, an analysis of 545 investment-intensive businesses (Value Added/Investment ratio of less than or equal to 1.01) in the PIMS data base showed that, regardless of the market share and relative product quality associated with such businesses, their

Copyright © 1987 by Balaji S. Chakravarthy, The Carlson School of Management, University of Minnesota

This case was prepared by Associate Professor Balaji S. Chakravarthy, with the cooperation of John Vrabel of the Dexter Corporation, as the basis for class discussion rather than to illustrate either effective or ineffective handling of an administrative situation.

Exhibit 1 **C. H. Dexter Products and Markets**

SBS	Products/Market	Remarks
Infusion—Worldwide	Specialty paper used in tea and coffee bags	Mature, slow growth
Casing—Worldwide	Specialty paper used in fibrous processed-meat casing base	Mature market
Sterilization Wrap—Worldwide	Nonwoven materials for disposable sterilization wrap for use in various medical delivery systems and industrial applications	Mature market
Drape, Pack, and Gown—Worldwide	Nonwoven and film materials for disposable medical products	Mature U.S. market; possible growth in Europe
Filtration Vac Bag—Worldwide	Nonwoven and paper materials used in the manufacture of vacuum cleaner bags for the OEM market	Stable, mature market
Porous Plug Wrap—Worldwide	Nonwoven porous plug-wrap materials used in the manufacture of low-tar cigarettes	Mature market
Textile Replacement Nonwoven Wall Cover Backing—Worldwide	Strippable, nonwoven wallcover backing for fabric-backed vinyl wallcoverings	Mature market
Hydraspun	Markets for process-proof Hydraspun fabric, in roll-goods form—including disposable apparel, wiping fabrics, vinyl fabric backing, and coolant filter media	
Electronic and Other Industrial Battery—Worldwide	Battery separators used in Sealed Lead Acid, Lithium, and Mercury batteries and Alkaline battery separators	High growth market

average pretax ROI was unlikely to exceed 25 percent (Exhibit 2). Furthermore, the probability of an investment-intensive SBS achieving or exceeding a pretax ROI of 25 percent was estimated by Patten at 14 percent.

Mayerhofer was struck by the fact that only one of his six capital-intensive businesses was able to equal or exceed a pretax ROI of 25 percent. This 16 percent ratio was frighteningly close to Patten's 14 percent. And yet Mayerhofer was confident that the strategic plans for his division were not overly optimistic in their profitability projections.

Exhibit 2   **Industrial Product Manufacturers Impact of Investment Intensity on Competitive Position (545 type-A[1] businesses)**

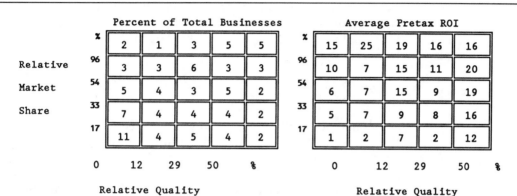

Percent of Total Businesses

Average Pretax ROI

¹A Type-A Business is one that has a Value Added/Investment ratio of 1.01 or less.

C. H. DEXTER'S STRATEGIC PLAN FOR INFUSION AND CASING SBSs

The division prepared detailed strategic plans and financial projections for each SBS as part of the company-wide strategic planning efforts. For purposes of illustration, only the strategic plans pertaining to the Infusion and Casing SBSs are briefly discussed in this case.

Infusion—Worldwide

The major product line of this SBS was specialty paper used in the manufacture of tea and coffee bags. The market for this product line was mature, and the SBS was designated a long-term cash generator for the company. Division management felt that Dexter had a leading market share in this market in the United States. The closest competitor, Bollore, was only one quarter of Dexter's size. Dexter's share in international markets was not as strong, but it was respectable. Its largest competitor in Europe was Crompton, which had a comparable market share; its largest competitor in the Far East was Nihon Shigyo, a price and quality leader in the Japanese heatseal tea market.

The Infusion SBS sought to protect its leadership position in the supply of a complete line of heatseal and nonheatseal filter papers to service the tea- and coffee-processing industry. A key strategy was to be a value leader—that is, to emphasize quality and service and to maintain strong and effective relationships at all customer levels. The proposed differentiation strategy was not without risks, as there was a growing consumer cost consciousness. Excess capacity that existed in the industry could easily spark a price war. However, C. H. Dexter planned to retain its market share and profitability by initiating product/process improvements aimed at offering new products with demonstrably superior performance characteristics and/or equivalent performance at a lower cost. The Index of Relative Quality[2] was planned to be raised threefold by 1990.

Casing—Worldwide

The major product line of this SBS was specialty paper used in fibrous processed-meat casing base. It was sold to producers who in turn serviced various markets throughout the world. Dexter was the inventor and the only true international supplier of this product line. The market for it was, however, mature. Less expensive alternative methods and reduction of red meat consumption had dampened growth in this market. The company consequently designated this SBS as a long-term cash generator. The company was the sole producer of this product in the United States and commanded a major share of the international market. Crompton in Europe and Nihon Shigyo in Japan offered some competition in world markets.

The Casing SBS sought to protect its leadership position through the selective use of multiyear supply contracts with world casing producers. Its strategic plan also called for supporting and initiating programs with customers to improve their efficiencies, quality, and costs. Dexter's own quality was judged to be superior, and the major thrust here was to retain this quality leadership. Special attention was aimed at fundamental research that would develop new bonding methods that could help reduce investment in plant pollution-control devices.

VALUE-BASED PLANNING

The two SBSs referred to above were rolled into a single entity called the food segment for purposes of the company's value-based planning system ("Naïve" Valuation.[3]) The ratio of naïve value to investment for the food entity had grown steadily from 1.6 in the second half of 1984 to 2.0 in the last half of 1986. The sales growth assumed in this computation was 2 percent, a figure consistent with the relative maturity of the Infusion and Casing SBSs.

Despite this positive endorsement by the company's latest planning tool and notwithstanding the great deal of effort that had gone into preparing the strategic plan for the two SBSs, Mayerhofer seemed to be haunted by Patten's warning about high-investment-intensive businesses. He requested PIMS to analyze his strategic plans.

THE PIMS ANALYSIS

The PIMS tests of the division's plans for the Infusion and Casing SBSs are summarized in Exhibit 3. The first column is the actual performance of the Infusion and Casing SBSs in the immediate past year, 1985. The next column refers to the performance planned by the C. H. Dexter Division in 1990.

The three columns to the right of the 1990 column represent three PIMS tests of the Dexter business plan for 1986–1990. The tests use a PIMS model that tests the reasonableness of the Dexter Plan's financial forecast and the relationship between suggested tactics and expected results. The first test (Plan A) assumes that the market share objectives and the value-added levels of the Dexter Plan are achieved in the final year of the five-year plan. All other data items, including sales, are developed by the PIMS model, including ROI levels, investment levels, tactics (working capital, quality, and new products levels), and cash flow and market values discounted to present values.

The second test (Plan B) assumes that the market share objectives and the value-added levels of the Dexter Plan are achieved in the final year of the five-year plan and that the planned tactics (working capital, quality, new products, marketing, and research levels) also are achieved. This test attempts to replicate the

---

Exhibit 3   **Strategic Plans and the PIMS Test[1]**

	1985 (Actual)	1990 (Plan)[2]	PIMS Test (1990)		
			A	B	C
SBS: Infusion [Growth: 2% (unit), 0% (price)]					
Index of relative quality (%)	45		49	48	53
Value added/ investment	0.62		0.75	0.62	0.77
ROI (%) (index)	100		167	138	167
Market value (index)	100		178	152	189
SBS: Casing [Growth: 1% (unit), 1% (price)]					
Index of relative quality (%)	15		−14	10	47
Value added/ investment	0.87		1.16	0.87	1.19
ROI (%) (index)	100		142	138	185
Market value (index)	100		143	157	186

[1]Numbers in this table are illustrative and do not reflect either the actuals or the plan for the two SBSs.
[2]Details of the plan have been omitted from the Exhibit.

Dexter Plan. The ROI, DCF, and market values, however, are developed by the PIMS model.

The third test (Plan C) disregards the Dexter Plan except for the market growth and selling price forecasts. This test uses the PIMS data base and models to suggest what an average PIMS business situated in the planning base year with the Dexter business characteristics would do (within certain constraints) to maximize shareholder value.

The purpose of the three tests was to see if the proposed five-year plan was financially attractive, consistent with suggested tactics, reasonable in its financial and investment projections, and consistent with maximizing shareholder value.

Based on these three tests, Patten advised the following:

> For the Infusion SBS, the most aggressive plan would be to improve relative quality to gain market share while minimizing additional investment in this slow growth market.
> For the Casing SBS, the PIMS optimization strategy supports a more aggressive value added plan and a considerable improvement in perceived quality.

DIVISIONAL PRESIDENT'S REACTIONS

Mayerhofer's initial reactions to Patten's recommendations were ones of disbelief:

> I could not believe that we were paying Joe to come here and insult the division. I think it is naive to argue that just because we are investment intensive and a mature business that we are losers. We were always investment intensive and until last year we met all our profitability goals. Our 1985 performance was hurt by lower priced foreign imports. Our European competitors took full advantage of the strong dollar and our need to maintain our domestic prices. Our capacity utilization fell and our profits suffered. I will grant you that investment intensive businesses are more prone to profit swings because of their high break even points. But our profitable history argues that we are winners and that there are other investment intensive winners out there as well.

At Mayerhofer's request, Patten did further analysis on the PIMS data base. Exhibit 4 presents the PIMS analysis of investment-intensive businesses that also had high relative quality and high relative market share (16 percent of all investment-intensive businesses). Mayerhofer felt that this additional analysis was clearly more appropriate to his division's SBSs. Commenting on this new analysis, Mayerhofer observed the following:

> It is definitely possible to generate a healthy Return on Investment (ROI) even in an investment intensive and mature business that has high market share and high relative quality like C. H. Dexter. Firms that do that have excellent control on their operating, selling, administrative and research costs. It is back to basics. Control your operations well and you can be profitable.

However, Mayerhofer felt that cost control alone would not be enough to fight foreign competitors, with their foreign-exchange-based cost advantages. He

Exhibit 4   **PIMS Analysis of Investment-Intensive, High Relative Quality, and High Market Share Businesses Grouped by ROI[1]**

As a Percentage of Sales	Low-ROI Business	Medium-ROI Business	High-ROI Business
Sales	100	100	100
Value added	53	55	55
Gross margin	21	26	34
Selling, administrative, and research expenses	20	17	15
Return on sales	1	9	19
Return on investment	1	14	31

[1]These are businesses with a relative market share of greater than 54 percent and a relative quality of higher than 29 percent in Exhibit 2.

had to find a way of maintaining price while giving commensurate value to the customer. He reasoned that customers would be willing to pay a premium price if they perceived the division's products to be of superior quality. It was important, however, to ensure that this superior quality was not accomplished by increasing the division's operating costs. To accomplish these objectives, the division launched a total quality effort called Partners in Dexter Quality (PDQ). In fact, C. H. Dexter's experience with PDQ has shown that cost reduction and quality improvement are very compatible goals and key to its profits growth plans. Mayerhofer noted this on the investment-intensity issue:

> Quality improvement can require additional investment. Sometimes you cannot increase R (return) without increasing I (investment). The proper approach is not to abandon all investment because a business is investment intensive, but to leverage such investment for cost reduction and quality improvement programs that contribute returns that increase the business' Return on Investment (ROI).

Mayerhofer felt that the added PIMS analysis was helpful, even though it had merely reaffirmed the division's earlier strategies for its infusion and casing businesses of total quality with increasing operating cost effectiveness. Reflecting on his experiences with PIMS and value-based planning for these two SBSs, Mayerhofer noted this:

> The "naïve" value projections for these two businesses showed an upward trend. We were presumably creating value for the stockholders, even when PIMS kept showing us as a loser. The models were contradicting each other. And again, much of our variation could have been influenced by foreign exchange gains/losses. Given the increasing globalization of our businesses, this has to be a significant issue in the "naïve" value computation.
>
> Analytical models to be useful must be comprehensible, must deal with variables

that a manager can control, and above all must show causation. I don't think the "naïve" value model can accurately track a company's stock price. It certainly didn't predict Black Monday (October 19, 1987); and the PIMS model is not really tailored to the industry context of a SBS. I believe that they are both useful diagnostic tools, but it is important that we recognize their limitations. For example, in an integrated manufacturing operation, like ours, assets are shared by several SBSs. Allocation of investments, overheads, and shared costs across the SBSs is critical to how a SBS is judged by an analytical model. If we modify a machine to take on products of a new SBS, where we show the additional investment is critical to how a business is valued. Moreover, a PIMS consultant may deny investment for a SBS based on his model. What the consultant may not know, however, is that a bulk of the proposed investment is to satisfy EPA or OSHA. Failure to invest is equivalent to saying we want to go out of that business. We must, therefore, be prepared to quantify all effects of an investment decision.

Finally, I believe it is very important to ask of ourselves whether the benefits from the models used outweigh the costs of supporting them. Filling out the PIMS questionnaires and providing the inputs for the "naive" valuation model take time and effort. The division, group, and corporation must get commensurate benefits.

The value of all models is to make explicit the implicit assumptions in the system. By challenging the models in a macro sense we were able to reaffirm our feelings that our pursuit of total quality and operating cost effectiveness were the keys to sustaining attractive levels of profitability in a mature and investment intensive business.

NOTES

1. See Case 13 for a description of the PIMS data base.
2. The Index of Relative Quality is a weighted average percentage measure of the perceived relative superiority (+) or inferiority (−) of an SBS's products over those of its competitors on all attributes of product quality that are important to the SBS's customers.
3. See Case 13 for a description of the "Naïve" Valuation System.

Texas Instruments Incorporated: Challenges in the 1980s

Texas Instruments (TI) was at the peak of its glory in 1978. Analysts considered it to be one of the best-managed companies in the United States. It was touted as an example for others on how to foster innovation and boost productivity. With all the hype then about the potency of Japanese management practices, many academicians took pride in Texas Instruments' unique organization structure and management system as a home-grown model of excellence.

The company itself had set ambitious sales goals, striving to achieve $10 billion of sales by 1988–1989 from $2.5 billion at the end of 1978. Capital expenditures in 1978 amounted to $300 million, of which about $120 million was devoted to research and development. A special report in *Business Week* stated this with admiration:

> Today the Dallas electronics giant leads the world in such fast-moving, high-technology markets as semiconductors, calculators, and digital watches. [Texas Instruments] has accomplished what 100 or more other U.S. companies tried and failed to do in recent years: It has built a flourishing, profitable business in consumer electronics. In doing so, TI has beaten the Japanese at their own game and probably is now No. 1 in worldwide revenues in both calculators and digital watches. Some experts believe that Texas Instruments has more potential in consumer electronics than any company in the world. The company's rapidly building momentum, orchestrated by one of the world's most finely tuned managements, is causing some observers to point to Texas Instruments as the prototype of what a U.S. company must be to compete in the surging, worldwide electronics markets of the 1980s.[1]

The subsequent history of the company unfortunately did not live up to these high expectations. By the early 1980s, Texas Instruments was faced with serious problems in some of its new businesses, such as home computers and digital watches. The digital watch business was discontinued in early 1981. In 1983, a year that Texas Instruments called "the most difficult period in Texas Instruments' history," the company withdrew from the home computer business after taking $660 million in writeoffs and posting a net loss of $145 million. The experience was traumatic for everyone in Texas Instruments. Exhibit 1 provides a summary description of the company's financial performance from 1976 to 1985.

The structure and the management systems that were praised in 1978 were blamed by some for Texas Instruments' failures in the 1980s. This case describes the problems faced by Texas Instruments since its heyday in the late 1970s and outlines some of the corrective actions that were initiated by the company.

THE SEMICONDUCTOR BUSINESS

At the end of the 1970s and the beginning of the 1980s, Texas Instruments worked hard to consolidate its leadership in several segments of the fast-growing semiconductor industry.

At that time, the U.S. semiconductor industry still dominated the expanding world markets for computers and semiconductor devices, while Japan was the world leader in consumer electronics products. The Japanese, however, realized that in order for their export earnings to grow in the 1980s, they had to surpass U.S. companies in the computer market worldwide. In order to achieve this, major Japanese companies worked intensively on a $300-million program sponsored by their government to develop a new generation of semiconductor chips. These chips were intended to leapfrog U.S. products and to provide the necessary building blocks for a new class of very low-cost, powerful computers. Although it was concerned, Texas Instruments had confidence that it would not be swept away by Japanese competition. After all, like the Japanese manufacturers, Texas Instruments understood and used the learning curve extensively. The concept of the learning curve suggests that as the cumulative volume produced by a manufacturer increases, the unit cost of manufacturing drops exponentially.

Dramatic improvements in product technology led to lower costs for performing several electronic functions. In 1960, two transistors and five other parts were needed to make the simplest functional circuit. By 1978, 20,000 functions could fit on a single silicon chip. This tremendous growth in circuit density reduced the cost of an electronic function from nearly $10 in 1950 to less than $.01 in 1978. This trend, reflecting both technology and manufacturing improvements, continued through the 1980s. It was estimated that by 1990 a single chip would contain 10 million functions or more and cost less than a hundredth of a cent per function. The radically changing semiconductor technology was responsible for the reduction of the retail price of an electronic calculator from $1,600 to $10 in a decade. It was also

Exhibit 1   **Summary of Selected Financial Data (Millions of Dollars)**

Year Ended December 31	1985	1984	1983	1982	1981	1980	1979	1978	1977	1976
Net sales billed	$4,924.5	$5,741.6	$4,579.8	$4,326.6	$4,206.0	$4,074.7	$3,224.1	$2,549.9	$2,046.5	$1,658.6
Operating costs and expenses	4,952.3	5,215.8	4,867.9	4,090.9	3,953.1	3,656.0	2,904.8	2,296.4	1,835.7	1,496.0
Profit (loss) from operations	(27.8)	525.8	(288.1)	235.7	252.9	418.7	319.3	253.5	210.8	162.6
Other income (expense) net	(46.8)	9.6	.9	10.5	(36.6)	4.6	8.9	12.3	9.3	23.8
Interest on loans	(40.4)	(48.9)	(36.0)	(33.1)	(41.3)	(44.3)	(19.5)	(8.4)	(9.2)	(8.3)
Income (loss) before provision (credit) for income taxes	(115.0)	486.5	(323.2)	213.1	175.0	379.0	308.7	257.4	210.9	178.1
Provision (credit) for income taxes	3.7	170.5	(177.8)	69.1	66.5	166.8	135.8	117.1	94.3	80.7
Net income (loss)	(118.7)	316.0	(145.4)	144.0	108.5	212.2	172.9	140.3	116.6	97.4
Earnings (loss) per common share (average outstanding during year)	$(4.76)	$13.05	$(6.09)	$6.10	$4.62	$9.22	$7.58	$6.15	$5.11	$4.25
Cash dividends declared per common share	2.00	2.00	2.00	2.00	2.00	2.00	2.00	1.76	1.41	1.08
Common shares (average shares outstanding during year, in thousands)	24,948	24,210	23,862	23,609	23,483	23,021	22,799	22,794	22,842	22,933

December 31	1985	1984	1983	1982	1981	1980	1979	1978	1977	1976
Working capital	$ 401.8	$ 446.2	$ 221.2	$ 568.2	$ 432.1	$ 327.9	$ 200.7	$ 304.3	$ 365.7	$ 364.8
Property, plant, and equipment (net)	1,450.0	1,481.1	1,199.0	1,096.3	1,105.5	1,097.4	812.5	572.7	394.1	302.9
Total assets	3,076.1	3,423.4	2,713.3	2,631.4	2,310.5	2,413.7	1,908.2	1,494.1	1,234.3	1,110.2
Long-term debt	381.9	380.7	225.1	214.0	211.7	211.7	17.6	19.1	29.7	38.2
Stockholders' equity	1,427.7	1,540.5	1,202.7	1,360.8	1,260.1	1,164.5	952.9	821.3	723.9	642.8
Employees	77,872	86,563	80,696	80,007	83,714	89,875	85,779	78,571	68,521	66,162
Stockholders of record	34,456	30,701	32,856	28,994	31,460	28,370	28,405	26,247	24,438	22,425

Source: Texas Instruments, annual report, 1985.

401

responsible for the transformation of the 3-ton computer, which cost $200,000 in the mid-1950s, into a 12-ounce hand-held unit priced at $300 in 1978. The power of this rapidly changing semiconductor technology was the primary force behind the "electronics revolution."

According to Texas Instruments' predictions at that time, the world electronics industry would grow from about $100 billion in 1977 to $325 billion in the late 1980s as reductions in the cost of electronic logic continued. This growth could reach even $400 billion if the next generation of chips, called VLSI (very large-scale integrated) circuits, could be introduced. That would make electronics the world's fourth-largest industry in a decade. Automobiles, steel, and chemicals would be the only larger ones because each was expected to generate about $500 billion in revenue.

One important area of growth in the semiconductor industry was memory. The metal-oxide semiconductor (MOS) memory was considered the most important semiconductor device. By 1978, these memory components accounted for $820 million in sales, or nearly 12 percent of the total worldwide semiconductor market. The growth in sales was expected to continue because of high demand aided by the decreasing prices of memory. In 1978, Intel was the memory leader. Texas Instruments decided to challenge Intel's position and launched a major program to supply the market with several new MOS memory products. However, Intel, which was a pioneer in memories and microprocessors, remained a strong competitor because its systems background and orientation were more suited to the industry's demands.

Intel understood that the growing complexity of circuits had transformed the products of the semiconductor industry from mere components to systems. The new company was able to grow fast because the large semiconductor manufacturers had not yet changed their component orientation. Even Texas Instruments found it hard to adjust to the systems culture, despite the corporation's systems background.

Another important development in the technology of memory was the creation of the random access memory (dynamic RAM), which took the computer mainframe memory business away from magnetic cores by 1973. The first two such memory devices were 4-kilobit (4K) and 16-kilobit (16K). The competition for dominance in the sales of this product was strong. Mostek, the market leader, lost its leadership to Texas Instruments because it did not expand its manufacturing capacity fast enough to meet the demands when the market took off. Texas Instruments' management considered it very important to be a leader and volume producer of 16K memories because "it is extremely difficult to go to the next big product if you haven't made it in the previous big part."[2] The next big product for the industry was the powerful 64K-memory chip, capable of sorting 65,536 bits of data. This was the basic memory size of a minicomputer in the early 1970s. Texas Instruments announced its 64K memory on September 8, 1978, several months ahead of its competitors. Being first to market was thought to improve the odds of being profitable and offered a good chance of the product becoming the industry standard.

Microprocessors, which permitted the construction of a computer on a chip, were the next major development in the industry. Intel dominated this business since the mid-1970s with a medium performance (8-bit) microprocessor. Ironically Texas Instruments had already introduced in the mid-1970s a new computer family that tied together microcomputers and high-performance (16-bit) microprocessors. The product, however, was too advanced for the market at that time, and it did not become a standard. Moreover, Intel and Motorola were able to surpass Texas Instruments in complex microprocessors because they made firm commitments to customers with regard to delivery times and disclosed details about their production costs and future prices. The customers thus had time and information to design their product strategies accordingly.

Distributed computing was another area of strong competition. The availability of software and product diversity were critical success factors in this business. Texas Instruments, IBM, and some major Japanese companies were expected to be the primary forces in this segment.

In mid-1981, the worldwide semiconductor business began stagnating. Profits diminished as a result of rapidly falling prices. The weakened European currencies sharpened the problem of U.S. semiconductor makers in European markets. One U.S. company executive admitted that his company's business was down 25 percent in Europe in terms of currency conversions alone. The economic recession in the United States and Europe caused the demand for computer parts to drop sharply, and the resulting overcapacity in the industry led to fierce price competition. The situation deteriorated when the Japanese introduced the 64K RAM memory. Texas Instruments developed this device in the 1970s but was not successful with its product launch. Japanese companies—including Hitachi, Nippon Electric, and Fujitsu—succeeded in capturing about 70 percent of the market for this product. Although Texas Instruments did not lose its leadership in the semiconductor business, its strength was tested severely in Europe.

One more problem appeared when the company discovered that the magnetic bubble memories on which considerable research effort had been expended, at an investment of nearly $100 million, would not catch on with enough computer makers. For a decade, Texas Instruments had done research on these memory devices because they promised to be a cheap and reliable replacement for mechanical rotating-disk memories.

In 1984, the industry situation improved. Sales increased 54 percent to reach $20.6 billion, and manufacturers invested about $6 billion in plant and equipment, increasing capacity by 60 percent. Texas Instruments was among them. Committed to pioneering technology, Texas Instruments introduced a new generation of 256K dynamic random access memory chip. Capital investment made in the transition from 16K chips to 64K chips proved to be very useful in the production of 256K chips.

In 1985, it became clear that much of the sales growth that prompted this massive investment was simply the result of an overheated computer industry. After the shakeout in the computer industry, the survivors scaled back production, and the semiconductor makers found themselves plunged in overcapacity. New semiconductor orders were running at only 72 percent of shipments, one of the lowest levels since the industry began keeping records in the mid-1970s. The severe price cutting that followed resulted in a significant decrease in earnings for several semiconductor companies. The selling prices for semiconductors dropped as much as 88 percent, causing sales of integrated circuits to sink 19 percent in 1985. Although it was expected that an increase in demand would raise the price especially for certain devices that could be manufactured only in specialized factories, the total capacity had to shrink.

The Japanese firms were again accused for the worldwide overcapacity. Their rate of investment in semiconductor plants (27 percent) was much higher than that of U.S. firms (18 percent). It is believed that the Japanese investments were made in order to dominate the electronics industry through the domination of its main supply—the chips. In 1985, the Japanese captured a significant share of the $500-million-a-year market for dynamic random access memory (D-RAM) chips, which were used to temporarily store data being processed by a computer. The erasable, programmable, read-only memory (E-PROM)—a chip that remembers 256,000 bits of information—was another area of interest to the Japanese. Their entrance into this market resulted in a price drop from $17 to $4 within 11 months. According to U.S. chipmakers, the chip had to be sold by them for at least $6.85 to make a profit.

American manufacturers, feeling threatened, decided to take several measures that would help them remain competitive, including legal and political actions against certain Japanese practices that were considered as dumping. Despite the fact that some Japanese companies were found responsible for dumping, the punishment meted out to them did not hurt. Only half of the revenues of the leading Japanese chipmakers came from chips; the rest came from products that used the chips. Forward integration was a major advantage to the leading Japanese chipmakers.

American semiconductor companies also started forming alliances in order to counter the Japanese threat, and they shared research and development, marketing, and even manufacturing. For example, in 1984, Advanced Micro Devices agreed to give LSI Logic some of its own chip designs in exchange for access to LSI Logic's software for designing chips. Most semiconductor companies forged partnerships or other agreements with several U.S. and Japanese companies. Intel had about 17 arrangements of this kind. Although few of the alliances extended to sharing production, this was changing. LSI Logic started a joint venture with Kawasaki Steel to produce the silicon wafers on which advanced integrated circuits were etched. Advanced Micro Devices planned to subcontract or share some production. A few companies tried forward integration, but this did not prove to be a successful strategy because the most talented engineers and managers of the chipmakers left the company after it was acquired. Fairchild, acquired by Schlumberger, and Mostek, acquired by United Technologies and Thomson, became two of the biggest money losers in the semiconductor business.

Several semiconductor companies began focusing on the design and production of complex chips for very specific applications. However, because the number of companies pursuing this strategy was increasing, the expensive development effort in application-specific chips was not very profitable overall, even if a particular application was very profitable. A compromise strategy that seemed more economical and less risky was to produce semicustom chips. These chips were half finished so that the customer still needed to use computer-aided engineering systems to add the final touches. In this way, the chipmaker avoided the risk of investing large sums in the design and production of an application-specific chip that might fail in the market. According to one estimate, semicustom chips accounted for $320 million, or 5.5 percent of the total chip market, in 1985 and was estimated to reach an annual sales of $8.3 billion in 1990.[3]

When it became apparent that the pioneering small companies, such as LSI Logic, had success with the semicustom chips, every major chipmaker decided to enter this market. Motorola and Texas Instruments seized significant market shares for certain types of semicustom chips, and it was expected that in two or three years they would drive out about 40 small firms in the semiconductor business.

Survival was not an issue for the big five semiconductor manufacturers—Texas Instruments, Intel, Motorola, Advanced Micro Technologies, and National Semiconductor—but they were challenged to handle successfully the transition from profitable standard products to application-specific and semicustom chips. Coping with the change involved paying closer attention to their customers' needs and responding to these needs fast by revamping their factories to emphasize quick turnaround times.

THE CONSUMER ELECTRONICS BUSINESS

Texas Instruments' history in the consumer electronics market went back to the early 1970s. It decided to enter this market at a strategy meeting in December 1971. For the following two to three years, the company placed most of its development into the consumer business rather than into computer memories and microprocessors (as its competitors did) and compromised an early leadership in semiconductor memories and microcomputers. At that time, industry analysts regarded Texas Instruments' entry into the consumer electronics market with great skepticism. In late 1978, however, Texas Instruments proved that it had won its big gamble.

The strategy that made Texas Instruments very successful in this market in the late 1970s was cost leadership. The Texas Instruments strategy was best illustrated by the calculator and digital watch. Pursuing this strategy, Texas Instruments succeeded in building a flourishing, profitable business in consumer electronics; in fall 1978, it probably had the highest worldwide revenues in both calculators and digital watches. Pretax profits from Texas Instruments' consumer electronics business were estimated at $28 million in 1978.

Texas Instruments, according to a major 1978 market study, had become "the most feared competitor in the consumer electronics business," and an industry analyst predicted that Texas Instruments and the Japanese "were going to share the huge, consumer electronics business in the 1980s, being the two major suppliers."[4]

Although Texas Instruments seemed unwilling to communicate and explain its strategy, Fred Bucy, its President, ordered in 1978 a major push to promote the company's image as a leader in technology. Bucy admitted that the image of a high-technology innovator was key to the company's strategy. He explained that Texas Instruments' fundamental strategy was not to be the second to enter a market and then overwhelm the competition with its manufacturing power. This was consistent with how the company was then perceived. One of its competitors described Texas Instruments as "an innovator in applying technology and exploiting it." In fact, Texas Instruments was considered in late 1978 to be the only semiconductor producer that was building end-user products and developing new applications for all market areas—consumer, military, and computers. According to an industry expert, the company's driving force seemed to be in innovating markets.

Texas Instruments' strategy in the consumer electronics business was, in several instances, compared with that of its Japanese competitors. According to Bruce Henderson, the President and founder of the Boston Consulting Group, "Texas Instruments follows the same underlying competitive approach the Japanese have used. It combines scale, technology, and capital intensity"—three important factors whose combination made it hard for the competitors to catch up. In addition to these factors, Texas Instruments adopted a long-term orientation. The company built new plants while its first plant was not yet fully utilized. The reasoning behind this action was, again, according to Henderson, to take advantage of declining unit costs in order to price its product below the price of those of competitors and thereby capture a big share of a growth market.

However, the consumer electronics bubble burst for Texas Instruments in the early 1980s, and 1981 proved to be a difficult year. The price of its stock plunged 50 percent from $150 to $75. On May 29, the company laid off 2,890 employees, or 3 percent of its workforce. In addition to the unfavorable conditions prevailing in the semiconductor business internationally, Texas Instruments experienced problems in some segments of its consumer electronics business. Specifically the firm faced strong competition from Hewlett-Packard in the high-priced end of its calculators business and from Japanese companies in the low-priced end of the same business. This resulted in a loss of market share in both ends.

Texas Instruments' attempt to enter the home computer market also failed. Its target customer was the ordinary American family to whom the firm offered its model 99/4. This model could be used to play games, teach children vocabulary, or keep track of household finances. However, with a price of over $1,000, it was too expensive for most families. Business professionals and skilled hobbyists, on the other hand, found the product to be unsophisticated. Although Texas Instruments placed emphasis on home computers, it appeared to have ignored the market for personal computers designed for professionals and very small businesses, computers that could sell in the $1,000-to-$10,000 range. During that time, the dominant companies in that market were Tandy and Apple Computer. IBM was planning to join them soon. It is interesting to note that Texas Instruments had designed such a personal computer two years earlier. However, an intracompany rivalry between the consumer group and the computer group for presence in the same market eliminated two personal computer models aimed at professionals and small businesses.

A third problematic area was the digital watch business. At the time when Texas Instruments started shipping the first all-electronic analog watch, the bulk of the watch market was still dominated by analog-style models. The new watch used a display to create the image of "hands." The product had good market penetration in the late 1970s—especially because of the company's aggressive pricing strategy— but it had some "user-hostile" features, such as a push button and a display that was impossible to read in bright sunlight. Later, the company failed to adapt to market demands for more fashionable features and remained firm in its commitment to producing low-end, low-margin watches. Keeping a close eye solely on production costs with a total disregard to consumer preferences, it produced watches with cheap plastic bands. These watches were soon replaced by competitors' watches that showed time continuously on liquid crystal displays. A one-time member of the digital watch group recalled the following:

> Fred [Bucy] and Mark [Shepherd] kept pushing to slash the price to $9.95. This meant having a plastic case and band. We kept telling them consumers didn't want that, but they wouldn't listen.[5]

After initial success, the firm reported losses of $10 million a year in the watch market for two consecutive years.

The company responded to all these problems with what it called "a partial, strategic restructuring of its business priorities," which basically meant a modification of its strategy in several areas. In the professional calculators business, Texas Instruments emphasized an extremely aggressive pricing strategy that consisted of two rebate offers and the launching of a new line of calculators that started at under $10. In programmable calculators, it challenged Hewlett-Packard by discounting its top-of-the-line TI-59 by 40 percent. Another $20 cash rebate was planned to bring the product within reach of the student market.

Similar tactics were employed in the home computer business that Texas Instruments and Atari were pioneering. Texas Instruments repositioned its product by decreasing its price and adding a wide array of software packages. It also extended its retail network by adding outlets and by attempting to sell through mass merchandisers, such as J. C. Penney. The company also decided to target personal computers to professionals and very small businesses at a point in time when industry experts believed that it was too late. Texas Instruments' argument, as expressed by Grant Dore, the Senior Vice President of Marketing, was that "there's very low penetration in the small-business market at this point in time, and quite a bit of disenchantment by disgruntled users," so "there's plenty of opportunity there."[6]

The losses in the digital watch business and the lack of impressive results in the magnetic memories business forced the company to completely pull out of the two markets that it had pioneered. The products themselves were not a significant fraction of corporate sales because they amounted to no more than $150 million annually. Although the short-term effects of these cutbacks seemed to be positive because they would help the earnings picture the next year, the long-range implications worried industry observers. These abrupt cancellations of products after large investments and extensive research shook the financial market's confidence in Texas Instruments. The response of the stock market to these announcements was a quick 10 percent tumbling of the company's stock.

Competitors expected these product withdrawals by Texas Instruments without early notice to have repercussions on Texas Instruments' calculator business because retailers who carried watches carried calculators as well. Texas Instruments' officers had a different opinion, which was expressed by William Sick, Jr., the Vice President of the Consumer Products Division. Giving up digital watches freed resources that were needed for the company to keep up with the semiconductor industry's fast-rising capital demands. Additionally, pulling out of the digital watch market not only would not hurt Texas Instruments, but also would strengthen its consumer business, because "for the same investment in the areas where we have a leading position—calculators and educational products—the payoff will be greater. It would have taken a tremendous additional investment to get a major position in the watch market and to make the profits the company expects."[7]

The one big success story for Texas Instruments in the consumer electronics business was in educational electronics. Since its 1978 introduction of a learning aid called Speak and Spell, Texas Instruments dominated the educational products market. This revolutionary new product was used to teach children how to speak and spell. It was built around a voice synthesizer on a single chip. The idea of the voice synthesizer materialized through a 1973 program that the company started to encourage innovation. Texas Instruments decided to establish annual $20,000 grants that would be distributed to employees who had new ideas on how to improve a product or a process. Every year, $1 million was split among 40 Senior Technical Officers who evaluated competing ideas and distributed the grants. If an employee's idea was rejected by an evaluator, the employee had the option of pursuing his or her idea with another evaluator. One of the employees, Gene Frantz, conceived the idea of a low-cost speech synthesizer built on a single chip with a voice quality equal to that of the telephone system. His team was awarded a $20,000 grant, through which it developed a breakthrough technology whose first application was a talking learning aid to teach spelling. The first Speak and Spell machine led to the development of other, similar learning aids for children, and the firm had an overwhelming success.

In early 1982, Texas Instruments decided not to increase its commitment to the consumer products division but rather to phase it out—with the exception of personal computers and the Speak and Spell learning aids.

Texas Instruments always followed the strategy of being a price leader in the market. By offering a low price to consumers, it attempted to achieve high volume of sales with associated reduction in manufacturing costs. This strategy had been successfully tested in the government and the industrial sectors. On the consumer sector, however, the policy of tying introductory price to estimates of future volumes, a policy called forward pricing, did not have the same success. After losses in the watch and computer markets, Texas Instruments chose to depart from this long-standing policy. Two of the changes in the pricing policy were an inclusion of a premium in the price to reflect new technological capabilities and the 1984 application of a different method for establishing a cost basis.

According to the new method, the expenses for introducing a consumer product into the market would not be charged against the manager's operating budget but rather would be considered strategic expenses and charged to the OST system.[8] This relieved project managers from the responsibility of quickly recovering product introduction expenses.

The price sensitivity of the consumers, on which Texas Instruments based its strategy, did not prove to be the most important factor in consumers' purchasing decisions. Customers appeared also to be sensitive to the product's style and prestige, and they had clear ideas about its use.

In an attempt to improve the company's marketing resources and skills, Texas Instruments assigned the marketing responsibilities to Senior Vice President Grant Dore, a long-time Texas Instruments executive who was also a member of the company's policy and corporate development committee. In fall 1980, it also replaced 26 different advertising agencies with New York's McCann-Erickson, which would handle the company's worldwide advertising. Dore's goal was twofold: first to "institutionalize marketing" inside the company by putting into practice the idea of design-to-market cost and second to increase the company's awareness in the public "as a technological leader whose products have value and quality."[9] The design-to-market cost used in the strategic plans included not only the costs of manufacturing and design but also the cost of bringing the product to the market. Dore also emphasized support and advertising costs.

At the same time, Texas Instruments instituted some changes in its policies with regard to personal computers. It improved the equipment itself, started offering more software, decreased the price by two thirds, and started selling through general retailers instead of computer shops. Also, it improved its relations with distributors of electronic components in 1981 by abolishing its relatively small, wholly owned distributor—the TI Supply—which took business away from independent distributors. Another improvement was the reduction of the paperwork and time needed by a distributor to fill a large customer's order for different Texas Instruments products. Specifically the distributor had to receive separate price quotes from the different product customer centers (PCCs) that manufactured each product. This was time consuming and prevented the distributor from winning a price break in exchange for a big order of diverse items. To correct this situation, Texas Instruments offered to centralize the process and let its distributors use Texas Instruments terminals to determine product availability and price discounts. In another attempt to better itself in the minicomputer business, Texas Instruments launched its first machine for small businesses priced at $7,500 in late 1981; in

August 1982, it announced another model. It also developed an elaborate new marketing program for signing up authorized dealers—who, after training in computer sales and service and with generous trade terms and financing from Walter E. Heller and Co., would be able to lease machines to their customers. The cost of this and other marketing programs was partly responsible for depressed minicomputers earnings in 1981.

In May 1982, in a new effort to enhance the company's marketing position, the top management appointed Stewart Carrell to a senior post that combined strategic planning, technology development, and marketing responsibilities. He also was the first to direct a corporate-wide marketing staff.

Despite all these changes, 1983 was "the most difficult period in TI history" and the year in which it decided to withdraw from the home computer business. The company took $660 million in writeoffs on home computers and posted a net loss of $145.4 million on sales of $4.6 billion for the year. Texas Instruments, which had 20 percent share of the home computer market, was not expected to drop its 99/4A computer. Until September 1983, it emphatically declared that it intended to support the home computer operation. However, as Bucy explained, "our 99/4A business did pick up but not at a sufficient rate. It was a bitter pill to swallow. But how much blood can you lose?"[10] According to Chairman Mark Shepherd, Texas Instruments would continue to support and service the 99/4A. Part of the write-down amount was used to set up reserves that would protect retailers from losses resulting from Texas Instruments' actions. The company also promised to build some peripheral products to fulfill commitments to retailers, to manufacture software for an unspecified time, and to continue the model's television advertising throughout the Christmas season. It would continue to provide one-year warranties on the 99/4A equipment and would repair out-of-warranty machines.

In late 1983, Texas Instruments decided to introduce marketing to the management ranks by hiring as President of its Consumer Group a veteran marketing executive from Procter and Gamble. Peter Field was the General Manager of Procter and Gamble's Coffee Division before he joined TI. That was the first time that Texas Instruments had chosen to hire at this level a marketing executive without a degree or background in engineering.

EVOLUTION OF THE PLANNING SYSTEM

The formal Objectives, Strategies, and Tactics (OST) system[11] had changed very little since its full implementation in the late 1960s and early 1970s. From its inception, OST was designed to stimulate creativity and innovation at all levels of the organization by requiring lower management involvement in the long-run strategic planning process. Strategic and operating resources remained separated through the reporting process. Many managers had dual responsibilities for the strategic and operating functions. The four-loop system for OST implementation also remained intact.

However, the utilization of the system changed markedly under Bucy and Shepherd. The process of decentralized strategic decision making was replaced by an informal top-down planning system.

A further change was the increase in formal reporting and financial analysis to cope with the organizational growth. Even top management realized that as the firm grew bigger, the planning exercise became a number crunching instead of a thinking exercise.[12] Texas Instruments' response was the "brain wave" program, a financial-planning tool to take care of the number crunching, thus giving managers more time to think about long-term strategies.[13]

Another modification to the OST framework was the establishment of Strategic Business Units (SBUs) headed by group Vice Presidents or Assistant Vice Presidents. A SBU combined several product/customer centers (PCCs) for strategic analysis.

Moreover, Texas Instruments' difficulties in the early 1980s caused it to rethink its matrix structure. The functional departments had grown in size and power. The PCC managers were sometimes unable to get their products manufactured to meet the demands of the market or to make the changes necessary to keep up with technology because of the dependence on powerful functional managers who differed on the allocation of resources. To rectify the situation, the PCCs were restructured in 1982. They were made bigger and their managers were given control of all resources: dollars, personnel, and facilities to create, manufacture, and market their products. By bringing production under the direct control of the PCC managers and placing them under SBU general managers, Texas Instruments moved further away from its dual structure planning and closer to a planning structure followed by other large, diversified corporations.

CHANGING FORTUNES AND SHIFTING CULTURE

A Culture with Some Notable Similarities to the Japanese

The organizational culture at Texas Instruments, in its heyday of the 1970s, received favorable attention from both the business and the academic press. In the company, culture was a religion. The climate polarized people—either you were incorporated into the culture or you were rejected, was the conclusion of one scholar.[14]

Texas Instruments had much of the style of a Japanese company. Like Japanese companies, Texas Instruments stressed a strong spirit of belonging, a strong work ethic, competitive zeal, company loyalty, and rational decision making. More than 83 percent of all Texas Instruments employees were organized into "people involvement teams" that sought ways to improve their own productivity. But some Texas Instruments employees perceived themselves as subservient to the success of the corporate entity and as completely interchangeable as auto parts.[15]

As in Japanese companies, the employees at Texas Instruments did not normally get fired—particularly those who had worked for the company five years or more, because company officials believed that five years were necessary to train a full-fledged Texas Instruments manager. Although firing was not the punishment for a manager who did not meet the goals that he or she had set, Texas Instruments was not compassionate with such a manager. He or she was moved to the side, down, or to a special assignment.

Corporate loyalty was another important feature of the Texas Instruments culture. A means to ensure it was to hire college graduates and train them in the company's ways. The efforts to cover other aspects of the employees' lives included the maintenance of a big recreation center with super-modern facilities and a seventy-five-acre recreation area on Lake Texoma. The experienced professionals that Texas Instruments hired from other companies were often misfits. Lack of loyalty to the company was cited as an important reason for their lack of success.

Work ethic was a cornerstone of the Texas Instruments culture. Overtime work was common, and so were 5:30 P.M. meetings. A forty-two-and-a-half-hour week usually included work on Saturday mornings.

The importance of seniority was another common feature with the Japanese. Instead of having badges on which color denoted levels of authority, as in other companies, Texas Instruments used badge color to indicate the number of years an employee was with the company.

Changing Times

Because of the changing fortunes at Texas Instruments, reorganization became frequent. In the hard-pressed computer memory operations, for example, executives were shifted at least once a year since 1979. Former employees ascribed such shifts to a company theory of "motivation through anxiety." According to the theory, when one has 10 tons of canaries—or executives—in a 5-ton truck, one has to beat on the roof from time to time to make sure at least half of them are up and flying.[16]

However, the reorganization did not always prove successful. Texas Instruments' top executives created an informal power structure and set values and unwritten rules that fostered a culture that could not easily respond to environmental changes. Also, because its U.S. semiconductor operations were based in Texas—far from the other centers of this technology, such as Silicon Valley in California and Massachusetts on the East Coast—Texas Instruments developed an insularity that was not conducive to fast acquisition of information about manufacturing processes in other companies. It should be noted that insularity refers to attitude rather than to location. The company appeared to have an unshakeable faith in its own ideas. When these ideas were contradicted by facts and forecasts appeared to be disappointing, a substantial effort was put forth by the executives to present unfavorable facets in a favorable way. As one executive recalled, "We spent more time saying what we thought Fred [Bucy] and Mark [Shepherd] wanted to hear than saying what we thought."[17]

The company's deteriorating performance led to what an analyst called "management by fear."[18] It would appear that top management was reluctant to delegate authority. An ex-employee said the following:

> Lower level managers had lost a great deal of authority. Much of their control had been shifted into the North building [Texas Instruments' headquarters]. Proposed products were defined and redefined there ad infinitum. Eventually you were just given a product that was a square peg and told to fit it into the round hole of a market.

Communications inside the company tended to be difficult.[19] That was partly attributed to the perceived reputation of the two top officers, Mark Shepherd and Fred Bucy, as "very autocratic, very powerful, and very intent on controlling things." The communication problem was compounded by the style of the division managers, who were used to driving rather than motivating people. As a 17-year Texas Instruments veteran recalled, "it got to the point where projects were just numbers and people along with them."[20]

Although the environment at Texas Instruments had grown more intense and emotional, it could hardly be described as totalitarian and repressive. Shepherd, then the company's CEO, said this:

> We get so damned intense sometimes on a problem, and pound the table and holler at one another, that people that are not used to us think we're about to let blood. That's where some of this dictatorial crap comes from. Some of the biggest arguments I've ever had were with Pat [Pat Haggerty, his predecessor] and with Fred. But the purpose behind all this is really to have a very open and participative corporate society. People will set tougher goals for themselves than you would dare set, and most of the time they'll make them.

A plaque on the wall of Shepherd's small, cluttered office summed up his attitude: "Nothing is ever accomplished by a reasonable man."[21]

A NEW PRESIDENT CHANGES TEXAS INSTRUMENTS' STRATEGIC FOCUS

In April 1984, an important management change took place at Texas Instruments. Fred Bucy, the President, replaced Mark Shepherd as the CEO. Shepherd, who had been CEO since 1969, remained Chairman and kept control of Texas Instruments' strategic planning, communications, legal, and finance departments as its "chief corporate officer." Bucy had been in the new post for just over a year when he abruptly resigned in May 1985. He was succeeded by Executive Vice President Jerry Junkins, who was elected President and CEO on May 24, 1985.

Junkins placed emphasis on military contracting, which had always been important to the company's sales. High hopes were placed on the HARM missile, which used hundreds of Texas Instruments' most sophisticated electronic components. In 1985, a $522-million contract was signed with the U.S. Navy for the building of 1,571 of these missiles. The contract had the long-term potential of generating an additional $5 billion in revenues. Not only was defense work more predictable than industrial semiconductors, but also it seemed that Texas Instruments was more comfortable selling to a customer who required detailed technical analyses rather than to customers who had to be persuaded by marketing techniques.[22]

Junkins also changed the way Texas Instruments did business in civilian markets by switching the focus from high-volume to high-profit products. He opened the company to more technology sharing and insisted on the memory-chip business despite strong Japanese competition. He believed that the ability to make smaller memory circuits was useful in making faster and more powerful logic circuits. In 1985, Texas Instruments built a computer memory chip that could store four million units of information. This was a technological leap that gave Texas Instruments competitive advantage in the advanced artificial intelligence market segment.

The new CEO acknowledged that marketing had been one of Texas Instruments' notable shortcomings. "We have to listen to what the consumer wants," he said. "As the market evolves, a lot of other people will have good technology. It's important we make a balanced shift to a market-driven customer relationship."[23]

In an attempt to improve marketing practices in the semiconductor business, he assigned 55 percent of the field sales engineers to give support and advice to the designers of new electronic products. That was a task on which only a few sales engineers had specialized in the past. They had mostly concentrated on selling mass quantities of inexpensive commodity electronic devices. Marketing improvements included a joint effort with Wyle Electronics Distribution Group, a unit of Wyle Laboratories, to build three centers at which Wyle would test and program semifinished Texas Instruments logic chips using equipment supplied by Texas Instruments. Because Wyle kept big supplies of chips on hand, the centers enabled Texas Instruments to shorten its delivery lead time from six weeks to three days.[24]

Junkins' goal in taking these steps was to make half of Texas Instruments' semiconductor sales by 1990 consist of more complicated, higher-profit semiconductors—including customized and specialized logic chips, chips for military applications, and very large-scale integrated chips. In 1986, these products constituted about 15 percent of its semiconductor sales. Because competitors were pursuing similar strategies, the senior executives and Junkins himself undertook sales calls on major customers. In order to encourage the exchange of marketing ideas among the employees, he introduced roundtable talks involving managers, engineers, and line workers. Although Texas Instruments had helped create pioneering technologies—such as in digital watches, personal computers, and hand-held calculators—it finally lost market share to others who had a better understanding of the marketplace and customers' needs. Junkins was determined to cure Texas Instruments' marketing myopia.

NOTES

1. "TI Shows U.S. Business How to Survive in the 1980's," *Business Week* (Sept. 18, 1978): 66.

2. Ibid., 71.

3. B. Uttal, "Who Will Survive the Microchip Shakeout?" *Fortune* 113 (June 6, 1986): 85.

4. "TI Shows U.S. Business," 67.

5. B. Uttal, "Texas Instruments Regroups," *Fortune* 106 (Aug. 9, 1982): 42.

6. "When Marketing Failed at Texas Instruments," *Business Week* (June 22, 1981): 93.

7. Ibid., 92.

8. For the details of the OST system, see R. F. Vancil, "Texas Instruments Incorporated: Management Systems in 1972," Harvard Business School case 9-172-054 (Boston: Harvard Graduate School of Business Administration, 1972).

9. "When Marketing Failed at Texas Instruments," 91.

10. "Why TI May Well Return to Home Computers," *Business Week* (November 14, 1983): 48–49.

11. Vancil, "Texas Instruments Incorporated: Management Systems in 1972."

12. "Texas Instruments Cleans Up Its Act: The Electronics Giant Is Slashing Its Own Red Tape," *Business Week* (Sept. 19, 1983): 57.

13. See Case 5 for other planning aids that Texas Instruments introduced to minimize the drudgery of analysis.

14. "TI Shows U.S. Business," 68.

15. Ibid.

16. Uttal, "Texas Instruments Regroups," 40.

17. Ibid., 44.

18. C. Alexander, "A Computer Whiz Short-Circuits," *Time* (Dec. 7, 1981): 59.

19. Uttal, "Texas Instruments Regroups," 44.

20. "TI Shows U.S. Business," 70.

21. S. N. Chakravarty, "Recovering from the Trauma," *Forbes* 133 (Apr. 23, 1984): 41.

22. Ibid., 64.

23. "Texas Instruments: New Boss, Big Job," *Fortune* 112 (July 8, 1985): 64.

24. Ibid.

Alfa-Laval

After leading Alfa-Laval through four years of major strategic and administrative changes, Harry Faulkner, the Chief Executive Officer, braced for the challenges ahead:

> We are now at a crossroads. We are back to the old question—is there growth potential in our old businesses, or do we have to diversify further? We have divested most of our nonprofitable 'dogs.' We now have the cash to do something else. In fact, 25 percent of our turnover is in cash. Should we stick to our old knitting, or use our cash resources to become some sort of a holding company? We have reached our short term goals. . . . What should our new long term goals be?

Alfa-Laval, a Swedish multinational corporation, was a world market leader in high-speed separators, compact heat exchangers, oil purifiers and heat exchangers for ships, milking systems, barn equipment, and turnkey dairies. In 1984, the Alfa-Laval Group consisted of approximately 140 companies with 40 plants in 35 countries. It employed nearly 16,000 persons, of whom 6,000 worked in Sweden. Its sales turnover in 1983 was 9.3 billion Swedish Kronor (SEK), or approximately $1.1 billion in U.S. dollars, and its income before special adjustments and taxes was approximately $96 million in U.S. dollars.[1]

The company celebrated its centennial in 1983. This case briefly describes Alfa-Laval's history, its impressive technical and business accomplishments of the past 100 years, and Faulkner's attempts to ensure its continued success in the future.

THE FIRST ONE HUNDRED YEARS

The forerunner of Alfa-Laval was AB Separator, a private limited company. In 1878, Gustav de Laval and his friend, financier Oscar Lamm, formed a partnership to capitalize on the former's new invention, the continuously functioning centrifugal separator. The invention was of immediate interest to the dairy industry and was used for separating milk from cream.

Lamm realized that the Swedish market for separators was rather small. He therefore appointed sales agents in Germany, France, and the United Kingdom to sell the new separator. Subsequently the company set up its own sales subsidiaries in a number of foreign countries. In 1883, the company formed its first overseas manufacturing subsidiary, De Laval Separator Company (Lavalco) in the United States. The Austrian subsidiary was formed in 1897, and the Germany subsidiary was established in 1907. The demand for separators remained strong during the early years of the twentieth century. Increased butter consumption throughout the world gave farmers increased purchasing power and the incentive to invest in their own separators.

Lamm left the company in 1886 over differences with de Laval. De Laval, the inventor, tried to expand the company's product line and was successful in designing a commercially successful hand-operated separator. In 1889, the company also acquired the Alfa patent for conical metal discs. By the time de Laval stepped down as Chairman of the Board in 1908, the company had begun development work on a milking machine. The milking machine, however, was not successful until 1918.

The superior quality of products marketed by AB Separator, together with its aggressive sales promotion policy, helped the company withstand the intense competition that developed, especially after its Alfa patent expired. Because of its high-quality image, AB Separator was not pressured into slashing its prices. This early emphasis on a differentiated high-quality product, sold at a premium price, set the tone for Alfa-Laval's business strategy in subsequent years.

During World War II, AB Separator was cut off from many of its business partners by the Skagerak blockade. The overseas marketing subsidiaries of AB Separator found it difficult to import machines and spare parts from Sweden and so began manufacturing some of these products on their own. The company's overseas factories, on the other hand, were forced to gear up for munitions production. Both of these circumstances proved fortuitous in hindsight. AB Separator came out of the war with a more diversified manufacturing base as well as more versatile engineering skills.

After the war, milking machines replaced separators as the hottest selling items in the dairy farming sector. Separators were then adapted to a variety of new industrial uses. By 1950, industrial sales represented over 50 percent of the company's total sales. Acquisitions and increased R&D expenditures helped the company to diversify its product line further. The Alfa-Laval product line in the early 1960s included plate heat exchangers, milk plant equipment, and industrial separators.

The pace of growth quickened in the mid-1960s, as the company—now called Alfa-Laval—continued to expand its product, customer, and geographic base. Although the dairy industry remained Alfa-Laval's stronghold, the company also developed expertise in other industrial sectors. Its high-quality centrifugal separator and heat exchange equipment for ships, for example, set the standards for the marine industry. Alfa-Laval soon became a global market leader in these products.

In the late 1960s, Alfa-Laval began to alter its business mission. It formerly considered itself solely a developer and manufacturer of machines, but it began to see itself as a provider of system solutions to industrial problems. This new strategy called for the sale of integrated industrial production systems, not just individual machines. In the food-processing sector, for example, Alfa-Laval began to sell complete milk-processing plants and utilized a number of the firm's own machines, together with bought-out products as needed.

By the 1970s, Alfa-Laval was a truly multinational corporation with 70 affiliates in 32 countries worldwide. As of 1976, the company had about 7,000 employees in Sweden and 11,000 in other countries. It served a variety of industries: agricultural, food, marine, chemical engineering, metal production, and pollution control. In the dairy, food-processing, and marine industries, it was the market leader. Exhibit 1 tracks the evolution of Alfa-Laval's product lines. Exhibit 2 shows the changes in its product groups over its first 100 years.

REVAMPING THE ORGANIZATIONAL STRUCTURE

By 1977, the company had a well-established international position, but top management felt that there were urgent problems that needed attention. Although the market shares were very high in several product lines (between 40 to 50 percent in separators, milking machines, and compact heat exchangers) and the gross margins were good, profitability and return on equity (ROE) were declining. For example, return on operating capital declined from 16.8 percent in 1974 to 12.7 percent in 1977; in the same period, ROE dropped from 12.8 percent to 9.5 percent. In addition, the company began experiencing unhealthy internal conflicts.

The company's organization chart at that time is shown in Exhibit 3. "Market companies" were subsidiaries in Sweden and abroad that marketed Alfa-Laval products. "Other companies and units" were autonomous Swedish subsidiaries that engaged in a number of diverse businesses. There were in all 60 different subsidiaries that directly reported to the President. The company was so decentralized that its subsidiaries could market the products of its competitors, in preference to those supplied by its own divisions. The "divisions" of Alfa-Laval were composed of both independent manufacturing companies and autonomous overseas operations. Although there was a central R&D function, each division was free to de-

Exhibit 1 **Alfa-Laval: Evolution of Product Lines (1880–1970)**

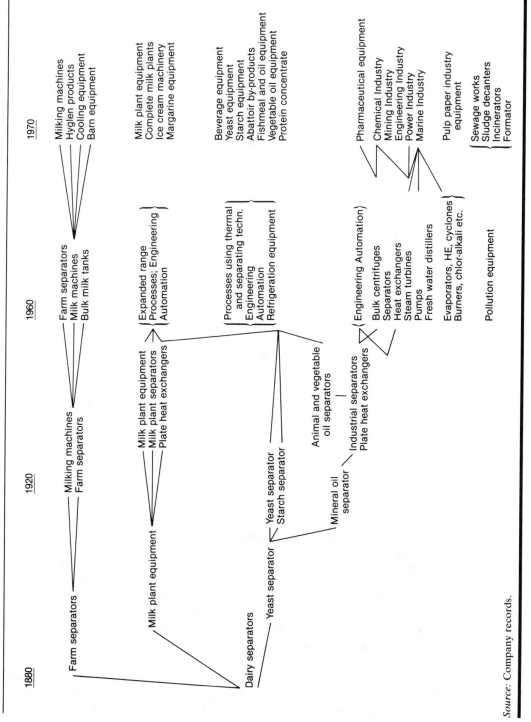

Source: Company records.

Exhibit 2   Sales as a Percent of Total, by Product Groupings (1890–1983)

Product Grouping	Year					
	1890	1900	1950	1960	1970	1983
Farming (%)	52.5	80.6	30.5	22.5	29.0	32.0
Dairy (%)	47.5	19.4	17.8	12.5	18.0 ⎫	
Industrial (%)	—	—	16.8	17.2	47.5 ⎬	54.0
Automotive Products and Turbines (%)	—	—	24.6	36.1	—	—
Other (%)	—	—	10.3	11.7	5.5	14.0

Source: Company records.

velop its own products. Faulkner described the confusion caused by this highly decentralized structure:

> Reporting relationships were very unclear. I was an executive vice president then, and yet I am sure that managers of some of the subsidiaries and divisions thought of me more as an assistant to the President. Relationships between managers in the divisions and daughter companies [subsidiaries] were equally unclear. The coordination between functions and across product line was poor.

Alfa-Laval's top management appointed a Swedish consultant to help resolve the company's organizational problems. The consultant confirmed that the reporting relationships between the divisions, daughter companies, and group management were not clear. In addition, he pointed out that Alfa-Laval was really comprised of three distinct businesses—agricultural, industrial, and a "conglomerate"—and that the competitive environment for each of these businesses was different. He also concluded that although the company had a complex and sophisticated accounting system, it did not generate the right information for management control; for example, the company did not readily have data available on the profitability of various product lines in different markets.

Following this study, Alfa-Laval underwent a major reorganization and was restructured into three separate business groups: the Agri-Group, consisting of daughter companies that marketed to only the agricultural sector; the Industrial Group, consisting of companies selling equipment to the industrial sector; and the Conglomerate Group, consisting of a number of companies that had limited relationships with each other and with other members of the group. At the same time, the "VL," or Executive Group Management team, was reorganized to include the CEO and six Executive Vice Presidents (EVPs). Three EVPs were appointed to head the newly defined business groups (Agri-Group, Industrial Group, and Conglomerate Group), and the remaining three were assigned staff responsibilities

Exhibit 3 Group Organization (1976)

		Executive Group Management: Hans Stahle, President Harry Faulkner, Exec VP Two Other Exec VPs		
Group Staffs	**Divisions**		**Market Companies**	**Other Companies**
Controller	Farm Equipment		Africa	AB Zander and Ingestrom
Corporate Development and Plan-	Rosenblads		South Africa	AB Pump-Separators Gjuterier
ning	AB Rosenblads Patenter		Asia	AB Profila
Finance	AB Celleco		Malaysia	Olofstroms Kraft AB
Internal Auditing	Separation		Iran	Alfa-Laval Automarine
Legal Matters	Thermal & Dairy		Japan	STAL Refrigeration AB
Personnel			Australia	Eskilstrums Manufacturing Unit
Research and Development			Australia	
Organization & Administrative Effi-			New Zealand	
ciency			Europe	
			Austria	
Group Staff Departments			Belgium	
			France	
Public Relations			West Germany	
Buildings and Plants			Ireland	
Purchasing			Italy	
Materials Administration			The Netherlands	
Production			Spain	
Quality Assurance			Switzerland	
			United Kingdom	
			Sweden	
			Norway	
			Denmark	
			Finland	
			North and Central America	
			Canada	
			United States of America	
			Mexico	
			Latin America	
			Argentina	
			Brazil	
			Chile	
			Peru	
			Venezuela	

Source: Company records.

(Marketing for State Economy and Developing Countries, Product/R&D, and Finance/Control). Each member of the Executive Group Management team also was expected to act as an "ambassador" for all of the daughter companies in a cluster of countries. The resulting structure was a matrix with a product focus. Harry Faulkner, for example, was made the Executive Vice President in charge of the Conglomerate Group, with country responsibility for South Africa, the United Kingdom, Canada, and the United States.

Alfa-Laval's organization structure did not undergo major changes since its 1977 reorganization. Its 1983 organization is shown in Exhibit 4. The five Deputy Managing Directors—together with Faulkner, who became CEO in 1980—formed the Executive Group Management, a top management team that made all strategic decisions for the company.

BUILDING A NEW IMAGE AND REITERATING OLD VALUES

Harry Faulkner brought a participative management style to Alfa-Laval. Soon after he took charge in 1980, he invited a business school professor, whom he had known for nearly two decades, to help him and his top management team reach a consensus on the key priorities for the firm. The discussion covered a number of topics, including defining the Group Management's role and the CEO's role within Group Management. This meeting resolved many substantive issues, and it was also invaluable for team building. Two of the contenders for Faulkner's job not only stayed on at Alfa-Laval but also became important members of the Group Management team. This top management conference has since been institutionalized and is held annually in Switzerland.

One of the first priorities for Faulkner and his top management team was to change the image of Alfa-Laval. Although the firm had branched into new products and markets during the 1970s, Alfa-Laval was still perceived as being stodgy and unimaginative. The management team wanted Alfa-Laval to be seen not only as financially sound and dependable but also as exciting and dynamic. They sought to turn Alfa-Laval into a "great company, as perceived by shareholders, employees, customers, etc.," so they launched a corporate advertising campaign. This campaign emphasized the firm's new products and technologies and also helped convey the new dynamism within the company.

Alfa-Laval's top management believed very strongly that the corporate communication effort directed at the company's external stakeholders had to be complemented by a similar effort aimed internally at key employees—they needed to know what Alfa-Laval stood for. After several discussions among the company's managers, the following core values were identified:

1. *Creating and nurturing team spirit.* Each manager was indeed responsible for the cohesiveness and competitiveness of his or her group or department but plays for only one team, Alfa-Laval. The manager must make decisions in the

Exhibit 4 **Alfa-Laval Group Organization, 1983**

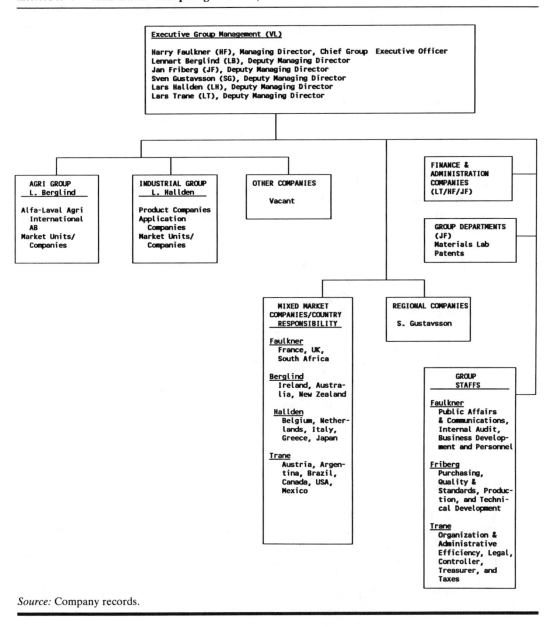

Source: Company records.

interest of Alfa-Laval as a whole and therefore must endeavor to talk to his or her colleagues and not about them. He or she must praise rather than criticize a colleague and must actively discourage "us versus them" thinking among subordinates. It is useful to remember that as far as customers, suppliers, and the public was concerned, each manager was Alfa-Laval.

2. *Working with integrity toward others.* Every manager at Alfa-Laval must be fair and honest toward subordinates, colleagues, and superiors. He or she must remember that good manners and politeness are still virtues. The manager must discuss with subordinates their development and future opportunities and let people express their ideas; each employee is a potential resource for improving company performance. He or she must never cheat in work and never pass the buck, but it was permissible for the manager to make a mistake occasionally.

3. *Keeping it simple.* A manager must avoid "bureaucratic" procedures and must not complicate matters unnecessarily.

4. *Providing quality performance.* Quality always will be the watchword for Alfa-Laval. Quality was a broad concept that neither began nor ended with the physical products sold but was an attitude, a way in which the company related to its markets. A manager must therefore endeavor to do things right the first time.

5. *Making sure customers come first.* Customers were entitled to impose their demands because they paid the bills. The decisive factor in their choice of Alfa-Laval was that the company gave them more value for their money than any other competing company—more quality in terms of products, service, punctuality, and operating reliability.

A little blue book discussing these values was distributed to all Alfa-Laval managers, with the following preface by Faulkner:

> Shared values for leadership are not rigid tenets. Rather, they should be regarded as a statement of objectives, as guidelines and as an initial joint effort. Naturally, you would probably like to add some items and delete others. But the important thing right now is that we set out towards a common goal, using our common resources.

CONSOLIDATING OLD BUSINESSES

Despite the distinguished careers enjoyed by the senior managers of Alfa-Laval, these managers were overwhelmed by the growing size and diversity of the company's businesses. In order to help his senior managers perform a strategic audit of their diverse businesses, Faulkner retained the Boston Consulting Group (BCG) in 1980. The first task of the BCG consultants was to help the company identify the SBUs within each of its three groups. At Faulkner's insistence, this was done primarily by Alfa-Laval managers, with senior BCG consultants acting as coaches.

After a series of deliberations, Alfa-Laval managers agreed on 22 Strategic Business Units (SBUs) (Exhibit 5). Manufacturing units and marketing subsidiaries were reorganized into appropriate SBUs, and the SBUs were then delegated sub-

Exhibit 5   Strategic Framework

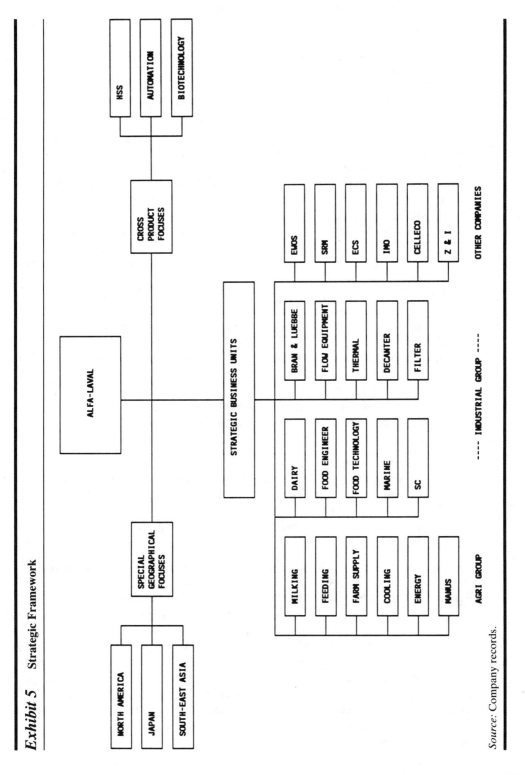

Source: Company records.

425

stantial authority by top management for making strategic decisions. The corporate headquarters staff was correspondingly shrunk.

Within each SBU, several distinct product/market segments were further identified. Many of these SBUs were earlier thought to be fairly homogeneous. However, after the strategic audit exercise, the managers were better able to pinpoint segments where competitive threats were beginning to emerge. In the marine heat-exchanger business, for example, classifying ships by their tonnage helped differentiate two distinct market segments. Despite being the largest supplier of marine heat exchangers in the world, Alfa-Laval found itself losing market share to the Japanese in the fastest-growing segment in the industry—heat exchangers for small-tonnage ships.

The next step was to position each SBU on the BCG growth-share matrix and to identify an appropriate mission for it. In the BCG terminology, businesses with high relative market share in high-growth markets are termed "stars" worthy of further investment; as the market matures and the market growth declines, they become "cash cows" or net generators of cash. Businesses that have a low market share in a high-growth market are called "question marks" (referring to their questionable attractiveness for investment); businesses with both low growth and low market share are called "dogs," and these are serious candidates for divestiture. Although a few businesses in Alfa-Laval's portfolio fell in the desirable "star" category, the majority were in the "cash cow" and "dog" categories. Three of these latter businesses together accounted for 65 percent of the company's cash flow.

Based on this analysis, the Executive Management Group began reshaping the company's business portfolio by deciding the following:

1. The company had to divest some of its unprofitable "dogs" that could not be turned around.
2. Although many of Alfa-Laval's businesses were in a mature stage, they still had some opportunities for internal growth. These had to be nurtured.
3. It was essential to protect some of the "cash cows." Cash could become a problem constraint in the future if only growth areas were funded and all the "cash cows" were harvested.

Operations representing 15 percent of turnover, with 3,000 employees, were then divested. In 1983, Alfa-Laval divested its evaporator and refrigeration equipment businesses. The remaining operations were consolidated.

In addition to emphasizing SBUs as the building blocks for its planning systems, Alfa-Laval also selected six major areas of focus that cut across the 22 SBUs (see Exhibit 5). Three of these were geographic areas targeted for growth: North America, Japan, and Southeast Asia. Despite Alfa-Laval's long history as a multinational company, its sales were primarily concentrated in Europe (65 percent). The new geographic focus was meant to highlight opportunities for international growth. Similarly the company sought to exploit synergies that it had in high-speed separators (HSS), automation, and biotechnology. These were designated as the three technology focus areas.

Faulkner and his top management team also tried to match managerial style with SBU mission in their choice of managers to head the newly created SBUs. Faulkner observed the following:

> I would have said in the past that a good leader can be used in any situation. But I now recognize that some of us are entrepreneurs, and some of us are cost cutters. If you ask an entrepreneur, say, to manage a dog business, he is bound to suggest "invest for the future." And if you put an experienced cost cutter in a high growth area, you won't grow with the market. So we've taken some hard nosed decisions based on this.
>
> Take for example our business manager in Brazil. He had been there for five years, and he had grown sales to record levels. He was naturally shocked when I did not renew his contract. He did not understand then that the situation in Brazil had changed. We needed an experienced administrator to pull things together. This entrepreneur, on the other hand, was needed in Singapore to grow our business there.

INSTITUTIONALIZING STRATEGIC MANAGEMENT

Not only did the BCG portfolio analysis shape the content of Alfa-Laval's consolidation and diversification strategies, but also it forced managers to think strategically. Alfa-Laval previously used a long-range planning system, which was abandoned because it seemed a futile numbers exercise to the participants. Recalling how the current planning process started, Faulkner observed this:

> I demanded that each daughter company should identify its businesses, and the growth possibilities for their portfolio. What started as a top-down demand very quickly became a bottom-up exercise. The firm's strategy is now based on what the operating units want to do, with subsequent evaluation by us as to whether they can do it or not. In general, they have to meet a number of broad objectives, minimum return of 18 percent, present targets for solidity ratio,[2] cash position, etc.

The BCG analysis became a catalyst for change. The BCG consultants went to each subsidiary to outline its format. However, the managers in those subsidiaries were the ones who gathered and analyzed information, segmented the businesses, and drew conclusions about their own data. Because of their heavy involvement, these subsidiaries showed a real commitment to the new bottom-up planning process. The planning cycle in use at Alfa-Laval began each year in early spring with Faulkner and the Executive Management Group outlining their objectives for each SBU. Each SBU then used a five-stage planning process to translate its objectives into action plans. These are the five stages:

1. *Definition*. This stage referred to the definition of the new SBUs and redefinition of old SBUs as well as their further subdivision into an appropriate number of product-market segments. It was completed before the objectives were set by the Executive Management Group for each SBU. It was also the SBU manager's responsibility to translate SBU objectives into targets for individual

product-market segments. This was usually completed within a few weeks after the SBU received its objectives.

2. *Documentation.* Each SBU was then required to provide a detailed analysis of its environment and its own strengths and weaknesses, describe its strategic alternatives, defend its chosen strategy, and request for resources needed to fulfill the assigned mission. Each SBU used a reporting format that was most appropriate to its particular circumstances but fell within the guidelines offered by the Group Management staff (Exhibits 6–8). This stage was the most time consuming and was typically completed by early April. All planning documentation was in English.

3. *Consolidation.* The third stage was the consolidation by the Group Management staff (of the financial data submitted by the SBUs) and the preparation of financial forecasts for the company as a whole. This was completed by the end of April.

4. *Presentation.* The next stage was the presentation of SBU plans to the concerned group managers in the Executive Management Group. This was done concurrently with Stage 3.

5. *Analysis.* The fifth stage was the analysis by the Group Management staff of the plans submitted by the SBU (after the scrutiny of their group managers) and the formulation of suitable corporate strategies. This was typically completed by June.

(*Text continues on page 432*)

Exhibit 6   **Guidelines for Preparing SBU Plans**

Structure of Documentation

With the experience of previous strategic studies, we have found the following topics particularly useful.

1. Business Mission for the SBU

2. Segmentation

Definition and description of segments
Changes from the segmentation last time and why

3. Market Analyses per Segment

Structural changes in the market
Market size and development
Market growth analyses—volume
real price changes
inflation
Objectives (related to the market)

4. Competitor Analyses per Segment

Description of the main competitors (or competitor groups)
competitive position: for example, their relative price, relative quality, and relative cost
position
strengths and weaknesses of the competitors
anticipated moves by the competitors (strategic moves—for example, major investments
in R&D, marketing, and facilities)

financial data: sales, market share, performance
Objectives (related to the competitors)

5. Cost Structure Analyses per Segment

Cost structure and evolution
Objectives (related to the cost structure and cost development)

6. R&D Projects Analyses

R&D priority per segment
Description of how the R&D efforts support the strategic thrust
Objectives (related to the R&D projects)

7. Business Strategy for the SBU

Key success factors
The business strategy for the SBU (to be followed during this planning period)
Critical strategic issues and actions to be implemented

8. The Segments Position in the Growth Share Matrix

1981's position (as presented in the previous study)
1985's position (as presented in the previous study)
1984's position
1988's position

9. Financial Summary per Segment

Sales
Real growth
Operating result
ROC
Cash flow

10. Financial Plan for the SBU

See Exhibit 7 for an illustration.
Objectives

11. Follow-Up of the Previous Plan

Strategic decisions planned to be taken in 1981–1983
Strategic decisions taken 1981–1983
Major changes in the strategy
Financial outcome of the previous plan

12. Summary of Selected Strategies and Objectives

See Exhibit 8 for the suggested format.

13. Executive Summary of the Strategic Plan

Two to three typed pages for VL that should contain—Business Mission
Segmentation
Business Strategy
Objectives

The SBUs are free to add or expand topics as they think suits their particular situation best. The focus should always though be on the business strategy part (see number 7).

Source: Group management staff, Alfa-Laval, 1984.

Exhibit 7   **Financial Plan for the SBU: An Illustration**

				Name of SBU			
Income	**A81**	**A82**	**A83**	**B84**	**F85**	**F86**	**F87**
Net invoicing	270	280	330	340	370	390	450
Cost of goods sold	150	190	230	200	220	230	270
Gross margin	120	90	100	140	150	160	180
Overheads	60	70	75	80	90	95	110
Profits	60	20	25	60	60	65	70
Calc. interest	29	31	33	34	35	36	39
Operating result	31	−11	−8	26	25	29	31
Gross margin (%)	44	32	30	41	41	41	40
Overheads/sales (%)	22	25	23	24	24	24	24
ROS (%)	22	7	8	18	16	17	16
Capital	**A81**	**A82**	**A83**	**B84**	**F85**	**F86**	**F87**
Working capital	150	160	170	175	180	185	195
Fixed capital	30	35	35	40	40	45	50
Operating capital	180	195	205	215	220	230	245
WCT[1]	1.8	1.8	1.9	1.9	2.1	2.1	2.3
OCT[2]	1.5	1.4	1.6	1.6	1.7	1.7	1.8
Cash Flow	**A81**	**A82**	**A83**	**B84**	**F85**	**F86**	**F87**
Operating result	31	−11	−8	26	25	29	31
Calculated interest	29	31	33	34	35	36	39
Change in operating capital	−10	−15	−10	−20	−15	−15	−15
Adjustments	0	0	−5	0	0	0	0
Cash flow	50	5	10	40	45	50	55
Cash flow margin[3] (%)	28	3	5	19	20	22	22
Real growth (%)	12	−5	8	−4	3	0	10
ROC (%)	33	10	12	28	27	28	29

A = actual, B = budget, F = forecast

[1]Net invoicing divided by working capital.

[2]Net invoicing divided by operating captial.

[3]Cash flow as percentage of operating capital.

Source: Group management staff, Alfa-Laval, 1984.

Exhibit 8 **Summary of Alfa-Laval's Business Portfolio: The Suggested Format**

SBU/Segment	Main Strategy				Objectives			Life Cycle Position[1]		Growth Mainly Through				
	Grow	Hold	Milk	Divest	Growth (Real)	ROC	Sales (SS Cur.)	83	88	Present Market	Prod. Line Extens.	New Markets	R&D	Acquis.

[1]The position of the SBU/segment or its life cycle was plotted in these two columns.

Source: Group management staff, Alfa-Laval, 1984.

431

After the SBU's plans and their implications for the marketing companies were analyzed by Group Management staff, a series of meetings were scheduled from June through October to discuss the business plan for each market company, business group, and division. Budget instructions were issued in June, and managers prepared the final budgets required to support their business plans by November. Budgets meetings run from November 1 through December 15, following a tightly structured schedule (Exhibit 9).

Progress vis-à-vis the business plan and budget was monitored frequently, and critical environmental assumptions were reviewed with the SBU manager. This review process took place both on-site in the subsidiaries and at the corporate headquarters. There was no formal schedule for these progress reviews because it frequently varied from SBU to SBU, depending on its mission.

Bonuses were awarded to managers based on their performance against their budgets. Alfa-Laval's incentive systems were, however, not tied to output alone and not based on any clear-cut formulas. Faulkner pointed out the following:

> We don't believe in that. Such systems can be manipulated. Besides, one year when profits are down the manager may still have to be rewarded because he was not responsible for the downturn. So we have a subjective system. We sit down in Group Management and evaluate the performance of each daughter company manager every year. A manager who runs an emerging business can get as high a bonus as another who runs a cash cow.
>
> Moreover, in Sweden we have a marginal tax of 80 percent. Monetary compensation as an incentive is, therefore, ineffective. The government has taken the carrot away. They have also taken away the stick. We cannot fire people. In fact, our employees at all levels take part in important decisions of the company. That is Swedish law. When I was appointed, for example, our union leader came and patted me on the shoulder and said, "We have approved you."
>
> We are looking for other ways of motivating people than the traditional monetary incentives. A little pat on the back helps sometimes. We often forget to tell our subordinates how good a job they are doing. We only focus on their problems.

NURTURING CREATIVITY FROM WITHIN

Alfa-Laval had a strong tradition of in-house creativity. R&D funding had averaged 3.5 percent of sales in the last decade. Faulkner was therefore convinced that the company could successfully diversify from within, but he realized that the company would have to do a better job of integrating technology planning with strategic planning. In August 1983, he appointed Jan Friberg from Sandvik as the first Deputy Managing Director for Technology and gave him the responsibility for strengthening the link between technology and strategy.

(*Text continues on page 436*)

Exhibit 9 Agenda for Budget Presentations

( )	=	Indicate possible participation or participation at certain parts of the presentation
X	=	Follow-up of the budget
T, L	=	Presentation at Tumba or Lund
D	=	Presentation at daughter company

NOTE! 1983-11-15—Last date for budgets to be in Tumba

One week before the budget presentation date or at the latest by the above indicated date the budget proposal should be handed over to the reviewers. The written comments included in your proposal must lead to a problem-oriented budget presentation!

Company	HF	LT	JF	LB	LH	SG	Repr KE	Day	Time	Place	Notes concerning board meeting, etc.
AL Corporate	T	T					JDG	30/11	0.900–12.30	Board room	
Alfa-Banken + KF	T	T						1/12	13.30–16.30	Board room	
AL Credit		T						29/11	09.00–12.30		
AL International		T						29/11	09.00–12.30		
Alfa-Data + KA		T						29/11	13.00		
AL Overseas/Unimex	T			T	T	T	JDG	22/12	09.00–12.30	Board room	
AL Energy and Cooling Systems					T		JDG	22/12	13.30–16.30		
AL Licens	X										
AL Automation					L		JDG	1/12	09.00–12.30	Lund F	
AL Agri International	T			T			JDG	8/11	09.00–13.00	Board room	
ALE, Sahlström											
AL Lantbruk Norden				T				14/10	09.00	C 4013	
incl. Denmark, Finland, Norway, Odin				T							
AL Separation AB					T		JDG	14/11	13.00–17.00	K 1181	
AL Thermal					L		JDG	30/11		Lund T	
AL Marine & Power Engineering					T		JDG	14/11	10.00–12.30		
incl. Nirex											
AL Food & Dairy Engineering	L				L		JDG	28/11	09.00	Lund F	
incl. Boyer, Danmaid, Danice, Tebel,											
Atmos., Square, Meat-By Prod.,								29/11	09.00	Lund F	
Cheddar											

(continued)

Exhibit 9 (continued)

Flow Equipment incl. LKM, LKM GmbH, AL Flow Equipm... Ibex, Jean Pagès						JDG	15/11	09.00–15.00	Kolding	
Flow Equipment					D	JDG	15/11	09.00–15.00	Kolding	Board meeting
AL Contracting	D		D				16/11			
AL Mejeri Norden					L	JDG	1/12	13.00–17.00	Lund F	
Manus Group			T				14/11 / 31/10	13.30–16.30		H. Gisel-Ekdahl
KB, KE, KT			T			JDG	31/10			
KI, KQ, KR, OB, OL, OM, OP, OT	T			T			1/11	13.30		Board meeting (T)
KC, KD, KM, KP						JDG	1/11	15.00		Board meeting
Olofströms Kraft						JDG	24/11			Board meeting
Profila					T	JDG	8/11	10.00		Board meeting
Rotor	D									Board meeting
Zander & Ingeström group incl Celleco	D			D	D		8/12	14.00		Board meeting
Ewos group		D			D		18/11	p.m.		
ARGENTINA		D			X		5–9/12			5–9/12 LT visit
AUSTRALIA incl Hamilton	T			T				09.00–12.30		
AUSTRIA — Alfa-Laval					D	JDG	14/12			
BELGIUM						JDG	19/12		Board room	5–9/12 LT visit
BRAZIL	T	T		D		JDG	14/12			14/12 prel, LT visit
CANADA	D									
CHILE					X		3–4/10			
DENMARK — Separation					D	JDG	22/11	09.00		
FRANCE — Elevage	D						2–3/11			
Agri Cool	D						2–3/11			
Diabolo Manus	D						2–3/11			
Export			X							
Industrie	D				D					
Total	D			D	D		17/11			Board meeting
GERMANY — Agrar	D					JDG	31/10–1/11			
Industrietechnik	D					JDG	20/12			Board Meeting
Atmos	D					JDG	20/12			
Bran & Lübbe	T					JDG	19–20/12			
GREECE	T					JDG	16/12	09.00–12.30		LH visit Jan.
INDIA	X			X						
IRAN	X						12/10			
IRELAND	D									

434

Country	Unit						Date	Time	Room	
ITALY					D	JDG	12/12	08.00–12.30	Board room	
JAPAN	Total	T			T	JDG	8/12		K 1235	
MALAYSIA			D			JDG	21/12			
MEXICO			X							
NETHERLANDS	Alfa-Laval				D	JDG	5–6/12			
	Tebel			X	D	JDG	5–6/12			
NEW ZEALAND				X						
PERU					X					
SINGAPORE					T	JDG	21/12	13.30	K 1235	
SOUTH AFRICA		T					29/9	08.30	Board room	
SPAIN	Equipos Agricolas									Terry Blanks
	Alfa-Laval				D	JDG	11–12/1			
SWITZERLAND	Industriegesellschaft				D	JDG	13/12			
	AL Sursee			D			10/10			
UK	Alfa-Laval	D		D			16/11			Board meeting
	Consolidated	T	T	T	T	JDG	2/12	09.00–12.30	Board room	
USA										
VENEZUELA		T			X					
AGRI GROUP		T		T	T	JDG	9/12	09.00	Board room	
INDUSTRIAL GROUP		T		T	T	JDG	27/12	09.00–16.30	Board room	
GROUP TOTAL + ALAB		T	T	T	T	JDG	23/1	09.00–16.30	Board Room	

Note: The members of the VL that review a particular budget are identified by their initials. For example, HF is Harry Faulkner.

Source: Alfa Laval Group Management Staff.

Friberg's efforts at integrating technology planning with strategic planning were channeled in these three major programs:

1. *Creating a technology orientation.* SBUs were encouraged to submit action plans and budgets aimed not only at profitability but also at future growth. The Executive Management Group assured the SBU that its proposals would not be evaluated on both the return on investment criterion and the future strategic options that they helped create.

Friberg encouraged frequent meetings between the SBU managers and their technologists. He attended many of these meetings himself to provide the necessary catalysis. He also invited several consulting firms—including McKinsey and Company, the Boston Consulting Group, Arthur D. Little, Stanford Research Institute, and Booz-Allen—to help the SBU managers assess and develop capabilities for strategically managing technology within their SBUs.

2. *A fund for innovation.* A central fund (initially $2 million) was established to fund worthwhile R&D projects throughout the company. Many of these were rejected by the SBUs because of their size or their riskiness. A high-powered screening committee consisting of four members of the Group Management team—Harry Faulkner, Sven Gustavsson, Jan Friberg, and Lars Trane—was set up to evaluate each proposal. Friberg noted this optimistically: "We would like to give all the money away during the first month of the fiscal year, and then try to get more if there are worthy projects."

3. *Joint ventures.* Alfa-Laval sought to participate in joint venture partnerships when they were potentially attractive for strengthening the company's technology base.

SEARCHING FOR EXTERNAL INVESTMENT OPPORTUNITIES

Despite its vigorous efforts at diversification through in-house research, Alfa-Laval's Group Management realized that the company's predominantly mature business portfolio (Exhibit 10) would have to be modified, at least in part, through selective acquisitions.

Furthermore, having its headquarters in Sweden posed additional challenges for Alfa-Laval. Not only was Swedish business closely regulated by the government, but also the personal tax rate was the highest among developed countries—with the marginal tax rate going as high as 80 percent. This made it nearly impossible to attract good managerial talent from outside the country and difficult to retain good Swedish managers. These factors made growth within Sweden less attractive.

Consequently Faulkner began to look for investment opportunities outside Sweden. In 1982, as part of a group of Swedish investors, he acquired a 6.4 percent minority interest in a U.S. biotechnology firm, Genentech. Faulkner was invited to join the Genentech board.

Exhibit 10   **Alfa-Laval's Growth Share Matrix (1983)**

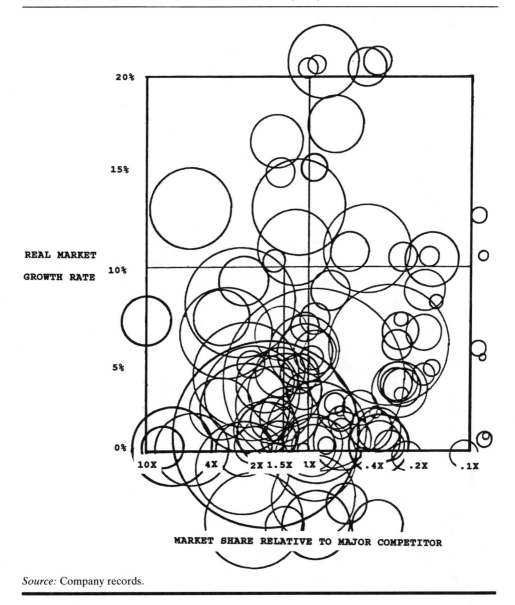

REAL MARKET GROWTH RATE

MARKET SHARE RELATIVE TO MAJOR COMPETITOR

Source: Company records.

Exhibit 11 **Alfa-Laval Group Activities in Summary**

As originally stated except for 1976, which is restated in accordance with accounting principles adopted in 1977 (amounts in MSEK)

	1983	1982	1981	1980	1979	1978	1977	1976	1975	1974
Net sales by Business Group										
Agri group	2,959	2,142	1,978	1,922	1,805	1,530	1,329	1,127	1,023	960
Industrial group	4,998	4,338	3,650	3,135	2,562	2,443	1,899	1,795	1,701	1,506
Other companies	1,293	1,760	1,645	1,445	1,119	1,013	980	834	817	708
Income data										
Net sales	9,250	8,240	7,273	6,502	5,486	4,986	4,208	3,756	3,541	3,174
Income after net financial items	803	662	516	479	391	322	306	303	264	249
As percentage of net sales	8.6	8.0	7.1	7.4	7.1	6.5	7.3	8.0	7.5	7.8
Adjusted income per share (SEK)[1]	27.3	23.8	18.5	17.2	14.1	11.6	11.0	10.9	10.6	10.0
Tax	285	142	143	102	108	114	90	89	77	68
Net result after tax	422	235	106	195	167	98	82	64	62	56
Balance sheet data										
Liquid assets	2,169	1,948	1,347	1,056	1,138	1,278	1,228	935	572	334
Inventories	2,637	3,054	2,706	2,313	2,023	1,790	1,656	1,486	1,295	1,108
Other current assets	2,838	2,730	2,318	1,833	1,754	1,677	1,309	1,139	1,131	1,048
Long-term assets	2,005	1,916	1,695	1,485	1,350	1,175	996	855	546	456
Current liabilities	3,904	4,719	3,810	2,754	2,666	2,587	2,230	1,678	1,440	1,200
Long-term liabilities	1,445	1,442	1,153	1,010	978	954	821	694	645	515
Untaxed reserves	1,891	1,940	1,689	1,454	1,282	1,151	1,034	910	544	431
Equity capital	2,409	1,547	1,434	1,459	1,339	1,228	1,104	1,133	933	800
Total assets	9,649	9,648	8,066	6,687	6,265	5,920	5,189	4,415	3,562	2,946
Number of employees										
Sweden	5,632	7,019	7,409	7,363	7,081	6,875	6,895	6,781	6,739	6,464
Outside Sweden	10,352	10,924	11,116	10,711	10,815	10,888	10,890	11,039	11,269	11,258
Profitability										
Return (%):										
On average operating capital before taxes[2]	17.8	17.1	15.1	14.8	13.0	12.0	12.8	13.7	15.5	16.8

On equity capital after standard deduction for taxes[3]	13.7	13.8	11.6	11.5	10.3	9.4	9.6	10.2	11.9	12.8
On equity capital after actual tax charges[4]	14.6	15.8	12.4	13.6	11.3	9.2	10.4	12.2	13.8	15.6

Ratios

Current assets to current liabilities[5]	1.9	1.6	1.7	1.9	1.8	1.8	1.9	2.1	2.1	2.1
Solidity ratio[6]	34.8	26.1	28.1	32.8	31.6	30.5	31.2	36.0	33.8	34.5
Solidity ratio (excl. advances from customers)	37.7	29.6	31.5	35.0	34.0	33.2	34.6	40.2	36.3	36.8
Interest coverage[7]	3.5	3.2	3.3	3.7	3.7	3.8	3.9	4.2	3.9	4.4

Other data

Dividend

As percent of earnings[8]	33.0	31.5	28.1	26.1	25.5	31.0	27.3	27.5	25.5	22.0
SEK per share[8]	9.0	7.5	5.2	4.5	3.6	3.6	3.0	3.0	2.7	2.2
Capital stock, December 31	734	521	521	521	417	417	417	417	333	267
Share price, December 31, SEK[9]	270	198	150	102	73	86	88	91	79	59
Price/earnings ratio, per share[10]	10	8	8	6	5	7	8	8	8	6

[1] Adjusted income is Group income after net financial items, less a standard 50 percent tax.

In calculating adjusted earnings per share and dividends per share, the number of shares outstanding in each year has been adjusted to reflect new and bonus issues of shares.

[2] Return on average operating capital before taxes consists of Group income before extraordinary income, special adjustments and taxes, plus interest expense (including interest on pension liabilities) divided by the Group's average assets less commercial liabilities.

[3] Return on equity capital after taxes consists of the Group's adjusted income divided by average adjusted equity capital. Adjusted equity capital consists of equity capital shown in the balance sheet plus 50 percent of average untaxed reserves.

[4] Return on equity capital after actual tax charges consists of the Group's income after net financial items after actual tax charges, divided by average equity capital. Equity capital is made up of the average equity capital shown in the balance sheet, plus 100 percent of average untaxed reserves.

[5] Liquidity is calculated as total current assets divided by current liabilities.

[6] Solidity ratio is calculated as adjusted equity capital as a percentage of total assets. Adjusted equity capital is defined in note 3 above.

[7] Interest coverage is defined as income after depreciation, plus dividends and interest income, as a percentage of interest expense.

[8] For 1983 the proposed dividend is shown. The 1982 dividend includes an anniversary bonus.

[9] The prices of Alfa-Laval shares on the Stockholm Stock Exchange at the respective year ends have been adjusted to reflect new and bonus issues of shares.

[10] The price/earnings ratio per share represents the adjusted stock-exchange price of an Alfa-Laval share divided by adjusted income per share.

Source: Annual report, 1983.

Although the investment in Genentech was small, it represented a new direction for Alfa-Laval. There were several underlying factors that persuaded Faulkner to invest in Genentech. A major reason was the opportunity to be at the forefront of a new, exciting technology—perhaps even more revolutionary than electronics. Faulkner expected biotechnology to become a major growth industry within a decade. Because so many of Alfa-Laval's markets were mature, it was important for the company to get a position in a growth market. Moreover, Faulkner believed that there was an attractive financial argument as well.

> We have a fairly low price/earnings ratio because of the mature fields we operate in. What I wanted to do was to acquire companies that give at least the image of high-tech so that we could get a higher price-earnings ratio, and then use our own equity to acquire more high-tech firms.

Another reason for the acquisition was that Alfa-Laval's centrifugal separators, with some modification, were well-suited for important tasks in genetic engineering. Faulkner speculated the following:

> [Bioengineering] would affect us as a company. A lot of Alfa-Laval equipment is involved. Separation technology is crucial as companies move to commercial scale production, and we want to be in a position to work closely to adapt our equipment to their needs. And Genentech is a leading company. . . . It will be a survivor.

CHALLENGES BEYOND 1984

By 1984, most of the financial targets the Group Management set for the firm were met (Exhibit 11). Also, the organization was streamlined: The reporting relationships had been clarified, and interunit coordination and cooperation had considerably improved. The company's planning process, coupled with its new initiative on technology planning, had strengthened its strategic orientation. Much had been accomplished in Faulkner's first four years as CEO. Commenting on these changes, he remarked this: "My role as Chief Executive Officer is really to be a guardian of change and to see that the attitude to change always remains positive."

Nevertheless, the company's portfolio remained mature, and its cash surplus confirmed the lack of attractive internal investment opportunities. But Faulkner wondered what further changes needed to be made.

Appendix _____
COMMENTS ON SWEDISH RULES AND REGULATIONS FOR A BETTER UNDERSTANDING OF ALFA-LAVAL'S FINANCIAL STATEMENTS

When analyzing Alfa-Laval Group results on an international basis you should observe that income after financial income and expenses but before special adjustments and taxes is the key figure. The reason for this is that Swedish tax laws have an important influence on the financial statements of the Swedish companies of the Group. An explanation of these rules and regulations is provided below.

Swedish tax laws have an important influence on the financial statements of the Swedish companies of the Group.

Fiscal law carries to the extreme the basic rule of Swedish taxation that taxable income is principally based on book income. This has been extended to a requirement that taxpayers who wish to claim several or more important tax incentives available in Sweden must record changes in their books equivalent to the pretax amount of these incentives.

INVENTORIES

Inventories are stated at the lower of FIFO cost and market. In some instances average cost is used when it approximates FIFO.

Unless a higher provision is required, 5 percent is set aside for inventory obsolescence. This is the standard amount permitted by the tax law.

In addition to this, 15 to 60 percent (depending on type of inventory) can be set aside to an inventory reserve. This charge is made for tax purposes only, and appears under the heading "Special adjustments" in the Income Statement.

Long-term construction and installation contracts are accounted for on a completed-contract basis.

DEPRECIATION

Depreciation charges are shown at two levels in the Income Statement.

The charge on operating income, planned depreciation, is computed on a straight-line basis over the estimated useful lives of the various classes of assets. The charge is based on original cost.

The difference between the charge to operating income and the total amount claimed for tax purposes is shown as a transfer to/from untaxed reserves under the heading "Special adjustments."

Source: Alfa-Laval annual report (1983).

UNTAXED RESERVES

The untaxed reserves are shown as a separate item in the Balance Sheet. The untaxed reserves are:

- Inventory reserves
- Accumulated additional depreciation
- Investment reserves
- Compulsory investment reserves

All these reserves represent the accumulation of charges which are allowed for tax purposes but are not required for fair presentation purposes. Swedish tax law nonetheless requires they be recorded in the books in order to be qualified for deduction.

Inventory reserves have existed for many years as a means whereby manufacturing industry could defer taxes and/or even out taxable income.

Reserves for future investment are, in effect, advance additional depreciation on unspecified fixed assets yet to be acquired.

Compulsory investment reserves were introduced in 1980 as a means of reducing excess corporate liquidity through the related compulsory deposits. These reserves can be used in the same way as reserves for future investment.

Blocked accounts with the Bank of Sweden, which appear as a separate item between current assets and long-term assets, relate to the compulsory deposits associated with reserves for future investments.

PENSION PROVISIONS

The allocation to pension funds is recorded under long-term liabilities. An independent body computes the total actuarial liability which the company has to provide for.

RETURN ON EQUITY CAPITAL

The taxable income is based on the net income in the Income Statement. As this income has been obtained after the deduction of the above-mentioned special adjustments for tax purposes only, it is not a valid measure of the net income of the company. The net income is therefore calculated as the income after financial income and expenses minus an approximate charge of 50 percent for income tax.

Fifty percent of the untaxed reserves are considered as equity capital, and 50 percent as a long-term tax liability.

The return on equity capital is calculated as the income after financial income and expenses minus a 50 percent charge for income tax divided by the equity capital plus 50 percent of the untaxed reserves.

Following the same logic, earnings per share and the P/E ratio are based on the net income as defined above.

NOTES

1. The Swedish Krona equals $0.12 in U.S. dollars. Income before adjustments and taxes is the key figure. Swedish tax laws have an important influence on net income. The appendix provides some comment on Swedish rules and regulations in order to clarify Alfa-Laval's financial statement.

2. See Exhibit 11 for the definition of solidity ratio.

ANALYTICAL AIDS FOR EVALUATING STRATEGY

In this Appendix, we briefly review various analytical approaches that can assist top management in evaluating business and corporate strategies. In the first section, we present these four types of analytical models that are available for evaluating business strategies:

1. The classic business policy framework first proposed by K. R. Andrews and his colleagues at Harvard.
2. Analytical models developed by such management consultants as the Boston Consulting Group, McKinsey and Company, and Arthur D. Little.
3. Inductive models, such as the PIMS model, derived from the collective experience of several businesses.
4. Frameworks based on industrial organization economics, such as those developed by M. E. Porter at Harvard.

We then move on to a discussion of approaches that facilitate the evaluation of corporate strategy and review three such approaches:

1. Models developed by management consultants for evaluating the quality of a firm's business portfolio.
2. Analytical approaches that are helpful when evaluating synergies between a firm's businesses.
3. Analytical approaches that are helpful in ensuring that the strategies pursued by the firm create value for its stockholders.

EVALUATING BUSINESS STRATEGY

Business Policy Framework

The framework proposed by Andrews[1] (Figure A-1) requires top management to assess both the opportunities and threats facing a business unit in its chosen environ-

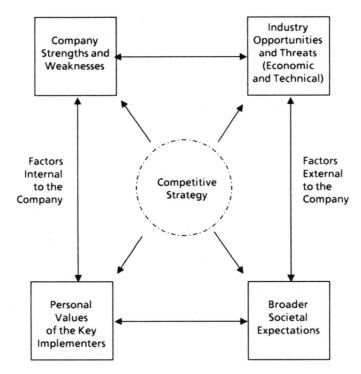

Figure A-1   **The Andrews Framework for Evaluating Strategy**

ment and the firm's strengths and weaknesses in adapting to that environment. The strategy proposed by a business unit manager must be consistent with these two assessments. This approach is popularly called the SWOT analysis because it seeks to analyze the firm's *s*trengths, *w*eaknesses, *o*pportunities, and *t*hreats.

In addition, the proposed strategy must be consistent with the personal values of the firm's senior managers and with what they believe to be the firm's obligations to the society at large. Finally, the framework suggests that a viable strategy should be internally consistent. The various functional plans that are proposed in support of a business strategy must be realistic and mutually congruent.

This is a general framework that is applicable to any business context. Its strength lies in its simplicity. However, apart from pointing to the right questions to ask, the framework does not provide any specific approach for evaluating business strategy.

Management Consultant's Models

A number of models have been proposed by management consultants to locate the competitive position of a business unit relative to its competitors and to suggest what type of generic strategy is appropriate to the unit's position. One of the earliest models of this genre was proposed by B. D. Henderson[2] of the Boston Consulting Group. The BCG growth-share matrix, as it is popularly called, uses two dimensions for positioning a particular business relative to its competitors:

1. The attractiveness of the industry segment in which the business participates, as measured by the growth rate enjoyed by that segment.
2. The relative market share of the firm compared to its major competitor or competitors, as a proxy for its competitive position in the chosen industry segment. If the relative market share of a firm is high, the firm is presumed to enjoy corresponding scale advantages and lower unit costs compared to its competitors.

A business can have one of four positions in the resulting matrix, as shown in Figure A-2. A "question mark" business will typically be a net user of cash, given the investments needed to grow this business. A "cash cow" business, in contrast, will typically generate a positive cash flow. A "star" business may be either a small net user or a net generator of cash, depending on its stage of development. A "dog" business is a cash trap and so must be avoided.

The model in Figure A-2 provides a useful way of picturing which type of strategy is appropriate for a business based on its setting and what kinds of strategic

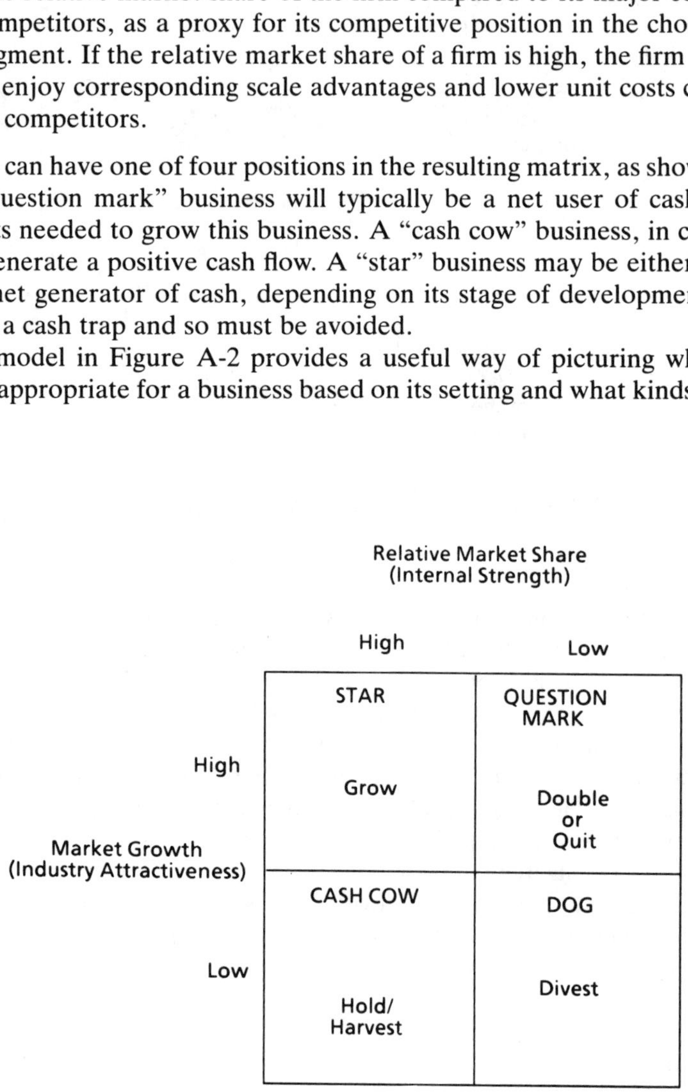

Figure A-2 **The BCG Growth-Share Matrix for Evaluating Business Strategy**

programs may assist its implementation. It also suggests the desired evolution of various businesses. For instance, a "question mark" business should be grown into a "star," a "star" business should be maintained, a "cash cow" business should be selectively harvested, and a "dog" business should be divested. Case 12 on the Norton Company provides an illustration of how such an approach can be used to evaluate business strategies.

We should point out, however, that Figure A-2 is merely a decision aid. The cash flows predicted for different strategies in Figure A-2 are valid only on an average. For this reason, labels such as "cash cow" and "dog" can be misleading, suggesting that such businesses should be milked or divested from the firm's portfolio. Several studies[3] have shown, for instance, how such "dog" businesses can be managed for profitability and even for growth through product extensions. In general, the predominant emphasis on low cost as a necessary prerequisite for a winning strategy has been challenged. A specialized business can be profitable, despite its low market share. It is therefore critically important that all businesses pursue opportunities for growth and not resign themselves to the dictates of this or any other analytical model. Similarly, a "star" business is not worthy of unlimited investment. There are inherent risks in these businesses, which a mechanical interpretation of the BCG model may ignore. Unless a "star" business generates returns that are commensurate with the high risks associated with it, it may not be worthy of investment.

Finally, we should point out that the model assumes that the sources of funds are all internal when it is clear that most firms have access to external financing. Also, funds are not the only strategic resource that should influence strategic choice. Other resources, such as technological and managerial resources, may be equally important. These additional factors may lead to a strategy different from that prescribed by the BCG model.

General Electric and McKinsey and Company have expanded on the initial BCG concept by their nine-cell industry attractiveness/business strength matrix.[4] A number of factors besides growth rate are considered for determining industry attractiveness. It is a composite of several factors, such as market size, market growth rate, cyclicality, competitive structure, barriers to entry, industry profitability, technology, inflation, regulation, personnel ability, social and environmental issues, and political and legal issues. Similarly business strength is measured in a far richer manner than merely using relative market share. It is a composite of several factors, including market share, strength of sales force, marketing and distribution strengths, manufacturing and R&D strengths, image, breadth of product line, quality/reliability, and managerial competence. As shown in Figure A-3, depending on the position of a business on this grid, its strategy can be determined.

We should note, however, that since each dimension of the matrix incorporates a number of factors, these factors will have to be subjectively weighted in order to position a business within the matrix. Again, as long as the model is not used mechanically as a prescriptive tool, the subjective aspects of the GE/McKinsey model may in fact facilitate a better understanding of the context of a business unit.

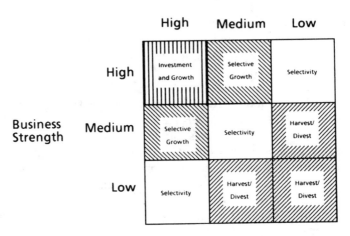

Figure A-3   **The General Electric/McKinsey Industry Attractiveness-Business Strength Matrix**

Arthur D. Little provides an even more finely grained model for positioning a business unit. It seeks to map a business based on what stage of the life cycle it is in and on its competitive position (Figure A-4). An advantage of this approach is that it helps underscore the transient nature of business strategy.[5] This model facilitates a discussion of how a business unit should evolve as its industry matures. Case 6 on Becton Dickinson and Company provides an illustration of this facility.

The evolution of a business strategy is not solely a function of its industry environment. It is also influenced significantly by the organization's own willingness to make the business strategy succeed. Although models, such as the ADL model, are useful stimulants for discussion in the strategy process, they should not be viewed as decision-making tools. Their primary contribution is in generating a realistic set of strategic alternatives.

PIMS Model

The PIMS model (Profit Impact of Market Strategy) is based on a large data base of more than 3,000 businesses belonging to 450 companies.[6] For a detailed discussion of the various technical aspects of the PIMS model, see Case 13 on Dexter Corporation and Case 12 on Norton Company. The PIMS model attempts to compare a business unit with the average profile of the companies represented in the PIMS data base. It also offers useful strategy prescriptions. The strengths of the PIMS model are these:

1. It provides a benchmark for comparing a business with the profile of an "average" business; it is a measure of the quality of a firm's businesses.
2. It offers suggestions for strengthening business strategy, based on what has worked, on the average, for many other businesses in the past.
3. Through the very task of preparing the input data required for each business, the business unit manager has a chance to audit his or her business.
4. It facilitates a comparison not only with other businesses in the entire PIMS data base but also with specific parts of the data base, thereby helping the firm identify to which strategic group it may belong.

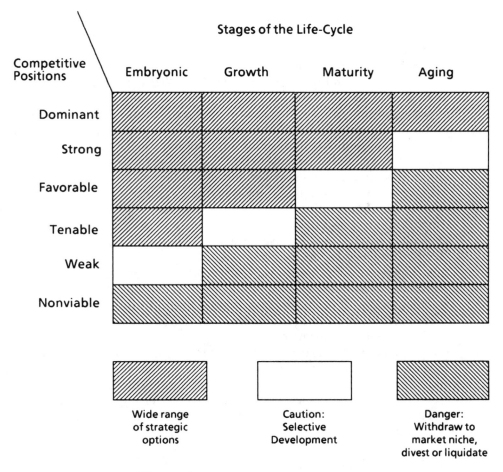

Figure A-4   **The Arthur D. Little Matrix**

The PIMS approach also has its limitations.[7] Above all, it is important to keep in mind that its recommendations are based on historical data, without any "guarantee" that the future will be the same as the past. Also, because the data are self-reported by a large number of different firms, they are subject to reporting biases. Finally, despite the strict guidelines provided by the PIMS administrators, the respondent has flexibility in defining a business unit. Thus the model may be comparing entities that are not consistently defined.

A major benefit of the PIMS model, however, is that it can answer a number of "what if" questions about a firm's business strategy. Although these answers are limited by the experiences of other firms, they are useful in delimiting the prudent set of strategic alternatives that a business unit should consider.

Industry Analysis

The analytical models discussed above primarily looked at business strategy without particular reference to the industry to which the business belongs. Research from industrial economics suggests that industry structure plays a fundamental role in determining which strategy is the most appropriate to the firm.[8]

M. Porter and others have pointed out that the strategy of a business unit should be delineated within the context of the particular industry to which the unit belongs. Figure A-5 describes the five competitive forces that can impact a business. The five major forces are the rivalry among existing firms, the bargaining power of suppliers, the bargaining power of buyers, the threat of substitutes, and the threat of potential entrants to the industry. The framework suggests that competition in an industry goes well beyond the established players. Also, the implied assumption in the analytical models presented earlier—that cost leadership is the only enduring competitive advantage—is questioned in this framework. Depending on the strategy chosen by a business unit, other competencies of the firm can provide a stronger competitive advantage. Thus, for example, in a specialized or focused strategy, having a large market share and thus enjoying the related scale and experience effects is not very important; rather, the success of these strategies will be predicated on the business unit's brand image, technological know-how, and relationships with distributors. As long as these distinctive competencies allow a business strategy to be defended from the five competitive forces, they provide it with a competitive advantage.

Within a particular industry, a number of rivals may face a similar array of competitive forces. They belong to a common strategic group. The strategy proposed by a business unit should enable the firm to counter the competitive forces successfully in its chosen strategic group. A strategic group consists of firms that seek to pursue a similar strategy and compete for the same customers. It is also distinguished by the unique competencies that are required to be a member.

In addition, however, a business unit should recognize, along with other members of its group, that it competes with other strategic groups. It is not enough

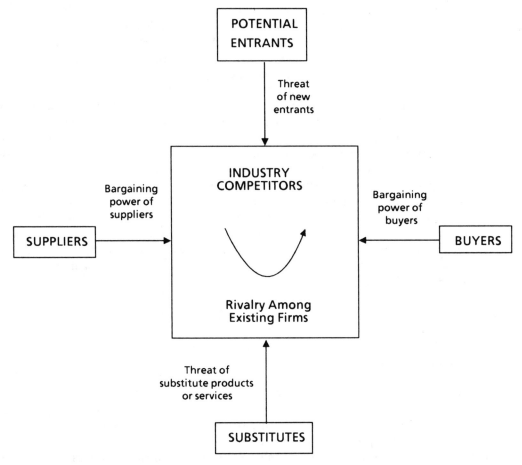

Figure A-5   **Competitive Forces in an Industry**

Source: Adapted with permission of The Free Press, a Division of Macmillan, Inc., from *Competitive Strategy: Techniques for Analyzing Industries and Competitors* by Michael E. Porter. Copyright © 1980 by The Free Press.

to have a winning strategy within one's own strategic group; the business unit should also attempt to migrate to a strategic group that is advantageous in terms of its configuration of competitive forces. A critical issue in evaluating business strategy is to assess the chances of a business unit's successful transition to a strategic group that is more desirable. Some of the important mobility barriers are the brand name, reputation, manufacturing or logistical capacities, R&D capabilities, and scale or scope economies that are enjoyed by incumbent firms in the strategic group targeted for entry. Transitioning from the present strategic group may not be easy because of the exit barriers faced by the business unit. These include the explicit or implicit commitments to the existing stakeholders, the specialization of the assets currently used in operations that may be made obsolete by the move, and the reluctance of the firm's employees to make the desired transition.

In summary, industry analysis helps identify the attractiveness of a given strategic group, the nature of the competition within that group and with other adjacent groups, the barriers to mobility that restrict the movement of a firm to a more-attractive group, and the competitive forces that shape the evolution of an industry. Such a comprehensive analysis is more informative in evaluating strategy than the simplistic analytical models that were proposed earlier. The one serious limitation of the framework is its tendency to view the stakeholders of a business unit solely in a competitive light. In business contexts where there are well-developed cooperative structures among a business unit's stakeholders, such as in Japan,[9] the Porter framework may not be very useful.

All of the models that we reviewed in this section help evaluate business strategies. The use of several analytic models will encourage an eclectic blend of viewpoints to emerge in the strategy process. However, if they are used in a dogmatic manner, analytical models will end up stifling creative thinking in the strategy process.

EVALUATING CORPORATE STRATEGY

Business Portfolio Models

The business portfolio models that were discussed earlier (see Figures A-2, A-3, and A-4) also can be used at the corporate level. The aggregate picture from plotting the positions of various businesses can provide a snapshot of the quality of the firm's overall portfolio. It was such an assessment that led to the major restructuring of the firm's business portfolio in Becton Dickinson (see Case 6), Norton Company (see Case 12), and Alfa-Laval (see Case 16).

With the help of these models, top management can provide a better *balance* among the firm's various businesses: growth matched by maturity, cyclicality matched by stability, domestic matched by foreign, and so on. A related requirement is to ensure that the businesses in the portfolio fit together in terms of specific synergies.

Evaluating Opportunities for Synergy

Figure A-6 provides an example of a value chain.[10] The value chain attempts to delineate how a firm chooses to add value through its business strategy. Thus, a business unit pursuing a low-cost strategy may try to focus its attention on operations and logistics, in contrast with a business unit that seeks to pursue a differentiated strategy with emphasis on R&D, marketing, sales, and service. The value chains for the two strategies will look different, with greater value being added in

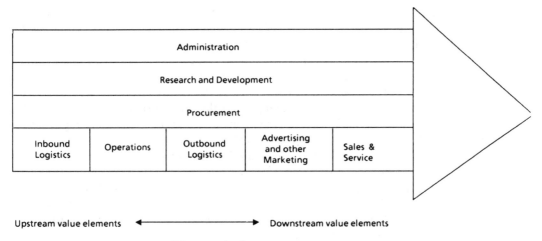

Figure A-6   **A Typical Value Chain**

Source: Adapted with permission of The Free Press, a Division of Macmillan, Inc., from *Competitive Advantage: Creating and Sustaining Superior Performance* by Michael E. Porter. Copyright © 1985 by Michael E. Porter.

the activities that are important to the strategy. When the value chains of the various businesses are looked at simultaneously (as in Figure 7-1), opportunities to coordinate either the upstream activities—such as operations—or the downstream activities—such as marketing, sales, and service—become evident.

Such synergies often are difficult to achieve. Businesses that are preoccupied with their own competitive pressures may not want to see the broader picture. Additionally there might be strong internal organizational rivalries between various business entities, discouraging attempts to embark on cooperative activities. As we discussed in Chapter 2, it is important that the strategy process highlights opportunities for economies of both scale and scope, so that top management can take necessary steps to exploit them. It may be useful in this regard to view the pursuit of synergy as an *internal* strategic alliance and apply the same principles to the formation of these as we discussed in Chapter 7 for external joint ventures (see Figure 7-2).

Strategic field analysis is another approach for managing potential synergies in a diversified firm. This analysis uses the value chain for each business as a point of departure. It then provides a mapping or clustering of businesses that can each improve its competitive position by collaborating with others.[11] If the value chains of a firm's diversified businesses can be juxtaposed on a single map, potential economies of scope and scale across these value chains can readily be discerned.

Value-Based Planning

Acquisition and Divestiture Planning.   Acquisitions and divestitures have become increasingly popular options for restructuring a firm's portfolio.[12] The value implications of either an acquisition or a divestiture can be assessed by examining the relationship between prices paid or received and the intrinsic value of the business unit acquired or divested. The valuation of target firms and the bidding strategy chosen by the acquirer are two important aspects of such an assessment.

The first step in planning an acquisition is to compute V_A, the estimated intrinsic value of the target firm to the new bidder (Figure A-7). V_A should incorporate all the potential synergies realizable after the target firm is properly integrated with the acquiring firm. These synergies include potential gains resulting from the joint use of shared resources and from extensions in the product lines of the acquirer. Moreover, there are costs associated with the integration of the target firm that should also be incorporated in its valuation. These costs are significant and are estimated at 10 to 15 percent of the prior value of the target firm.[13] Since V_A is an estimated figure, it is subject to variations depending on the assumptions made. It may be prudent therefore to construct for V_A alternate scenarios that are associated with each set of critical assumptions.

The value of an acquisition is only partially influenced by V_A. Typically the acquisition price, P_A represents a premium over the prior market value, M, of the target firm (Figure A-7). The premium paid for gaining control of the target firm is another important element in assessing the value of an acquisition. Acquisition premiums have varied on an average from 15 percent over prior market value in 1967–1972 to an average of 40 percent in 1979–1985. The premium eventually paid in the transaction is based on both the competition for the target firm and the intensity with which the winner seeks the target.

The net appropriable gain, NG_A, from the acquisition transaction is the difference between V_A and the price paid, P_A. It is influenced by both the intrinsic value of the target to the acquirer (firm-specific synergistic gain) and the market-wide determination of the premium paid for the acquisition. The appropriable gain, NG_A, represents the strategic gains to the acquirer from the acquisition.

Although the estimated post-acquisition value of the target firm is typically incorporated in acquisition planning, the decision on what premium to pay for gaining control often is delegated to intermediaries involved in the transaction. Yet we note in Figure A-7 that the premium paid has just as great an effect on the net appropriable gain from the transaction as the estimated post-acquisition value of the target firm. Top management of the diversifying firm should therefore pay close attention to both the value of the target firm and the bidding strategy used in its acquisition.

Divestiture is the mirror image of an acquisition decision. The appropriate gain in a divestiture, NG_D, is equal to the difference between the price obtained for the divested unit, P_D, and the estimated value of the unit to the divestor, V_{DU} (Figure A-8). The computation is similar to that in an acquisition decision. Clearly the divestor should determine whether the price obtained in selling the unit is likely to be higher than its value as part of the divestor's operations. The gain from divestiture is influenced by the potential synergies of the unit with other acquirers,

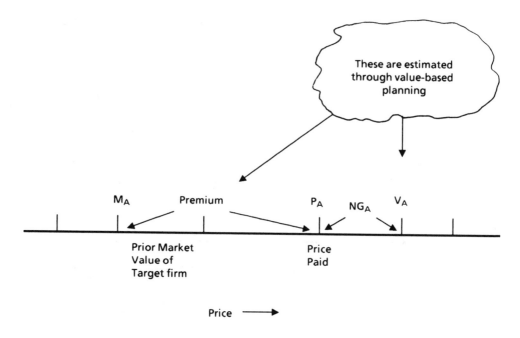

$P_A - M_A$ = Premium paid to gain control of the target firm

V_A = Acquirer-specific value of the target firm
Net appropriable gain $NG_A = V_A\text{-}P_A = V_A - M_A$ - Premium

Figure A-7 **Evaluating Acquisitions**

Source: B. S. Chakravarthy and H. Singh, "Value-Based Planning: Applications and Limitation," in *Advances in Strategic Management,* R. Lamb and P. Shrivastava, eds. (Greenwich, CT: JAI Press, 1990), 171.

the current synergies (or lack thereof) with the seller firm, and the number of potential bidders for the divested unit.

The divesting firm has some important strategic advantages that can potentially increase the gains from the transaction (except in distress sales and divestitures, where the relative bargaining power of the buyer over the seller is higher). First, the divesting firm has on the unit being divested very high-quality information that can provide a better estimate of its intrinsic value to the divestor than to a potential buyer. Second, the divestor has some degrees of freedom in determining the timing and process of divestiture. This allows the divestor to influence the premium received from the transaction. For instance, the divestor can negotiate privately with several potential acquirers, pitting one against the other. Care has to

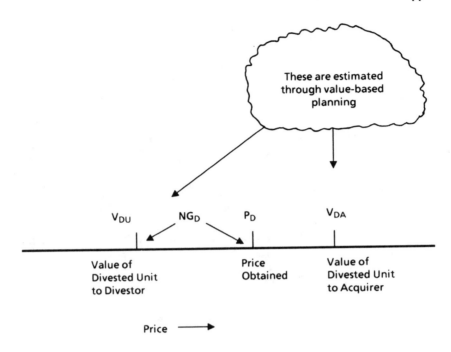

V_{DU} = Value of the unit to divesting firm when part of existing operations

V_{DA} = Value of the divested unit to the acquirer

Net appropriable gain on Divestiture
$NG_D = P_D - V_{DU}$

Figure A-8   **Evaluating Divestitures**

Source: B. S. Chakravarthy and H. Singh, "Value-Based Planning: Applications and Limitation," in *Advances in Strategic Management,* R. Lamb and P. Shrivastava, eds. (Greenwich, CT: JAI Press, 1990), 174.

be exercised, however, that leaks about such discussions do not demoralize the management of the unit targeted for divestiture.

Value-Based Control

The analytical approach used to evaluate acquisitions and divestitures has recently been extended to an ongoing assessment of the effects of various strategic programs on the value of the firm.[14] This recent approach, called value-based control, considers the firm as a portfolio of funds-generating businesses, analogous to a portfolio of stocks with expected future earnings flows. Models for assessing stock market portfolios have been modified for evaluating the firm's portfolio of businesses.[15] The first Dexter study (see Case 13) provides a detailed description of this approach as used by one company. Value-based strategic control can lead both to the restructuring of the firm's business portfolio and to the firm's capital structure.

Value-based control does not suffer from some of the limitations that other business portfolio matrices do, because it accepts the possibility of business renewal even in mature and declining industries. It is primarily concerned with future cash flows from a business and its riskiness, regardless of its position on the growth-share matrix. It is therefore potentially an attractive technique for auditing a firm's business portfolio.

Another advantage of this approach is that it allows the simultaneous consideration of the risks and returns associated with a strategy. For example, despite the potentially high returns from investments made in a "star" business, it may not be attractive when it is compared against the higher cost of the equity required to finance it.

An important limitation of value-based control is that projections of future cash flows cannot be made with accuracy. Users of the technique face substantial variations between the future income projections offered by line managers who are close to their businesses and the greater objectivity claimed by staff managers when they make their projections. Following the first set of numbers may subject the technique to self-serving manipulations without external controls; on the other hand, exclusively using the advice of staff may reduce the technique to a numbers game, since business expertise presumably rests with line managers. A difficult but important exercise in value-based control is the reconciliation of different projections by questioning the assumptions associated with each. As we discussed in the Dexter studies (see Cases 13 and 14), other limitations of value-based control have to do with the assumptions that have to be made for determining a business unit's capital structure and its cost of capital. These are open to debate.

Despite the above limitations, value-based control can be a potent aid in the periodic audit of a firm's business portfolio. It provides a logical screening device for identifying businesses whose actual returns are below the stockholder's expectations. Portfolio restructuring decisions can be initiated with the help of such an analysis. Value-based control is, however, only as good as the financial projections on which it is based. If it is used as one of several analytical tools for aiding strategic decisions, it can be quite helpful.

SUMMARY

This Appendix discussed various analytical approaches that are available to evaluate strategy. These approaches not only support the strategy process by strengthening the quality of the dialogue between managers but also help bring a sense of "objectivity" to the process. There is no contention between strategic analysis and the strategy process. In our opinion, good strategic analysis is essential for an effective strategy process, but it is useful to remember that analytical approaches can evaluate strategy only *after* it is formed. Forming and implementing strategy are two primary responsibilities of top management. These have been the focus of this book.

NOTES

1. K. R. Andrews, *The Concept of Corporate Strategy* (Homewood, IL: Richard D. Irwin, 1980).
2. B. D. Henderson, "The Product Portfolio," in *Perspectives* (Boston: Boston Consulting Group, 1970).
3. See C. Y. Woo and A. C. Cooper, "Strategies of Effective Low Share Businesses," *Strategic Management Journal* 4 (1983): 123–135.
4. See A. C. Hax and N. S. Majluf, *Strategic Management: Integrative Perspective* (Englewood Cliffs, NJ: Prentice Hall, 1984).
5. See R. A. Wright, *A System for Managing Diversity* (Cambridge, MA: Arthur D. Little, Inc., 1974).
6. R. Buzzell and B. Gale, *PIMS Principles* (New York: Free Press, 1987).
7. See C. R. Anderson and F. T. Paine, "PIMS: A Re-examination," *Academy of Management Review* 3 (1978): 602–611.
8. M. E. Porter, *Competitive Strategy* (New York: Free Press, 1980).
9. For a detailed contrast of the Japanese and U.S. business contexts, see W. M. Fruin, *Cooperative Structures and Competitive Strategies* (London: Oxford University Press, forthcoming). The EEC may play an important role in building cooperative structures within Europe as well. Even within the U.S. business environment, there is a growing recognition of the importance of strategic alliances. Consequently the competitive analysis framework has to be complemented by a cooperative perspective.
10. M. E. Porter, *Competitive Advantage* (New York: Free Press, 1985).
11. See Hax and Majluf, *Strategic Management.*
12. M. Rock, *The Mergers and Acquisitions Handbook* (New York: McGraw-Hill, 1987).
13. J. Kitching, *Acquisitions in Europe: Causes of Corporate Successes and Failures* (Geneva: Business International, 1973).
14. A. Rappaport, *Creating Shareholder Value* (New York: Free Press, 1986).
15. See B. S. Chakravarthy and H. Singh, "Value-Based Planning: Applications and Limitation," in *Advances in Strategic Management,* Vol. 6, ed. R. Lamb and P. Shrivastava (Greenwich, CT: JAI Press, 1990).

REFERENCES

Abernathy, W. J., and K. Wayne, "Limits of the Learning Curve," *Harvard Business Review* 52 (Sept.–Oct. 1974): 109–119.
Bettis, R. A., and W. K. Hall, "The Business Portfolio Approach—Where It Falls Down in Practice," *Long Range Planning* 16 (Apr. 1983): 95–104.
Buzzell, R. D., T. Gale, and R. G. M. Sultan, "Market Share—A Key to Profitability," *Harvard Business Review* 53 (Jan.–Feb. 1975): 97–108.

Caves, R. E., and M. E. Porter, "Market Structure, Oligopoly, and the Stability of Market Shares," *Journal of Industrial Economics* 26 (1978): 285–308.

————, "From Entry Barriers to Mobility Barriers: Conjectural Decisions and Contrived Deterrence to New Competition," *Quarterly Journal of Economics* 91 (May 1977): 241–261.

Ghemawat, P., "Building Strategy on the Experience Curve," *Harvard Business Review* 63 (Mar.–Apr. 1985): 143–149.

Harrigan, K. R., "The Strategic Exit Decision: Additional Evidence," in *Competitive Strategic Management,* ed. R. B. Lamb (Englewood Cliffs, NJ: Prentice Hall, 1984), 488–497.

Haspeslagh, P. C., "Portfolio Planning Approaches and the Strategic Management Process in Diversified Industrial Companies" (DBA dissertation, Graduate School of Business Administration, Harvard University, 1983).

Hax, A. C., and N. S. Majluf, "The Use of the Industry Attractiveness-Business Strength Matrix in Strategic Planning," *Interfaces* 13 (April 1983): 54–71.

————, "Competitive Cost Dynamics: The Experience Curve," *Interfaces* 12 (Oct. 1982): 50–61.

Lubatkin, M., and M. Pitts, "PIMS: Fact or Folklore," *The Journal of Business Strategy* 3 (Winter 1983): 38–43.

Porter, M. E., "Strategic Interaction: Some Lessons from Industry Histories for Theory and Antitrust Policy," in *Competitive Strategic Management,* ed. R. B. Lamb (Englewood Cliffs, NJ: Prentice Hall, 1984), 415–445.

Rumelt, R. P., "Towards a Strategic Theory of the Firm," in *Competitive Strategic Management,* ed. R. B. Lamb (Englewood Cliffs, NJ: Prentice Hall, 1984), 556–570.

Schoeffler, S., R. D. Buzzell, and D. F. Heany, "Impact of Strategic Planning on Profit Performance," *Harvard Business Review* 52 (Mar.–Apr. 1974): 137–145.

Wensley, R., "PIMS and BCG: New Horizon or False Dawn?" *Strategic Management Journal* 3 (Apr.–June 1982): 147–158.

Wind, Y., V. Mahajan, and D. Swire, "An Empirical Comparison of Standardized Portfolio Models," *Journal of Marketing* 47 (Spring 1983): 89–99.

BIBLIOGRAPHY

Abell, D. F., *Defining the Business: The Starting Point of Strategic Planning* (Englewood Cliffs, NJ: Prentice-Hall, 1980).

Abernathy, W. J., *The Productivity Dilemma: Roadblocks to Innovation in the Automobile Industry* (Baltimore: Johns Hopkins University Press, 1978).

———, K. B. Clark, and A. M. Kantrow, *Industrial Renaissance* (New York: Basic Books, 1983).

Ackerman, R. W., *The Social Challenge to Business* (Cambridge, MA: Harvard University Press, 1975).

Ackoff, R. L., *A Concept of Corporate Planning* (New York: Wiley-Interscience, 1970).

Aguilar, F. J., *General Managers in Action* (New York: Oxford University Press, 1988).

———, *Scanning the Business Environment* (New York: Macmillan, 1965).

Aldrich, H. E., *Organizations and Environment* (Englewood Cliffs, NJ: Prentice-Hall, 1979).

Allison, G. T., *Essence of Decision* (Boston: Little, Brown, 1971).

Andrews, K. R., *The Concept of Corporate Strategy* (Homewood, IL: Richard D. Irwin, 1980).

Ansoff, H. I., *Implanting Strategic Management* (Englewood Cliffs, NJ: Prentice Hall, 1985).

———, *Strategic Management* (New York: John Wiley, 1979).

———, *Corporate Strategy: Business Policy for Growth and Expansion* (New York: McGraw-Hill, 1965).

Anthony, R., and J. Dearden, *Management Control Systems* (Homewood, IL: Richard D. Irwin, 1980).

Anthony, R. N., *Planning and Control Systems: A Framework for Analysis* (Boston: Harvard Business School, 1965).

Ashby, W. R., *An Introduction to Cybernetics* (London: Chapman Hall and University Paperback, 1971).

Barnard, C. I., *The Functions of the Executive* (Cambridge, MA: Harvard University Press, 1938).

Bartlett, C., and S. Ghoshal, *Beyond Global Management: Transnational Solution* (Boston: Harvard Business School Press, 1989).

Beer, M., B. Spector, P. R. Lawrence, D. Quinn Mills, and R. E. Walton, *Managing Human Assets* (New York: Free Press, 1987).

Beer, S., *Brain of the Firm* (New York: Herder and Herder, 1972).

Bennis, W., and B. Nanus, *Leaders* (New York: Free Press, 1985).

Berg, N. A., *General Management: An Analytical Approach* (Homewood, IL: Richard D. Irwin, 1984).

Berle, A. A., and G. C. Means, *The Modern Corporation and Private Property* (New York: Commerce Clearing House, 1932).

Bower, J. L., *Managing the Resource Allocation Process* (Boston: Harvard Business School, 1968).

Brealey, R. A., and S. Myers, *Principles of Corporate Finance,* 2d ed. (New York: McGraw-Hill, 1984).

Burns, T., and G. M. Stalker, *The Management of Innovation* (London: Tavistock Publications, 1961).

Camillus, J. C., *Strategic Planning and Management Control: Systems for Survival and Success* (Lexington, MA: D. C. Heath, 1986).

Carlzon, J., *Moments of Truth* (New York: Harper and Row, 1987).

Caves, R. E., *Multinational Enterprise and Economic Analysis* (Cambridge, MA: Cambridge University Press, 1982).

Chakravarthy, B. S., *Managing Coal: A Challenge in Adaptation* (New York: State University of New York Press, 1982).

Chandler, A. D., *The Visible Hand: The Managerial Revolution in American Business* (Cambridge, MA: Belknap Press of Harvard University, 1977).

Christenson, C. R., K. R. Andrews, J. L. Bower, R. G. Hamermesh, and M. E. Porter, *Business Policy: Text and Cases,* 5th ed. (Homewood, IL: Richard D. Irwin, 1982).

Contractor, F., and P. Lorange, eds., *Cooperative Strategies in International Business* (Lexington, MA: Lexington Books, 1988).

Cyert, R. M., and J. G. March, *A Behavioral Theory of the Firm* (Englewood Cliffs, NJ: Prentice Hall, 1963).

de Bono, E., *Tactics: The Art and Science of Success* (Boston: Little, Brown, 1984).

Deal, T. E., and A. A. Kennedy, *Corporate Cultures* (Reading, MA: Addison-Wesley, 1982).

Donaldson, G., and J. W. Lorsch, *Decision Making at the Top: The Shaping of Strategic Direction* (New York: Basic Books, 1983).

Doz, Y., *Strategic Management in Multinational Companies* (London: Pergamon Press, 1986).

Drucker, P. F., *Innovation and Entrepreneurship* (New York: Harper and Row, 1985).

———, *Management* (New York: Harper and Row, 1982).

———, *Management: Tasks, Responsibilities, Practices* (New York: Harper and Row, 1974).

———, *The Practice of Management* (New York: Harper and Row, 1954).

Evan, W., *Organization Theory: Structures, Systems, and Environments* (New York: John Wiley, 1976).

———, ed., *Interorganizational Relations* (Philadelphia: University of Pennsylvania Press, 1976).

Freeman, R. E., *Strategic Management: A Stakeholder Approach* (Marsfield, MA: Pittman, 1984).

———, and D. R. Gilbert, *Corporate Strategy and the Search for Ethics* (Englewood Cliffs, NJ: Prentice Hall, 1988).

Fruin, W. M., *Cooperative Structures, Competitive Strategies: The Japanese Enterprise System* (London: Oxford University Press, forthcoming).

Galbraith, J., *Organization Design* (Reading, MA: Addison-Wesley, 1977).

———, and D. A. Nathanson, *Strategy Implementation: The Role of Structure and Process* (St. Paul, MN: West Publishing, 1978).

Gilbert, D. R., E. Hartman, J. J. Mauriel, R. E. Freeman, *A Logic for Strategy* (Cambridge, MA: Ballinger, 1988).

Godet, M., *Scenarios and Strategic Management* (London: Butterworths, 1987).

Goold, M., and A. Campbell, *Strategies and Styles: The Role of the Center in Managing Diversified Corporations* (Cambridge, MA: Basil Blackwell, 1987).

Grant, J. H., and W. R. King, *The Logic of Strategic Planning* (Boston: Little Brown, 1982).

Grinyer, P. H., and J. C. Spender, *Turnaround—Management Recipes for Strategic Success* (New York: Associated Business Press, 1979).

Hamermesh, R. G., *Making Strategy Work* (New York: John Wiley, 1986).

Harrigan, K. R., *Managing for Joint Venture Success* (Lexington, MA: Lexington Books, 1986).

————, *Strategic Flexibility: A Management Guide for Changing Times* (Lexington, MA: Lexington Books, 1985).

Harvey-Jones, P., *Making It Happen* (London: Collins, 1988).

Haspeslagh, P.C., and D. B. Jemison, *Managing Acquisitions: Creating Value Through Strategic Renewal* (New York: Free Press, forthcoming).

Hax, A. C., and N. S. Majluf, *Strategic Management: An Integrative Perspective* (Englewood Cliffs, NJ: Prentice Hall, 1984).

Hayes, R. H., and S. C. Wheelwright, *Restoring Our Competitive Edge: Competing through Manufacturing* (New York: John Wiley, 1984).

Heenan, D., and H. V. Perlmutter, *Multinational Organizational Development* (Reading, MA: Addison-Wesley, 1979).

Helmer, O., *Looking Forward: A Guide to Futures Research* (San Francisco: Sage, 1983).

Henderson, B. D., *Henderson on Corporate Strategy* (Cambridge, MA: Abt Books, 1979).

Hirschman, A. O., *Exit, Voice, and Loyalty* (Cambridge, MA: Harvard University Press, 1970).

Hrebiniak, L. G., and W. F. Joyce, *Implementing Strategy* (New York: Macmillan, 1984).

Jacobson, G., and J. Hillkirk, *Xerox: American Samurai* (New York: Macmillan, 1986).

Janis, I. L., *Victims of Groupthink* (Boston: Houghton Mifflin, 1972).

————, and L. Mann, *Decision Making* (New York: Free Press, 1977).

Kahneman, D., P. Slovic, and A. Tversky, *Judgement Under Uncertainty: Heuristics and Biases* (Cambridge, England: Cambridge University Press, 1982).

Kamien, M. I., and N. L. Schwartz, *Market Structure and Innovation* (Cambridge, England: Cambridge University Press, 1982).

Kanter, R. M., *The Change Masters* (New York: Simon and Schuster, 1983.

Kitching, J., *Acquisitions in Europe: Causes of Corporate Successes and Failures* (Geneva: Business International, 1973).

Kobrin, S. J., *Managing Political Risk Assessment* (Berkeley: University of California Press, 1982).

Kotter, J. P., *The General Managers* (New York: Free Press, 1982).

Lamb, R., *Running American Business* (New York: Basic Books, 1987).

Lawrence, P. R., and J. Lorsch, *Organization and Environment* (Boston: Harvard Business School, 1967).

————, and D. Dyer, *Renewing American Industry* (New York: Free Press, 1983).

Lenway, S. A., *The Politics of U.S. International Trade Protection, Expansion and Escape* (Cambridge, MA: Ballinger, 1985).

Lindblom, C. E., *The Policy-Making Process* (Englewood Cliffs, NJ: Prentice-Hall, 1968).

Lorange, P., *Corporate Planning: An Executive Viewpoint* (Englewood Cliffs, NJ: Prentice-Hall, 1980).

————, and R. F. Vancil, *Strategic Planning Systems* (Englewood Cliffs, NJ: Prentice-Hall, 1977).

————, M. S. Scott-Morton, and S. Ghoshal, *Strategic Control* (St. Paul, MN: West Publishing, 1987).

Lorsch, J. W., and S. A. Allen, *Managing Diversity and Interdependence* (Boston: Division of Research, Harvard Business School, 1973).

Mansfield, E., *Research and Innovation in the Modern Corporation* (New York: Norton, 1971).

Mason, R., and I. Mitroff, *Challenging Strategic Planning Assumptions* (New York: John Wiley, 1981).

Miles, R. E., and C. C. Snow, *Organizational Strategy, Structure, and Process* (New York: McGraw-Hill, 1978).

Miles, R. H., *Coffin Nails and Corporate Strategy* (Englewood Cliffs, NJ: Prentice Hall, 1982).

Miller, D., and P. H. Friesen, *Organizations: A Quantum View* (Englewood Cliffs, NJ: Prentice Hall, 1984).

Mintzberg, H., *The Nature of Managerial Work* (New York: Harper and Row, 1982).

———, *The Structuring of Organizations* (Englewood Cliffs, NJ: Prentice-Hall, 1979).

Nelson, R. R., and S. G. Winter, *An Evolutionary Theory of Economic Change* (Cambridge, MA: Belknap Press, 1982).

Normann, R., *Management for Growth* (New York: John Wiley, 1977).

Ohmae, K., *The Mind of the Strategist* (New York: McGraw-Hill, 1982).

———, *Triad Power: The Coming Shape of Global Competition* (New York: Free Press, 1985).

Ouchi, W., *The M-Form Society* (Reading, MA: Addison-Wesley, 1984).

Peters, T. J., and R. H. Waterman, *In Search of Excellence: Lessons from America's Best-Run Companies* (New York: Harper and Row, 1980).

Pettigrew, A. M., *The Politics of Organizational Decision Making* (London: Tavistock, 1973).

———, ed., *The Management of Strategic Chance* (Oxford: Basil Blackwell, 1987).

———, *The Awakening Giant* (Oxford: Basil Blackwell, 1985).

Pfeffer, J., and G. R. Salancik, *The External Control of Organizations: A Resource Dependence Perspective* (New York: Harper and Row, 1978).

Pinchot III, G., *Intrapreneuring* (New York: Harper and Row, 1985).

Porter, M. E., *Competitive Advantage* (New York: Free Press, 1985).

———, *Competitive Strategy* (New York: Free Press, 1980).

———, *The Competitive Advantage of Nations* (New York: Free Press, 1990).

Prahalad, C. K., and Y. Doz, *The Multinational Mission: Balancing Local Demands and Global Vision* (New York: Free Press, 1987).

Pyhrr, P. A., *Zero-Base Budgeting* (New York: John Wiley, 1973).

Quinn, J. B., *Strategies for Change: Logical Incrementalism* (Homewood, IL: Richard D. Irwin, 1980).

———, H. Mintzberg, and R. M. James, *The Strategy Process: Concepts, Contexts, and Cases* (Englewood-Cliffs, NJ: Prentice Hall, 1988).

Rappaport, A., *Creating Shareholder Value* (New York: Free Press, 1986).

Rawls, J., *A Theory of Justice* (Cambridge, MA: Harvard University Press, 1971).

Reich, R. B., *The Next American Frontier* (New York: Times Books, 1983).

Rock, M. (Ed.), *The Mergers and Acquisitions Handbook* (New York: McGraw-Hill, 1987).

Romiti, C., *Questi Anni Alla Fiat* (Milan: Rizzoli Libri, 1988).

Rothschild, W. E., *Strategic Alternatives: Selection, Development and Implementation* (New York: AMACOM, 1979).

———, *Putting It All Together: A Guide to Strategic Thinking* (New York: AMACOM, 1976).

Rumelt, R. P., *Strategy, Structure, and Economic Performance* (Boston: Division of Research, Harvard Business School, 1974).

Salter, M. S., and W. A. Weinhold, *Diversification through Acquisitions* (New York: Free Press, 1979).

Schein, E. H., *Organizational Culture and Leadership* (San Francisco: Jossey-Bass, 1985).

Schendel, D. E., and C. W. Hofer, eds., *Strategic Management: A New View of Business Policy and Planning* (Boston: Little, Brown, 1979).

Scherer, F. J,. *Industrial Market Structure and Economic Performance* (Boston: Houghton Mifflin, 1980).

Selznick, P., *Leadership in Administration* (New York: Harper and Row, 1957).

Simon, H. A., *Administrative Behavior: A Study of Decision-Making Processes in Administrative Organization* (New York: Free Press, 1976).

Steiner, G. A., *Strategic Planning: What Every Manager Must Know* (New York: Free Press, 1979).

Stonich, P. J., *Zero-Base Planning and Budgeting* (Homewood, IL: Richard D. Irwin, 1977).

Teece, D. J., ed., *The Competitive Challenge: Strategies for Industrial Innovation and Renewal* (Cambridge, MA: Ballinger, 1987).

Thompson, J., *Organizations in Action* (New York: McGraw-Hill, 1978).

Tichy, N., *Managing Strategic Change* (New York: John Wiley, 1983).

Tregoe, B., and J. W. Zimmerman, *Top Management Strategy* (New York: Simon and Schuster, 1980).

Tsurumi, Y., *Multinational Management: Business Strategy and Government Policy* (Cambridge, MA: Ballinger, 1977).

Urban, G. L., and J. R. Hauser, *Design and Marketing of New Products* (Englewood Cliffs, NJ: Prentice-Hall, 1980).

Vancil, R. F., *Decentralization: Managing Ambiguity by Design* (Homewood, IL: Dow Jones-Irwin, 1979),

———, *Implementing Strategy: The Role of Top Management* (Boston: Harvard Business School, 1982).

———, *Passing the Baton* (Boston: Harvard Business School, 1988).

Van de Ven, A. H., H. L. Angle, and M. S. Poole, *Research on the Management of Innovation: The Minnesota Studies* (New York: Harper and Row, 1989).

Von Hippell, E., *The Sources of Innovation* (New York: Oxford University Press, 1988).

Weick, K. E., *The Social Psychology of Organizing* (Reading, MA: Addison-Wesley, 1969).

Woodward, J., *Industrial Organization: Theory and Practice* (Oxford, England: Oxford University Press, 1965).

Wright, R. A., *A System for Managing Diversity* (Cambridge, MA: Arthur D. Little, 1974).

NAME INDEX

SUBJECT INDEX